D1559523

THE UPANISHADS – I

ISHA UPANISHAD

Sri Aurobindo

THE UPANISHADS – I

Isha Upanishad

Sri Aurobindo Ashram
Pondicherry

First edition 2003
Fifth impression 2017

Rs 290
ISBN 978-81-7058-749-1

© Sri Aurobindo Ashram Trust 2003
Published by Sri Aurobindo Ashram Publication Department
Pondicherry 605 002
Web http://www.sabda.in

Printed at Sri Aurobindo Ashram Press, Pondicherry
PRINTED IN INDIA

Publisher's Note

This volume contains Sri Aurobindo's translations of and commentaries on the Isha Upanishad. His translations of and commentaries on other Upanishads and Vedantic texts, and his writings on the Upanishads and Vedanta philosophy in general, are published in *Kena and Other Upanishads*, volume 18 of THE COMPLETE WORKS OF SRI AUROBINDO.

The present volume is divided into two parts. The first consists of Sri Aurobindo's final translation and analysis of the Isha Upanishad. This is the only work in this volume that was published during his lifetime. It contains his definitive interpretation of the Isha Upanishad.

Before publishing this final translation and analysis, Sri Aurobindo wrote ten incomplete commentaries on the Isha Upanishad. These appear in approximate chronological order in Part Two. Ranging in length from a few pages to more than a hundred, they show the development of his interpretation of this Upanishad from around 1900 to the middle of 1914, when he began work on his final translation and analysis.

The texts in both parts have been checked against the relevant manuscript and printed versions.

Guide to Editorial Notation

The contents of Part Two of this volume were never prepared by Sri Aurobindo for publication. They have been transcribed from manuscripts that sometimes present textual difficulties. In this edition these problems have been indicated as far as possible by means of the notation shown below.

Notation	Textual Problem
[.......]	Word(s) lost through damage to the manuscript (at the beginning of a piece, sometimes indicates that a page or pages of the manuscript have been lost)
[word]	Word(s) omitted by the author or lost through damage to the manuscript that are required by grammar or sense, and that could be supplied by the editors
[*note*]	Situations requiring textual explication; all such information is printed in italics

CONTENTS

Part One

Translation and Commentary
Published by Sri Aurobindo

Isha Upanishad

Isha Upanishad

ईशा वास्यमिदं सर्वं यत् किञ्च जगत्यां जगत् ।
तेन त्यक्तेन भुञ्जीथा मा गृधः कस्यस्विद् धनम् ॥ १ ॥

1. All this is for habitation[1] by the Lord, whatsoever is individual universe of movement in the universal motion. By
that renounced thou shouldst enjoy; lust not after any man's
possession.

कुर्वन्नेवेह कर्माणि जिजीविषेच्छतं समाः ।
एवं त्वयि नान्यथेतोऽस्ति न कर्म लिप्यते नरे ॥ २ ॥

2. Doing verily[2] works in this world one should wish to live
a hundred years. Thus it is in thee and not otherwise than
this; action cleaves not to a man.[3]

---

[1] There are three possible senses of *vāsyam*, "to be clothed", "to be worn as a garment"
and "to be inhabited". The first is the ordinarily accepted meaning. Shankara explains
it in this significance, that we must lose the sense of this unreal objective universe in
the sole perception of the pure Brahman. So explained the first line becomes a contradiction of the whole thought of the Upanishad which teaches the reconciliation, by the
perception of essential Unity, of the apparently incompatible opposites, God and the
World, Renunciation and Enjoyment, Action and internal Freedom, the One and the
Many, Being and its Becomings, the passive divine Impersonality and the active divine
Personality, the Knowledge and the Ignorance, the Becoming and the Not-Becoming,
Life on earth and beyond and the supreme Immortality. The image is of the world either
as a garment or as a dwelling-place for the informing and governing Spirit. The latter
significance agrees better with the thought of the Upanishad.
[2] *Kurvanneva*. The stress of the word *eva* gives the force, "doing works indeed, and
not refraining from them".
[3] Shankara reads the line, "Thus in thee — it is not otherwise than thus — action
cleaves not, a man." He interprets *karmāṇi* in the first line in the sense of Vedic sacrifices
which are permitted to the ignorant as a means of escaping from evil actions and their
results and attaining to heaven, but the second *karma* in exactly the opposite sense, "evil
action". The verse, he tells us, represents a concession to the ignorant; the enlightened
soul abandons works and the world and goes to the forest. The whole expression and
construction in this rendering become forced and unnatural. The rendering I give seems
to me the simple and straightforward sense of the Upanishad.

असूर्या नाम ते लोका अन्धेन तमसावृताः ।
तांस्ते प्रेत्याभिगच्छन्ति ये के चात्महनो जनाः ॥ ३ ॥

3. Sunless[4] are those worlds and enveloped in blind gloom whereto all they in their passing hence resort who are slayers of their souls.

अनेजदेकं मनसो जवीयो नैनद् देवा आप्नुवन् पूर्वमर्षत् ।
तद् धावतोऽन्यानत्येति तिष्ठत् तस्मिन्नपो मातरिश्वा दधाति ॥ ४ ॥

4. One unmoving that is swifter than Mind, That the Gods reach not, for It progresses ever in front. That, standing, passes beyond others as they run. In That the Master of Life[5] establishes the Waters.[6]

तदेजति तन्नैजति तद् दूरे तद्वन्तिके ।
तदन्तरस्य सर्वस्य तदु सर्वस्यास्य बाह्यतः ॥ ५ ॥

---

[4] We have two readings, *asūrya*, sunless, and *asurya*, Titanic or undivine. The third verse is, in the thought structure of the Upanishad, the starting-point for the final movement in the last four verses. Its suggestions are there taken up and worked out. The prayer to the Sun refers back in thought to the sunless worlds and their blind gloom, which are recalled in the ninth and twelfth verses. The sun and his rays are intimately connected in other Upanishads also with the worlds of Light and their natural opposite is the dark and sunless, not the Titanic worlds.

[5] *Mātariśvan* seems to mean "he who extends himself in the Mother or the container" whether that be the containing mother element, Ether, or the material energy called Earth in the Veda and spoken of there as the Mother. It is a Vedic epithet of the God Vayu, who, representing the divine principle in the Life-energy, Prana, extends himself in Matter and vivifies its forms. Here, it signifies the divine Life-power that presides in all forms of cosmic activity.

[6] *Apas*, as it is accentuated in the version of the White Yajurveda, can mean only "waters". If this accentuation is disregarded, we may take it as the singular *apas*, work, action. Shankara, however, renders it by the plural, works. The difficulty only arises because the true Vedic sense of the word had been forgotten and it came to be taken as referring to the fourth of the five elemental states of Matter, the liquid. Such a reference would be entirely irrelevant to the context. But the Waters, otherwise called the seven streams or the seven fostering Cows, are the Vedic symbol for the seven cosmic principles and their activities, three inferior, the physical, vital and mental, four superior, the divine Truth, the divine Bliss, the divine Will and Consciousness, and the divine Being. On this conception also is founded the ancient idea of the seven worlds in each of which the seven principles are separately active by their various harmonies. This is, obviously, the right significance of the word in the Upanishad.

5. That moves and That moves not; That is far and the same is near; That is within all this and That also is outside all this.

यस्तु सर्वाणि भूतानि आत्मन्येवानुपश्यति ।
सर्वभूतेषु चात्मानं ततो न विजुगुप्सते ॥ ६ ॥

6. But he who sees everywhere the Self in all existences and all existences in the Self, shrinks not thereafter from aught.

यस्मिन् सर्वाणि भूतानि आत्मैवाभूद् विजानतः ।
तत्र को मोहः कः शोक एकत्वमनुपश्यतः ॥ ७ ॥

7. He in whom it is the Self-Being that has become all existences that are Becomings,[7] for he has the perfect knowledge, how shall he be deluded, whence shall he have grief who sees everywhere oneness?

स पर्यगाच्छुक्रमकायमव्रणमस्नाविरं शुद्धमपापविद्धम् ।
कविर्मनीषी परिभूः स्वयम्भूर्याथातथ्यतोऽर्थान् व्यदधाच्छाश्वतीभ्यः
समाभ्यः ॥ ८ ॥

8. It is He that has gone abroad — That which is bright, bodiless, without scar of imperfection, without sinews, pure, unpierced by evil. The Seer, the Thinker,[8] the One who becomes everywhere, the Self-existent has ordered objects perfectly according to their nature from years sempiternal.

---

[7] The words *sarvāṇi bhūtāni*, literally, "all things that have become", are opposed to Atman, self-existent and immutable being. The phrase means ordinarily "all creatures", but its literal sense is evidently insisted on in the expression *bhūtāni abhūt* "became the Becomings". The idea is the acquisition in man of the supreme consciousness by which the one Self in him extends itself to embrace all creatures and realises the eternal act by which that One manifests itself in the multiple forms of the universal motion.

[8] There is a clear distinction in Vedic thought between *kavi*, the seer, and *manīṣī*, the thinker. The former indicates the divine supra-intellectual Knowledge which by direct vision and illumination sees the reality, the principles and the forms of things in their true relations, the latter the labouring mentality which works from the divided consciousness through the possibilities of things downward to the actual manifestation in form and upward to their reality in the self-existent Brahman.

अन्धं तमः प्रविशन्ति येऽविद्यामुपासते ।
ततो भूय इव ते तमो य उ विद्यायां रताः ॥ ९ ॥

9. Into a blind darkness they enter who follow after the Ignorance, they as if into a greater darkness who devote themselves to the Knowledge alone.

अन्यदेवाहुर्विद्यया अन्यदाहुरविद्यया ।
इति शुश्रुम धीराणां ये नस्तद् विचचक्षिरे ॥ १० ॥

10. Other, verily,[9] it is said, is that which comes by the Knowledge, other that which comes by the Ignorance; this is the lore we have received from the wise who revealed That to our understanding.

विद्याञ्च अविद्याञ्च यस्तद् वेदोभयं सह ।
अविद्यया मृत्युं तीर्त्वा विद्ययामृतमश्नुते ॥ ११ ॥

11. He who knows That as both in one, the Knowledge and the Ignorance, by the Ignorance crosses beyond death and by the Knowledge enjoys Immortality.

अन्धं तमः प्रविशन्ति येऽसम्भूतिमुपासते ।
ततो भूय इव ते तमो य उ सम्भूत्यां रताः ॥ १२ ॥

12. Into a blind darkness they enter who follow after the Non-Birth, they as if into a greater darkness who devote themselves to the Birth alone.

अन्यदेवाहुः सम्भवादन्यदाहुरसम्भवात् ।
इति शुश्रुम धीराणां ये नस्तद् विचचक्षिरे ॥ १३ ॥

13. Other, verily, it is said, is that which comes by the Birth,

---

[9] *Anyadeva* — *eva* here gives to *anyad* the force, "Quite other than the result described in the preceding verse is that to which lead the Knowledge and the Ignorance." We have the explanation of *anyad* in the verse that follows. The ordinary rendering, "Knowledge has one result, Ignorance another", would be an obvious commonplace announced with an exaggerated pompousness, adding nothing to the thought and without any place in the sequence of the ideas.

other that which comes by the Non-Birth; this is the lore we have received from the wise who revealed That to our understanding.

सम्भूतिश्च विनाशश्च यस्तद् वेदोभयं सह ।
विनाशेन मृत्युं तीर्त्वा सम्भूत्यामृतमश्नुते ॥ १४ ॥

14. He who knows That as both in one, the Birth and the dissolution of Birth, by the dissolution crosses beyond death and by the Birth enjoys Immortality.

हिरण्मयेन पात्रेण सत्यस्यापिहितं मुखम् ।
तत् त्वं पूषन्नपावृणु सत्यधर्माय दृष्टये ॥ १५ ॥

15. The face of Truth is covered with a brilliant golden lid; that do thou remove, O Fosterer,[10] for the law of the Truth, for sight.

पूषन्नेकर्षे यम सूर्य प्राजापत्य व्यूह रश्मीन् समूह ।
तेजो यत् ते रूपं कल्याणतमं तत् ते पश्यामि
योऽसावसौ पुरुषः सोऽहमस्मि ॥ १६ ॥

16. O Fosterer, O sole Seer, O Ordainer, O illumining Sun, O power of the Father of creatures, marshal thy rays, draw together thy light; the Lustre which is thy most blessed form

---

10 In the inner sense of the Veda Surya, the Sun-God, represents the divine Illumination of the Kavi which exceeds mind and forms the pure self-luminous Truth of things. His principal power is self-revelatory knowledge, termed in the Veda "Sight". His realm is described as the Truth, the Law, the Vast. He is the Fosterer or Increaser, for he enlarges and opens man's dark and limited being into a luminous and infinite consciousness. He is the sole Seer, Seer of Oneness and Knower of the Self, and leads him to the highest Sight. He is Yama, Controller or Ordainer, for he governs man's action and manifested being by the direct Law of the Truth, *satyadharma*, and therefore by the right principle of our nature, *yāthātathyatah*. A luminous power proceeding from the Father of all existence, he reveals in himself the divine Purusha of whom all beings are the manifestations. His rays are the thoughts that proceed luminously from the Truth, the Vast, but become deflected and distorted, broken up and disordered in the reflecting and dividing principle, Mind. They form there the golden lid which covers the face of the Truth. The Seer prays to Surya to cast them into right order and relation and then draw them together into the unity of revealed truth. The result of this inner process is the perception of the oneness of all beings in the divine Soul of the Universe.

of all, that in Thee I behold. The Purusha there and there,
He am I.

वायुरनिलममृतमथेदं भस्मान्तं शरीरम् ।
ॐ क्रतो स्मर कृतं स्मर क्रतो स्मर कृतं स्मर ॥ १७ ॥

17. The Breath of things[11] is an immortal Life, but of this body
ashes are the end. OM! O Will,[12] remember, that which was
done remember! O Will, remember, that which was done
remember.

अग्ने नय सुपथा राये अस्मान् विश्वानि देव वयुनानि विद्वान् ।
युयोध्यस्मज्जुह्वराणमेनो भूयिष्ठां ते नमउक्तिं विधेम ॥ १८ ॥

18. O god Agni, knowing all things that are manifested, lead us
by the good path to the felicity; remove from us the devious
attraction of sin.[13] To thee completest speech of submission
we would dispose.[14]

---

[11] Vayu, called elsewhere Matarishwan, the Life-Energy in the universe. In the light of
Surya he reveals himself as an immortal principle of existence of which birth and death
and life in the body are only particular and external processes.

[12] The Vedic term *kratu* means sometimes the action itself, sometimes the effective
power behind action represented in mental consciousness by the will. Agni is this power.
He is divine force which manifests first in matter as heat and light and material energy
and then, taking different forms in the other principles of man's consciousness, leads
him by a progressive manifestation upwards to the Truth and the Bliss.

[13] Sin, in the conception of the Veda, from which this verse is taken bodily, is that which
excites and hurries the faculties into deviation from the good path. There is a straight
road or road of naturally increasing light and truth, *rjuḥ panthāḥ, ṛtasya panthāḥ*,
leading over infinite levels and towards infinite vistas, *vītāni pṛṣṭhāni*, by which the law
of our nature should normally take us towards our fulfilment. Sin compels it instead
to travel with stumblings amid uneven and limited tracts and along crooked windings
(*duritāni, vṛjināni*).

[14] The word *vidhema* is used of the ordering of the sacrifice, the disposal of the offerings
to the God and, generally, of the sacrifice or worship itself. The Vedic *namas*, internal
and external obeisance, is the symbol of submission to the divine Being in ourselves and
in the world. Here the offering is that of completest submission and the self-surrender
of all the faculties of the lower egoistic human nature to the divine Will-force, Agni,
so that, free from internal opposition, it may lead the soul of man through the truth
towards a felicity full of the spiritual riches, *rāye*. That state of beatitude is intended,
self-content in the principle of pure Love and Joy, which the Vedic initiates regarded as
the source of the divine existence in the universe and the foundation of the divine life
in the human being. It is the deformation of this principle by egoism which appears as
desire and the lust of possession in the lower worlds.

Analysis

Plan of the Upanishad

THE UPANISHADS, being vehicles of illumination and not of instruction, composed for seekers who had already a general familiarity with the ideas of the Vedic and Vedantic seers and even some personal experience of the truths on which they were founded, dispense in their style with expressed transitions of thought and the development of implied or subordinate notions.

Every verse in the Isha Upanishad reposes on a number of ideas implicit in the text but nowhere set forth explicitly; the reasoning also that supports its conclusions is suggested by the words, not expressly conveyed to the intelligence. The reader, or rather the hearer, was supposed to proceed from light to light, confirming his intuitions and verifying by his experience, not submitting the ideas to the judgment of the logical reason.

To the modern mind this method is invalid and inapplicable; it is necessary to present the ideas of the Upanishad in their completeness, underline the suggestions, supply the necessary transitions and bring out the suppressed but always implicit reasoning.

The central idea of the Upanishad, which is a reconciliation and harmony of fundamental opposites, is worked out symmetrically in four successive movements of thought.

FIRST MOVEMENT

In the first, a basis is laid down by the idea of the one and stable Spirit inhabiting and governing a universe of movement and of the forms of movement. (*Verse 1, line 1*)

On this conception the rule of a divine life for man is founded, — enjoyment of all by renunciation of all through the exclusion of desire. (*Verse 1, line 2*)

There is then declared the justification of works and of the physical life on the basis of an inalienable freedom of the soul, one with the Lord, amidst all the activity of the multiple movement. (*Verse 2*)

Finally, the result of an ignorant interference with the right manifestation of the One in the multiplicity is declared to be an involution in states of blind obscurity after death. (*Verse 3*)

SECOND MOVEMENT

In the second movement the ideas of the first verse are resumed and amplified.

The one stable Lord and the multiple movement are identified as one Brahman of whom, however, the unity and stability are the higher truth and who contains all as well as inhabits all. (*Verses 4, 5*)

The basis and fulfilment of the rule of life are found in the experience of unity by which man identifies himself with the cosmic and transcendental Self and is identified in the Self, but with an entire freedom from grief and illusion, with all its becomings. (*Verses 6, 7*)

THIRD MOVEMENT

In the third movement there is a return to the justification of life and works (the subject of verse 2) and an indication of their divine fulfilment.

The degrees of the Lord's self-manifestation in the universe of motion and in the becomings of the one Being are set forth and the inner law of all existences declared to be by His conception and determination. (*Verse 8*)

Vidya and Avidya, Becoming and Non-becoming are reconciled by their mutual utility to the progressive self-realisation which proceeds from the state of mortality to the state of Immortality. (*Verses 9–14*)

FOURTH MOVEMENT

The fourth movement returns to the idea of the worlds and under the figures of Surya and Agni the relations of the Supreme Truth and Immortality (*Verses 15, 16*), the activities of this life (*Verse 17*), and the state after death (*Verse 18*) are symbolically indicated.

I

The Inhabiting Godhead: Life and Action

Verses 1–3*

THE BASIS OF COSMIC EXISTENCE

God and the world, Spirit and formative Nature are confronted and their relations fixed.

COSMOS

All world is a movement of the Spirit in Itself and is mutable and transient in all its formations and appearances; its only eternity is an eternity of recurrence, its only stability a semblance caused by certain apparent fixities of relation and grouping.

Every separate object in the universe is, in truth, itself the whole universe presenting a certain front or outward appearance of its movement. The microcosm is one with the macrocosm.

Yet in their relation of principle of movement and result of movement they are continent and contained, world in world, movement in movement. The individual therefore partakes of the nature of the universal, refers back to it for its source of activity, is, as we say, subject to its laws and part of cosmic Nature.

---

* 1. All this is for habitation by the Lord, whatsoever is individual universe of movement in the universal motion. By that renounced thou shouldst enjoy; lust not after any man's possession.

2. Doing verily works in this world one should wish to live a hundred years. Thus it is in thee and not otherwise than this; action cleaves not to a man.

3. Sunless are those worlds and enveloped in blind gloom whereto all they in their passing hence resort who are slayers of their souls.

SPIRIT

Spirit is lord of Its movement, one, immutable, free, stable and eternal.

The Movement with all its formed objects has been created in order to provide a habitation for the Spirit who, being One, yet dwells multitudinously in the multiplicity of His mansions.

It is the same Lord who dwells in the sum and the part, in the Cosmos as a whole and in each being, force or object in the Cosmos.

Since He is one and indivisible, the Spirit in all is one and their multiplicity is a play of His cosmic consciousness.

Therefore each human being is in his essence one with all others, free, eternal, immutable, lord of Nature.

TRANSITIONAL THOUGHT

AVIDYA

The object of habitation is enjoyment and possession; the object of the Spirit in Cosmos is, therefore, the possession and enjoyment of the universe. Yet, being thus in his essence one, divine and free, man seems to be limited, divided from others, subject to Nature and even its creation and sport, enslaved to death, ignorance and sorrow. His object in manifestation being possession and enjoyment of his world, he is unable to enjoy because of his limitation. This contrary result comes about by Avidya, the Ignorance of oneness: and the knot of the Ignorance is egoism.

EGO

The cause of ego is that while by Its double power of Vidya and Avidya the Spirit dwells at once in the consciousness of multiplicity and relativity and in the consciousness of unity and identity and is therefore not bound by the Ignorance, yet It can, in mind, identify Itself with the object in the movement, absorbingly, to the apparent exclusion of the Knowledge which remains behind, veiled at the back of the mentality. The movement of Mind in Nature is thus able to conceive of the object as the reality and the Inhabitant as limited and determined by the appearances of the object. It conceives of the object, not as the universe in one of its frontal appearances, but as itself a separate existence standing out from the Cosmos and different in being from all the rest of it. It conceives similarly of the Inhabitant. This is the illusion of ignorance which falsifies all realities. The illusion is called *ahaṁkāra*, the separative ego-sense which makes each being conceive of itself as an independent personality.

The result of the separation is the inability to enter into harmony and oneness with the universe and a consequent inability to possess and enjoy it. But the desire to possess and enjoy is the master impulse of the Ego which knows itself obscurely to be the Lord, although owing to the limitations of its relativity, it is unable to realise its true existence. The result is discord with others and oneself, mental and physical suffering, the sense of weakness and inability, the sense of obscuration, the straining of energy in passion and in desire towards self-fulfilment, the recoil of energy exhausted or disappointed towards death and disintegration.

Desire is the badge of subjection with its attendant discord and suffering. That which is free, one and lord, does not desire, but inalienably contains, possesses and enjoys.

THE RULE OF THE DIVINE LIFE

Enjoyment of the universe and all it contains is the object of world-existence, but renunciation of all in desire is the condition of the free enjoyment of all.

The renunciation demanded is not a moral constraint of self-denial or a physical rejection, but an entire liberation of the spirit from any craving after the forms of things.

The terms of this liberation are freedom from egoism and,

consequently, freedom from personal desire. Practically, this renunciation implies that one should not regard anything in the universe as a necessary object of possession, nor as possessed by another and not by oneself, nor as an object of greed in the heart or the senses.

This attitude is founded on the perception of unity. For it has already been said that all souls are one possessing Self, the Lord; and although the Lord inhabits each object as if separately, yet all objects exist in that Self and not outside it.

Therefore by transcending Ego and realising the one Self, we possess the whole universe in the one cosmic consciousness and do not need to possess physically.

Having by oneness with the Lord the possibility of an infinite free delight in all things, we do not need to desire.

Being one with all beings, we possess, in their enjoyment, in ours and in the cosmic Being's, delight of universal self-expression. It is only by this Ananda at once transcendent and universal that man can be free in his soul and yet live in the world with the full active Life of the Lord in His universe of movement.

THE JUSTIFICATION OF WORKS

This freedom does not depend upon inaction, nor is this possession limited to the enjoyment of the inactive Soul that only witnesses without taking part in the movement.

On the contrary, the doing of works in this material world and a full acceptance of the term of physical life are part of its completeness.

For the active Brahman fulfils Itself in the world by works and man also is in the body for self-fulfilment by action. He cannot do otherwise, for even his inertia acts and produces effects in the cosmic movement. Being in this body or any kind of body, it is idle to think of refraining from action or escaping the physical life. The idea that this in itself can be a means of liberation, is part of the Ignorance which supposes the soul to be a separate entity in the Brahman.

Action is shunned because it is thought to be inconsistent with freedom. The man when he acts, is supposed to be necessarily entangled in the desire behind the action, in subjection to the formal energy that drives the action and in the results of the action. These things are true in appearance, not in reality.

Desire is only a mode of the emotional mind which by ignorance seeks its delight in the object of desire and not in the Brahman who expresses Himself in the object. By destroying that ignorance one can do action without entanglement in desire.

The Energy that drives is itself subject to the Lord, who expresses Himself in it with perfect freedom. By getting behind Nature to the Lord of Nature, merging the individual in the Cosmic Will, one can act with the divine freedom. Our actions are given up to the Lord and our personal responsibility ceases in His liberty.

The chain of Karma only binds the movement of Nature and not the soul which, by knowing itself, ceases even to appear to be bound by the results of its works.

Therefore the way of freedom is not inaction, but to cease from identifying oneself with the movement and recover instead our true identity in the Self of things who is their Lord.

THE OTHER WORLDS

By departing from the physical life one does not disappear out of the Movement, but only passes into some other general state of consciousness than the material universe.

These states are either obscure or illuminated, some dark or sunless.

By persisting in gross forms of ignorance, by coercing perversely the soul in its self-fulfilment or by a wrong dissolution of its becoming in the Movement, one enters into states of blind darkness, not into the worlds of light and of liberated and blissful being.

II

[1]

Brahman:
Oneness of God and the World

Verses 4 – 5*

BRAHMAN — THE UNITY

The Lord and the world, even when they seem to be distinct, are not really different from each other; they are one Brahman.

"ONE UNMOVING"

God is the one stable and eternal Reality. He is One because there is nothing else, since all existence and non-existence are He. He is stable or unmoving, because motion implies change in Space and change in Time, and He, being beyond Time and Space, is immutable. He possesses eternally in Himself all that is, has been or ever can be, and He therefore does not increase or diminish. He is beyond causality and relativity and therefore there is no change of relations in His being.

---

* 4. One unmoving that is swifter than Mind; That the Gods reach not, for It progresses ever in front. That, standing, passes beyond others as they run. In That the Master of Life establishes the Waters.

5. That moves and That moves not; That is far and the same is near; That is within all this and That also is outside all this.

"SWIFTER THAN MIND"

The world is a cyclic movement (*saṁsāra*) of the Divine Consciousness in Space and Time. Its law and, in a sense, its object is progression; it exists by movement and would be dissolved by cessation of movement. But the basis of this movement is not material; it is the energy of active consciousness which, by its motion and multiplication in different principles (different in appearance, the same in essence), creates oppositions of unity and multiplicity, divisions of Time and Space, relations and groupings of circumstance and Causality. All these things are real in consciousness, but only symbolic of the Being, somewhat as the imaginations of a creative Mind are true representations of itself, yet not quite real in comparison with itself, or real with a different kind of reality.

But mental consciousness is not the Power that creates the universe. That is something infinitely more puissant, swift and unfettered than the mind. It is the pure omnipotent self-awareness of the Absolute unbound by any law of the relativity. The laws of the relativity, upheld by the gods, are Its temporary creations. Their apparent eternity is only the duration, immeasurable to us, of the world which they govern. They are laws regularising motion and change, not laws binding the Lord of the movement. The gods, therefore, are described as continually running in their course. But the Lord is free and unaffected by His own movement.

"THAT MOVES, THAT MOVES NOT"

The motion of the world works under the government of a perpetual stability. Change represents the constant shifting of apparent relations in an eternal Immutability.

It is these truths that are expressed in the formulae of the one Unmoving that is swifter than Mind, That which moves and moves not, the one Stable which outstrips in the speed of its effective consciousness the others who run.

TRANSITIONAL THOUGHT

THE MANY[1]

If the One is pre-eminently real, "the others", the Many are not unreal. The world is not a figment of the Mind.

Unity is the eternal truth of things, diversity a play of the unity. The sense of unity has therefore been termed Knowledge, Vidya, the sense of diversity Ignorance, Avidya. But diversity is not false except when it is divorced from the sense of its true and eternal unity.

Brahman is one, not numerically, but in essence. Numerical oneness would either exclude multiplicity or would be a pluralistic and divisible oneness with the Many as its parts. That is not the unity of Brahman, which can neither be diminished nor increased, nor divided.

The Many in the universe are sometimes called parts of the universal Brahman as the waves are parts of the sea. But, in truth, these waves are each of them that sea, their diversities being those of frontal or superficial appearances caused by the sea's motion. As each object in the universe is really the whole universe in a different frontal appearance, so each individual soul is all Brahman regarding Itself and world from a centre of cosmic consciousness.

For That is identical, not single. It is identical always and everywhere in Time and Space, as well as identical beyond Time and Space. Numerical oneness and multiplicity are equally valid terms of its essential unity.

These two terms, as we see them, are like all others, representations in Chit, in the free and all-creative self-awareness of

---

[1] The series of ideas under this heading seem to me to be the indispensable metaphysical basis of the Upanishad. The Isha Upanishad does not teach a pure and exclusive Monism; it declares the One without denying the Many and its method is to see the One in the Many. It asserts the simultaneous validity of Vidya and Avidya and upholds as the object of action and knowledge an immortality consistent with Life and Birth in this world. It regards every object as itself the universe and every soul as itself the divine Purusha. The ensemble of these ideas is consistent only with a synthetic or comprehensive as opposed to an illusionist or exclusive Monism.

the Absolute regarding itself variously, infinitely, innumerably and formulating what it regards. Chit is a power not only of knowledge, but of expressive will, not only of receptive vision, but of formative representation; the two are indeed one power. For Chit is an action of Being, not of the Void. What it sees, that becomes. It sees itself beyond Space and Time; that becomes in the conditions of Space and Time.

Creation is not a making of something out of nothing or of one thing out of another, but a self-projection of Brahman into the conditions of Space and Time. Creation is not a making, but a becoming in terms and forms of conscious existence.

In the becoming each individual is Brahman variously represented and entering into various relations with Itself in the play of the divine consciousness; in being, each individual is all Brahman.

Brahman as the Absolute or the Universal has the power of standing back from Itself in the relativity. It conceives, by a subordinate movement of consciousness, the individual as other than the universal, the relative as different from the Absolute. Without this separative movement, the individual would always tend to lose itself in the universal, the relative to disappear into the Absolute. Thus, It supports a corresponding reaction in the individual who regards himself as "other" than the transcendent and universal Brahman and "other" than the rest of the Many. He puts identity behind him and enforces the play of Being in the separative Ego.

The individual may regard himself as eternally different from the One, or as eternally one with It, yet different, or he may go back entirely in his consciousness to the pure Identity.[2] But he can never regard himself as independent of some kind of Unity, for such a view would correspond to no conceivable truth in the universe or beyond it.

These three attitudes correspond to three truths of the

---

[2] The positions, in inverse order, of the three principal philosophical schools of Vedanta, Monism, Qualified Monism and Dualism.

Brahman which are simultaneously valid and none of them entirely true without the others as its complements. Their co-existence, difficult of conception to the logical intellect, can be experienced by identity in consciousness with Brahman.

Even in asserting Oneness, we must remember that Brahman is beyond our mental distinctions and is a fact not of Thought that discriminates, but of Being which is absolute, infinite and escapes discrimination. Our consciousness is representative and symbolic; it cannot conceive the thing-in-itself, the Absolute, except by negation, in a sort of void, by emptying it of all that it seems in the universe to contain. But the Absolute is not a void or negation. It is all that is here in Time and beyond Time.

Even oneness is a representation and exists in relation to multiplicity. Vidya and Avidya are equally eternal powers of the supreme Chit. Neither Vidya nor Avidya by itself is the absolute knowledge. (See verses 9 – 11.)

Still, of all relations oneness is the secret base, not multiplicity. Oneness constitutes and upholds the multiplicity, multiplicity does not constitute and uphold the oneness.

Therefore we have to conceive of oneness as our self and the essential nature of Being, multiplicity as a representation of Self and a becoming. We have to conceive of the Brahman as One Self of all and then return upon the Many as becomings of the One Being (*bhūtāni . . . ātman*). But both the Self and the becomings are Brahman; we cannot regard the one as Brahman and the others as unreal and not Brahman. Both are real, the one with a constituent and comprehensive, the others with a derivative or dependent reality.

THE RUNNING OF THE GODS

Brahman representing Itself in the universe as the Stable, by Its immutable existence (Sat), is Purusha, God, Spirit; representing Itself as the Motional, by Its power of active Consciousness (Chit), is Nature, Force or World-Principle (Prakriti, Shakti,

Maya).[3] The play of these two principles is the Life of the universe.

The Gods are Brahman representing Itself in cosmic Personalities expressive of the one Godhead who, in their impersonal action, appear as the various play of the principles of Nature.

The "others" are *sarvāṇi bhūtāni* of a later verse, all becomings, Brahman representing itself in the separative consciousness of the Many.

Everything in the universe, even the Gods, seems to itself to be moving in the general movement towards a goal outside itself or other than its immediate idea of itself. Brahman is the goal; for it is both the beginning and the end, the cause and the result of all movement.

But the idea of a final goal in the movement of Nature itself is illusory. For Brahman is Absolute and Infinite. The Gods, labouring to reach him, find, at every goal that they realise, Brahman still moving forward in front to a farther realisation. Nothing in the appearances of the universe can be entirely That to the relative consciousness; all is only a symbolic representation of the Unknowable.

All things are already realised in Brahman. The running of the Others in the course of Nature is only a working out (Prakriti), by Causality, in Time and Space, of something that Brahman already possesses.

Even in Its universal being Brahman exceeds the Movement. Exceeding Time, It contains in Itself past, present and future simultaneously and has not to run to the end of conceivable Time. Exceeding Space, It contains all formations in Itself coincidently

---

[3] Prakriti, executive Nature as opposed to Purusha, which is the Soul governing, taking cognizance of and enjoying the works of Prakriti. Shakti, the self-existent, self-cognitive, self-effective Power of the Lord (Ishwara, Deva or Purusha), which expresses itself in the workings of Prakriti. Maya, signifying originally in the Veda comprehensive and creative knowledge, Wisdom that is from of old; afterwards taken in its second and derivative sense, cunning, magic, Illusion. In this second significance it can really be appropriate only to the workings of the lower Nature, *aparā prakṛti*, which has put behind it the Divine Wisdom and is absorbed in the experiences of the separative Ego. It is in the more ancient sense that the word Maya is used in the Upanishads, where, indeed, it occurs but rarely.

and has not to run to the end of conceivable Space. Exceeding Causality, It contains freely in Itself all eventualities as well as all potentialities without being bound by the apparent chain of causality by which they are linked in the universe. Everything is already realised by It as the Lord before it can be accomplished by the separated Personalities in the movement.

THE PRINCIPLE OF LIFE

MATARISHWAN AND THE WATERS

What then is Its intention in the movement?

The movement is a rhythm, a harmony which That, as the Universal Life, works out by figures of Itself in the terms of conscious Being. It is a formula symbolically expressive of the Unknowable, — so arranged that every level of consciousness really represents something beyond itself, depth of depth, continent of continent. It is a play[4] of the divine Consciousness existing for its own satisfaction and adding nothing to That, which is already complete. It is a fact of conscious being, justified by its own existence, with no purpose ulterior to itself. The idea of purpose, of a goal is born of the progressive self-unfolding by the world of its own true nature to the individual Souls inhabiting its forms; for the Being is gradually self-revealed within its own becomings, real Unity emerges out of the Multiplicity and changes entirely the values of the latter to our consciousness.

This self-unfolding is governed by conditions determined by the complexity of consciousness in its cosmic action.

For consciousness is not simple or homogeneous, it is septuple. That is to say, it constitutes itself into seven forms or grades of conscious activity descending from pure Being to physical being. Their interplay creates the worlds, determines all activities, constitutes all becomings.

---

[4] This is the Vaishnava image of the Lila applied usually to the play of the Personal Deity in the world, but equally applicable to the active impersonal Brahman.

Brahman is always the continent of this play or this working. Brahman self-extended in Space and Time is the universe.

In this extension Brahman represents Itself as formative Nature, the universal Mother of things, who appears to us, first, as Matter, called Prithivi, the Earth-Principle.

Brahman in Matter or physical being represents Itself as the universal Life-Power, Matarishwan, which moves there as a dynamic energy, Prana, and presides effectively over all arrangement and formation.

Universal Life establishes, involved in Matter, the septuple consciousness; and the action of Prana, the dynamic energy, on the Matrix of things evolves out of it its different forms and serves as a basis for all their evolutions.

TRANSITIONAL THOUGHT

THE WATERS

There are, then, seven constituents of Chit active in the universe.

We are habitually aware of three elements in our being, Mind, Life and Body. These constitute for us a divided and mutable existence which is in a condition of unstable harmony and works by a strife of positive and negative forces between the two poles of Birth and Death. For all life is a constant birth or becoming (*sambhava, sambhūti* of verses 12 – 14). All birth entails a constant death or dissolution of that which becomes, in order that it may change into a new becoming. Therefore this state of existence is called Mrityu, Death, and described as a stage which has to be passed through and transcended. (*Verses 11, 14*)

For this is not the whole of our being and, therefore, not our pure being. We have, behind, a superconscious existence which has also three constituents, Sat, Chit-Tapas and Ananda.

Sat is essence of our being, pure, infinite and undivided, as opposed to this divisible being which founds itself on the constant changeableness of physical substance. Sat is the divine counterpart of physical substance.

Chit-Tapas is pure energy of Consciousness, free in its rest or its action, sovereign in its will, as opposed to the hampered dynamic energies of Prana which, feeding upon physical substances, are dependent on and limited by their sustenance.[5] Tapas is the divine counterpart of this lower nervous or vital energy.

Ananda is Beatitude, the bliss of pure conscious existence and energy, as opposed to the life of the sensations and emotions which are at the mercy of the outward touches of Life and Matter and their positive and negative reactions, joy and grief, pleasure and pain. Ananda is the divine counterpart of the lower emotional and sensational being.

This higher existence, proper to the divine Sachchidananda, is unified, self-existent, not confused by the figures of Birth and Death. It is called, therefore, Amritam, Immortality, and offered to us as the goal to be aimed at and the felicity to be enjoyed when we have transcended the state of death. (*Verses 11, 14, 17, 18*)

The higher divine is linked to the lower mortal existence by the causal Idea[6] or supramental Knowledge-Will, Vijnana. It is the causal Idea which, by supporting and secretly guiding the confused activities of the Mind, Life and Body, ensures and compels the right arrangement of the universe. It is called in the Veda the Truth because it represents by direct vision the truth of things both inclusive and independent of their appearances; the Right or Law, because, containing in itself the effective power of Chit, it works out all things according to their nature with a perfect knowledge and prevision; the Vast, because it is of the nature of an infinite cosmic Intelligence comprehensive of all particular activities.

Vijnana, as the Truth, leads the divided consciousness back

---

[5] Therefore physical substance is called in the Upanishads Annam, Food. In its origin, however, the word meant simply being or substance.

[6] Not the abstract mental idea, but the supramental Real-Idea, the Consciousness, Force and Delight of the Being precipitated into a comprehensive and discriminative awareness of all the truths and powers of its own existence, carrying in its self-knowledge the will of self-manifestation, the power of all its potentialities and the power of all its forms. It is power that acts and effectuates, as well as knowledge master of its own action.

to the One. It also sees the truth of things in the multiplicity. Vijnana is the divine counterpart of the lower divided intelligence.

These seven powers of Chit are spoken of by the Vedic Rishis as the Waters, they are imaged as currents flowing into or rising out of the general sea of Consciousness in the human being.[7]

They are all coexistent in the universe eternally and inseparably, but capable of being involved and remanifested in each other. They are actually involved in physical Nature and must necessarily evolve out of it. They can be withdrawn into pure infinite Being and can again be manifested out of it.

The infolding and unfolding of the One in the Many and the Many in the One is therefore the law of the eternally recurrent cosmic Cycles.

THE VISION OF THE BRAHMAN

The Upanishad teaches us how to perceive Brahman in the universe and in our self-existence.

We have to perceive Brahman comprehensively as both the Stable and the Moving. We must see It in eternal and immutable Spirit and in all the changing manifestations of universe and relativity.

We have to perceive all things in Space and Time, the far and the near, the immemorial Past, the immediate Present, the infinite Future with all their contents and happenings as the One Brahman.

We have to perceive Brahman as that which exceeds, contains and supports all individual things as well as all universe, transcendentally of Time and Space and Causality. We have to perceive It also as that which lives in and possesses the universe and all it contains.

This is the transcendental, universal and individual Brahman, Lord, Continent and Indwelling Spirit, which is the object of all knowledge. Its realisation is the condition of perfection and the way of Immortality.

---

[7] *Hṛdya samudra*, Ocean of the Heart. R.V. IV. 58. 5.

III

[2]

Self-Realisation

Verses 6 – 7*

SELF-REALISATION

Brahman is, subjectively, Atman, the Self or immutable existence of all that is in the universe. Everything that changes in us, mind, life, body, character, temperament, action, is not our real and unchanging self, but becomings of the Self in the movement, *jagatī*.

In Nature, therefore, all things that exist, animate or inanimate, are becomings of the one Self of all. All these different creatures are one indivisible existence. This is the truth each being has to realise.

When this unity has been realised by the individual in every part of his being, he becomes perfect, pure, liberated from ego and the dualities, possessed of the entire divine felicity.

ATMAN

Atman, our true self, is Brahman; it is pure indivisible Being, self-luminous, self-concentrated in consciousness, self-concentrated in force, self-delighted. Its existence is light and bliss. It is timeless, spaceless and free.

---

* 6. But he who sees everywhere the Self in all existences and all existences in the Self, shrinks not thereafter from aught.

7. He in whom it is the Self-Being that has become all existences that are Becomings, for he has the perfect knowledge, how shall he be deluded, whence shall he have grief who sees everywhere oneness?

THE THREEFOLD PURUSHA[1]

Atman represents itself to the consciousness of the creature in three states, dependent on the relations between Purusha and Prakriti, the Soul and Nature. These three states are Akshara, unmoving or immutable; Kshara, moving or mutable; and Para or Uttama, Supreme or Highest.

Kshara Purusha is the Self reflecting the changes and movements of Nature, participating in them, immersed in the consciousness of the movement and seeming in it to be born and die, increase and diminish, progress and change. Atman, as the Kshara, enjoys change and division and duality; controls secretly its own changes but seems to be controlled by them; enjoys the oppositions of pleasure and pain, good and bad, but appears to be their victim; possesses and upholds the action of Nature, by which it seems to be created. For, always and inalienably, the Self is Ishwara, the Lord.

Akshara Purusha is the Self standing back from the changes and movements of Nature, calm, pure, impartial, indifferent, watching them and not participating, above them as on a summit, not immersed in these Waters. This calm Self is the sky that never moves and changes looking down upon the waters that are never at rest. The Akshara is the hidden freedom of the Kshara.

Para Purusha or Purushottama is the Self containing and enjoying both the stillness and the movement, but conditioned and limited by neither of them. It is the Lord, Brahman, the All, the Indefinable and Unknowable.

It is this supreme Self that has to be realised in both the unmoving and the mutable.

PURUSHA IN PRAKRITI[2]

Atman, the Self, represents itself differently in the sevenfold movement of Nature according to the dominant principle of the consciousness in the individual being.

---

[1] Gita XV. 16, 17. See also XIII passim.
[2] Taittiriya Upanishad II. 1–6.

In the physical consciousness Atman becomes the material being, *annamaya puruṣa.*

In the vital or nervous consciousness Atman becomes the vital or dynamic being, *prāṇamaya puruṣa.*

In the mental consciousness Atman becomes the mental being, *manomaya puruṣa.*

In the supra-intellectual consciousness, dominated by the Truth or causal Idea (called in Veda Satyam, Ritam, Brihat, the True, the Right, the Vast), Atman becomes the ideal being or great Soul, *vijñānamaya puruṣa* or *mahat ātman.*[3]

In the consciousness proper to the universal Beatitude, Atman becomes the all-blissful being or all-enjoying and all-productive Soul, *ānandamaya puruṣa.*

In the consciousness proper to the infinite divine self-awareness which is also the infinite all-effective Will (Chit-Tapas), Atman is the all-conscious Soul that is source and lord of the universe, *caitanya puruṣa.*

In the consciousness proper to the state of pure divine existence Atman is *sat puruṣa,* the pure divine Self.

Man, being one in his true Self with the Lord who inhabits all forms, can live in any of these states of the Self in the world and partake of its experiences. He can be anything he wills from the material to the all-blissful being. Through the Anandamaya he can enter into the Chaitanya and Sat Purusha.

SACHCHIDANANDA

Sachchidananda is the manifestation of the higher Purusha; its nature of infinite being, consciousness, power and bliss is the higher Nature, *parā prakṛti.* Mind, life and body are the lower nature, *aparā prakṛti.*

The state of Sachchidananda is the higher half of universal existence, *parārdha,* the nature of which is Immortality, Amritam. The state of mental existence in Matter is the lower half,

---

[3] The *mahat ātman* or Vast Self is frequently referred to in the Upanishads. It is also called *bhūmā,* the Large.

aparārdha, the nature of which is death, Mrityu.

Mind and life in the body are in the state of Death because by Ignorance they fail to realise Sachchidananda. Realising perfectly Sachchidananda, they can convert themselves, Mind into the nature of the Truth, Vijnana, Life into the nature of Chaitanya, Body into the nature of Sat, that is, into the pure essence.

When this cannot be done perfectly in the body, the soul realises its true state in other forms of existence or worlds, the "sunlit" worlds and states of felicity, and returns upon material existence to complete its evolution in the body.

A progressively perfect realisation in the body is the aim of human evolution.

It is also possible for the soul to withdraw for an indefinable period into the pure state of Sachchidananda.

The realisation of the Self as Sachchidananda is the aim of human existence.

THE CONDITION OF SELF-REALISATION[4]

Sachchidananda is always the pure state of Atman; it may either remain self-contained as if apart from the universe or overlook, embrace and possess it as the Lord.

In fact, it does both simultaneously. (*Verse 8*)

The Lord pervades the universe as the Virat Purusha, the Cosmic Soul (*paribhū* of the eighth verse, the One who becomes everywhere); He enters into each object in the movement, to the Knowledge as Brahman supporting individual consciousness and individual form, to the Ignorance as an individualised and limited being. He manifests as the Jivatman or individual self in the living creature.

From the standpoint of our lower state in the kingdom of death and limitation Atman is Sachchidananda, supra-mental,

---

[4] I have collected under this and the preceding headings the principal ideas of the Upanishads with regard to the Self, although not expressly mentioned or alluded to in our text, because they are indispensable to an understanding of the complete philosophy of these Scriptures and to the relations of the thought which is developed in the Isha.

but reflected in the mind. If the mind is pure, bright and still, there is the right reflection; if it is unpurified, troubled and obscured, the reflection is distorted and subjected to the crooked action of the Ignorance.

According to the state of the reflecting mind we may have either purity of self-knowledge or an obscuration and distortion of knowledge in the dualities of truth and error; a pure activity of unegoistic Will or an obscuration and deflection of Will in the dualities of right and wrong action, sin and virtue; a pure state and unmixed play of beatitude or an obscuration and perversion of it in the dualities of right and wrong enjoyment, pleasure and pain, joy and grief.

It is the mental ego-sense that creates this distortion by division and limitation of the Self. The limitation is brought about through the Kshara Purusha identifying itself with the changeable formations of Nature in the separate body, the individual life and the egoistic mind, to the exclusion of the sense of unity with all existence and with all existences.

This exclusion is a fixed habit of the understanding due to our past evolution in the movement, not an ineffugable law of human consciousness. Its diminution and final disappearance are the condition of self-realisation.

The beginning of wisdom, perfection and beatitude is the vision of the One.

THE STAGES OF SELF-REALISATION

THE VISION OF THE ALL

The first movement of self-realisation is the sense of unity with other existences in the universe. Its early or crude form is the attempt to understand or sympathise with others, the tendency of a widening love or compassion or fellow-feeling for others, the impulsion of work for the sake of others.

The oneness so realised is a pluralistic unity, the drawing together of similar units resulting in a collectivity or solidarity rather than in real oneness. The Many remain to the consciousness as the real existences; the One is only their result.

Real knowledge begins with the perception of essential oneness, — one Matter, one Life, one Mind, one Soul playing in many forms.

When this Soul of things is seen to be Sachchidananda, then knowledge is perfected. For we see Matter to be only a play of Life, Life a play of Mind energising itself in substance, Mind a play of Truth or causal Idea representing truth of being variously in all possible mental forms, Truth a play of Sachchidananda, Sachchidananda the self-manifestation of a supreme Unknowable, Para-Brahman or Para-Purusha.

We perceive the soul in all bodies to be this one Self or Sachchidananda multiplying itself in individual consciousness. We see also all minds, lives, bodies to be active formations of the same existence in the extended being of the Self.

This is the vision of all existences in the Self and of the Self in all existences which is the foundation of perfect internal liberty and perfect joy and peace.

For by this vision, in proportion as it increases in intensity and completeness, there disappears from the individual mentality all *jugupsā*, that is to say, all repulsion, shrinking, dislike, fear, hatred and other perversions of feeling which arise from division and personal opposition to other beings or to the objectivities that surround us. Perfect equality[5] of soul is established.

THE VISION OF THE SELF IN ITS BECOMINGS

Vision is not sufficient; one must become what inwardly one sees. The whole inner life must be changed so as to represent perfectly in all parts of the being what is understood by the intellect and seen by the inner perception.

---

[5] The state described in the Gita as *samatva*. *Jugupsā* is the feeling of repulsion caused by the sense of a want of harmony between one's own limited self-formation and the contacts of the external with a consequent recoil of grief, fear, hatred, discomfort, suffering. It is the opposite of attraction which is the source of desire and attachment. Repulsion and attraction removed, we have *samatva*.

In the individual soul extending itself to the All by the vision of unity (*ekatvam anupaśyataḥ*, seeing everywhere oneness), arranging its thoughts, emotions and sensations according to the perfect knowledge of the right relation of things which comes by the realisation of the Truth (*vijānataḥ*, having the perfect knowledge), there must be repeated the divine act of consciousness by which the one Being, eternally self-existent, manifests in itself the multiplicity of the world (*sarvāṇi bhūtāni ātmaiva abhūt*, the Self-Being became all Becomings).

That is to say, the human or egoistic view is that of a world of innumerable separate creatures each self-existent and different from the others, each trying to get its utmost possible profit out of the others and the world, but the divine view, the way in which God sees the world, is Himself, as the sole Being, living in innumerable existences that are Himself, supporting all, helping all impartially, working out to a divine fulfilment and under terms fixed from the beginning, from years sempiternal, a great progressive harmony of Becoming whose last term is Sachchidananda or Immortality. This is the view-point of the Self as Lord inhabiting the whole movement. The individual soul has to change the human or egoistic for the divine, supreme and universal view and live in that realisation.

It is necessary, therefore, to have the knowledge of the transcendent Self, the sole unity, in the equation *so'ham*, I am He, and in that knowledge to extend one's conscious existence so as to embrace the whole Multiplicity.

This is the double or synthetic ideal of the Isha Upanishad; to embrace simultaneously Vidya and Avidya, the One and the Many; to exist in the world, but change the terms of the Death into the terms of the Immortality; to have the freedom and peace of the Non-Birth simultaneously with the activity of the Birth. (*Verses 9–14*)

All parts of the lower being must consent to this realisation; to perceive with the intellect is not enough. The heart must consent in a universal love and delight, the sense-mind in a sensation of God and self everywhere, the life in the comprehension of all aims and energies in the world as part of its own being.

THE ACTIVE BEATITUDE

This realisation is the perfect and complete Beatitude, embracing action, but delivered from sorrow and self-delusion.

There is no possibility of self-delusion (*moha*); for the soul, having attained to the perception of the Unknowable behind all existence, is no longer attached to the Becoming and no longer attributes an absolute value to any particularity in the universe, as if that were an object in itself and desirable in itself. All is enjoyable and has a value as the manifestation of the Self and for the sake of the Self which is manifested in it, but none for its own.[6] Desire and illusion are removed; illusion is replaced by knowledge, desire by the active beatitude of universal possession.

There is no possibility of sorrow; for all is seen as Sachchidananda and therefore in the terms of the infinite conscious existence, the infinite will, the infinite felicity. Even pain and grief are seen to be perverse terms of Ananda, and that Ananda which they veil here and for which they prepare the lower existence (for all suffering in the evolution is a preparation of strength and bliss) is already seized, known and enjoyed by the soul thus liberated and perfected. For it possesses the eternal Reality of which they are the appearances.

Thus it is possible, by the realisation of the unity of God and the world (*īś* and *jagatī*) in the complete knowledge of the Brahman, to renounce desire and illusion through the ascent to the pure Self and the Non-Becoming and yet to enjoy by means of all things in the manifestation God in the universe through a free and illuminated self-identification with Sachchidananda in all existences.

CONCLUSION

We have, therefore, in the second movement the explanation of the first verse of the Upanishad. The first line, asserting that all

---

[6] Brihadaranyaka Upanishad.

souls are the one Lord inhabiting every object in the universe and that every object is universe in universe, movement in the general movement, has been explained in the terms of complete oneness by the Brahman, transcendental and universal even in the individual, One in the Many, Many in the One, Stable and Motional, exceeding and reconciling all opposites. The second line, fixing as the rule of divine life universal renunciation of desire as the condition of universal enjoyment in the spirit, has been explained by the state of self-realisation, the realisation of the free and transcendent Self as one's own true being, of that Self as Sachchidananda and of the universe seen as the Becoming of Sachchidananda and possessed in the terms of the right knowledge and no longer in the terms of the Ignorance which is the cause of all attraction and repulsion, self-delusion and sorrow.

IV

[1]

The Lord

Verse 8*

"HE"

In its third movement the Upanishad takes up the justification of works already stated in general terms in its second verse and founds it more precisely upon the conception of Brahman or the Self as the Lord, — Ish, Ishwara, Para Purusha, Sa (He) — who is the cause of personality and governs by His law of works the rhythm of the Movement and the process of the worlds that He conceives and realises throughout eternal Time in His own self-existence.

It is an error to conceive that the Upanishads teach the true existence only of an impersonal and actionless Brahman, an impersonal God without power or qualities. They declare rather an Unknowable that manifests itself to us in a double aspect of Personality and Impersonality. When they wish to speak of this Unknowable in the most comprehensive and general way, they use the neuter and call It *Tat*, That; but this neuter does not exclude the aspect of universal and transcendent Personality acting and governing the world (cf. Kena Upanishad III). Still, when they intend to make prominent the latter idea they more often prefer to use the masculine Sa, He, or else they employ the

---

* 8. It is He that has gone abroad — That which is bright, bodiless, without scar of imperfection, without sinews, pure, unpierced by evil. The Seer, the Thinker, the One who becomes everywhere, the Self-existent has ordered objects perfectly according to their nature from years sempiternal.

term Deva, God or the Divine, or Purusha, the conscious Soul, of whom Prakriti or Maya is the executive Puissance, the Shakti.

The Isha Upanishad, having declared the Brahman as the sole reality manifesting itself in many aspects and forms, having presented this Brahman subjectively as the Self, the one Being of whom all existences are Becomings, and as that which we have to realise in ourselves and in all things and beyond all things, now proceeds to assert the same Brahman more objectively as the Lord, the Purusha who both contains and inhabits the universe.

It is He that went abroad. This Brahman, this Self is identical with the Lord, the Ish, with whose name the Upanishad opens, the Inhabitant of all forms: and, as we shall find, identical with the universal Purusha of the 16th verse, — "The Purusha there and there, He am I." It is He who has become all things and beings, — a conscious Being, the sole Existent and Self-existent, who is Master and Enjoyer of all He becomes. And the Upanishad proceeds to formulate the nature and manner, the general law of that becoming of God which we call the world. For on this conception depends the Vedic idea of the two poles of death and immortality, the reason for the existence of Avidya, the Ignorance, and the justification of works in the world.

TRANSITIONAL THOUGHT

THE DIVINE PERSONALITY

The Vedantic idea of God, "He", Deva or Ishwara, must not be confused with the ordinary notions attached to the conception of a Personal God. Personality is generally conceived as identical with individuality and the vulgar idea of a Personal God is a magnified individual like man in His nature but yet different, greater, more vast and all-overpowering. Vedanta admits the human manifestation of Brahman in man and to man, but does not admit that this is the real nature of the Ishwara.

God is Sachchidananda. He manifests Himself as infinite existence of which the essentiality is consciousness, of which again the essentiality is bliss, is self-delight. Delight cognizing variety of itself, seeking its own variety, as it were, becomes the universe. But these are abstract terms; abstract ideas in themselves cannot produce concrete realities. They are impersonal states; impersonal states cannot in themselves produce personal activities.

This becomes still clearer if we consider the manifestation of Sachchidananda. In that manifestation Delight translates itself into Love; Consciousness translates itself into double terms, conceptive Knowledge, executive Force; Existence translates itself into Being, that is to say, into Person and Substance. But Love is incomplete without a Lover and an object of Love, Knowledge without a Knower and an object of Knowledge, Force without a Worker and a Work, Substance without a Person cognizing and constituting it.

This is because the original terms also are not really impersonal abstractions. In delight of Brahman there is an Enjoyer of delight, in consciousness of Brahman a Conscient, in existence of Brahman an Existent; but the object of Brahman's delight and consciousness and the term and stuff of Its existence are Itself. In the divine Being Knowledge, the Knower and the Known and, therefore, necessarily also Delight, the Enjoyer and the Enjoyed are one.

This Self-Awareness and Self-Delight of Brahman has two modes of its Force of consciousness, its Prakriti or Maya, — intensive in self-absorption, diffusive in self-extension. The intensive mode is proper to the pure and silent Brahman; the diffusive to the active Brahman. It is the diffusion of the Self-existent in the term and stuff of His own existence that we call the world, the becoming or the perpetual movement (*bhuvanam, jagat*). It is Brahman that becomes; what He becomes is also the Brahman. The object of Love is the self of the Lover; the work is the self-figuration of the Worker; Universe is body and action of the Lord.

When, therefore, we consider the abstract and impersonal aspect of the infinite existence, we say, "That"; when we consider the Existent self-aware and self-blissful, we say, "He". Neither conception is entirely complete. Brahman itself is the Unknowable beyond all conceptions of Personality and Impersonality. We may call it "That" to show that we exile from our affirmation all term and definition. We may equally call it "He", provided we speak with the same intention of rigorous exclusion. "Tat" and "Sa" are always the same, One that escapes definition.

In the universe there is a constant relation of Oneness and Multiplicity. This expresses itself as the universal Personality and the many Persons, and both between the One and the Many and among the Many themselves there is the possibility of an infinite variety of relations. These relations are determined by the play of the divine existence, the Lord, entering into His manifested habitations. They exist at first as conscious relations between individual souls; they are then taken up by them and used as a means of entering into conscious relation with the One. It is this entering into various relations with the One which is the object and function of Religion. All religions are justified by this essential necessity; all express one Truth in various ways and move by various paths to one goal.

The Divine Personality reveals Himself in various forms and names to the individual soul. These forms and names are in a sense created in the human consciousness; in another they are eternal symbols revealed by the Divine who thus concretises Himself in mind-form to the multiple consciousness and aids it in its return to its own Unity.[1]

HE THAT WENT ABROAD

It is He that has extended Himself in the relative consciousness whose totality of finite and changeable circumstances dependent on an equal, immutable and eternal Infinity is what we call the Universe. *Sa paryagāt.*

In this extension we have, therefore, two aspects, one of pure infinite relationless immutability, another of a totality of objects

---

[1] It would be an error to suppose that these conceptions are in their essence later developments of philosophical Hinduism. The conception of the many forms and names of the One is as old as the Rig Veda.

in Time and Space working out their relations through causality. Both are different and mutually complementary expressions of the same unknowable "He".

To express the infinite Immutability the Upanishad uses a series of neuter adjectives, "Bright, bodiless, without scar, without sinews, pure, unpierced by evil." To express the same Absolute as cause, continent and governing Inhabitant of the totality of objects and of each object in the totality (*jagatyāṁ jagat*) it uses four masculine epithets, "The Seer, the Thinker, the One who becomes everywhere, the Self-existent" or "the Self-Becoming".

The Immutable is the still and secret foundation of the play and the movement, extended equally, impartially in all things, *samaṁ brahma*,[2] lending its support to all without choice or active participation. Secure and free in His eternal immutability the Lord projects Himself into the play and the movement, becoming there in His self-existence all that the Seer in Him visualises and the Thinker in Him conceives. *Kavir manīṣī paribhūḥ svayambhūḥ.*

THE PURE IMMUTABLE

The pure immutability of the Lord is "bright". It is a luminosity of pure concentrated Self-awareness, not broken by refractions, not breaking out into colour and form. It is the pure self-knowledge of the Purusha, the conscious Soul, with his Power, his executive Force contained and inactive.

It is "bodiless", — without form, indivisible and without appearance of division. It is one equal Purusha in all things, not divided by the divisions of Space and Time, — a pure self-conscious Absolute.

It is without scar, that is, without defect, break or imperfection. It is untouched and unaffected by the mutabilities. It supports their clash of relations, their play of more and less, of increase and diminution, of irruption and interpenetration.

---

2 "The equal Brahman." — Gita.

For Itself is without action, *acalaḥ sanātanaḥ*,[3] "motionless, sempiternal".

It is without sinews. The reason for Its being without scar is that It does not put out Power, does not dispense Force in multiple channels, does not lose it here, increase it there, replenish its loss or seek by love or by violence its complementary or its food. It is without nerves of force; It does not pour itself out in the energies of the Pranic dynamism, of Life, of Matarishwan.

It is pure, unpierced by evil. What we call sin or evil, is merely excess and defect, wrong placement, inharmonious action and reaction. By its equality, by its inaction even while it supports all action, the conscious Soul retains its eternal freedom and eternal purity. For it is unmodified; It watches as the Sakshi, the witness, the modifications effected by Prakriti, but does not partake of them, does not get clogged with them, receives not their impression. *Na lipyate*.

THE SOUL INALIENABLY FREE

What is the relation of the active Brahman and of the human soul to this pure Inactive? They too are That. Action does not change the nature of the Self, but only the nature of the diverse forms. The Self is always pure, blissful, perfect, whether inactive or participating in action.

The Self is all things and exceeds them. It exceeds always that in which the mind is engrossed, that which it takes in a particular time and space as a figure of itself. The boundless whole is always perfect. The totality of things is a complete harmony without wound or flaw. The view-point of the part taken for a whole, in other words the Ignorance, is the broken reflection which creates the consciousness of limitation, incompleteness and discord. We shall see that this Ignorance has a use in the play of the Brahman; but in itself it appears at first to be only a parent of evil.

Ignorance is a veil that separates the mind, body and life

---

[3] Gita II. 24.

from their source and reality, Sachchidananda. Thus obscured the mind feels itself pierced by the evil that Ignorance creates. But the Active Brahman is always Sachchidananda using for its self-becoming the forms of mind, body and life. All their experiences are therefore seen by It in the terms of Sachchidananda. It is not pierced by the evil. For It also is the One and sees everywhere Oneness. It is not mastered by the Ignorance that It uses as a minor term of its conception.

The human soul is one with the Lord; it also is in its completeness Sachchidananda using Ignorance as the minor term of its being. But it has projected its conceptions into this minor term and established there in limited mind its centre of vision, its view-point. It assumes to itself the incompleteness and the resultant sense of want, discord, desire, suffering. The Real Man behind is not affected by all this confusion; but the apparent or exterior Man is affected. To recover its freedom it must recover its completeness; it must identify itself with the divine Inhabitant within, its true and complete self. It can then, like the Lord, conduct the action of Prakriti without undergoing the false impression of identification with the results of its action. It is this idea on which the Upanishad bases the assertion, "Action cleaveth not to a man."

To this end it must recover the silent Brahman within. The Lord possesses always His double term and conducts the action of the universe, extended in it, but not attached to or limited by His works. The human soul, entangled in mind, is obscured in vision by the rushing stream of Prakriti's works and fancies itself to be a part of that stream and swept in its currents and in its eddies. It has to go back in its self-existence to the silent Purusha even while participating in its self-becoming in the movement of Prakriti. It becomes, then, not only like the silent Purusha, the witness and upholder, but also the Lord and the free enjoyer of Prakriti and her works. An absolute calm and passivity, purity and equality within, a sovereign and inexhaustible activity without is the nature of Brahman as we see it manifested in the universe.

There is therefore no farther objection to works. On

the contrary, works are justified by the participation or self-identification of the soul with the Lord in His double aspect of passivity and activity. Tranquillity for the Soul, activity for the energy, is the balance of the divine rhythm in man.

THE LAW OF THINGS

The totality of objects (*arthān*) is the becoming of the Lord in the extension of His own being. Its principle is double. There is consciousness; there is Being. Consciousness dwells in energy (*tapas*) upon its self-being to produce Idea of itself (*vijñāna*) and form and action inevitably corresponding to the Idea. This is the original Indian conception of creation, self-production or projection into form (*sṛṣṭi, prasava*). Being uses its self-awareness to evolve infinite forms of itself governed by the expansion of the innate Idea in the form. This is the original Indian conception of evolution, prominent in certain philosophies such as the Sankhya (*pariṇāma, vikāra, vivarta*). It is the same phenomenon diversely stated.

In the idea of some thinkers the world is a purely subjective evolution (*vivarta*), not real as objective fact; in the idea of others it is an objective fact, a real modification (*pariṇāma*), but one which makes no difference to the essence of Being. Both notions claim to derive from the Upanishads as their authority, and their opposition comes in fact by the separation of what in the ancient Vedanta was viewed as one, — as we see in this passage.

Brahman is His own subject and His own object, whether in His pure self-existence or in His varied self-becoming. He is the object of His own self-awareness; He is the Knower of His own self-being. The two aspects are inseparable, even though they seem to disappear into each other and emerge again from each other. All appearance of pure subjectivity holds itself as an object implicit in its very subjectivity; all appearance of pure objectivity holds itself as subject implicit in its very objectivity.

All objective existence is the Self-existent, the Self-becoming, "Swayambhu", becoming by the force of the Idea within it. The Idea is, self-contained, the Fact that it becomes. For Swayambhu sees or comprehends Himself in the essence of the Fact as "Kavi", thinks Himself out in the evolution of its possibilities as "Manishi", becomes form of Himself in the movement in Space and Time as "Paribhu". These three are one operation appearing as successive in the relative, temporal and spatial Consciousness.

It follows that every object holds in itself the law of its own being eternally, *śāśvatībhyaḥ samābhyaḥ*, from years sempiternal, in perpetual Time. All relations in the totality of objects are thus determined by their Inhabitant, the Self-existent, the Self-becoming, and stand contained in the nature of things by the omnipresence of the One, the Lord, by His self-vision which is their inherent subjective Truth, by His self-becoming which, against a background of boundless possibilities, is the Law of their inevitable evolution in the objective Fact.

Therefore all things are arranged by Him perfectly, *yāthā-tathyataḥ*, as they should be in their nature. There is an imperative harmony in the All, which governs the apparent discords of individualisation. That discord would be real and operate in eternal chaos, if there were only a mass of individual forms and forces, if each form and force did not contain in itself and were not in its reality the self-existent All, the Lord.

THE PROCESS OF THINGS

The Lord appears to us in the relative notion of the process of things first as Kavi, the Wise, the Seer. The Kavi sees the Truth in itself, the truth in its becoming, in its essence, possibilities, actuality. He contains all that in the Idea, the Vijnana, called the Truth and Law, Satyam Ritam. He contains it comprehensively, not piecemeal; the Truth and Law of things is the Brihat, the Large. Viewed by itself, the realm of Vijnana would seem a realm of predetermination, of concentration, of compelling seed-state. But it is a determination not in previous Time, but in perpetual Time; a Fate compelled by the Soul, not compelling it, compelling rather the action and result, present in the expansion of the movement as well as in the concentration of the Idea.

Therefore the truth of the Soul is freedom and mastery, not subjection and bondage. Purusha commands Prakriti, Prakriti does not compel Purusha. *Na karma lipyate nare.*

The Manishi takes his stand in the possibilities. He has behind him the freedom of the Infinite and brings it in as a background for the determination of the finite. Therefore every action in the world seems to emerge from a balancing and clashing of various possibilities. None of these, however, are effective in the determination except by their secret consonance with the Law of that which has to become. The Kavi is in the Manishi and upholds him in his working. But viewed by itself the realm of the Manishi would seem to be a state of plasticity, of free-will, of the interaction of forces, but of a free-will in thought which is met by a fate in things.

For the action of the Manishi is meant to eventuate in the becoming of the Paribhu. The Paribhu, called also Virat, extends Himself in the realm of eventualities. He fulfils what is contained in the Truth, what works out in the possibilities reflected by the mind, what appears to us as the fact objectively realised. The realm of Virat would seem, if taken separately, to be that of a Law and Predetermination which compels all things that evolve in that realm, — the iron chain of Karma, the rule of mechanical necessity, the despotism of an inexplicable Law.

But the becoming of Virat is always the becoming of the self-existent Lord, — *paribhūḥ svayambhūḥ.* Therefore to realise the truth of that becoming we have to go back and re-embrace all that stands behind; — we have to return to the full truth of the free and infinite Sachchidananda.

This is the truth of things as seen from above and from the Unity. It is the divine standpoint; but we have to take account of the human standpoint which starts from below, proceeds from the Ignorance, and perceives these principles successively, not comprehensively, as separate states of consciousness. Humanity is that which returns in experience to Sachchidananda, and it must begin from below, in Avidya, with the mind embodied in Matter, the Thinker imprisoned and emerging from the objective Fact. This imprisoned Thinker is Man, the "Manu".

He has to start from death and division and arrive at unity and immortality. He has to realise the universal in the individual and the Absolute in the relative. He is Brahman growing self-conscious in the objective multiplicity. He is the ego in the cosmos vindicating himself as the All and the Transcendent.

V

THIRD MOVEMENT

[2]

Knowledge and Ignorance

Verses 9 – 11 *

VIDYA AND AVIDYA

All manifestation proceeds by the two terms, Vidya and Avidya, the consciousness of Unity and the consciousness of Multiplicity. They are the two aspects of the Maya, the formative self-conception of the Eternal.

Unity is the eternal and fundamental fact, without which all multiplicity would be unreal and an impossible illusion. The consciousness of Unity is therefore called Vidya, the Knowledge.

Multiplicity is the play or varied self-expansion of the One, shifting in its terms, divisible in its view of itself, by force of which the One occupies many centres of consciousness, inhabits many formations of energy in the universal Movement. Multiplicity is implicit or explicit in unity. Without it the Unity would be either a void of non-existence or a powerless, sterile limitation to the state of indiscriminate self-absorption or of blank repose.

But the consciousness of multiplicity separated from the true knowledge in the many of their own essential oneness, — the

---

* 9. Into a blind darkness they enter who follow after the Ignorance, they as if into a greater darkness who devote themselves to the Knowledge alone.

10. Other, verily, it is said, is that which comes by the Knowledge, other that which comes by the Ignorance; this is the lore we have received from the wise who revealed That to our understanding.

11. He who knows That as both in one, the Knowledge and the Ignorance, by the Ignorance crosses beyond death and by the Knowledge enjoys Immortality.

view-point of the separate ego identifying itself with the divided form and the limited action, — is a state of error and delusion. In man this is the form taken by the consciousness of multiplicity. Therefore it is given the name of Avidya, the Ignorance.

Brahman, the Lord, is one and all-blissful, but free from limitation by His unity; all-powerful, He is able to conceive Himself from multiple centres in multiple forms from which and upon which flow multiple currents of energy, seen by us as actions or play of forces. When He is thus multiple, He is not bound by His multiplicity, but amid all variations dwells eternally in His own oneness. He is Lord of Vidya and Avidya. They are the two sides of His self-conception (Maya), the twin powers of His Energy (Chit-Shakti).

Brahman, exceeding as well as dwelling in the play of His Maya, is Ish, lord of it and free. Man, dwelling in the play, is Anish, not lord, not free, subject to Avidya. But this subjection is itself a play of the Ignorance, unreal in essential fact (*paramārtha*), real only in practical relation (*vyavahāra*), in the working out of the actions of the divine Energy, the Chit-Shakti. To get back to the essential fact of his freedom he must recover the sense of Oneness, the consciousness of Brahman, of the Lord, realise his oneness in Brahman and with the Lord. Recovering his freedom, realising his oneness with all existences as becomings of the One Being who is always himself (*so'ham asmi*, He am I), he is able to carry out divine actions in the world, no longer subject to the Ignorance, because free in the Knowledge.

The perfection of man, therefore, is the full manifestation of the Divine in the individual through the supreme accord between Vidya and Avidya. Multiplicity must become conscious of its oneness, Oneness embrace its multiplicity.

THE EXTREME PATHS

The purpose of the Lord in the world cannot be fulfilled by following Vidya alone or Avidya alone.

Those who are devoted entirely to the principle of multiplicity and division and take their orientation away from oneness enter into a blind darkness of Ignorance. For this tendency is one of increasing contraction and limitation, disaggregation of the gains of knowledge and greater and greater subjection to the mechanical necessities of Prakriti and finally to her separative and self-destructive forces. To turn away from the progression towards Oneness is to turn away from existence and from light.

Those who are devoted entirely to the principle of indiscriminate Unity and seek to put away from them the integrality of the Brahman, also put away from them knowledge and completeness and enter as if into a greater darkness. They enter into some special state and accept it for the whole, mistaking exclusion in consciousness for transcendence in consciousness. They ignore by choice of knowledge, as the others are ignorant by compulsion of error. Knowing all to transcend all is the right path of Vidya.

Although a higher state than the other, this supreme Night is termed a greater darkness, because the lower is one of chaos from which reconstitution is always possible, the higher is a conception of Void or Asat, an attachment to non-existence of Self from which it is more difficult to return to fulfilment of Self.

THE GAINS IN EITHER PATH

Pursued with a less entire attachment the paths of Vidya and Avidya have each their legitimate gains for the human soul, but neither of these are the full and perfect thing undertaken by the individual in the manifestation.

By Vidya one may attain to the state of the silent Brahman or the Akshara Purusha regarding the universe without actively participating in it or to His self-absorbed state of Chit in Sat from which the universe proceeds and towards which it returns. Both these states are conditions of serenity, plenitude, freedom from the confusions and sufferings of the world.

But the highest goal of man is neither fulfilment in the movement as a separate individual nor in the Silence separated from the movement, but in the Uttama Purusha, the Lord, He who went abroad and upholds in Himself both the Kshara and the

Akshara as modes of His being. The self of man, the Jivatman, is here in order to realise in the individual and for the universe that one highest Self of all. The ego created by Avidya is a necessary mechanism for affirming individuality in the universal as a starting-point for this supreme achievement.

By Avidya one may attain to a sort of fullness of power, joy, world-knowledge, largeness of being, which is that of the Titans or of the Gods, of Indra, of Prajapati. This is gained in the path of self-enlargement by an ample acceptance of the multiplicity in all its possibilities and a constant enrichment of the individual by all the materials that the universe can pour into him. But this also is not the goal of man; for though it brings transcendence of the ordinary human limits, it does not bring the divine transcendence of the universe in the Lord of the universe. One transcends confusion of Ignorance, but not limitation of Knowledge, — transcends death of the body, but not limitation of being, — transcends subjection to sorrow, but not subjection to joy, — transcends the lower Prakriti, but not the higher. To gain the real freedom and the perfect Immortality one would have to descend again to all that had been rejected and make the right use of death, sorrow and ignorance.

The real knowledge is that which perceives Brahman in His integrality and does not follow eagerly after one consciousness rather than another, is no more attached to Vidya than to Avidya. This was the knowledge of the ancient sages who were *dhīra*, steadfast in the gaze of their thought, not drawn away from the completeness of knowledge by one light or by another and whose perception of Brahman was consequently entire and comprehensive and their teaching founded on that perception equally entire and comprehensive (*vicakṣire*). It is the knowledge handed down from these Ancients that is being set forth in the Upanishad.

THE COMPLETE PATH

Brahman embraces in His manifestation both Vidya and Avidya and if they are both present in the manifestation, it is because they are both necessary to its existence and its accomplishment. Avidya subsists because Vidya supports and embraces it; Vidya depends upon Avidya for the preparation and the advance of the soul towards the great Unity. Neither could exist without the other; for if either were abolished, they would both pass away into something which would be neither the one nor the other, something inconceivable and ineffable beyond all manifestation.

In the worst Ignorance there is some point of the knowledge which constitutes that form of Ignorance and some support of Unity which prevents it in its most extreme division, limitation, obscurity from ceasing to exist by dissolving into nothingness. The destiny of the Ignorance is not that it should be dissolved out of existence, but that its elements should be enlightened, united, that which they strive to express delivered, fulfilled and in the fulfilment transmuted and transfigured.

In the uttermost unity of which knowledge is capable the contents of the Multiplicity are inherent and implicit and can any moment be released into activity. The office of Vidya is not to destroy Avidya as a thing that ought never to have been manifested but to draw it continually towards itself, supporting it the while and helping it to deliver itself progressively from that character of Ignorance, of the oblivion of its essential Oneness, which gives it its name.

Avidya fulfilled by turning more and more to Vidya enables the individual and the universal to become what the Lord is in Himself, conscious of His manifestation, conscious of His non-manifestation, free in birth, free in non-birth.

Man represents the point at which the multiplicity in the universe becomes consciously capable of this turning and fulfilment. His own natural fulfilment comes by following the complete path of Avidya surrendering itself to Vidya, the Multiplicity to the Unity, the Ego to the One in all and beyond all, and of Vidya accepting Avidya into itself, the Unity fulfilling the Multiplicity, the One manifesting Himself unveiled in the individual and in the universe.

MORTALITY AND IMMORTALITY

MORTALITY

By Avidya fulfilled man passes beyond death, by Vidya accepting Avidya into itself he enjoys immortality.

By death is meant the state of mortality which is a subjection to the process of constant birth and dying as a limited ego bound to the dualities of joy and sorrow, good and evil, truth and error, love and hatred, pleasure and suffering.

This state comes by limitation and self-division from the One who is all and in all and beyond all and by attachment of the idea of self to a single formation in Time and Space of body, life and mind, by which the Self excludes from its view all that it verily is with the exception of a mass of experiences flowing out from and in upon a particular centre and limited by the capacities of a particular mental, vital and bodily frame. This mass of experiences it organises around the ego-centre in the mind and linking them together in Time by a double action of memory, passive in state, active in work, says continually, "This is I."

The result is that the soul attributes to itself a certain portion only of the play of Prakriti or Chit-Shakti and consequently a certain limited capacity of force of consciousness which has to bear all the impact of what the soul does not regard as itself but as a rush of alien forces; against them it defends its separate formation of individuality from dissolution into Nature or mastery by Nature. It seeks to assert in the individual form and by its means its innate character of Ish or Lord and so to possess and enjoy its world.

But by the very definition of the ego its capacity is limited. It accepts as itself a form made of the movement of Nature which cannot endure in the general flux of things. It has to form it by the process of the movement and this is birth, it dissolves it by the process of the movement and this is death.

It can master by the understanding only so much of its experiences as assimilate with its own view-point and in a way which must always be imperfect and subject to error because it is not the view of all or the view-point of the All. Its knowledge is partly error and all the rest it ignores.

It can only accept and harmonise itself with a certain number of its experiences, precisely because these are the only ones it can understand sufficiently to assimilate. This is its joy; the rest is sorrow or indifference.

It is only capable of harmonising with the force in its body, nerves and mind a certain number of impacts of alien forces. In these it takes pleasure. The rest it receives with insensibility or pain.

Death therefore is the constant denial by the All of the ego's false self-limitation in the individual frame of mind, life and body.

Error is the constant denial by the All of the ego's false sufficiency in a limited knowledge.

Suffering of mind and body is the constant denial by the All of the ego's attempt to confine the universal Ananda to a false and self-regarding formation of limited and exclusive enjoyments.

It is only by accepting the oneness of the All that the individual can escape from this constant and necessary denial and attain beyond. Then All-being, All-force, All-consciousness, All-truth, All-delight take possession of the individual soul. It changes mortality for immortality.

MORTALITY AND AVIDYA

But the way of attaining to immortality is not by the self-dissolution of the individual formation into the flux of Prakriti, neither is it by prematurely dissolving it into the All-soul which Prakriti expresses. Man moves towards something which fulfils the universe by transcending it. He has to prepare his individual soul for the transcendence and for the fulfilment.

If Avidya is the cause of mortality, it is also the path out of mortality. The limitation has been created precisely in order that the individual may affirm himself against the flux of Prakriti in order eventually to transcend, possess and transform it.

The first necessity is therefore for man continually to enlarge himself in being, knowledge, joy, power in the limits of the ego so that he may arrive at the conception of something which progressively manifests itself in him in these terms and becomes more and more powerful to deal with the oppositions of Prakriti and to change, individually, more and more the terms of ignorance, suffering and weakness into the terms of knowledge, joy and power and even death into a means of wider life.

This self-enlargement has then to awaken to the perception of something exceeding itself, exceeding the personal manifestation. Man has so to enlarge his conception of self as to see all in himself and himself in all (*verse* 6). He has to see that this "I" which contains all and is contained in all, is the One, is universal and not his personal ego. To That he has to subject his ego, That he has to reproduce in his nature and become, That is what he has to possess and enjoy with an equal soul in all its forms and movements.

He has to see that this universal One is something entirely transcendent, the sole Being, and that the universe and all its forms, actions, egos are only becomings of that Being (*verse* 7). World is a becoming which seeks always to express in motion of Time and Space, by progression in mind, life and body what is beyond all becoming, beyond Time and Space, beyond mind, life and body.

Thus Avidya becomes one with Vidya. By Avidya man passes beyond that death, suffering, ignorance, weakness which were the first terms he had to deal with, the first assertions of the One in the birth affirming Himself amid the limitations and divisions of the Multiplicity. By Vidya he enjoys even in the birth the Immortality.

IMMORTALITY

Immortality does not mean survival of the self or the ego after dissolution of the body. The Self always survives the dissolution of the body, because it always pre-existed before the birth of the body. The Self is unborn and undying. The survival of the ego is only the first condition by which the individual soul is able to continue and link together its experiences in Avidya so as to pursue with an increasing self-possession and mastery that process of self-enlargement which culminates in Vidya.

By immortality is meant the consciousness which is beyond birth and death, beyond the chain of cause and effect, beyond all bondage and limitation, free, blissful, self-existent in conscious-being, the consciousness of the Lord, of the supreme Purusha, of Sachchidananda.

IMMORTALITY AND BIRTH

On this realisation man can base his free activity in the universe.

But having so far attained, what further utility has the soul for birth or for works? None for itself, everything for God and the universe.

Immortality beyond the universe is not the object of mani-festation in the universe, for that the Self always possessed. Man exists in order that through him the Self may enjoy Immortality in the birth as well as in the non-becoming.

Nor is individual salvation the end; for that would only be the sublime of the ego, not its self-realisation through the Lord in all.

Having realised his own immortality, the individual has yet to fulfil God's work in the universe. He has to help the life, the mind and the body in all beings to express progressively Immortality and not mortality.

This he may do by the becoming in the material body which we ordinarily call birth, or from some status in another world or even, it is possible, from beyond world. But birth in the body is the most close, divine and effective form of help which the liberated can give to those who are themselves still bound to the progression of birth in the lowest world of the Ignorance.

VI

THIRD MOVEMENT

[3]

Birth and Non-Birth

Verses 12 – 14*

THE BIRTH AND THE NON-BIRTH

The Self outside Nature does not become; it is immutable as well as eternal. The Self in Nature becomes, it changes its states and forms. This entry into various states and forms in the succession of Time is Birth in Nature.

Because of these two positions of the Self, in Nature and out of Nature, moving in the movement and seated above the movement, active in the development and eating the fruits of the tree of Life or inactive and simply regarding, there are two possible states of conscious existence directly opposed to each other of which the human soul is capable, the state of Birth, the state of Non-Birth.

Man starts from the troubled state of Birth, he arrives at that tranquil poise of conscious existence liberated from the movement which is the Non-Birth. The knot of the Birth is the ego-sense; the dissolution of the ego-sense brings us to the Non-Birth. Therefore the Non-Birth is also called the Dissolution (Vinasha).

---

* 12. Into a blind darkness they enter who follow after the Non-Birth, they as if into a greater darkness who devote themselves to the Birth alone.

13. Other, verily, it is said, is that which comes by the Birth, other that which comes by the Non-Birth; this is the lore we have received from the wise who revealed That to our understanding.

14. He who knows That as both in one, the Birth and the dissolution of Birth, by the dissolution crosses beyond death and by the Birth enjoys Immortality.

Birth and Non-Birth are not essentially physical conditions, but soul-states. A man may break the knot of the ego-sense and yet remain in the physical body; but if he concentrates himself solely in the state of dissolution of ego, then he is not born again in the body. He is liberated from birth as soon as the present impulse of Nature which continues the action of the mind and body has been exhausted. On the other hand if he attaches himself to the Birth, the ego-principle in him seeks continually to clothe itself in fresh mental and physical forms.

THE EVIL OF THE EXTREMES

Neither attachment to Non-Birth nor attachment to Birth is the perfect way. For all attachment is an act of ignorance and a violence committed upon the Truth. Its end also is ignorance, a state of blind darkness.

Exclusive attachment to Non-Birth leads to a dissolution into indiscriminate Nature or into the Nihil, into the Void, and both of these are states of blind darkness. For the Nihil is an attempt not to transcend the state of existence in birth, but to annul it, not to pass from a limited into an illimitable existence, but from existence into its opposite. The opposite of existence can only be the Night of negative consciousness, a state of ignorance and not of release.

On the other hand, attachment to Birth in the body means a constant self-limitation and an interminable round of egoistic births in the lower forms of egoism without issue or release. This is, from a certain point of view, a worse darkness than the other; for it is ignorant even of the impulse of release. It is not an error in the grasping after truth, but a perpetual contentment with the state of blindness. It cannot lead even eventually to any greater good, because it does not dream of any higher condition.

THE GOOD OF THE EXTREMES

On the other hand each of these tendencies, pursued with a certain relativeness to the other, has its own fruit and its own good.

Non-Birth pursued as the goal of Birth and a higher, fuller and truer existence may lead to withdrawal into the silent Brahman or into the pure liberty of the Non-Being. Birth, pursued as a means of progress and self-enlargement, leads to a greater and fuller life which may, in its turn, become a vestibule to the final achievement.

THE PERFECT WAY

But neither of these results is perfect in itself nor the true goal of humanity. Each of them brings its intended portion into the perfect good of the human soul only when it is completed by the other.

Brahman is both Vidya and Avidya, both Birth and Non-Birth. The realisation of the Self as the unborn and the poise of the soul beyond the dualities of birth and death in the infinite and transcendent existence are the conditions of a free and divine life in the Becoming. The one is necessary to the other. It is by participation in the pure unity of the Immobile (Akshara) Brahman that the soul is released from its absorption in the stream of the movement. So released it identifies itself with the Lord to whom becoming and non-becoming are only modes of His existence and is able to enjoy immortality in the manifestation without being caught in the wheel of Nature's delusions. The necessity of birth ceases, its personal object having been fulfilled; the freedom of becoming remains. For the Divine enjoys equally and simultaneously the freedom of His eternity and the freedom of His becoming.

It may even be said that to have had the conscious experience of a dissolution of the very idea of Being into the supreme Non-Being is necessary for the fullest and freest possession of Being itself. This would be from the synthetic standpoint the justification of the great effort of Buddhism to exceed the conception of all positive being even in its widest or purest essentiality.

Thus by dissolution of ego and of the attachment to birth the soul crosses beyond death; it is liberated from all limitation in the dualities. Having attained this liberation it accepts becoming as a process of Nature subject to the soul and not binding upon it and by this free and divine becoming enjoys Immortality.

THE JUSTIFICATION OF LIFE

Thus, the third movement of the Upanishad is a justification of life and works, which were enjoined upon the seeker of the Truth in its second verse. Works are the essence of Life. Life is a manifestation of the Brahman; in Brahman the Life Principle arranges a harmony of the seven principles of conscious being by which that manifestation works out its involution and evolution. In Brahman Matarishwan disposes the waters, the sevenfold movement of the divine Existence. That divine Existence is the Lord who has gone abroad in the movement and unrolled the universe in His three modes as All-Seer of the Truth of things, Thinker-out of their possibilities, Realiser of their actualities. He has determined all things sovereignly in their own nature, development and goal from years sempiternal.

That determination works out through His double power of Vidya and Avidya, consciousness of essential unity and consciousness of phenomenal multiplicity.

The Multiplicity carried to its extreme limit returns upon itself in the conscious individual who is the Lord inhabiting the forms of the movement and enjoying first the play of the Ignorance. Afterwards by development in the Ignorance the soul returns to the capacity of Knowledge and enjoys by the Knowledge Immortality.

This Immortality is gained by the dissolution of the limited ego and its chain of births into the consciousness of the unborn and undying, the Eternal, the Lord, the ever-free. But it is enjoyed by a free and divine becoming in the universe and not outside the universe; for there it is always possessed, but here in the material body it is to be worked out and enjoyed by the divine Inhabitant under circumstances that are in appearance the most opposite to its terms, in the life of the individual and in the multiple life of the universe.

Life has to be transcended in order that it may be freely

accepted; the works of the universe have to be overpassed in order that they may be divinely fulfilled.

The soul even in apparent bondage is really free and only plays at being bound; but it has to go back to the consciousness of freedom and possess and enjoy universally not this or that but the Divine and the All.

VII

FOURTH MOVEMENT

[1]

The Worlds — Surya

Verses 15–16*

THE WORLDS AFTER DEATH

In the third verse the Upanishad has spoken of sunless worlds enveloped in blind gloom. In its third movement it also speaks twice of the soul entering into a blind gloom, but here it is a state of consciousness that seems to be indicated and not a world. Nevertheless, the two statements differ little in effect; for in the Vedantic conception a world is only a condition of conscious being organised in the terms of the seven constituent principles of manifested existence. According to the state of consciousness which we reach here in the body, will be our state of consciousness and the surroundings organised by it when the mental being passes out of the body. For the individual soul out of the body must either disappear into the general constituents of its existence, merge itself into Brahman or persist in an organisation of consciousness other than the terrestrial and in relations with the universe other than those which are appropriate to life in the body. This state of consciousness and the relations belonging to it are the other worlds, the worlds after death.

---

* 15. The face of Truth is covered with a brilliant golden lid; that do thou remove, O Fosterer, for the law of the Truth, for sight.

  16. O Fosterer, O sole Seer, O Ordainer, O illumining Sun, O power of the Father of creatures, marshal thy rays, draw together thy light; the Lustre which is thy most blessed form of all, that in Thee I behold. The Purusha there and there, He am I.

THE THREE STATES

The Upanishad admits three states of the soul in relation to the manifested universe, — terrestrial life by birth in the body, the survival of the individual soul after death in other states and the immortal existence which being beyond birth and death, beyond manifestation can yet enter into forms as the Inhabitant and embrace Nature as its lord. The two former conditions appertain to the Becoming; Immortality stands in the Self, in the Non-Birth, and enjoys the Becoming.

The Upanishad, although it does not speak expressly of rebirth in an earthly body, yet implies that belief in its thought and language, — especially in the 17th verse. On the basis of this belief in rebirth man may aim at three distinct objects beyond death, — a better or more fortunate life or lives upon earth, eternal enjoyment of bliss in an ultra-terrestrial world of light and joy or a transcendence exclusive of all universal existence, merged in the Supreme as in one's true self, but having no relation with the actual or possible contents of its infinite consciousness.

REBIRTH

The attainment of a better life or lives upon earth is not the consummation offered to the soul by the thought of the Upanishad. But it is an important intermediate object so long as the soul is in a state of growth and self-enlargement and has not attained to liberation. The obligation of birth and death is a sign that the mental being has not yet unified itself with its true supramental self and spirit, but is dwelling "in Avidya and enclosed within it".[1] To attain that union the life of man upon earth is its appointed means. After liberation the soul is free, but may still participate in the entire movement and return to birth no longer for its own sake but for the sake of others and according to the will in it of its divine Self, the Lord of its movement.

---

[1] *Avidyāyām antare vartamānāḥ.* — Katha Upanishad I. 2. 5; Mundaka I. 2. 8.

HEAVEN AND HELL

The enjoyment of beatitude in a heaven beyond is also not the supreme consummation. But Vedantic thought did not envisage rebirth as an immediate entry after death into a new body; the mental being in man is not so rigidly bound to the vital and physical, — on the contrary, the latter are ordinarily dissolved together after death, and there must therefore be, before the soul is attracted back towards terrestrial existence, an interval in which it assimilates its terrestrial experiences in order to be able to constitute a new vital and physical being upon earth. During this interval it must dwell in states or worlds beyond and these may be favourable or unfavourable to its future development. They are favourable in proportion as the light of the Supreme Truth of which Surya is a symbol enters into them, but states of intermediate ignorance or darkness are harmful to the soul in its progress. Those enter into them, as has been affirmed in the third verse, who do hurt to themselves by shutting themselves to the light or distorting the natural course of their development. The Vedantic heavens are states of light and the soul's expansion; darkness, self-obscuration and self-distortion are the nature of the Hells which it has to shun.

In relation to the soul's individual development, therefore, the life in worlds beyond, like the life upon earth, is a means and not an object in itself. After liberation the soul may possess these worlds as it possesses the material birth, accepting in them a means towards the divine manifestation in which they form a condition of its fullness, each being one of the parts in a series of organised states of conscious being which is linked with and supports all the rest.

TRANSCENDENCE

Transcendence is the goal of the development, but it does not exclude the possession of that which is transcended. The soul need not and should not push transcendence so far as to aim at its own extinction. Nirvana is extinction of the ego-limitations, but not of all possibility of manifestation, since it can be possessed even in the body.

The desire of the exclusive liberation is the last desire that the soul in its expanding knowledge has to abandon; the delusion that it is bound by birth is the last delusion that it has to destroy.

SURYA AND AGNI

On the basis of this conception of the worlds and the relation of these different soul-states to each other the Upanishad proceeds to indicate the two lines of knowledge and action which lead to the supreme vision and the divine felicity. This is done under the form of an invocation to Surya and Agni, the Vedic godheads, representative one of the supreme Truth and its illuminations, the other of the divine Will raising, purifying and perfecting human action.

THE ORDER OF THE WORLDS

To understand entirely the place and function of Surya we must enter a little more profoundly into the Vedic conception of the seven worlds and the principles of consciousness they represent.

All conscious being is one and indivisible in itself, but in manifestation it becomes a complex rhythm, a scale of harmonies, a hierarchy of states or movements. For what we call a state is only the organisation of a complex movement. This hierarchy is composed by a descending or involutive and an ascending or evolutive movement of which Spirit and Matter are the highest and lowest terms.

Spirit is Sat or pure existence, pure in self-awareness (Chit), pure in self-delight (Ananda). Therefore Spirit can be regarded as a triune basis of all conscious being. There are three terms, but they are really one. For all pure existence is in its essence pure self-conscience and all pure self-conscience is in its essence pure self-delight. At the same time our consciousness is capable of separating these three by the Idea and the Word and even of creating for itself in its divided or limited movements the sense of their apparent opposites.

An integral intuition into the nature of conscious being shows us that it is indeed one in essence, but also that it is capable of an infinite potential complexity and multiplicity in self-experience. The working of this potential complexity and multiplicity in the One is what we call from our point of view manifestation or creation or world or becoming — (*bhuvana, bhāva*). Without it no world-existence is possible.

The agent of this becoming is always the self-conscience of the Being. The power by which the self-conscience brings out of itself its potential complexities is termed Tapas, Force or Energy, and, being self-conscious, is obviously of the nature of Will. But not Will as we understand it, something exterior to its object, other than its works, labouring on material outside itself, but Will inherent in the Being, inherent in the becoming, one with the movement of existence, — self-conscious Will that becomes what it sees and knows in itself, Will that is expressed as Force of its own work and formulates itself in the result of its work. By this Will, Tapas or Chit-Shakti, the worlds are created.

THE HIGHER WORLDS

All organisation of self-conscient being which takes as its basis the unity of pure existence belongs to the world of the highest creation, *parārdha,* — the worlds of the Spirit.

We can conceive three principal formations.

When Tapas or energy of self-conscience dwells upon Sat or pure existence as its basis, the result is Satyaloka or world of true existence. The soul in Satyaloka is one with all its manifestations by oneness of essence and therefore one in self-conscience and in energy of self-conscience and one also in bliss.

When Tapas dwells upon active power of Chit as its basis, the result is Tapoloka or world of energy of self-conscience. The soul in Tapoloka is one with all manifestations in this Energy and therefore enjoys oneness also in the totality of their bliss and possesses equally their unity of essence.

When Tapas dwells upon active Delight of being as its basis, the result is Janaloka, world of creative Delight. The soul in Janaloka is one in delight of being with all manifestation and through that bliss one also in conscious energy and in essence of being.

All these are states of consciousness in which unity and multiplicity have not yet been separated from each other. All is in all, each in all and all in each, inherently, by the very nature of conscious being and without effort of conception or travail of perception. There is no night, no obscurity. Neither is there, properly speaking, any dominant action of illuminating Surya. For the whole of consciousness there is self-luminous and needs no light other than itself. The distinct existence of Surya is lost in the oneness of the Lord or Purusha; that luminous oneness is Surya's most blessed form of all.

THE LOWER CREATION

In the lower creation also there are three principles, Matter, Life, and Mind. Sat or pure existence appears there as extended substance or Matter; Will or Force appears as Life which is in its nature creative or manifesting Force and that Force is in its nature a self-conscient will involved and obscure in the forms of its creation. It is liberated from the involution and obscurity by delight of being struggling to become conscious of itself in desire and sensation; the result is the emergence of Mind. So at least it appears to us in the ascending or evolutive movement.

Wherever there is Matter, Life and Mind are present involved or evolving. So also, Life and Mind have some kind of material form as the condition of their activities. These three appear not as triune, owing to their domination by the dividing principle of Avidya, but as triple.

In the organisation of consciousness to which we belong, Tapas dwells upon Matter as its basis. Our consciousness is determined by the divisibility of extended substance in its apparent forms. This is Bhurloka, the material world, the world of formal becoming.

But we may conceive of a world in which dynamic Life-force with sensation emergent in it is the basis and determines without the gross obstacle of Matter the forms that it shall take. This organisation of consciousness has for its field Bhuvarloka, the worlds of free vital becoming in form.

We may conceive also of an organised state of consciousness in which Mind liberates itself from subjection to material sensation and becoming dominant determines its own forms instead of being itself determined by the forms in which it finds itself as a result of life evolution. This formation is Swarloka or world of free, pure and luminous mentality.

In these lower worlds consciousness is normally broken up and divided. The light of Surya, the Truth, is imprisoned in the night of the subconscient or appears only reflected in limited centres or with its rays received by those centres and utilised according to their individual nature.

THE INTERMEDIATE WORLD

Between these two creations, linking them together, is the world or organisation of consciousness of which the infinite Truth of things is the foundation. There dominant individualisation no longer usurps the all-pervading soul and the foundation of consciousness is its own vast totality arranging in itself indi-vidualised movements which never lose the consciousness of their integrality and total oneness with all others. Multiplicity no longer prevails and divides, but even in the complexity of its movements always refers back to essential unity and its own integral totality. This world is therefore called Maharloka or world of large consciousness.

The principle of Maharloka is Vijnana, the Idea. But this Vijnana is intuitional or rather gnostic Idea,[2] not intellectual

---

[2] Intuition (revelation, inspiration, intuitive perception, intuitive discrimination) is Vijnana working in mind under the conditions and in the forms of mind. Gnosis or true supermind is a power above mind working in its own law, out of the direct identity of the supreme Self, his absolute self-conscious Truth knowing herself by her own power of absolute Light without any need of seeking, even the most luminous seeking.

conception. The difference is that intellectual conception not only tends towards form, but determines itself in the form of the idea and once determined distinguishes itself sharply from other conceptions. But pure intuitional or gnostic Idea sees itself in the Being as well as in the Becoming. It is one with the existence which throws out the form as a symbol of itself and it therefore carries with it always the knowledge of the Truth behind the form. It is in its nature self-conscience of the being and power of the One, aware always of its totality, starting therefore from the totality of all existence and perceiving directly its contents. Its nature is *dṛṣṭi*, seeing, not conceiving. It is the vision at once of the essence and the image. It is this intuition or gnosis which is the Vedic Truth, the self-vision and all-vision of Surya.

THE LAW OF THE TRUTH

The face of this Truth is covered as with a brilliant shield, as with a golden lid; covered, that is to say, from the view of our human consciousness. For we are mental beings and our highest ordinary mental sight is composed of the concepts and percepts of the mind, which are indeed a means of knowledge, rays of the Truth, but not in their nature truth of existence, only truth of form. By them we arrange our knowledge of the appearances of things and try to infer the truth behind. The true knowledge is truth of existence, *satyam*, not mere truth of form or appearance.

We can only arrive at the true Truth, if Surya works in us to remove this brilliant formation of concepts and percepts and replaces them by the self-vision and all-vision.

For this it is necessary that the law and action of the Truth should be manifested in us. We must learn to see things as they are, see ourselves as we are. Our present action is one in which self-knowledge and will are divided. We start with a fundamental falsehood, that we have a separate existence from others and we try to know the relations of separate beings in their separateness and act on the knowledge so formed for an individual utility. The law of the Truth would work in us if we saw the totality of our existence containing all others, its forms created by the action of the totality, its powers working in and by the action of the totality. Our internal and external action would then well naturally and directly out of our self-existence, out of the very truth of things and not in obedience to an intermediate principle which is in its nature a falsifying reflection.

THE FULFILMENT OF SURYA IN MAN

Nevertheless even in our ordinary action there is the beginning or at least the seed of the Truth which must liberate us. Behind every act and perception there is an intuition, a truth which, if it is continually falsified in the form, yet preserves itself in the essence and works to lead us by increasing light and largeness to truth in the manifestation. Behind all this travail of differentiation and division there is an insistent unifying tendency which is also continually falsified in the separate result, but yet leads persistently towards our eventual integrality in knowledge, in being and in will.

Surya is Pushan, fosterer or increaser. His work must be to effect this enlargement of the divided self-perception and action of will into the integral will and knowledge. He is sole seer and replacing other forms of knowledge by his unifying vision enables us to arrive finally at oneness. That intuitive vision of the totality, of one in All and All in one, becomes the ordainer of the right law of action in us, the law of the Truth. For Surya is Yama, the Ordainer or Controller who assures the law, the dharma. Thus we arrive at the fullness of action of the Illuminer in us, accomplish the entirety of the Truth-Consciousness. We are then able to see that all that is contained in the being of Surya, in the Vijnana which builds up the worlds is becoming of existence in the one existence and one Lord of all becoming, the Purusha, Sachchidananda. All becoming is born in the Being who himself exceeds all becomings and is their Lord, Prajapati.

By the revelation of the vision of Surya the true knowledge is formed. In this formation the Upanishad indicates two successive actions. First, there is an arrangement or marshalling of the rays of Surya, that is to say, the truths concealed behind our concepts and percepts are brought out by separate intuitions of the image and the essence of the image and arranged in their true relations to each other. So we arrive at totalities of intuitive knowledge and can finally go beyond to unity. This is the drawing together of the light of Surya. This double movement is necessitated by the constitution of our minds which cannot, like the original Truth-consciousness, start at once from the totality and perceive its contents from within. The mind can hardly conceive unity except as an abstraction, a sum or a void. Therefore it has to be gradually led from its own manner to that which exceeds it. It has to carry out its own characteristic action of arrangement, but with the help and by the operation of the higher faculty, no longer arbitrarily, but following the very action of the Truth of existence itself. Afterwards, by thus gradually correcting the manner of its own characteristic action it can succeed in reversing that characteristic action itself and learn to proceed from the whole to the contents instead of proceeding from "parts"[3] mistaken for entities to an apparent whole which is still a "part" and still mistaken for an entity.

THE ONE EXISTENT

Thus by the action of Surya we arrive at that light of the supreme superconscient in which even the intuitive knowledge of the truth of things based upon the total vision passes into the self-luminous self-vision of the one existent, one in all infinite complexities of a self-experience which never loses its unity or its self-luminousness. This is Surya's goodliest form of all. For it is the supreme Light, the supreme Will, the supreme Delight of existence.

This is the Lord, the Purusha, the self-conscient Being. When we have this vision, there is the integral self-knowledge, the perfect seeing, expressed in the great cry of the Upanishad, *so'ham.* The Purusha there and there, He am I. The Lord manifests Himself in the movements and inhabits many forms, but it is One

---

[3] There are really no parts, existence being indivisible.

who inhabits all. This self-conscient being, this real "I" whom the mental being individualised in the form is aware of as his true self — it is He. It is the All; and it is that which transcends the All.

VIII

FOURTH MOVEMENT

[2]

Action and the Divine Will

Verses 17–18*

THE SIDE OF ACTION

Through Surya then, through the growth of the illumination in the mind which enables it eventually to pass beyond itself, we have the first principle of progress from mortality to immortality. It is by the Sun as a door or gate[1] that the individual, the limited consciousness attains to the full consciousness and life in the one, supreme and all-embracing Soul.

Both consciousness and life are included in the formula of Immortality; Knowledge is incomplete without action. Chit fulfils itself by Tapas, Consciousness by energy. And as Surya represents the divine Light, so Agni to the ancient Rishis represented divine Force, Power or Will-in-Consciousness. The prayer to Agni completes the prayer to Surya.

THE INDIVIDUAL WILL

As in knowledge, so in action, unity is the true foundation. The individual, accepting division as his law, isolating himself

---

* 17. The Breath of things is an immortal life, but of this body ashes are the end. OM! O Will, remember, that which was done remember! O Will, remember, that which was done remember.

18. O god Agni, knowing all things that are manifested, lead us by the good path to the felicity; remove from us the devious attraction of sin. To thee completest speech of submission we address.

[1] *Sūryadvāreṇa.* — Mundaka Upanishad I. 2. 11.

in his own egoistic limits, is necessarily mortal, obscure and ignorant in his workings. He follows in his aims and in his methods a knowledge that is personal, governed by desire, habits of thought, obscure subconscious impulses or, at best, a broken partial and shifting light. He lives by rays and not in the full blaze of the Sun. His knowledge is narrow in its objectivity, narrow in its subjectivity, in neither one with the integral knowledge and the total working and total will in the universe. His action, therefore, is crooked, many-branching, hesitating and fluctuating in its impulsion and direction; it beats about among falsehoods to find the Truth, tosses or scrapes fragments together to piece out the whole, stumbles among errors and sins to find the right. Being neither one-visioned nor whole-visioned, having neither the totality of the universal Will nor the concentrated oneness of the transcendent, the individual will cannot walk straight on the right or good path towards the Truth and the Immortality. Governed by desire, exposed to the shock of the forces around it with which its egoism and ignorance forbid it to put itself in harmony, it is subject to the twin children of the Ignorance, suffering and falsehood. Not having the divine Truth and Right, it cannot have the divine Felicity.

AGNI, THE DIVINE WILL

But as there is in and behind all the falsehoods of our material mind and reason a Light that prepares by this twilight the full dawn of the Truth in man, so there is in and behind all our errors, sins and stumblings a secret Will, tending towards Love and Harmony, which knows where it is going and prepares and combines our crooked branchings towards the straight path which will be the final result of their toil and seeking. The emergence of this Will and that Light is the condition of immortality.

This Will is Agni. Agni is in the Rig Veda, from which the closing verse of the Upanishad is taken, the flame of the Divine Will or Force of Consciousness working in the worlds. He is described as the immortal in mortals, the leader of the journey, the divine Horse that bears us on the road, the "son of crookedness" who himself knows and is the straightness and the Truth. Concealed and hard to seize in the workings of this world because they are all falsified by desire and egoism, he uses them to transcend them and emerges as the universal in Man or universal Power, Agni Vaishwanara, who contains in himself all the gods and all the worlds, upholds all the universal workings and finally fulfils the godhead, the Immortality. He is the worker of the divine Work. It is these symbols which govern the sense of the two final verses of the Upanishad.

THE IMMORTAL LIFE-PRINCIPLE

Life is the condition from which the Will and the Light emerge. It is said in the Veda that Vayu or Matarishwan, the Life-principle, is he who brings down Agni from Surya in the high and far-off supreme world. Life calls down the divine Will from the Truth-consciousness into the realm of mind and body to prepare here, in Life, its own manifestation. Agni, enjoying and devouring the things of Life, generates the Maruts, nervous forces of Life that become forces of thought; they, upheld by Agni, prepare the action of Indra, the luminous Mind, who is for our life-powers their Rishi or finder of the Truth and Right. Indra slays Vritra, the Coverer, dispels the darkness, causes Surya to rise upon our being and go abroad over its whole field with the rays of the Truth. Surya is the Creator or manifester, Savitri, who manifests in this mortal world the world or state of immortality, dispels the evil dream of egoism, sin and suffering and transforms Life into the Immortality, the good, the beatitude. The Vedic gods are a parable of human life emerging, mounting, lifting itself towards the Godhead.

Life, body, action, will, these are our first materials. Matter supplies us with the body; but it is only a temporary knot of the movement, a dwelling-place of the Purusha in which he presides over the activities generated out of the Life-principle. Once it is thrown aside by the Life-principle it is dissolved; ashes are its end. Therefore the body is not ourselves, but only an outer tool and instrument. For Matter is the principle of obscurity and division, of birth and death, of formation and dissolution. It is the assertion of death. Immortal man must not identify himself with the body.

The Life-principle in us survives. It is the immortal Breath[2] or, as the phrase really means, the subtle force of existence which is superior to the principle of birth and death. At first sight it may appear that birth and death are attributes of the Life, but it is not really so: birth and death are processes of Matter, of the body. The Life-principle is not formed and dissolved in the formulation and dissolution of the body; if that were so, there could be no continuity of the individual existence and all would go back at death into the formless. Life forms body, it is not formed by it. It is the thread upon which the continuity of our successive bodily lives is arranged, precisely because it is itself immortal. It associates itself with the perishable body and carries forward the mental being, the Purusha in the mind, upon his journey.

WILL AND MEMORY

This journey consists in a series of activities continued from life to life in this world with intervals of life in other states. The Life-principle maintains them; it supplies their material in the formative energy which takes shape in them. But their presiding god is not the Life-principle; it is the Will. Will is Kratu, the effective power behind the act. It is of the nature of consciousness; it is energy of consciousness, and although present in all forms, conscious, subconscious or superconscious, vital, physical or mental, yet comes into its kingdom only when it emerges in Mind. It uses the mental faculty of memory to link together and direct consciously the activities towards the goal of the individual.

In man the use of consciousness by the mental will is imperfect, because memory is limited. Our action is both dispersed and circumscribed because mentally we live from hour to hour in the current of Time, holding only to that which attracts or

2 *Anilam amṛtam.*

seems immediately useful to our egoistic mind. We live in what we are doing, we do not control what has been done, but are rather controlled by our past works which we have forgotten. This is because we dwell in the action and its fruits instead of living in the soul and viewing the stream of action from behind it. The Lord, the true Will, stands back from the actions and therefore is their lord and not bound by them.

The Upanishad solemnly invokes the Will to remember the thing that has been done, so as to contain and be conscious of the becoming, so as to become a power of knowledge and self-possession and not only a power of impulsion and self-formulation. It will thus more and more approximate itself to the true Will and preside over the co-ordination of the successive lives with a conscious control. Instead of being carried from life to life in a crooked path, as by winds, it will be able to proceed more and more straight in an ordered series, linking life to life with an increasing force of knowledge and direction until it becomes the fully conscious Will moving with illumination on the straight path towards the immortal felicity. The mental will, *kratu*, becomes what it at present only represents, the divine Will, Agni.

WILL AND KNOWLEDGE

The essentiality of the divine Will is that in it Consciousness and Energy, Knowledge and Force are one. It knows all manifestations, all things that take birth in the worlds. It is Jatavedas, that which has right knowledge of all births. It knows them in the law of their being, in their relation to other births, in their aim and method, in their process and goal, in their unity with all and their difference from all. It is this divine Will that conducts the universe; it is one with all the things that it combines and its being, its knowledge, its action are inseparable from each other. What it is, it knows; what it knows, that it does and becomes.

But as soon as egoistic consciousness emerges and interferes, there is a disturbance, a division, a false action. Will becomes an impulsion ignorant of its secret motive and aim, knowledge becomes a dubious and partial ray not in possession of the will, the act and the result, but only striving to possess and inform them. This is because we are not in possession of our self,[3] our true being, but only of the ego. What we are, we know not; what we know, we cannot effect. For knowledge is real and action in harmony with true knowledge only when they proceed naturally out of the conscious, illumined and self-possessing soul, in which being, knowledge and action are one movement.

SURRENDER TO THE DIVINE WILL

This is the change that happens when, the mental will approximating more and more to the divine, Agni burns out in us. It is that increasing knowledge and force which carries us finally into the straight or good path out of the crookedness. It is the divine Will, one with the divine knowledge, which leads us towards felicity, towards the state of Immortality. All that belongs to the deviations of the ego, all that obscures and drives or draws us into this or that false path with its false lures and stumblings are put away from us by it. These things fall away from the divinised Will and cease to find lodging in our consciousness.

Therefore the sign of right action is the increasing and finally the complete submission of the individual to the divine Will which the illumination of Surya reveals in him. Although manifested in his consciousness, this Will is not individual. It is the will of the Purusha who is in all things and transcends them. It is the will of the Lord.

Knowledge of the Lord as the One in the fully self-conscious being, submission to the Lord as the universal and transcendent in the fully self-conscious action, are the two keys of the divine gates, the gates of Immortality.

And the nature of the two united is an illuminated Devotion which accepts, aspires to and fulfils God in the human existence.

---

[3] *Ātmavān.*

CONCLUSION

Thus the fourth movement indicates psychologically the double process of that attainment of Immortality which is the subject of the third movement, the state of bliss and truth within and the worlds of Light after death culminating in the identity of the self-luminous One. At the same time it particularises under the cover of Vedic symbols the process of that self-knowledge and identification with the Self and all its becomings which is the subject of the second movement and of that liberated action in the assertion of which the first culminates. It is thus a fitting close and consummation to the Upanishad.

Conclusion and Summary

T HE ISHA Upanishad is one of the more ancient of the Vedantic writings in style, substance and versification, subsequent certainly to the Chhandogya, Brihadaranyaka and perhaps to the Taittiriya and Aitareya, but certainly the most antique of the extant metrical Upanishads. Upanishadic thought falls naturally into two great periods; in one, the earlier, it still kept close to its Vedic roots, reflected the old psychological system of the Vedic Rishis and preserved what may be called their spiritual pragmatism; in the other and later, in which the form and thought became more modern and independent of early symbols and origins, some of the principal elements of Vedic thought and psychology begin to be omitted or to lose their previous connotation and the foundations of the later ascetic and anti-pragmatic Vedanta begin to appear. The Isha belongs to the earlier or Vedic group. It is already face to face with the problem of reconciling human life and activity with the Monistic standpoint and its large solution of the difficulty is one of the most interesting passages of Vedantic literature. It is the sole Upanishad which offered almost insuperable difficulties to the extreme illusionism and anti-pragmatism of Shankaracharya and it was even, for this reason, excised from the list of authoritative Upanishads by one of his greatest followers.

THE PRINCIPLE OF THE UPANISHAD

The principle it follows throughout is the uncompromising reconciliation of uncompromising extremes. Later thought took one series of terms, — the World, Enjoyment, Action, the Many, Birth, the Ignorance, — and gave them a more and more secondary position, exalting the opposite series, God, Renunciation, Quietism, the One, Cessation of Birth, the Knowledge, until this trend of thought culminated in Illusionism and the idea of existence in the world as a snare and a meaningless burden imposed inexplicably on the soul by itself, which must be cast aside as soon as possible. It ended in a violent cutting of the knot of the great enigma. This Upanishad tries instead to get hold of the extreme ends of the knots, disengage and place them alongside of each other in a release that will be at the same time a right placing and relation. It will not qualify or subordinate unduly any of the extremes, although it recognises a dependence of one on the other. Renunciation is to go to the extreme, but also enjoyment is to be equally integral; Action has to be complete and ungrudging, but also freedom of the soul from its works must be absolute; Unity utter and absolute is the goal, but this absoluteness has to be brought to its highest term by including in it the whole infinite multiplicity of things.

So great is this scruple in the Upanishad that having so expressed itself in the formula "By the Ignorance having crossed over death by the Knowledge one enjoys Immortality" that Life in the world might be interpreted as only a preliminary to an existence beyond, it at once rights the balance by reversing the order in the parallel formula "By dissolution having crossed over death by birth one enjoys Immortality", and thus makes life itself the field of the immortal existence which is the goal and aspiration of all life. In this conclusion it agrees with the early Vedic thought which believed all the worlds and existence and non-existence and death and life and immortality to be here in the embodied human being, there evolvent, there realisable and to be possessed and enjoyed, not dependent either for acquisition or enjoyment on the renunciation of life and bodily existence. This thought has never entirely passed out of Indian philosophy, but has become secondary and a side admission not strong enough to qualify seriously the increasing assertion of the extinction of mundane existence as the condition of our freedom and our sole wise and worthy aim.

THE OPPOSITES

The pairs of opposites successively taken up by the Upanishad and resolved are, in the order of their succession:
1. The Conscious Lord and phenomenal Nature.
2. Renunciation and Enjoyment.
3. Action in Nature and Freedom in the Soul.
4. The One stable Brahman and the multiple Movement.
5. Being and Becoming.
6. The Active Lord and the indifferent Akshara Brahman.
7. Vidya and Avidya.
8. Birth and Non-Birth.
9. Works and Knowledge.
These discords are thus successively resolved:

GOD AND NATURE

1. Phenomenal Nature is a movement of the conscious Lord. The object of the movement is to create forms of His consciousness in motion in which He as the one Soul in many bodies can take up his habitation and enjoy the multiplicity and the movement with all their relations.[1]

ENJOYMENT AND RENUNCIATION

2. Real integral enjoyment of all this movement and multiplicity in its truth and in its infinity depends upon an absolute renunciation; but the renunciation intended is an absolute renunciation of the principle of desire founded on the principle of egoism and not a renunciation of world-existence.[2] This solution depends on the idea that desire is only an egoistic and vital deformation of the divine Ananda or delight of being from which the

---

[1] This is also the view of the Gita and generally accepted.
[2] This again is the central standpoint of the Gita, which, however, admits also the renunciation of world-existence. The general trend of Vedantic thought would accept the renunciation of desire and egoism as the essential but would hold that renunciation of egoism means the renunciation of all world-existence, for it sees desire and not Ananda as the cause of world-existence.

world is born; by extirpation of ego and desire Ananda again becomes the conscious principle of existence. This substitution is the essence of the change from life in death to life in immortality. The enjoyment of the infinite delight of existence free from ego, founded on oneness of all in the Lord, is what is meant by the enjoyment of Immortality.

ACTION AND FREEDOM

3. Actions are not inconsistent with the soul's freedom. Man is not bound by works, but only seems to be bound. He has to re-cover the consciousness of his inalienable freedom by recovering the consciousness of unity in the Lord, unity in himself, unity with all existence.[3] This done, life and works can and should be accepted in their fullness; for the manifestation of the Lord in life and works is the law of our being and the object of our world-existence.

THE QUIESCENCE AND THE MOVEMENT

4. What then of the Quiescence of the Supreme Being and how is persistence in the Movement compatible with that Quiescence which is generally recognised as an essential condition of the supreme Bliss?

The Quiescence and the Movement are equally one Brah-man and the distinction drawn between them is only a phe-nomenon of our consciousness. So it is with the idea of space and time, the far and the near, the subjective and the objective, in-ternal and external, myself and others, one and many. Brahman, the real existence, is all these things to our consciousness, but in itself ineffably superior to all such practical distinctions. The Movement is a phenomenon of the Quiescence, the Quiescence itself may be conceived as a Movement too rapid for the gods, that is to say, for our various functions of consciousness to follow in its real nature. But it is no formal, material, spatial, temporal

---

[3] This truth would, again, be generally admitted, but not the conclusion that is drawn from it.

movement, only a movement in consciousness. Knowledge sees it all as one, Ignorance divides and creates oppositions where there is no opposition but simply relations of one consciousness in itself. The ego in the body says, "I am within, all else is outside; and in what is outside, this is near to me in Time and Space, that is far." All this is true in present relation; but in essence it is all one indivisible movement of Brahman which is not material movement but a way of seeing things in the one consciousness.

BEING AND BECOMING

5. Everything depends on what we see, how we look at existence in our soul's view of things. Being and Becoming, One and Many are both true and are both the same thing: Being is one, Becomings are many; but this simply means that all Becomings are one Being who places Himself variously in the phenomenal movement of His consciousness. We have to see the One Being, but we have not to cease to see the many Becomings, for they exist and are included in Brahman's view of Himself. Only, we must see with knowledge and not with ignorance. We have to realise our true self as the one unchangeable, indivisible Brahman. We have to see all becomings as developments of the movement in our true self and this self as one inhabiting all bodies and not our body only. We have to be consciously, in our relations with this world, what we really are, — this one self becoming everything that we observe. All the movement, all energies, all forms, all happenings we must see as those of our one and real self in many existences, as the play of the Will and Knowledge and Delight of the Lord in His world-existence.

We shall then be delivered from egoism and desire and the sense of separate existence and therefore from all grief and delusion and shrinking; for all grief is born of the shrinking of the ego from the contacts of existence, its sense of fear, weakness, want, dislike, etc.; and this is born from the delusion of separate existence, the sense of being my separate ego exposed to all these contacts of so much that is not myself.

Get rid of this, see oneness everywhere, be the One manifesting Himself in all creatures; ego will disappear; desire born of the sense of not being this, not having that, will disappear; the free inalienable delight of the One in His own existence will take the place of desire and its satisfactions and dissatisfactions.[4] Immortality will be yours, death born of division will be overcome.

THE ACTIVE AND INACTIVE BRAHMAN

6. The Inactive and the Active Brahman are simply two aspects of the one Self, the one Brahman, who is the Lord. It is He who has gone abroad in the movement. He maintains Himself free from all modifications in His inactive existence. The inaction is the basis of the action and exists in the action; it is His freedom from all He does and becomes and in all He does and becomes. These are the positive and negative poles of one indivisible consciousness. We embrace both in one quiescence and one movement, inseparable from each other, dependent on each other. The quiescence exists relatively to the movement, the movement to the quiescence. He is beyond both. This is a different point of view from that of the identity of the Movement and Quiescence which are one in reality; it expresses rather their relation in our consciousness once they are admitted as a practical necessity of that consciousness. It is obvious that we also by becoming one with the Lord would share in this biune conscious existence.[5]

VIDYA AND AVIDYA

7. The knowledge of the One and the knowledge of the Many are a result of the movement of the one consciousness, which

---

[4] In the ordinary view all this would be admitted, but the practical possibility of maintaining this state of consciousness and birth in the world together would be doubted.

[5] In the ordinary view the Jiva cannot exist in both at the same time; his dissolution is into the Quiescence and not into unity with the Lord in the action and inaction.

sees all things as One in their truth-Idea but differentiates them in their mentality and formal becoming. If the mind (Manishi) absorbs itself in God as the formal becoming (Paribhu) and separates itself from God in the true Idea (Kavi), then it loses Vidya, the knowledge of the One, and has only the knowledge of the Many which becomes no longer knowledge at all but ignorance, Avidya. This is the cause of the separate ego-sense.

Avidya is accepted by the Lord in the Mind (Manishi) in order to develop individual relations to their utmost in all the possibilities of division and its consequences and then through these individual relations to come back individually to the knowledge of the One in all. That knowledge has remained all along unabrogated in the consciousness of the true seer or Kavi. This seer in ourselves stands back from the mental thinker; the latter, thus separated, has to conquer death and division by a developing experience as the individual Inhabitant and finally to recover by the reunited knowledge of the One and the Many the state of Immortality. This is our proper course and not either to devote ourselves exclusively to the life of Avidya or to reject it entirely for motionless absorption in the One.

BIRTH AND NON-BIRTH

8. The reason for this double movement of the Thinker is that we are intended to realise immortality in the Birth. The self is uniform and undying and in itself always possesses immortality. It does not need to descend into Avidya and Birth to get that immortality of Non-Birth; for it possesses it always. It descends in order to realise and possess it as the individual Brahman in the play of world-existence. It accepts Birth and Death, assumes the ego and then dissolving the ego by the recovery of unity realises itself as the Lord, the One, and Birth as only a becoming of the Lord in mental and formal being; this becoming is now governed by the true sight of the Seer and, once this is done, becoming is no longer inconsistent with Being, birth becomes a means and not an obstacle to the enjoyment of immortality by

the lord of this formal habitation.[6] This is our proper course and
not to remain for ever in the chain of birth and death, nor to
flee from birth into a pure non-becoming. The bondage does not
consist in the physical act of becoming, but in the persistence
of the ignorant sense of the separate ego. The Mind creates the
chain and not the body.

WORKS AND KNOWLEDGE

9. The opposition between works and knowledge exists as long
as works and knowledge are only of the egoistic mental character. Mental knowledge is not true knowledge; true knowledge
is that which is based on the true sight, the sight of the Seer,
of Surya, of the Kavi. Mental thought is not knowledge, it is
a golden lid placed over the face of the Truth, the Sight, the
divine Ideation, the Truth-Consciousness. When that is removed,
sight replaces mental thought, the all-embracing truth-ideation,
Mahas, Veda, Drishti, replaces the fragmentary mental activity.
True Buddhi (Vijnana) emerges from the dissipated action of the
Buddhi which is all that is possible on the basis of the sense-
mind, the Manas. Vijnana leads us to pure knowledge (Jnana),
pure consciousness (Chit). There we realise our entire identity
with the Lord in all at the very roots of our being.

But in Chit, Will and Seeing are one. Therefore in Vijnana
or truth-ideation also which comes luminously out of Chit, Will
and Sight are combined and no longer as in the mind separated
from each other. Therefore when we have the sight and live in
the truth-consciousness, our will becomes the spontaneous law
of the truth in us and, knowing all its acts and their sense and
objective, leads straight to the human goal, which was always
the enjoyment of the Ananda, the Lord's delight in self-being,
the state of Immortality. In our acts also we become one with
all beings and our life grows into a representation of oneness,

---

[6] This is the stumbling-block to the ordinary philosophies which are impregnated with
the idea of the illusoriness of the world, even when they do not go the whole way with
the Mayavada. Birth, they would say, is a play of ignorance, it cannot subsist along with
entire knowledge.

truth and divine joy and no longer proceeds on the crooked path of egoism full of division, error and stumbling. In a word, we attain to the object of our existence which is to manifest in itself whether on earth in a terrestrial body and against the resistance of Matter or in the worlds beyond or enter beyond all world the glory of the divine Life and the divine Being.

Part Two

Incomplete Commentaries
from Manuscripts

Isha Upanishad

All that is world in the Universe

The Sanscrit word जगत् is in origin a reduplicated & therefore frequentative participle from the root गम् to go. It signifies "that which is in perpetual motion", and implies in its neuter form the world, universe, and in its feminine form the earth. World therefore is that which eternally vibrates, and the Hindu idea of the cosmos reduces itself to a harmony of eternal vibrations; form as we see it is simply the varying combination of different vibrations as they affect us through our perceptions & establish themselves to the concept. So far then Hinduism has reached by analysis to the last & simplest material expression of this complex universe. The question then arises, "Does anything lie beyond? If matter is all, then this is the last & there is no beyond. But is matter all?"

Our first verse is the answer of the Upanishad to this question. "All that is world in the Universe by the Lord must be pervaded." The very object of our existence is to pierce beyond this last & thinnest veil of matter to Spirit, the Lord who is behind every manifestation of matter, even the simplest & therefore is he the Lord, he is the Self of all things, matter being merely the body. When we have realised that all this universe of vibration is full of the Spirit, we have set our feet on the right road that will lead us to the goal of existence. This is what we "must" do, in other words to realise God in the universe is the object of our existence. But why does the Upanishad say "must be pervaded"; why does it not say simply "is pervaded"? Is this pervasion then not a fact, but a possibility which each individual soul has to turn into a fact for itself? In what sense is it said that the object of the individual soul is to pervade the Universe with the Lord? We must remember that according to the Upanishad there are only two entities in existence which are not phenomena or manifestations, but eternal facts, and these two are in reality not two but one, the illimitable & infinite Self behind phenomena, and the finite self which perceives phenomena. The Adwaita or Monistic Vedanta affirms the entire unity of these two & explains their apparent separation by Maya, Illusion or Ignorance, in other words by the theory that the Indivisible Eternal has deliberately imagined himself as divisible (I speak in metaphors, the only way of approaching such subtle inquiries) & hence created an illusion of multiplicity where the only real fact is Unity. We may take the metaphor of a sea & its waves; if each wave were to imagine itself separate from all other waves & from the sea of which it is a part, that would be an illusion similar to that of the finite self when it imagines itself as different from other finite selves and from the Infinite. The wave is not really different from the sea but is sea (not *the* sea) and the next moment will be indistinguishable from sea; in fact the word "wave" merely expresses a momentary perception, an idea of change or modification which the next moment we perceive not to exist, and not a real object; the only real object is the sea.

The Visishta Adwaita or modified-Monistic Vedanta on the other hand recognises that the infinite Self & the finite Self are eventually One, but still there is a distinction, a certain limitation of the Oneness. The finite Self is of & in the infinite Self & therefore one with it but it does not coincide with it or disappear into it; the goal of its existence is the delight of feeling its oneness with the Eternal, but still the very feeling of delight implies a limitation, a difference, & this limitation is not temporary but eternal. An image may be taken from the phenomenon of Light & its vibrations; it is all light, there is no real difference, & yet each of the vibrations is in a sense separate & continues its own existence on its own line for ever through infinity. Lastly the Dwaita or Dualistic Vedanta affirms, on the contrary, that the finite selves & the Infinite are for ever different & the whole riddle of the world lies in their difference & in their attraction to each other. To become one with the Eternal is here also the goal of the finite but the oneness is emotional & not essential; it is Union & not fusion. It is difficult to find a close image here, but for want of a better we may take that of a river & the sea to which it is hasting. It is water hasting to water & the whole aim of the river is to fling itself into the sea & towards that it strives with all its might & with all its soul; & finally it reaches the sea & mixes with it. And yet there it is still, a river & not the sea. So the two live in a perpetual embrace, ever united & yet ever different & feeling their separate existence. Now these three philosophies really image three different states of soul & three different roads to the realisation of God. There is the intellectual state of soul which reaches God through knowledge; this naturally attaches itself to Monism, for it seeks only the knowledge of its identity with God & its tendency is to discourage all action & emotion which interfere with this aim. Then there is the actional state of soul which reaches God through action leading to knowledge & inspired by emotion; this aims at the knowledge of its identity with God, but its actional state requires a certain sense of difference from God without which action becomes meaningless; its tendency therefore, if the knowledge-impulse predominates over the emotional, is to rest for a time in modified Monism, though it recognises pure Monism as a far goal beyond; but if the emotional impulse predominates over the intellectual, its tendency is to adopt modified Monism as a final solution. Lastly there is the emotional state of soul which reaches God through divine love; this naturally attaches itself to Dualism; for the only desire of love is to attain the loved one & go on loving for ever; an impossibility unless the feeling of difference in Union goes on for ever. The three philosophies are therefore simply three different standpoints from which we envisage one single truth, that nothing eventually matters in the world except God & the goal of existence is to attain Him. And I may add my own conviction that all three are necessary soul-stages. By pausing too long in Dualism or even in modified Monism, we debar ourselves too long from our final emancipation; but by leaping too quickly to Monism we fall into a dangerous tendency towards the premature dissolution of phenomena which if largely followed upsets the fine balance of the world. The right progress of the soul is first to realise its difference from God, so that we may feel attracted towards Him, then to realise that that difference is a temporary or at least not an entire difference, that there is unity beyond, so that we may advance towards Him by the right road & under the laws of that phenomenal existence through which he reveals himself to us, and finally to perceive that we and God are One & all phenomena temporary & illusory, so that escaping from name & form we may lose ourselves in Him and attain our soul's salvation. Well then, here are three standpoints; which is the standpoint of the Upanishads? They do not, in fact, confine themselves to any, but regarding them as three necessary stages, speak now from one, now from another, now from a third. Here it is speaking in a spirit of very slightly modified Monism. There are two nonphenomenal existences, the Infinite Self & the Finite Self; from the point of view of the Infinite, Eternal Self, the universe is already pervaded with God; but we must also consider the point of view of the Finite Self, — which is really Infinite but considers itself to be Finite. To this Finite Self the Universe is only the mass of its own perceptions. If it perceives the Universe as mere matter, then for its purposes the Universe is Matter & not pervaded by the Lord; if I consider yonder tree as so much wood & pith & sap & leaves, such it is & no more so far as I am concerned; if I look within & perceive God there then it is I who have put him there; for the moment before He was not there for me & now He is. In more Monistic language the Self at first imagines itself to be confined within its own body, but as it grows in thought it looks into object after object & perceives itself there & so it goes on putting itself into everything until it has pervaded all that is in the world with itself; it then realises that there is no self or non-self but all is God. We see that it is merely a difference of language, of outlook, of perception; but these are the things through which human thought proceeds & they must be given their due place. To recognize the differences they involve & yet to perceive the unity into which they merge, is the law & goal of all Hindu thought.

But whatever the standpoint we take, for dualist, monist or semimonist the Vedanta lays this down as the great essential step to realise that when we have resolved this universe of forms

& names into a great harmony of vibrations, we must still go beyond & perceive that the whole is but the material expression of one pervading Spirit. And when we have realised this, what is the practical result; for it must be remembered that the Vedanta is always profoundly practical[.]

The Ishavasyopanishad

with a commentary in English

1.

With God all this must be invested, even all that is world in this
moving universe; abandon therefore desire and enjoy and covet
no man's possession.

THE GURU

The Upanishad sets forth by pronouncing as the indispensable basis of its revelations the universal nature of God. This
universal nature of Brahman the Eternal is the beginning and
end of the Vedanta and if it is not accepted, nothing the Vedanta
says can have any value, as all its propositions either proceed
from it or at least presuppose it; deprived of this central and
highest truth, the Upanishads become what Mleccha scholars &
philosophers think them to be, — a mass of incoherent though
often sublime speculations; with this truth in your hand as a
lamp to shed light on all the obscurest sayings of the Scriptures,
you soon come to realise that the Upanishads are a grand harmonious and perfectly luminous whole, expressing in its various
aspects the single and universal Truth; for under the myriad
contradictions of phenomena (prapancha) there is one Truth
and one only. All the Smritis, the Puranas, the Darshanas, the
Dharmashastras, the writings of Shaktas, Shaivas, Vaishnavas,
Sauras, as well as the whole of Buddhism and its Scriptures
are merely so many explanations, comments and interpretations
from different sides, of these various aspects of the one and only
Truth. This Truth is the sole foundation on which all religions
can rest as on a sure and impregnable rock; — and more than a
rock, for a rock may perish but this endures for ever. Therefore
is the religion of the Aryas called the Sanatana Dharma, the Law
Sempiternal. Nor are the Hindus in error when they declare the
Sruti to be eternal and without beginning and the Rishis who

composed the hymns to be only the witnesses who saw the truth and put it in human language; for this seeing was not mental sight, but spiritual. Therefore the Vedas are justly called Sruti or revelation. Of these the Rig, Yajur, Sama & Atharvan are the fertilising rain which gave the plant of the Truth nourishment and made it grow, the Brahmanas are the forest in which the plant is found, the Aranyakas are the soil in which it grows, the Upanishads are the plant itself, roots, stalk, leaves, calix and petals, and the flower which manifests itself once and for ever is the great saying SO AHAM — I AM HE which is the culmination of the Upanishads. Salutation to the SO AHAM. Salutation to the Eternal who is without place, time, cause or limit, Salutation to my Self who am the Eternal.

THE STUDENT

   I salute the Eternal and my Self who am the Eternal. Swaha!

THE GURU

   The Upanishad therefore begins by saying that all this must be clothed or invested with the Lord. By this expression it is meant that the individual Jivatman or human soul in order to attain salvation must cover up all this universe with the Lord, as one might cover the body with a garment. By the Lord we mean obviously not the Unknowable Parabrahman, for of the Unknowable we cannot speak in terms of place, time or difference, but the Brahman knowable by Yoga, the luminous shadow of the One put forth by the Shakti of the One, which by dividing itself into the Male and Female, Purusha and Prakriti, has created this world of innumerable forms and names. Brahman is spoken of as the Lord; that is, we best think of Him as the Ruler & Sovran of the Universe. He is the still ocean of spiritual force, its mere presence sets working the creative, preservative, and destructive Shakti or Will of the Eternal Parabrahman. By her means he forms the Ocean of Prakriti, which is the substratum of all form or matter. Of these two, the Ocean of spiritual force and the Ocean of material form, the latter is contained in the other & could not be without it. It may be said to be surrounded by it or clothed by it. The Lord himself is present on the Ocean in various forms, Prajna, Hiranyagarbha & Virat, or Vishnu, Brahma and Maheshwara. This is what the Puranas represent as Vishnu on the Serpent of Time & Space in the Causal Ocean & Brahma growing out of the lotus in his navel etc. This is the Lord, the King & Ruler. We must therefore realise all things in this universe to be the creation of that ocean of Brahman or spiritual force which surrounds them as a robe surrounds its wearer.

THE STUDENT

Surely all things [are] Brahman himself; why then should he be said to surround all things as if he were different from them?

THE GURU

It is meant by this expression that the universal & undivided consciousness which we call Brahman, surrounds and includes all the limited individual consciousnesses which present themselves to us in the shape of things.

THE STUDENT

Still I do not understand. How can the one indivisible consciousness be divided, or if it is divided how can it at the same time remain one and surround its own parts? A thing cannot be at the same time one and indivisible and yet divisible and multifold.

THE GURU

On the contrary this is precisely the nature of consciousness to be eternally one & indivisible, & yet always divisible at will. A man's consciousness has often been split up into two states, each with its own history and memory, so that when he is in one state, he does not know what he has been thinking and doing in the other. Persons ignorant of the Truth imagine from this circumstance that a man's consciousness must be not single and homogeneous but a bundle of different personalities, just as the Sankhyas & others imagine that there must be an infinite number of Purushas, souls & not One, for otherwise, they say,

all would have the same knowledge, the same pleasure & pain
etc. (This is so in a sense, as his present personality contains also
in a submerged state the personalities of his previous births, and
an unwise hypnosis may throw him back into a bygone state of
personality.) But this is merely Avidya, Ignorance, & when the
apparently individual Purusha puts himself into the complete
state of Yoga with the Eternal he discovers that all the time there
was only One Purusha who was cognizant of & contained the
others, in the sense that they were simply projections (सृष्टिs) from
him. These states of split consciousness are only different states
of one personality and not separate personalities. This will at
once be clear if a skilful and careful hypnotiser put the man in the
right state of sleep; for then a third state of personality will often
evolve which has known all along what the other two were doing
and saying & is in itself sufficient proof that all along the unity
of consciousness was there, submerged indeed but constant and
subliminally active. The division of this one consciousness into
two separate states results from a particular & unusual action
of Avidya, the same universal Nescience which in its general
& normal action makes men imagine that they are a different
self from the Universal Consciousness and not merely states or
conditions projected (सृष्ट) of that consciousness. We see here then
an established example of the one and indivisible consciousness
becoming divided and multifold, yet remaining one and indivisible all the time. This single consciousness itself, the I of the
waking man, is only a division or rather a state of a still wider
consciousness more independent of gross matter which gets
some play in the condition of dream (and of dream hypnosis is
only a particular and capricious form), but is more permanently
& coherently liberated from the gross body at or after death.
This wider consciousness is called the Dream Condition and
the body or upadhi in which it works is called the Subtle Body.
The Dream Consciousness may be said to surround the waking
consciousness and its body as a robe surrounds its wearer, for
it is wider & less trammelled in its nature & range; it is the
selecting agency from which & by which a part is selected for
waking purposes in the material life. The Dream Consciousness

is itself [surrounded] by a still wider consciousness which we call the Sleep Condition or the Causal Body and from this & by this it is selected for life before birth & after death. This Sleep Condition is again surrounded by Brahman from whom & by whom it is selected for causal purposes, — just as a robe surrounds its wearer. Thus you will realise that Brahman is a wide eternally one & indivisible Consciousness which yet limits itself at will and yet remains illimitable surrounding like a robe all its various states or illusory limitations.

THE STUDENT

True but that which surrounds is always a separate thing from that which is surrounded, the robe is different from its wearer.

THE GURU

Let us consider a nut with the kernel in it, we see that ether in the form or *upadhi* of the nut, surrounds ether in the *upadhi* of the kernel as a robe surrounds its wearer; but the two are the same; there is one ether, not two.

THE STUDENT

Now I understand.

THE GURU

Consider next what the Upanishad goes on to indicate more definitely as the thing to be clothed or invested — whatever is *jagat* in *jagati*, or literally whatever is moving thing in her that moves. Now *jagati*, she who moves, is an old name for Earth, Prithivi, and afterwards for the whole *wide* universe, of which the Earth with which alone we human beings are at present concerned, is the type. Why then is the universe called *jagati*, she that moveth? Because it is a form of Prakriti whose essential characteristic is motion; for by motion she creates this material world, and indeed all object-matter is only a form, that is to say a visible, audible or sensible result of motion; every material object is *jagat*, full of infinite motion, — even the stone, even the clod. This material world, our senses tell us, is the only existing reality; but the Upanishad warns us against the false evidence of our senses and bids us realise in our hearts and minds Brahman the Ocean of spiritual force, drawing him in our imaginations like a robe round each sensible thing.

THE STUDENT
But the Upanishad does not say that the material world is itself Brahman.

THE GURU
It will yet say that. It tells us next by abandonment of this (all that is in the world) to enjoy and not covet any man's wealth. We are to enjoy the whole world, but not to covet the possessions of others. How is this possible? If I, Devadatta, am told to enjoy all that is in the world, but find that I have very little to enjoy while my neighbour Harischandra has untold riches, how can I fail to envy him his wealth and why should I not try to get it for my own enjoyment, if I safely can? I shall not try, because I cannot, because I have realized that there is nothing in this world but Brahman manifesting the universe by his Shakti, and that there is no Devadatta, no Harischandra, but only Brahman in various states of consciousness to which these names are given. If therefore Harischandra enjoys his riches, then it is I who am enjoying them, for Harischandra is myself, — not my body in which I am imprisoned or my desires by which my body is made miserable, but my true self, the Purusha within me who is the witness & enjoyer of all this sweet, bitter, tender, grand, beautiful, terrible, pleasant, horrible and wholly wonderful and enjoyable drama of the world which Prakriti enacts for his delectation. Now if as the Sankhyas and other philosophies and the Christians and other religions declare, there are innumerable Purushas and not one, there would be no ground for the Christian injunction to love others as oneself or for the description by the Sruti & Smriti of the perfect sage as सर्वभूतहितरत:, busied with and delighting in the good of all creatures; for then Harischandra would be in no way connected with me and there would be no point of contact

between us except the material, from which hatred & envy are far more ready to arise than love and sympathy. How then could I prefer him to myself? But from the point of view of Vedanta, such preference is natural, right and in the end inevitable.

THE STUDENT
That is a large view.

THE GURU
And a true view.

THE STUDENT
How is the preference of others to myself inevitable, natural, right?

THE GURU
It is inevitable because as I have risen from the beast to the man, so must I rise from the man to the God & of Godhead this preference is the perennial well & fountain, evolution meaning simply the wider and wider revelation of Brahman, the universal spirit, the progress from the falsehood of matter to the truth of spirit; — and this progress, however slow, is inevitable. It is natural because I am not really preferring another to myself, but my true self to my false, God who is in all to my single body and mind, myself in Devadatta and Harischandra, to myself in Devadatta alone. It is right because it is better for me to enjoy the enjoyment of Harischandra than to enjoy my own, since in this way I shall make my knowledge of Brahman a reality and not a mere intellectual conception or assent; I shall turn it into an experience — anubhav, and anubhav, the Smritis tell us, is the essence of true Jnana. For this reason perfect love, by which I do not mean the mere sensual impulse of man towards woman, is a great and ennobling thing, for by its means two separated conditions of the Universal Consciousness come together and become one. Still nobler and more ennobling is the love of the patriot who lives & dies for his country, for in this way he

becomes one with millions of divine units and still greater, nobler, more exalting the soul of the philanthropist, who without
forgetting family or country lives and dies for mankind or for all
creatures. He is the wisest Muni, the greatest Yogi, who not only
reaches Brahman by the way of Jnana, not only soars to Him
on the wings of Bhakti, but becomes He through God-devoted
Karma, who gives himself up utterly for his family and friends,
for his country, for all humanity, for the world, yes & when he
can, the solar system & systems upon systems, — for the whole
universe.

Therefore the Upanishad tells us that we must enjoy by
abandonment, by *tyaga* or renunciation. This is a curious expression, तेन त्यक्तेन भुञ्जीथा:; it is a curious thing to tell a man
that he must abandon & what he has abandoned enjoy by the
very sacrifice. The natural man shrinks from the statement as a
dangerous paradox. Yet the seer of the Upanishad is wiser than
we, for his statement is literally true. Think what it means. It
means that we give up our own petty personal joy and pleasure,
to bathe up to the eyes in the joys of others; and the joys of one
man may be as great as you please, the united joys of a hundred
must needs be greater. By renunciation you can increase your
enjoyments a hundredfold; if you are a true patriot, you will feel
the joys, not of one man, but of three hundred millions; if you
are a true philanthropist, all the joys of the countless millions
of the earth will flow through your soul like an ocean of nectar.
But, you say, their sorrows will flow there too? That too is an
agony of sweetness which exalts the soul to Paradise, that you
can turn into joy, the unparalleled joy of relieving and turning
into bliss the woes of the nation for which you sacrifice yourself
or of the humanity in whom you are trying to realise God. Even
the mere continuous patient resolute effort to do this is a joy
unspeakable; even defeat in such a cause is a stern pleasure
when it strengthens the soul for new and ceaseless endeavour.
And the souls worthy of the sacrifice, derive equal strength from
defeat & victory. Remember that [it] is not the weak in spirit to
whom the Eternal gives himself wholly; it is the strong heroic
soul that reaches God. Others can only touch His shadow from

afar. In this way the man who renounces the little he can call his own for the good of others, gets in return and can utterly enjoy all that is world in this moving universe.

If you cannot rise so high, still the words of the Upanishad are true in other ways. You are not asked necessarily to give up the objects of your enjoyments physically; it is enough if you give them up in your heart, if you enjoy them in such spirit that you will neither be overjoyed by gain nor cast down by loss. That enjoyment is clear, deep and calm; fate cannot break it, robbers cannot take it away, enemies cannot overwhelm it. Otherwise your enjoyment is chequered and broken with fear, sorrow, trouble & passion, the passion for its increase, the trouble of keeping it, the sorrow of diminution, the fear of its utter loss. It is far better by abandoning to enjoy. If you wish to abandon physically, that too is well, so long as you take care that you are not cherishing the thought of the enjoyment in your mind. Nay, it will often be a quicker road to enjoyment. Wealth and fame and success naturally flee from the man who pursues them; he breaks his heart or perishes without gaining them; or if he gains them, it is often after a very hell of difficulty, a very mountain of toil. But when a man turns his back on wealth & glory, then, unless his past actions forbid, they come crowding to lay themselves at his feet. And if they come, will he enjoy or reject them? He may reject them — that is a great path & the way of innumerable saintly sages — but you need not reject them, you may take & enjoy them. How will you enjoy them then? Not for your personal pleasure, certainly not for your false self; for you have already abandoned that kind of enjoyment in your heart; but you may enjoy God in them and them for God. As a king merely touching the nuzzerana, passes it on into the public treasury, so you may, merely touching the wealth that comes to you, pour it out for those around you, for the country, for humanity, seeing Brahman in these. Glory again he may conceal with humility, but use the influence it gives him in order to lead men upwards to the divine. Such a man will quickly rise above joy & sorrow, victory & defeat; for in sorrow as in joy he will feel himself to be near God, with God, like God and finally God himself. Therefore the Upanishads go on to say

कुर्वन्नेवेह कर्माणि जिजीविषेच्छतं समा: ।

Do thy deeds in this world and wish to live thy hundred years. A
hundred years is the full span of man's natural life according to
the Vedas. The Sruti therefore tells us that we must not turn our
backs on life, must not fling it from us untimely or even long for
early release from our body but willingly fill out our term, even
be most ready to prolong it to the full period of man's ordinary
existence so that we may go on doing our deeds in this world.
Mark the emphasis laid on the word कुर्वन् by adding to it *eva*.
Verily we must *do* our deeds in the world and not avoid doing
them; there is no need to flee to the mountains in order to find
the Self, since He is here, in you and in all around you. And if
you flee there, not to find Him, but to escape from the misery &
misfortune of the world which you are too weak to face, then
you lose the Self for this life and perhaps many to come. I repeat
to you that it is not the weak and the coward who can climb
up to God, but the strong and brave alone. Every individual
Jivatman must become the perfect Kshatriya before he can be
the Brahmin.

THE STUDENT
     All this is opposed to what the wisest men have taught and
those we most delight to revere, still teach and practise.

THE GURU
     Are you sure that it is? What do they teach?

THE STUDENT
     That *vairagya*, disgust with the world is the best way and
its entry into a man's soul is his first call to the way of *mukti*,
which is not by action but by knowledge.

THE GURU
     Vairagya is a big word and it has come to mean many things,
and it is because these are confused and jumbled together by the

men of Aryavarta, that tamas and Anaryan cowardice, weakness & selfishness have spread over this holy & ancient land, covering it with a thick pall of darkness. There is one vairagya, the truest and noblest, of the strong man who having tasted the sweets of this world finds that there is no permanent and abiding sweetness in them, that they are not the true and immortal joy which his true and immortal self demands and turns to something in himself which is deeper, holier and imperishable. Then there is the vairagya of the weakling who has lusted and panted and thirsted for the world's sweets but has been pushed & hustled from the board by fate or by stronger men than himself; and would use Yoga and Vedanta as the drunkard uses his bottle and the opium-maniac his pill or his laudanum. Not for such ignoble uses were these great things meant by the Rishis who disclosed them to the world. If such a man came to me for initiation, I would send him back with the fiery rebuke of Srikrishna to the son of Pritha

कुतस्त्वा कश्मलमिदं विषमे समुपस्थितम् ।
अनार्यजुष्टमस्वर्ग्यमकीर्तिकरमर्जुन ॥
क्लैब्यं मा स्म गमः पार्थ नैतत् त्वय्युपपद्यते ।

Truly is such weakness unworthy of one who is no other than Brahma, the Eternal, the Creator and Destroyer of the worlds. Yet I would not be understood to decry the true vairagya of sorrow and disappointment; for sometimes when men have tried in ignorance for ignoble things and failed, not from weakness but because these things were beneath their true greatness and high destiny, then their eyes are opened and they seek meditation, solitude and samadhi not as a dram to drown their sorrow and still unsated longing, but to realise their divine strength and use it for divine purposes; sometimes great spirits seek the way of the Sannyasin, because in the solitude alone with God and the Guru, they can best develop Brahmatejah. Once attained they pour it in a stream over the world; such was Shankaracharya; and sometimes it is the sorrow of others or the misery of the world that finds them in ease & felicity & drives them out, as Buddha was driven out, to seek help for sufferers in the depths of their own being. True Sannyasins are the greatest of all men because they are the strongest unto work, the most mighty in God to do the works of God.

THE STUDENT

I repeat that all this is opposed to the teaching of the great Adwaitavadin Acharyas, Sri Shankara and the rest.

THE GURU

It is not opposed to the teaching of Srikrishna who is the greatest of all teachers and the best of Jagatgurus. For he tells Sanjay in the Mahabharata that between the creed of salvation by works and the creed of salvation by no works, that of salvation by works is the true creed and he condemns the other as the idle talk of a weakling; and again and again in the Bhagavadgita he lays stress on the superiority of works.

THE STUDENT

This is true, but he also says that Jnana is superior to all things and there is nothing equal to it.

THE GURU

Nor is there; for Jnana is indispensable. Jnana is first & greatest; works without Jnana will not save a man but only plunge him deeper and deeper into bondage. The works of which the Upanishad speaks are to be done after you have invested all this universe with God; after, that is to say, you have realised that all is the one Brahman and that your actions are but the dramatic illusions unrolled by Prakriti for the delight of the Purusha. You will then do your works तेन त्यक्तेन; or as Srikrishna tells you to do, after giving up the desire for the fruits of your works and devoting all your actions to Him, — not to your lower not-self which feels pleasure & pain but to the Brahman in you which works only लोकसंग्रहार्थं that instead of the uninstructed multitudes being bewildered and led astray by your inactivity, the world may rather be helped, strengthened and maintained by the godlike nature of your works. This is what the Upanishad goes on to say

"Thus to you there is no other way than this, action clingeth not to a man." This means that desireless actions, actions performed after renunciation and devoted to God, — these & these only — do not cling to a man, do not bind him in their invisible chains but fall from him as the water from the wings of the swan. They cannot bind him, because he is freed from the woven net of causality. Causality springs from the idea of duality, the idea of sorrow & happiness, love & hate, heat & cold which arises from Avidya and he, having renounced desire and realised Unity, is above Avidya and above duality. Bondage has no meaning for him. It is not in reality he that is doing the actions, but Prakriti inspired by the presence of the Purusha in him.

THE STUDENT

Why then does Shankara say that it is necessary to give up works in order to attain absolute unity? Those who do works, in his opinion, only reach सालोक्य with Brahman, relative and not absolute unity.

THE GURU

There was a reason for what Shankara said and it was necessary in his age that Jnana should be exalted at the expense of works; for the great living force with which he had to struggle, was not the heresies of later Buddhism — Buddhism decayed and senescent, but the triumphant doctrines of the Karmakanda which made the faithful performance of Vedic rites & ceremonies the one path and heaven the only goal. In his continual anxiety to show that works — of which these rites & ceremonies were a part, — could not be the one path to heaven, he bent the bow as far as he could the other way and argued that works were not the path to the last and greatest *mukti* at all. Let us however consider what the depreciation of the Karmamarga means in the mouths of Shankara and other Jnanamargis. It may mean that Karma in the sense of Vedic rites & ceremonies are not the way to Mukti and if this is the meaning, then Shankara has done his work effectually; for I think no one of authority will now try to maintain the opposite thesis. We all agree that Swarga,

the sole final result of the Karmakanda, is not Mukti, is much
below Mukti and ends as soon as its cause is exhausted. We all
agree also that the only spiritual usefulness of Vedic ceremonies
is to purify the mind and fit it for starting on the true path of
Mukti which lies through Jnana. But if you say that works in
the sense of कर्तव्य कर्म are not a path to Mukti, then I demur;
for I say that Karma is not different from Jnana, but is Jnana, is
the necessary fulfilment and completion of Jnana; that Bhakti,
Karma and Jnana are not three but one and go inseparably
together. Therefore Srikrishna says that Sankhya (Jnanayog) and
Yoga (Bhakti Karma Yoga) are not two but one and only बाला:,
undeveloped minds, make a difference.

THE STUDENT
    But how can Shankaracharya be called an undeveloped
mind?

THE GURU
    He was not an undeveloped mind, but he was dealing with
undeveloped minds and had to speak their language. If he had
given his sanction to Karma, however qualified, the general run
of people would not have understood him and would have clung
to their rites and ceremonies; it is indeed to this difficulty of
language, its natural imperfection and the imperfection of the
minds that employ language, to which all the confusion and
sense of difference in religion & philosophy is due, for religion
& philosophy are one & above difference. Nor was Shankara
so entirely opposed to Karma as is ordinarily imagined from
the vehemence of his argument in some places. For what do
you mean when you say that Karma is no path to Mukti? Is
it that Karma prompted by desire is inconsistent with *mukti*,
because it necessarily leads to bondage and must therefore be
abandoned? On this head there is no dispute. We all agree that
works prompted by desire, lead to nothing but the fulfilment of
desire followed by fresh works in another life. Is it that Karma
without desire is inconsistent with Mukti, prevents *mukti* by
fresh bondage and must be abandoned? This is not consistent

with reason, for bondage is the result of desire & ignorance and disappears with desire & ignorance; therefore in *nishkam karma* there can be no bondage. It is inconsistent with Sruti त्रिणाचिकेतस्त्रिभिरेत्य सन्धिं त्रिकर्मकृत्तरति जन्ममृत्यू इत्यादि. It is inconsistent with facts for Srikrishna did works, Janaka and others did works, but none will say that they fell into the bondage of their works; for they were जीवन्मुक्त. Is it meant that *nishkam karma* may be done as a step towards ब्रह्मप्राप्ति by Jnan but must be abandoned as soon as Jnan is acquired? This also will not stand because Janaka and the others did works after they had acquired Jnan as well as before. For the same reason Shankara's argument that कर्म must cease as a matter of sheer necessity as soon as one gains Brahma, because Brahma is अकर्ता, will not stand; for Janaka gained Brahma, Srikrishna *was* Brahma, and yet both did works; nay, Srikrishna in one place speaks of him as doing works; for indeed Brahman is both अकर्ता as Purusha and कर्ता as Prakriti; and if it be said that Parabrahman the Turiya Atma in whom all *bhed* disappears is अकर्ता, I answer that he is neither कर्ता nor अकर्ता, He is नेति नेति, the Unknowable and the Jivatma does not merge finally in Him while it is in the body; though it may do so at any time by Yoga. लय takes place आदेहनिपातात्, that is to say by the Muktatma after leaving its body, not willing to return to another; the Jivanmukta is made one with the luminous shadow of Parabrahman which we call the Sacchidananda. If it be said that this is not Mukti, I answer that there can be no greater Mukti than becoming the Sacchidananda, and that *laya* in the Parabrahman is स्वेच्छाधीन to the Jivatman when it has ceased to be Jivatman and become Sacchidananda; for Parabrahman can always & at will draw Sacchidananda into Itself and Sacchidananda can always and at will draw into Parabrahman; since the two are in no sense two but one, in no sense subject to Avidya but on the other side of Avidya. Then if it be said that निष्काम कर्म can only lead to Brahmaloka and not mukti, I still answer that in that case we must suppose that Srikrishna after he left his body, remained separate from the Supreme and therefore was not Bhagavan at all but only a great philosopher & devotee, not wise enough to attain Mukti, and that Janak and other Jivanmuktas were falsely called muktas or only in the sense of the आपेक्षिक *mukti*. This however would contradict Scripture and the uniform teaching of Sruti and Smriti, and cannot therefore be upheld by any Hindu, still less by any Vedantin; for if there is no authority in Sruti, then there is no truth in Vedanta, and the doctrine of the Charvakas has as much force as any. Moreover it would contradict reason, since it would make mukti which is a spiritual change, dependent on a mere mechanical & material change like death, which is absurd. Shankara himself therefore admits that in these cases निष्काम कर्म was not inconsistent with मुक्ति or with being the Brahman; and he would have admitted it still more unreservedly if he had not been embarrassed by his relations of intellectual hostility to the Purvamimansa. It is proved therefore that कर्म is not inconsistent with मुक्ति but that on the contrary both the teaching and practice of the greatest Jivanmuktas and of Bhagavan himself have combined Jnana and निष्काम कर्म as one single path to *mukti*.

One argument, however, remains; it may be said that कर्म may be not inconsistent with *mukti*, may be one path to *mukti*, but in the last stage it is not necessary to *mukti*. I readily admit that particular works are not necessary to *mukti*; it is not necessary to continue being a householder in order to gain *mukti*. But no one who possesses a body, can be free of karma. This is clearly and incontrovertibly stated by Srikrishna in the Bhagavadgita.

[न हि कश्चित्क्षणमपि जातु तिष्ठत्यकर्मकृत् ।
कार्यते ह्यवशः कर्म सर्वः प्रकृतिजैर्गुणैः ॥]

And this statement in the Gita is perfectly consistent with reason; for the man who leaves the world behind him and sits on a mountaintop or in an asram has not therefore, it is quite clear, got rid of Karma; if nothing else, he has to maintain his body, to eat, to walk, to move his limbs or to sit in *asan* and meditate; and all this is Karma. If he is not yet mukta, this karma will moreover bind him and bear its fruits in relation to himself as well as to others; even if he is mukta, his body & mind are not free from Karma until his body is dropped off, but go on under the impulse of prarabdha until the prarabdha & its fruit are complete. Nay even the greatest Yogi by his mere bodily presence in the phenomenal world, is pouring out a stream of spiritual force on all sides, and this action though it does not bind him, has a stupendous influence on others. He is सर्वभूतहिते रत: though he wills it not; he too with regard to his body is अवश: and must let the gunas of prakriti work. Since this is so, let every man who wishes to throw his कर्तव्य कर्म behind him, see that he is not merely postponing the completion of his प्रारब्ध to a future life and thereby condemning himself to the rebirth he wishes to avoid.

THE STUDENT

But how can this be that the jivanmukta is still bound by his past deeds? Does not *mukti* burn up one's past deeds as in a fire? For how can one be at the same time free and yet bound?

THE GURU

Mukti prevents one's future deeds from creating bondage; but what of the past deeds which have already created bondage? The Jivanmukta is not indeed bound, for he is one with God and God is the Master of His *prakriti*, not its slave; but the Prakriti attached to this Jivatman has created causes while in the illusion of bondage and must be allowed to work out its effects, otherwise the chain of causation is snapped and the whole economy of nature is disturbed and thrown into chaos. उत्सीदेयुरिमे लोका: etc. In order to maintain the worlds therefore, the Jivanmukta remains working like a prisoner on parole, not bound indeed by others, but detained by himself until the period previously appointed for his captivity shall have elapsed.

THE STUDENT

This is indeed a new light on the subject.

THE GURU

It is no new light but as old as the sun; for it is clearly laid down in the Gita and of the teaching of the Gita, Srikrishna says that it was told by him to Vivasvan, the Vishnu of the solar system and by him to Manou, the original Thinker in man, and by Manou handed down to the great king-sages, his descendants. Nay, it plainly arises from the nature of things. The whole confusion in this matter proceeds from an imperfect understanding of *mukti*; for why do men fly from action and shun their कर्तव्य कर्म in the pursuit of mukti? It is because they dread to be cast again into bondage, to lose their chance of मुक्ति. Yet what is mukti? It is release, — from what? From Avidya, from the great Nescience, from the belief that you are limited & bound, who are illimitable Brahman and cannot be bound. The moment you have realised that Avidya is an illusion, that there is nothing but Brahman and never was nor will be anything but Brahman, realised it, I say, had अनुभव of it, not merely intellectually grasped the idea, from that moment you are free and always have been free. Avidya consists precisely in this that the Jivatman thinks there is something beside himself, he himself being other than Brahman, something which binds him; but in reality He, being Brahman, is not bound, never was bound nor could be bound and never will be bound. Once this is realised, the Jivatman can have no farther fear of *karma*; for he knows that there is no such thing as bondage. He will be quite ready to do his deeds in this world; nay, he will even be ready to be reborn, as Srikrishna himself has promised to be reborn again and again; for of rebirth also he has no farther fear, since he knows he cannot again fall under the dominion of Avidya, unless he himself deliberately wills it; once free, always free. Even if he is reborn, he will be reborn with full knowledge of what he really is, of his past lives and of the whole future and will act as a Jivanmukta.

THE STUDENT

But if this statement once free, always free hold, what of the statements about great Rishis & Yogis falling again under the dominion of Avidya?

THE GURU

A man may be a great Rishi or Yogi without being Jivan-mukta. Yog and spiritual learning are means to Mukti, not Mukti itself. For the Sruti says नायमात्मा प्रवचनेन लभ्यो न मेधया न बहुना श्रुतेन ।

THE STUDENT

Will then the Jivanmukta actually wish to live a hundred years, as the Sruti says? Can one who is मुक्त have a desire?

THE GURU

The Jivanmukta will be perfectly ready to live a hundred years or more if needs be; but this recommendation is given not to the Jivanmukta or to any particular class of person but generally. You should desire to live your allotted term of life, because you in the body are the Brahman who by the force of His own Shakti is playing for Himself by Himself this *lila* of creation, preservation and destruction; in this view Brahman is Isha, the Lord, Creator & Destroyer; and you also are Isha, Creator & Destroyer; only for your own amusement, to use a violent metaphor, you have imagined yourself limited by a particular body for the purposes of the play, just as an actor imagines himself to be Dushyanta or Rama or Ravana; and often the actor loses himself in the part and really feels himself to be what he is playing, forgetting that he is really not Dushyanta or Rama, but that Devadatta who plays a hundred parts besides. Still when he shakes off this illusion & remembers that he is Devadatta, he does not therefore walk off from the stage and by refusing to act, break up the play but goes on playing his best till the proper time for the curtain to fall. And so we should all do, whether as householder or Sannyasi, as Jivanmukta or as mumukshu, remembering always that the object of this *sansara* is creation and that it is our business so long as we are in this body to create. The only difference is this, that so long as we forget our Self, we create like servants under the compulsion of our Prakriti or Nature, and are, as it were, slaves & bound by her actions which we imagine to be ours; but when we know the Self and experience our true Self, then we are masters of our Prakriti and not bound by her creations; our soul becomes the Sakshi, the silent spectator, of the actions of our Nature; thus are we both spectator & actor, and yet because we know the whole to be merely the illusion of an action and not action itself, because we know that Rama is not really killing Ravana nor Ravana being killed, for indeed Ravana lives as much after the supposed death as before; so are we neither actor nor spectator but the Self only and all we see only visions of the Self — as indeed the Sruti frequently uses the word ऐक्षद्, saw, in preference to any other for those conceptions with which the Brahman peoples with Himself the Universe of Himself. The mumukshu therefore will not try or wish to leave his life before the time, just as he will not try or wish to leave actions in this life, but only the desire for their fruit. For if he breaks impatiently the thread of his life before it is spun out, he will be no Jivanmukta but a mere suicide and attain the very opposite result of what he desires. The Upanishad says

असुर्या नाम ते लोका अन्धेन तमसावृताः ।
तांस्ते प्रेत्याभिगच्छन्ति ये के चात्महनो जनाः ॥

Shankara takes this verse in a very peculiar way. He interprets आत्महनो as slayers of the Self, and since this is obviously an absurdity, for the Self is eternal and unslayable, he says that it is a metaphor for casting the Self under the delusion of ignorance which leads to birth. Now this is a very startling and violent metaphor and quite uncalled for, since the idea might easily have been expressed in any other natural way. Still the Sruti is full of metaphor and we shall therefore not be justified in rejecting Shankara's interpretation on that ground only. We must see whether the rest of the verse is in harmony with the interpretation. Now we find that in order to support his view Shankara is obliged to strain astonishingly the plain meaning of other words in the sentence also; for he takes लोका as meaning various kinds of birth, so that असुर्या लोका means the various births as man, animal etc, called आसुरा because Rajas predominates in them and they are accompanied with Asuric dispositions.[1] All this is a curious and unparalleled meaning for Asuric worlds. The expression लोका is never applied to the various kinds of forms the Jivatman assumes, but to the various surroundings of the different conditions through which it passes, of which life in this world is one; we say इहलोक or मर्त्यलोक, परलोक or स्वर्गलोक, ब्रह्मलोक, गोलोक etc, but we do not say पशुलोक, पक्षिलोक, कीटलोक. If we say आसुर लोक we can mean nothing but the regions of Asuric gloom as opposed to the divine लोकs, Brahmalok, Golok, Swarga. This is the ordinary meaning when we speak of going to a world after death, and we must not take it in any other sense here just to suit our own argument. Moreover the expression ये के loses its peculiar force if we apply it to all living beings except the few who obtain mukti partial or complete; it obviously means some out of many. We must therefore refuse to follow even Shankara, when his interpretation involves so many violences to the language of Sruti and so wide a departure from the recognized meaning of words.

The ordinary sense of the words gives a perfectly clear and consistent meaning. The Sruti tells us that it is no use taking refuge in suicide or the shortening of your life, because those who kill themselves instead of finding freedom, plunge by death into a worse prison of darkness — the Asuric worlds enveloped in blind gloom.

THE STUDENT

Are then worlds of Patala beneath the earth a reality and do the souls go down there after death? But we know now that there is no beneath to the earth, which is round & encircled by nothing worse than air.

---

[1] *Another version which duplicates some of the last part of this sentence reads as follows, beginning after "other words in the sentence also;"* —
for he says that असुर्या लोका means the various kinds of birth; even the Devas being considered Asuric births as opposed to the Paratman; but this is a misuse of words because the Devas cannot be Asura births as opposed to the Daiva birth of Paratman, Paratman is above birth & above Devahood. Asurya can only mean Asuric as opposed to Devic.

THE GURU

Do not be misled by words. The Asuric worlds are a reality, the worlds of gloom in the nether depths of your own being. A world is not a place with hills & trees & stones, but a condition of the Jivatman, all the rest being only circumstances & details of a dream; this is clear from the language of the Sruti when it speaks of the spirit's *lok* in the next world, अमुष्मिन् लोके, as being good or otherwise. Obviously लोक means state or condition. मर्त्यलोक is not essentially this Earth we see, for there may & must be other abodes of mortal beings but the condition of mortality in the gross body, Swargalok is the condition of bliss in the subtle body, Narak the condition of misery in the subtle body, Brahmalok the condition of being near to Hiranyagarbha in the causal body. Just as the Jivatman like a dreamer sees the Earth & all its features when it is in the condition of mortality, and regards itself as in a particular place, so when it is in a condition of complete *tamas* in the subtle body, it believes itself to be in a place surrounded by thick darkness, a place of misery unspeakable. This world of darkness is imagined as being beneath the earth, beneath the condition of mortality, because the side of the earth turned away from the Sun is regarded as the nether side, while Swarga is above the Earth, because the side of earth turned to the Sun is considered the upper side, the place of light & pleasure. So the worlds of utter bliss begin from the Sun and rise above the Sun to Brahmalok. But these are all words & dreams, since Hell & Patal & Earth & Paradise & Heaven are all in the Jivatma itself and not outside it. Nevertheless while we are still dreamers, we must speak in the language & terms of the dream.

THE STUDENT

What then are these worlds of nether gloom?

THE GURU

When a man dies in great pain, or in great grief or in great agitation of mind and his last thoughts are full of fear, rage, pain or horror, then the Jivatman in the Sukshmasharir is unable to shake off these impressions from his mind for years, sometimes for centuries. The reason of this is the law of death; death is a moment of great concentration when the departing spirit gathers up the impressions of its mortal life, as a host gathers provender for its journey, and whatever impressions are predominant at that moment, govern its condition afterwards. Hence the importance, even apart from Mukti, of living a clean and noble life and dying a calm & strong death. For if the ideas & impressions then uppermost are such as associate the self with this gross body and the vital functions, ie to say, with the lower upadhi, then the soul remains long in a tamasic condition of darkness & suffering, which we call Patal or in its worst forms Hell. If the ideas & impressions uppermost are such as associate the self with the mind and the higher desires then the soul passes quickly through a short period of blindness to a rajaso-sattwic condition of light & pleasure and wider knowledge, which we call Paradise, Swarga or Behesta, from which it will return to birth in this world; if the ideas & impressions are such as to associate the self with the higher understanding & the bliss of the Self, the soul passes quickly to a sattwic condition of highest bliss which we call Heaven or Brahmaloka and thence it does not return. But if we have learned to identify for ever the self with the Self, then before death we become God and after death we shall not be other. For there are three states of Maya, tamasic illusion, rajasic illusion, & sattwic illusion; and each in succession we must shake off to reach that which is no illusion, but the one and only truth.

The Sruti says then that those who slay themselves go down into the nether world of gloom, for they have associated the Self with body and fancied that by getting rid of this body, they will be free, but they have died full of impressions of grief, impatience, disgust and pain. In that state of gloom they are continually repeating the last scene of their life, its impressions and its violent disquiet, and until they have worn off these, there is no possibility of *shanti* for their minds. Let no man in his folly or impatience court such a doom.

THE STUDENT

I understand then that these three verses form a clear &
connected exposition. But in the next verse the Upanishad goes
on suddenly to something quite disconnected.

THE GURU

No. It says

अनेजदेकं मनसो जवीयो नैनद्देवा आप्नुवन् पूर्वमर्षत् ।
तद्धावतोऽन्यानत्येति तिष्ठत्तस्मिन्नपो मातरिश्वा दधाति ॥

The Sruti has said that you must invest all things with the Lord.
But of course that really means, you must realise how all things
are already invested with Him. It now proceeds to show how this
is and to indicate that the Lord is the Brahman, the One who,
regarded in his creative activity through Purusha & Prakriti, is
called the Lord. Therefore it now uses the neuter form of the
pronoun, speaking of Him as That and This; because Brahman
is above sex & distinction. He is One, yet he is at once unmoving
& swifter than mind. He is both Purusha & Prakriti, and yet at
the same time He is neither, but One and indivisible; Purusha
& Prakriti being merely conceptions in His mind deliberately
raised for the sake of creating multiplicity. As Prakriti, He is
swifter than the mind; for Prakriti is His creative force making
matter & its forms through motion. All creation is motion, all
activity is motion. All this apparently stable universe is really in
a state of multifold motion, everything is whirling with inconceivable rapidity through motion, and even thought which is the
swiftest thing we know, cannot keep pace with the velocity of the
cosmic stir. And all this motion, all this ever evolving Cosmos
& Universe is Brahman. The Gods in their swiftest movements,
the lords of the senses, cannot reach him, for He rushes far in
front. The eye, the ear, the mind, nothing material can reach or
conceive the inconceivable creative activity of the Brahman. We
try to follow Him pouring as light through the solar system and
lo! while we are striving He is whirling universes into being far
beyond the reach of eye or telescope, far beyond the farthest
flights of thought itself. Material senses quail before the thought

of the wondrous stir and stupendous unimaginable activity that the existence of the Universe implies. And yet all the time He who outstrips all others, is not running, but standing. While we are toiling after Him, He is all the time here, at our side, before, behind us, with us, *in* us. Really He does not move at all; all this motion is the result of our own Avidya which by persuading us to imagine ourselves as limited, subjects our thoughts to the conditions of Time & Space. Brahman in all his creative activity is really in one place; He is at the same time in the Sun & here; but we in order to realise Him have to follow Him from the Sun to the Earth; and this motion of our thoughts, this sensory impression of a space covered & a time spent we attribute not to our thought, but to Brahman, just as a man in a railway-train has a sensory impression that everything is rushing past, but that the train is still. Vidya, Knowledge tells him that this is not so. So that the stir of the Cosmos is really the stir of our own minds — and yet even our own mind does not really stir. What we call mind is simply the play of conception sporting with the idea of multiplicity which is in form the idea of motion. The Purusha is really unmoving; he is the motionless & silent spectator of a drama of which He himself is the stage, the theatre, the scenery, the actors and the acting. He is the poet Shakespeare watching Desdemona & Othello, Hamlet & the murderous Uncle, Rosalind & Jacques & Viola and all the other hundred multiplicities of himself acting & talking & rejoicing & suffering, all Himself & yet not himself, who sits there a silent witness, their Creator who has no part in their actions and yet without Him not one of them could exist. This is the mystery of the world and its paradox, yet its one plain, simple & easy truth.

THE STUDENT

Now I see. But what is this suddenly thrown in about Matariswun & the waters? Shankara interprets अपः as actions. Will not this bring it more into harmony with the rest of the verse?

THE GURU

Perhaps; waters is the proper sense of अप: but let us see first
whether by taking it in its proper sense we cannot arrive at a
clear meaning. The Sruti says that this infinitely motionless yet
infinitely moving Brahman is that in which Matariswun setteth
the waters. Now we know the conception which the Scripture gives us of this Universe. Everything that we call creation,
putting forth & Science calls evolution is in reality a limitation,
a *srishti*, as we say, that is a letting loose of a part from the
whole, or a selection, as the Scientists say, a natural selection
they call it or, as we should put it, selection by the action of
Prakriti, of a small portion from a larger stock, of the particular
from the general. Thus we have seen that the Sleep Condition
or Prajna is a letting loose or let us say selection of one part
of consciousness from the wider Universal Consciousness; the
Dream Consciousness or Hiranyagarbha is a selection from the
wider Sleep Consciousness, and the Waking Consciousness Virat
or Vaisvanor is a selection from the wider Dream Consciousness;
similarly each individual consciousness is only a selection from
the wider Universal Waking Consciousness, each step involving a
narrower & ever narrowing consciousness until we come to that
extremely narrow bit of consciousness which is only conscious
of a bit out of the material & outward world of phenomena.
It is the same with the process of material creation. Out of the
unformed Prakriti which the Sankhya calls Pradhana or primary
idea, substance, plasm or what you will, of matter, one aspect
or force is selected which is called Akash and of which ether is
the visible manifestation; this *akash* or ether is the substratum
of all form & material being. Out of ether a narrower force
is selected or let loose which is called Vaiou or Matariswun,
the Sleeper in the Mother, because he sleeps or rests directly in
the mother-principle, Ether. This is the great God who in the
Brahman setteth the waters in their place.

THE STUDENT

You speak of it as a God, I think, metaphorically. Science
has done away with the Gods of the old crude mythology.

THE GURU

The Gods are; — they are the Immortals and cannot be done away with by Science however vehemently she denies them; only the knowledge of the One Brahman can do away with them. For behind every great & *elemental* natural phenomenon there is a vast living force which is a manifestation, an aspect of Brahman and can therefore be called nothing less than a God. Of these Matariswun is one of the mightiest.

THE STUDENT

Is Air then a God or Wind a God? But it is only a conglomeration of gases.

THE GURU

That and nothing more in the terms of material analysis, but look beyond to the synthesis; matter is not everything and analysis is not everything. By material analysis you can prove that man is nothing but a conglomeration of animalcules, and so materialism with an obstinate and learned silliness persists in asseverating; but man will never consent to regard himself as a conglomeration of animalcules, because he knows that he is more. He looks beyond the analysis to the synthesis, beyond the house to the dweller in the house, beyond the parts to the force that holds the parts together. So with the Air, which is only one of the manifestations of Matariswun proper to this earth, one of the houses in which he dwells; but Matariswun is in all the worlds and built all the worlds; he has numberless houses for his dwelling. The principle of his being is *motion* materially manifested, and we know that it is by motion creation becomes possible. Matariswun therefore is the Principle of Life, the universal and all pervading ocean of Prana, of which the most important manifestation in man is the force which presides over that distribution of gases in the body to which we give the name of Breath.

THE STUDENT

Still, most people would call this a natural force, not a God.

THE GURU

Call him what you like, only realise that Matariswun is a force of Brahman, nay, Brahman Himself, who in himself setteth the waters to their places. Now just as Matariswun was a selection from Akasha or ether, so is Agni, Fire, a selection from Matariswun and the Waters a selection from fire. Now notice that it is the plural word अप: which is used; just as often you find the Sruti instead of the name Agni of the presiding principle, using the plural *jyotinshi*, lights, splendours, shining things, of the various manifestations of Agni, so it uses आप:, all fluidities, of the various manifestations of Varouna, the presiding force behind them. You must not think that the waters of the ocean or of the rain are the only manifestations of this principle, just as you must not suppose that the fire in yonder brazier or the sun in heaven is the only manifestation of the fiery principle. All the phenomena of light and everything from which heat proceeds have their immediate basis or substratum in Agni. So with the waters which are selected out of Agni by the operations of heat etc. So again all *earth*, all forms of solidity have their basis or substratum in Prithivi, the earth-force, which is again a selection out of Jala or Varouna, the fluid principle. Now life proceeds in this way; it arises on the substratum of ether with Matariswun or the Air Force as its principle & essential condition, by the operation of the fiery or light principle through heat, out of the fluid to solidity which is its body. The material world is therefore often said in the Sruti to be produced out of the waters, because so long as it does not emerge from the fluid state, there is as yet no Cosmos. When Science instead of following the course of Nature upstream by analysis, resolving the solid into fluid, the fluid into the fiery, and the fiery into the aerial, shall begin to follow it downstream, imitating the processes of Prakriti, and especially studying & utilising critical stages of transition, then the secret of material creation will be solved, and Science will be able to create material *life* and not as now merely destroy it. We can now understand what the Sruti means when it says that Matariswun in Brahman setteth the waters to their places. Brahman is the reality behind all material life, and the operations of creation are only a limited part of His universal consciousness and cannot go on without that consciousness as its basis. Shankara is not perhaps wrong when he reads the meaning "actions" into अपः; for the purposes of mankind, actions are the most important of all the various vital operations over which Matariswun presides. Remember therefore that all you do, create, destroy you are doing, creating & destroying in Brahman, that He is the condition of all your deeds; the more you realise & intensify in yourself Brahman as an ocean of spiritual force, the mightier will be your creation & your destruction, you will approach nearer and nearer to Godhead. For the Spirit is all & not the body, of which you should only be careful as a vehicle of the Spirit, for without the presence of Spirit, which gives Prakriti the force to act, Prakriti would be inert, nay could not exist. For what is Prakriti itself but the creation of the mighty Shakti, who is without end & without beginning, the Shakti of the Eternal? Without some Jnana, some knowledge & feeling of the Spirit within you, your work cannot be great; and the deeper your Jnana the greater your work. All the great creators have been men who felt powerfully God within them, whether they were Daivic, of the Olympian type like Shankara, or Asuric, of the Titanic type like Napoleon; only the Asura, his Jnana being limited and muddied, is always confusing the Eternal with the grosser & temporary manifestations of Prakriti such as his own vital passions of lust & ambition; the Deva, being sattwic & a child of light, sees clearer. When Napoleon cried out, "What is the French Revolution? I am the French Revolution," he gave utterance to that sense of his being more than a mere man, of his being the very force & power of God in action, which gave him such a stupendous energy & personality; but his mind being muddied by rajas, passion & desire, he could not see that the very fact of his being the French Revolution should have pointed him to higher & grander ideals than the mere satisfaction of his vital part in empire & splendour, that it should have spurred him to be the leader of insurgent humanity, not the trampler down of the immortal spirit of nationality, which was a yet greater and more energetic manifestation of the Eternal Shakti than himself. Therefore he fell; therefore the Adyashakti, the mighty Devi Chandi Ranarangini Nrimundamalini, withdrew from him her varabhaya and fought against him till she had crushed and torn him with the claws of her lion. Had he fallen as the leader of humanity, — he could not have fallen then, but yet if he had fallen, — his spirit would have conquered after his death and ruled & guided the nations for centuries to come. Get therefore Jnana, the pure knowledge of Brahman within you and show it forth in nishkam karma, in selfless work for your people, for your country, for humanity, for the world, then will you surely become Brahman even in this mortal body and by death take upon yourself eternity.

The Sruti then having set forth the nature of the Lord & identified Him with the Brahman, proceeds to sum up the apparent paradoxes attending his twofold aspect as the Unknowable Parabrahman and the Master of the Universe, as the Self within the Universe and the Self within your body. That moveth and That moveth not, — as has already been explained; That is far and the same That is quite near, That is within all this and the same That is without all this.

THE STUDENT
There is no difficulty in this statement.

THE GURU
No, there is no difficulty, once you have the key. But try to realise what it means. Lift your eyes towards the Sun; He is there in that wonderful heart of life & light and splendour. Watch at night the innumerable constellations glittering like so many solemn watchfires of the Eternal in the limitless silence which is no void but throbs with the presence of a single calm and tremendous existence; see there Orion with his sword and belt shining as he shone to the Aryan fathers ten thousand years ago at the beginning of the Aryan era, Sirius in his splendour, Lyra sailing billions of miles away in the ocean of space. Remember that these innumerable worlds, most of them mightier than our own, are whirling with indescribable speed at the beck of that

Ancient of Days whither none but He knoweth, and yet that they are a million times more ancient than your Himalaya, more steady than the roots of your hills and shall so remain until He at his will shakes them off like withered leaves from the eternal tree of the Universe. Imagine the endlessness of Time, realise the boundlessness of Space; and then remember that when these worlds were not, He was, the Same as now, and when these are not, He shall be, still the Same; perceive that beyond Lyra He is and far away in Space where the stars of the Southern Cross cannot be seen, still He is there. And then come back to the Earth & realise who this He is. He is quite near to you. See yonder old man who passes near you crouching & bent, with his stick. Do you realise that it is God who is passing? There a child runs laughing in the sunlight. Can you hear Him in that laughter? Nay, He is nearer still to you. He is in you, He is you. It is yourself that burns yonder millions of miles away in the infinite reaches of Space, that walks with confident steps on the tumbling billows of the ethereal sea; it is you who have set the stars in their places and woven the necklace of the suns not with hands but by that Yoga, that silent actionless impersonal Will which has set you here today listening to yourself in me. Look up, O child of the ancient Yoga, and be no longer a trembler and a doubter; fear not, doubt not, grieve not; for in your apparent body is One who can create & destroy worlds with a breath.

Yes, He is within all this as a limitless ocean of spiritual force; for if He were not, neither this outer you nor this outer I nor this Sun nor all these worlds could last for even a millionth part of the time that is taken by a falling eyelid. But He is outside it too. Even in His manifestation, He is outside it in the sense of exceeding it, अत्यतिष्ठद्दशांगुलं, in His unmanifestation, He is utterly apart from it. This truth is more difficult to grasp than the other, but it is necessary to grasp it. There is a kind of Pantheism which sees the Universe as God and not God as the Universe; but if the Universe is God, then is God material, divisible, changeable, the mere flux & reflux of things; but all these are not God in Himself, but God in His shadows & appearances; they are, to repeat our figure, the shadows and figments of Shakespeare's mind, Shakespeare is not only vaster than all his drama-world put together, he is not only both in it and outside it, but apart from it and other than it.

THE STUDENT
Do you mean that these are emanations from His Mind?

THE GURU
I do not. Emanation is a silly word and a silly idea. God is not a body emitting vapours. If they have emanated from Him, where, pray, have they emanated to? Which is their locality and where is their habitation? You cannot go anywhere where you will be outside God; you cannot go out of your Self. For though you flee to the uttermost parts of space, He is there. Are Hamlet & the rest of them emanations from Shakespeare's mind? Will you tell me then where they have emanated to? Is it on to those pages, those corruptions of pulp which are made today and destroyed tomorrow? Is it into those combinations of those letters of the English alphabet with which the pages are covered? Put them into combinations of any other alphabet, or relate them in any language to a man who knows not what letters are, and still Hamlet will live for him. Is it in the sounds that the letters represent? sounds that are heard this moment and forgotten the next? But Hamlet is not forgotten — he lives on in your mind for ever. Is it in the impressions made on the material brain by the forgotten sounds? Nay the Sleep Self within you, even if you have never heard or read the play of Hamlet, will, if it is liberated by any adequate process of Yoga or powerful hypnosis, tell you about Hamlet. Shakespeare's drama-world never emanated from Shakespeare's mind, because it was in his mind and is in his mind; and you can know of Hamlet because your mind is part of the same universal mind as Shakespeare's — part, I say, in appearance, but in reality that mind is one and indivisible. All knowledge belongs to it by its nature perpetually and from perpetuity, and the knowledge that we get in the waking condition through such vehicles as speech & writing are mere fragments created (let loose) from it & yet within it, just as the worlds are mere

fragments created (let loose) from the Brahman, in the sense of being consciousness selected & set apart from the Universal Consciousness, but always within the Brahman. Emanation is a metaphor, like the metaphor in the Sruti about the spider & his web, — convenient for certain purposes, but not the truth, very poor ground therefore on which to build a philosophy.

To realise God in the Universe & in yourself, is true Pantheism and it is the necessary step for approaching the Unknowable, but to mistake the Universe for God, is a mistaken & inverted Pantheism. This inverted Pantheism is the outer aspect of the Rigveda, and it is therefore that the Rigveda unlike the Upanishad may lead either to the continuation of bondage or to Brahmaloka, while the Upanishad can lead only to Brahmaloka or to the Brahman Himself.

THE STUDENT

But the new scholarship tells us that the Rigveda is either henotheistic or polytheistic, not real Pantheism.

THE GURU

Nay, if you seek the interpretation of your religion from Christians, atheists and agnostics, you will hear more wonderful things than that. What do you think of Charvak's interpretation of Vedic religion as neither pantheistic nor polytheistic but a plutotheistic invention of the Brahmins? An European or his disciple in scholarship can no more enter into the spirit of the Veda than the wind can blow freely in a closed room. And pedants especially can never go beyond the manipulation of words. Men like Max Muller presume to lecture us on our Veda & Vedanta because they know something of Sanscrit grammar; but when we come to them for light, we find them playing marbles on the doorsteps of the outer court of the temple. They had not the adhikar to enter, because they came in a spirit of arrogance with preconceived ideas to teach & not to learn; and their learning was therefore not helpful towards truth, but only towards grammar. Others ignorant of the very rudiments of Sanscrit, have seen more deeply than they, — even if some *have* seen more than there was to see. What for instance is this *henotheism*, this new word, the ill begotten of pedantry upon error? If it is meant that various sections of the Aryas consider different Gods as *the* God above all & the others false or comparatively false Gods, there would have been inevitably violent conflicts between the various sects and perpetual wars of religion but such there were not. If on the other hand, it is meant that different worshippers preferred to worship the Lord of the Universe in different particular forms, then are we still henotheist; for there is hardly one of us who has not his ishta-devata, Vishnou, Siva, Ganapati, Maruti, Rama, Krishna or Shakti; yet we all recognize but one Lord of the Universe behind the form we worship. If on the other hand the same man worshipped different nature-forces, but each in its turn as the Lord of the Universe, then is this Pantheism, pure and simple. And this was indeed the outer aspect of the Vedic religion; but when the seers of the Veda left their altars to sit in meditation, they perceived that Brahman was neither the Visvadevas nor the synthesis of the Visvadevas but something other than they; then was the revelation made that is given us in the Upanishads. ते ध्यानयोगानुगता अपश्यन् देवात्मशक्तिं स्वगुणैर्निगूढाम् । This is what is meant by saying that Brahman is outside all this; he is neither the synthesis of Nature nor anything that the Universe contains, but himself contains the Universe which is only a shadow of His own Mind in His own Mind.

THE STUDENT
   I understand.

THE GURU
   If you really understand, then are you ready for the next step which the Sruti takes when it draws from the unity of the Brahman, the sublimest moral principle to be found in any religion.

यस्तु सर्वाणि भूतान्यात्मन्येवानुपश्यति ।
सर्वभूतेषु चात्मानं ततो न विजुगुप्सते ॥

To man finding himself in the midst of the paradoxes created by the twofold nature of the Self, of himself, the Shakti that knows & the Shakti that plays at not knowing, the Sruti gives an unfailing guide, a sure staff and a perfect ideal. See all creatures in thy Self.[2] Yes, all; wife, children, friends, enemies, joy, sorrow, victory, defeat, beauty and ugliness, animation and inanimation — all these are but moods of One Consciousness and that Consciousness is our own. If you come to think of it, you have no friends or enemies, no joys or sorrows but of your own making. Scientists tell you that it is by the will to adapt itself in a particular way to its surroundings, one species differentiates itself from another. That is but one application of an universal principle. The Will is the root of all things; you will to have wife & children, friends & enemies and they arise. You will to be sick & sorry and sickness & sorrow seize you; you will to be strong & beautiful and happy, and the world becomes brighter with your radiance. This whole Universe is but the result of One universal Will which having resolved to create multitude in itself has made itself into all the forms you see within it.

THE STUDENT
        The idea is difficult to grasp, too vast & yet too subtle.

THE GURU
        Because Avidya, the sense of difference is your natural condition in the body. Think a little. This body is built by the protoplasm multiplying itself; it does not *divide* itself, for by division it could not grow. It produces another itself out of itself, the same in appearance, in size, in nature and so it builds up the body which is only itself multiplied in itself. Take that as an imperfect example, which may yet help you to understand.

---

[2] *Here the following sentences which occur again in a rewritten form twelve pages later are found in the manuscript, enclosed within parentheses but not cancelled:*
If thy mind fails thee, if the anguish of thy coverings still conceals the immortal Spirit within, dash away tears, ay be they very tears of blood, wipe them from thy eye and look out on the Universe. There is thy Self, that is Brahman, and all these things, thy self, thy joy, thy sorrow, thy friends & enemies are in Him. तत्र को मोह: क: शोक एकत्वमनुपश्यत:.

THE STUDENT

But it multiplies not in itself, but out of itself, as a man &
woman create a son out of themselves.

THE GURU

So it appears to you because it is working in Time & Space,
— for the same reason that there seem to you [to] be many
Jivatmans outside each other, while deeper knowledge shows
you one only, or that you imagine two separate consciousnesses
in one man, while more skilful hypnosis shows you that they are
one consciousness working variously within itself. In one sense
the One seems to us to multiply himself like the protoplasm, because the One Jivatman is the same in all, hence the fundamental
similarity of consciousness in all beings; in one sense He seems
to divide himself like the human consciousness because He is the
unit & all seem to be partial expressions of the comprehensive
unit; again he seems to add pieces of Himself together, because
you the consciousness who are He add yourself to your wife
the consciousness who is again He and become one, and so the
process goes on till of the vyashti, analysis in parts, you get the
samashti or synthesis of all; finally He seems to subtract Himself
from Himself, because as I have told you, each step in creation
is a letting loose or separating of part from a wider entity. All
these are however figures and appearances and whatever He
does, it must be in Himself, because He has nowhere else to
do it in, since He is all Space & all Time. Realise therefore
that all these around you, wife, children, friends, enemies, men,
animals, animate things & inanimate are in you, the Universal
Mind, like actors on a stage, and seem to be outside you only for
appearance' sake, for the convenience of the play. If you realise
this, you will be angry with none, therefore you will hate none
& therefore you will try to injure none. For how can you be
angry with any; if your enemies injure you, it is yourself who
are injuring yourself; whatever they are, you have made them
that; whatever they do, you are the root of their action. Nor will
you injure them, because you will be injuring none but yourself.
Why indeed should you hate them & try to injure them any more

than Shakespeare hated Iago for injuring Othello; do you think that Shakespeare shared the feelings of [Lodovico] when he condemned the successful villain to death & torture? If Shakespeare did hate Iago, you would at once say that it was illusion, Avidya, on the part of Shakespeare — since it is Shakespeare himself who set Iago there to injure Othello, since indeed there is no Othello or Iago, but only Shakespeare creating himself in himself. Why then should you consider your hatred of yourself made enemy more reasonable than Shakespeare's hatred of his own creation? No, all things being in yourself, are your own creation, are yourself, and you cannot hate your own creation, you cannot loathe yourself. Loathing and hatred are the children of illusion, of ignorance. This is the negative side of morality; but there is a positive for which the Sruti next proceeds to lay down the basis. You must for the purpose of withdrawing yourself from unrealities see all creatures in the Self; but if you did that only, you would soon arrive at the Nirvana of all action and ring down the curtain on an unfinished play. For the purpose of continuing the play till the proper time for your final exit, you must also see yourself in all creatures. The nature of the Self in a state of Vidya is bliss; now the state of Vidya is a state of self-realisation, the realisation of oneness & universality. The nature of the Self in the state of Avidya, the false sense of diversity and limitation is a state not of pure bliss but of pleasure & pain, for pleasure is different from bliss, as it is limited & involves pain, while the nature of bliss is illimitable and above duality; it is when pain itself becomes pleasure, is swallowed up in pleasure, that bliss is born. Every thing therefore which removes even partially the sense of difference and helps towards the final unity, brings with it a touch of bliss by a partial oblivion of pain. But that which brings you bliss, you cannot help but delight in ecstatically, you cannot help but *love*. If therefore you see yourself in another, you spontaneously love that other; for in yourself you must delight. If you see yourself in all creatures, you cannot but love all creatures. Universal love is the inevitable consequence of the realisation of the One in Many, and with Universal Love how shall any shred of hate, disgust, dislike, loathing coexist? They dissolve in it like the night mists in the blaze of the risen sun. Take it in another way and we get a new facet of the one truth. All hatred & repulsion arises from the one cause, Avidya, which begot Will, called Desire, which begot Ahankar, which begot desire called Hunger. From Desire-Hunger are born liking & dislike, liking for whatever satisfies or helps us to our desire, dislike for whatever obstructs or diminishes the satisfaction of desire. This liking in this way created is the liking of the protoplasmic sheath for whatever gives it sensual gratification, the liking of the vital sheath for whatever gives it emotional gratification, the liking of the mind sheath for whatever gives it aesthetic gratification, the liking of the knowledge sheath for whatever gives it intellectual gratification. But beyond these there is something else not so intelligible, beyond my liking for the beautiful body of a woman or for a fine picture or a pleasant companion or an exciting play or a clever speaker or a good poem or an illuminative and well-reasoned argument there is my liking for somebody which has no justification or apparent reason. If sensual gratification were all, then it is obvious that I should have no reason to prefer one woman over another and after the brute gratification liking would cease; I have seen this brute impulse given the name of love; perhaps I myself used to give it that name when the protoplasmic animal predominated in me. If emotional gratification were all, then I might indeed cling for a time to the woman who had pleased my body, but only so long as she gave me emotional pleasure, by her obedience, her sympathy with my likes & dislikes, her pleasant speech, her admiration or her answering love. But the moment these cease, my liking also will begin to fade away. This sort of liking too is persistently given the great name and celebrated in poetry & romance. Then if aesthetic gratification were all, my liking for a woman of great beauty or great charm might well outlast the loss of all emotional gratification, but when the wrinkles began to trace the writing of age on her face or when accident marred her beauty, my liking would fade or vanish since the effect would lose the nutrition of a present cause. Intellectual gratification seldom enters into the love of a man for a woman; even if it did so, more frequently the intellectual gratification to be derived from a single mind is soon exhausted in daylong and nightlong companionship. Whence then comes that love which is greater than life and stronger than death, which survives the loss of beauty and the loss of charm, which defies the utmost pain & scorn the object of love can deal out to it, which often pours out from a great & high intellect on one infinitely below it? What again is that love of woman which nothing can surpass, which lives on neglect and thrives on scorn & cruelty, whose flames rise higher than the red tongues of the funeral pyre, which follows you into heaven or draws you out of hell? Say not that this love does not exist and that all here is based on appetite, vanity, interest or selfish pleasure, that Rama & Sita, Ruru & Savitri are but dreams & imaginations. Human nature conscious of its divinity throws back the libel in scorn, and poetry blesses & history confirms its verdict. That Love is nothing but the Self recognizing the Self dimly or clearly and therefore seeking to realise oneness & the bliss of oneness. What again is a friend? Certainly I do not seek from my friend the pleasure of the body or choose him for his good looks; nor for that similarity of tastes & pursuits I would ask in a mere comrade; nor do I love him because he loves me or admires me, as I would perhaps love a disciple; nor do I necessarily demand of him a clever brain, as if he were only an intellectual helper or teacher. All these feelings exist, but they are not the soul of friendship. No, I love my friend for the woman's reason, because I love him, because in the old imperishable phrase, he is my *other self*. There by intuition the old Roman hit on the utter secret of Love. Love is the turning of the Self from its false self in the mind or body to its true Self in another; I love him because I have discovered the very Self of me in him, not my body or mind or tastes or feelings, but my very Self of love & bliss, of the outer aspect of whom the Sruti has beautifully said "Love is his right side" etc. So is it with the patriot; he has seen himSelf in his nation & seeks to lose his lower self in that higher national Self; because he can do so, we have a Mazzini, a Garibaldi, a Joan of Arc, a Washington, a Pratap Singh or a Sivaji; the lower material self could not have given us these; you do not manufacture such men in the workshop of utility, on the forge of Charvaka or grow them in the garden of Epicurus. So is it with the lover of humanity, who loses or seeks to lose his lower self in mankind; no enlightened selfishness could have given us Father Damien or Jesus or Florence Nightingale. So is it finally with the lover of the whole world, of whom the mighty type is Buddha, the one unapproachable ideal of Divine Love in man, he who turned from perfect divine bliss as he had turned from perfect human bliss that not he alone but all creatures might be saved.

To see your Self in all creatures and all creatures in your Self — that is the unshakeable foundation of all religion, love, patriotism, philanthropy, humanity, of everything which rises above selfishness and gross utility. For what is selfishness? it is mistaking the body & the vital impulses for your true self and seeking their gratification, a gross, narrow and transient pleasure, instead of the stainless bliss of your true self which is the whole Universe & more than the Universe. Selfishness arises from Avidya, from the great fundamental ignorance which creates Ahankara, the sense of your individual existence, the pre-occupation with your own individual existence, which at once leads to Desire, to Hunger which is Death, death to yourself and death to others. The sense that this is I and that is you, and that I must take this or that, or else you will take it, that is the basis of all selfishness; the sense that this I must eat that you, in order to live & avoid being eaten, that is the principle of material existence from which arises strife and hatred. And so long as the difference between I and you exists, hatred cannot cease, covetousness cannot cease, war cannot cease, evil & sin cannot cease, and because sin cannot cease, sorrow & misery cannot cease. This is the eternal Maya that makes a mock of all materialistic schemes for a materialistic Paradise upon earth. Paradise cannot be made upon the basis of food and drink, upon the equal division of goods or even upon the common possession of goods, for always the *mine* & *thine*, the greed, the hate, will return again if not between this man & that man, yet between this community and that community. Christianity hopes to make men live together like brothers — a happy family, loving and helping each other; perhaps it still hopes, though there is little in the state of the modern world to flatter its dreams. But that millennium too will not come, not though Christ should descend with all his angels and cut the knot, after banishing the vast majority of mankind to the outer darkness where there is wailing and gnashing of teeth, by setting up this united family of mankind with the meagre remnants of the pure and faithful. What a mad dream of diseased imaginations that men could be really and everlastingly happy while mankind was everlastingly suffering! How would the everlasting hatred breathing out from the innumerably-peopled furnaces of pain blast & mar with unconquerable smoke of Hell the light & peace of the saints! And how strangely was the slight, but sweet and gracious shadow of Buddhism distorted in the sombre & cruel minds of those fierce Mediterranean races, when they pictured the saints as drawing added bliss from the contemplation of the eternal tortures in which those they had lived with and perhaps loved, were agonizing. Divine love, divine pity, the nature of the Buddha, that was the message which India sent to Europe through the lips of Jesus, and this is how the European mind interpreted divine love & divine pity! The fires of Hell aptly and piously anticipated on earth by the fires of Smithfield, the glowing splendours of the Auto-da-fé, the unspeakable reek of agony that steams up thro' history from the dungeons of the Holy Office — nay, there are wise men who find an apology for these pious torturers; it *was* divine love after all seeking to save the soul at the cost of the perishable body! But the Aryan spirit of the East, the spirit of Buddha struggles for ever with European barbarism and surely in the end it shall conquer. Already Europe does homage to humanity with her lips and in the gateways of her mind; perhaps some day she will do so with her heart also. At any rate the millennium of Tertullian is out of date. But still it is the Christian ideal, the Syrian interpretation of the truth and not the truth itself, which dominates the best European thought and the Christian ideal is the ideal of the *united family*.

THE STUDENT
    Surely it is a noble ideal.

THE GURU
    Very noble and we have it among ourselves in a noble couplet वसुधैव कुटुम्बकं; but everything which implies difference is based upon Avidya and the inevitable fruits of Avidya. Have you ever watched a big united family, a joint-family in Bengal especially in days when the Aryan discipline is lost? Behind its outward show of strength and unity, what jarring, what dissensions, what petty malice & hatred, what envy & covetousness! And then finally one day a crash, a war, a case in the law-courts, a separation for ever. What the joint-family is on a small scale, that on a big scale is an united nation, Russia or Austria or Germany or the *United* Kingdom. Mankind as an united family would mean in practice mankind as an united nation. How much would you gain by it? You would get rid of war, — for a time — of the mangling of men's bodies by men, but the body though to be respected as the chosen vehicle or the favourite dress of Brahman, is not of the first importance. You would not get rid of the much more cruel mangling of the human Self by hatred, greed and strife. The Europeans attach too much importance to the body, shrink too much from physical sin and are far too much at their ease with mental sin. It is enough for them if a woman abstain from carrying out her desire in action, if a man abstain from physical violence, then is the one chaste, the other self-controlled. This if not sheer unAryanism or Mlecchahood is at best the half baked virtue of the semi-Aryanised. Be you who are born in the Aryan discipline, however maimed by long bondage, an Aryan indeed, chaste in mind & spirit, & not merely careful in speech & body, gentle in heart & thought and not merely decent in words & actions. That is true self-control and real morality. No Paradise therefore can exist, no Paradise even if it existed, can last, until that which makes sin and hell is conquered. We may never have a Paradise on earth, but if it is ever to come, it will come not when all mankind are as brothers, for brothers jar and hate as much & often more than mere friends or strangers,

but when all mankind has realised that it is one Self. Nor can that be until mankind has realised that all existence is oneself, for if an united humanity tyrannise over bird & beast & insect, the atmosphere of pain, hatred & fear breathing up from the lower creation will infect & soil the purity of the upper. The law of Karma is inexorable, and whatever you deal out to others, even such shall be the effect on yourself, in this life or in another. Do you think then that this strange thing will ever come about that mankind in general, will ever come to see in the dog and the vulture, nay, in the snake that bites and the scorpion that stings, their own Self, that they will say unto Death my brother & to Destruction my sister, nay that they will know these things as themself? सर्वभूतेषु चात्मानं, the Sruti will not spare you the meanest insect that crawls or the foulest worm that writhes.

THE STUDENT
   It does not seem possible.

THE GURU
   It does not; and yet the impossible repeatedly happens. At any rate, if you must have an ideal, of the far-off event to which humanity moves, cherish this. Distrust all Utopias that seek to destroy sin or scrape away part of the soil in which it grows while preserving intact the very roots of sin, Ahankar born of Ignorance & Desire. For once Ahankar is there, likes and dislikes are born, रागद्वेषौ the primal couple of dualities, liking for what farthers the satisfaction of desire, dislike for what hinders it, the sense of possession, the sense of loss, attraction, repulsion, charm, repugnance, love, hatred, pity, cruelty, kindness, wrath, — the infinite and eternal procession of the dualities. Admit but one pair, and all the others come tumbling in in its wake. But the man who sees himself in all creatures, cannot hate; he shrinks from none, he has neither repulsion nor fear. ततो न विजुगुप्सते. Yonder leper whom all men shun — but shall I shun him, who know that from this strange disguise the Brahman looks out with smiling eyes? This foeman who comes with a sword to pierce me through the heart, — I look beyond the sharp threatening sword,

beyond the scowling brow and the eyes of hate, and I recognize the mask of my Self; thereafter I shall neither fear the sword nor hate the bearer. O myself who foolishly callest thyself mine enemy, how canst thou be my enemy unless I choose; friend & enemy are but creations of the Mind that myriad-working magician, that great dreamer & artist; and if I will not to regard thee as my enemy, thou canst no more be such than a dream or shadow can, as indeed thy flashing sword is but a dream and thy scowling brow but a shadow. But thou wilt divide me with thy sword, thou wilt slay me, pierce me with bullets, torture me with fire, blow me from the mouth of thy cannon? Me thou canst not pierce, for I am unslayable, unpierceable, indivisible, unburnable, immovable. Thou canst but tear this dress of me, this foodsheath or multiplied protoplasm which I wear — *I* am what I was before. I will not be angry with thee even, for who would trouble himself to be angry with a child because in its play or little childish wrath it has torn his dress? Perhaps I valued the dress and would not so soon have parted with it; I will try then to save it, if I may, and even punish thee without anger so that thou mayst not tear more dresses; but if I cannot — well, it was but a cloth and another can soon be had from the merchant; nay, have I not already paid the purchase-money? O my judge, thou who sittest pronouncing that I be hanged by the neck till I be dead, because I have broken *thy* laws perchance to give bread to starving thousands, perchance to help the men of my country whom thou wouldst keep as slaves for thy pleasure — Me wilt thou hang? When thou canst shake the sun from heaven or wrap up the skies like a garment, then shall power be given thee to hang me. Who or what is this thou deemest will die by hanging? A bundle of animalculae, no more. This outward thou & I are but stage masks; behind them is One who neither slayeth nor is slain. Mask called a judge, play thou thy part; I have played mine. O son of the ancient Yoga, realise thy Self in all things; fear nothing, loathe nothing; dread none, hate none, but do thy part with strength and courage; so shalt thou be what thou truly art, God in thy victory, God in thy defeat, God in thy very death & torture, — God who will not be defeated & who cannot die.

Shall God fear any? shall He despair? shall He tremble & shake? Nay 'tis the insects that form thy body & brain which shake & tremble; Thou within them sittest looking with calm eyes at their pain & terror; for they are but shadows that dream of themselves as a reality. Realise the Self in all creatures, realise all creatures in the Self; then in the end terror shall flee from thee in terror, pain shall not touch thee, lest itself be tortured by thy touch; death shall not dare to come near to thee lest he be slain.

यस्मिन् सर्वाणि भूतान्यात्मैवाभूद्विजानतः ।
तत्र को मोहः कः शोक एकत्वमनुपश्यतः ॥

He who discerneth, in whom all creatures have become himSelf, how shall he be deluded, whence shall he have sorrow, in whose eyes all things are One. That is the realisation of the mighty ideal, the moral and practical result of perfected Vedanta, that in us all things will become ourself. There, says the Sruti, in the man whose Self has become all creatures, what delusion can there be or what sorrow, for wherever he looks (अनुपश्यतः), he sees nothing but the great Oneness, nothing but God, nothing but his own Self of love and bliss. Delusion (मोह) is the mistaking of the appearance for the reality, bewilderment by the force of Maya. "This house that my fathers had was mine and alas, I have lost it." "This was my wife whom I loved, and she is lost to me for ever." "Alas, how has my son disappointed me from whom I hoped so much." "This office for which I hoped and schemed, my rival, the man I hated has got it." All these are the utterances of delusion and the result of delusion is शोक, sorrow. But to one whose Self has become all creatures, there can be no delusion and therefore no sorrow. He does not say "I, Devadatta, have lost this house. What a calamity!" He says "I, Devadatta, have lost this house, but it has gone to me, Harischandra. That is fortunate." *I* can lose nothing except to myself. Nor shall I weep because my wife is dead & lost, who is not lost at all, but as near to me as ever, since she is still my Self, in my Self, with my Self, as much after death as when her body was underneath my hands. *I* cannot lose my Self. My son has disappointed me? He has taken his own way & not mine, but he has not disappointed himSelf who is my Self, he has only disappointed the sheath, the case, the mental cell in which I was imprisoned. The vision of the One Self dispels all differences; an infinite calm, an infinite love, an infinite charity, an infinite tolerance, is the very nature of the strong soul that has seen God. The sin, the stain, the disease, the foulness of the world cannot pollute his mind nor repel his sympathy; as he stoops to lift the sinner from the dung heap in which he wallows, he does not shrink from the ordure that stains his own hands; his eyes are not bedimmed by tears, when he lifts up the shrieking sufferer out of his pit of pain; he lifts him as a father lifts his child who has tumbled in the mire and is crying; the child chooses to think he is hurt & cries; the father knows he is not really hurt, therefore he does not grieve, but neither does he chide him, rather he lifts him up & soothes the wilful imaginary pain. Such a soul has become God, mighty & loving to help and save, not weak to weep and increase the ocean of human tears with his own. Buddha did not weep when he saw the suffering of the world; he went forth to save. And surely such a soul will not grieve over the buffets the outward world seems to give to his outward self; for how can He grieve who is all this Universe? The pain of his petty personal Self is no more to his consciousness than the pain of a crushed ant to a king as he walks musing in his garden bearing on his shoulders the destiny of nations. He cannot feel sorrow for himself even if he would, for he has the sorrow of a whole world to relieve; his own joy is nothing to him, for he has the joy of the whole Universe at his command.

There are two ways of attaining to Jnana, to the Vision. One is the way of Insight, the other the way of World-Sight. There are two ways of Bhakti, one by devotion to the Self as Lord of all concentrated within you, the other by devotion to the Self as Lord of all extended in the Universe. There are two ways of Karma, one by Yoga, quiescence of the sheaths & the ineffable unacting, yet all-enveloping omnipotence of the Self within; the other by quiescence of desire and selfless activity of the sheaths for the wider Self in the Universe. For the first you must turn your eyes within instead of without, put from you the pleasures of contact & sense, hush the mind & its organs and rising above the dualities become One in yourself, आत्मतुष्टिरात्मारामः. Is this too difficult for thee? Does thy mind fail thee, the anguish of thy coverings still conceal the immortal Spirit within? Dash the tears from thine eyes; though they be tears of blood, still persist in wiping them away as they ooze out and look *out* on the Universe. That is thy self, that is Brahman. Realise all this Cosmic Stir, this rolling of the suns, this light, this life, this ceaseless activity. It is thou thyself that art stirring through all this Universe, thou art this Sun and this moon and these Constellations. The Ocean rolls in thee, the storm blows in thee, the hills stand firm in thee. If thou wert not, these things would not be. Canst thou grieve over the miseries of this little speck in the Brahman, this little insect-sheath, of whose miseries thou art the maker and thou canst be the ender? Is the vision too great for thee? Look round thee then, limit the vision there. These men & women and living things that are round thee, their numberless joys & sorrows, amongst which what are thine? they are all thy Self and they are all in Thee. Thou art their Creator, Disposer & Destroyer. Thou canst break them if thou wilt and thou canst rescue them from their griefs and miseries if thou wilt, for power infinite is within thee. Thou wilt not be the Asura to injure thyself in others? Be then the Deva to help thy Self in others. Learn the sorrows of those who live near thee and remove them; thou wilt soon feel what a joy has been so long lost to thee, a joy in which thy own sorrows grow like an unsubstantial mist. Wrestle with mighty wrongdoers, succour the oppressed, free the slave and the bound and thou shalt soon know something of the joy that is more than any pleasure, thou shalt soon be initiated into the bliss of the One who is in all. Even in death thou shalt know that ecstasy and rejoice in the blood as it flows from thee.

THE STUDENT

These ideals are too high. Where is the strength to follow them and the way to find that strength?

THE GURU

The strength is in yourself and the way to find that strength has been laid down from the times of old. But accept that ideal first or you will have no spur to help you over the obstacles in the way.

THE STUDENT
    But how many will accept the ideal, when there are so many easier ideals to give them strength & comfort?

THE GURU
    But are those ideals true? Delusions may give you strength & comfort for a while, but after all they break down & leave you tumbling through Chaos. Truth alone is a sure & everlasting rock of rest, an unfailing spear of strength. The whole universe rests upon Truth, on the Is, not on the Is Not. To be comfortable in delusion is the nature of man in his tamasic covering of gross matter-stuff; it is the business of philosophy & religion to dispel his delusion & force him to face the truth.

THE STUDENT
    But many wise men are of the opinions that these smaller ideals are the truth, not religion and philosophy which are a delusion.

THE GURU
    Tell me one of these newborn truths that profess to dispel the knowledge that is without end & without beginning; for you know more of the science of the West than I.

THE STUDENT
    There is the doctrine of the greatest good of the greatest number, which has something finite, certain and attainable about it — nothing metaphysical, nothing abstract.

THE GURU
    We have heard something about it in this country, a system of morality by arithmetic called utilitarianism which would have man pass his life with a pair of scales in his hand weighing good

& evil. It did good in its time, but it was not true, and could not last.

THE STUDENT
    In what is it not true?

THE GURU
    It is not true, because it is not in human nature; no human being ever made or ever will make an arithmetical calculation of the pain & pleasure to result from an action and the numbers of the people diversely affected by them, before doing the action. This sort of ethical algebra, this system of moral accounts needs a different planet for its development; a qualified accountant has yet to be born on the human plane. You cannot assess pleasure & pain, good and evil in so many ounces & pounds; human feelings, abstract emotions are elusive and variable from moment to moment. Utilitarianism with all its appearance of extreme practicality and definiteness, is really empty of any definite truth and impotent to give any sound and helpful guidance; it is in itself as barren of light as of inspiration, a creed arid, dry and lifeless, and what is worse, *false.* Whatever it has of value, it has copied or rather caricatured from altruism. It gives us standards of weight & measure which are utterly impossible to fix; and it fails to provide any philosophical justification for self-sacrifice nor any ardent inspiration towards it. Utilitarian hedonism — is not that the phrase — suggests, I think, that by doing good to others, we really provide a rarer and deeper pleasure for ourselves than any purely self-limited gratification can give us. Most true — and a truth we needed not to learn from either hedonist or utilitarian. The Buddhists knew it 2000 years ago and the Aryans of India practised it before that; the whole life of Srikrishna was a busy working for the good of others, of his friends, his country and the world, and Srikrishna never knew grief or pain. But there are three kinds of pleasure to be had from charity and beneficence; there is the satisfaction of vanity, the vanity of hearing oneself praised, the vanity of feeling "How very good I am." This, I think, is at the bottom

of much charity in India and more in Europe, and it is here that hedonism comes most into play, but it is a poor spring and will break down under any strain; it may lead to charity but never to self-sacrifice. Then there is the joy of having done a good work and brought oneself nearer to heaven which used to be and perhaps still is the most common incentive to beneficence in Aryaland. That is a more powerful spring, but it is narrow and does not reach the true self; its best value is that it is helpful towards purification. Then there are the natures born for love & unselfishness who in the mere joy of helping others, of suffering for others, of seeing the joy return to tear-worn faces & pain-dimmed eyes, feel the bliss that comes from the upsurging of God within. To these hedonism is as vanity and the babbling of children. The hedonistic element in utilitarianism is an imperfect & blundering effort to grope for a great truth which it has neither been able to grasp itself nor set forth with scientific accuracy. That truth is found only in the clear & luminous teaching of the Vedanta; it is this, that the compound result we call man *is* a compound result and not the single simple homogeneous being our senses would believe; he is composed of several elements, corporeal, vital, mental, intellectual and essential; and his true self is none of these heterogeneous factors of the element the Self lives in, but something beyond & transcendent. Pain & pleasure, good & evil are therefore not permanent and definite entities; the former are a heterogeneous conglomeration, sometimes a warring agglomeration of the feelings & impulses belonging to the various husks in which the true Self is wrapped. Good & evil are relative & depend on the standpoint we take with reference to the true locality of Self in this little cosmos of man; if we locate that Self low down our "good" will be a poor thing, of the earth, earthy, little distinguishable from evil; if we locate it in its true place, our good will be as high, vast & pure as the heavens. All pain & pleasure, all good & evil have their birth, their existence and their end in the Self. It follows therefore that even the highest love & altruism are bounded by the Self. Altruism is not the sacrifice of self to others, but the sacrifice of our false self to our true Self, which unless we are Yogins we can best see in others. True love is not the love of others but the love of our Self; for we cannot possibly love what is not ourself. If we love what is not ourself, it must be as a result of contact; but we cannot love by स्पर्श, by mere contact; because contact is temporary in its nature and in its results, and cannot give rise to a permanent feeling such as love. Yajnavalkya well said, "We desire the wife, not for the sake of the wife but for the sake of the Self." Only if we mistake things for the Self which are not the true Self, we shall, as a result, mistake things for love which are not real love. If we mistake the food-husk for Self, we shall desire the wife for corporeal gratification; if we mistake the vital emotion-husk for Self we shall desire the wife for emotional gratification; if we mistake the mind husk for the self we shall desire the wife for aesthetic gratification & the pleasurable sense of her presence, her voice, looks etc about the house; if we mistake the intellect husk for the self, we shall desire the wife for her qualities & virtues, her capacities & mental gifts, for the gratification of the understanding. If we see the Self, in the bliss Sheath, where the element of error reaches the vanishing point, we shall then desire the wife for the gratification of the true Self, the bliss of the sense of Union, of becoming One. And if we have seen & understood our true Self without husk or covering, we shall not desire her at all, because we shall possess her, we shall know that she is already our Self and therefore not to be desired in her sheaths, since *She* is already possessed. It follows that the more inward the sheath with which we confuse the Self, the purer the pleasure, the more exalted the conception of Good, until in the real naked Self we rise beyond good & evil because we have no longer any need of good or any temptation to evil. Emotional pleasure is higher than corporeal, aesthetic than emotional, intellectual than aesthetic, ethical than intellectual, spiritual than ethical. This is the whole truth and the whole philosophy of ethics; all else is practical arrangement and balancing of forces, economising of energies for the purposes of social stability or some other important but impermanent end.

Utilitarianism gets a partial & confused view of the truth and being unable properly to correlate it, groping about for some law, some standard and principle of order, thinks it has found it in utility. But what utility? I, this perfected animal, with desires, thoughts, sensations and a pressing need for their gratification, can very well understand what is personal utility; utility for this vital, sensational, conceptual me. My utility is to get as much sensual, emotional & intellectual gratification as I may out of life consistent with my own ease & safety; if utility is to be my standard of ethics, that is my ethics. But when you ask me in the name of utility & rationalism to sacrifice these things for some higher or wider utility, for others, for the greater number, for society, I no longer follow you. So much as is necessary to keep up government, law & order and a good police, I can understand, for these things are necessary to my safety & comfort; society has given me these & I must see to & pay for their maintenance by myself & others. That is businesslike, both utilitarian & rational. But beyond this society has not any claim on me; society exists for me, not I for society. If then I have to sacrifice what I perhaps most deeply cherish for society, my life, my goods, my domestic peace, my use for society ceases; I regard society then as a fraudulent depositor who wishes to draw from my ethical bank more than he has deposited. So might argue the average man who is neither immoral nor deeply moral but only respectable; and utilitarianism can give him no satisfactory answer.

Moreover, if I have other instincts than those of the respectable citizen, and ability to carry them out, why should I refrain? What holds me? If I can earn a huge fortune rapidly by some safe form of swindling, by gambling, by speculation or by the merciless methods of the American capitalist, why should I refrain? The charge of anti-social conduct; but that has no terrors for an egotist of strong character; he knows well that he can hush the disapproval of society under a shower of gold coin. Morality with the vital sensational man becomes in an utilitarian age merely the *fear* of social or legal punishment, and strong men do not fear; nor unless their acts shake the social framework will an utilitarian society care to condemn them, for they are breaking no powerful sanctions, outraging no deep-rooted sentiments — utilitarianism deliberately parts company with sentiment and except force & fear it has no sanctions to replace those of religion & ancient prejudice which it has destroyed. It is useless to tell these people that they will find a deeper & truer bliss in good moral conduct and altruism than in their present selfish and anti-social career. Where is the proof or even the philosophic justification of what these philosophers allege? Their own experience? That is not valid for the average sensational man; *his* deepest pleasure is necessarily vital and sensational; it is only valid for the men who make the statement, they being the intellectual self with an ethical training that has survived from a dead Christianity. In order for it to be true of the sensational man, he must cease to be sensational, he must undergo a process of spiritual regeneration to which utilitarian philosophy cannot give him either the key or even the motive-impulse. For in the mouth of the utilitarian, this statement of the deeper & truer bliss, is a piece of secondhand knowledge; not his own earning, but part of that store of ethical coin rifled by rationalism from the coffers of Christianity on which European civilisation is precariously living at the present day. One trembles to think of the day when that coin shall be exhausted — already we see some signs of growing moral vulgarity, coarseness, almost savagery in the European mind, which, if it increases, if the open worship of brutal force & unscrupulous strength which is rampant in politics & in commerce taint, as it must eventually do, the deeper heart of society, may lead to an orgy of the vital & sensational impulses such as has not been since the worst days of the Roman Empire.

THE STUDENT

But Lecky has proved that the moral improvement of Europe was due entirely to the rise of rationalism.

THE GURU

My son, there is one great capacity of the learned & cultured mind both in Europe & Asia which one should admire without imitating — it is the capacity of dextrous juggling with words. If you choose to give an extension of meaning to a particular word, a meaning it cannot & ought not to have, you can easily build on it a very glittering edifice of theory, which will charm the eye until someone comes by with a more effective word more effectively extended in meaning and knocks down the old house to build a newer & more glittering mansion. Thus the old eternal truths are overlaid by trashy superstructures until some day some salutary earthquake swallows up the building & builders & reveals the old truth which no change or chance can injure. Amid the giddy round of ever shifting theories Europe gives us, there are only two fundamental truths, often misapplied, but nevertheless true in the sphere of phenomena, — Evolution, which is taught in different ways by our Sankhya & Vedanta, and the Law of Invariable Causality, which is implied in our theories of Kal & Karma. These receive & hold fast to, — for it is by working them out not always well, but always suggestively that Europe has made her real contribution to the eternal store of knowledge. But in their isms and schisms trust not — they contain scant grain of truth hidden in a very bushelful of error.

THE STUDENT
Still it seems to me that Lecky is not altogether wrong.

THE GURU
On the contrary he is entirely right, — if we consent to lump together all enlightenment without regard to its nature & source, as rationalism; that the moral improvement of Europe was due to increasing enlightenment is entirely true, for Knowledge, by which I mean not the schoolmaster's satchelful of information or even the learning of the Universities, but Jnana, the perception & realisation of truth, is the eternal enemy and slayer of sin; for sin is descended of ignorance through her child, egoism. It is true that the so-called Christian ages in Europe were times of sin and darkness; Europe had accepted Christ only to crucify him afresh; she had entombed him alive with his pure & gracious teaching and over that living tomb she had built a thing called the Church. What we know as Christendom was a

strange mixture of Roman corruption, German barbarism and fragments of ancient culture all bathed in the pale light that flowed upward from the enhaloed brows of the entombed and crucified Christ. The great spiritual hoard he had opened to the West was kept locked up and unavailable except to individuals whose souls were too bright to be swallowed up in the general darkness. All knowledge was under taboo, not because there was any natural conflict between Religion & Science, but because there was natural & irreconcilable antipathy between the obscurantism of political ecclesiastics & resurgent knowledge. Again Asia came to the rescue of Europe and from the liberal civilisation of the Arabs, Science was reborn into her mediaeval night, and the light of Science, persecuted & tortured, struggled up until the darkness was overpowered & wounded to death. The intellectual history of Europe has outwardly been a struggle between Science & the Church, with which has been confounded the Christian religion which the Church professed with its lips & attempted to strangle with its hands; inwardly it was the ancient struggle between Deva and Asura, sattwa & tamas. Now Religion is sattwic with a natural impulse towards light, it cannot be tamasic, it can have no dealings with the enemies of the Devas; and if something calling itself religion, attempts to suppress light, you may be sure it is not religion but an impostor masquerading in her name. Consider what were the ideas under which as under a banner, the modern spirit overthrew the mediaeval Titan; the final uprush of those ideas we see in the French revolution. The motto of the Revolution we know, liberty, equality & fraternity; the spirit it professed but could not attain we know, humanity. In liberty the union of the individual moral liberty of Christianity with the civic liberty of Greece; in equality, the democratic spiritual equality of Christianity applied to society; fraternity, the aspiration to universal brotherhood, which is the peculiar and distinguishing idea of Christianity; in humanity, the Buddhistic spirit of mercy, pity, love, of which Europe knew nothing till Christianity breathed it forth over the Mediterranean and with greater purity over Ireland, mingled with the sense of the divinity in man, borrowed from India through the old Gnostics

& Platonists, these are the ideas which still profoundly influence Europe, many of which Scientific materialism has been obliged to borrow or tolerate, none of which it has as yet availed entirely to root out. Rationalism did not create these ideas, but found and adopted them. Rationalism is the spirit which subjects all beliefs & opinions to the test of logic from observed facts, it is indeed the intellectual sheath, mostly the lower or merely logical half of the intellectual sheath attempting to establish itself as the Self. This is what we call Science and the scientific spirit. Wherever it has been able to work in the light of pure dry intellect, not distorted by irruptions of the lower selves in the shape of interest, vanity, passions, prejudices, it has produced invaluable results; in the sphere therefore of the passionless observation, classification and correlation of facts we may follow Science without distrust or fear of stumbling; but whenever it tries to theorize from what it has observed about human nature, human affairs & spiritual development, Science is always tumbling into the pits of the lower selves; in attempting to range things above the material level under the law of the material self, it is trying to walk upon water, to float upon air; it is doing something essentially unscientific. Still more is this the case when it deals with the higher things of the spirit in the same terms; its theories then become so amazingly paradoxical, one stands astonished at the wilful blindness to facts to which prejudice & prepossession can lead the trained observers of facts. Follow them not there, there are the blind leading the blind who go round and round battering themselves like a blind bird at night against the same eternal walls and never seeing the window open to it for its escape.

THE STUDENT

But you have said that Evolution is an eternal truth. On the basis of Evolution the scientists have discovered a moral sanction, which does replace the old religious sanctions, the paramount claim of the race upon the individual.

THE GURU

What race? The English or German or Russian or the great

Anglo-Saxon race, which it appears is to inherit the world, God's Englishmen and, we must now add, God's Americans — or is it the whole white race? To whom must the individual bow his head as the head & front of Evolution?

THE STUDENT

I mean the whole human race. The individual is ephemeral, the species endures, the genus lasts almost for ever. On this basis your duty to yourself, your duty to society, your duty to your country, your duty to mankind, all fall into a beautifully ranged, orderly & symmetrical arrangement. All morality is shown to be a historical inevitable evolution, and you have only to recognise it and farther that evolution by falling into its track instead of going backward on the track.

THE GURU

And getting called atavistic and degenerate and other terrible names? Still I should like to be better satisfied as to the basis of this symmetrical and inevitable arrangement; for if I were convinced that I am an ephemeral animal, I should like to enjoy myself during my day like other ephemeral animals and cannot see why I should trouble myself about the eternal future; & even tho' science should hurl the most formidable polysyllables in its vocabulary at me, I do not know that I should greatly care, and I think Messrs Rockefeller & Jay Gould & millions more were or are in hearty agreement with me. You say the genus is eternal? But I believe this is not the teaching of Science. As I understand it, man is only an animal, a particular sort of monkey which developed suddenly for some inexplicable reason & shot forward 10,000 miles ahead of every animal yet born upon earth. If this is so, there is no reason why some other animal, say, some particular kind of ant, should not suddenly for some inexplicable reason develop & shoot forward 100,000 miles ahead and make as short work of man as man made of the mammoth. Or in some other way the human race will certainly be replaced. Now what good is it to the mammoth whose bones science has recently disinterred, that a race has developed which can disinter him and dissertate in numerous polysyllables upon his remains? And if a scientific mammoth in his days had placed before him this prospect and bid him give up in the interest of the mammoth race, his unsocial & selfish ways, would that have seemed even to the most reasonable tusker a sufficient motive for his self-sacrifice? Where would his *benefit* in the affair come in?

THE STUDENT

It is not precisely a question of personal benefit; it is a question of inevitable law. You would be setting yourself against the inevitable law.

THE GURU

Verily? and what do I care, if my opposition to the inevitable brings me no harm, but rather content & prosperity in my day? After my death nothing can injure me, if I am but clay.

THE STUDENT

The individual may be immoral, but morality progresses inevitably.

THE GURU

Truly? I do not think the present state of Europe favourable to that conception. Why, we had thought that Science would make the cultured nations dominate & people the earth. And we find them stationary or absolutely retrograding in population, degenerating in nerve & hardiness, losing in the true imperial qualities. We had thought that sacking of cities, massacre, torture & foul rape were blotted by civilisation from the methods of war. The enlightened peoples of Europe march into China and there takes place an orgy of filth & blood & cold delight in agony which all but the most loathsome savages would shrink from in disgust. Is that the inevitable moral advance or Red Indian savagery improved upon? We had thought that with increasing education & intellectuality must come increasing chastity or at least refinement. In a great American city the police sweeps the brothels and gathers in its net hundreds of educated, cultured, gracious & stately women who had carried their education, beauty and culture *there*. Is that the inevitable moral advance, or rather the days of Messalina returned? These are not isolated phenomena but could be multiplied infinitely. Europe is following in the footsteps of ancient Rome.

THE STUDENT
There are these periods of retrogression. Evolution advances in a curve, not in a straight line.

THE GURU
And mark that these retrogressions are most inevitable when the world, abandoning religion, plunges into philosophic materialism. Not immediately do they come; while the spirit of the old religion still survives the death of its body, the nations seem perhaps to gain in strength & power; but very soon the posthumous force is exhausted. All the old nations perished because in the pride of intellect they abandoned their *dharma*, their religion. India, China still live. What was the force that enabled India beaten down & trampled by mailed fist & iron hoof ever to survive immortally, ever to resist, ever to crush down the conqueror of the hour at last beneath her gigantic foot, ever to raise her mighty head again to the stars? It is because she never lost hold of religion, never gave up her faith in the spirit. Therefore the promise of Srikrishna ever holds good; therefore the Adyashakti, the mighty Chandi, ever descends when the people turn to her and tramples the Asura to pieces. Times change and a new kind of outer power rules over India in place of the Asuras of the East. But woe to India if she cast from her her eternal *dharma*. The fate of the old nations shall then overtake her, her name shall be cast out from the list of nations and her peoples become a memory and a legend upon the earth. Let her keep true to her Self, and the *Atmashakti*, the eternal Force of the Self shall again strengthen & raise her. Modern Science has engaged itself deeply in two cardinal errors; it has built out of the Law of Causation a new and more inexorable fate than Greek or Hindu or Arab ever imagined. Engrossed

with this predestination, Science has come to believe that the human will is a mere servant, nay, a mere creation of eternal inanimate forces. Science is mistaken & unless it widen its view it may easily be convinced of its mistake in a very ugly fashion before long. The Will is mightier than any law, fate or force. The Will is eternal, omnipotent, it has created the law of causation and governs it; it has made the laws of matter and it can override them; it is itself all the forces which seem to govern and bind it. There is no compulsion on the human will to evolve towards progression; if it chooses to regress, back it will go and all the world reeling and shrieking with it into barbarism and chaos; if it chooses to go forward, no force can stop it. The other mistake Science has made, it borrows from Christianity; it is that action and emotion can be directed towards beings distinct from oneself; all action and emotion are for the self, in the self. But if Science teaches men to regard themselves as distinct and purely corporeal beings, with no connection with others except such as may be created by physical contact and the communication of the senses, it is obvious that the human Will under the obsession of this belief, will inevitably shape its action & thought in accordance passing over the more shadowy moral generalities of evolutionary theorists or play with them only as intellectual marbles. And that spells in the end a colossal selfishness, an increasing sensuality, lust of power, riches, comfort & dominion, a monstrous & egoistic brutality like that of a hundred-armed Titan wielding all the arms of the Gods in those hundred hands. If man believes himself to be an animal he will act like an animal & exalt the animal impulse into his guide. That Europe does not approach more swiftly to this condition is due to the obstinate refusal of Jnana, Religion, true enlightenment, maimed & wounded tho' it be, to perish and make an end; it will not allow the human Will to believe that it is no more than nerve & flesh & body, animal & transitory. It persists & takes a hundred forms to elude the pursuit of materialistic Science, calling upon the Eternal Mother to come down and save; and surely before long she shall come. All bases of morality which do not go back to the original divine

and sempiternal nature of man, must be erroneous and fleeting.
Not from the instincts & customs of the ape & savage did the
glories of religion & virtue arise, — they are the perennial light
of the concealed godhead revealing themselves ever with clearer
lines, with floods of more beautiful rainbow lustre, to culminate
at last in the pure white light of the supreme realisation, when
all creatures have become our Self and our Self realises its own
Unity.

यस्मिन् सर्वाणि भूतान्यात्मैवाभूद्विजानतः ।
तत्र को मोहः कः शोक एकत्वमनुपश्यतः ॥

The Upanishad having posited this Unity which is at once
the justification of all religion & morality and the culmination
in which religion & morality disappear into something higher
than either, proceeds again to sum up and describe the Eternal
under this new light. In the fourth verse He has been described
only as the mighty Force which creates & surrounds all this
universe; He is now to be described as the mighty Unity which
in its unmanifestation is the source of all existence and in its
manifestation governs these innumerable worlds.

स पर्यगाच्छुक्रमकायमव्रणमस्नाविरं शुद्धमपापविद्धम् ।
कविर्मनीषी परिभूः स्वयंभूर्याथातथ्यतोऽर्थान्व्यदधाच्छाश्वतीभ्यः
समाभ्यः ॥

This is He that went round, the brightness, unbodied, unscarred,
without sinews, pure, untouched by sin; He is the Seer, the
Thinker, the Selfborn that pervadeth; He from years sempiternal
hath ordered perfectly all things.

The verse begins by repeating a position already taken, of the
Lord surrounding all things as a robe surrounds its wearer, creating all things by the appearance of motion, which is however
an appearance, a phenomenon and not a reality of the Eternal.
"This is He that went round." In other words the whirl of motion
which the manifested Eternal set at work created the worlds; he
poured forth from himself as Prajna the Eternal Wisdom and
entered & encompassed each thing as he created it. But who is
this He? In answering this question the Sruti immediately reverts

to the neuter gender, because it has to go back to the luminous Parabrahman who is beyond the idea of sex or characteristic. He the Creator of the Worlds is in reality That Brightness, the luminous shadow of the Unknowable of which we can only speak in negatives. That has not a body or form, form being created by Him and therefore this side of Him; He has no scars or imperfections, but is one faultless & perfect light; He has no sinews or muscles; ie He is that side of matter and creation is produced from him not by physical means or physical strength & skill, but by the mere flowing forth of his Shakti or Will. Finally He is not only that side of Matter, but He is that side of Mind also, for He is pure and untouched by evil. It is mind that creates impurity & evil, by desire which produces duality; but the Eternal is not subject to desire. What is evil or Sin? It is merely the preference of the more gross to the more subtle, of tamas to rajas and of rajas to sattwa; it operates therefore in the sphere of the *gunas* and the Eternal being above the *gunas* cannot be touched by Sin. Having established the identity of the Lord who creates & rules, with the pure luminous Parabrahman, who is neither lord nor subject, the Sruti describes the Lord in his capacity of the All-wise Governor; he is the Seer & Poet, who by his illumined inspirations creates as Hiranyagarbha the whole world in His own infinite Mind, He is the Thinker, Prajna, the Wise One, from whose essential mass of equipoised consciousness all existence and its laws draw their perennial strength and being and flow forth to their works, and He is also that which flows forth, Virat, the pervading spirit which enters into all things and encompasses. In all these capacities He is selfborn; for He is Prajna who came forth by His own strength from the luminous Parabrahman & is Parabrahman, He is Hiranyagarbha who comes forth by His own strength from Prajna & is Prajna; He is Virat who comes forth by His own strength from Hiranyagarbha & is Hiranyagarbha. He is the Self born out of the Self by the Self. In other words all these are merely names of the One Spirit in different aspects or states of universal & infinite consciousness. Why then is the Lord spoken of, unlike Parabrahman, in the masculine gender? Because he is now considered in His capacity as the great ruler & ordainer, not in His capacity as the source from which all things flow. As the source, substratum & container of things He is the Trinity, Prajna-Hiranyagarbha-Virat, in whom the Male & Female, Spirit & Matter, the Soul & its Shakti are still one & undivided. He is therefore best spoken of in the neuter. But when we see Him as the Ruler & Ordainer, the Manifested Brahman dealing with a world of phenomena already created, then division has taken place, the Shakti has gone forth to its works, and the great male Trinity, Brahma-Vishnu-Maheshwara, filled with the force of that Shakti are creating, preserving & destroying the countless worlds and the innumerable myriads of their inhabiting forms. Both these Trinities are in reality one Trinity, it is only the point of view that makes the difference. From this standpoint the Sruti goes on then to describe the Lord. He is *kavi*, the great seer & *poet* in the true sense of the word poet; the *kavi* is he who divines things luminously & distinctly by sheer intuition and whose divinations become, by their own overflow, creations. Paramatman as Sat-Brahma-Hiranyagarbha has this divine quality of poethood, — which men call the power of creation and it is therefore that his Shakti is described as Saraswati. Then the Lord is described as *manishi*, the Thinker. It is the thought of the Lord that is the basis or substratum of all this creation; it is therefore that the inanimate object forms faultlessly, that the tree grows unerringly, that the animal acts with infallible instinct towards his dominant needs, that the star moves in its course & the mountain holds to its base. All the creations of the great Kavi would be inconstant in their relations and clash & collide till they destroyed each other if there were not this imperative Wisdom, with stability & equipoise as its characteristic, underlying all things & keeping them to their places, actions & nature. This Wisdom, be it noted, is the very nature of things; it is no deliberate invention, no thing of afterthoughts, adjustments & alterations, but unchangeable & the essential basis of existence from the beginning. Whatever form it take, of gravitation, or of attraction and repulsion, or of evolution, it is an eternal presence & the very nature of the world, प्रज्ञानं ब्रह्म. This power of divine instinctive thought is one capacity of Paramatman as Chit-Mahadev-Prajna (Tamas, Sthanu). His other capacity is that of destruction, for He is the Spirit of immobility to whom the deep sleep of perfect unconditioned thought is the culmination (Chit) and if it were not for the activity of the Kavi in the Eternal, if the Thinker in Him were to blot out the Poet, all this pulsating world of phenomena would be stilled & resolve by inaction into the womb of undetermined condensed existence. Then again He is *paribhu*, He who exists all round, the great pervading Bliss of existence (Ananda). For the works of the Poet even though upheld by the Thinker, could not last, if it were not that the bliss of existence [is] poured through all created things like a stream of heavenly nectar & makes life, being, their first imperative need. This is that Will to Live of the German philosopher, which because like all Europeans, he could see Truth only in one of her limbs and not as a divine whole, gave so pessimistic a note to his thought. All things are supported & eternalized by this Bliss, for it is the unchanging & eternal Paramatman. Manifesting as the will to live finitely, it must be broadened into the will to live infinitely in order to fulfil itself & recover its own deepest & essential nature. We will first to live as individuals, then to live in the family, then to live in the tribe or clan, then to live in the race or nation, then to live in mankind, then to live in the Universe, then to live in God, the one Eternal; this is the natural evolution of humanity & its course is determined by the very nature of the Self. Science the Apara Vidya traces for us the course & byelaws of evolution, but it is only the Para Vidya that bases it for us, gives us its reason, source, law & culmination. This Bliss is the capacity of Vishnu-Virat who is Ananda. By his very existence in all beings the Lord preserves & saves. Remember that, though you cry out to the Heavens for help in your misery, it is not the blue sky that hears, it is nothing outside you that comes to save, but He within you alone can protect. Art thou oppressed, O man, by ogre & giant, by fiend & foeman? Seek His mighty Shakti, Bhavani Mahishamardini, in yourself and She will externalize armed with sword & trident to crush the triumphing Asura. This is the law & the gospel. The Poet, the Thinker, the Pervading

Presence, these three are the Swayambhu, the eternal Selfborn who is born by HimSelf out of HimSelf into HimSelf. The Gods are not different from each other, for they are all one God, & there is no other. This is He who has ordered from eternal years perfectly all things. याथातथ्यत:, each duly as it should be & must be because of its own nature, for the nature of a thing is its origin, its law, its destiny, its end; and harmony with its nature is its perfection. All this mighty universe where various things acting according to their various natures harmonise & melt into a perfect unity, all this wonderful Kingdom of a single Law in its manifold aspects He has ordered, व्यदधात्, he has arranged diversely; he has set each thing in its own place, working in its own orbit & according to its own overmastering & inexorable nature. All this He has done from years eternal, not in time, not at a particular date & season, but eternally, before Time was. The Law did not spring into being, but was, is & for ever shall be. The forms of objects, it is true, vary in Time, but the law of their nature is of eternal origin. In the act you do today, you are obeying a Law which has existed during the whole of eternity. Try to realise it, and you will see Time & Space vanishing into Infinity, you will hear the boom of the eternal waters & the great voice crying for ever on the waters "Tapas, tapas", and feel yourself in the presence of the One unchangeable & eternal God. Maya & her works have no ending, because they had no beginning, but the soul of Man can rise above Maya and her works & stand over her & free from her watching her as her master for whose joy she labours unto all eternity. For verily Man is God and as by his own Will he has cast himself into the illusory bonds of the Enchantress, so by His own will He can shake off the bonds & rule her. The play of the Soul with the Maya is the play of the lover & his beloved, one feigning to be the slave of the other, rejoicing in her favour or weeping at her feet in her anger, and now resuming his rightful rôle of lord & master, yea, turning away from her at will to a fairer & more wonderful face; and now Krishna wears the blue dress & shining jewels, and now Radha the yellow cloth & fragrant garlands of the green wood and the brilliant feather of the peacock; for He is She, and She is He; they are only playing at difference, for in real truth they have been and are one to all Eternity.

THE STUDENT
Here then the first part of the Upanishad seems to be ended and some very obscure & disconnected utterances follow.

THE GURU
The utterances of the Upanishad are never disconnected, but the connection is usually beneath the surface, not openly declared by explicit statement or grammatical construction. The Upanishad has said that the Eternal has arranged all objects of the Universe perfectly from years eternal. Maya therefore is eternal, Avidya is eternal. The question will at once be put, what then of Vidya & Avidya? the Eternal and the Transient? the Is & the Seems to Be? If Avidya is eternal, let us rejoice in her wonders & glories & never strive to escape from her bonds. But if Vidya alone be eternal, then is Avidya a curse and a bondage, what have we to do with it, but shake it off with disgust as soon as possible? These are the extremes of the Materialist and Nihilist, the Charvak & the Sunyavadin; but the Vedanta gives its sanction to neither. The Unconditioned Brahman is, but of the Conditioned also we cannot say that He is not and the Conditioned Brahman is what we call Maya. Brahman is eternal & Maya therefore is eternal; but the Conditioned Brahman obviously rests on the Unconditioned and cannot be except in Him. As are the reverse & obverse of a coin, so are the Conditioned and Unconditioned, and the aspirant to Knowledge must know both and not one only or he will know but little indeed of the true nature of the Eternal.

THE STUDENT
The followers of Adwaita will call this rank heresy. Maya is illusion, unreality and is slain by knowledge, it cannot therefore be eternal.

THE GURU
You cannot slay Maya; you can only slay Moha, the illusion

of Maya; her you can only conquer and put her under your feet. You remember that Shankara after conquering Ubhayabharati, made her living body his *asan* of meditation; that is the symbol of the Yogi and the wonderful twofold Maya of the Eternal. He has conquered her & put her beneath him, but it is still upon her that his *asan* is based even when he is unconscious of Her and in union with the Eternal. If this were not so, then the whole of phenomena would cease the moment a man becomes a Buddha and enters into Nirvana; for He & the Eternal are One. If Parabrahman therefore were limited either to Vidya or Avidya, obviously Avidya would cease the moment Vidya began and the salvation of one Jivatma would bring about the end of the world for all; just as the Christians say that the crucifixion of Christ saved the world. But this is not so. The power of Shakti of Brahman is twofold & simultaneous; He is able to exercise Vidya & Avidya at the same moment; he eternally realises His own transcendental nature; and at the very same time He realises this wonderful universe of His imagination. He is like a great poet who shadows forth a world of his own creation made in himself and of himself and yet knows that He is different from it & independent of it. It is for this reason only that the salvation of a particular Jivatman does not bring the world to an end. Nor does Shankara really say anything different; for he does not assert that Maya is unreal; he says it is a mysterious something of which you cannot say that it is and yet you cannot say that it is not. This indeed is the only description that the finite mind can make of this mysterious Shakti of the Illimitable, Unconditioned, Unknowable Brahman. Maya in its forms may be unreal & transitory but Maya in its essence as a Shakti of the Eternal, must itself be eternal, from of old & for ever.

The Karmayogin

A Commentary on the
Isha Upanishad

Sri Aurobindo modified the structure of *The Karmayogin: A Commentary on the Isha Upanishad* while he was working on it. He began with a two-tier division: "Chapters" and sections. Later he introduced a superior division, the "Part", and began calling the lowest-level divisions "Chapters". The intermediate divisions, earlier called "Chapters", became known as "Books". The numbering of these divisions is neither consistent nor complete. The table on the opposite page shows the structure as marked by Sri Aurobindo in the manuscript and printed in the text and, italicised and within square brackets, how it would be if the final three-tier division were applied consistently throughout.

In the right margin are indicated the places where the discussions of the first six verses begin. The other twelve verses were not discussed.

Chapter I.

The Law of Renunciation.

I. God All and God Everywhere

GURU

Salutation to the Eternal who is without place, time, cause or limit. Salutation to Him who rules the Universe, the Lord of the Illusion, the Master of manifold life. Salutation to the Self in me, who is the Self in all creatures. Brahman, Isha, Atman, under whatever aspect He manifests Himself or manifests not, to Him the One and Only Existence, Consciousness, Bliss, salutation.

The Upanishad begins; —

"With the Lord all this must be clothed (as with a garment), even all that is world in this moving universe; abandon the world that thou mayest enjoy it, neither covet any man's possessions."

The Upanishad first sets forth the universality of the Supreme Being; whatever we see, hear or are in any way sensible of, we must feel the presence of the Lord surrounding it. This tree that I am sitting under, I must not consider as only so many leaves, bark, pith, sap and roots encased in earth and air; I must realise that it is a manifestation in the Supreme who is the only reality. This voice that I am uttering, vibrates in the atmosphere of the Divine Reality; only because it vibrates there, is it capable of sound, articulation and meaning. No action I do or watch others do, but the Lord is there surrounding and upholding it; otherwise it could not be done. Whatever I see, I am seeing God; whatever I hear, I am hearing God; whatever I do, it is the Energy of God which is governing my actions. This is the first thing the Karmayogin has to realise and until he has set his mind on the realisation, Karmayoga is impossible. The Lord is everywhere; the Lord surrounds everything with His presence; the Lord is all. वासुदेवः सर्वमिति। This Karma that I do, I do it in the Lord; this subjective I who act, exist only in the Lord; this objective he, she, it to whom the action is done, exists only in the Lord. It is the omnipresent universality of the Supreme, that has first to be realized. When the Yogin has had spiritual experience of this universality, then only is he fit for Karmayoga; for not till then can he sink the constant feeling of I and thou and he in a single higher and wider Existence; not till then can he escape from apparent self to true Self, and without such escape Karmayoga cannot really begin. To clothe all things with the Supreme, to be conscious of Him in all you say, do, think, feel or are sensible of, — this experience is the beginning of Karmayoga. The transformation of this experience into the habitual condition of the soul, is the consummation of Karmayoga; for it leads straight to the knowledge of Brahman and the ecstasy of union with Him, Karma melting into and becoming one with Jnana and Bhakti. Karma, Bhakti, Jnana, — Action, Love, Knowledge, are the three paths which lead out of phenomenal existence to the eternal reality, and where the three meet & become one, is the end of the great journey, that highest home of Vishnu towards which it is the one object of the Upanishad to turn and guide us. The Isha Upanishad is the Scripture of the Karmayogin; of the three paths it teaches the way of Action, and therefore begins with this first indispensable condition of all Godward action, to see all things, creatures, causes, effects, changes & evolutions as so many transitory phenomena enveloped with the presence of the Supreme Being and existing in Him and by Him only. Not I but He, for He is my real self and what I call I is only so much covering and semblance, — this is Vedanta; the first feeling of this truth is the beginning of Jnana, the beginning of Bhakti, the beginning of Karma. सोऽहं. He is the true & only I.

II. Isha, the Lord.

Let us now look closely into the language of the Scripture, for in the Upanishad every word is of infinite importance and is chosen in preference to others for some profound and significant reason. *Ishâ* is the first word of the Upanishad; it is with the Lord that we must clothe all things in this Universe, it is the Lord whose presence, will, energy we must realize in whatever we see, feel, do or think. It is in other words the Supreme Being not in His aspect as the actionless, unknowable Parabrahman, transcendental and beyond realization by senses, mind or speech; it is not even Sacchidananda, that absolute self-centred Existence, Consciousness, Bliss with whom the Jnanayogin seeks to unite himself in Samadhi; it is the Eternal in His aspect as Ruler of the Universe, He who keeps the wheel of phenomena turning and guides its motions as the mechanician controls his machine. The Karmamargin aims at living disillusionized, but yet using the illusions of Maya as the materials of his Yoga; he seeks to free himself from phenomena while yet living among phenomena; it is therefore Isha, Maheshwara, the Lord of the Illusion, the Master of multiple phenomenal life whom he must seek and in whom he must lose his lower self. Since he works through actions, it is the Master of actions whom he must worship with the flowers and incense of a selfless life.

Is there then a difference between Parabrahman and Isha? Are there two Supreme Beings and not one? No difference, really; the distinction is one of appearance, of semblance. Parabrahman, the absolute, transcendental, eternal reality is unknowable to human reason; That which is above reason in man can reach Parabrahman and experience Parabrahman, because It is Parabrahman, but this is in the state of Samadhi and from the state of Samadhi the human understanding can bring back no record intelligible to the reason or explicable in terms of speech. Parabrahman in His Essence is therefore realizable but not intelligible; He can be experienced, He cannot be explained or understood. Still Parabrahman presents to the understanding two semblances or aspects by which He can be relatively though not absolutely known. These two aspects correspond to the two powers inherent in Parabrahman as the Knower of Himself, the powers of Vidya and Avidya, the power to know and the power not to know, the faculty of Knowledge and the faculty of Illusion. Parabrahman can know Himself as He really is; this is Vidya. He can also imagine

Himself as He is not; this is Avidya. In the first aspect He is
Sacchidananda, absolute Existence, Consciousness and Bliss;
He exists to Himself alone, because there *is* no other existence
but Himself; He is conscious of His own existence only, because
there *is* no other existence to be conscious of; He is the bliss
of His own self-conscious existence, because there is nothing
outside or other than Him to give Him external bliss. That is the
eternal reality, that is His aspect to Vidya or true Knowledge.
But there is also the eternal unreality, His aspect to Avidya
or False Knowledge. Then He is a great Will, Shakti or Force
pouring itself out in a million forms and names and keeping
for ever in motion the eternal wheel of phenomenal Evolution,
which He guides and governs. He is then Isha, the Lord or Ruler.
To use a human parallel, Shakespeare pouring himself out in a
hundred names and forms, Desdemona, Othello, Iago, Viola,
Rosalind, Macbeth, Hamlet, Lear, Cymbeline is using his power
of Avidya to become the lord and ruler of a wonderful imaginary
world. Shakespeare putting aside his works and returning to his
own single & sufficient existence is using his power of Vidya
to recover his own constant single reality. But there is one
Shakespeare and not two. Now the Karmamargin has to deal
with this great multifold phenomenal universe and when he
seeks to feel the presence of the Eternal round every single thing
it contains, it must necessarily be not in His unconditioned,
unphenomenal aspect of Sacchidananda but in His conditioned,
phenomenal aspect as Isha, Lord of the Universe. As Isha the
Karmayogin may worship Him in various sub-aspects. Isha is a
double being as Purusha-Prakriti; Purusha, the great male ocean
of spiritual force which sets Prakriti to produce and watches
her workings, and Prakriti, the mighty female energy which
produces and works unweariedly for the pleasure of Purusha.
He is the triple Being, Prajna, Hiranyagarbha, Virat; Prajna,
Lord of Sleep-Life, the intelligent force which lives and wakes in
what would otherwise seem inert and inanimate existence or the
mere blind play of mechanical forces; Hiranyagarbha, the Lord
of Dream-Life who takes from this ocean of subconsciously
intelligent spiritual being those conscious psychic forces which

He materializes or encases in various forms of gross living matter; and Virat, Lord of Waking-Life, who governs, preserves and maintains the sensible creation which Hiranyagarbha has shaped. He is triple again as Shiva, Brahma, Vishnu; Shiva, the destroyer, the Yogin, the Lord of brute or inert life; the Master of Samadhi, the Refuge of the outcast & of those who have no refuge; Brahma, the Creator, who puts forth life and stays not his hand for a moment; Vishnu, the Preserver & Saviour, the Master of Power & Love and Life and Light and Sweetness. With all these aspects of Isha, the Lord, Hindu worship has associated names & forms and in these names and forms He shows Himself to His worshippers. The Jnanayogin loves to worship Him as Shiva, the Master of utter Samadhi; to the Bhakta He appears in whatever form appeals most to the spiritual emotions of His devotee. But the Karmayogin should devote himself to those forms of the Supreme Lord in which His mighty Shakti, His Will to live and create has expressed itself in its highest, purest and most inspiring and energetic virility; for Karma is merely Shakti in motion and the Karmayogin must be a pure conductor of divine energy, a selfless hero and creator in the world. Isha Himself in His Avatars, Buddha, Rama, Srikrishna, has given us the highest types of this selfless divine energy and it is therefore to these mighty spirits, God-in-man, that the Karmayogin may well direct his worship. Or he may worship Isha in His Shakti, in the form of Durga-Kali, the most powerful realisation of His cosmic energy which the human mind has yet envisaged. If he is able to dispense with forms, he may worship the idea of Isha Himself, the Almighty Lord, whom the Hindu adores as Hari, the Christian as God, the Mahomedan as Allah. Even the atheist, if he recognizes a mighty Power at work in all life and existence and yields up his self and actions to the will and ends of that Power, or if he recognizes in men the godhead he refuses to recognize in the Universe and devotes himself to the selfless service of his kind, has set his foot on the path of Karmayoga and cannot fail to reach the Lord whom he denies. It is of no importance that the Karmayogin should recognize a particular name or form as the greater Self to win whom he must lose his smaller self; but it is of importance & essential that he should recognize the existence of a Power inside and outside himself to the law of whose Will and Workings he can sacrifice the self-will and self-worship of the natural man. Whatever name he gives to this Power or whether he gives it a name or not, it is Isha, the Lord, whose presence he must feel around every object and movement in the Universe.

III. Isha and His Universe.

Next let us take note of the word वास्यं. All this Universe must be clothed with Isha; we must draw the feeling of His presence round every object in the Universe and envelop it with Isha, as a robe is drawn round and envelops the wearer. For the Lord is greater than His universe. This tree is not the Lord, it is in the Lord. We must avoid the materialistic Pantheism which identifies the visible Universe with the Supreme Being. It is true that He is both the final and material Cause of the universe, and in one sense He is His Universe and His Universe is He, just as Shakespeare's creations are really Shakespeare himself, woven by him out of his own store of psychic material; and yet it would be obviously a mistake to identify, say, Iago with Shakespeare. This tree is evolved out of original ether, ether pervades it and surrounds it, but the tree cannot be described as ether, nor ether as the tree; so, going deeper down, we find it is evolved out of the existence of the Lord who pervades it and surrounds it with His presence; but the tree is not the Lord, nor the Lord the tree. The Hindu is no idolater; he does not worship stocks or stones, the tree as tree or the stone as stone or the idol as a material thing, but he worships the presence of the Lord which fills & surrounds the tree, stone or idol, and of which the tree, stone or idol is merely a manifestation or seeming receptacle. We say for the convenience of language and mental realization that God is in His creature, but really it is the creature who is in God, न त्वहं तेषु ते मयि. "I am not in them, they are in Me."

We find European scholars when they are confronted with the metaphors of the Sruti, always stumbling into a blunder which we must carefully avoid if we wish to understand our Scriptures. Their reason, hard, logical and inflexible, insists on fixing the metaphor to its literal sense and having thus done violence to the spirit of the Upanishad, they triumphantly point to the resultant incoherence and inconsistency of our revealed writings and cry out, "These are the guesses, sometimes sublime, generally infantile, of humanity in its childhood." But the metaphors of the Sruti are merely helps to a clearer understanding; you are intended to take their spirit and not insist on the letter. They are conveniences for the hand in climbing, not supports on which you are to hang your whole weight. Here is a metaphor वास्यं, clothe, as with a garment. But the garment is different from the wearer, & limited in the space it occupies: is the Lord then different from His creation and limited in His being? That would be the letter; the spirit is different. The presence of the Lord who is infinite, must be thought of as surrounding each object and not confined to the limits of the object, — this and no more is the force of वास्यं. When we see the tree, we do not say, "This is the Lord", but we say "Here is the Lord". The tree exists only in Him & by Him; He is in it and around it, even as the ether is.

All this, says the Sruti, is to be thought of as surrounded by the presence of the Lord, सर्वमिदं, all this that is present to our senses, all in fact that we call the Universe. But to avoid misunderstanding the Upanishad goes on to point out that it is not only the Universe as a whole, but each thing that is in the Universe which we must feel to be encompassed with the divine Presence, यत्किंच जगत्यां जगत्। everything and anything that is moving thing in Her who moves. *Jagati*, she that moves, in the ancient Sanscrit, was a word applied to the whole Universe; afterwards it meant rather this moving earth,[1] that part of the cosmos with which we human beings are mainly concerned and the neuter *jagat*, that which moves, came to be the ordinary expression for world or universe. But why is the universe called

[1] The ancient Rishis knew that the earth moves, चला पृथ्वी स्थिरा भाति, "The earth moves, but seems to be still".

"she that moves"? Because it is the result of the working of Prakriti, the visible form of Prakriti, the great female material energy of the Lord, and the essence of Prakriti is motion; for by motion she creates this material world. Indeed all object matter is only a form, that is to say a visible, audible or in some way sensible result of motion. Every material object is what it is here called, *jagat*, a world of infinite motion; even the stone, even the clod. Our senses tell us that the material world is the only reality, the only steadfast thing of whose rule and order we can be sure and by which we can abide; but our senses are in error and the Upanishad warns us against their false evidence. The material world is a transitory and changing whirl of motion on the surface of Brahman, the great ocean of spiritual existence, who alone is, in His depths, eternal, real and steadfast. It is He who as the Lord gives order, rule and abidingness to the infinite motion we call the Universe; and if we wish to be in touch with reality, we must train our souls to become aware of His presence sustaining, pervading and surrounding this moving Prakriti and every objective form to which her varying rates of vibration have given rise. Thus placed in constant touch with reality, the Karmayogin will escape from the false shows and illusions of Prakriti; Karma or action which also is merely her motion, energy at work, will not master him and drive him as a storm drives a ship, but he will rather be the master of action, both his own and that of others. For it is only by understanding practically the reality of a thing and its law of working that one can become its master and make use of it for his own purposes.

IV. God in Man and in all Creatures.

But when the Karmayogin has seen the Lord surrounding all things with His presence and all things existing only as transitory manifestations, idols or images in this divine Reality, what follows? It follows that just as this tree or that mountain exists only as an image or manifestation in the divine Reality, so also all creatures, men included, are merely images or manifestations in the same divine Reality. In other words what is real, living, eternal in you and me, is not our body, nor our vitality & its desires, nor our mind, nor our reason and understanding, but just the divine presence which pervades me and you as much as it pervades the tree and the mountain. And it is not the body, vitality, mind, reason or understanding which constitutes the presence of the Lord within us; for my body differs from yours, my vitality differs from yours, my mind differs from yours, my reason and understanding differ from yours; they differ even from themselves according to time and circumstances; but the Lord is one and unchanging. There must therefore be something deeper hidden within us than any of these things, something which is alone real, living and eternal. This something is called in the Vedanta the Self; it is Brahman or the Lord within each of his creatures. The Self is in the microcosm what Sacchidananda is in the macrocosm; it is the great pure luminous existence, self-conscious and self-blissful, which acts not, neither desires, but watches the infinite play of Prakriti in the life of the creature It informs. And just as by the power of Avidya Sacchidananda takes the semblance of a mighty Will or Force, Isha, creating endless multiplicity and governing, guiding and rejoicing in the interplay of worlds, so by the same power this Self or Witness in Man takes the semblance of a sublime Will creating for itself action and inaction, pleasure & pain, joy & sorrow, victory & defeat, guiding, governing & rejoicing in the activity of the apparent creature it informs, but unaffected and unbound by his works. This Will, which the Vedanta calls Ananda or Bliss and not will, must not be confused with mere volition or desire, for volition belongs to the outer & apparent man and not to the inner and real. This Self is in me, it is also in you and every other being and in all it is the same Self, only the Will or Shakti manifests in different degrees, with a different intensity and manner of working and so with different qualities & actions in each separate creature. Hence the appearance of diversity and divisibility in what is really One and indivisible.

This divisibility of the Indivisible is one of those profound paradoxes of Vedantic thought which increasing Knowledge will show to be deep and far-reaching truths. It used to be implicitly believed that human personality was a single and indivisible thing; yet recently a school of psychologists has grown up who consider man as a bundle of various personalities rather than a single, homogeneous and indivisible consciousness. For it has been found that a single man can divide himself or be divided into several personalities, each living its own life and unconscious of the other, while yet again another personality may emerge in him which is conscious of the others and yet separate from all of them. This is true; nevertheless, the *man* all through remains one and the same, not only in body but in his psychical existence; for there is a deeper substratum in him which underlies all these divided personalities and is wider than all of them put together. The truth is that the waking personality is only the apparent man, not the real. Personality is the creation of memory, for memory is its basis and pedestal. If the pedestal, then, be divided and put apart, the superstructure also must be in the same act divided and put apart. But the waking memory is only a part, a selection of a wider latent memory which has faithfully recorded all that happens not in the man's present life only, but in all his past. The personality which corresponds with this latent unerring memory is the true personality of the man; it is his soul, one infinite and indivisible, and its apparent divisions are merely the result of Avidya, false knowledge, due to defective action of the waking memory. So the apparent division of the divine Self into many human selves, of the indivisible Paramatman into many Jivatmans, is simply the result of Avidya due to the action of the Maya or self-imposed illusion of Isha, the great Force who has willed that the One by this force of Maya should become phenomenally manifold. In reality, there is no division and the Self in me is the same as the Self in you and the same as the Self up yonder in the Sun. The unity of spiritual existence is the basis of all true religion and true morality. We know indeed that as God is not contained in His universe, but the universe is in Him, so also God is not contained within a man. When the Sruti says elsewhere that the Purusha lies hidden in the heart of our being and is no larger than the size of a man's thumb, it simply means that to the mind of man under the dominion of Avidya his body, vitality, mind, reason bulk so largely, the Spirit seems a small and indistinguishable thing indeed inside so many and bulky sheaths and coverings. But in reality, it is body, vitality, mind & reason forming the apparent man that are small and trifling and it is the Spirit or real man that is large, grandiose & mighty. The apparent man exists in & by the real, not the real in the apparent; the body is in the soul, not the soul in the body. Yet for the convenience of language and our finite understanding we are compelled to say that the soul is in the body and that God is within the man; for that is how it naturally presents itself to us who use the mental standpoint and the language of a finite intelligence. The Lord, from our standpoint, is within all His creatures and He is the real self of all His creatures. My self and yourself are not really two but one. This is the second truth proceeding logically from the first, on which the Karmayogin has to lay fast hold.

V. Selflessness, the Basic Rule of Karma-Yoga

From the fundamental truth of one divine Reality pervading and surrounding all phenomenal objects and from its implied corollary, the identity of my Self with your Self, the Upanishad deduces a principle of action which holds good for all Karmayogins. "Abandon the world that thou mayst enjoy it, neither covet any man's possession." He that would save his soul, must first lose it. He who would enjoy the world, must first abandon it. Thus from an intellectual paradox the Upanishad proceeds to a moral paradox, and yet both are profound and accurate statements of fact. At first the reason revolts against an assertion so self-contradictory. If I put my food away from me, how can I enjoy it? If I throw away the sovereign in my hand, another may have the joy of it but how can I? I, Devadatta, am told to enjoy the world, yes, all that is in the world; yet I find that I have little enough to enjoy while my neighbour Harischandra has untold wealth. If I am to enjoy the world, how shall I proceed to my object? Not surely by abandoning the little I have, but by keeping fast hold on it and adding to it the much that Harischandra has. So would argue the natural man, rationally enough from his point of view, but so would not argue the Karmayogin. He will covet no man's possession, because he knows such terms as possession, mine, thine, to be false and illusory in the light of the secret tremendous truth he has got hold of, that there is nothing in this world real, desirable and worth calling by the name of bliss except Brahman, the eternal reality of things. Self-gratification and the possession of wealth and its enjoyments are transitory, illusory and attended with inevitable trouble and pain, but the enjoyment of one's identity with Brahman and the possession of Brahman are pure and undisturbed bliss. The more I possess of Him, the wider and nearer perfection will be my enjoyment. Brahman then is the only wealth the Karmayogin will covet. But how can we possess Brahman? By surrounding all things in the world with Him, by realizing Him in all things. If I am wealthy, the Lord is there in my wealth, but if I am poor, the Lord is there too in my poverty; because of His presence I can enjoy my poverty as much as I did my wealth. For it is not the wealth and the poverty which matter or are real, but only the feeling of the presence of the Lord in all things. That is one way in which I can enjoy the world by abandoning it; for the world is Brahman, the world is the Lord, and to him who has experience of it, all things are bliss, all things are enjoyment. What ground then is there left for coveting another man's possessions? Harischandra possesses merely so much gold, estates, houses, Government paper; but I, Devadatta, in my cottage, possess the Lord of the Universe and am the master & enjoyer of the whole world. It is I who am rich and not Harischandra. That is the fulfilment of his discipline for the Karmayogin.

But let us go down many steps lower. I have not yet ascended the ladder, but am still climbing. I have not yet acquired the habitual consciousness of the presence of the Lord surrounding all things as the only reality for whose sake alone transitory phenomena are precious or desirable. How in this imperfect stage of development can the Karmayogin escape from covetousness and the desire for other men's possessions? By realising more &

more the supreme bliss of a selfless habit of mind and selfless work. This is the way to his goal; this is his ladder. Unselfishness is usually imagined as the abnegation of self, a painful duty, a "mortification", something negative, irksome and arduous. That is a Western attitude, not Hindu; the European temperament is dominated by the body and the vital impulses; it undertakes altruism as a duty, a law imposed from outside, a standard of conduct and discipline; it is, in this light, something contrary to man's nature, something against which the whole man is disposed to rebel. That is not the right way to look at it. Unselfishness is not something outside the nature, but in the nature, not negative but positive, not a self-mortification and abnegation but a self-enlargement and self-fulfilment; not a law of duty but a law of self-development, not painful, but pleasurable. It is in the nature, only latent, and has to be evolved from inside, not tacked on from outside. The lion's whelp in the fable who was brought up among sheep, shrank from flesh when it was placed before him, but once he had eaten of it, the lion's instincts awoke and the habits of the sheep had no more delight for him. So it is with man. Selflessness is his true nature, but the gratification of the body and the vital impulses has become his habit, his second or false nature, because he has been accustomed to identify his body & vital impulses with himself. He, a lion, has been brought up to think himself a sheep; he, a god, has been trained to be an animal. But let him once get the taste of his true food, and the divinity in him awakes; the habits of the animal can please him no longer and he hungers after selflessness and selfless work as a lion hungers after his natural food. Only the feeling has to be evolved as a fulfilment of his nature, not painfully worked up to as a contravention of his nature. The man who regards selflessness as a duty, has not yet learned the alphabet of true altruism; it is the man who feels it as a delight and a natural craving, who has taken the right way to learn. The Hindu outlook here is the true outlook. The Hindu does not call the man who has risen above the gratification of desire a selfless man; he calls him आत्मवान्, the selfful man; that man is अनात्मवान्, that man has not found himself who still clings to the gratification of his body & vital impulses. Read that great drama of self-sacrifice, the Nagananda, and you will feel how different is the Hindu outlook from the Western; there self-sacrifice is not a painful and terrible struggle but a glorious outpouring of the nature, a passionate delight. "It is only human nature," we say indulgently of any act of selfishness. But that is an error and thrice an error. It is not human nature, but animal nature; human nature is divine & selfless and the average selfish man is selfish not because of his humanity, but because his humanity is as yet undeveloped & imperfect. Christ, Buddha, these are the perfect men; Tom, Dick & Harry are merely animals slowly shaping into men.

VI. The Philosophical Justification of Altruism

The philosophical justification for this outlook is provided for in the fundamental position of Vedanta. सोऽहं, I am He; Thou too art He; there is therefore no I and Thou, but only He. Brahman, Isha is my true self, the real Devadatta; Brahman, Isha is the true self of my neighbour, the real Harischandra. There is therefore really no Devadatta, no Harischandra, but my Self in the mental and bodily case called Devadatta and my Self in the mental and bodily case called Harischandra. If therefore Harischandra enjoys untold riches, it is I who am enjoying them; for Harischandra is my Self, — not my body in which I am imprisoned or my desires by which my body is made miserable, but my true self, the Purusha or real Man within me, who is the witness and enjoyer of all this sweet, bitter, tender, grand, beautiful, terrible, pleasant, horrible and wholly wonderful and enjoyable drama of the world which Prakriti enacts for his delectation. Once I experience this truth, I can take as much pleasure in the riches of Harischandra as if I myself were enjoying them; for I can thenceforth go out of my own self and so enter into the self of Harischandra, that his pleasure becomes my own. To do that I have simply to break down the illusory barrier of associations which confines my sense of self to my own body, mind & vitality. That this can be done, is a common experience of humanity, to which the name of love is given. Human evolution rises through love and towards love. This truth is instinctively recognised by all the great religions, even when they cannot provide any philosophical justification for a tenet to which they nevertheless attach the highest importance. The one law of Christianity which replaces all the commandments is to love one's neighbour as oneself, the moral ideal of Buddhism is selfless benevolence & beneficence to others; the moral ideal of Hinduism is the perfect sage whose delight and occupation is the good of all creatures (सर्वभूतहितरतः). It is always the same great ideal expressed with varying emphasis. But love in the sense which religion attaches to the word, depends on the realization of oneself in others. If, as Sankhya and Christian theology say, there are millions of different Purushas, if the real man in me is different and separate from the real man in another, one in kind but not in essence, there can be no feeling of identity; there can only be mental or material contact. From material contact nothing but animal feelings of passion & hatred can arise; from mental contact repulsion is as likely to arise as attraction. A separate individual Self will live its own life, pursue its own gratification or its own salvation; it can have no ground, no impulse to love another as itself, because it cannot feel that the other is itself. The Vedanta provides in the realisation of a single Self and the illusory character of all division the only real explanation of this higher or spiritual love. Altruism in the light of this one profound revealing truth becomes natural, right and inevitable. It is natural because I am not really preferring another to myself, but my wider truer self to my narrower false self, God who is in all to my single mind and body, myself in Devadatta and Harischandra to myself in Devadatta alone. It is right because by embracing in my range of feelings the enjoyment of Harischandra in addition to my own I shall make my knowledge of the universality of Brahman an experience, and not merely an intellectual conception or assent; for experience and not intellectual conception is true knowledge. It is inevitable because that is my way of evolution. As I have risen from the animal to the man, so must I rise from the man to the God; but the basis of godhead is the realisation of oneself in all things. The true aim and end of evolution is the wider and wider realisation of the universal Brahman. Towards that goal we progress, with whatever tardiness, with whatever lapses, yet inevitably, from the falsehood of matter to the truth of spirit. We leave behind, first, the low animal stage of indolence, brutishness, ignorance, wrath, lust, greed and beast violence, or as we call it in our philosophy the *tamasic* condition and rise to various human activity and energy, the *rajasic* condition; from that again we must rise to the *sattwic* condition of divine equipoise, clarity of mind, purity of soul, high selflessness, pity, love for all creatures, truth, candour, tranquillity. Even this divine height is not the highest; we must leave it behind and climb up to the peak of all things where sits the bright and passionless Lord of all, lighting up with a single ray of His splendour a million universes. On that breathless summit we shall experience the identity of our Self not only with the Self of others, but with the All-Self who is the Lord and who is Brahman. In Brahman our evolution finds its vast end and repose.

VII. The Meaning of Renunciation

The Karmayogin therefore will abandon the world that he may enjoy; he will not seek, as Alexander did, to possess the whole world with a material lordship, but, as Gods do, to possess it in his soul. He will lose himself in his own limited being, that he may find himself illimitably in the being of others. The abandonment of the world means nothing less than this, that we give up our own petty personal joy and pleasure to bathe up to the eyes in the joy of others; and the joys of one man may be as great as you please, the united joys of a hundred must needs be greater. By renouncing enjoyment you can increase your enjoyment a hundredfold. That was ever the privilege of the true lover. If you are [a] true lover of a woman, it is her joys far more than your own that make your happiness; if you are a true lover of your friends, their prosperity and radiant faces will give you a delight which you could never have found in your own small and bounded pleasures; if you are a true lover of your nation, the joy, glory and wealth of all its millions will be yours; if you are a true lover of mankind, all the joys of the countless millions of the earth will flow like an ocean of nectar through your soul. You will say that their sorrows too will be yours. But is not the privilege of sharing the sorrows of those you love a more precious thing than your own happiness? Count too the other happinesses which that partnership in sorrow can bring to you. If you have power, — and Yoga always brings some power with it, — you may have the unsurpassable joy of solacing or turning into bliss the sorrow of your friend or lover, or the sufferings and degradation of the nation for which you sacrifice yourself or the woes of the humanity in whom you are trying to realize God. Even the mere continuous patient resolute effort to do this is a joy unspeakable; even defeat in such a cause is a stern pleasure that strengthens you for new and invincible endeavour. And if you have not the power to relieve or the means to carry on the struggle, there is still left you the joy of suffering or dying for others. "Greater love than this has no man, that he should die for his friend." Yes, but that greatest love of all means also the greatest joy of all. "It is a sweet and noble thing to die for one's country." How many a patriot in his last moments has felt that this was no empty poetical moralising, but the feeble understatement of a wonderful and inexpressible reality. They say that Christ suffered on the cross! The body suffered, doubtless, but did Christ suffer or did he not rather feel the joy of godhead in his soul? The agony of Gethsemane was not the agony of the coming crucifixion, the cup which he prayed might be taken from his lips, was not the cup of physical suffering, but the bitter cup of the sins of mankind which he had been sent to drink. If it were not so, we should have to say that this Jesus was not the Christ, not the Son of God, not the avatar who dared to say "I and my Father are one", but a poor weak human being who under the illusion of Maya mistook his body for himself. Always remember that it is not the weak in spirit to whom the Eternal gives himself wholly; it is the strong heroic soul that reaches God. Others can only touch his shadow from afar. नायमात्मा बलहीनेन लभ्यो न च प्रमादात्तपसो वाप्यलिङ्गात्।

The abandonment of the world which is demanded of the

Karmayogin is not necessarily a physical abandonment. You are not asked to give up your house and wealth, your wife, your children, your friends. What you have to give up is your selfish desire for them and your habit of regarding them as your possessions and chattels who are yours merely in order to give you pleasure. You are not asked to throw away the objects of your desire, but to give them up in your heart. It is the desire you have to part with and not the objects of the desire. The abandonment demanded of you is therefore a spiritual aban-donment; the power to enjoy your material possessions in such spirit of detachment that you will not be overjoyed by gain, nor cast down by loss, is the test of its reality, — not the mere flight from their presence, which is simply a flight from temptation. The Karmayogin has to remain in the world & conquer it; he is not allowed to flee from the scene of conflict and shun the battle. His part in life is the part of the hero, — the one quality he must possess, is the lionlike courage that will dare to meet its spiritual enemies in their own country and citadel and tread them down under its heel. A spiritual abandonment then, — for the body only matters as the case of the spirit; it is the spirit on which the Karmayogin must concentrate his effort. To purify the body is well, only because it makes it easier to purify the spirit; in itself it is of no importance; but if the soul is pure, the body cannot be touched by uncleanness. If the spirit itself is not stained by desire, the material enjoyment of the objects of desire cannot stain it. For if my spirit does not lust after new wealth or cling to the wealth I have, then my use of riches must necessarily be selfless and without blame; and having parted with them in spirit and given them into the treasury of God, I can then truly enjoy their possession. That enjoyment is clear, deep and calm; fate cannot break it, robbers cannot take it away, enemies cannot overwhelm it. All other joy of possession is chequered and broken with fear, sorrow, trouble and passion, — the passion for its increase, the trouble of keeping it unimpaired, the sorrow for its diminution, the fear of its utter loss. Passionless enjoyment alone is pure & unmixed delight. If indeed you choose to abandon riches physically as well as in spirit, that too is well, provided you take care that you are not cherishing the thought of them in your mind. There is another curious law of which many who follow the path of spiritual renunciation, have had experience. It is this that such renunciation is often followed by a singular tendency for wealth to seek him who has ceased to seek wealth. A strong capable will bent on money-making, will doubtless win its desire, but at least as often wealth, fame and success flee from the man who longs after them and come to him who has conquered his longing. Their lover perishes without winning them or reaches them through deep mire of sin or a hell of difficulty or over mountains of toil, while the man who has turned his back on them, finds them crowding to lay themselves at his feet. He may then either enjoy or reject them. The latter is a great path and has been the chosen way of innumerable saintly sages. But the Karmayogin may enjoy them, not for his personal pleasure certainly, not for his false self, since that sort of enjoyment he has abandoned in his heart, but God in them and them for God. As a king merely touching the nazzerana passes it on to the public treasury, so shall the Karmayogin, merely touching the wealth that comes to him, pour it out for those around him, for the poor, for the worker, for his country, for humanity because he sees Brahman in all these. Glory, if it comes to him, he will veil in many folds of quiet and unobtrusive humility and use the influence it gives not for his own purposes but to help men more effectively in their needs or to lead them upward to the divine. Such a man will quickly rise above joy and sorrow, success and failure, victory and defeat; for in sorrow as in joy he will feel himself to be near God. That nearness will deepen into continual companionship and by companionship he will grow ever liker God in his spiritual image until he reaches the last summit of complete identity when man, the God who has forgotten his godhead, remembers utterly and becomes the Eternal. Selflessness then is the real & only law of renunciation; in the love of one's wider self in others, it has its rise; by the feeling of the divine presence in all earthly objects, it becomes rooted & unshakeable; the realization of the Brahman is its completion and goal.

Chapter II

Salvation through Works

I

The law of spiritual abandonment in preference to mere physical abandonment, is the solution enounced by Srikrishna, the greatest of all teachers, for a deep and vexed problem which has troubled the Hindu consciousness from ancient times. There are, as we know, three means of salvation; salvation by knowledge, the central position in Buddhism; salvation by faith & love, the central position in Christianity; salvation by faith & works, the central position in Mahomedanism. In Hinduism, the Sanatandharma, all these three paths are equally accepted. But in all three the peculiar and central religious experience of Hinduism, — the reality & eternity of the Self, the transience & unreality of all else, — is insisted upon as the guiding principle & indispensable idea. This is the bridge which carries you over to immortality; this is the gate of salvation. The Jnanamargin envisages only one reality, the Brahman, and by turning away from all that is phenomenal and seeking the One reality in himself, enters into the being of the Eternal. The Bhakta envisages only two realities, God & himself, and by the ecstatic union of himself with God through love and adoration, enters into the pure and unmixed presence of the Eternal. The Karmamargin envisages three realities which are one; the Eternal in Itself, pure and without a second, the Eternal as a transcendent Will or Force manifesting Himself phenomenally but not really in cosmic work & the Eternal in the Jivatman, manifesting Himself similarly in individual work in a finite body; and he too, by abandoning desire and laying his works upon God, attains likeness to the Eternal and through that gate enters into identity with the Eternal. In one thing all these agree, the transience & unreality of phenomenal existence. But if phenomenal existence is unreal, of what use is it to remain in the world? Let us abandon house and wealth and wife and friends and children; let us flee from them to the solitude of mountain & forest and escape as soon as possible by knowledge & meditation from the world of phenomena. Such was the cry that arose in India before and after the days of Buddha, when the power of the Jnanamarga was the strongest on the Hindu consciousness. The language of the Bhakta is not very different; "Let us leave the things of the world," he cries, "let us forget all else and think and speak only of the name of Hari." Both have insisted that works and the world are a snare & a bondage from which it is best to flee. The Karmayogin alone has set himself against the current and tried to stand in the midmost of the cosmic stir, in the very surge and flux of phenomena without being washed away in the tide. Few, he has said, who remain in the world, can be above the world and live in communion with the Eternal; but few also who flee to the mountains, really attain Him, and few of those who spend their days in crying Lord, Lord, are accepted by Him to whom they cry. It is always the many who are called, the few who are chosen. And if Janak could remain in the world and be ever with God in the full luxury, power & splendour of the life of a great king, if Rama & Srikrishna lived in the world and did the works of the world, yet were God, who shall say that salvation cannot be attained in the midst of actions, nay, even through the instrumentality of actions? To this dispute the answer of Srikrishna is the one solution. To abandon desire in the spirit is the one thing needful; if one fail to do this, it is vain for him to practise Yoga in mountain or forest solitude, it is vain to sing the name of Hari and cry Lord, Lord, from morn to night, it is vain to hope for safety by "doing one's duty in the world". The man unpurified of desire, whatever way he follows, will not find salvation. But if he can purify his spirit of desire, then whether on solitary mountain and in tiger-haunted forest, or in Brindavun the beautiful, or in the king's court, the trader's shop or the hut of the peasant, salvation is already in his grasp. For the condition of salvation is to leave the lower unreal self and turn to the real Self; and the stain & brand of the lower self is desire. Get rid of desire and the doors of the

Eternal stand wide open for your soul to enter in. The way of
the Sannyasin who leaves the world and devotes all himself to
Jnana or Bhakti, is a good way, and there is none better; but
the way of the Tyagin who lives among sense-objects and in the
whirl of action without cherishing the first or yielding to the
rush of the second, is the right way for the Karmayogin. This is
what the Upanishad with great emphasis proceeds to establish
as the second rule of conduct for the Karmamargin.

"Do, verily, thy deeds in this world and wish to live thy
hundred years, for thus to thee and there is no other way than
this, action cleaveth not to a man."

A hundred years is the full span of a man's natural life when
he observes all the laws of his nature and keeps his body and
mind pure by the use of pure food, by pure ways of living, by
purity of thought and by self-restraint in the satisfaction of his
desires. The term is ordinarily diminished by heedlessness, sin,
contamination or the effects of our past action in other lives;
it may, on the other hand, be increased to hundreds of years
by Yoga. But the Karmayogin will neither desire to increase
his term of life nor to diminish it. To increase his term of life
would show a desire for and clinging to phenomenal existence
quite inconsistent with that abandonment of desire which we
have seen to be the fundamental law of Karmayoga. A few
great Yogis have prolonged their lives without personal desire
merely to help the world by their presence or example. These
are exceptional cases which the ordinary Karmamargin need not
keep in view. On the other hand we must not turn our backs
on life; we must not fling it from us untimely or even long for
an early release from our body, but willingly fill out our term
and even be most ready to prolong it to the full period of man's
ordinary existence so that we may go on doing our deeds in this
world. Mark the emphasis laid on the word कुर्वन् "doing" by
adding to it the particle एव, the force of which is to exclude any
other action, state, person or thing than the one expressed by the
word to which it is attached. Verily we must do our deeds in this
world and not avoid doing them. There is no need to flee to the
mountains in order to find God. He is not a hill-man or a serpent

that we should seek for Him only in cave & on summit; nor a
deer or tiger that the forest only can harbour Him. He is here,
in you and around you; He is in these men and women whom
you see daily, with whom you talk & pass your life. In the roar
of the city you can find Him and in the quiet of the village, He
is there. You may go to the mountains for a while, if the din of
life deafens you & you wish to seek solitude to meditate; for to
the Karmayogin also Jnana is necessary and solitude is the nurse
of knowledge. You may sit by the Ganges or the Narmada near
some quiet temple or in some sacred asram to adore the Lord;
for to the Karmayogin also *bhakti* is necessary, and places like
these which are saturated with the *bhakti* of great saints and
impassioned God-lovers best feed and strengthen the impulse
of adoration in the soul. But if Karmayoga be your path, you
must come back and live again in the stir of the world. In no
case flee to solitude and inaction as a coward and weakling,
— not in the hope of finding God, but because you think you
can by this means escape from the miseries and misfortunes of
your life which you are too weak to face. It is not the weak
and the coward who can climb up to God, but the strong and
brave alone. Every individual Jivatman must become the perfect
Kshatriya before he can become the Brahmin. For there is a
caste of the soul which is truer and deeper than that of the body.
Through four soul-stages a man must pass before he can be
perfect; first, as a Sudra, by service and obedience to tame the
brute in his being; then, as a Vaishya to satisfy within the law
of morality the lower man in him and evolve the higher man
by getting the first taste of delight in well-doing to others than
himself and his; then, as the Kshatriya, to be trained in those first
qualities without which the pursuit of the Eternal is impossible,
courage, strength, unconquerable tenacity and self-devotion to
a great task; last, as the Brahmin, so to purify body & mind
and nature that he may see the Eternal reflected in himself as
in an unsoiled mirror. Having once seen God, man can have no
farther object in life than to reach and possess Him. Now the
Karmayogin is a soul that is already firmly established in the
Kshatriya stage and is rising from it through an easily-attained

Brahminhood straight & swift to God. If he loses hold of his courage & heroism, he loses his footing on the very standing-ground from which he is to heighten himself in his spiritual stature until his hand can reach up to and touch the Eternal. Let his footing be lost, & what can he do but fall?

II. Vairagya.

Disgust with the world, the shrinking from the phenomenal life and the desire to escape from it to the Eternal, is called, in our terminology, *vairagya*. *Vairagya* is the turning of the soul to its salvation; but we must be on our guard against the false shows and imitations of it to which our minds are subject. "I am continually battered with the siege of sorrows & miseries; I cannot cope with the world; let me therefore get away from the world, put on the saffron robe and be at peace from anxiety and grief"; that is not the language of real *vairagya*. Just as you recognize a genuine article from the imitation by its trademark, so there is a mark by which you recognize the true Sannyasin. Not weariness of the phenomenal world by itself, but this world-weariness accompanied by a thirst for the Eternal, that is the real *vairagya*. The thirst for the Eternal is the trademark; look for it always and see that it is the real trademark, not an imperfect & fraudulent reproduction. The saffron robe nowadays covers a great deal of selfishness, a great deal of idleness, a great deal of hypocrisy. It is not the robe which is the trademark, but the longing for the Eternal. Nor is it the talk and the outward action which is the trademark, for that may be a mere imitation. Look in the eyes, watch the slighter, less observed habits, wait for a light on the face; then you will find the trademark. Apply the same test to yourself. When you think you have *vairagya*, ask yourself, "Is this mere weariness & disgust, a weak fainting of the soul, or can I detect in it even in a slight degree an awakening of the Self and a desire for that which is not transient but eternal, not bound to sin and chequered with sorrow, but pure and free?" If after severe self-examination, you can detect this desire in yourself, know that your salvation has begun.

There are many kinds of *vairagya*, some true, some false. There is one *vairagya*, deep, intense & energetic, when the strong man having tasted the sweets of the world finds that there is in them no permanent and abiding sweetness; they are not the true and immortal joy which his true and immortal self demands, so he turns from them to something in his being which is deeper and holier, the joy of the inexhaustible and imperishable spirit within. Then there is the *vairagya*, false or transient, of the hypocrite or weakling, who has lusted and panted and thirsted for the world's sweets, but has been pushed and hustled from the board by Fate or by stronger men than himself, and seeks in the outward life of the Sannyasin a slothful and thornless road to honour and ease and the satisfaction of greed, or else would use Yoga and Sannyas as the drunkard uses his bottle or the slave of opium his pill or his daily draught. Not for such ignoble purpose were these great things meant by the Rishis who disclosed them to the world. Beware of such weakness. क्लैब्यं मा स्म गमः पार्थ नैतत्त्वय्युपपद्यते। Truly is such base weakness unworthy of one who is no other than Brahman, the Eternal, the Creator, Protector and Destroyer of worlds. But on the other hand there is a true *vairagya* of sorrow and disappointment; sometimes men have tried in their ignorance for ignoble things and failed, not from weakness but because these things were not in their nature, were unfit for them and below their true greatness and high destiny. The sorrow and disappointment were necessary to open their eyes to their true selves; then they seek solitude, meditation & Samadhi, not as a dram to drown their sorrow and yet unsated longing, but because their yearning is no longer for unworthy things but for the love of God or the knowledge of the Eternal. Sometimes great spirits enter the way of the Sannyasin, because in the solitude alone with the Eternal they can best develop their divine strength (*Brahmatej*) to use it for divine purposes. Once attained they pour it in a stream of divine knowledge or divine love over the world; such were Shankaracharya and Ramakrishna. Sometimes it is the sorrows & miseries of the world that find them in ease & felicity and drive them out, as Buddha & Christ were driven out, to seek light for the ignorant and help for sufferers in the depths of their own being. True Sannyasins are the greatest of all workers, because they have the most unalloyed & inexhaustible strength and are the mightiest in God to do the works of God.

Whatever be the precise nature of the *vairagya* or its immediate & exciting cause, if the thirst for the Eternal mingle in it, know that it is real *vairagya* and the necessary impulse towards your salvation. You must pass through this stage if you are to reach the Eternal at all. For if you do not get weary of the phenomenal, your mind cannot turn to the Eternal; the attraction of the phenomenal, keeps your eyes turned downward & not upward, outward & not inward. Welcome therefore the first inrush of *vairagya* into your life, but remember it is a first stage on the road, not the goal. Swami Bhaskarananda was driven into Sannyas by a keen & overmastering disgust of life in the world, but when he had attained *mukti*, the state of his mind so changed that if his wife had been living, he would have lived with her in the world as one in the world; an idea shocking to priestly & learnèd orthodoxy, but natural to the Jivanmukta. Sri Ramakrishna, when he had attained identity with the Lord, could not indeed return to the world as a householder or bear the touch of worldly things, — for he was the incarnation of utter Bhakti, — but he took as much delight in the Eternal manifested in phenomena & especially in man as in the pure actionless Brahman with whom he became one in Samadhi. The Karmamargin must pass through the condition of Vairagya, but he will not abide in it. Or to speak more accurately he will retain the spiritual element in it and reject the physical. The spiritual element of *vairagya* is the turning away from the selfish desire for phenomenal objects and actions; the physical element is the fear of and shrinking from the objects & actions themselves. The retention of the spiritual element is necessary to all Yogins; the retention of the physical element, though often a sign of great physical purity and saintliness, is not essential to salvation.

Do not be shaken by the high authority of many who say that to leave the world is necessary to the seeker after Brahman and that salvation cannot come by works. For we have a greater authority than any to set against them, the teaching of Srikrishna himself. He tells Sanjay in the Mahabharata that as between the gospel of action and the gospel of inaction, it is the former that is to his mind and the latter strikes him as the idle talk of a weakling. So too, in the Gita, while laying stress on Jnana & Bhakti, he will by no means banish Karma nor relegate it to an inferior place; the most significant portion of the Gita is its eulogy of Karmayoga and inspired exposition of its nature & principles. Jnana, of course, is indispensable; Jnana is first & best. Works without knowledge will not save a man but only plunge him deeper & deeper into bondage. The Upanishad, before it speaks of the necessity of works, takes care first to insist that you must realise the presence of the Lord enveloping this universe & each object that it contains. When you have got this Jnana that all is the One Brahman and your actions are but the dramatic illusions unrolled by Prakriti for the delight of the Purusha, you will then be able to do works without desire or illusion, abandoning the world that you may enjoy it, as the Upanishad tells you, or as Sri Krishna advises, giving up all hankering for the fruits of your work. You will devote all your actions to the Lord; not to the lower false self, which feels pleasure & pain in the results of your actions, but to the Brahman in you which works लोकसंग्रहार्थं, for the keeping together of the peoples, so that instead of the uninstructed multitudes being bewildered and led astray by your inactivity, the world may be rather helped, strengthened and maintained by the godlike character of your works. And your works must be godlike if they are done without desire or attachment to their fruits. For this is how God works. The world is His *lila*, His play & sport, not a purposeful stir and struggle out of which He is to gain something and be benefited. The great empire in which you glory & think it is to be eternal, is to Him no more than the house of sand which a child has built in his play. He has made it and He will break it, and, one day, it will be as if it had never been. The very Sun and its glorious wheeling planets are but momentary toys in His hands. Once they were not, now they are, a day will come & they will no longer be. Yet while

He works on these things, He works like the boy when he is building his castle of sand, as if the work were to be permanent and for all time.

न च मां तानि कर्माणि निबध्नन्ति धनञ्जय ।
उदासीनवदासीनमसक्तं तेषु कर्मसु ॥

"And yet these actions bind Me not, Dhanunjoy, for I sit as one unconcerned and I have no attachment to these My works." Actions performed after renunciation, actions devoted to God, these only do not cling to a man nor bind him in their invisible chains, but rather fall from him as water from the wings of a swan. They cannot bind him because he is free from the woven net of causality. Cause and effect exist only in the idea of duality which has its root in Avidya; the Yogin when he has renounced desire and experienced unity, rises above Avidya & her children, and bondage has no farther meaning for him. This is the goal of the Karmayogin as of all Yoga, but the path for him is through spiritual Vairagya, the renunciation of desire, not through physical separation from the objects of desire. This the Upanishad emphasizes in the second line of the verse. "Thus to thee; and there is no other way than this, action clingeth not to a man." एवं त्वयि नान्यथेतोऽस्ति न कर्म लिप्यते नरे। This is conclusive and beyond appeal.

III. One Road and not Three.

"There is no other way than this." By this expression it is not intended that Karmayoga is the only path of salvation for all men, but that the renunciation of desire is essential to salvation; every Yogin, be he Jnani, Bhakta, or Karmi, must devote whatever work he may be doing to the Eternal. To the Karmayogin indeed this path is the only possible way; for it is the *swabhava* or nature of a man which decides the way he shall take. If a born Jnani becomes the disciple of a great Bhakta, however submissively he may accept his Master's teachings, however largely he may infuse his Jnana with Bhakti, yet eventually it is the way of Jnana he must take and no other. For that is his *swabhava* or nature, his *dharma* or the law of his being. If the Brahmin predominates in him, he will be drawn into Jnana; if the Kshatriya, into works; if the Sudra or Vaisya, the child or woman, to Bhakti. If he is born saint or avatar, he will harmonize all three, but still with one predominant over the others and striking the main note of his life and teaching. It is always the predominance of one or other, not its unmixed control, which decides the path; for as with the Karmayogin, the devotion of works to God brings inevitably the love of God, and love gives knowledge, so it is with the Bhakta; the love of God will of itself direct all his works to God and bring him straight to knowledge. So it is even with the Jnani; the knowledge of the Brahman means delight in Him, and that is Bhakti; and this love & knowledge cannot let him live to himself but will make him live to Brahman, and that is divine Karma. The three paths are really one, but the Jnani takes the right hand, the Bhakta the left hand and the Karmayogin walks in the middle; while on the way each prefers his own choice as best and thinks the others inferior, but when they reach the goal, they find that none was inferior or superior, but it was one road they were following which only seemed to be three.

The Jnani & Bhakta shrink from the idea of Karma as a means of salvation. Unillumined Karma is such a stumbling block in the path of the seeker that they can hardly regard even illumined & desireless Karma as anything but a subordinate discipline whose only value is to prepare a man for Bhakti or Jnan. They will not easily concede that *karma* can be by itself a direct and sufficient road to Brahman. So Shankaracharya disparages *karma*, and Shankaracharya's is an authority which no man can dare to belittle. Nevertheless even the greatest are conditioned by their nature, by the times they work in and by the kind of work they have come to do. In the age that Shankara lived in, it was right that Jnana should be exalted at the expense of works. The great living force with which he had to deal, was not the heresies of later Buddhism, Buddhism decayed and senescent, but the triumphant Karmakanda which made the faithful performance of Vedic ceremonies the one path and heaven the highest goal. In his continual anxiety to prove that these ceremonies could not be the path, he bent the bow as far as he could in the other direction and left the impression that works could not be the path to salvation at all. Had he laid stress on Karma as one of the ways to salvation, the people would not have understood him; they would have thought that they had one more authority for their belief in rites and ceremonies as all-sufficient for salvation. These things must be remembered when we find Shankara and Ramanuja and Madhwa differing so widely from each other in their interpretation of the Upanishad. It was necessary that the Scripture should be interpreted by Shankara wholly in the light of Adwaita, the Monistic conception of the Eternal, so that the Monistic idea might receive its definite and consummate philosophical expression; for a similar reason it was necessary that Madhwa should interpret them wholly in the light of the Dwaita or dualistic conception and that Ramanuja should find a reconciliation in Visishtadwaita, a modified Monism. All these conceptions of the Eternal have their own truth and their own usefulness to the soul in its effort to reach Him. But the Upanishad is not concerned only with the ultimate reality of the Brahman to Himself, but also with His reality in His universe and His reality to the Jivatman or individual self. It is therefore sometimes Adwaitic, sometimes Dwaitic, sometimes Visishtadwaitic, and we should have the courage now to leave the paths which the mighty dead have trod out for us, discharge from our mind all preconceived philosophies and ask only, "What does the Upanishad actually say?" Never mind whether the interpretation arrived at seems to be self-contradictory to the logician or incoherent to the metaphysical reasoner; it will be enough if it is true in the experience of the seeker after God. For the Eternal is infinite and cannot be cabined within the narrow limits of a logical formula.

IV. The denial of salvation by works

What is it, after all, to which the denial of salvation by works amounts, when looked at not from the standpoint of logic only but of actual spiritual experience? Some people when they talk of Karma or works, think only of rites and ceremonies, Vedic,

Puranic or Tantric. That kind of works, certainly, do not bring us to salvation. They may give success & great joy, power and splendour in this world. Or they may lead to enjoyment after death in Paradise; but Paradise is not salvation; it is a temporary joyous condition of the soul, the pleasure of which ceases when the cause is exhausted. Or these rites may lead to the conscious possession and use of occult powers, latent in ordinary men, by which you may help or harm others; but the possession of occult powers cannot be an assistance, it is indeed often a hindrance to salvation. Or rites and ceremonies may purify and prepare the mind and fit it for starting on one of the paths to salvation. This indeed is their only helpfulness for the true aim of our existence. They are no more than an infant or preparatory class in the school of Brahmavidya.

It is evident again that works done with desire, works done without knowledge and not devoted to God, cannot lead to salvation, but only to continued bondage. Works prompted by desire, lead only to the fulfilment of desire; nor do they disappear in that consummation. For all work that we do, has, besides its effect on ourselves, infinite effects on others and on the general course of phenomena; these in their turn become causes and produce fresh effects; so the ripple continues widening till we lose sight of it in the distance of futurity. For all the effects of our action we are responsible and by each new thing we do, we are entering into so many debts which we must discharge before we can be released from the obligation of phenomenal existence. Existence in phenomena may be imaged as a debtor's prison in which the soul is detained by a million creditors not one of whom will forgive one farthing of his claims. But those claims we can never discharge; each sum we get to pay off our old creditors, we can only procure by entering into fresh debts which put us at the mercy of new and equally implacable claimants. Nature, the great judge and gaoler, is ever giving fresh decrees against us, for her law is inexorable and will not admit of remission or indulgence. We can obtain our release only by escaping from her jurisdiction into the divine sanctuary where the slave of Nature, by his very entry, becomes free and her master.

But the works of the Karmayogin are works done with knowledge and without desire. These certainly cannot prevent release or lead to fresh debt and fresh bondage. For bondage is the result of desire and ignorance and disappears with desire and ignorance. Desire & ignorance are indeed the boundaries of Nature's jurisdiction and once we have left them behind, we have passed out of her kingdom; we have taken sanctuary from her pursuit and are freemen released from the action of her laws. To deny the innocence of works without desire would be to deny reason, to deny Sruti, to deny facts. For Janaka and others did works, Srikrishna did works, but none will say that either the *avatar* or the *jivanmukta* were bound by his works; for their *karma* was done with knowledge and without desire. Works without desire, then, cannot prevent salvation or lead to fresh bondage.

It may be argued, however, that if they do not prevent salvation, neither do they help towards salvation. The works of the Bhakta or Jnani do not bind him because he has attained the Eternal and by the strength of that attainment becomes free from desire and ignorance; but works done before attainment can be nothing but means of bondage; only the pursuit of God-knowledge and the worship & adoration of God, to which the name of works does not properly apply, are free from responsibility. But this reasoning too is not consistent with divine teaching, with experience or with reason. For divine teaching distinctly tells us that works done after abandonment of the world and devoted to God only, do lead to salvation. We know also that a single action done without desire and devoted to the Lord, gives us strength for fresh actions of the same kind, and the persistent repetition of such works must form the habit of desirelessness & self-devotion to Him, which then become our nature and atmosphere. We have already seen that desirelessness necessarily takes us outside the jurisdiction of Nature, and when we are outside the jurisdiction of Nature, where can we be if not in the presence of the Eternal? Nor can self-devotion to the Lord be reasonably said not to lead to the Lord; for where else can it lead? It is clear therefore that works without desire not only do not prevent salvation but are a mighty help towards salvation.

It may still be argued that works without desire help only because they lead to devotion and knowledge and there their function ceases; they bring the soul to a certain stage but do not carry it direct to God. It is therefore devotion and knowledge, bhakti and jnana, which alone bring us to God. As soon as either of these takes him by the hand, karma must leave him, just as rites & ceremonies must leave him, and its function is therefore not essentially higher than that of rites & ceremonies. But if this were good reasoning, the Karmayogin might equally well say that Bhakti leads to knowledge and the devotion of one's works to the Lord; therefore knowledge and works without desire bring a man to the Eternal and *bhakti* is only a preliminary means; or that *jnana* leads to adoration of the Eternal and devotion of all one does to him, therefore *bhakti* and works without desire alone bring the soul direct to God and *jnana* is only a preliminary means. Or if it is said that works must cease at a certain stage while Bhakti and Jnana do not cease, this too is inconsistent with experience. For Janaka and others did works after they attained the Eternal and while they were in the body, did not cease from works. It cannot even be said that works though they need not necessarily cease after the attainment of the Eternal, yet need not continue. Particular works need not continue; rites & ceremonies need not continue; the life of the householder need not continue. But work continues so long as the body gross or subtle continues; for both the gross body and the subtle body, both the physical case & the soul-case are always part of Prakriti, and whatever is Prakriti, must do work. The Gita says this plainly

न हि कश्चित्क्षणमपि जातु तिष्ठत्यकर्मकृत् ।
कार्यते ह्यवशः कर्म सर्वः प्रकृतिजैर्गुणैः ॥

"For no man verily remaineth even for a moment without doing works, for all are helplessly made to do work by the moods to which Nature has given birth." And again सदृशं चेष्टते स्वस्याः प्रकृतेर्ज्ञानवानपि। "Even the Jnani moveth & doeth after the semblance of his own nature; for created things follow after their

nature and what can forcing it do?" A man works according to
his nature and cannot help doing work; but he can choose to
what he shall direct his works, whether to his lower self or his
higher, whether to desire or to God. The man who leaves the
world behind him and sits on a mountaintop or in an asram,
has not therefore got rid of works. If nothing else he has to
maintain his body, to eat, to walk, to move his limbs, to sit
in *asan* and meditate; all this is work. And not only his body
works; his mind is far more active than his body. If he is not
released from desire, his work will bind him and bear fruit in
relation to himself and others. Even if he is released from desire,
his body & mind are not free from Karma until he is able to get
rid of them finally, and that will not be till his *prarabdha karma*
has worked itself out and the debts he has written against his
name are wiped off. Even the greatest Yogi by his mere bodily
presence in the world, is pouring out a stream of spiritual force
on all sides; this action does not bind him, it is true, yet it is work
and work which exercises a stupendous influence on others. He
is सर्वभूतहितरत:, busy doing good to all creatures by his very
nature, even though he does not lift a finger or move a step. He
too with regard to his body, gross & subtle, is अवश:, he must
let the gunas, the moods of Nature, work. He may control that
work, for he is no longer the slave of Prakriti, but he cannot
stop it except by finally leaving his body & mind through Yoga
with the Eternal. Work therefore does not cease any more than
Bhakti or Jnana.

Shankara indeed says that when we have got Jnana, we
necessarily cease to do works, for Jnana makes us one with the
Eternal who is actionless अकर्ता. Yet Janaka knew the Eternal
and did works; Sri Krishna was the Eternal and did works. For
Brahman the Eternal, is both कर्ता and अकर्ता; He works and He
does not work. As Sacchidananda, He is above works, but He is
also above knowledge and above devotion. When the Jivatman
becomes Sacchidananda, devotion is lost in Ananda or absolute
bliss, knowledge is lost in Chit or absolute Consciousness, works
are lost in Sat or absolute Existence. But as Isha or Shakti, He
does works by which He is not bound and the Jivatman also

when he is made one with Isha or Shakti continues to do works without being bound.

Works therefore do not cease in the body, nor do they cease after we have left the body except by union with the action-less Sacchidananda or *laya* in the Unknowable Brahman, where Jnana and Bhakti also are swallowed up in unfathomable being. Even of the Unknowable Parabrahman too it cannot be said that It is actionless; It is neither कर्ता nor अकर्ता. It is néti, néti, not this, not that, unexplicable and inexpressible in terms of speech and mind. We need not therefore fear that works without desire will not lead us straight to the Eternal; we need not think that we must give up works in order that we may develop the love of God or attain the knowledge of God.

V. Mukti and the Jivanmukta.

The ideal of the Karmayogin is the Jivanmukta, the self who has attained salvation but instead of immediately passing out of phenomenal existence, remains in it, free from its bondage. There are three kinds of salvation which are relative & partial; *salokya* or constant companionship with the Lord, *sadrishya*, or permanent resemblance to Him in one's nature & actions, and *sayujya* or constant union of the individual self with the Eternal. It is supposed by some schools that entire salvation consists in *laya* or absorption into the Eternal, in other words entire self-removal from phenomena and entrance into the utter being of the unconditioned and unknowable Parabrahman. Such *laya* is not possible in the body, but can only begin, *adehanipatat*, as soon as the Self throws away all its bodies and reenters into its absolute existence. It is not indeed the mere mechanical change of death that brings about this result, but the will of the Self to throw aside all its bodies and never returning to them pass rather out of that state of consciousness in the Eternal in which He looks upon Himself as a Will or Force. This, however, is an extreme attitude. Complete self-identification with the Eternal, such as we find in the Jivanmukta, is complete *mukti*; for the Jivanmukta can at will withdraw himself in Samadhi into the being of Sacchidananda, who is actionless and turned away from phenomena; and can at will look again towards phenomena, dealing with them as their Lord who puts them to work without being touched by their stir and motion. For the Jivanmukta *laya*, absorption into the Unknowable, can be accomplished at his will; but he does not will it.

The reason for his not willing this utter departure brings us to the very essence of Mukti. Why do men hanker after complete absorption into the unphenomenal? why do they flee from Karma and dread lest it should interfere with their salvation? Because they feel that phenomenal life and works are a bondage and they desire to be free and not bound. This state of mind can only last so long as the seeker is the *mumukshu*, the self desirous of freedom, but when he is actually *mukta*, the free self, the terror of Maya and her works cannot abide with him. *Mukti*, which we have to render in English by salvation, means really release. But release from what bondage, salvation from what tyranny? From the bondage of Maya, from the tyranny of Avidya which will have us believe that we are finite, mortal and bound, who are not finite, but infinite, not mortal, but deathless & immutable, not bound, but always free. The moment you have realised that Avidya is illusion and there is nothing but the Eternal, and never was anything but the Eternal and never will be anything but the Eternal, the moment you have not merely intellectually grasped the idea but come to have habitual experience of the fact, from that moment you will know that you are not bound, never were bound and never will be bound. Avidya consists precisely in this that the Jivatman thinks there is something else than the Eternal which can throw him into bondage and that he himself is something else than the Eternal and can be bound. When the Jivatman shakes off these illusory impressions of Avidya, he realises that there is nothing but Brahman the Eternal who is in His very nature *nityamukta*, from ever and forever free. He can therefore have no fear of Karma nor shrink from it lest it should bind him, for he knows that the feeling of bondage is itself an illusion. He will be ready not only to do his deeds in this world and live out his hundred years, but to be reborn as Srikrishna himself has promised to be reborn again and again and as other avatars have promised to be reborn. For however often he may enter into phenomenal life, he has no farther terror of Maya and her bondage. Once free, always free.

Even if he does not will to be reborn, he will be careful not to leave the world of phenomena until his *prarabdha karma* is worked out. There are certain debts standing against his name in the ledger of Nature and these he will first absolve. Of course the Jivanmukta is not legally bound by his debts to Nature, for all the promissory notes he has executed in her name have been burned up in the fire of Mukti. He is now free and lord, the master of Prakriti, not its slave. But the Prakriti attached to this Jivatman has created, while in the illusion of bondage, causes which must be allowed to work out their effects; otherwise the chain of causation is snapped and a disturbance is brought about in the economy of Nature. उत्सीदेयुरिमे लोकाः. In order therefore to maintain the law of the world unimpaired, the Jivanmukta remains amid works like a prisoner on parole, not bound by the fetters of Prakriti, but detained by his own will until the time appointed for his captivity shall have elapsed.

The Jivanmukta is the ideal of the Karmayogin and though he may not reach his ideal in this life or the next, still he must always strive to model himself upon it. Do therefore your deeds in this world and wish to live your hundred years. You should be willing to live your allotted term of life not for the sake of long living, but because the real you in the body is Brahman who by the force of His own Shakti is playing for Himself and by Himself this dramatic *lila* of creation, preservation and destruction. He is Isha, the Lord, Creator, Preserver and Destroyer; and you also in the field of your own Prakriti are the lord, creator, preserver and destroyer. You are He; only for your own amusement you have imagined yourself limited to a particular body for the purposes of the play, just as an actor imagines himself to be Dushyanta, Rama or Ravana. The actor has lost himself in the play and for a moment thinks that he is what he is acting; he has forgotten that he is really not Dushyanta or Rama, but Devadatta who has played & will yet play a hundred parts besides. When he shakes off this illusion and remembers that he is Devadatta, he does not therefore walk off the stage and by refusing to act, break up the play, but goes on playing his best till the proper time comes for him to leave the stage. The object of this phenomenal world is creation and it is our business, while we are in the body, to create. Only, so long as we forget our true Self, we create like servants under the compulsion of Prakriti and are slaves and bound by her actions which we falsely imagine to be our own. But when we know and experience our true Self, then we are masters of Prakriti and not bound by her creations. Our Self becomes the Sakshi, the silent spectator of the actions of our Nature which she models in the way she thinks would best please it. So are we at once spectator and actor; and yet because we know the whole to be merely an illusion of apparent actions, because we know that Rama is not really killing Ravana, nor Ravana being killed, for Ravana lives as much after the supposed death as before, so are we neither spectator nor actor, but the Self only and all we see nothing but visions of the Self. The Karmamargin therefore will not try or wish to abandon actions while he is in this world, but only the desire for their fruits; neither will he try or wish to leave his life in this world before its appointed end. The man who violently breaks the thread of his life before it is spun out, will obtain a result the very opposite to what he desires. The Karmamargin aims at being a Jivanmukta, he will not cherish within himself the spirit of the suicide.

VI. Suicide and the other World.

In the early days of spiritualism in America, there were many who were so charmed by the glowing description of the other world published by spiritualists that they committed suicide in order to reach it. It would almost seem as if in the old days when the pursuit of the Eternal dominated the mind of the race and disgust of the transitory was common, there were many who rather than live out their hundred years preferred a self-willed exit from the world of phenomena. To these the Upanishad addresses a solemn warning. "Godless verily are those worlds and with blind gloom enveloped, thither they depart when they have passed away, whatso folk are slayers of self." One has to be peculiarly careful in rendering the exact words of the Upanishad, because Shankara gives a quite unexpected and out-of-the-way interpretation of the verse. He does not accept आत्महनो, self-slayers, in the sense of suicides, the natural and ordinary meaning, but understands it to signify slayers of the eternal Self within them. Since this is a startlingly unnatural & paradoxical sense, for the Self neither slays nor is slain, he farther interprets his interpretation in a figurative sense. To kill the Self means merely to cast the Self under the delusion of ignorance which leads to birth and rebirth; the Self is in a way killed because it is made to disappear into the darkness of Maya. Farther लोकाः has always the sense of worlds as in गोलोक ब्रह्मलोक द्युलोक but Shankara forces it to mean births, for example birth as a man, birth as a beast, birth as a God. Then there is a third and equally violent departure from the common & understood use of words; असुर्या or आसुरा would mean ordinarily Asuric of the Daityas in opposition to Daivic of the Devas; Shankara takes आसुरा as Rajasic and applicable to birth in the form of men, beasts and even of gods in opposition to दैव which is pure Sattwic and applicable only to Parabrahman. He thus gets the verse to mean, "Rajasic verily are those births and enveloped with blind darkness to which those depart when they pass away, whoso are slayers of the Self." All those who put themselves under the yoke of Ignorance, lose hold of their true Self and are born as men, beasts or gods, instead of returning to the pure existence of Parabrahman.

The objections to this interpretation are many and fatal. The rendering of आत्महनो substitutes a strained and unparalleled interpretation for the common and straightforward sense of the word. The word लोकः cannot mean a particular kind of birth but either a world or the people in the world; and in these senses it is always used both in the Sruti and elsewhere. We say स्वर्गलोक, द्युलोक, मर्त्यलोक, इहलोक, परलोक; we do not say कीटलोक, पशुलोक, पक्षिलोक. We say indeed मनुष्यलोक, but it means the world of men & never birth as a man. The word असुर्या may very well mean

Rajasic but not in the way Shankara applies to it; for असुर्या लोका cannot signify the births of beasts, men, gods as opposed to the divine birth of Parabrahman, who is above birth and above condition. Moreover, Daivic and Asuric are always opposed terms referring to the gods and Titans, precisely as Titanic and Olympian are opposed terms in English. For instance in the Gita

मोघाशा मोघकर्माणो मोघज्ञाना विचेतसः ।
राक्षसीमासुरीं चैव प्रकृतिं मोहिनीं श्रिताः ॥
महात्मानस्तु मां पार्थ दैवीं प्रकृतिमाश्रिताः ।
भजन्त्यनन्यमनसो ज्ञात्वा भूतादिमव्ययम् ॥

In this passage Asuric and Rakshasic nature are rajasic nature as of the Titans and tamasic nature as of the Rakshasa; daivic nature implies sattwic nature as of the Gods. Such is always the sense wherever the terms are opposed in Sanscrit literature. It may be urged, in addition, that the expression ये के loses its strong limiting force if it is applied to all beings but the very few who have found salvation. There are other flaws besides the straining of word-senses. The verse as rendered by Shankara does not logically develop from what went before and the fault of incoherence is imported into the Upanishad which, if taken in its straightforward sense, we rather find to be strictly logical in its structure and very orderly in the development of its thought. On the other hand, the plain rendering of the words of the Upanishad in their received and ordinary sense gives a simple and clear meaning which is both highly appropriate in itself and develops naturally from what has gone before. Shankara's rendering involves so many and considerable faults, that even his authority cannot oblige us to accept it. We will therefore take the verse in its plain sense: it is a warning to those who imagine that by the self-willed shortening of their days upon earth they can escape from the obligation of phenomenal existence.

The Asuric or godless worlds to which the suicide is con-demned, are the worlds of deep darkness & suffering at the other pole from the worlds of the gods, the world of light and joy which is the reward of virtuous deeds. Patala under the earth, Hell under Patala, these are Asuric worlds: Swarga on the mountaintops of existence in the bright sunshine is a world of the gods. All this is of course mythology and metaphor, but the Asuric worlds are a reality; they are the worlds of gloom and suffering in the nether depths of our own being. A world is not a place with hills, trees and stones, but a condition of the Jivatman, all the rest being only circumstances and details of a dream. The Sruti speaks of the spirit's *loka* in the next world, अमुष्मिन् लोके लोक:, where the word is used in its essential meaning of the spirit's state or condition and again in its figurative meaning of the world corresponding to its condition. The apparent surroundings, the sum of sensible images & appearances into which the spirit under the influence of Illusion materializes its mental state, makes the world in which it lives. *Martyaloka* is not essentially this Earth we men live in, for there may be other abodes of mortal beings, but the condition of mortality in the gross body; Swargaloka is the condition of bliss in the subtle body; Narak, Hell, the condition of misery in the subtle body; Brahmalok the condition of abiding with God in the causal body. Just as the Jivatman like a dreamer sees the Earth and all it contains when it is in the condition of mortality and regards itself as in a particular region with hills, trees, rivers, plains, so when it is in a condition of complete *tamas* in the subtle body, it believes itself to be in a place surrounded by thick darkness, a place of misery unspeakable. This world of darkness is imaged as under the earth on the side turned away from the sun; because earth is our mortal condition and this world is a state lower than our mortal condition; it is a world of thick darkness because the light created by the splendour of the Eternal in the consciousness of the Jivatman is entirely eclipsed with the extreme thickening of the veil of Maya which intercepts from us the full glory of His lustre. Hell, Patal, Earth, Paradise, the Lunar & Solar Worlds, Golok, Brahmalok, — these are all imagery and dreams, since they are all in the Jivatman itself and exist outside it only as pictures & figures: still while we are dreamers, let us speak in the language and think the thoughts of dream.

This then is the Asuric world. When a man dies in great pain or in great grief or in fierce agitation of mind and his last thoughts are full of fear, rage, pain or horror, then the Jivatman in the Sukshmasharir is unable to shake off these impressions from his mind for years, perhaps for centuries. So it is with the suicide; he sinks into this condition because of the feelings of disgust, impatience and pain or rage & fear which govern his last moments; for suicide is not the passionless & divine departure at his appointed time of the Yogin centred in samadhi, but a passionate and disgustful departure; and where there is disturbance or bitterness of the soul in its departure, there can be no tranquillity & sweetness in the state to which it departs. This is the law of death; death is a moment of intense concentration when the departing spirit gathers up the impressions of its mortal life as a host gathers provender for its journey, and whatever impressions are dominant at the moment, govern its condition afterwards.

यं यं वापि स्मरन्भावं त्यजत्यन्ते कलेवरम् ।
तं तमेवैति कौन्तेय सदा तद्भावभावितः ॥

"Or indeed whatever (collective) impressions of mind one remembering leaveth his body at the last, to that state and no other it goeth, O son of Kunti, and is continually under the impress of those impressions." Hence the importance, even apart from Mukti, of living a clean and noble life and dying a calm and strong death. For if the ideas and impressions then uppermost are such as to associate the self with this gross body and the vital functions or the base, vile & low desires of the mind, then the soul remains long in a *tamasic* condition of darkness and suffering which we call Patala or in its acute forms Hell. If the ideas and impressions uppermost are such as to associate the self with the higher desires of the mind, then the soul passes quickly to a rajasic condition of light & pleasure which we call Swarga, Behesta or Paradise and from which it will return to the state of mortality in the body. If the ideas and impressions uppermost are such as to associate the self with the higher understanding and bliss of the Self, the soul passes quickly to a condition of highest bliss which we call variously Kailas, Vaikuntha, Goloka or Brahmaloka, from which it does not return in this aeon of the universe. But if we have learned to identify for ever the self with the Self, then before death we become the Eternal and after death we shall not be other. There are three states of Maya, tamasic illusion, rajasic illusion, sattwic illusion, and each in succession we must surmount before we reach utterly that which is no illusion but the one eternal truth and, leaving our body in the state of Samadhi, rise into the unrevealed & imperishable bliss of which the Lord has said, "That is my highest seat of all."

VII. Retrospect

The Isha Upanishad logically falls into four portions, the first of which is comprised in the three verses we have already explained. It lays down for us those first principles of Karmayoga which must govern the mental state and actions of the Karmamargin in his upward progress to his ideal. In the next five verses we shall find the Upanishad enunciating the final goal of the Karmamargin and the ideal state of his mind and emotional part when his Yoga is perfected and he becomes a Yogin in very truth, the Siddha or perfected man and no longer the Sadhak or seeker after perfection.

While he is still a seeker, his mind must be governed by the idea of the Eternal as the mighty Lord and Ruler who pervades and encompasses the Universe. He must see him in all and around all, informing each object and encompassing it. On all that he sees, he must throw the halo of that presence; around all creatures and things, he must perceive the nimbus and the light.

His mind being thus governed by the idea of the divine omnipresence, he must not and cannot covet or desire, for possessing the Lord, what is it that he does not possess? what is it he needs to covet or desire? He cannot wish to injure or deprive others of their wealth, for who are others? are they other than himself? The Karmamargin must strive to abandon desire and make selflessness the law of his life and action. Seeing God in others, he will naturally love them and seek to serve them. By abnegation of desire he will find the sublime satisfaction the divinity in him demands and by the abandonment of the world in spirit, he will enjoy the whole world as his kingdom with a deep untroubled delight instead of embracing a few limited possessions with a chequered and transient pleasure.

Whatever others may do, the Karmamargin must not remove himself from the field of action and give up work in the world; he is not called upon to abandon the objects of enjoyment, but to possess them with a heart purified of longing and passion. In this spirit he must do his work in this world and not flee from the struggle. Neither must he shrink from life as a bondage. He must realise that there is no bondage to him who is full of God, for God is free and not bound. He must therefore be ready to live out his life and work out his work calmly and without desire, seeking only through his life and actions to get nearer to Him who is the Lord of life and Master of all actions.

Least of all will he allow disgust of life and work so to master him as to make him seek release by shortening his days upon earth. For the suicide does not escape from phenomenal being in this world but passes into a far darker & more terrible prison of Maya than any that earthly existence can devise for the soul.

If his nature can expand to the greatness of this discipline, if his eyes can avail never to lose sight of God, if he can envisage the godhead in his fellowmen, if he can empty his soul of its lust & longing, if he can feel all the glory & joy & beauty of the world passionlessly & disinterestedly as his own, if he can do his works in the world however humble or however mighty not for himself but for God in man and God in the world, if he can slay the sense of egoism in his works and feel them to be not his own but the Lord's, if he can put from him alike the coward's shrinking from death and the coward's longing for death, suffering neither the lust of long life nor impatience of its vanities & vexations, but live out his full term bravely, modestly, selflessly and greatly, then indeed he becomes the Karmayogin who lives ever close to the eternal & almighty Presence, moving freely in the courts of God, admitted hourly to His presence and growing always liker & liker in his spiritual image to the purity, majesty, might and beauty of the Lord. To love God in His world and approach God in himself is the discipline of the Karmayogin; to embrace all created things in his heart and divinely become God in his spirit, is his goal and ideal.

Part II

Karmayoga; the Ideal

Chapter IV
The Eternal in His Universe

अनेजदेकं मनसो जवीयो नैनद्देवा आप्नुवन्पूर्वमर्षत् ।
तद्धावतोऽन्यानत्येति तिष्ठत्तस्मिन्नपो मातरिश्वा दधाति ॥

I. ETERNAL TRUTH THE BASIS OF ETHICS

"There is the One and It moveth not, yet is It swifter than thought, the Gods could not overtake It as It moved in front. While It standeth still, It outstrippeth others as they run. In It Matariswan ordereth the waters."

I
The Root of Ethical Ideals

Everything that has phenomenal existence, takes its stand on the Eternal and has reality only as a reflection in the pure mirror of His infinite existence. This is no less true of the affections of mind and heart and the formations of thought than of the affections of matter and the formations of the physical ether-stuff out of which this material Universe is made. Every ethical ideal and every religious ideal must therefore depend for its truth and permanence on its philosophical foundation; in other words, on the closeness of its fundamental idea to the ultimate truth of the Eternal. If the ideal implies a reading of the Eternal which is only distantly true and confuses Him with

His physical or psychical manifestations in this world, then it is a relatively false and impermanent ideal. Of all the ancient nations the Hindus, for this reason only, attained to the highest idea and noblest practice of morality. The Greeks confused the Eternal with His physical manifestations and realised Him in them on the side of beauty; beauty therefore was the only law of morality which governed their civilization. Ethics in their eyes was a matter of taste, balance and proportion; it hinged on the avoidance of excess in any direction, of excessive virtue no less than of excessive vice. The fine development of personality under the inspiration of music and through the graceful play of intellect was the essential characteristic of their education; justice, in the sense of a fine balance between one's obligations to oneself and one's obligations to others, the ideal of their polity; decorum, the basis of their public morality; the sense of proportion the one law of restraint in their private ethics. Their idea of deity was confined to the beautiful and brilliant rabble of their Olympus. Hence the charm and versatility of Greek civilisation; hence also its impermanence as a separate culture. The Romans also confused the Eternal with His manifestations in physical Nature, but they read Him on the side not of beauty but of force governed by law; the stern and orderly restraint which governs the Universe, was the feature in Nature's economy which ruled their thought. Jupiter was to them the Governor & great Legislator whose decrees were binding on all; the very meaning of the word religion which they have left to the European world was "binding back" and indicated as the essence of religion restraint and tying down to things fixed and decreed. Their ethics were full of a lofty strength & sternness. Discipline stood as the keystone of their system; discipline of the actions created an inelastic faithfulness to domestic & public duties; discipline of the animal impulses an orderly courage and a cold, hard purity; discipline of the mind a conservative practical type of intellect very favourable to the creation of a powerful and well ordered State but not to the development of a manysided civilization. Their type too, though more long lived than the Greek, could not last, because of the imperfection of the ideal on which it was based.[1] The Chinese seem to have envisaged the Eternal in a higher aspect than these Mediterranean races; they found Him not in the manifested physical Universe itself, but in its origination and arrangement out of the primal material from which it arose. Heaven, Akasha or the Eternal in the element of Ether, creates in the womb of Earth or formal Matter which is the final element developed out of Ether, this arranged and orderly Universe, — He is therefore the Father, Originator, Disposer and Arranger. Veneration for parents and those who stand in the place of parents became the governing idea of their ethics; orderly disposition, the nice care of ceremony, manners, duties the law of their daily life; origination and organization the main characteristics of their intellectual activity. The permanence and unconquerable vitality of their civilization is due to their having seized on an interpretation of the Eternal which, though not His ultimate truth to humanity, is at least close to that truth and a large aspect of it. It is really Himself in his relation to the Universe, but not the whole of Himself. But the ancient Aryans of India raised the veil completely and saw Him as the Universal Transcendent Self of all things who is at the same time the particular present Self in each. They reached His singleness aloof from phenomena, they saw Him in every one of His million manifestations in phenomena. God in Himself, God in man, God in Nature were the "ideas" which their life expressed. Their civilisation was therefore more manysided and complete and their ethical and intellectual ideals more perfect and permanent than those of any other nation. They had in

---

[1] *The following passage was written in the top margin of the manuscript page. Its place of insertion was not marked:*

Beauty is not the ultimate truth of the Eternal but only a partial manifestation of Him in phenomena which is externalised for our enjoyment and possession but not set before us as our standard or aim, and the soul which makes beauty its only end is soon cloyed & sated and fails for want of nourishment and of the growth which is impossible without an ever widening & progressive activity. Power & Law are not the ultimate truth of the Eternal, but manifestations of Himself in phenomena which are set within us to develop and around us to condition our works, but this also is not set before us as our standard or aim. The soul which follows Power as its whole end must in the long run lose measure and perish from hardness and egoism and that which sees nothing but Law wither for dryness or fossilise from the cessation of individual expansion.

full measure the sense of filial duty, the careful regulation of ceremony, manners and duties, the characteristics of origination and organization which distinguished the Chinese. They had in full measure the Roman discipline, courage, purity, faithfulness to duty, careful conservatism; but these elements of character & culture which in the Roman were hard, cold, narrow and without any touch of the spirit in man or the sense of his divine individuality, the Hindus warmed & softened with emotional & spiritual meaning and made broad and elastic by accepting the supreme importance of the soul's individual life as overriding and governing the firm organization of morals and society. They were not purely devoted to the worship and culture of beauty like the Greeks and their art was not perfect, yet they had the sense of beauty & art in a greater degree than any other ancient people; unlike the Greeks they had a perfect sense of spiritual beauty and were therefore able to realise the delight & glory of Nature hundreds of years before the sense of it developed in Europe. On the ethical side they had a finer justice than the Greeks, a more noble public decorum, a keener sense of ethical & social balance, but they would not limit the infinite capacities of the soul; they gave play therefore to personal individuality but restrained and ordered its merely lawless ebullitions by the law of the type (caste). In addition to these various elements which they shared with one civilization or another they possessed a higher spiritual ideal which governed & overrode the mere ethics (*mores* or customary morality) which the other nations had developed. Humanity, pity, chivalry, unselfishness, philanthropy, love of and self-sacrifice for all living things, the sense of the divinity in man, the Christian virtues, the modern virtues were fully developed in India at a time when in all the rest of the world they were either non-existent or existent only in the most feeble beginnings. And they were developed, because the Aryan Rishis had been able to discover the truth of the Eternal and give to the nation the vision of the Eternal in all things and the feeling of His presence in themselves and in all around them. They had discovered the truth that morality is not for its own sake, nor for the sake of society, but a preparation and purification of the soul

by which the limited human self must become fit to raise itself
out of the dark pit of bodily, mental and emotional selfishness
into the clear heaven of universal love and benevolence and
enlarge itself until it came into conscious contact, entered into
and became one with the Supreme and Sempiternal Self. Some
hold the aim of morality to be a placing of oneself in harmony
with the eternal laws that govern the Universe, others hold it to
be the fulfilment under self-rule and guidance of man's nature,
others a natural evolution of man in the direction of his highest
faculties. The Hindus perceived that it was all these at once but
they discovered that the law with which the soul must put itself
in relation was the law of the Eternal Self, that man's nature
must seek its fulfilment in that which is permanent & eternal
in the Universe and that it is to which his evolution moves.
They discovered that his higher self was the Self of his Universe
and that by a certain manner of action, by a certain spirit in
action, man escaped from his limitations and realised his higher
Self. This way of Works is Karmayoga and Karmayoga therefore
depends on the Hindu conception of Brahman, the Transcendent
Self and its relations to the Universe. From this all Hindu ethics
proceeds.[2]

Chapter I. Brahman.

The first four verses of the Upanishad have given the general
principle of Karmayoga; the next four provide its philosophical justification and of these four the first two express in a
few phrases the Vedantic philosophy of God and Cosmos as a
necessary preliminary to the formation of a true and permanent
ethical ideal.

The close dependence of ethical ideals on the fundamental
philosophy of the Eternal and Real to which they go back, is a
law which the ancient Yogins had well understood. Therefore
the Upanishad when it has to set forth an ethical rule or ethical

---

[2] *The last six sentences of this paragraph, beginning "They had discovered the truth",
were written separately. They seem to have been intended for insertion here. — Ed.*

ideal or intellectual attitude towards life, takes care to preface it with that aspect of the Eternal Reality on which its value and truth depend. The first principles of Karmayoga arise from the realization of the Eternal as a great and divine Presence which pervades and surrounds all things, so that it is impossible to direct one's thought, speech or actions to thing or person without directing them to Him. With the declaration of the Eternal as the Universal and Omnipresent Lord the Upanishad must, therefore, begin. Now it is about to take a step farther & set forth the ideal of the Karmayogin and the consummation of his yoga. It preludes the new train of thought by identifying Isha the Lord with Parabrahman the Eternal and Transcendent Reality. Not only does He surround and sustain as the supreme Will by which and in which alone all things exist, but He is really the immutable and secret Self in all things which is ultimately Parabrahman. This Isha whose Energy vibrates through the worlds, is really the motionless and ineffable Tranquillity towards which the Yogins & the sages strive.

"There is One and It unmoving is swifter than thought; the gods could not reach It moving in front; standing still It passes others as they run; 'tis in This that Matariswan setteth the waters. It moves, It moveth not; It is far, the same It is near; It is within everyone, the same It is also outside everyone."

There is only One existence, one Reality in apparent multiplicity. The unimaginable Presence which is manifest in the infinite variety of the Universe, is alone and alone Is. The variety of things is in fact merely the variety of forms which the play or energy of the Will only seems, by its rapidity of motion, to create; so when the blades of an electric fan go whirling with full velocity, round & round, there seem to be not four blades or two, but a whole score; so, also, when Shiva in His mood begins His wild dance and tosses His arms abroad, He seems to have not two arms but a million. It is the motion of the play of Will, it is the velocity of His Energy vibrating on the surface of His own existence which seems to create multiplicity. All creation is motion, all activity is motion. All this apparently stable universe is really in a state of multifold motion; everything is whirling with inconceivable rapidity in its own orbit, and even thought which is the swiftest thing we know, cannot keep pace with the velocity of the cosmic stir. And all this motion, all this ever evolving cosmos and universe is Brahman the Eternal. The Gods in their swiftest movements, the lords of the mind & senses cannot reach Him, for He rushes far in front. The eye, the ear, the mind, nothing material can reach or conceive the inconceivable creative activity of this Will which is Brahman. We try to follow Him pouring as light through the solar system and lo! while you are striving He is whirling universes into being far beyond reach of eye or telescope, far beyond the farthest flights of thought itself. तन्मनसो जवीयो। Material senses quail before the thought of the wondrous stir and stupendous unimaginable activity that the existence of the Universe implies. And yet all the time He does not really move. All the time He who outstrips all others, is not running but standing. It is the others, the forms and things His Energy has evolved, who are running and because He outstrips them, they think that He too moves. While we are toiling after Him, He is all the time here, at our side, before us, behind us, with us, in us, His presence pervading us like the ether, clothing us like a garment. "Standing still, He outstrips others as they run." It is our mind & senses that are running and this universal motion is the result of the Avidya to which they are subject; for Avidya by persuading us to imagine ourselves limited, creates the conditions of Time, Space & Causality and confines us in them as in a prisoning wall beyond which our thoughts cannot escape. Brahman in all His creative activity is really standing still in His own being outside and inside Time & Space. He is at the same time in the Sun and here, because neither here nor the Sun are outside Himself; He has not therefore to move any more than a man has to move in order to pass from one thought to another. But we in order to realise His creative activity have to follow Him from the Sun to the Earth and from the Earth to the Sun; and this motion of our limited consciousness, this sensory impression of a space covered and a time spent, we cannot dissociate from Brahman and must needs attribute the limitations of our own thought to Him; just as a man in a railway-train has a sensory impression that everything is rushing past him and the train is still. The stir of the Cosmos is really the stir of our own minds, and yet even that is a mere phenomenon. What we call mind is simply one play of the Will sporting with the idea of multiplicity which is, in form, the idea of motion. The Purusha, the Real Man in us and in the world, is really unmoving; He is the motionless and silent spectator of a drama of which He himself is the stage, the theatre, the scenery, the actors and the acting. He is the poet Shakespeare watching Desdemona and Othello, Hamlet and the murderous Uncle, Rosalind and Jacques and Viola, and all the other hundred multiplicities of himself acting and talking and rejoicing and suffering, all himself and yet not himself, who sits there a silent witness, their Creator who has no part in their actions, and yet without Him not one of them could exist. This is the mystery of the world and its paradox and yet its plain and easy truth.

But what really is this Will which as Purusha watches the motion and the drama and as Prakriti is the motion and the drama? It is the One motionless, unconditioned, inexpressible Parabrahman of whom, being beyond mark and feature, the Upanishad speaks always as It, while of Isha, the Lord, it speaks as He; for Isha as Purusha is the male or spiritual presence which generates forms in Prakriti the female or material Energy. The spiritual entity does not work, but merely is and has a result; it is the material Energy, the manifestation of Spirit, which works or ceases from work. Eventually however Spirit and Matter are merely aspects of each other & of something which is behind both; that something is the motionless, actionless It. This which without moving is swifter than thought, is It; this which mind & senses cannot reach, for it moves far in front, is It; this which stands still & yet outstrips others as they run is It. Will, Energy, Isha, the play of Prakriti for Purusha, are all merely the manifestation of that unmanifested It. What we envisage as the manifested Brahman is, in His reality to Himself, the unmanifest Parabrahman. It is only in His reality to us that He is the manifested Brahman. And according as a man comes nearer to the truth of Him or loses himself in Him, so will be his spiritual condition. While we think of Him as Isha, the one in innumerable aspects, the idea of difference remains though it can be subordinated to the idea of Oneness; that is the beginning of Yoga. When we realize Isha as one with Parabrahman, the idea of Oneness has sway & rules; that is the culmination of Yoga. When we realize Parabrahman Itself, that is the cessation of Yoga; for we depart utterly from Oneness & difference and no longer envisage the world of phenomena at all; that is Nirvana.

Chapter II. Spiritual Evolution in Brahman

It is in this infinitely motionless, yet infinitely moving Brahman that Matariswan or Prana, the great Breath of things, the mighty principle of Life, disposes forms and solidities rescuing them out of the undifferentiated state from which the world arose. To understand these two verses it is necessary to grasp clearly the ideas of creation & evolution which the Upanishads seek to formulate. What in Europe is called creation, the Aryan sages preferred to call *srishti*, projection of a part from the whole, the selection, liberation and development of something that is latent and potentially exists. Creation means the bringing into existence of something which does not already exist; *srishti* the manifestation of something which is hidden and unmanifest. The action of Prakriti proceeds upon the principle of selection leading naturally to development; she selects the limited out of the unlimited, the particular out of the general, the small portion out of the larger stock. This limited, particular & fractional having by the very nature of limitation a *swabhav*, an own-being or as it is called in English a nature, which differentiates it from others of its kind, develops under the law of its nature; that is its *swadharma*, its own law & religion of being, and every separate & particular existence, whether inanimate thing or animal or man or community or nation must follow & develop itself under the law of its nature and act according to its own *dharma*. It cannot follow a nature or accept a *dharma* alien to itself except on peril of deterioration, decay and death. This nature is determined by the balance in its composition of the three *gunas* or essential qualities of Prakriti, passivity, activity and equipoise, which reveal themselves under different shapes in the animate as well as the inanimate, in the mind as well as in the body. In matter they appear as passive reception, reaction and retention, in human soul as the brutal animal, the active, creative man and the calm, clear-souled god. It must always be remembered that Prakriti is no other than Avidya, the great Illusion. She is that impalpable indeterminable source of subtle and gross matter, Matter in the abstract, the idea of difference and duality, the impression of Time, Space and Causality. The limited is limited not in reality, but by walls of Avidya which shut it in and give it an impression of existence separate from that of the illimitable, just as a room is shut off from the rest of the house by walls and has its separate existence and its separate nature small or large, close or airy, coloured white or coloured blue. Break down the walls and the separate existence and separate nature disappear; the very idea of a room is lost and there is nothing left but the house. The sense of limitation and the consequent impulse towards development & self-enlargement immediately create desire which takes the form of hunger and so of a reaching after other existences for the satisfaction of hunger; and from desire & the contact with other existences there arise the two opposite forces of attraction and repulsion which on the moral plane are called liking and dislike, love and hatred. Thus [the] necessity of absorbing mental and aesthetic food for the material of one's works; this too is hunger. The instinct of self-enlargement shows itself in the physical craving for the absorption of other existences to strengthen oneself, in the emotional yearning to other beings, in the intellectual eagerness to absorb the minds of others and the aesthetic desire to possess or enjoy the beauty of things & persons, in the spiritual passion of love & beneficence, and all other activity which means the drawing of the self of others into one's own self and pouring out of oneself on others. Desire is thus the first principle of things. Under the force of attraction and repulsion hunger begins to differentiate itself & develop the various senses in order the better to master its food and to feel & know the other existences which repel or attract it. So out of the primal consciousness of Will dealing with matter is developed form and organism, vitality, receptive mind, discriminating mind, Egoism. Out of this one method of Prakriti, selection, liberation and development, the whole evolution of the phenomenal world arises. Creation therefore is not a making of something where nothing existed, but a selection and new formation out of existing material; not a sudden increase, but a continual rearrangement and substitution; not an arbitrary manufacture, but an orderly development.

The idea of creation as a selection and development from preexisting material which is common to the Upanishads & the Sankhya philosophy, is also the fundamental idea of the modern theory of Evolution. The theory of Evolution is foreshadowed in the Veda, but nowhere clearly formulated. In the Aitareya Upanishad we find a luminous hint of the evolution of various animal forms until in the course of differentiation by selection the body of man was developed as a perfect temple for the gods and a satisfactory instrument for sensational, intellectual and spiritual evolution. When the Swetaswatara sums up the process of creation in the pregnant formula "One seed developed into many forms", it is simply crystallizing the one general idea on which the whole of Indian thought takes its stand and to which the whole tendency of modern science returns. The opening of the Brihadaranyakopanishad powerfully foreshadows the theory that hunger & the struggle for life (ashanaya mrityu) are the principle agents in life-development. But it was not in this aspect of the law of creation that the old Hindu thought interested itself. Modern Science has made it its business to investigate and master the forces and laws of working of the physical world; it has sought to know how man as a reasoning animal developed into what he is, how he is affected in detail by the laws of external nature and what is the rule of his thought and action in things physical & psycho-physical whether as an individual or in masses. Outside the limits of this inquiry it has been sceptical or indifferent. Hindu thought, on the contrary, has made it its business to investigate the possibilities of man's escape from the animal and physical condition, from his subjection to the laws of external nature and from his apparent limitations as a mere creature of surroundings & sensational impact from outside. Its province has been the psychical and spiritual world. It has not concerned itself minutely with man's physical sheath, but rather with what is vital & elemental in the matter of which he is made, the law of the workings of the breath and the elemental forces within him, the relation of the various parts of his psychical anatomy to each other, and the law of his thought and action as a spiritual being having one side of itself turned to phenomena and this transient life in society and the world, the other to the single and eternal verity of things.

Speculating and experimenting on these psychical and spiritual relations, the ancient Rishis arrived at what they believed to be the fundamental laws respectively of spiritual, psychical and elemental evolution. Spiritually, the beginning of all things is the Turiya Atman, spirit in its fourth or transcendental state, intellectually unknowable and indefinable, infinite, indivisible, immutable and supra-conscious. This Turiya Atman may be imaged as the infinite ocean of spirit which evolves in itself spiritual manifestations and workings by that process of limitation or selection on which all creation or manifestation depends. By this Turiya Atman there is conceived or there is selected out of its infinite capacity a state of spirit less unknowable and therefore less indefinable, in which the conceptions of finity and division preexist in a potential state and in which consciousness is self-gathered and as yet inoperative. This state of Spirit is called variously Avyakta, the unmanifestation, or the seed-condition or the condition of absolute Sleep, because as yet phenomena and activity are not manifest but preexist gathered-together and undeveloped, just as all the infinite potentialities of organic life upon earth preexist gathered-together and undeveloped in the protoplasm; just as leaf and twig, trunk and branches, sap and pith and bark, root and flower and fruit preexist, gathered-together and undeveloped in the seed. The State of Sleep may be envisaged as Eternal Will and Wisdom on the brink of creation, with the predestined evolution of a million universes, the development of sun & star and nebula and the shining constellations and the wheeling orbits of satellite and planet, the formation of

metals and the life of trees, the motions and actions of fish and
bird and beast and the infinite spiritual, mental and physical stir
& activities of man already pre-ordained, pre-arranged and preexistent, before Time was or Space existed or Causality began.
Spirit in this state of Sleep is called Prajna, the Wise One or
He who knows and orders things beforehand. The next state
of Spirit, evolved out of Prajna, is the pure psychical or Dream
State in which Spirit is in a condition of ceaseless psychical activity imagining, willing, selecting out of the matter which Prajna
provides, and creating thought-forms to clothe the abundant
variety of its multitudinous imaginations. The Dream-State is
the psychical condition of Spirit and operates in a world of subtle matter finer and more elastic than gross physical matter and
therefore not subject to the heavy restrictions and slow processes
with which the latter is burdened. For this reason while physical
workings are fixed, slow and confined by walls within walls,
thought, psychical manifestation and other operations in subtle
matter are in comparison volatile, rapid and free, reacting more
elastically against the pressure of Time, Condition and Space.
This State of Dream may be envisaged as Eternal Will and Energy
in the process of creation with the whole activity of the Universe
teeming and fructuating within it; it is that psychical matrix out
of which physical form and life are evolved and to which in
sleep it partially returns so that it may recuperate and drink in
a fresh store of psychical energy to support the heavy strain of
physical processes in gross matter. Spirit in the middle or Dream-
State is called Taijasa or Hiranyagarbha, the Shining Embryon.
It is Taijasa, Energy of Light, and Hiranya the Shining because
in psychical matter luminous energy is the chief characteristic,
colour and light predominating over fluid or solid form. It is
Garbha, Embryon, because out of psychical matter physical life
and form are selected and evolved into the final or Waking State
in which Spirit manifests itself as physically visible, audible &
sensible form and life, and arrives at last at an appearance of
firm stability & solidity in gross matter. Spirit in the Waking
State is called Vaisvanor, the Universal Male, He who informs
and supports all forms of energy in this physical universe; for

it is a root idea of Hindu philosophy that Spirit is the Male which casts its seed into Matter and Matter the female Energy which receives the seed and with it creates and operates. Spirit and Matter are not different entities, but simply the positive and negative poles in the creative operation of the All-Self or Universal which evolves in Itself and out of Itself the endless procession of things.

All things in the Universe are of one texture & substance and subject to a single law; existence is a fundamental unity under a superficial diversity. Each part of the Universe is therefore a little Universe in itself repeating under different conditions and in different forms the nature and operations of the wider Cosmos. Every individual man must be in little what the Cosmos is in large. Like the Cosmos therefore each individual man has been created by the evolution of Spirit from its pure essence through the three states of Sleep, Dream and Waking. But this evolution has been a downward evolution; he has descended spiritually from pure Spirit into physical matter, from self-existent, self-knowing, self-delighting God into the reasoning animal. In other words each new condition of Spirit, as it evolved, has overlaid and obscured its predecessor. In the physical condition, which is the ultimate term of the downward evolution, man realizes himself as a body moving among and affected by other bodies and he readily understands, masters and employs physical organs, physical processes and physical forces, but he finds it difficult to understand, master or employ psychical organs, psychical processes and psychical forces, — so difficult that he has come to be sceptical of the existence of the psychical and doubt whether he is a soul at all, whether he is not merely an animal body with an exceptional brain-evolution. In his present state any evolution of the psychical force within is attended with extraordinary disturbances of the physical instruments; such as the development of delusions, hallucinations, eccentricities, mania and disease side by side with the development of genius or exceptional mental & spiritual powers in family or individual. Man has not yet discovered his soul; his main energies have been directed towards realizing and mastering the physical world in which he moves.

It is indeed, as some are beginning dimly to perceive, the soul within him which has all along been using the body for its own ends on the physical plane, but the soul has been working from behind the veil, unrealized and unseen. The Waking-State has overlaid and obscured the Dream-State. When he has mastered, as in the course of his evolution he must master, the psychical world within him, man will find that there is another & deeper self which is overlaid and obscured by the psychical, — the Sleep-world within or as it is called, the causal self. At present, even when he admits the existence of the soul, he sees nothing beyond his psychical self and speaks of soul and spirit as if they were identical. In reality, there are three spirit-states, spirit, soul and body, the sleep-state, the dream-state and the waking-state. Body has overlaid and obscured soul, soul overlays & obscures spirit, spirit in its turn obscures & overlays the pure self from which & towards which the circle of evolution moves.

Creation, then, has been a downward evolution which has for its object to create a body fit for an upward evolution into the region of pure spirit. It is in this direction that the future of human evolution lies. When man has mastered the physical world and its forces, when the earth is his and the fullness thereof, he must turn his efforts towards mastering the world within himself. Instead of allowing the soul to use the body for its own ends, he must learn to master both soul and body and use them consciously for the purposes of the spirit, that Eternal Will & Wisdom which at present operates in secrecy, veiled with darkness within darkness and seeming even to be blind and hidden from itself. In the end he will be master of spirit, soul and body, a Jivanmukta using them at will for cosmic purposes or transcending them to feel his identity with the Self who is pure and absolute existence, consciousness and bliss.

Chapter III. Psychical evolution — downward to matter

In their enquiry into the spiritual nature of man the ancient thinkers and Yogins discovered that he has not only three spiritual states but three bodies or cases of matter corresponding to the spiritual states. This was in accordance with the nature of phenomenal existence as determined by their inquiries. Spirit and matter, the inner inspiring presence and outward acting substance-energy, are the two necessary terms of this existence. When phenomena are transcended we come to a Self independent of Spirit or Matter; but the moment Self descends into phenomenal existence, it must necessarily create for itself a form or body and a medium in which it manifests and through which it acts. Directly, therefore, the pure transcendent Self evolves one aspect of itself as a definable spiritual condition, it must in the nature of things evolve also a form or body and a medium through and in which Spirit in that condition can manifest itself. Matter, in other words, evolves coevally and coincidently with Spirit. As soon as the Sleep-State appears, Spirit surrounds itself with matter in that most refined & least palpable condition, to which the name of causal matter may be given, — the material seed state, single and elemental in its nature, from which the material universe is evolved. With the evolution of the Dream-State matter also evolves from the causal into the subtle, a condition compound, divisible and capable of definite form but too fine to be perceived by ordinary physical senses. It is only when the Waking-State is evolved that matter concentrates into that gross physical condition which is all that Science has hitherto been able to analyse and investigate.

In man also as in the larger Cosmos each spiritual State lives in and uses its corresponding medium of matter and out of that matter shapes for itself its own body or material case. He has therefore a causal body for his Sleep-State or causal self, a subtle body for his Dream-State or psychical self and a gross body for his Waking-State or physical self. When he dies, what happens is simply the disintegration of the physical body and the return of the Waking into the Dream-State from which it was originally projected. Death, in the ordinary view, is a delivery from matter; body is destroyed and only spirit or soul remains: but this view is rejected by Hindu philosophy as an error resulting from confused and inadequate knowledge of man's psychical nature. The Waking-State having disappeared

into the Dream-State and no longer existing, the physical body
must necessarily disintegrate since it has no longer a soul to
support it and keep naturally together the gross material atoms
out of which it is constructed. But because the physical body
is destroyed or dropped off, it does not follow that no body is
left. Man goes on existing after death in his Dream-State and
moves & acts with his subtle body; it is this dream-state in the
subtle body to which the name soul or spirit is popularly given.
Even the disintegration of the subtle body and the return of the
Dream-State into the Sleep-State from which it was projected,
would not imply a release from all restrictions of matter; for the
causal body would still remain. It is only when the Sleep-State is
also transcended, that phenomenal existence with its necessary
duality of Spirit-Matter is left behind and transcended. Then
spirit & body are both dissolved into pure and transcendent
self-existence.

In examining and analysing these spiritual conditions in
their respective bodies the Rishis arrived at a theory of psychical
evolution contained within and dependent on the spiritual evolution already described. The basis of psychical as of spiritual
existence is the pure Self called the Paramatman or Supreme Self
when it manifests in the Cosmos and the Jivatman or individual
Self when it manifests in man. The Self first manifests as Will or
as the Rishis preferred to call it Ananda, Bliss, Delight. Ananda
is the pure delight of existence and activity and may be identified
in one of its aspects with the European Will-to-live, but it has
a double tendency, the Will to be phenomenally and the Will to
be transcendentally, the Will to live and the Will to cease from
phenomenal life. It is also the Will to know and the Will to
enjoy and in each aspect the double tendency is repeated. The
Will to know eternal reality is balanced by the Will to know
phenomenal diversity; the Will to absolute delight by the Will
to phenomenal delight. Will must be clearly distinguished from
volition which is only one of the operations of Will acting in
phenomena. The impacts from external things upon the mind
result in sensations and the reactions of the Will upon these sensations when conveyed to it, take the form of desires. Volition is

simply the impulse of the Will operating through the intelligence to satisfy or curb the desires created in the medium between itself and the mind. But the Will itself is antecedent to mind and intelligence and all the operations of body, mind and intelligence are ultimately operations of material energy ordained by the Will. Self manifesting as Will or Bliss is, spiritually, the Sleep-State and operates absolutely & directly in the Causal body as the creative force behind Nature, but indirectly & under limitations in the subtle & gross bodies as the cause of all thought, action and feeling.

The next evolutionary form of Will, put forth by itself from itself as an instrument or operative force in the creation of the worlds, is Buddhi or Supra-intelligence, an energy which is above mind and reason and acts independently of any cerebral organ. It is Will acting through the Supra-intelligence that guides the growth of the tree and the formation of the animal and gives to all things in the Universe the appearance of careful and abundant workmanship and orderly arrangement from which the idea of an Almighty Artificer full of fecund and infinite imaginations has naturally grown up in the human mind; but from the point of view of the Vedanta Will and Supra-Intelligence are not attributes of an anthropomorphic Deity endowed with a colossal brain but aspects of a spiritual presence manifesting itself cosmically in phenomenal existence. Will, through Buddhi, creating and operating on phenomena in subtle matter evolves Mind, which by reception of external impacts & impressions evolves sensation; by reaction to impressions received, evolves desire and activity; by retention of impressions with their reactions, evolves memory; by coordination of impressions & reactions memorized, evolves the sense of individuality; by individual arrangement of impressions and reactions with the aid of memory evolves understanding; and by the action of supra-intelligence on developed mind evolves reason. Mind & Supra-intelligence with reason as an intermediate link are, spiritually, the Dream-State and operate absolutely and directly in the subtle body but indirectly, under limitations and as a governing and directing force in the gross body.

So far spirit and soul only have been evolved; the evolution of the Will has not manifested itself in physical forms. But in Mind Will has evolved a grand primal sense by which it is able to put itself into conscious relations with external objects; before the development of mind it has been operating by methods of self-contained consciousness through the supra-intelligence. Mind is in a way the one true and real sense; it is Mind that sees, Mind that hears, Mind that smells, Mind that feels, Mind that acts; but for the purposes of varied experience Mind evolves from itself ten potencies, five potencies of knowledge, sight, hearing, smell, touch and taste by which the Will receives impressions of external objects and five potencies of action, grasp, locomotion, utterance, emission and ecstasy, by which it reacts on what it receives; and for each of these potencies it evolves an instrument of potency or sense-organ, making up the ten *indriyas* with the Mind, which is alone self-acting and introspective, as the eleventh. So far however the Mind acts with rapidity and directness under the comparatively light restrictions of subtle matter in the Dream State; it is a psychical sense, an instrument of the soul for knowing and dealing with life in the psychical world of subtle matter. Only in the physical evolution of gross matter do the sense-organs receive their consummate development and become of supreme importance; for Will in the Waking State acts mainly through them and not directly through the Mind. Soul-evolution precedes physical evolution. This theory directly contradicts those conclusions of modern Science which make soul an evolution of physical life and activities, not an all-important and enduring evolution, but merely their temporary efflorescence and dependent on them for its existence. Arguing from the facts of physical evolution which alone it has studied and excluding all possibilities outside this limit, Science is justified in coming to this conclusion, and, as a logical corollary, it is justified in denying the immortality of the soul. For if psychical activities are merely a later and temporary operation of physical life and dependent on the physical for their own continuance, it follows that when physical life ceases with the arrest of bodily operations by the mysterious agency of death, human personality which is a psychical activity must also come to an end. When the body dies, the soul dies also; it can no more outlast the body than the flower can outlast the plant on which it grows or a house survive the destruction of its foundations. Body is the stem, soul the flower; body the foundation, soul a light and temporary superstructure. To all this Hindu thought gives a direct denial. It claims to have discovered means of investigating psychical life as thoroughly as Science can investigate physical nature and in the light of its investigations it declares that soul exists before body and outlasts it. It is physical life that is an evolution from psychical, and no more than a later and temporary operation of psychical activities. Body is the flower, soul the stem; soul is the foundation, body the fragile and transient superstructure.

For the purposes of physical evolution Will evolves a new aspect of itself which is called Prana or vital energy. Prana exists in the physical state also, but there it is simple, undifferentiated, gathered up in mind and not acting as a separate agent. Prana in gross matter is an all-pervading energy which subsists wherever there is physical existence and is the principle agent in maintaining existence and furthering its activities. It is present in what seems inert and inanimate no less than in what is manifestly endowed with life. It lives concealed in the metal and the sod, it begins to emerge in the plant, it reveals itself in the animal. Prana is the agent of Will in all physical evolution. It is the mainspring of every hunger-impulse and presides over every process of alimentation. It creates life, it fills it with vital needs, desires, longings; it spurs it to the satisfaction of its needs & desires; and it evolves the means and superintends and conducts the processes of that satisfaction. In the course of evolution it reveals itself with an ever-rounding fulness, vibrates with an ever swifter and more complex energy, differentiates and enriches its activity with a more splendid opulence until the crescendo reaches its highest note in man. In this, the noblest type of physical evolution, Prana manifests itself in five distinct vital powers, to which the names, Prana, Samana, Vyana, Apana and Udana have been given by the ancient writers. Prana, the vital force *par excellence* has its seat in the upper part of the body and conducts all mental operations, the indrawing and the outdrawing of the breath and the induction of food. Samana, seated centrally in the body, balances, equalizes and harmonizes the vital operations and is the agent for the assimilation of food. Vyana pervades the whole body; on it depends the circulation of the blood and the distribution of the essential part of the food eaten and digested throughout the body. Apana, situated in the lower part of the trunk, presides over the lower functions, especially over the emission of such parts of the food as are rejected by the body and over procreation, it is intimately connected with the processes of decay and death. Udana is the vital power which connects bodily life with the spiritual element in man. As in the purely vital operations, so also in the motional and volitional Prana is still the great agent of Will, and conducts such operations of Mind also as depend on the sense-organs for their instruments. Prana is the regent of the body, ministering to the Mind and through that great intermediary executing the behests of the concealed sovereign of existence, the Will.

As Prana is the first term in the physical evolution of the Self, so Anna, Food or gross visible matter is the second term. "I am food that devours the eater of food" says the Taittiriya Upanishad, and no formula could express more pregnantly and tersely the fundamental law of all phenomenal activity especially on the physical plane. The fundamental principle of vitality is hunger and all gross matter forms the food with which Prana satisfies this, its root-impulse. Hence the universality of the struggle for life. This hungry Prana first needs to build up a body in which it can subsist and in order to do so, it devours external substances so as to provide itself with the requisite material. This body once found it is continually eating up by the ceaselessness of its vital activity and has to repair its own ravages by continually drawing in external substances to form fresh material for an ever-wasting and ever-renewing frame. Unable to preserve its body for ever under the exhausting stress of its own activity, it has to procreate fresh forms which will continue vital activity and for the purpose concentrates itself in a part of its material which it throws out of itself to lead a similar but independent life even after the parent form decays. To satisfy its hunger it is ever evolving fresh means and new potencies for mastery & seizure of its food. Dissatisfied with the poor sustenance a stationary existence can supply, it develops the power & evolves various means of locomotion. To perceive its food more & more thoroughly & rapidly it develops the five senses and evolves the organs of perception through which they can act. To deal successfully with the food perceived, it develops the five potencies of action and evolves the active organs which enable them to work. As a centre of all this sensational and actional activity it evolves the central mind-organ in the brain and as channels of communication between the central & the outer organs it develops a great nerve-system centred in seven plexuses, through which it moves with a ceaseless stir and activity, satisfying hunger, satisfying lust, satisfying desire. At the base of all is the impulse of Life to survive, to prolong itself for the purposes of the Will-to-live of which it is the creature and the servant. Prana & Anna, Vitality and physical form are, spiritually, the Waking-State and operate entirely in gross matter, — the last term of that downward evolution which is the descent of Spirit from the original purity of absolute existence into the impurity and multiplicity of matter.

Chapter IV. Psychical Evolution — Upward to Self.

In this downward psychical evolution, as in the downward spiritual evolution, each succeeding and newly-evolved state of the original Self obscures and overlays that which preceded it, until the last state of the Self appears to be an inert brute and inanimate condition of gross physical matter devoid of life, mental consciousness or spiritual possibilities. From this state of inert and lifeless matter the upward evolution starts and, as in our spiritual evolution the course set down for us is to recover from a firm footing in the Waking State mastery over the obscured and latent Dream and Sleep States and so return into the presence of that pure and unimaginable Self from whom the process of our evolution began, so in our psychical evolution we have to recover out of the inertia of gross physical materiality Life, Mind, Supra-Intelligence, Will until we know our infinite and eternal Self who is one with the Supreme Self of the Universe.

With inanimate matter the world began, says evolutionary Science; but in inanimate matter there is no evidence of life or mind or spirit, no apparent possibility of the evolution of animate conscious existence. Into this inanimate world at some unknown period, by some unknown means, perhaps from some unknown source, a mysterious thing called Life entered or began to stir and all this mighty evolution we have discovered became in a moment possible. Grant one infinitesimal seed of life and everything else becomes possible, but life itself we cannot explain nor can we discover as yet how it came originally into being. We can only suppose that life is some chemical process or develops from some chemical process we shall ultimately discover. Even what life is, has not been satisfactorily settled. The term is sometimes rigidly confined to animal life, — surely a crude and unscientific limitation, since the peculiarities of animal life, — consciousness and organic growth —, exist quite as evidently in the highest forms of plant-life as in the animalcule or the jelly-fish. Or if we confine life to organic growth, we do so arbitrarily, for recent discoveries have shown the beginning of one element of vital activity, the one which forms the very basis of consciousness, viz. reception of & reaction to outward impressions and the phenomena of vigour and exhaustion, in a substance so apparently inanimate as metal. So obscure is the whole subject that many are inclined to regard life as a divine mystery, breathed by God into the world or introduced, as if it were a sort of psychical meteoric dust, from some other planet. Upanishadic philosophy accounts for the appearance of Life in a more calm and rational manner. Life, it would say, is in a sense a divine mystery but no more and no less so than the existence of inanimate matter. God did not breathe it from outside into an inert and created body, neither did it drift hither from some mystic and superior planet. Nor did it come into sudden being by some fortuitous chemical process which marked off suddenly all existences into two rigidly distinct classes, animate and inanimate, organic and inorganic. All such ideas are, when carefully examined, irrational and inconsistent with the unity and harmonious development of the world under fixed and invariable laws. Life is evolved naturally and not mysteriously out of matter itself, because it is already latent and preexistent in matter. Prana is involved in anna, matter cannot exist without latent life, and the first step in evolution is the liberation of the latent life out of the heavy obscuration of matter in its grossest and densest forms. This evolution is effected by the three gunas, the triple principle of reception, retention and reaction to outward impacts; as fresh forms of matter are evolved in which the power of retaining impacts received in the shape of impressions becomes more and more declared, consciousness slowly and laboriously develops; as the power of reacting on external objects becomes more pronounced and varied, organic life-growth begins its marvellous career; and the two, helping and enriching each other, evolve complete, well-organized and richly-endowed Life.

Prana receives its perfect development in animal life and when man, the highest term of animal life, has been reached, there is no farther need for its development. The true evolution of Man therefore lies not in the farther development of vitality, but in the complete & triumphant liberation of mind out of the overlaying obscuration of the vital energies. Just as Prana is involved in Anna and has to be evolved out of it, so Mind is involved in Prana and has to be evolved out of it. The moment Life begins to liberate itself from the obscuration of gross matter, the first step has been taken towards the evolution of Mind. We see the gradual development of Mind in animal evolution; the highest animal forms below man seem to possess not only memory and individuality, but a considerable degree of understanding and even the rudiments of reason. In man the development is much more rapid and triumphant, but it is by no means, as yet, complete or perfect. Prana still to an immense extent obscures Mind, the gross body dominates the subtle. Mind is dominated by the instruments which Prana has created for it; the body, the nerve-system, the sense-organs, the brain hamper and hinder its operations even more than they help them; for the Mind is bound within the narrow circle of their activity and limited by their deficiencies. The continual stir of the vital energies in the brain and throughout the whole system, disturb the Mind, the continual siege of external impressions distract it, the insistent urgency of the senses towards the external world impede the turning of the energies inward; calm and purity, concentration and introspection are rendered so difficult that the majority of men do not attempt them or only compass them spasmodically and imperfectly. Any powerful and unusual development of mind, in its intellectual and spiritual tendencies, is apt to be resented by the vital part of man and to impair or seriously disturb his vital energies and physical health. Along with the intellectual development of the race, there has been a marked deterioration of vital vigour & soundness and of the bodily organs. Moral and spiritual development is continually at war with the needs of our physical life, our hungers, desires, lusts, longings and the insistent urgency of the instincts of self-preservation and self-gratification. It is therefore towards the conquest and control of Prana and the free development of Mind that the energies of Man ought in future to be directed. He must arrive at some arrangement of his social and individual life which, while satisfying the legitimate demands of his body and his vital impulses, will admit of the extreme and unhampered perfection of his intellectual, moral and spiritual being. He must discover and practise some method of maintaining the harmony and soundness of the vital and bodily instruments and processes without for a moment allowing the care for them to restrict the widest possible range, the most bold and powerful exercise and the most intense and fiery energisms of which the higher principle in his being is capable. He must learn how to transcend the limitations and errors of the physical senses and train his mind to act even in the physical body with the rapidity, directness and unlimited range proper to a psychical organ whose function is to operate in subtle as well as in gross matter. To see where the physical eye is blind, to hear where the physical ear is deaf, to feel where the physical sense is callous, to understand thoughts unexpressed, are legitimate functions of the mind; but they must be exercised, not as a rare power or in moments of supreme excitation, but as a regular and consciously willed operation, the processes of which have been mastered and known. Reason, at present fallible, imperfect and enslaved to desire and prejudice, must be trained into its highest possibilities of clarity, sanity and calm energy. The Mind must be tranquillised and purified by control of the senses and the five Pranas, and trained to turn itself wholly inward, excluding at will all outward impressions, so that Man may become master of the inner world no less than of the outer, a conscious soul using the body and no longer a body governed by a self-concealing and self-guiding psychical entity. We think we have done wonders in the way of mental evolution; in reality we have made no more than a feeble beginning. The infinite possibilities of that evolution still lie unexplored in front.

As Mind is involved in Prana, so is Supra-Intelligence involved and latent in all the operations of Mind. With the evolution of the Mind, some rudimentary beginnings have been unconsciously made towards the liberation of this higher & far grander force. As the mental development foreshadowed above proceeds to its goal, man will begin to evolve and realize himself as a mighty and infinite Intelligence, not limited by sense-perception or the laborious and clumsy processes of the reason, but capable of intuitive and infinite perception. And when the evolution of Mind is complete and the evolution of Supra-Intelligence proceeds, the liberation of the Will involved in its operations will lead man to the highest evolution of all when he realizes himself as a potent and scient Will, master of creation and not its slave, whose infinite delight in its own existence is lifted far beyond the thraldom of pain and pleasure and uses them with as unalloyed a pleasure as the poet when he weaves joy and sorrow, delight and pain and love and fear and horror into one perfect and pleasurable masterpiece or the painter when he mixes his colours and blends light and shade to create a wedded harmony of form and hue. This state of unfettered Will and infinite Delight once realized, he cannot fail to know his real Self, absolute and calm, omnipotent and pure, the eternal Brahman in whom this evolution has its root and resting-place.

VII. Elemental Evolution.

The evolution of the cosmos has not only spiritual and psychical aspects; it has also from the moment of its inception a material element. Spirit exists from the beginning and was before any beginning, infinite and sempiternal; but Matter also is an eternal entity. In the Parabrahman, the absolute inconceivable Self, Spirit and Matter are one and undifferentiated, but the moment evolution begins Spirit and Matter manifest equally and coevally. We have seen that the first spiritual evolution from the pure self-existent Atman is Prajna of the Sleep-State, Eternal Wisdom, a supporting spiritual presence which contains in itself the whole course of cosmic evolution even as a single seed contains in itself the complete banyan-tree with all its gigantic progeny. We have seen that corresponding to this Eternal Wisdom, there is a first psychic evolution, Ananda or Will, an inspiring psychical force in man & the cosmos which makes all the workings of Nature possible. Spirit however, even when operating as Will, is not a working force in the sense that it itself carries on the operations of Nature; it is an inspiring, impelling force, whose function is to set in motion a powerful material energy of the Self; and it is this material energy which under the inspiration of Will and at the bidding of Prajna sets about the evolution of the Cosmos. Self in its dealings with the Cosmos is a dual entity, underlying spiritual presence and superficially active material energy, or as they are called in the terminology of the Sankhya philosophy, Purusha and Prakriti; — Purusha, that which lies concealed in the Vast of universal existence, Prakriti, active or operative energy thrown forward from the concealed spiritual source. The whole of Evolution spiritual, psychical, material, is the result of Purusha and Prakriti acting upon each other; the three evolutions are really one, coincident and coeval, because throughout it is one Reality that is manifesting and not three. It is Self manifesting as spirit, Self manifesting as soul, Self manifesting as matter or body. The three manifestations are coincident in Time and Space and each condition of phenomena is a triple state with Spirit and Matter for its extreme terms and Soul for its middle. In the evolution of the spirit-states Purusha determines itself so as to inform and support the progressive manifestations of Self as soul and body; in the evolution of the psychic states Prakriti worked on by Purusha creates for the manifestations of Self as spirit psychic sheaths or coverings which will at the same time inform and support the manifestations of Self as matter; in the evolution of the causal, subtle and gross bodies Prakriti shapes itself so as to create the material out of which the psychical coverings of Self as spirit may be made and the medium in which the Self as soul may operate. The three evolutions are dependent on each other, and that it is really one entity and not three which is evolving, is shown by the fact that while in the first stage of the downward evolution and the last of the upward Matter seems so refined as to appear identical with Spirit, in the last of the downward and first of the upward Spirit seems so densified as to appear identical with Matter. This possibility of evolution from and involution into each other would not be conceivable if they were not in essence one entity; and we may legitimately deduce from the oneness of such diverse phenomena that they *are* no more than phenomena, merely apparent changes in one unchanging reality.

In the first stage of evolution Matter appears as an aspect or shadow of Spirit, and like Spirit it is infinite, unanalysable, undifferentiated. Just as Spirit then has only three positive attributes, infinite and undefinable existence, consciousness and bliss, so original Matter has only three positive attributes, infinite and undefinable Time, Space and Causality — or, as Hindu thought phrases it, Condition. For the essence of Condition being change from one state to another, and each change standing in the relation of cause or origin to the one that follows it, Condition and Causality become convertible terms. From this indefinable noumenal condition of Prakriti the Self forms for its uses matter in its most refined and simple form, undifferentiated and undeveloped, but pregnant with the whole of material evolution. The causal state is called by the Sankhyas Pradhana, the first state or arrangement of matter and its essential principle. The relation of Spirit and Matter in this causal or seed-state is admirably expressed in the Puranic image of Vishnu, the eternal Purusha, asleep on the waveless causal ocean with the endless coils of the snake Ananta, the Infinite, for his couch. The sea of causal matter is then motionless and it is only when Vishnu awakes, the snake Ananta stirs and the first ever widening ripples are created on the surface of the waters that the actual evolution of matter has begun. The first ripple or vibration in causal matter creates a new & exceedingly fine and pervasive condition of matter called akasha or ether; more complex motion evolves out of ether a somewhat intenser condition which is called Vayu, Air; and so by ever more complex motion with increasing intensity of condition for result, yet three other matter-states are successively developed, Agni or Fire, Apah or Water and Prithivi or Earth. These are the five *tanmatras* or subtle elements of Sankhya philosophy by the combination of which subtle forms in subtle matter are built.

Here it is necessary to enter a caution against possible misunderstandings to which the peculiar nomenclature used by the Rishis & the common rendering of *tanmatra* & *bhuta* by the English word elements may very easily give rise. When we speak of elements in English in a scientific sense, we always imply elemental *substances*, those substances which when analysed by chemical processes, cannot be resolved into substances simpler than themselves. But when Hindu philosophy speaks of the five elements, it is not dealing with substances at all but with elemental states or conditions of matter, which are not perceptible or analysable by chemical inquiry but underlie substances and forms as basic principles of material formation. The old thinkers accepted the atomic theory of the formation of objects and substances but they did not care to carry the theory farther and inquire by what particular combinations of atoms this or that substance came into being or by what variations and developments in detail bodies animate or inanimate came to be what they are. This did not seem to them to be an inquiry of the first importance; they were content with laying down some main principles of material evolution and there they left the matter. But they were anxious to resolve not substances into their original atoms but matter into its original condition and so discover its ultimate relations to the psychical and spiritual life of man. They saw that perpetual motion involving perpetual change was the fundamental characteristic of matter and that each new motion was attended by a new condition which stood to the immediately preceding condition in the relation of effect to cause or at least of a new birth to the matrix in which it had been enembryoed. Behind the solid condition of matter, they found a condition less dense which was at the basis of all fluid forms; behind the fluid condition, another still less dense which was at the basis of all igneous or luminous forms; behind the igneous, yet another and finer which was at the basis of all aerial or gaseous forms; and last of all one finest and most pervasive condition of all which they called Akash or Ether. Ether was, they found, the primary substance out of which all this visible Universe is evolved and beyond ether they were unable to go without matter losing all the characteristics associated with it in the physical world and lapsing into a quite different substance of which the forms and motions were much more vague, subtle, elastic and volatile than any of which the physical world is aware. This new world of matter they called subtle matter and analysed the subtle as they had analysed the gross until by a similar procession from denser to subtler they came to a finest condition of all which they described as subtle ether. Out of this subtle ether a whole world of subtle forms and energies are evolved which constitute psychical existence. Beyond subtle ether matter lost its subtle characteristics and lapsed into a new kind which they could not analyse but which seemed to be the matrix out of which all material evolution proceeded. This they termed causal matter.

In the course of this analysis they could not help perceiving that consciousness in each world of matter assumed a different form and acted in a different way corresponding to the characteristics of the matter in which it moved. In its operations in

gross matter the forms it assumed were more firm, solid and
durable but at the same time more slow, difficult and hampered,
just as are the motions and acts of a man in his waking state as
compared with what he does in his dreams. In its operations in
subtle matter the forms consciousness assumed were freer and
more rapid, but more volatile, elastic & swiftly mutable, as are
the motions and acts of a man in a dreaming state compared to
the activities of his waking condition. To consciousness acting on
gross matter they gave therefore the name of the Waking State,
to consciousness acting on subtle matter the name of the Dream
State. In causal matter they found that consciousness took the
shape merely of the pure sense of blissful existence; they could
discover no other distinguishing sensation. This therefore they
called the Sleep State. They farther discovered that the various
faculties and functions of man belonged properly some to one,
some to another of the three states of consciousness and its
corresponding state of matter. His vital and physical functions
operated only in gross matter, and they determined accordingly
that his physical life was the result of consciousness working in
the Waking State on gross matter. His mental and intuitional processes were found to operate freely and perfectly in subtle matter,
but in gross matter with a hampered and imperfect activity; they
considered therefore that man's mental life belonged properly to
the Dream State and only worked indirectly and under serious
limitations in the Waking State. They determined accordingly
that mental life must be the result of Consciousness working
in the Dream State on subtle matter. There remained the fundamental energy of consciousness, Will-to-be or shaping Delight of
existence: this, they perceived, was free and pure in causal matter, but worked if consciously, yet through a medium and under
limitations in subtle matter, in hampered & half effectual fashion
when the subtle self acted through the gross and sub-consciously
only in gross matter. They considered therefore that man's causal
faculty or spiritual life belonged properly to the Sleep State and
worked indirectly and through less & less easy mediums in the
Dream and Waking States; and accordingly determined that it
must be the result of Consciousness working in the Sleep State

on causal matter. The whole of creation amounted therefore to a natural outcome from the mutual relations of Spirit and Matter; these two they regarded as two terms — call them forces, energies, substances, or what you will, — of phenomenal existence; and psychical life only as one result of their interaction. They refused however to accept any dualism in their cosmogony and, as has been pointed out, regarded Spirit and Matter as essentially one and their difference as no more than an apparent duality in one real entity. This one entity is not analysable or intellectually knowable, yet it is alone the real, immutable and sempiternal Self of things.

It will be clear even from this brief and condensed statement of the Vedic analysis of existence that the elements of the Upanishad are not the elementary substances of modern chemistry but five general states of matter to which all its actual or substantial manifestations belong. It will also be clear that the names of the five elements have a conventional, not a literal value, but it may be as well to indicate why these particular names have been chosen. The first and original state of subtle matter is the pure ethereal of which the main characteristics are extreme tenuity and pervasiveness and the one sensible property, sound. Sound, according to the Vedic inquirers, is the first evolved property of material substance; it precedes form and has the power both to create it and to destroy it. Looking around them in the physical universe for a substance with these characteristics they found it in Akash or Vyom (sky), implying not our terrestrial atmosphere but that which is both beyond it and pervades it, — the fine pervasive connecting substance in which, as it were, the whole universe floats. They therefore gave this name, Akash, to the ethereal condition of matter.

The next matter-condition evolved from Ether and moving in it, was the pure aerial or gaseous. Here to pervasiveness was added a new potency of sensible and varied motion bringing with it, as increased complexity of motion necessarily must do, increased differentiation and complexity of substance. All the variety and evolutions of gaseous matter with their peculiar activities, functions and combinations have this second state or power of matter as their substratum; it is the basis also of that universal Prana or vital energy, starting from action, retention and reaction and culminating in organized consciousness, which we have seen to be so all-important an agent in the Vedic theory of the Cosmos. In this second power of matter a new property of material substance is evolved, touch or contact, which was not fully developed in pure ether owing to its extreme tenuity and primary simplicity of substance. Seeking for a physical substance gaseous in nature, sensible by sound and contact, but without form and characterized chiefly by varied motion and an imperfect pervasiveness, the Rishis found it in Vayu, Wind or Air. Vayu, therefore, is the conventional term for the second condition of matter.

Evolved out of the pure gaseous state and moving in it is the third or pure igneous condition of matter, which is also called Tejah, light and heat energy. In the igneous stage pervasiveness becomes still less subtle, sensible motion no longer the paramount characteristic, but energy, especially formative energy, attains full development and creation and destruction, formation and new-formation are at last in readiness. In addition to sound and contact matter has now evolved a third property, form, which could not be developed in pure Air owing to its insufficient density and the elusive vagueness and volatility of gaseous manifestations. The third power of matter is at the basis of all phenomena of light and heat and Prana by its aid so develops that birth and growth now become possible; for light and heat are the necessary condition of animate life-development and in their absence we have the phenomenon of death or inert and inanimate existence: when the energy of light and heat departs from a man, says the Upanishad, then it is that Prana, the vital energy, retires into mind, his subtle or psychical part, and withdraws from the physical frame. The physical substance which seemed to the Rishis to typify the igneous state was fire; for it is sensible by sound, contact and form and, less pervasive than air, is distinguished by the utmost energy of light and heat. Fire therefore is the conventional or symbolic name of the third power of matter.

Next upon the igneous state follows the liquid or fluid, less pervasive, less freely motional or energetic, and distinguishingly marked by a kind of compromise between fixity and volatility. In this state matter evolves a fourth property, taste. The liquid state is the substratum of all fluid forms and activities, and in its comparative fixity life-development finds its first possibility of a sufficiently stable medium. All life is gathered out of "the waters" and depends on the fluid principle within it for its very sustenance. Water as the most typical fluid, half-volatile, half-fixed, perceptible by sound, contact, form and taste, has given a symbolical name to the fourth condition of matter.

The solid state is the last to develop in this progression from tenuity to density, for in this state pervasiveness reaches its lowest expression and fixity predominates. It is the substratum of all solid forms and bodies and the last necessity for the development of life; for it provides life with a fixed form or body in which it can endure and work itself out and which it can develop into organism. The last new property of matter evolved in the solid state is odour; and since earth is the typical solid substance, containing all the five properties sound, contact, form, taste and smell, Earth is the conventional name selected for the fifth and final power of matter.

These five elemental states are only to be found in their purity and with their characteristic qualities distinct and unblended in the world of subtle matter. The five elemental states of gross matter are impure; they are formed out of subtle matter by the combination of the five subtle elements in certain fixed proportions, that one being given the characteristic name of ether, air, fire, water or earth in which the subtle ethereal, gaseous, igneous, fluid or solid element prevails overwhelmingly over the others. Even the last and subtlest condition to which gross matter can be reduced is not a final term; when realised into its constituents, the last term of gross matter disintegrates and matter reaches a stage at which many of the most urgent and inexorable laws of physics no longer operate. It is at this point where chemical analysis and reasoning can no longer follow Nature into her recesses that the Hindu system of Yoga by getting behind the five Pranas or gross vital breaths through which Life manifests in gross physical matter, is able to take up the pursuit and investigate the secrets of psychic existence in a subtler and freer world.

VIII. Matariswan and the Waters.

We are now in a position to consider what may [be] the precise meaning of the Upanishad when it says that in It Matariswan ordereth the waters. Shankara takes *apah* in a somewhat unusual and peculiar sense and interprets, "Air orders or arranges actions"; in other words, all the activity in the Cosmos is dependent upon the aerial or gaseous element in matter which enters into and supports all objects and, as Prana, differentiates and determines their proper functions. Prana, as we have seen, is the great vital energy breathing and circulating through all existence whose activity is the principal instrument of Will in the evolution of the Universe and whose mediation is necessary for all the operations of mind and body in gross matter. In psychic life also Prana is inherent in mind and supports those activities of subtle matter which are necessary for psychic existence. The intimate connection between Prana and vital activity may be best illustrated in its most obvious and fundamental function in the living organism, the regulation of breathing. So important is this function that Breath and Prana are generally identified; the usual signification of the word Prana is, indeed, breath and the five differentiated vital energies supporting the human frame are called the five breaths. So important is it, that even the searching analysis of modern science has not been able to get behind it, and it is held as an incontrovertible fact that the maintenance of respiration is necessary to the maintenance of life. In reality, this is not so. Ordinarily, of course, the regular inhalation of oxygen into the system and exhalation of corrupted breath out of it, is so necessary to the body that an abrupt interruption of the process, if continued for two minutes will result in death by suffocation. But this is merely due to a persistent vital habit of the body. It needs only a careful training in the regulation of the breath to master this habit and make respiration subservient to the will.

Anyone who has for a long time practised this art of breath-regulation or Pranayam can suspend inhalation and exhalation for many minutes and some not only for minutes but for hours together without injury to the system or the suspension of bodily life; for internal respiration and the continuance of the vital activities within the body still maintain the functions necessary to life. Even the internal respiration may be stopped and the vital activities entirely suspended without subjecting the body to the process of death and disintegration. The body may be kept intact for days, months and years while all the functions of breath and vitality are suspended, until the Will in its psychical sheaths chooses to resume its interrupted communications with the world of gross matter and recommence physical life at the precise point at which it was discontinued. And this is possible because Prana, the vital energy, instead of being allowed to circulate through the system under the necessary conditions of organic physical activity, can be gathered up into the mind-organ and from there in its simple undifferentiated form support and hold together the physical case.

But if respiration is not necessary to the maintenance of life, it certainly is necessary to the maintenance of activity. The first condition of Pranayam is the suspension of conscious physical activity and the perfect stillness of the body, which is the primary object of the various *asans* or rigidly set positions of the body assumed by the Yogin as a necessary preliminary in the practice of his science. In the first stages of Yoga the sub-conscious activity of the body due to the life of the cells, continues; in the later stages when internal respiration and vital activities are suspended, even this ceases, and the life of the body becomes like that of the stone or any other inert object. It is held together and exists by the presence of Prana in its primary state, the only connection of Will with the physical frame being the will to subsist physically. This is the first outstanding fact of Yoga which proves that Prana is the basis of all physical activity; the partial or complete quiescence of Prana brings with it the partial or complete quiescence of physical activity, the resumption of its functions by Prana is inevitably attended by the resumption of physical activity. The second outstanding fact is the peculiar effect of Pranayam and Yoga on mental activity. The first condition of Yogic exercises is, as has been said, the stillness of the body, which implies the suspension of the five *indriyas* or potencies of action, grasp, locomotion, utterance, emission and physical ecstasy. It is a significant fact that the habit of suspending these *indriyas* is attended by an extraordinary activity of the five *indriyas* of knowledge, sight, hearing, smell, touch and taste, and an immense heightening of mental power and energy. In its higher stages this increase of power intensifies into clairvoyance, clairaudience, the power of reading other minds and knowing actions distant in space and time, conscious telepathy and other psychical powers. The reason for this development is to be found in the habit of gathering Prana or vitality into the mind-organ. Ordinarily the psychical life is overlaid and hampered by the physical life, the activity of Prana in the physical body. As soon as this activity becomes even partially quiescent, the gross physical obstruction of Anna and Prana is rarefied and mind becomes more self-luminous, shining out through the clouds that concealed it; vital energy is not only placed mainly at the service of the mind as in the concentration of the poet and the thinker, but is so much subtilised by the effect of Pranayam that the mind can operate far more vigorously and rapidly than in ordinary conditions. For mind operates freely and naturally in subtle matter only and the subtler the matter, the freer the workings of the mind. At an intenser stage of Yogic exercise all the vital functions are stilled and Prana entirely withdrawn from bodily functions into mind which can then retire into the subtle world and operate with perfect freedom and detachment from physical matter. Here again we see that just as Prana, differentiated and working physically, was the basis of all physical activity, so Prana, intermediate and working psycho-physically, is at the basis of all mental activity, and Prana, pure and working psychically is at the basis of all psychical activity.

The third outstanding fact of Yoga is that while in its earlier processes it stimulates mental activity, in its later stages it overpasses mental activity. At first the mind drawn inward from active reactions to external impacts, is able to perfect its passive reactions or powers of reception and its internal reactions or powers of retention and combination. Next it is drawn inward from external phenomena altogether and becomes aware of the internal processes and finally succeeds in concentrating entirely within itself. This is followed by the entire quieting of the subtle or psychical *indriyas* or sense-potencies followed by the entire quiescence of the mind itself. The reception of psychical impacts and the vibrations of subtle thought-matter are suspended; mind concentrates on a single thought and finally thought itself is surmounted and the Supra-Intelligence is potent, free and active. It is at this stage that Yoga develops powers which are so unlimited as to appear like omnipotence. The true Yogin, however, does not linger in this stage which is still within the confines of psychical existence, but withdraws the Will beyond Supra-Intelligence entirely into itself. The moment the Will passes out of subtle matter, activity ceases. Will has then three courses open to it; either to realize itself as the eternal Sakshi or witness and behold the vision of the Universe as a phenomenon within itself which it *sees but does not enact*; or to disappear into the Sunya Brahman, Supreme Nothingness, the great Void of unconscious mere-existence with which the Parabrahman is veiled; or to return into the Self and, liberated from even the vision of phenomena, exist in its own infinity of pure consciousness and supreme bliss. If we follow Prana through this process of Yogic liberation, we shall find that Prana ends where activity ceases. For Prana is a material entity arising out of the aerial state of subtle matter and as soon as that state is overpassed, Prana is impossible. Throughout there is this close identification of Prana with activity. It may well be said, therefore, that Matariswan is that which arranges actions.

Matariswan is the philosophical expression for Vayu, the aerial principle. It means that which moves in the mother or matrix and the word implies the three main characteristics of the aerial element. It is evolved directly out of ether, the common matrix, which is therefore its own mother and ultimately the mother of all elements, forces, substances, objects; its predominant characteristic is motion, and this characteristic of motion operates in the matrix, ether. Moving in ether, developing, combining, it creates the substances out of which sun and nebula and planet are made; it evolves fire and water and atmosphere, earth, stone and metal, plant, fish, bird and beast. Moving in ether, acting and functioning through its energy Prana, it determines the nature, motions, powers, activities of all those infinite forms which it has created. By the combinations & operations of this aerial element the sun is built up, fire is struck forth, clouds are formed, a molten globe cools and solidifies into earth. By the energy of the aerial element the sun gives light and heat, fire burns, clouds give rain, earth revolves. Not only all animate, but all inanimate existence owes its life and various activity to Matariswan and its energy Prana.

But it owes not only its life and activity, but the very materials out of which it is made. Here lies the insufficiency of Shankara's interpretation. The word *apah* naturally and usually signifies "waters", and it is a law of interpretation not lightly to be set aside that when the natural and usual meaning of a word gives a satisfactory or even a possible and not unsuitable sense, it should be preferred to an artificial and unusual meaning. In this case "waters" may have two meanings one of which gives a sense possible and not unsuitable, the other a sense even more satisfactory than Shankara's interpretation. By waters may be indicated the various fluid forms which are evolved by the fluid element, and, involved in the solid, sustain organic life; for the word *apah* is commonly used to indicate the fourth element of matter. Prana, the vital energy, may be said so to dispose these "waters" as to originate, sustain and develop all solidities and all forms of organic life. But this would be a narrow interpretation out of harmony with the vast sweep and significance of this verse which sums up the Supreme Entity in its aspects as the stable substratum of cosmic existence, the mighty sum of cosmic motion and energy and the infinite continent of cosmic energy. It is better therefore to take *apah* in the sense of the original ocean of cosmic matter, a figure which is so common as to have become a commonplace of Hindu thought. In It, in Brahman, Matariswan, the aerial element took and disposed the infinite supply of causal matter so as to provide the substance, evolve the forms and coordinate the activities of this vast and complex Universe.

IX. Spirit and Matter

But Matariswan does not conduct these numberless cosmic operations vast and minute by virtue of its own intrinsic and unborrowed power. Otherwise we might well ask, If there is a material substance which provides all the wherewithal necessary for the evolution of this Universe and a material energy by whose existence all the operations implied in its evolution can be explained, then the whole Universe can be understood as a development out of eternal Matter with its two properties substance and energy, and no second term of existence other than Matter need be brought in to account for the evolution of Consciousness. But the Upanishad emphatically negatives the material origination of things by stating that it is in Brahman, the Supreme Entity, that Matariswan orders the waters. By this, as Shankara points out, it is meant that only so long as the Supreme Self is there, can the activity of Matariswan be conceived as possible. As ether, the matrix, is the continent and condition of Matariswan and his works, so is Brahman the continent and condition of ether and its evolution. Matariswan is born out of ether and works in ether, but ether is itself only an intermediate evolution; in reality, Matariswan is born out of Brahman the Self and works in Brahman the Self.

The materialistic theory of cosmic origins has a great superficial plausibility of its own and it is popular with scientists because analytical Science knows thoroughly the evolutions of matter and does not know thoroughly the evolutions of soul and spirit; it is therefore inevitably led to explain what it knows imperfectly or not at all by what it does know and understand. The materialistic tendency is immensely assisted by the universal interdependence of Spirit, Soul and Matter. Every spiritual and psychical activity involves a material operation and this Science has clearly seen. It is natural therefore for the Scientist to argue that the material operation is the cause of the spiritual and psychical activity, nay, that the material operation is the activity and spirit and soul do not exist, but are essentially matter. It is equally true that every material operation involves a spiritual and psychical activity, but this Science has not yet seen. When therefore idealistic philosophies argue in precisely the opposite sense and urge that the spiritual activity is the cause of the material operation, nay that the activity is the material operation and matter does not exist but is essentially spirit, it is natural for Science to brush aside the argument as metaphysical, mystical and irrational. I argue from the firm basis of well-tested certainties, thinks the Scientist, my opponent from mere ideas the truth of which cannot be demonstrated by definite evidence or actual experiment.

All Hindu philosophies, however, not only the Vedantic, but Sankhya and Buddhism agree in rejecting the materialistic reading of the Universe and oppose to the well-tested certainties of Science certainties as well-tested of their own. Hindu thought has its own analysis of the Universe arrived at by processes and experiments in which its faith is as assured and unshakeable as the confidence of the Scientist in his modern methods of analysis and observation. To a certain extent Hindu philosophy goes hand in hand with the materialistic. Prakriti or Nature, an original energy manifesting in substance is the origin, the material and the agent of evolution. This original energy is not Prana, the vital energy, for Prana is not original but a later evolution, arising out of the aerial condition of matter and subsequent in time to the ethereal; there must therefore have been a previous energy which evolved ether out of causal matter. To this original Matter Sankhya gives the name of Prakriti, while Vedanta & Buddhism, admitting the term Prakriti, prefer to call it Maya. But Prakriti is not in itself sufficient to explain the origin of the universe; another force is required which will account for the activity of Prakriti in Pradhana or original substance. This force is Purusha or Spirit. It is the presence of Purusha and Prakriti together, says Sankhya, that can alone account for cosmic evolution.

Vedanta agrees and emphasizes what Sankhya briefly assumes,
— that Purusha & Prakriti are themselves merely aspects, obverse and reverse sides, of a single Supreme entity or Self of
Things. Buddhism, still more trenchant, does away with the
reality of Purusha and Prakriti altogether and regards Cosmic
Evolution as a cosmic illusion.

The necessity for positing another force than Prakriti arises
from the very nature of Prakriti and its operations. The fundamental characteristic of Prakriti as soon as it manifests is eternal motion, — motion without beginning, without end, without
limit, without cessation or respite. Its cosmic stir is like an
eternally troubled ocean, a ceaseless rush, foam and clamour
of perpetual restlessness, infinite activity. And the rapidity, the
variability, the unimaginably complex coincidence and simulta-
neousness of different rates and forms of motion in the same material, in the same limits of space and time, are such as to baffle
realization. We can only realize it in sections by picking the web
of Nature to pieces and regarding as separable and self-sufficient
what are really simultaneous and coincident motions. The first
result of this infinite complexity of motion is an infinite mutability. Wherever we turn our eyes, there is something evolving and
developing, something decaying and disintegrating. Nothing at
this moment is precisely what it was the moment before; every
ripple in the sea of Time means a disturbance however small in
the coincident sea of Space, a change however infinitesimal in
the condition of the largest or most apparently stable parts of
Nature as well as of the minutest or most volatile. Causality,
infinite and without beginning or end, cannot cease from its
perpetuity of persistent action, its infinite progression of effects
which are the causes of other effects, causes which are the effects
of other causes; it is an endless chain, moving through Space &
Time, working in Substance, forged by an eternal and indefinable
Energy. And this eternal motion and mutability means inevitably
an infinite multiplicity. Every inch of Space is thronged with an
infinite variety of animate and inanimate existences, countless in
number, multitudinous in kind, myriadly various in motion and
action. An infinite multiplicity of motions make up the world

creating endless variety of substance, form, function; an infinite multiplicity of change is the condition of its activity. Remove this eternal motion, eternal mutability, eternal multiplicity from the idea of Prakriti and we arrive at something we cannot recognize, an inactive energy, an immaterial substance. Without motion, Time, Space, Causality, as things in themselves, cease to be. We are face to face with blank void and nothingness — or else, since this is unimaginable and impossible, we must suppose something which cannot cease to be, an absolute Infinity undivided by Space or Time, an absolute Immutability unconditioned by cause and effect, an absolute Stillness unaffected by the illusive mobilities of Energy, an absolute Spirit ultimately real behind the phenomenon of substance.

If we do not accept this transcendental reality, we must suppose that an eternal Prakriti with eternal motion, mutability, multiplicity as its characteristics is the Alpha & Omega of existence. But a consideration of the Universe does not justify our resting secure in that hypothesis. In this eternal motion there is something perpetually stable, in this eternal mutability a sum and reality which is immutable; in this eternal multiplicity an initial, persistent and final Unity. Eternal motion in itself would lead to nothing but eternal chaos and confusion. We know that the Cosmos is made up of an infinite number of motions simultaneously occupying the same Space and simultaneously existent in the same substance; but the result is not clash or confusion, but harmony. In other words, the condition of this unending motion is an eternal stability. Everywhere we see variety of motion resulting in a harmonious balance, in the orbits of the revolving planets round the moving sun woven into one solar system we have a striking instance out of myriads of this law which governs every object and every organism. There is therefore not only the mobile Prakriti, but something else which is eternally stable.

Eternal mutability, likewise, can lead to nothing but eternal unrest and disorder. What is it that imposes an unchanging law of persistence and orderly development on this mass of infinitely shifting, unquiet and impermanent parts and combines into one harmony this confused strife of changing and interchanging phenomena? In its details the universe is restlessly mutable, momentarily changing, in its broad masses it is more fixed and permanent, in its sum it is immutable. The class is less mutable and impermanent than the man, the community than the class, the race than the community, mankind than the race; and so it is with all existences. The parts change, the whole persists. And it is well known that while matter goes through infinite changes of form, its sum never changes; unincreasing it develops, undiminishing it disintegrates. But not only is the sum of things immutable, the laws of their development are immutable; phenomena vary but the law governing them remains the same, and for this reason that the nature of things is immutable. Whatever the variety of forms, the thing in itself preserves its characteristics and remains unchanged. Electricity works in various shapes and in many activities, but it is always electricity preserving its true characteristics whatever work it may do or whatever body it may wear and always working and changing under the fixed laws of its being which cannot change. Electricity again is only one form and function of the igneous element which takes many forms, but in all of them preserves its true characteristics and its own law of work. We see therefore that the parts are impermanent, the whole permanent; forms of things change, the reality is immutable. The condition of this unending mutability and impermanence is an eternal immutability and permanence. There is therefore not only this mutable Prakriti, but something else which is eternally immutable.

The apparent multiplicity of the Universe is equally deceptive. For the very condition of this infinite multiplicity, is a persistent Unity which precedes it and towards which it moves. There are many substances, but they are all evolutions from one substance; one seed disposes itself in many forms. There are many laws governing the workings of that substance in its evolution but they resolve themselves into one law to which all existence is subject. As substances and forms develop, there seem to be many things with many natures, but they go back into one thing with one nature. There are many forms of electricity, but all resolve themselves into the one substance electricity; there are many forms of the igneous element, of which electricity is one, but they all resolve themselves into one igneous element; there are many elements besides the igneous, but they all resolve themselves into one causal and universal substance. This is the bottom fact of the universe; all complexities and varieties resolve themselves into a precedent simplicity, and all simplicities into an original Unity. There is therefore not only this ever-multiplying Prakriti, but something else which is eternally One. In this mobile, mutable, multitudinous Prakriti, there is then a persistent element which is stable, immutable and one. We have arrived again at that One infinitely Immutable, Immobile Sum and Reality of Things which is Parabrahman.

Materialistic Analysis insists however that the eternal unity, immutability and immobility supporting and making possible the eternal multiplicity, mutability and motion are themselves characteristics of Eternal Matter. They are the two opposing lines of force whose action and reaction preserve the equibalance of cosmic existence, but the eternal reality in which they act is not spiritual but material. For material energy working in material substance is quite enough to explain all the evolutions of Nature and these in themselves make Eternal Matter. Hindu thought, however, has always been unable to accept this conclusion because its analysis of cosmic existence has convinced it that substance and energy are not things in themselves, but merely phenomena. Substance increases with density until it reaches its highest expression in solid physical matter; but as it is analysed and resolved nearer and nearer to its origin, its density becomes less and less, its tenuity increases, it becomes more and more unsubstantial, until, on the farther brink of causal matter, it disappears into something which is not substance. Moreover, when examined it appears that substance is really another term for energy; the conditions of density and tenuity which constitute material substance, correspond with the conditions of motional intensity and vagueness which constitute material energy. As, therefore, matter is resolved nearer and nearer to its origins, energy like substance becomes less and less intense, its vagueness increases until it comes to a standstill or rather dissipates in something which is not energy. The conclusion is irresistible that substance and energy are merely a single phenomenon with a double aspect, and that in the origin of things this phenomenon, to which we may give the name of Matter, does not exist. The question remains, into what do substance and energy disappear? out of what were they born? We are confronted again with the necessity of choosing between the unimaginable impossibility of blank void and nothingness, for which we have no warrant in reason or experience, or the One, Immutable, Immobile, Infinite and Eternal Reality which is Parabrahman. This Supreme Entity is not matter, we have seen. But it may be argued that it cannot be certainly called Spirit, since it is so absolute an entity as to be indefinable except by negatives. Vedanta concedes this caution, asserting only that Parabrahman is not a negative entity, but an eternal and positive Reality, defined by negatives simply because it is not expressible to the finite intellect, and containing in itself the unity of Spirit and Matter, which is neither material nor spiritual.

One argument remains open to material Analysis. Granted Parabrahman as the reality of things, yet phenomenal existence itself is purely material and there is no need to call in the assistance of any other and different entity. For material energy in material substance is sufficient to explain all phenomena. Hindu thought holds however that it is not sufficient to explain the ultimate phenomena of Consciousness. At the beginning of material evolution matter is in itself inanimate, consciousness, to all appearance, non-existent. How and whence, then, did it appear? By the interaction of the three *gunas* inherent in Prakriti, reception, reaction, retention. But the interaction of the three *gunas* did not create Consciousness, they only liberated it from the dense obscuration of gross matter. For if consciousness were not involved in Matter, it could never be evolved from it. For if it be evolved from matter as an entirely new birth, it must be either some already existent material substance in a new form — say, some kind of gas or electricity, or it must be a new substance formed by the union of two or more substances, just as water is formed out of hydrogen and oxygen. No such gas or electricity has been discovered, no such new substance exists. Indeed the evolution of a mighty, reasoning, aspiring, conquering, irrepressible Consciousness, capable of something like omnipotence and omniscience, out of mere material gases and chemical substance is a paradox so hardy, so colossally and impossibly audacious that mankind has rightly refused to accept it even when advanced with the prestige of Science and her triumphant analysis and the almost irresistible authority of her ablest exponents to support the absurdity. Christian theology was inconsistent enough when it degraded man to the dust as a worm and clod, yet declared him capable of divinity by the easy process of belief in an irrational dogma; but the materialistic paradox, which lodges no hidden angel in the flesh, is even more startling, more naked, more inexorably irrational. Man, says materialistic Science, is an utterly insignificant unit in the universe; the infinitesimal creature of a day, he lives his short span of life and is then decomposed into the gases out of which he was made. He derives his mind, body and moral nature from his brother the chimpanzee and his father the gorilla. In his organism he is merely a mass of animalculae which belong individually to the lowest stage of animal life; but by combining into a republic with the cells of the brain as a sort of despotic senate or council, these undeveloped forms of life have been able to master the world. What has not this republic of animalculae, this Rome of protoplasms, been able to effect? It has analysed the elements; it has weighed the suns and measured the orbits of the stars; it has written the dramas of Shakespeare, the epics of Valmekie and Homer and Vyasa, the philosophies of Kant and Shankara; it has harnessed the forces of Nature to do its bidding; it has understood existence and grasped the conception of infinity. There is something fascinatingly romantic and interesting in the conception and it is not surprising that the human intellect should have been captured for a while by its cheerful audacity. But how long can unreason prevail? Even if we regard man as a limited being and take what the race has done for the utmost measure of what the individual can do, the disproportion between the results achieved and the means supplied by this theory is too great to be overlooked. It was inevitable that the religions formerly crushed down and almost smothered by the discoveries of Science, — even those creeds most philosophically insufficient and crude, — should be raising their heads and showing an unexpected vitality. Science prevailed for a time over religion by exposing the irrationalities and prejudices which had overgrown and incrusted spiritual truth. But when it sought to replace them by a more astounding irrationality than any religion had been guilty of and began to contract its own hard crust of dogmas and prejudices, it exposed itself to an inevitable reaction. Mankind for a time believed because it was incredible at the bidding of theologians who ruled reason out of court; the experiment is not likely to be repeated for long on the authority of scientists who profess to make reason their judge.

If it be still contended that, however paradoxical, consciousness is the result of impressions and vibrations in the brain, or that consciousness is merely a material energy manifested at a particular intensity of ethereal vibration, like light or sound, the answer is that consciousness operates more powerfully when the brain is quiescent and unimpressed from without and survives cellular decomposition, and that when energy is quiescent and ether dissolved into its origin, consciousness abides. To the Hindu mind this is an insuperable obstacle to the acceptance of the material origin of consciousness. From its long acquaintance with Yoga and the results of Yoga, it has learned that conscious Will in the human body can not only override the laws of gross physical matter and come appreciably nearer, within its sphere, to omnipotence and omniscience, but that this conscious Will can impose absolute quietude on and detach itself from the animalcule republic which is erroneously supposed to originate and contain it and that it does, as a habitual law of Nature, survive the disintegration of the body. These two facts are fatal to the materialistic theory and, so long as the practice of Yoga subsists in India, the Hindu mind will never accept materialism. For they show that, although undeniably consciousness is evolved out of gross matter, it can only be because it was involved into gross matter by a previous downward evolution; it is not being created, it is being merely liberated from its prison. Neither can consciousness be taken as a function of subtle matter; for just as it can exist apart from and survives the disintegration of its gross body, so also it can exist apart from and survives the disintegration of its subtle body. Before subtle matter evolves, consciousness preexists in causal matter; and after subtle matter dissolves, consciousness survives in causal matter. And since matter at the stage of causality neither functions, nor evolves, consciousness is not a function or evolution of causal matter, but other and different from it. It is clear therefore that from the first appearance of matter, consciousness operates coevally with it, but is not dependent on it for its origin.

X.

Original consciousness, as distinct from Matter, is termed Spirit. Spirit must never be confused with the apparent manifestations of it, which are merely the action and reaction of Matter and Spirit on each other. The characteristics of true Spirit can be determined by distinguishing what is essential, characteristic and permanent in consciousness throughout all its stages from what is merely condition, form or function of consciousness affected by the medium in which it is working. There are three such characteristics which appear rudimentarily the moment consciousness itself appears and seem more and more pronounced as liberated Spirit develops to its highest self-expression. The first of the trio is the impulse of existence, the will to preserve self, to survive and be, not merely temporarily but unendingly. Showing itself at first physically in the instinct of self-preservation and the instinct of self-reproduction, it develops psychically in the desire to outlast death and become "immortal" by whatever way, by a book, a song, a picture, a statue, a discovery, an invention, an immortal act or remembered career no less than by psychical persistence of personality after the death of the body, and it culminates spiritually in the Will to surmount both death and life and persist eternally and transcendentally. The second characteristic of consciousness is the capacity of knowledge or awareness, the Will to know. Showing itself at first physically in sensation and response to external objects, it develops psychically in personality with memory, its basis, and understanding, reason and intuition, its superstructure, and culminates spiritually in self-knowledge and the awareness of one's own eternal and unabridged reality. The third characteristic of consciousness is the emotion of pleasure in existence, primarily in one's own, sympathetically in all existence, the Will to enjoy. This is the most powerful and fundamental of emotions, — so powerful as to persistently outlast all the pain and struggle which the hampered existence of Spirit in Matter brings to the personality. Showing itself physically at first in mere sense-pleasure and the clinging to life, it develops psychically in the emotions of love and joy, and culminates spiritually in the delight of our psychical personality in contact with or entering into the impersonal existence of our real and infinite Self. These three characteristics constitute the conception of Spirit, which by throwing its will-to-be, its power of awareness and its delight in existence into the medium of Matter sets evolution going. This is what Sankhya philosophy means when it says that Purusha imparts activity to Prakriti by its mere presence or propinquity without thereby becoming itself active. Spirit remains what it essentially is, pure existence, consciousness and delight; it is Prakriti that vibrating to the touch of this conscious delight in existence, begins to act, to move, change and evolve. The limitations of consciousness, the phenomena of consciousness are merely phenomenal results of the vibrations of Prakriti in Consciousness and not changes in Spirit itself. Purusha is the eternally immutable, immobile and singly real condition of Universal Evolution; Prakriti in action is its eternal motion, mutability, multiplicity.

Sankhya does not go beyond this conclusion which it finds sufficient for its purposes; it considers Purusha and Prakriti to be both ultimate eternal entities in the Supreme Reality and their propinquity a satisfactory explanation of the Universe. Vedic philosophy, going deeper, was driven both by philosophical reasoning and the ultimate experience of Yoga to the conception of the one Supreme Entity transcending the distinction between

Spirit and Matter, Purusha and Prakriti, which are merely its
noumenal self-expressions. Nor could Vedanta be satisfied with
mere propinquity as a sufficient explanation of the manner in
which immutability, stability and unity continually interpene-
trate, surround and govern the infinite motion, mutability and
multiplicity of Matter, still less of the manner in which Purusha
identifies itself with the merely phenomenal changes of consciousness. But if Spirit informs, conditions and governs Matter,
just as energy informs, conditions and governs substance, it
would be possible for it to impress its own nature on the motions
of Prakriti at every point of its evolutions without itself moving
and acting. And if Spirit and Matter are not entirely different
and separate entities but various expressions of a single supreme
Ens, Matter a noumenon of apparent self phenomenally evolving
as substance and energy, Spirit, a sense of Its real self supporting and therefore pervading and conditioning phenomena, it is
then not only possible but inevitable that Spirit should be so
constantly and closely aware of the perpetual activity of Matter
as to attribute that activity to itself. In this interpretation of the
Universe Vedanta consummated its analysis.

Time, Space, Condition reposing in the sense of actual Infinity and Immutability, — this is Prakriti, Origin-of-Matter working in Spirit; and all philosophic analysis of existence must
inevitably culminate in this noumenon; for without it the Universe as it is, cannot be conceived; it is the very condition of
thought and knowledge; it is the ultimate fact of cosmic existence. The triune noumenon of Time, Space, Condition or, in one
word, Prakriti, immediately generates the noumenon of motion
characterized by change and relation of parts and we have at
once motion, mutability, multiplicity operating in the Infinite
and Immutable. The triune noumenon of motion, mutability,
multiplicity or, in one word, Energy generates the noumenon
of substance moving, changing, relatively shifting in the Infinity
and Immutability of Spirit. The noumenon of energy-substance
constitutes Pradhana, original matter, and nothing farther is
needed for the evolution of the cosmos. Prakriti with its evolution Pradhana is the material cause of the Universe; the presence

of Spirit containing, supporting and pervading Prakriti and its evolutions is the efficient cause of the Universe.

Noumenon leads naturally to phenomenon. Consciousness and Existence in the Eternal Self being one, every noumenon of Consciousness must translate itself into an Existence of which the Consciousness is aware. The conception of Time, Space, Condition creates the appearance of Time, Space, Condition by that fundamental power of Consciousness which shows itself physically as formation, psychically as imagination and spiritually as Avidya, the power of conceiving what is Not-Self. The conception of motion creates the appearance of energy at work. The conception of motion-intensity as substance creates the appearance of matter worked upon. All Matter is phenomenal; all evolution the result of Avidya. Spirit is not phenomenal, but owing to its continual immanency in matter, attributes phenomenal existence to itself, so creating the phenomenon of soul or spirit working in matter. Thus Cosmos originates.

It will be seen that in this explanation of the Universe Spirit is taken as nearer to the Supreme Reality of things than Matter; it is not absolutely the real Self of things, but it is the noumenon or sense of the real Self persisting throughout all the obscurations of Avidya. This view is triply necessitated by the truths of elemental, psychical & spiritual evolution. When we consider the relations of Spirit to elemental matter, we see that as the obscuration of Matter thickens, Spirit becomes more and more concealed until, in gross inanimate matter, it is utterly covered in; but as the obscuration of Matter lessens, Spirit is more and more liberated until in the origin of things Matter seems a mere appearance in the reality of Spirit. It is therefore through Spirit and not through Matter that we are likely to get nearest to the Supreme Reality. So too, when we study our psychical evolution and follow Consciousness in its progressive liberation until it becomes Will in causal matter, we find it characterized in this last stage by the Will to be, the Will to know, the Will to enjoy; and when we get behind will and matter to our pure unconditioned Self, we still envisage Consciousness as pure existence, awareness and bliss. But our pure unconditioned Self is, we have seen, the

Reality of Things unaffected by Prakriti or its phenomena. We may therefore safely conclude that so far as the Supreme Reality can be positively envisaged by us in its purity, it is envisaged as existence, awareness, bliss, — in terms of Spirit and not of Matter. Lastly, when we analyse the evolution of Purusha in its three States, we find that it consists in the reflection of Prakriti as if by the Spirit. Spirit follows Prakriti through her three stages of material evolution, informing and sustaining them and mirrors their changes in itself as the changes of the sky may be mirrored in a clear and motionless pool; but the changes of the sky are not changes in the water. Purusha is immutable, immobile and One, just as the Supreme Reality is immutable, immobile and One. Purusha or Spirit is therefore the noumenon of the true Self, Prakriti the noumenon of not-Self or apparent Self. It is in this true Self of Parabrahman that the evolutions of apparent Self take place. In It Matariswan ordereth the waters.

XI.

Long and difficult to follow as has been this account of the Nature of Things according to Vedic philosophy, it was necessary so that we might understand minutely and comprehensively the meaning of these two verses, which in the second chapter of this book we could only adumbrate. The verses describe Parabrahman in Its truth with respect to the Cosmos, not in the absolute reality which is Its truth in Itself, but at the same time they indicate that it is the absolute and real Self of things which manifests in the Cosmos and not any Other, for there is no Other. It is anejad Ekam, the *One* who moveth not. The root *ejri*, as Shankara points out, means to shake or vibrate, and the reference is obviously to those vibrations of Prakriti on the tranquil surface of Self which are the beginning and cause of matter and its evolutions. But the Self does not vibrate and is not affected by the vibrations of Prakriti, even when It is supporting the cosmos and seems to be moving in it. Throughout it remains the One and is not broken up into multiplicity; even when by its immanence in many forms it seems to be many. These opening words of the first verse identify the One Immutable Immobile Infinity called Self or Spirit in the Cosmos with the Supreme Entity, Parabrahman.

This Supreme Entity which, as Self or Spirit, is immobile and one, is yet, without moving, swifter than thought. Swiftness implies motion; but the motion of Spirit in Cosmos is the illusory motion we see in the landscape as it whirls swiftly past the quiet watcher in the railway-carriage. The individual Self in Man is the watcher in the train, the train is Prakriti, the landscape the Universal Self in the Cosmos. The watcher is not moving, the landscape is not moving; it is the train which is moving and carries the sitter with it. In this second phrase of the verse the Parabrahman is identified with the Supreme Will in the Cosmos which without lifting a finger or stirring a foot creates and encompasses the Universe. This Supreme Will is simply Self or Spirit envisaging itself as the immanent Cause and Director of cosmical evolution in matter. The Will does not move but causes and conditions the infinitely complex cosmic motions; the Will does not act, but causes and determines actions; the Will does not divide or multiply itself, but plays with the multiplicity of cosmic forms and energies and impresses or mirrors itself in each. Being essentially the Self, it is, like the Self, One and Immobile, but as seen in the moving Cosmos, pervading, informing and governing it, It is, even in its motionlessness, swifter than thought.

The Gods could not reach It going in front. In the terminology of the Upanishads the Gods are the Potencies of the Universe which govern the Mind and the Senses in the microcosm Man and the Elements and their manifestations in the macrocosm Universe. Brahman, the One, precedes all these multiple potencies. It existed before they came into being and is therefore beyond their grasp. The rapid and stupendous effects of Will, omnipotent and omniscient, are such that the Mind, Sight, Hearing, all the senses together cannot comprehend their origination; limited and finite, they cannot grasp that which transcends limit. To the finite intelligence reasoning within prescribed limits it appears that there is no Will in action; all that happens and becomes is the inevitable working of material cause and effect, or of the Elements combining and working on each other. But Will is the cause of Causation and the disposer of Effect; Will preceded and dictated the workings of the Elements and arranged their combinations beforehand. This is He that from years sempiternal hath ordered perfectly all things. But the mind and senses cannot come near to and apprehend the nature of the Will or realize the how of its workings, because the mind and the senses can only understand what is done through their instrumentality or within the elemental medium to which they are limited and confined. They can analyse the physical forces of Nature and formulate the laws under which they work; they can dissect thought and sentiment and classify the mental functions and the laws of reasoning. But Brahman, the Will, they cannot reach and analyse; for He does not work through them, nor does He act in phenomena. He has arranged the motions of Prakriti beforehand, from years sempiternal; He has mapped out the law of those motions before ever they began to stir; and He now abides concealed in them, not acting but simply by His presence necessitating that the Law shall be observed and His dispositions followed. Will creates effects, outside Time, Space and Condition in a way the Mind cannot comprehend, by *Iccha* or Wish, in other words, by Itself. Will by Will necessitates phenomena in Itself, atmanyatmana. But when Prakriti translates Will into phenomena in the terms of Time, Space, Causality, she does it under limitations and by limited instruments. The preordainment was immediate, unhindered and perfect, but the carrying out seems to be slow, imperfect and the result of ceaseless effort and struggle, a web of failures, incomplete realizations and transient successes, a maze of forces acting and reacting on each other, helping, hindering and repulsing and always with a partial and mechanical or only half-intelligent action. Somehow a result is worked out, progress is made, but nowhere is there any finality or completeness, nowhere the repose of consummation. This incompleteness is an illusion created by the nature of finite Consciousness. The Mind and the Senses, through whom we become aware of the workings of the Universe, are themselves limited and imperfect; functioning only under limits and with effort they cannot envisage the work accomplished except in parts and with a restricted, disturbed and broken vision. To see life steadily and see it whole is only permitted to a Perfect and Infinite Consciousness standing outside Time, Space and Conditions. To such a divine Vision the working out of preordainment may present itself as a perfect, immediate and unhindered consummation. God said, "Let there be Light" and, straightway, there was Light; and when the Light came into being, God saw that it was good. But to the imperfect finite consciousness, Light seems in its inception to have come into being by a slow material evolution completed by a fortuitous shock of forces; in its operation to be lavished with a prodigal wastefulness since only a small part is used for the purposes of life; in its presentation to be conveyed to a blinking and limited vision, hampered by obstacles and chequered with darkness. Limitation, imperfection, progression and retrogression are inseparable from phenomenal work, phenomenal intelligence, phenomenal pleasure and satisfaction. To Brahman the Will who measures all Time in a moment, covers all Space with one stride, embraces the whole chain of causation in one glance, there is no limitation, imperfection, progression or retrogression. He looks upon his work as a whole and sees that it is good. But the Gods cannot reach to His completeness, even though they toil after it; for ever He outruns their pursuit, moving far in front.

Brahman, standing still, overtakes and passes the others as they run. While the Mind and Senses pressing onward through Time, look before and after and see sections of the past and dim apparitions of the future from the standpoint of their moment in the present, the Will from its position beyond the beginning of the past speeds beyond them into the future and to the end of things. It has in that moment apprehended, decided and accomplished in Itself all that is to be and leaves the mind and senses to toil after It and work out the preordained ideas and forms left impressed on the mould of that future which to It already exists. It does this standing still, because to the Will Past, Present and Future are but one moment and It lives in all of them simultaneously; they do not contain Brahman but are contained in Him. The Mind and senses hasten through Space, measuring the distance between star and star; but the Will passes them, traverses Space from one end to the other, knows it as a Whole and creates in Itself all its forms present, past and future; it leaves the Mind and senses to gather slowly, toilfully and by parts the single comprehensive knowledge It acquired without any process and to experience under the law of Time the immediately complete Universe It has perfected without any labour. It does this also standing still, for to Brahman here and there do not exist; all is here, since He is not in Space, but Space is in Him. While the Mind and senses run in the winding & twisted line of causation, the Will from the beginning of the chain passes them and has in a moment formed and surveyed it to its very end; It leaves them to count out the chain link by link by the imperfect aid of reason, piecing what is past to what is to come, and to trace out by the slow and endless process of work generating work and life generating life the complete and single Evolution which is already a predestined and therefore an accomplished fact. This too It does standing still; for to Brahman there is no succession of cause and effect, since cause and effect exist simultaneously in the Will; cause does not precede Him nor effect follow, but are both embraced in the single and mere existence of Himself as Will.

In It Matariswan ordereth the waters. We have here Brahman in a third relation to Cosmos. Brahman is the stable and immutable Unity which is immanent in the Cosmos as its real self of existence, awareness and bliss and which supports all phenomenal objects and forces as their omnipresent substratum of reality. Secondly, Brahman, this immobile Unity, is also, as Will, that which stands still and is yet swifter than mind and the potencies of mind; for Will, the Ordainer, Disposer and Cause, traverses all Time, Space and Causation, without motion, by the mere fact of being. Lastly, Brahman, this Self and Omnipresent Lord of things, is also that which contains all evolution and determines every object and force evolved by Prana out of original matter. Brahman is Vaisvanor, the Waking Self, in whom is contained and by whom exists all this evolution of physical world; Brahman is Taijasa, the Dream Self, in whom is contained and by whom exists all the psychical evolution from which the physical draws its material; Brahman is Prajna, the Sleep Self, in whom all evolution psychical & physical is for ever self-existent and preordained; Brahman is the Turiya Atman in whom and by whom Prajna-Taijasa-Vaisvanor are. He pervades the Cosmos and contains the Cosmos, as ether pervades the earth and contains the earth, and not only the Cosmos as a whole but every particular object and force in the Cosmos. This tree is pervaded and surrounded by the Divine Presence, — not, be it clearly understood, by a part of It but by Brahman one and indivisible. The presence of God is as complete in one small flower as in the whole measureless Universe. So also the Spirit in man is not a fragment of Deity, but the Eternal Himself in His imminuable majesty. The Self in me is not merely a brother to the Self in you or of one kind with it but is completely and utterly yourself; for there is no you or I, but One Eternal Immutable in many names and forms, One Reality in many transient and perishable frames.

XII.

It moves, It moveth not; It is far, the same It is near; It is within all this, the same It is outside all.

This second verse only brings out more emphatically what is implied in the first or presents the same truth from a slightly different standpoint. Brahman moves or vibrates, and Brahman does not move or vibrate. As the One Immutable and Immobile, He does not move, but He moves as mobile and multiple Prakriti. When it is said that Brahman is One and Unmoving, it is not meant that the mobile and multiple element in the Universe is other than Brahman; the Gods who cannot reach Brahman, whom He precedes and outstrips, are yet appearances of Himself; Matariswan and the Waters, whom He contains, are also of His substance. Purusha alone is not Brahman, Prakriti also is Brahman; for He is not only the efficient cause of His Cosmos, but its material Cause as well. It is true that the motion and multiplicity of Prakriti are phenomenal and superficial, the stability and immutability of Purusha fundamental and real; but the phenomenal has a truth and existence of its own and is not utterly unreal. To take the suggestive human parallel, Shakespeare in himself is one and immutable, in his creations he is mutable and many; the personages of his dramas and their words and actions are not Shakespeare in the ultimate truth of himself, yet they are not other than Shakespeare; for they live in him, by him and are of his substance. It is easy to say they are unreal, but they have a reality of their own; they are true psychical images and live as phenomena in the consciousness of Shakespeare though not as separate and independent entities. So also the multiple Cosmos has a true phenomenal existence and reality in the Brahman, though no separate existence as independent entities. The tree and the river are not real as tree and river, but they are real as images, eidolons of the Brahman. In Himself He is calm, quiescent and unmoved, in them He moves and energises.

It is far and It is at the same time near. Physically near and far; the Sun and the distant constellations and Orion and Aldebaran and Lyra and whatever utmost star glitters on the outermost mesh of this network of suns and systems, all that is Brahman; and equally this earth which is our dwelling-place, and this country which is our mother and nurse, and this village or city in which we live and do business, and this house which shelters us, and these trees and tanks which were part of our childhood, and the faces we familiarly know and the voices we daily hear, all in which we habitually live and move, all this is Brahman. Emotionally & mentally near and far; for our love and our hatred, and what we love and hate, things forgotten and things remembered, things we cherish until death and things we put from us with loathing, friend and enemy, injurer and injured, our work and the daily web of our fears and hopes and longings, this is Brahman; and that which is so far from us that it cannot stir a single emotion or create a ripple of sensation in the mind, whether because it is remote in the distance of Time or hidden in the distance of Space or lost to the blindness of indifference, that too is Brahman. Intellectually near and far; for the unknown and the little known, that which is too vast or too small for us to perceive, or which our most powerful instruments cannot bring near to us or our keenest reasonings analyse or our widest comprehension embrace, that is Brahman; all we daily perceive and note, the myriad forms that Science analyses, the delight of the eye and ear and taste and smell and touch, this is Brahman; and the subjective world in ourselves which is nearest to us of all, thought and memory and sensation and feeling, volitions and aspirations and desires, these too are Brahman. Spiritually near and far; for the Omniscient and Omnipotent Cause and Ruler who creates universes with the indrawing of its breath and destroys universes with its out-throwing, beside whom we feel ourselves to be too vile and weak and feeble to partake even infinitesimally of His divine nature, that is Brahman; the ineffable and unimaginable Spirit whom our senses cannot perceive, nor our minds comprehend, nor our reason touch, that is Brahman; and our own Self who eternally enthroned in the cavern-heart of our being, smiles at our pleasures and pains, mighty in our strength, as mighty in our weakness, pure in our virtues, unstained by our sins, no less omniscient and omnipotent than Isha, no less calm, immutable and ineffable than the Supreme Being, — this our Self too is Brahman. The Karmayogin who has realised it, must hold all existence divine, all life a sacrament, all thought and action a self-dedication to the Eternal.

It is within all this, It too is without all. Brahman is within the whole Universe; every object however inanimate, every form of life however vile, is brim-full with the presence of God. The heathen who worships stocks and stones has come nearer to the truth of things, than the enlightened professor of "rational" religion, who declares God to be omnipresent and yet in the next breath pronounces the objects in which He is present to be void of anything that can command religious reverence. There is no error in "idolatry"; the error is in the mind of the idolater who worships the stone as stone and the stock as stock, thinking that is God, and forgets or does not realise that it is the Divine

Presence in them which is alone worship-worthy. The stock or
the stone is not God, for it is only an eidolon, a symbol of His
presence; but the worship of it as a symbol is not superstitious
or degrading; it is true and ennobling. Every ceremony which
reminds us of the presence of the Eternal in the transient, is,
if performed with a religious mind, a spiritual help and assists
in the purification of consciousness from the obscuration of
the senses. To the ordinary intelligence, however, the idea of
Brahman's omnipresence, if pushed home, becomes a stumbling-
block. How can that which is inert, senseless and helpless be full
of that which is divine and almighty? Is it not a sacrilege to
see Him in what is vile and repulsive? Is it not a blasphemy to
envisage Him in the vicious and the criminal? Hence the popular
Manicheanism which pervades every religion; hence the persistent idea of a twofold creative power, God and devil, Ormuzd
and Ahriman, Allah and Iblis, the one responsible for all that
is good, the other for all that is evil. This kind of spiritual and
intellectual weakness loves to see God in everything good and
pleasant and beautiful, but ignores Him in what is evil, ugly or
displeasing. But it is an imperfect religion which thus yields to the
domination of the mind and senses and allows them to determine
what is or is not God. Good is a mask and evil is a mask; both
are eidola, valid for the purposes of life in phenomena, but when
we seek that which is beyond phenomena, we must resolutely
remove the mask and see only the face of God behind it. To the
Karmayogin there should be nothing common or unclean. There
is nothing from which he has the right to shrink; there is none
whom he can dare to loathe. For God is within us all; as the
Self pure, calm and eternal, and as the Antaryamin or Watcher
within, the Knower with all thought, action and existence for
His field of observation, the Will behind every movement, every
emotion, every deed, the Enjoyer whose presence makes the pain
and pleasure of the world. Mind, Life and all our subjective
consciousness and the elements of our personal existence and
activity, depend on His presence for the motive-force of their
existence. And He is not only within us, but within all that is.
What we value within ourselves, we must not belittle in others;

what we cherish within ourselves, we must not hurt in others; what we love in ourselves, we must not hate in others. For that which is within us, is the Divine Presence, and that which is in others, is the same Divine Presence. To remember this is worth all the moral teachings and ethical doctrines in the world. Vedanta has been declared by those who have not chosen to understand it, a non-moral or even immoral philosophy. But the central truth of Vedanta enfolds in a single phrase all the highest ethics of the world. Courage, magnanimity, purity, justice, charity, mercy, beneficence, loving kindness, forgiveness, tolerance, all the highest demands that the most exalted ethical teacher can make on humanity are contained in that single doctrine; and find in it their one adequate philosophical justification and sole natural basis.

That is not only within all this, It is also outside all. We have already seen that Brahman is outside all in the sense of containing the Universe and not only pervading but surrounding every object with His presence. He is also outside in the sense that He is apart from it and other than it. He is not confined in Time, Space and Condition, but is quite above and outside Time, Space and Condition: Cosmos is within Him only as the shadow of a cloud is in the water; He is in Cosmos only as the water is in the shadow and causes and contains the shadow; but He is not the Cosmos in His nature or in His substance any more than the water is in nature or substance the shadow. The Cosmos exists in Him phenomenally and as a transient appearance, just as the shadow exists phenomenally in the water and after a time passes away. But there is this difference that the appearance in the water is the shadow of something else cast from outside, but the Cosmos is a shadow or eidolon of Himself created by Brahman in His own being. The materialistic Pantheism so natural to the sense-dominated intelligence of the West, is not Vedanta. God is not in nature or substance His Universe; but the Universe is He phenomenally and as a manifestation. Spirit-Matter is Brahman, but Brahman is not Spirit-Matter. This distinction must be carefully kept in mind or the doctrine of entire identity between Brahman and the Self of Things, may lead to disastrously false conclusions. The truth that Brahman is in all this, must be carefully balanced by the truth that Brahman is outside it all.

Yet to the Karmayogin the negative side of this dual truth is only necessary as a safeguard against error and confusion; it is the positive side which must be his inspiration. In its light the whole world becomes a holy place and all cause of fear or grief or hatred disappear, all reason for selfishness, grasping, greed and lust are eliminated, all excuses for ignoble desire or ignoble action are taken away. In their stead he receives the mightiest stimulus to self-purification and self-knowledge, which will lead him to the liberation of the divine in himself, to that subdual of the bodily and vital impulses which disciplines the body into the triune strength of purity, abstemiousness and quietude; to courage, magnanimity, justice, truth, the four elements of strength; and mercy, charity, love, beneficence, the four elements of sweetness, making that harmony of perfect sweetness & strength which is perfect character, to a mind, pure of passion and disturbance and prepared against the delusions of sense and the limitations of intellect, such a mind as is alone capable of self-knowledge. In this disciplined body, a perfect heart and a pure mind he will have erected a fitting temple for the Eternal within him in which he can offer the worship of works to the Lord and of selflessness to the Self. For by that worship he will become himself the Lord and find release from phenomenal life into the undisturbed tranquillity of the Spirit. The dictum, Theos ouk estin alla gignetai, God is not but is becoming, has been used to express the imperfect evolution of the cosmos but is better applied to the present spiritual progress of humanity. In the race the progress is still rudimentary, but each man has that within him which is empowered to fulfil his evolution and even in this life become no longer an animal, or a mind, a heart, an intellect, but the supreme and highest of all things — Himself.

Book III.

Chapter I.

"But he who sees all creatures in his very Self and the Self in all creatures, thereafter shrinketh not away in loathing. He who discerneth, in whom all creatures have become Himself, how shall he be deluded, whence shall he have sorrow in whose eyes all are one?"

In these two stanzas the Upanishad formulates the ethical ideal of the Karmayogin. It has set forth as its interpretation of life the universality of the Brahman as the sole reality and true self of things; all things exist only in Him and He abides in all as the Self. Every creature is His eidolon or manifestation and every body His temple and dwelling-place. From Him all things began, in Him they develop and mature themselves, to Him they must in their nature strive to return. The mutual relations of all beings to each other may be summed up in the single phrase, "One Self in all creatures, all creatures in one Self"; for He is both within all and contains all. But this Self exists in each creature not partially or fragmentarily but in Its indivisible completeness. Therefore the Self in one creature is precisely the same as the Self in another, not merely kin by origin as in the Christian theology, not merely of the same kind and nature as in the Sankhya teaching, but absolutely identical. The sense of personal separation in space and substance and difference in nature has been illusorily brought about by the play of Prakriti, the noumenon of false self, on the one eternal Reality, creating an illusion of multiplicity and mutability. Self identifies itself with the phenomena of the evolved universe; habitually feeling the play of the three gunas, the principles of material reception, reaction and retention, on the body, the vital impulses, the mind, the intellect, the supra-intelligence it mistakes the continuity of conscious impressions for the real self, forgetting that these are merely aspects of consciousness in relation to matter and not the true and eternal reality of consciousness. But the end of evolution is to liberate the permanent from the impermanent, the spiritual from the material, the Self from its bondage to the three gunas and the false conceptions which that bondage creates. This liberation or release must therefore be the final aim of religion and ethics, otherwise religion and ethics will be out of harmony with the truth of things and therefore false or imperfect. Religion and ethics must train the individual self in a man to discover its universality, to see himself in all creatures and all creatures in himself, and the ideal or ethically perfect man is the one who has attained to this vision and observes it habitually in his thoughts and actions as the one law of his life.

In order to realize this vision, it has been found by experience that a man must attain freedom from the lower impulses which identify the body and the vital impulses with self; he must practise cleanliness and purity in mind, body and speech, — abstinence from gross gratifications and freedom from the domination of passions and desires; indifference to cold, heat, hunger, thirst, fatigue and other affections from external influences. In other words he must be completely master of his own body. The Christian virtue of purity, the Pagan virtue of endurance, lie therefore at the very root of Vedantic morality.

To see oneself in others is impossible without completely identifying oneself with others; a perfect sympathy is essential and perfect sympathy brings with it perfect love, perfect charity and forgiveness, perfect pity for sin and suffering, perfect tolerance, a universal benevolence with its counterpart in action universal beneficence. The Jivanmukta, the Rishi, the sage must be, by their very nature, sarvabhutahitarata; men who make it their business and pleasure to do good to all creatures, not only all men, but all creatures, — the widest possible ideal of universal charity and beneficence. To do as one would be done by, to love your enemies and those who hate you, to return good for evil are the first ethical inferences from the Vedantic teaching; they were fully expressed in their highest and noblest form by Buddhism five hundred years before they received a passionately emotional and lyrical phrasing in Judaea and were put widely into practice in India more than two thousand years before Christian Europe took even slightly to heart what it had so long been professing with its lips. And not only perfect love and beneficence, but perfect justice with its necessary counterpart in action, honest dealing and faithful discharge of duty are the natural outcome of the Vedantic teaching. For if we see ourself in others, we shall not only be willing but delighted to yield them all that is due to them and must shrink from wronging or doing hurt to them as naturally as we would shrink from doing hurt to ourselves. The debts we owe to parents, family, friends, the caste, the community, the nation we shall discharge not as an irksome obligation, but as a personal pleasure. The Christian virtue of charity, the Pagan virtue of justice are the very sap and life of Vedantic morality.

Seeing the Self in all creatures, implies seeing the Lord everywhere. The ideal man of Vedanta will accept pain as readily as pleasure, hatred, wrong, insult and injustice as composedly as love, honour and kindness, death as courageously as life. For in all things he will see the mighty Will which governs the Universe and which wills not only his own good and pleasure and success, but the good and pleasure and success of others equally with his own; which decrees that his own good and the good of others shall be worked out not only by his victories and joys, but by his defeats and sufferings. He will not be terrified by the menace of misfortune or the blows dealt him by man or nature, nor even by his own sins and failures, but walk straight forward in the implicit faith that the Supreme Will is guiding his steps aright and that even his stumblings are necessary in order to reach the goal. If his Yoga is perfect, his faith and resignation will also be perfectly calm and strong; for he will then fully realize that the Supreme Will is his own Will. Whatever happens to me, it is I that am its cause and true doer and not my friend or enemy who is merely the agent of my own Karma. But the faith and resignation of the Karmayogin will not be a passive and weak submission. If he sees God in his sufferings and overthrow, he will also see God in his resistance to injustice and evil, a resistance dictated not by selfishness and passion, but undertaken for the sake of right and truth and the maintenance of that moral order on which the stability of life and the happiness of the peoples depend. And his resistance like all his actions will be marked by a perfect fearlessness, a godlike courage. For when a man sees God in all things and himself in all beings, it is impossible for him to fear. What is it that can cause him terror? Not danger or defeat, not death or torture, not hatred or ingratitude, not the worse death of humiliation and the fiercer torture of shame and disgrace. Not the apparent wrath of God Himself; for what is God but his own self in the Cosmos? There is nothing that he can fear. The Christian virtue of faith and resignation, the Pagan virtue of courage are the strong stem and support of Vedic morality.

The ignorant censure of Vedanta as an immoral doctrine because it confuses the limits between good and evil or rejects the one necessary motive to action and virtue, proceeds from unwillingness or inability to understand the fine truth and harmony of its teachings. Vedanta does indeed teach that virtue and vice, good and evil are relative terms, things phenomenal and not real; it does ask the seeker to recognize the Supreme Will in what is evil no less than in what is good; but it also shows how the progression of the soul rises out of the evil into the good and out of the good into that which is higher than good and evil. Vedanta does reject the lower self of desire as a motive to action and virtue, but it replaces it by the far more powerful stimulus of selflessness which is only the rising to our higher and truer Self. It does declare phenomenal life to be an illusion and a bondage, but it lays down the practice of courage, strength, purity, truth and beneficence as the first step towards liberation from that bondage, and it demands a far higher standard of perfection in these qualities than any other creed or system of ethics. What to many moralists is the highest effort of feeble human nature is to Vedanta only the first imperfect manifestation of the divine self in humanity. Vedanta embraces, harmonizes and yet overtops and exceeds all other moralities; as Vedic religion is the eternal and universal religion, so is Vedic ethics the eternal and universal morality. Esha dharmah sanâtanah.

II. Ethics in primitive society.

Every system of ethics must have a sanction to validate its scheme of morals and an aim which will provide man the stimulus he needs, if he is to surmount his anti-ethical instincts and either subdue them or eradicate. Man is not a purely ethical being; he has immoral and nonmoral impulses which are primarily stronger than his ethical tendencies. To check the former, to liberate, strengthen and train the latter is the first object of all practical ethics religious or non-religious. The first requisite to this end is a true knowledge of human nature and its psychology; for if an ethical system is psychologically untrue, if it is seriously mistaken in its view of human nature or fails to discern and reach his highest and noblest instincts, it will either be ineffective or possibly even do as much harm as good to the moral growth of humanity. But even a psychologically sound morality will not command general assent in practice unless there is a sanction behind it which the reason or the prejudices of mankind will accept as sufficiently strong to make a necessity of obedience. Armed with such a sanction it will influence the thoughts and the thoughts the actions of the race, but even then it will be only a repressive and disciplinary influence; to be an active stimulus or powerful moral lever it must be able to set in our front an aim which will enlist strong natural forces on the side of virtue or an ideal which will appeal to instincts deepseated and persistent in universal humanity.

In its origin it is more than probable that morality was a social growth and limited to communal habits and communal necessities. The aim set before the individual was the continued privilege of abiding in the community and enjoying all-important advantages of security, assistance and social life which membership of the community could alone provide. The sanction was again a communal sanction; the custom-code of the tribe or community commanded assent and obedience precisely because it was the tribe and community that commanded and could enforce them with severe social punishments, death, ostracism, excommunication. This origin of ethics from the customs of the tribe, themselves originating from the fundamental necessities of self-preservation, is warranted by the facts of sociology as rendered by modern investigation. It agrees also with the view of nature and evolution held by the Vedic inquirers. For if we consider the history of communities and nations so far as we know them, we shall find that it consists so far in a progression from the society to the individual in society, from a basis of tamas to an outgrowth of rajas in the tamasic basis; while sattwa perfected in a few individuals, is, as a social force, not yet emancipated.

We have seen that Prakriti or nature in all its operations works through three inherent *gunas* or qualities which repeat themselves in all stages and forms of her multifold activity; they are present as much in psychic and spiritual evolution as in the physical; and so all-important are they that all activity of any kind whatsoever, all life mental, vital, physical are said to be merely the natural operation of the three *gunas* interacting upon each other. These three *gunas* are called in the Sankhya terminology *sattwa, rajas, tamas*; comprehension, activity, passivity, or as they manifest in physical substance, retention, active reaction and passive reception. None of these *gunas* can exist or act by themselves; the activity of each involves the activity of the other two; but according as one or the other predominates, an action, a state of things, a substance, a character, is called tamasic, rajasic, or sattwic. In the early stages of upward evolution tamas predominates, in the medial rajas, in the final sattwa. In the early evolution of man it is inevitable, therefore, that the obscuration of tamas should be very heavy and that the characteristic of passive receptivity to outside surroundings should be markedly predominant. Early man is active only under the pressure of hunger, or when moved by the primitive impulses of sense and vitality and the needs of self-preservation. His senses are keen and his power of activity great because keen senses and a strong, hardy, agile body are necessary to self-preservation; but in the absence of necessity or stimulus he is profoundly indolent, even inert. His sensibility, physical or mental, is small, for sensibility depends on and increases with rajas, the power of reaction and this power is in the savage comparatively undeveloped. His emotional reactions are also weak and primitive; in their predominantly physical character and in the helpless spontaneousness of their response to impressions they reveal the domination of tamasic passivity. The centres of individuality, a characteristically sattwo-rajasic function, are too weak as yet to control, regulate and rationalize the response. Hence the emotional nature shows itself on one side in a childishly unruly gratification of the pleasure of pleasant impressions, — the savage is easily mastered by gluttony and drunkenness but also capable of childlike worship and doglike fidelity when brought into close contact with a higher nature; on the other it is manifested in a brutally violent response to unpleasant impressions. Anger is the primitive reaction to an unpleasant impact which is not unfamiliar, fear the primitive reaction to an unpleasant impact which is new and surprising. The savage is therefore prone to childish terror in presence of the unknown, to ferocious anger and vindictive cruelty when his hatred is aroused by injury or the presence of what, though not unfamiliar in form, is alien and therefore hateful in its features. The habit of self-indulgence in anger by an organization of great passivity and low physical and mental sensibility creates the characteristic of a quiet unimpassioned cruelty, — the savage is, as a rule, calmly cruel. The Red-Indian's stoicism, impassivity, immobility, quiet endurance of pain are merely the inertia of the tamasic mind and body systematized and become part of his tribal morality. But the height of passivity is reached in his intellectual organization of which the only strong reaction is the primitive mental response to outside impressions, curiosity. This curiosity is different from the desire to know, for it consists in a childish amused wonder and a desire merely to repeat the experience, not to learn from it. Such curiosity is at the root of the practice of torture; for the primitive mind finds a never-failing delight in the physical response evoked by intense and violent pain. This pleasure in crude physical, moral, aesthetic or intellectual reactions because of their raw intensity and violence is a sure sign of the undeveloped tamasic mind and is still common enough in the most civilized communities. Originality and independence of mind and character spring from a strong rajasic development and are therefore unknown to the savage who is the creature and slave of his environments. By far the most powerful and insistent of these environments is the community in which he lives and which is necessary to him at every turn for his security and his self-gratification. His passive mentality therefore not only accepts but welcomes rigid control by the community; it receives the hereditary custom-law of the tribe as an inviolable natural law, and has too weak an individuality to react against it or to desire change and progress. The primitive community is therefore stationary; the individual exists in it not as an individual, but as an undetachable fragment of the whole. The social organization, even at its best, is in type and level on a par with that of the beehive and the ant-hill.

The tamasic state of society reaches its highest development when the community, entirely outgrowing the attractions of the nomadic instinct, settles down to a fixed habitation for centuries and adds to its original reason for existence, — communal self-preservation, — the more fruitful impulse towards communal accumulation. It has then the necessary condition for progress from the tamasic stage to the sub-tamasic in which the individual first begins to emerge although he is still subordinated to the community and lives chiefly for the general advantage, not for his own. The settled state of society and the expansion of the community which a more prosperous and stable life brings with it, involve an increasing complexity of the social organization. Specialization of function becomes pronounced, for the larger needs of the community demand an increasing division of labour. Rank and private property begin to emerge; inequality has begun. The more various activities, the more varied experience, the less primitive range of desires and the need of a wider knowledge of things and men create a greater mental alertness and increased mental differentiation. This in its turn means the growth of individuality. Personality, we have seen, has memory for its basis and is determined by memory; individuality or difference of personality is originally created by difference in the nature and range of the impressions experienced and retained by the mind, which naturally results in different habits of emotional and mental reaction. The fundamental self in all men is the same, the action of external Prakriti in its broad masses is the same all over the world; therefore human personality is necessarily the same in its general nature wherever we meet it. Difference in personality arises purely from difference in the range of mental and emotional experience; from the different distribution of various kinds of experience, and from differently developed habits or ways of reaction to impressions received. For character is nothing but habit; and habit is nothing but an operation of memory. The mind remembers that it received this particular impact before and reacted on it in this particular way and it repeats the familiar experience. The repetition becomes a habit of the mind ingrained in the personality and so a permanent characteristic. Difference of experience thus creates difference of personality, and difference of experience depends on difference in life, pursuits, occupations. So long as life is bounded by the desires of alimentation, self-preservation and self-reproduction, there can be no real individuality within the species, for the processes required and the experiences involved in these functions are practically the same for each member of the species. Even the gratification of primitive sensuous desires does not involve anything more than minute and unnoticeable differences. Hence one savage very much resembles any other savage just as one animal of a species very much resembles another of the same species, and one savage community differs from another only as one animal sub-species differs from a kindred sub-species. It is only when desires and needs multiply, that difference of life and occupation can bring difference of experience and develop individuality. The increasing complexity of the community means the growth of individuality and the liberation of rajas in the human psychology.

Rajas is the principle of activity and increases with the intensity and rapidity of the reactions of Will upon external things; it is not content like tamas with passively receiving impressions and obeying its environments, but seizes on the impressions and strives ever to turn them to the service of individual personality, to master its environments and use them for its own enjoyment. Everything which it experiences, it utilizes for the pleasure and pain of the individuality. The rajasic man is the creator, the worker, the man of industry, enterprise, invention, originality, the lover of novelty, progress and reform. The growth of rajas therefore necessarily meant the inception of a great problem for society. In the tamasic and sub-tamasic states man develops the all-important faculty of conservatism, reverence for the past, fidelity to the communal inheritance, subordination of the interests and passions of the particular, be it class or individual, to the stability and safety of the whole. But here was a new element likely to disturb and upset the old state of things. The rajasic individuality was not likely to accept the traditional sanction, the communal aim as a satisfying aim and a binding sanction. The more and more he developed, the more and more strongly it would crave for the satisfaction of its expanding individual desires, ideas, activities with less and less regard to the paramount importance of social stability. How should society deal with this element? From that single difficulty arose the whole sociological problem involving difficulties of ethics, legislation and politics which after so many thousands of years mankind has not solved to its permanent satisfaction.

Chapter III. Social Evolution.

In the early stages of the sub-tamasic state the question was not so acute, for differentiation in the society was not at first very complex; it proceeded upon broad lines, and as soon as it took definite form, usually as a result of intermixture with alien elements, it developed classes or castes, the priest, the warrior, the people, — merchant, tiller or artisan — and the thrall or servant. Character developed at first more on these broad lines than by individual irregularities, in types rather than in persons; for each kind of life, each broad line of pursuits and occupations would naturally mean the same general range of experience and the same habits of reaction to external impressions and so evolve broad developments of character falling into caste-types, within whose general predominance personal idiosyncrasy would be at first comparatively ill-developed and of minor importance. The priest-type would develop favourably in the direction of purity, learning, intellectual ability and acuteness, unfavourably in the direction of jealous exclusiveness, spiritual and intellectual pride, a tendency to trade on the general ignorance. The warrior type would evolve courage, honour, governing power as its qualities, arrogance, violence and ruthless ambition as its defects. The earning class would develop on the one side honesty, industry and enterprise, on the other desire of gain. Obedience and fidelity would be the virtues of the thrall. Society accommodating itself to the altered circumstances modified its single and rigid social morality and admitted the validity of the newly-formed habits of mind and action as within the caste to which it properly belonged. Thus arose the ethical phenomenon of caste morality. Outside the limits of the caste ethics the general social code remained in full force. As the life of the individual in the community expanded in extent and became more varied and complex in content, the social custom-code also became more complex in its details and wider in its comprehensiveness, in its attempt to pursue him into every detail of his life and control not only his broad lines of life but his particular actions, allowing no distinction between private and public life. Its nature had not changed; it was as rigid and inexorable in its demands, as intolerant of individual originality and independence; its sanctions were unaltered, the ancestral tradition of the community and the fear of social punishments, death, ostracism, excommunication or other penalties which if less drastic were yet sufficiently formidable. The object to be fulfilled was still predominantly the same, the satisfaction of communal demands as the price of communal privileges.

In this attempt society could not permanently succeed and had either to abandon it or to call in the aid of other forces and stronger sanctions. The community grew into the nation; social divisions became more intricately complex, the priest-class breaking up into schools, the warriors into clans, the people into guilds and professions; the organization was growing too vast in size, too intricate in detail. Class began to push its individual claims against class, individuals began to question the old sanctions or doubt the sacredness of tradition. In small villages the old tyranny of society might be possible, in great towns it must necessarily become increasingly lax and ineffective. Above all, as the individual's mental life became enriched and vigorous, society found itself baffled by an insurmountable difficulty; it could control his outward acts by its rigour, but it could not ultimately control his mental and spiritual life, yet this inner life psychical and spiritual tended irresistibly to master and mould outer physical actions. No sanction by which society could enforce its decrees, is of any ultimate utility against the victorious advance of the individual life pressing forward in its irresistible demand for progress and freedom. Society may command the homage of conformance in speech and act to its fixed and conventional ideals; it may control a man's bodily organs; it has no jurisdiction over his heart and mind or only so much as he chooses to allow it. But speech and act cannot long remain divorced from the heart and mind without affecting the soundness of society itself by a dry rot of hypocrisy and falseness; the end of which is either the decay and death of the community or a purifying revolt. Society can save itself only by conceding within limits the claim for individual freedom; outside those limits it must persuade or compel him to conformity by influencing his mind and heart, not by direct coercion of his words and acts.

In the later stages of the subtamasic social period we find that society has to a less or greater extent contracted its demands on the individual. Over his inner life and a certain part of his conduct, it exercises no other coercive influence than that of social disapproval expressed but not enacted; over another part of his conduct it exercises the right of enacting that disapproval in the shape of ostracism or excommunication; but that part of his life which most strongly concerns the community, it still insists on regulating by the infliction or menace of social penalties more or less severe. Social disapproval unenacted is, however, an ineffective control over mind and spirit. Society therefore, by no means content to leave the inner life of the individual free from the demands of its moral code, since any such abdication of its rule would lead, it instinctively felt, to moral anarchy, sought to dominate the individual intellect and imagination by the more radical process of education. Its view of life and its unwritten code of customs, manners, traditions had always been naturally accepted as sacrosanct, now the individual was consciously habituated and trained from his childhood to retain this impression of venerable and inviolable sanctity. Social morality was no longer unwritten but gathered into codes and systems of life associated either with the names of the primitive makers of the nation or with the deified or half-deified historic individuals who first harmonised and perfected its traditionary ideals and routine of life and expressed the consciousness of the race in their political or ethico-legal systems. Such were Lycurgus, Confucius, Menes, Manu. For in those days individual greatness and perfection commanded a sacred reverence from the individual consciousness, because in each man it was to this greatness and perfection that individuality impelled to achieve its complete emancipation was painfully striving forward. Thus in the subtamasic state even at its highest development the social code retained its sacrosanct character in the new form of a consciously cherished and worshipped national tradition; and the repositories of that tradition became the dominant class of the community, whether an oligarchy as in Sparta and early republican Rome or a theocracy as in Egypt. For in order to control not only the heart and imagination but the deepest self in the individual society called in the aid of a spiritual force rapidly growing in its midst, the power of religion. In some communities, it strove even to give the religious sanction to all its own ideas, traditions, demands, sanctions.

In the older races and nations Mongolian, Dravidic, Mediterranean the subtamasic stage of social culture was of long duration and has left its impress in the only civilizations which have survived unbroken from that period, the Indian and Chinese. In the younger races, Aryan and Semitic, the development of the individual was far more rapid and urgent and left no time for the peculiarities of the later subtamasic period to crystallize and endure. Their evolution passed quickly into the rajaso-tamasic or even into the rajasic stage. In the rajasic state the individual forces himself into predominance and gets that emancipation and free play for his personality which his evolution demands, while the society degenerates into a mere frame for a mass of individuals. Social morality, once so rigid and compelling, dissolves into a loose bundle of superstitions and prejudices; tradition is broken into pieces by the desire for progress & novelty and free play of mind. The individual is governed in his conduct not by social sanctions or religious obligations and ideals, but by his personal idiosyncrasy and the stress of his own ideas, desires, passions, capacities and ambitions, which clamantly demand satisfaction. Individual originality being given free rein, there is an immense outburst of genius, talent, origination, invention or of splendid personal force and activity. Periods such as the revolutionary epoch in France when the rajasic element gets free play and communities like the Ionian democracies of which Athens was the head and type, are not only the most interesting from their fascinating abundance of stir, passion, incident, brilliance of varied personality, but also among the most fruitful and useful to humanity. In such periods, in the brief history of such communities the work of centuries is done in a few years or in a few decades and future ages are fertilized from the seeds of a single epoch. But the history of rajasic communities is necessarily brief, the course of rajasic periods is soon run. Rajas has in itself no principle of endurance; if it is to work steadily and enduringly, it must either be weighted down by a heavy load of tamas or sustained and uplifted by a great strength of sattwa. But sattwa as a social force has not yet liberated itself; it operates on society through a chosen and select few and is only rudimentary as yet in the many. For the preservation of a people tamas is absolutely necessary; a mass of blind conservatism, intolerance of innovations, prejudice, superstition, even gross stupidity are elements essential to the safety of society. The Athenian thinkers themselves dimly realized this, hence their dislike to the mobile spirit of old democracy and their instinctive preference for the Spartan constitution in spite of its rigid, unprogressive and unintellectual character. They felt the transience and insecurity of the splendid and brilliant life of Athens. Politically the predominance of the individual was dangerous to the state and the evil might be checked but could not be mended by occasional resort to ostracism; the excessively free and varied play of intellect turned out a corrodent which too rapidly ate away the old beliefs and left the people without any fixed beliefs at all; the old prejudices, predilections, superstitions were exposed to too rapid a tide of progress: for a time they acted as some feeble check on the individual, but when the merciless questioning of Socrates and his followers crumbled them to pieces, nothing was left for society to live by. Reason, justice and enlightened virtue which Socrates and his successors offered as a substitute, could not take their place because the world was not, nor is it yet sattwic enough for society to subsist entirely or mainly by the strength of reason, justice and enlightenment. The history of Athens may be summed up from the Vedic standpoint as rajas too rapidly developed destroying tamas and in its turn leading to a too rapid development of sattwa; till by an excess of the critical and judging faculty of sattwa, the creative activity of rajas was decomposed and came to an end. As a result the Athenian social organism lost its vitality, fell a prey to stronger organisms and perished.

Those communities have a better chance of survival which linger in the rajaso-tamasic stage. For that is a social period when the claims of the individual are being constantly balanced and adjusted in a manner which strongly resembles the replacement in the physical organism of waste tissue by sound, bad blood by good, corrupted breath by fresh inhalations; the individual is given legitimate scope, but those irreducible demands of society which are necessary to its conservation, are thoroughly enforced; progress is constantly made, but the past and its traditions are, as far as is consistent with progress, jealously preserved and cherished. England with its rapid alternations of progress safeguarded by conservatism and conservatism vivified by progress is an excellent example of the rajaso-tamasic community. The English race is preeminently rajaso-tamasic; tamasic by its irrational clinging to what it possesses not because it is inherently good or satisfying but simply because it is there, because it is part of its past and its national traditions; tamasic by its habit of changing not in obedience to any inner voice of ethical aspiration or sense of intellectual fitness but in answer to the pressure of environment; but rajasic by the open field it gives to individual character and energy, rajasic by its reliance on the conflicts and final balance of passions and interests as the main agents of progress and conservation political and social. Japan with her periods of splendid and magnificently fruitful progress and activity when she is absorbing new thoughts and new knowledge, followed by periods of calm and beautiful conservation in which she thoroughly assimilates what she has absorbed and suits it to her system, — Japan with the unlimited energy and personality of her individuals finely subservient to the life of the nation is an instance of a fundamentally rajaso-tamasic nation which has acquired by its assimilation of Indian and Chinese civilisation the immortalizing strength of sattwa.

Sattwa is present indeed in all communities as a natural force, for without it nothing could exist; but as a conscious governing strength, it exists only in India and China. Sattwa is physically the principle of retention which instead of merely reacting to impressions retains them as part of its inner life; it is therefore the natural force which most helps consciousness to develop. As rajogune is the basic principle of desire, so sattwagune is the basic principle of knowledge. It is sattwa that forms memory and evolves judgment. Morally it shows itself as selfless sympathy, intellectually as disinterested enlightenment and dispassionate wisdom, spiritually as a calm self-possessing peacefulness as far removed from the dull tamasic inertia as from the restless turbidity of rajas. The growth of sattwa in a community will show itself by the growing predominance of these characteristics. The community will be more peaceful and unaggressive than the ordinary rajasic race or nation, it will present a more calm and unbroken record of culture and enlightenment, it will record its life-history not in wars and invasions, not in conquests and defeats, not by the measure of the births and deaths of kings and the downfall of dynasties but by spiritual and intellectual evolutions and revolutions. The history of tamasic nations is a record of material impacts thrown out from the organism or suffered by it; its life is measured by the duration of dynasties or outward forms of government. The history of rajasic nations is a bundle of biographies; the individual predominates. The history of sattwic nations would be the story of the universal human self in its advance to knowledge and godhead. Most of all, the sattwic leaven will show itself in an attempt to order society not to suit material requirements or in obedience to outward environments or under the pressure of inward passions and interests, but in accordance with a high spiritual and intellectual ideal applied to life. And until *sattwa* is fully evolved, the community will try to preserve all the useful forces and institutions gathered by the past social evolution, neither destroying them nor leaving them intact, but harmonising and humanising them by the infusion of a higher ideal and vivifying them from time to time by a fresh review in the light of new experience and wider knowledge. The sattwic nation will avoid the dead conservatism of tamasic communities, it will avoid the restless progress of rajasic nations; it will endeavour to arrive at a living and healthy stability, high, calm and peaceful, in which man may pursue undisturbed his nobler destiny.

The true sattwic community in which life shall be naturally regulated by calm wisdom, enlightenment and universal sympathy, exists only as an Utopia or in the Aryan tradition of the Sattwayuga, the Golden Age. We have not evolved even the rajaso-sattwic community in which the licentious play of individual activity and originality will be restrained not by the heavy brake of tamasic indolence, ignorance and prejudice, but by the patient and tolerant control and guidance of the spirit of true science, sympathy and wisdom. The farthest advance made by human evolution is the sub-rajaso-tamasic stage in which sattwa partially evolved tries to dominate its companions. Of this kind of community China, India and more recently Japan are the only known instances. In China the tamasic element is very strong; the passionate conservatism of the race, the aggregativeness of the Chinese character which seems unable to live to itself and needs a guild, an organization or some sort of collective existence to support it, the low physical and emotional sensibility which permits the survival of a barbarous and senselessly cruel system of punishment, are striking evidences of prevalent tamas. The rajasic element is weaker but evident enough in the religious, intellectual and, in one sense, political liberty allowed to the individual and in the union of Mongolian industry and inventiveness with the democratic individualism which allows every man the chance his individual capacity and energy deserve. Sattwa finds its place in the high place immemorially assigned to wisdom, learning and culture and in the noble and perfect Buddhist-Confucian system of ethics and ideal of life which regulates Chinese politics, society and individual life. In India on the other hand, as we shall perceive, we have an unique and remarkable instance of sattwic, rajasic, tamasic influences acting upon the community in almost equal degrees and working at high pressure side by side; tamasic constraint and conservatism governs the arrangement of daily life, rajasic liberty, progress and originality brilliantly abound in the affairs of the mind and spirit, a high sattwic ideal and spirit dominate the national temperament, humanise and vivify all its life, social polity, institutions and return almost periodically, a fresh wave of life and strength, to save the community when it appears doomed to decay and oblivion.

From sattwa springs the characteristic indestructibility which Chinese and Indian society, alone of historic civilizations, have evinced under the pressure of the ages and the shocks of repeated, even incessant national disaster. Sattwa is the principle of conservation. The passive tamasic organism perishes by decay of its unrepaired tissues or disintegrates under the shock of outward forces against which it has not sufficient elasticity to react. The restless rajasic organism dies by exhaustion of its too rapidly expended vitality and vigour. But sattwic spirit in the rajaso-tamasic body is the nectar of the gods which makes for immortality. China and India have suffered much for their premature evolution of the sattwic element; they have repeatedly undergone defeat and subjugation by the more restless and aggressive communities of the world, while Japan by keeping its rajasic energy intact has victoriously repelled the aggressor. At present both these great countries are under temporary obscuration, they seem to be overweighted with tamas and passing through a process of disintegration and decay. In India especially long continuation of foreign subjection, a condition abhorred by Nature and accursed by Heaven, has brought about disastrous deterioration. Conquering Europe on the other hand, for the first time flooded with sattwa as a distinct social influence by the liberating outburst of the French Revolution, has moved forward. The sattwic impulse of the 18th century, though sorely abused and pressed into the service of rajasic selfishness and tamasic materialism, has yet been so powerful an agent to humanize and illuminate that it has given the world's lead to the European. But these two great Oriental civilizations are not likely to perish; always they have conquered their conquerors, asserted their free individuality and resumed their just place in the forefront of the nations, nor is the future likely to differ materially from the past. So long as the sattwic ideal is not renounced, it is always there to renew itself in extremity and to save. Preeminently sattwic is the Universal Self in man which if realized and held fast to, answers unfailingly the call for help and incarnating in its full season brings with it light, strength and healing. "For the deliverance of the good and the destruction of evil doers, for the restoration of righteousness I am born from age to age."

Chapter IV. The place of Religion in ethics.

If the view of human development as set forth in the last two chapters is correct, we shall have to part with several notions long cherished by humanity. One of these is the pristine perfection of man and his degradation from his perfect state by falling into the domination of sin; God made man perfect but man by his own fault brought sin and death into the world. This Semitic tradition passed from Judaism into Christianity and less

prominently into Mahomedanism became for a long time part
and parcel of the fixed beliefs of half humanity. Yet it is doubtful
whether the original legend which enshrined and prolonged this
tradition, quite bears the interpretation which has been put on
it. If rightly understood, it supports rather than conflicts with
the theory of trigunic development. The legend does not state
that man was unfailingly virtuous by choice, but that he was
innocent because he did not yet know good and evil. Innocence
of this kind is possible only in the primitive state of man and
the description of man as naked and unashamed shows that it
is precisely the primitive state of society before arts and civilization were developed, to which the legend alludes. Man was then
innocent, because being unable to distinguish between good and
evil he could not choose evil of free choice and therefore had
no sense of sin and no more responsibility for his actions than
the pure animal. His fall from the state of innocence was the
result of the growth of rajasic individuality in his mind which
led him to assert his own will and desires and disobey the law
imposed on him by an external Power. In this first stage of
his evolution he is not guided by a law within himself, but by
prohibitions which his environment imposes on him without
his either understanding or caring to understand the reason for
their imposition. Certain things are forbidden to him, and it is as
much a necessity for him to refrain from them as to refrain from
putting his hand in the fire lest he should be burned; all others
are allowed to him and he does them freely without questioning
whether, apart from their legality, they are bad or good. Sin
comes by disobedience and disobedience by the assertion of an
inner standard as against the external standard hitherto obeyed;
but it is still a standard not of right and wrong, but of licit
and illicit. "What I desire, what my individual nature demands,
should be allowed me", reasons the rajasic man; the struggle
is between an external negation and an internal assertion, not
between two conflicting internal assertions. But once the former
begins, the latter must in time follow; the physical conflict must
create its psychical counterpart. From the opposition of pun-
ished and unpunished evolves the opposition of licit and illicit;

from the opposition of licit and illicit evolves the opposition of right and wrong. Originally the sanction which punishes or spares, allows or disallows, approves or disapproves, is external and social; society is the individual's judge. Finally, in the higher stage of evolution, the sanction is internal and individual; the individual is his own judge. The indulgence of individual desire in disobedience to a general law is the origin of sin.

With the rejection of this theory of an originally perfect humanity, the tradition of an infallible inner conscience which reflects a divinely-ordained canon of absolute right and wrong must be also rejected. If morality is a growth, the moral sense is also a growth and conscience is nothing more than activity of the moral sense, the individual as judge of his own actions. If conscience be a divine and infallible judge, it must be the same in all men; but we know perfectly well that it is not. The conscience of the Red Indian finds nothing immoral in murder and torture; the conscience of the modern civilised man vehemently condemns them. Even in the same man conscience is an uncertain and capricious quantity changing and deciding inconsistently under the influence of time, place and circumstances. The conscience of one age or country varies from the conscience of another age or country. It is therefore contrary to all experience to assert the divinity or infallibility of conscience. A man must be guided ordinarily by his moral sense, not because it is infallible or perfect, but because moral growth depends upon development from within and to this end the independent use of the "inner monitor", when once evolved, is the first necessity.

Ish and Jagat

The Isha Upanishad in its very inception goes straight to the root of the problem the Seer has set out to resolve; he starts at once with the two supreme terms of which our existence seems to be composed and in a monumental phrase, cast into the bronze of eight brief but sufficient words, he confronts them and sets them in their right & eternal relation. Ishá vásyam idam sarvam yat kincha jagatyám jagat. Ish and Jagat, God and Nature, Spirit and World, are the two poles of being between which our consciousness revolves. This double or biune reality is existence, is life, is man. The Eternal seated sole in all His creations occupies the ever-shifting Universe and its innumerable whorls and knots of motion, each called by us an object, in all of which one Lord is multitudinously the Inhabitant. From the brilliant suns to the rose and the grain of dust, from the God and the Titan in their dark or their luminous worlds to man and the insect that he crushes thoughtlessly under his feet, everything is His temple and mansion. He is the veiled deity in the temple, the open householder in the mansion; for Him and His enjoyment of the multiplicity & the unity of His being, all were created and they have no other reason for their existence. For habitation by the Lord is all this, everything whatsoever that is moving thing in her that moves.

The problem of a perfect life upon earth, a life free from those ills of which humanity seems to be the eternal and irre-deemable prisoner & victim, can only be solved, in the belief of the Vedantins, if we go back to the fundamental nature of exis-tence; for there alone can we find the root of the evil and the hint of the remedy. They are here in the two words Ish & Jagat. The Inhabitant is the Lord; in this truth, in the knowledge of it by our minds, in the realisation of it by our whole nature and being is the key of escape for the victim of evil, the prisoner of limitation and death. On the other hand, Nature is a fleeting & inconstant motion preserved by the harmonious fixity of the laws which govern its particular motions. This subjection and inconstancy of Nature is the secret of our bondage, death, limitation and suffering. We who entangle ourselves in the modalities of Nature, must, if we would escape from her confounding illusions, realise the other pole of our existence, unqualified Spirit or God. By rising to the God within us, we become free, liberated from the bondage of the world and the snare of death. For God is freedom, God is immortality. Mrityum tírtwá amritam asnute. Crossing over death, we enjoy immortality.

This relation of Nature & Spirit, World & God, on which the Seer fixes, Nature the mansion, God the occupant, is their practical, not their essential relation. Conscious existence is Brahman, single & indivisible; Spirit & Nature, World and God are one; anejad ekam manaso javíyas, — they are One unmoving swifter than mind. But for life, whether bound or free, and for the movement from bondage to freedom, this One must always be conceived as a double or biune term in which God is the reverse side of Nature, Nature the obverse side of God. The distinction has been made by Spirit itself in its own being for the object which the Seer expresses in the single word vásyam. God has thrown out His own being in the spatial & temporal movement of the Universe, building up forms in His mobile extended self-consciousness which He conceives as different from His still & eternal, regarding, occupying & enjoying self-consciousness, so that He as soul, the subject, may have an objective existence which it can regard, occupy & enjoy, the householder of its self-mansion, the god of its self-temple, the king of its self-empire. In this cosmic relation of Spirit to Nature the word Ishá expresses the perfect and absolute freedom, eternally uninfringed, with which the Spirit envisages its objects and occupies its kingdom. World is not a material shell in which Spirit is bound, nor is Spirit a roving breath of things ensnared to which the object it inspires is a prison-house. The indwelling God is the lord of His creations and not their servant or prisoner; as a householder is lord of his dwelling-places to enter them and go forth from them at his will and to pull down what he has built up whenever it ceases to please him or be serviceable to his needs, so the Spirit is free to enter or go forth from its bodies and has power to build, destroy and rebuild whatever it pleases in this universe. The very universe itself It is free at any moment to destroy and recreate. God is not bound; He is the free and unopposed master of His creations.

This word Ishá, the Lord, is placed designedly at the opening of this great strain of Vedantic thought to rule as with a master-tone all its rhythms. It is the key to everything that follows in the eighteen verses of the Upanishad. Not only does it contradict all mechanical theories of the Universe and assert the preexistence, omnipotence, majesty and freedom of the transcendent Soul of things within, but by identifying the Lord of the universe with the Spirit in all bodies it asserts the greatness, freedom and secret omnipotence of the soul of man that seems here to wander thus painfully entangled and bewildered. Behind all the veils of his nature, the soul in man also is master, not slave, not bound, but free. Grief, death and limitation are instruments of some activity it is here to fulfil for its own delight, and the user is not bound to his instruments; he can modify them, he can reject, he can change. If, then, we appear as though bound, by the fixed nature of our minds and bodies, by the nature of the visible universe, by the dualities of grief & joy, pleasure and pain, by the chain of cause and effect or by any other chain, shackle or tie whatsoever, the bondage is a semblance and can be nothing more. It is Maya, a willed illusion of bondage, or it is Lila, a self-chosen play at bondage. Like a child pretending to be this or that and identifying itself with its role the Purusha, this divine inhabitant within, may seem to forget his freedom, but even when he forgets, the freedom is still there, self-existent, therefore inalienable. Never lost except in appearance, it is recoverable even in appearance. The game of the world-existence is not a game of bondage alone, but equally of freedom & the liberation from bondage.

The Secret of the Isha

It is now several thousands of years since men ceased to study Veda and Upanishad for the sake of Veda or Upanishad. Ever since the human mind in India, more & more intellectualised, always increasingly addicted to the secondary process of knowledge by logic & intellectual ratiocination, increasingly drawn away from the true & primary processes of knowledge by experience and direct perception, began to dislocate & dismember the manysided harmony of ancient Vedic truth & parcel it out into schools of thought & systems of metaphysics, its preoccupation has been rather with the later opinions of Sutras & Bhashyas than with the early truth of Scripture. Veda & Vedanta ceased to be guides to knowledge & became merely mines & quarries from which convenient texts might be extracted, regardless of context, to serve as weapons in the polemic disputes of metaphysicians. The inconvenient texts were ignored or explained away by distortion of their sense or by depreciation of their value. Those that neither helped nor hindered the polemical purpose of the exegete were briefly paraphrased or often left in a twilit obscurity. For the language of the Vedantic writers ceased to be understood; their figures, symbols of thought, shades of expression became antique & unintelligible. Hence passages which, when once fathomed, reveal a depth of knowledge & delicacy of subtle thought almost miraculous in its wealth & quality, strike the casual reader today as a mass of childish, obscure & ignorant fancies characteristic of an unformed and immature thinking. Rubbish & babblings of humanity's nonage an eminent Western scholar has termed them not knowing that it was not the text but his understanding of it that was rubbish & the babblings of ignorance. Worst of all, the spiritual & psychological experiences of the Vedic seekers were largely lost to India as the obscurations of the Iron Age grew upon her, as her knowledge contracted, her virtue dwindled & her old spiritual valiancy lost its daring & its nerve. Not altogether lost indeed for its sides of knowledge & practice still lived in cave & hermitage, its sides of feeling & emotion, narrowed by a more exclusive & self-abandoned fervour, remained, quickened even in the throbbing intensity of the Bhakti Marga and the violent inner joys of countless devotees. But even here it remained dim & obscure, shorn of its fullness, dimmed in its ancient and radiant purity. Yet we think, however it may be with the Vedas we have understood & possess the Upanishads! We have understood a few principal texts & even those imperfectly; but of the mass of the Upanishads we understand less than we do of the Egyptian hieroglyphics and of the knowledge these great writings hold enshrined we possess less than we do of the wisdom of the ancient Egyptians. Dabhram evapi twam vettha Brahmano rupam!

I have said that the increasing intellectualisation of the Indian mind has been responsible for this great national loss. Our forefathers who discovered or received Vedic truth, did not arrive at it either by intellectual speculation or by logical reasoning. They attained it by actual & tangible experience in the spirit, — by spiritual & psychological observation, as we may say, & what they thus experienced, they understood by the instrumentality of the intuitive reason. But a time came when men felt an imperative need to give an account to themselves & to others of this supreme & immemorial Vedic truth in the terms of logic, in the language of intellectual ratiocination. For the maintenance of the intuitive reason as the ordinary instrument of knowledge demands as its basis an iron moral & intellectual discipline, a colossal disinterestedness of thinking, — otherwise the imagination and the wishes pollute the purity of its action, replace, dethrone it and wear flamboyantly its name & mask; Vedic knowledge begins to be lost & the practice of life & symbol based upon it are soon replaced by formalised action & unintelligent rite & ceremony. Without tapasya there can be no Veda. This was the course that the stream of thought followed among us, according to the sense of our Indian tradition. The capacity for tapasya belongs to the Golden Age of man's fresh virility; it fades as humanity ages & the cycle takes its way towards the years that are of Iron, and with tapasya, the basis, divine knowledge, the superstructure, also collapses or dwindles. The place of truth is then taken by superstition, irrational error that takes its stand upon the place where truth lies buried builds its tawdry & fantastic palace of pleasure upon those concealed & consecrated foundations, & even uses the ruins of old truth as stones for its irregular building. But such an usurpation can never endure. For, since the need of man's being is truth & light, the divine law, whose chief article it is that no just demand of the soul shall remain always unsatisfied, raises up Reason to clear away Superstition. Reason arrives as the Angel of the Lord, armed with her sword of doubt & denial (for it is the nature of intellectual Reason that beyond truth of objective appearance she cannot confidently & powerfully affirm anything, but must always remain with regard to fundamental truth agnostic and doubtful, her highest word of affirmation "probably", her lowest "perhaps"), — comes & cuts away whatever she can, often losing herself in a fury of negation, denying superstition indeed, but doubting & denying also even Truth because it has been a foundation for superstition or formed with some of its stones part of the building. But at any rate she clears the field for sounder work; she makes tabula rasa for a more correct writing. The ancient Indian mind felt instinctively — I do not say it realised or argued consciously — the necessity, as the one way to avoid such a reign of negation, of stating to the intellectual reason so much of Vedic truth as could still be grasped and justifying it logically. The Six Darshanas were the result of this mighty labour. Buddhism, the inevitable rush of negation, came indeed but it was prevented from destroying spirituality as European negation destroyed it for a time in the eighteenth & nineteenth centuries by the immense & unshakeable hold the work of the philosophers had taken upon the Indian temperament. So firm was this grasp that even the great Masters of negation — for Brihaspati who affirmed matter was a child & weakling in denial compared with the Buddhists, — could not wholly divest themselves of this characteristic Indian

realisation that subjective experience is the basis of existence &
the objective only an outward term of that existence.

But admirable & necessary as was this vast work of intellectual systemisation, subtle, self-grasped & successful beyond
parallel, supreme glory as it is now held and highest attainment
of Indian mentality, it had from the standpoint of Vedantic truth
three capital disadvantages.

Chapters for a Work on the Isha Upanishad

[1]

The Isha Upanishad

The Puranic account supposes us to have left behind the last
Satya period, the age of harmony, and to be now in a period of
enormous breakdown, disintegration and increasing confusion
in which man is labouring forward towards a new harmony
which will appear when the spirit of God descends again upon
mankind in the form of the Avatara called Kalki, destroys all
that is lawless, dark and confused and establishes the reign of
the saints, the Sadhus, those, that is to say, — if we take the literal
meaning of the word Sadhu, who are strivers after perfection.
Translated, again, into modern language — more rationalistic
but, again, let me say, not necessarily more accurate — this
would mean that the civilisation by which we live is not the
result of a recent hotfooted gallop forward from the condition
of the Caribbee and Hottentot, but the detritus and uncertain
reformation of a great era of knowledge, balance and adjustment
which lives for us only in tradition but in a universal tradition,
the Golden Age, the Saturnia regna, of the West, our Satyayuga
or age of the recovered Veda. What then are these savage races,
these epochs of barbarism, these Animistic, Totemistic, Naturalistic and superstitious beliefs, these mythologies, these propi-
tiatory sacrifices, these crude conditions of society? Partly, the
Hindu theory would say, the ignorant & fragmentary survival
of defaced & disintegrated beliefs & customs, originally deeper,
simpler, truer than the modern, — even as a broken statue by
Phidias or Praxiteles or a fragment of an Athenian dramatist is

*The six chapters comprising this work have been numbered [1] to [6] by the editors. Sri
Aurobindo's own chapter divisions have been reproduced as written in the manuscript.*

at once simpler & nobler or more beautiful and perfect than the best work of the moderns, — partly, a reeling back into the beast, an enormous movement of communal atavism brought about by worldwide destructive forces in whose workings both Nature and man have assisted. Animism is the obscure memory of an ancient discipline which put us into spiritual communion with intelligent beings and forces living behind the veil of gross matter sensible to our limited material organs. Nature-worship is another side of the same ancient truth. Fetishism remembers barbarously the great Vedic dogma that God is everywhere and God is all and that the inert stone & stock, things mindless & helpless & crude, are also He; in them, too, there is the intelligent Force that has built the Himalayas, filled with its flaming glories the sun and arranged the courses of the planets. The mythologies are ancient traditions, allegories & symbols. The savage and the cannibal are merely the human beast, man hurled down from his ascent and returning from the sattwic or intelligent state into the tamasic, crumbling into the animal and almost into the clod by that disintegration through inertia which to the Hindu idea is the ordinary road to disappearance into the vague & rough material of Nature out of which we were made. The ascent of man, according to this theory, is not a facile and an assured march; on the contrary, it is a steep, a strenuous effort, the ascent difficult, though the periods of attainment & rest yield to us ages of a golden joy, the descent frightfully easy. Even in such a descent something is preserved, unless indeed we are entirely cut off from the great centres of civilisation, all energetic spirits withdrawn from our midst and we ourselves wholly occupied with immediate material needs. An advanced race, losing its intelligent classes and all its sources of intelligence and subjected to these conditions, would be in danger of descending to the same level as the Maori or the Basuto. On the other hand individuals of the most degraded race — a son of African cannibals, for instance — could under proper conditions develop the intellectual activity and high moral standard of the most civilised races. The spirit of man, according to the Vedic idea, is capable of everything wherever it is placed; it has an infinite capacity both for the highest and the lowest; but because he submits to the matter in which he dwells and matter is dominated by its surrounding contacts, therefore his progress is slow, uncertain and liable to these astounding relapses. Such is the Hindu explanation of the world and, so expressed, freed from the Puranic language & symbols which make it vivid & concrete to us, I can find nothing in it that is irrational. Western thought with its dogmatic materialism, its rigid insistence on its own hastily formed idea of evolution, its premature arrangements of the eras of earth, animal and man, may be impatient of it, but I see no reason why we Hindus, heirs of that ancient and wise tradition, should so long as there is no definite disproof rule it out of court in obedience to Western opinion. We can afford at least to suspend judgment. Modern research is yet in its infancy. We, a calm, experienced & thoughtful nation, always deep & leisurely thinkers, ought not to be carried away by its eager and immature conclusions.

I will take this Puranic theory as a working hypothesis and suppose at least that there was a great Vedic age of advanced civilisation broken afterwards by Time and circumstance and of which modern Hinduism presents us only some preserved, collected or redeveloped fragments; I shall suppose that the real meaning & justification of Purana, Tantra, Itihasa & Yoga can only be discovered by a rediscovery of their old foundation and harmonising secret in the true sense of the Veda, and in this light I shall proceed, awaiting its confirmation or refutation and standing always on the facts of Veda, Vedanta & Yoga. We need not understand by an advanced civilisation a culture or a society at all resembling what our modern notions conceive to be the only model of a civilised society — the modern European; neither need or indeed can we suppose it to have been at all on the model of the modern Hindu. It is probable that this ancient culture had none of those material conveniences on which we vaunt ourselves, — but it may have had others of a higher, possibly even a more potent kind. (Perfection of the memory and the non-accumulation of worthless books might have dispensed with the necessity of large libraries. Other means of receiving information and the habit of thinking for oneself might have prevented the growth of anything corresponding to the news-paper, — it is even possible that the men of those times would have looked down on that crude and vulgar organ. Possibly the power of telepathy organised — it seems to persist disorganised, — in some savage races, — might make the telegraph, even the wireless telegraph unnecessary.) The social customs of the time might seem strange or even immoral to our modern sanskaras, — just as, no doubt, many of ours will seem incredible and shocking to future ages. The organisation of Government may have been surprisingly different from our own and yet not inconsistent with civilisation; there may have been a simple communism without over-government, large armies or wars of aggression, or even an entire absence of government, a human freedom & natural coordination such as Tolstoy & other European idealists have seen again in their dreams, — for it is at least conceivable that, given certain spiritual conditions which would constitute, in the language of religion, a kingdom of Heaven on earth or a govern-ment of God among men, the elaborate arrangements of modern administration, — whose whole basis is human depravity & the needs of an Iron Age, — would become unnecessary. The old tradition runs that in the Satyayuga there was neither the desire nor the need of modern devices; the organised arrangement of men's actions, duties and institutions by an external compulsion representing the community's collective will began in the Bronze Age with the institution of government in Kingship. The Vishnu Purana tells us, conformably with this idea, that Vishnu in the Satya incarnates as Yajna, that is to say as the divine Master in man to whom men offer up all their actions as a sacrifice, reserving nothing for an egoistic satisfaction, but in the Treta he descends [as] the Chakravarti Raja, the King & standing forward as sustainer of society's righteousness, its sword of justice & defence, its preserver of the dharma gathers a number of human communities under his unifying sway. But it is unnecessary to my present purpose to consider these speculations, for which much might be said and many indications collected. It is sufficient that an ancient society might differ in every respect from our modern communities and yet be called advanced if it possessed a deep, scientific and organised knowledge and if it synthetised in the light of large & cultured conceptions all human institutions, relations and activities. This is all with which I am here and at present concerned. For I have only to inquire whether we have not at any rate some part of such a profound and organised knowledge in the surviving Upanishads and the still extant Sanhitas of the Veda; — written long afterwards, mostly in the Dwapara & Kali when, chiefly, men sought the aid of the written word & the material device to eke out their failing powers & their declining virility of mind & body, we need expect from them no picture of that ancient civilisation, nor even the whole of its knowledge, for the great mass of that knowledge has been lost to us with the other numberless Sanhitas of Veda. The whole of it we cannot reconstitute, since a great mass of Vedic material has been lost to us, possibly beyond hope of recovery until Vishnu descends once more as the Varaha into the sea of oblivion and lifts up the lost Veda on his mighty tusks into the light of our waking consciousness and on to the firm soil of our externalised knowledge.

Not therefore the conception of semi-savages or half civilised philosophers, but the disjecta membra of a profound spiritual culture, a high and complex Yogic discipline and a well-founded theory of our relations with the unseen is what we shall expect in Veda & Vedanta. It is here that Comparative Philology intervenes. For it professes to have fixed for the Vedas a meaning which will bring them well within the savage theory and for the Vedanta an ambiguous character, half of it barbarous foolishness and half of it sublime philosophy such as we might expect from a highly gifted nation emerging out of a very primitive culture into a premature and immature activity of the higher intellectual faculties. A worship of the personified Sun, Moon, Fire, Wind, Dawn, Sky and other natural phenomena by means of a system of animal sacrifices, this is the Veda; high religious thinking & profound Monistic ideas forcibly derived from Vedic Nature-worship marred by the crudest notions about physics, psychology, cosmology and material origins & relations generally and mixed up with a great mass of unintelligible mystical jargon, this is the Upanishads. If that be so, our preoccupation with these works is misplaced. We must put them away as lumber of the past, interesting records of the beginnings and crude origins of religion and philosophy but records only, not authorities for our thought or lamps for our steps in life. We must base ourself not on the Vedas and Upanishads, but, as for that matter many of us are well inclined to do, on Badarayana, Kapila, Shankara and Buddha, not on the ancient Rishis but on the modern philosophers and logicians.

Such an abandonment is only obligatory on us after we have fixed the precise scientific value of these philological conclusions, the view of this modern naturalistic interpretation of which so much is made. We are too apt in India to take the European sciences at their own valuation. The Europeans themselves are often more sceptical. In ethnology the evidence of philology is increasingly disregarded. The ethnologists tend to disregard altogether, for example, the philological distinction between Aryan and Dravidian with its accompanying corollary of an immigration from the sub-Arctic regions or the regions of the Hindu-Kush and to affirm the existence of a single homogeneous Indo-Afghan race in immemorial occupation of the peninsula. Many great scientific thinkers deny the rank of a science to philology or are so much impressed by the failure of this branch of nineteenth-century inquiry that they doubt or deny even the possibility of a science of language. We need not therefore yield a servile assent to the conclusions of the philologists from any fear of being denounced as deniers of modern enlightenment and modern science; for we shall be in excellent company, supported by the authority of protagonists of that enlightenment and science.

When we examine the work of the philologists, our suspicions will receive an ample confirmation; for we shall find no evidence of any true scientific method, but only a few glimpses of it eked out by random speculation sometimes of a highly ingenious and forcible character but sometimes also in the last degree hasty and flimsy. A long time ago European scholars comparing what are now called the Indo-Aryan tongues were struck by the close resemblance amounting to identity of common domestic and familiar terms in these languages. "Pitar, patêr, pater, vater, father", "mâtar, mêtêr, mater, mutter, mother", — here, they thought, was the seed of a new science and the proof of an affiliation of different languages to our parent source which might lead to the explanation of the whole development of human speech. And indeed there was a coincidence & a discovery which might have been as important to human knowledge as the fall of Newton's apple and the discovery of gravitation. But this great possibility never flowered into actuality. On the contrary the after results were disappointingly meagre. One or two bye-laws of the modification of sounds as between the Aryan languages were worked out, the identity of a certain number of terms as between these kindred tongues well-established and a few theories hazarded or made out as to the classification not scientific but empirical of the various extant dialects of man. No discovery of the laws governing the structure of language, no clear light on the associations between sound and idea, no wide, careful and searching analysis of the origins and development even of the Aryan tongues resulted from this brilliant beginning. Philology is an enquiry that has failed to result in the creation of a science.

In its application to the Vedas modern philology has followed two distinct methods, the philological method proper and the scholastic, derivation of words and the observation of the use of words. From comparative philology in its present imperfect & rudimentary condition all that Vedic research can gain is the discovery of a previously unsuspected identity of meaning as between some peculiarly Vedic words or forms or the Vedic use of Sanscrit words or forms and the sense of the same vocable or form, whether intact or modified, in other Aryan tongues. Wherever Philology goes beyond this limit, its work is conjectural, not scientific and cannot command from us an implicit assent. Unfortunately, also, European scholars permit themselves a licence of speculation and suggestion which may sometimes be fruitful but which renders their work continually unconvincing. I may instance — my limits forbid more detail

— Max Muller's extraordinary dealings in his Preface to the Rig Veda with the Vedic form uloka (for loka). He derives this ancient form without an atom or even a shadow of proof or probability from an original uruloka or urvaloka, rejecting cavalierly the obvious & fruitful Tamil parallel uloka — the same word with the same meaning — on the strength of an argument which proceeds from his ignorance of the Tamil tongue and its peculiar phonetic principles. The example is typical. These scholars are on firmer ground when they attempt to establish new meanings of words by legitimate derivation from Sanscrit roots and careful observation of the sense suitable to a particular word in the various contexts in which it occurs. But here also we may be permitted to differ from their arguments and reject their conclusions. For their work is conjectural; not only is the new meaning assigned to particular words conjectural but the interpretation of the context on which its correctness depends is also very often either doubtful or conjectural. We are moving in a field of uncertainty and the imposing careful method and systematisation of the European scholars must not blind us to the fact that it is a method of conjecture and a systematisation of uncertainties.

Is a more certain application of philology to the Veda at all possible? I believe it is. I believe that by following a different clue we can arrive at least at the beginnings of a true science which will explain in its principles & details the origin, structure and development first of the Sanscrit, and then of the other Aryan & Dravidian tongues, if not of human speech generally in its various families. The scholars erred because they took the identity "pitar, pater, vater, father" as the master-clue to the identities of these languages. But this resemblance of familiar terms is only an incident, a tertiary result of a much deeper, more radical, more fruitful identity. The real clue is not yet discovered, but I believe that it is discoverable. Until, however, it is found and followed up, a task which demands great leisure and a gigantic industry, I am content to insist on the inconclusiveness of the initial work of the philologists. I repeat, the common assumption in Europe and among English-educated Indians that the researches of European scholarship have fixed for us correctly, conclusively & finally the meaning of Veda and the origin & process of development of Vedanta, is an assumption not yet justified and until it is justified no one is bound by it who does not choose to be bound. The field is still open, the last word still remains to be pronounced. I refuse, therefore, at this stage, my assent to the European idea of Veda and Vedanta and hold myself free to propound another interpretation and a more searching theory.

[2]

Chapter [ ][1]

I have combated the supremacy of the European theory — not seeking actually to refute it but to open the door for other possibilities, because the notions generated by it are a stumbling block to the proper approach to Vedanta. Under their influence we come to the Upanishads with a theory of their origin and in a spirit hostile to the sympathetic insight to which alone they will render up their secret. The very sense of the word Vedanta indicates clearly the aim of the seers who composed the Upanishads as well as the idea they entertained, — the true & correct idea, I believe, of their relations to the Veda. They were, they thought, recording a fulfilment of Vedic knowledge, giving shape to the culmination to which the sacred hymns pointed, and bringing out the inner and essential meaning of the practical details of the Karmakanda. The word, Upanishad, itself meant, I would suggest, originally not a session of speculative inquirers (the ingenious & plausible German derivation) but an affirmation and arrangement of essential truths & principles. The sense, it would almost seem, was at first general but afterwards, by predominant practice, applied exclusively to the Brahmi Upanishad, in which we have the systematisation particularly of the Brahmavidya. In any case such a systematisation of Vedic Knowledge was what these Rishis thought themselves to be effecting. But the

---

[1] *Sri Aurobindo did not write a chapter number. — Ed.*

modern theory denies the claim and compels us to approach the Upanishads from a different standpoint and both to judge and to interpret them by the law of a mentality which is as far as the two poles asunder from the mentality of the writers. We shall therefore certainly fail to understand the workings of their minds even if we are right in our history.

But I am convinced that the claim was neither a pretence nor an error. I believe the Vedas to hold a sense which neither mediaeval India nor modern Europe has grasped, but which was perfectly plain to the early Vedantic thinkers. Max Muller has understood one thing by the Vedic mantras, Sayana has understood another, Yaska had his own interpretations of their antique diction, but none of them understood what Yajnavalkya and Ajatashatru understood. We shall yet have to go back from the Nature-worship and henotheism of the Europeans, beyond the mythology and ceremonial of Sayana, beyond even the earlier intimations of Yaska and recover — nor is it the impossible task it seems — the knowledge of Yajnavalkya and Ajatashatru. It is because we do not understand the Vedas that three fourths of the Upanishads are a sealed book to us. Even of the little we think we can understand, much has been insecurely grasped and superficially comprehended, so that these sublimest of all Scriptures have become, latterly, more often a ground for philosophic wranglings than an illumination to the soul. For want of this key profound scholars have fumbled and for want of this guidance great thinkers gone astray, — Max Muller emitted his wonderful utterance about the babblings of humanity's nonage, Shankara left so much of his text unexplained or put it by as inferior truth for the ignorant, Vivekananda found himself compelled to admit his non-comprehension of the Vedantins' cosmological ideas & mention them doubtfully as curious speculations. It is only Veda that can give us a complete insight into Vedanta. Only when we thoroughly know the great Vedic ideas in their totality shall we be able entirely to appreciate the profound, harmonious and grandiose system of thought of our early forefathers. By ignoring the Vedas we lose all but a few rays of the glorious sun of Vedanta.

But whether this view is sound or unsound, whether we decide that the sense of those ancient writings was best known to the ancient Hindus or to the modern Europeans, to Yajnavalkya or to Max Muller, two things are certain that the Vedantic Rishis believed themselves to be in possession of the system of their Vedic predecessors and that they surely did not regard this system as merely a minute collection of ritual practices or merely an elaborate worship of material Nature-Powers. Minds that saw the world steadily as a whole, they did not repel that worship or disown that ritual. Surya was to them the god of the Sun; Agni they regarded as the master of fire; but they were not — and this is the important point — simply the god of the sun and simply the master of fire. They were not even merely a Something behind both, unknown & vague, although deep, mighty & subtle; but because of the nature & origin of the sun, Surya was also a god of a higher moral & spiritual function & Agni possessed of diviner & less palpable masteries. I will cite the single example of the Isha Upanishad in support of my point. The bulk of this poem is occupied with the solution of problems which involve the most abstruse and ultimate questions of metaphysics, ethics and psychology; yet after a series of profound and noble pronouncements on these deep problems the Upanishad turns, suddenly, without any consciousness of descent, without any lowering of tone to appeal with passion and power not to some Supernal Power but to Surya, to Agni. Is it to the earthly Fire and the material Sun that the Rishi lifts his mighty song? Does he pray to Surya to give him the warmth of his beams or to drive away night from the sky? Does he entreat Agni to nourish the sacrificial fire or to receive for the gods on his flaming tongues the clarified butter and the Soma-juice? Not even for a moment, not even by allusion; but rather to Surya to remove — from the sight of his mind — the distracting brilliance which veils from mankind the highest truth and form of things, to enable him to realise his perfect identity with God and to Agni to put aside this siege of the devious attractions of ignorance and desire and raise our kind to that sublime felicity reserved for purified souls. It is for the fulfilment of the loftiest spiritual ends

that he calls upon Surya; it is for support in the noblest moral
victories that he appeals to Agni. This is not Helios Hyperion but
another Vivusvan, master of this sun & its beams (that is also
evident) but master too of the soul's illumination, sa no dhiyah
prachodayat; this is not the limping blacksmith Hephaistos, but
another Hiranyaretas, master no doubt of this fire and its helpful
& consuming flames, but master also of purified & illuminated
action and force, hota kavikratuh satyas chitrasravastamah —
agnih purvebhir rishibhir idyo nutanair uta, the priest, the seer,
the true, the full of rich inspirations, Agni adorable to the sages
of the past, adorable to the great minds of today. Here is no
lapse of a great philosophic mind into barbarous polytheistic
superstition, no material and primitive Nature-worship, no extraordinary intellectual compromise and vague henotheism. We
are in the presence of an established system of spiritual knowledge and an ordered belief in which matter, mind and spirit
are connected and coordinated by the common action of great
divine powers. When we know according to what idea of cosmic
principle Surya and Agni could be at once material gods and
great spiritual helpers, we shall have some clue to the system
of the early Vedantins and at the same time, as I believe, to the
genuine significance and spiritual value of that ancient & eternal
bedrock of Hinduism, the Vedas.

But European scholars have their own explanation of the
development of this remarkable speculative system out of the
superstitious ritual and unintelligent worship which is all they
find in the Vedas and, since the utmost respect in intellectual
matters ought to be paid to the king of the day even when we
seek to persuade him to abdicate, I must deal with it before I
close this introductory portion & pass to the methods & substance of the Upanishads. It is held that there was a development
of religious thought from polytheism to henotheism and from
henotheism to pantheism which we can trace to some extent
in the Vedas themselves and of which the Upanishads are the
culmination. Some, notably the Indian disciples of European
scholarship — interpreting these ancient movements by the light
of our very different modern intellectuality or pushed by the

besetting Occidental impulse to search in our Indian origins for parallels to European history — even assert that the Upanishads represent a protestant and rationalistic movement away from the cumbrous ritual, the polytheistic superstition and the blind primitive religiosity of the Vedas and towards a final rationalistic culmination in the six Darshanas, in the agnosticism of Buddha, in the atheism of Charvaka & in the loftiness of the modern Adwaita philosophy. It would almost seem as if this old Indian movement contains in itself at one & the same time the old philosophic movement of [the Greeks], Luther's Protestant reformation and the glories of modern free thought.[2] These are indeed exhilarating notions and they have been attractively handled — some of them can be read, developed with great lucidity and charm in that remarkable compilation of European discoveries and fallacies, M⸢r⸣ Romesh Chandra Dutt's History of Ancient Indian Civilisation. Nothing indeed can be more ingenious and inspiriting, nothing more satisfactory at once to the patriotic imagination and our natural human yearning for the reassuringly familiar. But are such ideas as sound as they are ingenious? are they as true as they are exhilarating? One may surely be permitted to entertain some doubt! I profess myself wholly unable to find any cry of revolutionary protest, any note of rationalism in the Upanishads. I can find something one might almost call rationalism in Shankara's commentary — but an Indian rationalism entirely different in spirit from its European counterpart. But in the Upanishads the whole method is suprarational; it is the method of intuition and revelation expressed in a language and with a substance that might be characterised rather as the language of mysticism than of rationality. These sages do not protest against polytheism; they affirm the gods.

---

[2] *The following sentence was written in the top margin of the manuscript page. Its place of insertion was not marked:*
One would sometimes almost think that this upheaval of thought anticipated at once Plato & Empedocles, Luther, Erasmus and Melanchthon, Kant, Hegel & Berkeley, Hume, Haeckel & Huxley — that we have at one fell blast Graeco-Roman philosophy, Protestant Reformation & modern rationalistic tendency anticipated by the single movement from Janaka to Buddha.

These spiritual Titans do not protest against ritual and ceremony, they insist on the necessity of ritual and ceremony. It is true that they deny emphatically the sufficiency of material sacrifices for the attainment of the highest; but where does the Rigveda itself assert any such efficacy? From this single circumstance no protestant movement against ritual and sacrifice can be inferred, but at the most we can imagine rather than deduce a spiritual movement embracing while it exceeded ritual and sacrifice. But even this seems to me more than we can either infer or hazard without more light on the significance of early Vedic worship & the attitude on the subject of the Vedic Rishis. It is also true that certain scattered expressions have been caught at by Theistic minds as significant of a denial of polytheistic worship. I have heard the phrase, nedam yad idam upasate, not this to which men devote themselves, of the Kena Upanishad given this sense by reading the modern sense of upasana, worship, into the old Vedantic text. It can easily be shown from other passages in the Upanishads that upasate here has not the sense of religious worship, but quite another significance. We have enough to be proud of in our ancient thought & speculation without insisting on finding an exact anticipation of modern knowledge or modern thought & religion in these early Scriptures written thousands of years ago in the dim backwards of our history.

The theory of a natural and progressive development of Pantheistic ideas is far more rational and probable than this adhyaropa of European ideas & history onto the writings of the ancient world. But that theory also I cannot accept. Because the clearly philosophical passages in the Vedas, — those that are recognised as such, — occur in the later hymns, — in which the language is nearest to modern Sanscrit, — it is generally supposed that such a development is proved. It is, however, at least possible that we do not find philosophical ideas in the more ancient hymns merely because we are not mentally prepared to find them there. Not understanding their obscure and antique diction we interpret conjecturally with a confidence born of modern theories, led by our preconceived ideas to grasp only at what, we conceive, ought to be the primitive notions of a half-savage humanity. Any indications of more developed religious motives, if they exist, will from this method get no chance of revealing themselves & no quarter even if they insisted on lifting their luminous heads out of the waves of oblivion. In hymns with an almost modern diction, we have on the contrary no choice but to recognise their presence.

We cannot then say that there was no philosophy in the earlier & obscurer hymns unless we are sure that we have rightly interpreted their difficult language. But there are also certain positive considerations. The Vedantic thinkers positively believed that they were proceeding on a Vedic basis. They quote Vedic authority, appeal to Vedic ideas, evidently thinking themselves standing on the secure rock of Veda. Either, then, they were indulging in a disingenuous fiction, inconsistent with spiritual greatness & that frank honesty, arjavam, on which the nation prided itself, — either they were consciously innovating under a pretence of Vedic orthodoxy or else quite honestly they were reading their own notions into a text which meant something entirely different, as has often been done even by great & sincere intellects. The first suggestion — it has, I think, been made, — is inadmissible except on conclusive evidence; the second deserves consideration.

If it were only a matter of textual citation or a change of religious notions, there would be no great difficulty in accepting the theory of an unconscious intellectual fiction. But I find in the Upanishads abounding indications of a preexisting philosophical system, minute & careful at least & to my experience profound as well as elaborate. Where is the indication of any other than a Vedic origin for this well-appointed metaphysics, science, cosmology, psychology? Everywhere it is the text of the Veda that is alluded to or quoted, the knowledge of Veda that is presupposed. The study of Veda is throughout considered as the almost indispensable preliminary for the understanding of Vedanta. How came so colossal, persistent & all-pervading a mistake to have been committed by thinkers of so high a capacity? Or when, under what impulse & by whom was this great & careful system originated & developed? Where shall we find any documents of that speculation, — its initial steps, its gradual clarifying, its stronger & more assured progress? The Upanishads are usually supposed themselves to be such documents. But the longer I study these profound compositions, the less I feel able to accept this common and very natural hypothesis. If we do not prejudge their more recondite ideas as absurd, if we try sympathetically to enter into the thoughts & beliefs of these Rishis, to understand what precise facts or experiences stand behind their peculiar language, especially if we can renew those experiences by the system they themselves used, the system of Yoga, — a method still open to us — it will, I think, very soon dawn upon our minds that these works are of a very different nature from the speculative experiments they are generally supposed to be. They represent neither a revolt nor a fresh departure. We shall find that we are standing at a goal, not assisting at a starting-point. The form of the Upanishads is the mould not of an initial speculation but of an ultimate thinking. It is a consummation, not a beginning, the soul of an existing body, not the breath of life for a body yet to come into being. Line after line, passage after passage indicates an unexpressed metaphysical, scientific or psychological knowledge which the author thinks himself entitled to take for granted, just as a modern thinker addressing educated men on the ultimate generalisations of Science takes for granted their knowledge of the more important data and ideas accepted by modern men. All this mass of thought so taken for granted must have had a previous existence and history. It is indeed possible that it was developed between the time of the Vedas and the appearance of these Vedantic compositions but left behind it no substantial literary trace of its passage and progress. But it is also possible that the Vedas themselves when properly under-stood, contain these beginnings or even most of the separate data of these early mental sciences. It is possible that the old teachers of Vedanta were acting quite rationally & understood their business better than we understand it for them when they expected a knowledge of Veda from their students, sometimes even insisting on this preliminary knowledge, not dogmatically, not by a blind tradition, but because the Veda contained that basis of experimental knowledge upon which the generalisations of Vedanta were built. There is a chance, a considerable chance — I must lay stress again and more strongly on a suggestion already hazarded, — that minds so much closer to the Vedas in time and in the possibility of spiritual affinity may have known better the meaning of their religion than the inhabitant of different surroundings and of another world of thought speculating millenniums afterwards in the light of possibly fanciful Greek and German analogies. So far as I have been able to study & to penetrate the meaning of the Rigvedic hymns, it seems to me that the Europeans are demonstrably wrong in laying so predominant a stress on the material aspects of the Vedic gods. I find Varuna and Mitra to be mainly moral and not material powers; Surya, Agni, Indra have great psychical functions; even Sarasvati, in whom the scholars insist on seeing, wherever they can, an Aryan river, presents herself as a moral and intellectual agency, — "Pâvakâ nah Sarasvatî Vâjebhir vâjinîvatî, Yajnam vashtu *dhiyâvasuh. Chodayitrî sûnritânâm Chetantî sumatînâm*, Yajnam dadhe Sarasvatî. Maho arnas Sarasvatî Prachetayati ketunâ, *dhiyo visvâ virâjati.*" If we accept the plain meaning of the very plain & simple words italicised, we are in the presence not of personified natural phenomena, but of a great purifying, strengthening and illuminating goddess. But every word in the passage, pavaka, yajnam dadhe, maho arnas, ketuna, it seems to me, has a moral or intellectual significance. It would be easy to multiply passages of this kind. I am even prepared to suggest that the Vritras of the Veda (for the Sruti speaks not of a single Vritra but of many) are not — at least in many hymns — forces either of cloud or of drought, but Titans of quite another & higher order. The insight of Itihasa and Purana in these matters informed by old tradition seems to me often more correct than the conjectural scholarship of the Europeans. But there is an even more important truth than the high moral and spiritual significance of the Vedic gods and the Vedic religion which results to my mind from a more careful & unbiassed study of the Rigveda. We shall find that the moral functions assigned to these gods are arranged not on a haphazard, poetic or mythological basis, but in accordance with a careful, perhaps even a systematised introspective psychology and that at every step the details suggested agree with the experiences of the practical psychology which has gone in India from time immemorial by the name of Yoga. The line Maho Arnas Sarasvati prachetayati ketuna dhiyo visva virajati is to the Yogin a profound and at the same time lucid, accurate and simple statement of a considerable Yogic truth and most important Yogic experience. The psychological theory & principle involved, a theory unknown to Europe and obscured in later Hinduism, depends on a map of human psychology which is set forth in its grand lines in the Upanishads. If I am right, we have here an illuminating fact of the greatest importance to the Hindu religion, a fact which will light up, I am certain, much in the Veda that European scholarship has left obscure and will provide our modern study of the development of Hindu Civilisation with a scientific basis and a principle of unbroken continuity; we may find the earliest hymns of the Veda linked in identity of psychological experience to the modern utterances of Vivekananda and Sri Ramakrishna. Meanwhile the theory I have suggested of the relations of Veda to Vedanta receives, I contend, from these Vedic indications a certain character of actuality.

But I have to leave aside for the present these great & interesting but difficult questions. Although I believe the knowledge of Veda to be requisite for a full understanding of Vedanta, although I have considered it necessary to lay great stress on that relation, I shall myself in this book follow a different method. I shall confine my inquiry principally to the evidence of the Upanishads themselves and use them to shed their light on the Veda, instead of using the light of the written Veda to illumine the Upanishads. The amount & quality of truth I shall arrive at by this process may be inferior in fullness and restricted in quantity; instead of the written mantras, authoritative to many and open to all, I shall have to appeal largely to Yogic experiences as yet accessible only to a few; but I shall have in compensation this advantage that I shall proceed from the less disputed to the more disputed, from the nearer & better known to the obscurer & more remote, advancing, therefore, by a path not so liberally set with thorns and strewn with impeding boulders. By the necessity of the times my object must be different from that of the mighty ones who went before us. The goal Shankara and other thinkers had in view was the intellectual assurance of the Brahmavada; ours will be the knowledge of the Veda. Mighty Jnanis and Bhaktas, they sought in the Upanishads only those metaphysical truths which base upon reason and Vedic authority the search for the Highest; all else they disregarded as mean or of little moment. From those secure & noble heights, facile of ascent to our ancestors, we of the present generation are compelled to descend. Obliged by the rationalistic assault to enquire into much which they, troubled only by internal & limited disputes, by Buddhism & Sankhya, could afford to take for granted, called upon by modern necessity to study the ideas of the Upanishads in their obscure details no less than in their clear & inspiring generalities, in their doubtful implications no less than in their definite statements, in physical and psychological limb and member no less than in their heart of metaphysical truth, we must seek to know not only the Brahman in Its Universality, but the special functions of Surya and the particular powers of Agni; devote thought to the minor & preliminary "Vyuha rashmin samuha" as well as to the ultimate and capital So'ham asmi; neglect neither the heavenly fire of Nachicatus nor the bricks of his triple flame of sacrifice nor his necklace of many colours. We have behind the Upanishads a profound system of psychology. We must find our way back into that system. We perceive indications of equally elaborate ideas about the processes underlying physical existence, human action and the subtle connections of mind, body and spirit. We must recover in their fullness these ideas and recreate, if possible, this ancient system of psychical mechanics & physics. We find also a cosmology, a system of gods and of worlds. We must know what were the precise origin and relations of this cosmology, on what experiences subjective or objective they rested for their justification. We shall then have mastered not only Vedantadarshana but Vedanta, not only the truth that Badarayana or Shankara arrived at but the revelation that Yajnavalkya & Ajatashatru saw. We may even be compensated for our descent by a double reward. By discovering the early Vedantic interpretation of Veda, we may pour out a great illumination on the meaning of Veda itself, — to be confirmed, possibly, by the larger & more perfect Nirukta which the future will move inevitably to discover. By recovering the realisations of Yajnavalkya & Ajatashatru, we shall recover perhaps the inspired thoughts of Vasishta and Viswamitra, of Ghora from whom perhaps Srikrishna heard the word of illumination, of Madhuchchhandas, Vamadeva and Atri. And we may even find ourself enriched in spiritual no less than in psychological knowledge; rejoice in the sense of being filled with a wider & more potent knowledge & energy, with jnanam, with tapahshakti, & find ourselves strengthened & equipped for the swifter pursuit & mightier attainment of the One whom both Veda & Vedanta aspire to know & who is alone utterly worth possessing.

[3]

Chapter V.

The Interpretation of Vedanta.

In an inquiry of this kind, so far as we have to use purely intellectual means — and I have not concealed my opinion that intellectual means are not sufficient and one has to trust largely the intuitions of a quiet and purified mind and the experiences of an illuminated and expanding soul, — but still, so far as we are to use purely intellectual means, the first, most important, most imperative must be a submissive acceptance of the text of the Sruti in its natural suggestion and in its simple and straightforward sense. To this submissiveness we ought to attach the greatest importance & to secure it think no labour or self-discipline wasted. It is the initial tapasya necessary before we are fit to approach the Sruti. Any temperamental rebellion, any

emotional interference, any obstinacy of fixed mental association, any intellectual violation of the text seems to me to vitiate
the work of the interpreter and deprive it, even when otherwise
noble and brilliant, of some of its value. It is for this reason that
the mind, that restless lake of sanskaras, preferences, prejudices,
prejudgments, habitual opinions, intellectual & temperamental
likes & dislikes, ought to be entirely silent in this matter; its role
is to be submissive and receptive, detached, without passion;
passivity, not activity, should be its state, na kinchid api chin-
tayet. For the Sruti carries with it, in its very words, a certain
prakash, a certain illumination. The mind ought to wait for that
illumination and receiving it, should not because it is contrary to
our expectation or our desire, labour to reject or alter what has
been seen. Our pitfalls are many. One man has an active, vital
& energetic temperament; he is tempted to read into Sruti the
praise of action, to slur over anything that savours of quietism.
Another is temperamentally quietistic; any command enjoining
action as a means towards perfection his heart, his nerves cannot
endure, he must get rid of it, belittle it, put it aside on whatever
pretext. This is the interference of temperamental preference
with the text of the Sruti. A man is attached to a particular
thinker or teacher, enamoured of a definite view of life & God.
Any contradiction of that thinker, teacher or view irritates his
heart & cannot be borne, even though the contradiction seems
to stand there plainly on the face of sacred writ; the mind at
once obeying the heart sets about proving to itself that the
words do not mean what they seem to mean. This is the interference of emotional preference. Or else the mind has always
been accustomed to a particular philosophy, mode of thinking,
idea of religion or dogma. Whatever contradicts these notions,
strikes our fixed mental idea as necessarily wrong. Surely, it
says, the philosophy, the thought, the dogma to which I am
accustomed must be the thought of the Scriptures; there cannot,
in the nature of things, be anything in them inconsistent with
what I believe; for what I believe is true and the Scriptures are
repositories of truth. So begins the interference which arises from
association & fixed opinions. There is, finally, the intervention

of the intellect when a speculative philosopher with a theory or a scholar reaching out after novelty or conscious of an opening for scholastic ingenuities, meddles powerfully with the plain drift of the text. All these interferences, however brilliantly they may be managed, are injuries to the truth of Veda; they diminish its universality and limit its appeal. It is for others to judge whether I have myself been able to avoid all of them, — especially the intellectual interference to which my temperament is most open, but I have had certainly the will to avoid it if not the power, the intention if not its successful performance.

I do not mean, however, that the received or dictionary sense of the word has to be always accepted. In dealing with these ancient writings such a scholastical puritanism would be less dangerous indeed than the licence of the philosophic commentators, but would still be seriously limiting. But in departing from the dictionary sense one must not depart from the native and etymological sense of the word; one ought to abide within its clear grammatical connotation as in a hedge of defence against one's own intellectual self-will and any superstructure of special sense or association must be consistent with that connotation and with the general usage of the Upanishads or of the Veda on which they rest. I have myself suggested that the scope of dhanam in the first verse of the Isha exceeds the contracted idea of material wealth and embraces all sorts of possessions; *eno* in the last verse still keeps to me its etymological association and is different from papa; the word vayunani meaning no doubt actions or activities, has been supposed by me to keep a colour of its proper etymological sense "phenomena" and to denote universal activities and not solely the individual or human; but none of these suggestions in the least meddle with the grammatical connotation, the etymological force or even the dictionary meaning of the words used; only a deeper or more delicate shade of meaning is made to appear than can ordinarily be perceived by a careless or superficial reader. A more serious doubt may arise when I suggest special associations for drishtaye and satya in the [fifteenth] verse. It will be seen however that in neither case do I depart from the basic meaning of the

words, sight for drishti, truth for satya. It will be seen also, as
I proceed in my larger task, that I have good Vedic warrant
for supposing these special senses to be applied sometimes &
indeed often to sight and to Truth in the Sruti and that they
agree with the whole drift & logical development of this &
other Upanishads.

For the fixing of the actual sense of separate words in Sruti is
not the only condition of the interpretation nor is the acceptance
of their natural sense the only standard for the interpreter. A
great value, indeed an immense value must be attached, in my
opinion, to the rhythm & structure and the logical connection
with each other in thought of the separate clauses & shlokas.
The language of the Upanishads is largely regarded by the modern readers as sublime and poetical indeed, full of imagery &
suggestion, but not to be too much insisted on, not always to
be pressed as having a definite meaning but often allowed to
pass vaguely as rather reaching out at truths than accurately
expressing them. My experience forbids me to assent to this
view, in itself very natural and superficially reasonable. I have
been forced to believe in the plenary inspiration of the Upanishads in word as well as in thought; I have been continually
obliged to see that the expressions they use are the inevitable
expression for the thought that has to be conveyed, and even
when using poetical language the Rishis use it with a definite
purpose, not vaguely reaching out at truth, but keeping before
their vision a clear and firm thought or experience which they
clearly & firmly express. No interpretation would impress me
with a sense of satisfaction which did not give its clear & due
weight to each word or account for the choice of one word over
another where the choice is unusual. In accordance with this fullness of inspiration is the perfection of the chhandas, the rhythm
& structure of verse & sentence which corresponds felicitously
with the rhythm & structure of the thought. I may instance
for this importance of the rhythm & structure of sentence such
a juxtaposition as jagatyam jagat in the first verse; while the
remarkable development & balance, supremely wedded to the
thought, of the six verses about Vidya & Avidya may stand as

an example of the importance of rhythm & structure of both sentence & verse. The jagatyam jagat of the first verse already alluded to, is a striking instance of the perfect & pregnant use of language, but there are numerous other examples such as the powerful collocation of kavir manishi paribhuh swayambhur in one of the most noble & profound of the revelatory shlokas, the [eighth]. It is easy for a careless translator or interpreter to accept kavir & manishi loosely as words with the same essential meaning used a little tautologically for a rhetorical effect. In reality, they differ widely in sense, are used in this passage with great correctness and pregnancy and on a right understanding of them depends our right understanding of the whole system of philosophy developed in the Isha. Much depends on whether we take the hiranmaya patra of the [fifteenth] shloka as mere vague poetical rhetoric or an image used with a definite intention and a lucid idea. But almost every step in the Isha will give us examples.

Even an observation of formal metre as an element of the rhythm is of some importance to the Vedantic interpreter. The writers of the Upanishads handle their metres, whether Anushtup or Tristubh, not entirely in the manner of the Vedic Rishis, but very largely on Vedic principles. They permit themselves to avoid elision even in the middle of a pada, eg vidyancha avidyancha, and always avoid it between the different padas; their principle is to keep not only the two lines of the shloka but all its four parts separate and not to run them into each other by sandhi. This peculiarity disappears in the manuscript & printed copies where the post-Vedic sandhi is observed usually though not with absolute consistency. But the disregard of Vedic practice is ruinous to the rhythm and sweetness of the verse, for it disregards the first conditions of the Vedic appeal to the ear. What for instance can be more clumsy than the junction of the padas in the seventh shloka, with its heavy obstruction & jar as of a carriage wheel jolting momentarily over a sudden obstacle,

yasmin sarvani bhutanyatmaivabhud vijanatah

or what can be more rhythmical, sweet & harmonious than the

same verse properly written & read with an observation of the pause between the padas

> yasmin sarvani bhutani atmaivabhud vijanatah?

There are other antique peculiarities, the use of two short matras as the equivalent of one long syllable, the occasional introduction of one or more excessive feet into a pada, resembling the use of the Alexandrine in English dramatic verse, the optional quantity of the vowel before a conjunct consonant of which the second element is a liquid, especially the semivowels y or v, and, — although this is more doubtful, — the Vedic use of these semivowels optionally as actual vowels which turns a dissyllable frequently into a trisyllable — a freedom possible only in a living language appealing to an ear tuned to the flexibility of living & daily intonations. It is possible that we have an example of this use in vidyancha avidyancha, but although it would introduce a very beautiful and delicate poetical effect, we cannot speak with certainty. These minutiae are not merely interesting to the literary critic and the philologist. Their importance will appear when we find that Max Muller would almost tempt us, for the sake of regularity of metre, to eject the important, if not indispensable yathatathyato, which gives such profundity, so many reverberations of meaning to the closing thought in the majestic [eighth] shloka, kavir manishi paribhuh swayambhur, yathatathyato'rthan vyadadhach chhaswatibhyah samabhyah; or that Shankara's desperate dealings with the line, from his point of view almost unmanageable,

> vinashena mrityum tirtwa sambhutyamritam asnute

his forcing of vinasha to mean sambhava and reading of tirtwa asambhutya are negatived by the metre & rhythm of the verse no less than by the rhythm & structure of the thought throughout these six crucial verses.

The ordinary view of the Upanishads ignores another equally important, if not more important characteristic, the closeness of their logical structure, the intimate subjective linking of clause with clause, the logical stride from shloka to shloka, the profound relations of passage to passage. The usual treatment

of these works seems to go on the assumption that this high
logical strenuousness does not exist. They might often be loose
collections of ill connected speculations, haphazard & illogical
structures, for all the importance that is given to this element of
their divine inspiration. I shall try to show how mighty are the
architectonics of thought in the Isha, how movement leads on to
movement, how intimately, for instance, the closing invocations
to Surya & Agni are related to the whole thought-structure and
how perfectly they develop from what precedes. The importance
of the logical relation in the interpretation will be manifest, if I
mistake not, at every step of our progress.[3]

[I have spoken so far of the intellectual tests that we can
employ. Before I pass from this subject, it may be well to in-
sert a word of explanation, of self-defence, almost of apology.
Among the intellectual interpreters of Sruti, Shankara towers
like an unreachable giant above his fellows. As a philosopher, as
a metaphysician, as a powerful logician & victorious disputant
his greatness can hardly be measured. For a thousand years and
more he has stood in the heavens of Indian thought, his head far
away in the altitudes of Adwaita, his feet firmly planted on the
lifeless remnants of crushed systems and broken philosophies,
the wreckage of his logical conquests, his mouth like Trishira's
swallowing up the world, lokan grasantam, annihilating it in the
white flame of the Mayavada, his shadow covering our intellects
& stunting the efforts of all who have dared to think originally
& dispute his conclusions. Not Madhwa, not even Ramanuja
can prevail against this colossal shadow. Yet I have ventured
throughout to differ from this king of commentators — almost
even to ignore this great & invincible disputant. If I have done
so, it is because I think the decree of our liberty has already
been pronounced by another giant of thought. When the great
Vivekananda, potent seedsower of the future, in answer to the
objection of the Pundits, "But Shankara does not say that,"
replied simply but finally, "No, but I, Vivekananda, say it," he
pronounced the decree of liberation not only for himself but for

---

[3] *The paragraph that follows was cancelled in the manuscript by Sri Aurobindo.—Ed.*

all of us from the yoke, the golden but heavy yoke, of the mighty Dravidian. For this was Vivekananda's mission to smite away all obstacles, however great & venerable, & open the path to the resurgence of Indian originality & the direct confrontation of the soul of man with the living Truth. He was our deliverer not only from ignorance & weakness, but from the systems of knowledge that would limit us and impose a premature finality.
    In truth,]

[4]

Part II.

The Instruments and Field of Vedanta.

Chapter I.

Textual Inference.

The three principal means of intellectual knowledge are anumana, pratyaksha and aptavakya. Anumana, inference from data, depends for its value on the possession of the right data, on the right observation of the data including the drawing of the right analogies, the unerring perception of true identity & rejection of false identity, the just estimate of difference & contrast, and finally on the power of right reasoning from the right data. Pratyaksha is the process by which the things themselves about which we gather data are brought into our ken; aptavakya is evidence, the testimony of men who have themselves been in possession of the knowledge we seek. An error in pratyaksha, an error committed by the apta, an error of data or of reasoning from the data may, if serious in its bearing or extent, vitiate all our conclusions even if all our other means are correct and correctly used. Especially is this danger present to us when we are reasoning not from things but from words; when we are using the often artificial counters of traditional logic & metaphysics, we are apt to lose ourselves in a brilliant cloud, to be lifted from the earth, our pratistha, into some nebulous region where even

if we win high victories we are not much advanced, since we
get thereby nothing but an intellectual satisfaction and cannot
apply our knowledge to life. This is the great advantage of the
scientist over the metaphysician that he is always near to facts
& sensible things which, when the truth of them is outraged
by the freaks of the mind, present a much more formidable &
tangible protest than words, those vague & flexible symbols of
things which have been habituated to misuse ever since human
thinking began. The metaphysician is too apt to forget that he
is dealing with the symbols of things and not with the things
themselves; he should but is not always careful to compare his
intellectual results with the verities of experience; he is apt to be
more anxious that his conclusions should be logical than that
they should be in experience true. Much of the argumentation
of the great Dravidian thinkers, though perfect in itself, seems
to be vitiated by this tendency to argue about words rather than
about the realities which alone give any value to words. On
the other hand scientists as soon as they go beyond the safe
limits of observation & classification of data, as soon as they
begin to reason & generalise on the basis of their science, show
themselves to be as much subject to the errors of the intellect as
ordinary mortals. They too like the metaphysicians use words
in a fixed sense established upon insufficient data and forge
these premature fixatures into fetters upon thought and inquiry.
We seem hardly yet to possess the right & sufficient data for a
proper understanding of the universe in which we find ourselves;
the habit & power of right reasoning from data, even if with
insufficient materials right reasoning were possible, seem yet to
be beyond the reach of our human weakness. The continued
wrangles of philosophy, dogmatisms of science and quarrels of
religion are so many proofs that we are yet unripe for the highest
processes of thought and inquiry. How few of us have even the
first elementary condition of truth-seeking, a quiet heart and a
silent, patient & purified understanding. For the Vedantins were
surely right in thinking that in order to be a discoverer & teacher
of truth one must first be absolutely dhira, — live that is to say
in a luminous calm of both heart & understanding.

[5]

Part II

The Field and Instruments of Vedanta

Chapter I

Historically, then, we have our Hindu theory of the Vedanta. It is the systematised affirmation, the reaffirmation, perhaps, of that knowledge of God, man and the universe, the Veda or Brahmavidya, on which the last harmony of man's being with his surroundings was effected. What the Vedanta is, intrinsically, I have already hinted. It is the reaffirmation of Veda or Brahmavidya, not by metaphysical speculation or inferential reasoning, but by spiritual experience and supra-intellectual inspiration. If this idea be true, then by interpreting correctly the Vedanta, we shall come to some knowledge of what God is, what man, of the nature and action of the great principles of our being, matter, life, mind, spirit and whatever else this wonderful world of ours may hold. In fact, this is my sole object in undertaking the explanation of the Upanishads. The essential relations of God & the world, so far as they affect our existence here, this is my subject. A philological enquiry into the meaning of ancient Hindu documents, an antiquarian knowledge of the philosophising of ancient generations, although in itself a worthy object of labour and a patriotic occupation, — since those generations were our forefathers and the builders of our race, — would not to me be a sufficient motive for devoting much time & labour out of a life lived in these pregnant & fruitful times when each of us is given an opportunity of doing according to our powers a great work for humanity. I hold with my forefathers that this is an age of enormous disintegration & reconstitution from which we look forward to a new Satyayuga. That Satyayuga can only be reconstituted by the efforts of the sadhus, the seekers after human perfection, by maintaining in however small a degree that harmony of man's being with his surrounding & containing universe which is the condition of our perfection. The knowledge

of the principles of that harmony is therefore man's greatest need
and should be the first preoccupation of his lovers and helpers.
This knowledge, this perfection is within us and must ultimately
be found and manifested by plunging into the depths of our own
being, into that karanasamudra or causal ocean from which our
beings emerge and bringing out from thence the lost Veda and
the already existing future. Within us is all Veda and all Vedanta,
within us is God & perfected humanity — two beatitudes that
are the same and yet different. But to effect this great deliverance,
to push aside the golden shield of our various thought from the
face of Truth, to rescue the concealed Purusha, future Man, out
of those waters in which he lies concealed and give him form
by the intensity of our tapas, let no man think that it is a brief
or an easy task in which we can dispense with the help that the
wisdom of the past still offers us. We must link our hands to the
sages of the past in order that we may pass on the sacred Vedic
fire, agnir idyah, to the Rishis of the future. The best beginning
for this great inquiry is, therefore, to know what the Vedanta has
to say on these profound problems. Afterwards we may proceed
to confirmation from other sources.

Three questions at the very beginning confront us. What is
the nature of the truth that the Vedanta sets out to teach, —
what, that is to say, are its relations to the actual thought and
labour of humanity? What are these methods of inspiration and
experience by which they arrive at the truths of which they are
the repositories? And granting that they are inspired in word &
thought, how are we to arrive at the right meaning of words
written long ago, in the Sanscrit language, by ancient thinkers
with ideas that are not ours and a knowledge from which we
have receded? Is it the method of the darshanik, the logical
philosopher, that we must follow? Shall we arrive by logic at this
knowledge of the Eternal? Or is [it] the scientist and scholar, who
must be our guides? Shall grammar and analysis from outside
help us? But the scientist does not admit inspiration, the logician
does not use it.

[6]

Part II

The Field and Instruments of Vedanta

Chapter I

Intellect and Revelation

If in the progression of the ages there are always golden periods in which man recovers self-knowledge and attunes the truth of himself to the truth of his surroundings — or may it not even be, may not this be the true secret of his evolution — attunes his surroundings to his fulfilled and triumphant self, not being merely determined by his environment, but using it freely for infinite purposes & determining it, and if the Veda keeps, even fragmentarily, the practical application and the Vedanta, the theoretical statement of that self-knowledge, the importance of the inner meaning of these books to the progress of humanity will be self-evident. It is perfectly true, or so at least the Indian Yogin has always held, that we have in ourselves the eternal Veda. Available by God's grace or our own effort there is always in each human being that hidden salvation. But it is hard to arrive at, harder to apply. Many of the greatest, not seeing how it can be applied to the conditions of phenomenal life, carry it away with them into the eternal Silence. They put away from them the Veda, they seek in the Vedanta or in their souls only so much knowledge as will help them to loosen the coils of thought & sense wound round them by the Almighty Magician. But the Vedanta is not useful only for the denial of life; it is even more useful for the affirmation of life. If it affirms the evil of bondage to the idea of this world, it also affirms the bliss of harmony between the world & God. Neither Shankara nor Schopenhauer have for us the entirety of its knowledge.

It is this supreme utility of Vedanta for life, for man's individual and racial evolution that I hope to rescue from the obscuration of quietistic philosophies born of the pessimism of the iron age. I have said that I do not deny the truth of these philosophies. The Asad Brahman, Nirvana, annihilation of the manifest soul in the unmanifest are all of them great truths and, if we regard them without the fear & shrinking of the ignorant existence-loving mind, they are not only great but also blissful truths; they are an eternal part of Vedanta and it is well that they should have been brought out though with exaggeration & the exclusion of other verities. But they are only a part, a side of Vedantic truth. There are other sides, in a way even greater and more blissful, and at any rate much more helpful to mankind as a whole. God & the World is my subject, — not the incompatibility of God with the world He has created in Himself, but the fulfilment of Himself in it for which it was created — the conditions in which the kingdom of heaven on earth can be converted from a dream into a possibility, — by the willed evolution in man of his higher nature, by a steady self-purification and a development in the light of this divine knowledge towards the fulfilment of his own supra-material, supra-intellectual nature. For that purpose he must know God and not only the physical laws of Nature. He must know his soul and not only the open or secret machinery of his body. This knowledge he can only get from his own soul or from Vedanta explained to him by the Master, the one who knows, and awakening by its contact the knowledge in his own soul. He cannot get it from Science or from speculative Philosophy, but only from God's revelation. Nayam atma pravachanena labhyah. If Vedanta had not this high utility, if it only brought a philosophical satisfaction or were good for logical disputation, I should not think it worth while to write a word about it, much less to delve deep for its meaning.

We wish to know, we enlightened moderns, what man is, what God, the nature & relation of matter, mind, life in order to satisfy an intellectual craving. If we can systematise our guesses about these things, if we can present the world with a theory intellectually interesting or logically flawless, we are satisfied. But the ancients wished to know these things because they thought they were of the greatest importance for man's life and being. Whether they had their knowledge by thought or by religion, from the judgment or from the heart, their first preoccupation was to live according to their knowledge, — the Stoic & the Epicurean quite as much as the Christian or the Jew held his knowledge as a means towards life, towards the highest fulfilment of his being. It has been left for enlightened Europe to profess a religion, yet avowedly separate its precepts from practical life, and it has been first the privilege of Teutonic thinkers to speculate in the void, using great words & high ideas as if these were ornaments of a bright lustre & great costliness but of no living utility. The Vedanta is above all a rule of life, a law of being and a determination of relation and conduct; for its ideas are sovereign, potent, insistent to remould a man's whole outlook upon existence; it is at once a philosophy & a religion and it owes this sovereign force & double mastery not only to the substance of its message, but to the instrumentality of that message, the sources from which it is drawn and the principles of knowledge & activity in our complex being to which it appeals.

For although the determination to live by the best light we have is important, it is equally important to know what that light is and how we came by it, whether by the inspiration of the heart & the satisfaction of the emotional being, as in ordinary religion, or by the working of the observation and the logical faculties as in ordinary Science or by intellectual revelation as Newton discovered gravitation or by spiritual intuition as in the methods of the great founders of religion or by a higher principle in us which sums up and yet transcends all these mighty channels of the Jnanam Brahma. It is such a higher undivided principle from which Vedanta professes to derive its knowledge. For the ancient Hindus, alone of earth's nations, seem to have not only trusted the internal revelation in preference to the external, which, however, they also recognized & highly valued, but to have known & commanded the psychological sources of internal revelation and mastered to a certain extent its secret, its science and its workings. They claim to have found a principle of knowledge as superior to reason as reason itself is to sensational perception and animal instinct — to have laid their grasp on workings and results which can satisfy the demands

of the intellect but transcend intellectual ideation, meet the test
of observation & logic but act in a sense wider, more direct
& more penetrating than observation & logic, and fulfil all
the demands of the heart while preserving our freedom from
the heart's vagaries. All existence is a staircase by which we are
climbing in God & through God Godwards. We start here at the
bottom rung, from the involution, the obscuration in matter and
ascend from the obscurer manifestation to the less obscure, from
an air in which light comes to us from above to emergence in the
very light itself. The spirit in the stone, clod and metal is at the
bottom of that ladder; tree & plant and all vegetable life a little
higher; animal life dwelling in vitality but using from below the
lower functions of mind and a reason which entirely depends
on memory & observation & almost consists in memory &
observation climbs yet higher; man dwelling in the lower mind
but using matter & vitality from above and from below taking
possession of reason and imagination, seems, of all beings on
earth, to be at the top. But above man's present position, above
the heart in which he dwells & the imagination & reason to
which he rises there opens out a wider atmosphere of life, there
shoots down on him a more full & burning splendour of strength
& knowledge, a more nectarous lustre of joy & beauty. There
there is another sun, another moon, other lightnings than ours.
To this the poet and the artist aspire in the intoxication of the
vision and the hearing, chakshush cha shrotran cha; from this the
prophet & the Pythoness draw the exaltation of their inspiration
or its frenzy; genius is a beggar at the doors of that bounty.
But all these are like men that dream and utter ill-understood
fragments of their dream. For man in his heart is awake; in his
reason & imagination, half awake, not yet buddha, but in that
higher principle he is asleep. It is to him a state of sushupti. Yet
secretly, subliminally, unknown to the egoistic mind he takes
from this slumber his waking thought & knowledge, though he
is compelled by the limitations of mind to mistake & misuse it.
For that slumber is the real waking and our waking is a state of
dream and delusion in which we use a distorted truth & establish a world of false relations. Therefore the Gita says, "Yasyam

jagrati bhutani sa nisha pashyato muneh." In that which is night to all creatures, he who has mastered his own being is awake; that in which these creatures are awake, is night to the eye of the awakened seer. The Vedantists call this principle by the name, vijnanam, an entire & pervading principle of knowledge which puts everything in its true light & its right relations. It is from vijnanam that Veda descends to us; the movement of this higher principle is the source of all internal revelation. It is the drishti of which the Veda is the result, it is the sruti which in its expression the Veda is, it is the smriti of the Rishi which gives to the intelligent part, the manishi in him a perfect account of the vision & inspired hearing of the seer in him, the Kavi.

For mankind although evolving towards vijnana yet dwells in the mind. He has to be fulfilled in mind before he can rise taking up mind with him into the vijnanamaya self, — the mahan atma, — just as, in his animal state, he had to be fulfilled in body & vitality before he could develop freely in mind. Thus it comes about that even when Veda manifests in the mental world, it has although the higher & truer, to give an account of itself to the lower & more fallible, to Science, to Philosophy & to Religion. It must answer their doubts & questions, it must satisfy all their right and permissible demands. For although from the ideal point of view it is an anomaly that the higher should be cross-questioned by the lower, the source of truth by the propagators of half-truth and error, yet from the evolutionary point of view an anomaly is often the one right and indispensable process. For if we act otherwise, if we deny for instance the claims of the reason in order to serve revelation only & exclusively — though we ought to serve her first and chiefly — we are in danger of defeating man's evolution, which consists in self-fulfilment and not, except as a temporary means to an end, in self-mortification. Otherwise, we are in danger of becoming by a one-sided exaggeration self-injurers, self-slayers, atmaha, and incurring that condemnation to the sunless & gloomy states beyond of which the Isha Upanishad speaks. Religion makes this mistake when she attempts to destroy the body & the vitality in order to satisfy the aspirations of the heart; philosophy, when she stifles the heart

in order to enthrone the pure intellect; Science when she denies
the power of vision of the heart and the pure intellect in order
to strengthen & serve solely the analytical reason — denying
herself thus the benefit of the great benediction "Blessed are the
pure in heart for they shall see God," denying herself the fullness
of the great secular effort of humanity summed up in the gnothi
seauton of the sages, binding herself to a barren Agnosticism,
urging mankind towards the gran rifiuto, the great refusal &
renunciation of its past and its future. Mayavada commits this
error when not content with trampling the tyranny of cosmic
Illusion underfoot, it seeks to deny and destroy the world in
order to attain That which has chosen to express itself through
the world. For God has expressed us in many principles & not
one. He has ranged them one over the other & commanded us
not to destroy one in order to satisfy another, not to sanction
internal civil war and perpetrate spiritual suicide, but to rise
from one principle to the other, taking it up with us as we go,
fulfilling the lower first in itself and then in the higher. We have
to dissociate our sense of being from body & vitality and become mind, to dissociate it from mind and become vijnanam, to
dissociate it from vijnanam and become divine bliss, awareness
& being, Sachchidanandam manifest in phenomenal existence,
to dissociate it from Sachchidanandam and become That which
is in the world Sachchidanandam, not in order to destroy body,
vitality, mind, knowledge, manifested bliss & being but to transcend and satisfy them more mightily, without being limited
by their conditions, to become through them yet beyond them
infinite, divine & universal. Destroy them we cannot without
blotting out ourselves and entering into the Sunyam Brahma; but
we can maim ourselves in the world by the attempt to destroy
them. For thus are we made and we can be no other, — evam
twayi nanyatheto'sti. "Thus is it in thee and it is not otherwise."
Purnata, fullness is the true law of our progression.

Therefore all attempts to deny and slaughter the reason are
reprehensible and should be strongly opposed & discouraged.
The revolt of Rationalism against the tyranny of the creeds & the
Churches is justified by God's law and truth. And not only the

Churches & creeds, but Veda must bend down from its altitudes
& justify itself before reason even as God descends from his
heavens of infinity to humour our weakness & limitations and
take us into His embrace. On the other hand, to deny Veda in
order to give reason a supremacy which its natural limitations,
its stumbling imperfections make impossible to it, is to go against
Nature and restrict our evolution. It has been well said that to
deny Veda by hetuvada, divine revelation by intellectual rationality, is, in the end, to become a pashanda, — a word which
has now acquired only the significance of an abusive epithet
but meant originally and etymologically a materialist, one who
denies his higher self in order to enthrone & worship the brute
matter in which he is cased. A harmony is needed in which the
higher shall illumine the lower, the lower recognise & rise to
the higher. The ancient Hindus, therefore, insisted on Veda as
the supreme authority, allowing Philosophy, Science & Religion
only as subordinate helps to knowledge, because they perceived
the danger of giving too unlicensed a freedom to these great
but inferior powers. Religion, putting Veda away into a sacred
oblivion, follows the impulses of the undisciplined heart, not
purified, but full of the vital impulses, chittam pranair otam, and
becomes spasmodic, ignorant, narrow, obscurantist, sectarian,
cruel, violent. Philosophy acknowledging Veda in theory but
relying instead on her own intellectual self-sufficiency, ends by
living in words, a thing of vain disputations & exultant logic-
splitting, abstract, unpractical and visionary. Science, denying
Veda altogether, arrogant & bigoted in her own conceit, makes
man a materialist, a pashanda. For all her analytical knowledge
she knows not that that in man which believes only in matter
is the beast in him, — the beast so long & with such difficulty
subdued & disciplined by Philosophy, Religion & Veda; she
keeps telling him, "Thou, O brute body & nerve system, art
Brahman," Annam vai Brahma, Prano vai Brahma, until his
whole nature begins to believe it. One day, while she yet reigns,
he is sure to rise, — the egoistic heartless lust of power & pleasure in man, — and demand that she shall be his servant with
her knowledge, her sophistries, her organisation, her appliances,

shall justify to him his selfishness, lusts & cruel impulses and arm them with engines of irresistible potency. Already the shadow of this terrible revival is cast upon the world; already Science is bowing her head to this tremendous demand. What the Hindus foresaw and dreaded and strove to organise their society against it, erecting barrier upon artificial barrier as their own knowledge & grasp upon Veda diminished, is now growing actual and imminent. The way to avoid it is not to deny the truth of Science, but to complete, correct and illuminate it. For the Veda also says with Science, Annam vai Brahma, Prano vai Brahma; it acknowledges the animal, the Pashu in man & God as the Master of the Animal, the Pashupati; but by completing the knowledge and putting it in its right relations, it completes him also & liberates him, lifts the Pashu to the Pashupati and enables him to satisfy himself divinely by enjoying even in matter the supramaterial and replacing egoistic and selfish power by an universal mastery & helpfulness and egoistic & unsatisfying pleasures by a bliss in which he can become one with his fellows, a bliss divine & universal.

   In any explanation, therefore, that we may offer of Veda and Vedanta we must give an account to Science, Philosophy & Religion in their own terms of that which we mean by Veda & Vedanta and our reasons for attaching a supreme importance to the conclusions we reach by them. In order that this satisfaction may be given the Vedantist must make it clear what he means by knowledge, what he holds to be the value of the criteria relied on respectively by Science, Philosophy & Religion and how he determines their relation to the standards used by Vedanta. Science takes her stand upon two means of knowledge only; she admits observation by the physical senses aided by physical instruments and she admits inference from this observation, or to use our Indian terms physical pratyaksha & anumana from physical pratyaksha. All else she puts by as misleading and unreliable. She admits neither aptavakya nor analogy, neither the statements of well-equipped & credible witnesses nor argument from the perception of like circumstances as between the various objects or movements observed. Aptavakya is in this system only an uncertain makeshift, a secondhand pratyaksha; analogy is only a doubtful and often a false inference. But the Vedantist in common with all Indian thinkers admits in intellectual reasoning aptavakya and analogy as well as pratyaksha and anumana.

At bottom all human thinking is some sort of perception; either perception by the mind of something that seems to be outside itself or of something that seems to be within itself, either, as we say, physical perception or mental perception. Logic itself is only the science of placing our perceptions in their proper order, — nothing more. If we take things physical with which alone the modern scientific method is really at home, it must be clear to us that the whole basis of knowledge is the right perception of objects. We have first to bring it under observation by the mind through some sense-organ usually or predominantly the eye, — we have to bring not only the eye, but the mind into concentrated contact with the object; for if only the eye dwells on it, the mind is likely to retain nothing in memory or only a vague impression of what has been seen. This process I may be allowed to call simply bodha or taking into the observation. Once I have the object in my mind's grasp, I proceed to separate it clearly in my observation from all surrounding object or circumstance foreign to it even if contiguous or attached — by separation in observation, by prithagbodha. Finally, I take it completely into my mind by a perfect observation of it in its parts, its circumstance & its entirety, by totality in observation, by samyagbodha. Only if I have accomplished these three movements of perception perfectly, can I be said to have properly or scientifically observed the object; only then can I be sure of its dwelling in my memory or of my power to reproduce it accurately before my imagination.

The Upanishad in Aphorism

THE ISHA UPANISHAD

For the Lord all this is a habitation whatsoever is moving thing in her that moves.

Why dost thou say there is a world? There is no world, only One who moves.

What thou callest world is the movement of Kali; as such embrace thy world-existence. In thy all-embracing stillness of vision thou art Purusha and inhabitest; in thy outward motion and action thou art Prakriti and the builder of the habitation. Thus envisage thy being.

There are many knots of the movement and each knot thy eyes look upon as an object; many currents and each current thy mind sees as force and tendency. Forces and objects are the forms of Kali.

To each form of her we give a name. What is this name? It is word, it is sound, it is vibration of being, the child of infinity & the father of mental idea. Before form can be, name & idea must have existed.

The half-enlightened say "Whatever form is built, the Lord enters to inhabit"; but the Seer knows that whatever the Lord sees in His own being, becomes Idea and seeks a form and a habitation.

The universe is a rhythmic vibration in infinite existence which multiplies itself into many harmonies and holds them well ordered in the original type of motion.

Thou lookest upon a stone and sayest, "It is still." So it is, but to the sense-experience only. To the eye that sees, it is built out of motion and composed of motion. In the ordered repetition of the atomic movements that compose it, consists its appearance of stillness.

All stability is a fixed equilibrium of rhythm. Disturb the rhythm, the stability dissolves & becomes unstable.

No single rhythm can be eternally stable; therefore the universe is an ocean always in flow, and everything in it is mutable & transient. Each thing in Nature endures till the purpose of Kali in it is fulfilled; then it is dissolved and changed into a constituent of some other harmony.

Prakriti is eternal, but every universe passes. The fact of universe endures for ever, but no particular world of things can last; for each universe is only one rhythm out of an infinite number of possible movements. Whatsoever system in Nature or of Nature is thoroughly worked out, must give place to a new harmony.

Nevertheless all world and everything in world is eternal in its essential being; for all essential existence is Brahman without end or beginning.

Forms and names are also Brahman and eternal; but, in world, theirs is an eternity of recurrence, not of unbroken persistence. Every form & every idea that has once been, exists still and can again recur; every form or idea that is to be, already exists and was from the beginning. Time is a convention of movement, not a condition of existence.

That which inhabits the forms of Kali is Self and Lord of the Movement. Purusha is master of Prakriti, not her subject; Soul determines Form & Action & is not determined by them. Spirit reflects in its knowledge the activity of Nature, but only those activities which it has itself compelled Nature to initiate.

The soul in the body is master of body and not subject to its laws or limited by its experiences.

The soul is not constituted by mind and its activities, for these also are parts of Nature and movements only.

Mind and body are instruments of the secret all-knowing and omnipotent Self within us.

The soul in the body is not limited in space by the body or

in experience by the mind; the whole universe is its habitation.

There is only one Self of things, one soul in multitudinous forms. By body & mind I am separated even from my brother or my lover, but by exceeding body & mind I can become one with all things in being & in experience, even with the stone & the tree.

My universal soul need no more be limited by my individual mind and body, than my individual consciousness is limited by the experiences of a single cell in my body. The walls which imprison us have been built up by Prakriti in her movement and exist only in her inferior kingdoms. As one rises higher they become conventional boundaries which we can always stride across and, on the summits, they merely mark off compartments in our universal consciousness.

The soul does not move, but motion of Nature takes place in its perfect stillness.

The motion of Nature is not real or material motion, but vibration of the soul's self-consciousness.

Nature is Chit-Shakti, the Lord's expressive power of self-awareness, by which whatever He sees in Himself, becomes in form of consciousness.

Every thing in Nature is a becoming of the one Spirit who alone is Being. We and all things in Nature are God's becomings, sarvabhutani.

Although there are to world-experience multitudinous souls (Purushas) in the universe, all these are only one Purusha masked in many forms of His consciousness.

Each soul in itself is God entirely, every group of souls is collectively God; the modalities of Nature's movement create their separation and outward differences.

God transcends world and is not bound by any law of Nature. He uses laws, laws do not use Him.

God transcends world and is not bound to any particular state of consciousness in the world. He is not unity-consciousness nor multiple consciousness, not Personality nor Impersonality, not stillness, nor motion, but simultaneously includes all these self-expressions of His absolute being.

God simultaneously transcends world, contains it and informs it; the soul in the body can arrive at the God-consciousness and at once transcend, contain and inform its universe.

God-consciousness is not exclusive of world-consciousness; Nature is not an outcast from Spirit, but its Image, world is not a falsity contradicting Brahman, but the symbol of a divine Existence.

God is the reverse side of Nature, Nature the obverse side of God.

Since the soul in the body is eternally & inalienably free, its bondage to egoism, law of bodily nature, law of mental nature, law of pleasure and pain, law of life and death, can only be an apparent & not a real bondage. Our chains are either a play or an illusion or both play & illusion.

The secret of our apparent bondage is the Spirit's play by which It consents to forget God-consciousness in the absorption of Nature's movement.

The movement of Nature is a sevenfold flow, each stream subject to its own law of motion but containing latent, expressed or half-apparent in itself its six sisters or companions.

Nature is composed of Being, Will or Force, Creative Bliss, Pure Idea, Mind, Life and Matter, — Sat, Chit or Tapas, Ananda, Vijnanam, Manas, Prana and Annam.

The Soul, Purusha, can seat itself in any of these principles and, according to its situation, its outlook changes and it sees a different world; all world is merely arranged and harmonised outlook of the Spirit.

What God sees, that exists; what He sees with order & harmony, becomes a world.

There are seven worlds, Satya, of pure being, Tapas, of pure will or force, Jana, of pure delight, Mahas, of pure idea, Swar, of pure mentality, Bhuvah, of pure vitality, Bhuh, of pure matter.

The soul in Sat is pure truth of being and perceives itself as one in the world's multiplicity.

The soul in Tapas is pure force of divine will & knowledge and possesses universe omnisciently and omnipotently as its extended self.

The soul in Ananda is pure delight and multiplies itself in universal self-creation and unmixed joy of being.

The soul in Mahas is pure idea, perceives itself in order and arrangement of comprehensive unity in multiplicity, all things in their unity & each thing in its right place, time and circumstance. It is not subject to the tyranny of impressions, but contains & comprehends the objects it knows.

The soul in Manas is pure mentality & receives the pure impression of separate objects & from their sum receives the impression of the whole. It is Manas that measures, limits & divides.

The soul in Prana is pure vitality & pours itself out in various life-energy.

The soul in Annam is pure matter & forgets force of consciousness in the form of consciousness.

Matter is the lowest rung of the ladder and the soul that has descended into Matter tends by its secret nature & inevitable self-impulsion to reemerge out of form towards the freedom of pure universal being. These are the two movements that govern world-existence, adhogati, the descent towards matter or mere form and urdhwagati, the ascent towards Spirit and God.

Man is a mental being, manu or manomaya purusha, who has entered into a vitalised material body and is seeking to make it capable of infinite mentality & infinite ideality so that it may become the perfect instrument, seat and temple of the manifest Sacchidananda.

Mind in the material world is attentive to two kinds of knowledge, impacts from outside, corporeal or mental, received into the individual mentality and translated into mental values and knowledge from within, spiritual, ideal or mental similarly translated.

Inert physical bodies receive all the impacts that the mind receives, but being devoid of organised mentality, retain them only in the involved mind in matter and are incapable of translating them into mental symbols.

Our bodies are naturally inert physical bodies moved by life & mind. They also receive all impacts, but not all of them are translated into mental values. Of those which are translated, some are rendered imperfectly, some perfectly, some immediately, some only after a longer or shorter incubation in the involved mind in matter. There are the same variable phenomena with the internal knowledge. All the knowledge translated here into mental values forms the stuff of our waking consciousness. This waking consciousness accepted by the manomaya purusha as itself & organised round a central I-sense is the waking ego.

The Jiva or embodied mental being is in its consciousness much wider than the waking ego; it has a wide range of knowledge & experience of the past, present and future, the near & the distant, this life & other lives, this world & other worlds which is not available to the waking ego. The waking ego fails to notice many things & forgets what it notices; the Jiva notices & remembers all experience.

That which goes on in our life-energy & bodies below the level of waking mind is our subconscious self in the world; that which goes on in our mind & higher principles above the level of our waking mind is our superconscious self. The waking ego often receives intimations, more or less obscure, from either source which it fails to trace to their origin.

Man progresses in proportion as he widens his consciousness & renders ever wider & finer experiences available for the perception & delight of the waking consciousness & in proportion as he can ascend to higher reaches of mind & beyond mind to ideality & spirit.

The swiftest & most effective means of his advance & self-fulfilment is to dissolve his waking ego in the enjoyment of an infinite consciousness, at first mental of the universal manomaya Purusha, but afterwards ideal and spiritual of the high vijnana & highest Sacchidananda.

The transcendence & dissolution of the waking mental ego in the body is therefore the first object of all practical Vedanta.

This transcendence & dissolution may result either in loss of the waking self & relapse into some sleepbound principle, undifferentiated Prakriti, sushupta Purusha, Sunyam Brahma (Nihil), etc or in loss of the world self in Parabrahman or in universalisation of the waking self & the joy of God's divine being in & beyond the world, Amritam. The last is the goal proposed for man by the Isha Upanishad.

The waking ego, identifying the Jiva with its bodily, vital & mental experiences which are part of the stream of Nature's movement & subject to Nature & the process of the movement, falsely believes the soul to be the subject of Nature & not its lord, anish and not Ish. This is the illusion of bondage which the manomaya Purusha either accepts or seeks to destroy. Those who accept it are called baddha Jivas, souls in bondage; those who seek to destroy it mumukshu Jivas, self-liberating souls, — those who have destroyed it are mukta Jivas, souls free from illusion & limitation.

In reality, no soul is bound & therefore none seeking liberation or liberated from bondage; these are all conditions of the waking mind and not of the self or spirit which is Ish, eternally lord & free.

The essence of bondage is limitation & the chief circumstances of limitation are death, suffering and ignorance.

Death, suffering & ignorance are circumstances of the mind in the vitalised body and do not touch the consciousness of the soul in vijnana, ananda, chit & sat. The combination of the three lower members, mind, life & body, is called therefore aparardha, the lower kingdom or in Christian parlance the kingdom of death & sin, the four higher members are called parardha, the higher kingdom, or in Christian parlance, the kingdom of heaven. To liberate man from death, suffering & ignorance and impose the all-blissful & luminous nature of the higher kingdom upon the lower is the object of the Seer in the Isha Upanishad.

This liberation is to be effected by dissolving the waking ego into the Lord's divine being and experiencing entirely our unity with all other existences & with Him who is God, Atman & Brahman.

All individual existences are jagat in jagati, object of motion in stream of motion & obey the laws & processes of that motion.

Body is an object of motion in the stream of material

consciousness, of which the principal law is birth & death. All bodies are subject therefore to formation and dissolution.

Life is a current of motion in the stream of vital consciousness composed of eternal life-energy. Life is not itself subject to death, — death not being a law of life-energy, — but only to expulsion from the form which it occupies and therefore to the physical experience of death of its body.

All matter here is filled with life-energy of a greater or less intensity of action, but the organisation of life in individual animation begins later in the process of the material world by the appearance first of the plant, then of the animal. This evolution of life is caused & supported by the pressure of the gods of the Bhuvar or life-world upon Bhu.

Life entering into body is dominated partly by the laws of body; it is therefore unable to impart its own full & uninterrupted energy to its form. Consequently there is no physical immortality.

The organisation of individual animated life tends to hasten the period of dissolution by introducing shocks of an intensity of force alien to matter which wastes the material form by its activity. Therefore the plant dissolves while the stone & metal endure in their own equilibrium.

Mind entering into the vitalised body tends still farther to hasten the period of dissolution by the higher demands of its vibrations upon the body.

Mind is a knot of motion in the stream of mental consciousness. Like life, it is not itself subject to death, but only to expulsion from the vitalised body it has occupied. But because the mental ego identifies itself with the body and understands by its life only this residence in its present perishable gross corporeal body, therefore it has the mental experience of a bodily death.

The experience of death is therefore combined of the apparently mortal mind's ignorance of its own true immortal nature and of the limitation of energy in the body by which the form we inhabit wears out under the shocks of vibrating life-energy & vibrating mentality. We mean by death not dissolution of life or of mind, but dissolution of the form or body.

The dissolution of body is not true death for the mental being called man; it is only a change of media & of the surroundings of consciousness. Matter of body changes its constituents and groupings, mental being persists both in essence and personality and passes into other forms & environments.

The Life Divine

A Commentary on the Isha Upanishad

[Draft A]

Foreword

Veda & Vedanta are the inexhaustible fountains of Indian spirituality. With knowledge or without knowledge, every creed in India, sect, school of philosophy, outburst of religious life, great or petty, brilliant or obscure, draws its springs of life from these ancient and ever flowing waters. Conscious or unwitting each Indian religionist stirs to a vibration that reaches him from those far off ages. Darshana and Tantra and Purana, Shaivism & Vaishnavism, orthodoxy & heresy are merely so many imperfect understandings of Vedic truth & misunderstandings of each other; they are eager half-illuminated attempts to bring some ray of that great calm & perfect light into our lives & make of the stray beam an illumination on our path or a finger laid on the secret & distant goal of our seeking. Our greatest modern minds are mere tributaries of the old Rishis. Shankara, who seems to us a giant, had but a fragment of their knowledge. Buddha wandered away on a bypath in their universal kingdom. These compositions of an unknown antiquity are as the many breasts of the eternal Mother of Knowledge from which our succeeding ages have been fed & the imperishable life in us fostered. The Vedas hold more of that knowledge than the Vedanta, hold it more amply, practically and in detail; but they come to us in a language we have ceased to understand, a vocabulary which often, by the change of meaning to ancient terms, misleads most where it seems most easy & familiar, a scheme of symbols of which the key has been taken from us. Indians do not understand the Vedas at all; Europeans have systematised a gross misunderstanding of them. The old knowledge in the Vedas is to us, therefore, as a river wandering in dark caverns inaccessible to the common tread. It is in the Upanishads that the stream first emerges into open country. It is there that it is most accessible to us. But even this stream flows through obscure forest & difficult mountain reaches and we only have it for our use at favourable points where the forest thins or the mountain opens. It is there that men have built their little artificial cities of metaphysical thought and spiritual practice, in each of which the inhabitants pretend to control the whole river. They call their dwelling places Vedanta or Sankhya, Adwaita or Dwaita, Shaivism or Vaishnavism, with a hundred names beside and boast that theirs is the way & theirs is the knowledge. But, in reality, each of us can only command a little of the truth of the Sanatana Dharma, because none of us understands more than a little of the Upanishads.

They become, indeed, easier to us as they come nearer to us in date & the modernity of their language — the stream more accessible as it draws farther away from the original sources and descends more into the plain and the lowlands. But even the secret of these more modern revelations is not wholly ours and we delude ourselves if we think we have understood them entirely & need not plunge deeper for their meaning. There is much gold in the sands of the bed which no man has thought of disinterring.

The Isha Upanishad is simpler in form & expression than such writings as the Chhandogya & Brihad Aranyaka which contain in their symbolic expressions, — to us obscure & meaningless, disparaged by many as violently bizarre in idea & language & absurd in substance, — more of the detail of old Vedic knowledge. The diction of the Upanishad is, for the most part, plain & easy; the ideas expressed by it, when they are not wrested from their proper sense, seem to be profound, yet lucid and straightforward. Yet even in the Isha the real import of the closing passage is a sealed book to the commentators, and I am convinced that the failure to understand this culminating strain in the noble progressive harmony of the thoughts has resulted for us in a failure to grasp the real & complete sense of the whole Upanishad. We understand, more or less clearly, the separate sense of the different slokas, but their true connection & relation of the thoughts to each other has been almost entirely missed. We have hold of some of its isolated truths; we have lost the totality of its purport.

For the Isha Upanishad is one of the most perfectly worked out, one of the most finely and compactly stated inspired arguments the world possesses — an argument not in the sense of a train of disputatious reasoning, logical not in the fashion of an intellectual passage from syllogism to syllogism, but a statement of inspired thought each part of which has been perfectly seen by the revelatory faculty & perfectly stated by inspired expression in itself, in relation to the others & to its place in the whole. Not only every sloka, but every word in each sloka has been perfectly chosen & perfectly placed. There is a consummate harmony in the rhythm of the thought as well as in the rhythm of the language & the verse. The result is a whole system of knowledge & spiritual experience stated with the utmost pregnant brevity, with an epic massiveness & dignity, but yet in itself full and free from omission. We have in this Upanishad no string of incoherent thoughts thrown out at random, no loose transitions from one class of ideas to another, but a single subject greatly treated, with completeness, with precision, with the inspiration of a poet possessed by divine truth & the skill of a consummate architect of thought & language. The Isha Upanishad is the gospel of a divine life in the world and a statement of the conditions under which it is possible and the spirit of its living.

It is this harmonious totality of meaning which it is the sole object of my commentary to bring to light. It has not been my object to support a particular philosophy or to read Adwaita or Dwaita or Visishtadwaita into its separate verses, and make it useful for metaphysical polemics. I hold firmly the belief that the truths of the Upanishads were not arrived at by intellectual speculation, cannot be interpreted by disputation according to the rules of logic and are misused when they are employed merely as mines & quarries for the building of metaphysical systems. I

hold them to have been arrived at by revelation & spiritual experience, to be records of things seen, heard & felt, drishta, sruta,
upalabdha, in the soul and to stand for their truth not on logic
which they transcend but on vision to which they aspire. Those
supra-intellectual faculties by which they received the Veda &
developed its implications, drishti, sruti & smriti, are also the
only means by which their thoughts can be perfectly understood.
What is it that the Upanishad reveals — this is the question I have
set myself to answer; I am indifferent for what set of warring
philosophical dogmas its texts can be made an armoury.

In the course of exegesis I have been compelled
to come into conflict with the opinions of the Mayavada. The
collision was inevitable rather than desired, for the Mayavada
was the opinion with which I commenced my study of Vedanta.
It is a system which still attracts the abstract intellectuality in me
and represents to me what I may call an intervening & mediary
truth of realisation which can never lose its validity. But when
it seeks to govern human thought & life, to perpetuate itself as
the sole truth of Vedanta, I feel that it is in conflict with the
old Vedanta, stultifies the Upanishad & endangers or sterilises
all our highest human activities without giving us the highest
spiritual truth in its place. Even so I would have preferred to
leave aside all negative criticism of it in these commentaries.
But that is not possible. For it has so possessed India's ideas
about the Upanishads that it has to be cleared away in order
that the true sense of this Upanishad at least may shine out
from the obscuration. For the Isha at least does not support
the Mayavada as is indeed evident from the struggle & sense
of difficulty in Shankara's own commentary which reduces its
fine thought & admirable expression to incoherence & slipshod
clumsiness. The error, however lofty, must be removed in order
that the plain & simple Truth may reveal itself.

In following the end I have had in view there are a few plain
and binding rules by which I have endeavoured always to be
guided. My method does not allow me to deal with the language
of the Upanishads in the spirit of the scholar, — not the pride of
the Pandit dealing with words as he chooses, but the humility of

the seeker after truth in the presence of one of its masters is, I have thought, the proper attitude of the exegete. In the presence of these sacred writings, so unfathomably profound, so infinitely vast in their sense, so subtly perfect in their language, we must be obedient to the text and not presume to subject it ignorantly to our notions. To follow the plain & simple meaning of the words has been therefore the first rule of my exegesis. Vidya & Avidya are plain words, with a well-ascertained sense; I cannot turn aside from it to interpret them as knowledge of the gods & ignorance. Sambhuti, asambhuti, vinasha are words with fixed meanings; my interpretation must arise directly & simply from those meanings. The rhythm and metre of the Upanishads, the balance of the sentences demand their place in the interpretation; for chhandas is of primary importance in all Veda, — I must not disturb that rhythm, metre & balance in order to get over a philosophical difficulty. The anustup of the Isha, for instance, is Vedic in its form & principle & not classical; it demands, that is to say, a stanza of two couplets and admits of sandhi in the middle of the pada but not between two padas: I must not take advantage of a possibility of sandhi between two padas possible only in the classical anustup in order to extract from the Upanishad the opposite of its apparent sense. And when the meaning of a verse is determined, when it stands without qualification as an integral part of the teaching, I am not at liberty to read in a gloss of my own "for the ignorant" in order to depreciate or annul the validity of the doctrine. I am bound by the thoughts of the Sage; I cannot force upon him any ideas of my own to govern & override his apparent meaning — all that I am allowed to do, is to explain his evident textual meaning in the light of my inward spiritual experience but I must not use that experience which may be imperfect to contradict the text.

Shankara has permitted himself all these departures from the attitude of subjection to the text. He has dealt with the Upanishad, and with this Upanishad more than any other, as a master of the Sruti & not its servant. He has sought to include it among his grandiose intellectual conquests. But the Sruti cannot be mastered by the intellect, and although the great Dravidian has enslaved men's thoughts about the Sruti to his victorious intellectual polemic, the Sruti itself still preserves its inalienable freedom, rising into its secret heights of knowledge & being superior to the clouds & lightnings of the intellect, awaiting & admitting only the tread of the spirit, opening itself only to experience in the soul & vision in the supra-intellectual faculty of ideal knowledge. I trust I shall not be considered as wanting in reverence for the greatest of Indian philosophers, — in my opinion, the greatest of all philosophers. Nevertheless the greatest have their limitations. In profundity, subtlety & loftiness Shankara has no equal; he is not so supreme in breadth & flexibility of understanding. His was a spirit visited with some marvellous intuitions & realisations, but it would be to limit the capacities of the human soul to suppose that his intuitions exclude others equally great or that his realisations are the only or final word of spiritual knowledge. Shankara of the Commentaries on the Upanishad, — although the greatest commentaries on them that we have, — is not so great as Shankara of the Bhashya on the Vedanta Sutras. In the latter he is developing in full freedom his own philosophy, which even those who disagree with it must recognise as one of humanity's most marvellous intellectual achievements; in the former he is attempting to conquer for his own system the entire & exclusive authority of the Sruti. A commentary on the Upanishads should be a work of exegesis; Shankara's is a work of metaphysical philosophy. He does not really approach the Sruti as an exegete; his intention is not to use the philosophical mind in order to arrive at the right explanation of the old Vedanta, but to use explanation of the Vedanta in order to support the right system of philosophy. His main authority is therefore his own preconceived view of Vedantic truth, — a standard external to the text & in so far illegitimate. Accordingly he leaves much of the text unexplained, because it does not either support or conflict with the conclusions which he is interested in establishing; he gives merely a verbal paraphrase or a conventional scholastic rendering. Where he is interested, he compels the Sruti to agree with him. Without going quite to the same extent of self-will as the Dwaita Commentator who does not hesitate to turn the famous Tat twam asi into Atat twam asi, "Thou art *not* that, O Swetaketu," he goes far enough & uses a fatal masterfulness. The Isha especially, it seems to me, is vitiated by the defects of his method, because in the Isha the clear & apparent meaning of the text conflicts most decisively with some of his favourite tenets. The great passage on Vidya & Avidya, Sambhuti & Asambhuti bristles for him with stumbling blocks. We find him walking amid these difficulties with the powerful but uneasy steps of Milton's angels striding over the burning marl of their prison house. I for my part am unwilling to keep to the trace of his footsteps. For, after all, no human intellect can be permitted to hold the keys of the Sruti & fix for us our gate of entrance & the paths of our passage. The Sruti itself is the only eternal authority on the Sruti.

I have also held it as a rule of sound interpretation that any apparent incoherence, any want of logical relation & succession of thought in the text must exist in my deficiency of understanding & not in the Seer's deficiency of thinking. This view I base upon my constant experience of the Upanishads; for I have always found in the end that the writers thought clearly & connectedly & with a perfect grasp of their subject & my own haste, ignorance & immaturity of spiritual experience has always been convicted in the end of the sole responsibility for any defect imputed by the presumption of the logical understanding to the revealed Scripture. The text has to be studied with a great patience, a great passivity, waiting for experience, waiting for light & then waiting for still more light. Insufficient data, haste of conclusions, wilful ramming of one's own favourite opinions into the text, wilful grasping at an imperfect or unfinished experience, wilful reading of a single narrow truth as the sole meaning of this complex harmony of thought, experience & knowledge which we call the Veda, — these are fruitful sources of error. But if a man can make his mind like a blank slate, if he can enter into the condition of bottomless passivity proper to the state of the calm all-embracing Chaitanya Atma, not attempting to fix what the Truth shall be, but allowing Truth to manifest herself in his soul, then he will find that it is the nature of the Sruti to reveal perfectly its own message.

For ultimately, as I have already insisted, we can know the subject of the Veda only by the soul & its pure faculty of knowledge, not by verbal scholarship, metaphysical reasoning or intellectual discrimination. By entering into communion with the soul of the thinker which still broods behind the inspired language, we come to realise what he saw, and what he put into his words, what waits there to make itself known to us. By communion with the soul of the Universe which is behind the soul of the thinker & one with it, we get those experiences which illumine & confirm or correct by amplifying our vision of truth in the Sruti. And since no man should lightly hope that he has been able always to think, act & know in this supreme method, it is fitting always to bow down in utter self-surrender to the Master of All, the Lord who as the Knower dwells in himself as name & form & offer to him the truth we have found in the Sruti & the error we have imported in it to do both with the truth & the error whatso He wills in His infinite power, love & wisdom for the purpose of His eternal & infinite Lila.

———

Chapter I
The Subject & Plan of the Upanishad.

The Upanishads have but one subject without a second and yet by the very nature of that subject they take all life & being & knowledge for their portion. Their theme is the One who is Many. It is an error which the Adwaitins have popularised to suppose that all the aim of the Upanishads is to arrive at the unconditioned Brahman. A very cursory examination of their contents reveals a much wider and more complex purpose. They strive rather to develop from various standpoints the identity of the One & the Many & the relations of the conditioned to the unconditioned. Granting the unconditioned One, they

show us how this conditioned & manifold existence consists
with, stands in and is not really different from the original unity.
Starting from the multitudinous world they resolve it back into a
single transcendental existence, starting back from the transcendental they show us its extension within itself in phenomena.
Both the multitudinousness & the Unity, the manifestation &
the Manifested they establish in the unknowable Absolute of
which nothing can be proposed except that in some way different from any existence conceivable to mind or transferable
to the symbols of speech, beyond all conception of Time &
Space & Circumstance, beyond Personality & Impersonality,
beyond Finite & Infinity It Is. They seek not only to tell us of
the way of withdrawal from life into unconditioned existence,
but also of the way to dwell here in the knowledge & bliss
of the Supreme. They show us the path to heaven & the true
joy of the earth. Dwelling on the origin of things & the secret
of life & movement, they have their parts of science, — their
physics, their theory of evolution, their explanation of heredity.
Proceeding from the human soul to the Universal, they have their
minutely scrupulous, subtle & profound system of psychology.
Asserting the existence of worlds & beings other than those that
live within the compass of our waking senses, they have their
cosmogony, theogony, philosophy of Nature & of mental &
material nature powers. The relations of mind to matter & soul
to mind, of men to the gods & the illimitable Master Soul to
the souls apparently limited in bodies, have all their authority
in the Upanishads. The philosophical analysis of Sankhya, the
practices of Tantra, the worship & devotion of Purana, the love
of the formed Divinity & the aspiration to the Formless, the
atomic structure of Vaisheshika & the cardinal principles of
Yoga, — whatever has been afterwards strong in development
& influential on the Indian Mind, finds here its authority &
sanction. Not the unmanifested & unconditioned alone but the
identity of the Transcendental & the phenomenal, their eternal
relations, the play of their separation & the might of their union,
is the common theme of the Upanishads. They are not only for
the anchorite but for the householder. They do not reject life

but embrace it to fulfil it. They build for mankind a bridge by which we can cross over from the limited to the illimitable, the recurrent & transitory to the persistent & eternal, but by which also we can recross & cross again with delight & without danger that once unfathomable & irremeable abyss. They are God's lamps that illumine the stairs by which we ascend & descend no longer bound but freely & at will the whole scale of existence, finding Him there in His ineffability, concealed in utter luminousness, but also here in the garden of light & shade, manifest in every being.

The Upanishads have therefore a common field of thought, experience & knowledge; but in that field each has its own peculiar corner or province. There is nothing vague or ill-connected in their contents, nothing random in their structure. Each sets out with a certain definite thought & aim which it progressively develops & brings to a perfect culmination. The Aitareya for instance has for its subject the workings of the Self in the world as creator and master of evolution; creation, evolution, birth, heredity, death, our present human development are the matter of its brief & pregnant sentences. The Taittiriya takes for its subject the Anandam Brahman, the constitution of the soul in relation to the Infinite Delight in Conscious Being which is God & the reality of existence & reveals the way & the result of its attainment; it develops for us our gospel of eternal Bliss. The Kena starting from the present constitution of consciousness in man affirms the universal Brahman & teaches knowledge & self-surrender to Him as the inscrutable Self & the ever-present Master. Similarly, the Isha has for its subject the nature of human life & action lived & done in the light of Vedantic knowledge & supreme realisation. It is the gospel of a divine life on earth, a consecration of works, the seed & foundation of Karmayoga.

The Upanishads are works of inspiration, not of reasoning; therefore we shall not find in them the development of thought or the logical connection of the sentences managed on the system of modern writers. The principle of our modern writing borrowed from the Greeks, who were the first nation to replace inspiration by intellect, resembles the progress of the serpent over a field, slow, winding, insinuating, covering perfectly every inch of the ground. The literary method of the ancients resembles the steps of a Titan striding from reef to reef over wide & unfathomable waters. The modern method instructs the intellect, the ancient illumines the soul. In the latter also there is a perfect logical sequence but this logic demands for our understanding & capacity to follow it something of the same illumination which presided at its construction. So profoundly characteristic is this difference that the Greek governs even his poetry by the law & style of the logical intellect, the Indian tends to subject even his prose to the law & style of the illuminated vision. The Sage of the Isha is an inspired poet writing of God & life in a style of clear, but massive & epic sublimity, lofty & grandiose, but without the European epical tendency to amplitude & period, exceedingly terse, pregnant, compactly decisive, — every word stored with meaning & leaving behind it a thousand solemn echoes. These conditions of his method of composition must be taken into full account when we try to interpret his thinking.

The theme which he has to develop arises from the fundamental doctrine of the Vedanta, Sarvam khalu idam Brahma, Verily all this is the Brahman. To realise that everything of which we have separate knowledge by the limited & dividing movement of the mind & senses, is limited & separate only in appearance, but in its reality transcends its appearance and is a manifestation, a form in consciousness, an eidolon, a mask of something absolute, transcendental & without limit, — this is the first necessity of true knowledge according to the early thinkers. But when we have realised it, when we know that earth is not earth except in form & idea but the Brahman, man is not man except in form & idea but the Brahman, what then? Can we live in the light of that knowledge or must we abandon life to possess it? For it is obvious that all actions are done through mind with its two great instruments of name & form and if we are to look beyond name & form we must transcend mind & ignore its limitations. How can we do that & still act & live in this world as men act & live? Can one keep one's eyes fixed on the transcendent & yet move with any ease or safety in the phenomenal? Must we not remove our thoughts from That (Tat) in order to deal with this (sarvam idam), — just as a man cannot walk safely on earth if he keeps his eyes fixed on the heavens, but must constantly be removing his gaze from the lofty object of his contemplation? And another & deeper question arises. Is life worth living when we know the Brahman? is there any joy & use in the phenomenal when we know the transcendent, in the recurrent & transient when we know the persistent & eternal, in the apparent when we know the real? Immense is the attraction of the infinite & unlimited, why should we take pleasure in the finite & fleeting? Does not the charm of phenomena disappear with the advent of this supreme knowledge & is it possible to busy ourselves with the phenomenal when its attraction & apparent necessity are removed? Is not persistence in life caused by ignorance and possible only if there is persistence in igno-rance? Must we not abandon the world, if we would possess God? forsake Maya if we would become one in the Atman? For who can serve at the same time two masters & such different masters? We know the answer of Shankara, the answer of the later Adwaitin, the Mayavadin; and the answer of most religious minds in India since Buddhism conquered our intellects has not been substantially different. To flee the world & seek God, sums up their attitude. There have been notable exceptions, but the general trend hardly varies. The majority of the pre-Buddhistic Hindus answered the question, if I am not mistaken, in a differ-ent sense & attained to a deeper consummation. They answered it in the sense of the Isha Upanishad & the Gita; they held divine life in the Brahman here to be a possibility.

The supreme importance of the question is apparent. If the theory of the Illusionist is true, life is an inexplicable breach of Truth, an unjustifiable disturbance in the silence & stillness of the Eternal. It is a freak to be corrected, a snare to be es-caped from, a delusion to be renounced, a mighty cosmic whim & blunder. The results upon the nation which produced this tremendous negation, have been prodigious. India has become the land of saints & ascetics, but progressively also of a decaying society and an inert, effete & helpless people. The indignant denunciation of the Vishnu Purana against the certain results to society of the Buddhist heresy has been fulfilled in the fate of our strongly Buddhicised Hindu nation. We see increasing upon it through the centuries the doom announced in the grave warnings of the Gita against the consequences of inaction, "utsideyur ime lokah . . sarirayatrapi akarmanah . . sankarasya cha karta syam upahanyam imah prajah . . buddhibhedam janayed ajnanam karmasanginam" etc. The religious life of this country has divided itself into two distinct & powerful tendencies, the Hinduism of the withdrawal from life which has organised itself in the monastery & the hermitage and the Hinduism of social life which has resolved itself into a mass of minute ceremony & unintelligent social practice. Neither is pure; both are afflicted with sankara, mixture & confusion of dharmas; for the life of the monastery is stricken with the tendency towards a return to the cares & corruptions of life, the life of society sicklied over & rendered impotent by the sense of its own illusion & worthlessness faced with the superiority of the monastic ideal. If a man or a nation becomes profoundly convinced that this phenomenal life is an illusion, its aims & tendencies of a moment & its values all false values, you cannot expect either the man or the nation to flourish here, whatever may be gained in Nirvana. For the nation any sustained & serious greatness of aim & endeavour becomes impossible. To get through the years of life, to maintain the body and propagate the race, since for some unreasonable reason that is demanded of us, but to get done with the business as soon as possible & escape by sannyasa into the unconditioned, this must obviously be the sole preoccupation of man in a society governed by this negative ideal. What is chiefly needed by it is an elaborate set of rules, the more minute & rigid the better, which will determine every action of life both social & religious, so as to save men the labour of thought & action & give them the assurance that they are doing only the nityakarma necessary to life in the body or the shastric karma which creates the least bondage for future lives & are not heaping up on themselves the burden of long continued existence in this terrible & inexplicable nightmare of

the phenomenal world. But the attachment to works remains &
it tends to satisfy itself by an excessive insistence on the petty
field still left to it. We see an exclusive preoccupation with a
petty money-getting, with the mere maintenance of a family,
with the sordid cares of a narrow personal existence. The great
ideals, the universalising & liberating movements which have
continually swept rajasic Europe & revivified it, have been more
& more unknown to us in the later history of our country.
We have had but one world-forgetting impulse & one world-
conquering passion, — the impulse of final renunciation & the
passion of self-devotion to the Master of all or to a spiritual
teacher. It is this habit of bhakti that alone has saved us alive;
preserving an imperishable core of strength in the midst of our
weakness & darkness it has returned upon us from age to age
and poured its revivifying stream always through our inert mass
and our petrifying society. But for all that our great fundamental
mistake about life has told heavily; it has cursed our rajasic
activity with continual inefficiency and our sattwic tendencies
with a perpetual weight of return to tamas. Andham tamah
pravishanti ye avidyam upasate. Tato bhuya iva te tamo ya u
vidyayam ratah. Both these sentences of gloom have weighed
upon us; we have divided ourselves into the exclusive seekers
after the unconditioned knowledge & the exclusive lingerers in
the phenomenal ignorance. We have made the life divine well
nigh impossible in the world, possible only in remote hermitage,
desolate forest or lonely mountain. We have not known the
harmony which the early Vedantins practised; we have given
ourselves instead to a great negation which, however inspiring
and strength giving by its positive side — for it has its strong
positive side — to a few exceptional spirits, cannot be grasped
by the ordinary soul even when it is accepted by the ordinary
intellect, is not man's swadharma, and must therefore tend only
to destroy his strength & delight in life by imposing upon him an
effort beyond our average human capacity, from which it sinks
back dispirited, weakened and nerveless. No nation, not even a
chosen race, can with impunity build its life on a fundamental
error about the meaning of life. We are here to manifest God in

our mundane existence; our business is to express & formulate in phenomenal activity such truth as we can command about the Eternal; and in order to do that effectively we must answer the riddle set for us of the coexistence of the eternal & the phenomenal — we must harmonise God & Nature on peril of our destruction. The European nations have invariably decayed after a few centuries of efflorescence because they have persisted in ignorance, & been obstinate in Avidya. We who possess the secret but misunderstand it, have taken two millenniums to decay, but in the end we have decayed & brought ourselves to the verge of actual death & decomposition. We can preserve ourselves only by returning to the full & harmonious truth of our religion, truth of Purana & Tantra which we have mistranslated into a collection of fables and of magic formulae, truth of Veda which we have mistranslated into the idea of vacant & pompous ceremonial & the truth of Vedanta which we have mistranslated into the inexplicable explanation, the baffling mystery of an incomprehensible Maya. Veda & Vedanta are not only the Bible of hermits or the textbook of metaphysicians, but a gospel of life and a guide to life for the individual, for the nation & for all humanity.

The Isha Upanishad stands first in the order of the Upanishads we should read as of a supreme importance for us & more almost than any of the others, because it sets itself with express purpose to solve that fundamental difficulty of life to which since Buddha & Shankara we have persisted in returning so lofty but so misleading an answer. The problem resolves itself into a few primary & fundamental questions. Since we have here a great unconditioned unity and a great phenomenal multitudinous manifestation, what is the essential relation between this unity & this manifestation? Given the coexistence & identity of the reality & the phenomenon where is the key to their identity? what is the principle which harmonises them? and wherein lies the purpose & justification of their coexistence & apparent differentiation? The essential relation being known, what is that practical aspect of the relation upon which we can build securely our life here in this world? Is it possible to do the

ordinary works of our human life upon earth consistently with
the higher knowledge or in such a way as to embody in our every
action the soul of the divine knowledge & the divine guna? What
is that attitude towards God & the world which secures us in
such a possibility? Or what the rule of life which we must keep
before us to govern our practice and what the practical results
that flow from its observance? The present curses of phenomenal
life seem always to have been the sorrowful trinity of pain, death
& limitation; will these practical results of a Vedantic life include
the acceptance of this great burden and this besetting darkness
or has mankind even here, even in this body & in this society, an
escape from death & sorrow? As human beings what is our aim
here or what our hope hereafter? These are the great questions
that arise from the obscured soul of man to the Infinite & the
conflicting & partial answers to them have eternally perplexed
humanity. But if they can once be answered, simply, embracingly,
satisfyingly — so as to leave no true demand of the God in man
upon the world unsatisfied, then the riddle of existence is solved.
The Isha Upanishad undertakes to answer them all. Setting out
with a declaration of God's purpose in manifestation for which
the world was made & the golden rule of life by which each
man individually can utterly consummate that divine purpose,
the mighty Sage to whom as an instrument & channel we owe
this wise & noble solution asserts the possibility of human works
without sin, grief & stain in the light of the one spiritual attitude
that is consistent with the conscious & true knowledge of things
& in the strength of the golden rule by which alone a divine
life here can be maintained. In explaining & justifying these
original positions he answers incidentally all the other great
human questions.

The structure of the Upanishad is built up, the harmony of
its thought worked out in four successive movements, with the
initial verse of each swelling passage linking it in the motion of
thought to the strain that precedes. Before we proceed to any
work of analysis or isolate each note in order to obtain its full
value, it will be convenient to have a synthetical understanding
of the main ideas that run through the symphony and perceive

something of the manner with which they pass into or help each other and build up by their agreement a great and harmonious philosophy of life.

II The First Movement

"For the Lord all this is a habitation, yea, whatsoever single thing is moving in this universe of motion: by that abandoned thou shouldst enjoy; neither do thou covet any man's possession. Doing verily works in this world thou should wish to live a hundred years, for thus it is with thee & not otherwise; action clingeth not to a man. Sunless, truly are those worlds and enveloped in blind gloom whither they passing hence arrive who are hurters of their own souls." So runs the first movement of the Upanishad.

In the very beginning the Rishi strikes the master note to which all the rest of the harmony vibrates, lays down the principle of which every Upanishad is an exposition. God & the World, — these are the two terms of all our knowledge. From their relation we start, to their relation in union or withdrawal from union all our life & activity return. When we have known what the world is, when we have exhausted Science & sounded all the fathomless void, we have still to know what God is, & unless we know what God is, we know nothing fundamental about the world. Tasmin vijnate sarvam vijnatam. He being known, all the rest is known. Material Philosophy & Science have to admit in the end that because they do not know the Transcendental, therefore they cannot be sure about the phenomenal. They can only say that there are these phenomena which represent themselves as acting in these processes to the thought & senses, but whether their appearance is their reality, no man can say. The end of all Science is Agnosticism.

The Rishi takes these two great terms, God, one, stable & eternal, the world shifting, multitudinous, transient. For this great flux of Nature, by which we mean a great cosmic motion & activity, shows us nowhere a centre of knowledge & intelligent control, yet its every movement, denoting law, pointing

to harmony, speaks of a centre somewhere of knowledge &
intelligent control. It shows nowhere any definite unity except
that of sum and process, yet every little portion of it the more
we analyse, cries out more loudly, "There is One & not many."
Every single thing in it is perishable & mutable, yet for ever its
ancient & inevitable movements thunder in our ears the chant
of the immutable & eternal. She is one term, Prakriti, jagati,
the ever moving, with every object, small or great, a mere knot
of motion, jagat; that which she obeys & worships & of which
she speaks to us always & yet seems always by the whirl of her
motions in mind & matter to conceal, is the Lord, the Purusha.
He is that One, Eternal & Immutable; it is He that is the centre of
knowledge & eternal control. He is Ish, the Lord. The relation
between the world & its Lord on which the Rishi bids us fix
as the one on whose constant & established realisation we can
best found the thoughts & activities of the Life Divine, is the
relation of the Inhabitant & His inhabitation. For habitation by
Him it was made, not only as a whole, but every object which
it has built up, is building or will build in the whirl & race of
its eternal movement, from the god to the worm, from the Sun
to the atom & the grain of dust to the constellations & their
group, each, small or great, mean or mighty, sweet or sombre,
beautiful or repulsive, is his dwelling place & that which dwells
in it, is the Lord.[1]

We start then with this truth. We have seen that the problem
of life involves two essential questions; first, the essential relation
between the Transcendent & the phenomenal, secondly, that
practical aspect of the relation on which we can build securely
our life & action in the world. The Rishi starts with the practical
relation. This is the knowledge which we must win, the attitude
which having attained we must guard & keep. Looking around
upon the multitude of objects in the world, we have to see so
many houses & in each an inhabitant, one inhabitant only, He

---

[1] *In the manuscript, the above paragraph is followed by one that is bracketed and
struck through. This is reproduced as piece [1] of the Appendix. Piece [2] of the
Appendix, a passage written separately, is related to the above paragraph in theme.—Ed.*

who has built also the whole & inhabits the whole, its Lord. When we see the infinite ether containing this multitude of suns & solar systems, we are not to forget or ignore what we see but we must look on infinity as a house of manifest being & in it one great infinite indwelling Consciousness, Allah, Shiva, Krishna, Narayana, God. When we see around us man & animal & leaf & clod, king & beggar, philosopher & peasant, saint & criminal, we must look on these names & forms as so many houses of being and within each the same great inhabitant, Allah, Shiva, Krishna, Narayana, the Lord. Manhood & animality, animation & inanimation, wealth & poverty, wisdom & ignorance, saint-hood & criminality are the robes he wears, but the wearer is One. In every man I meet, I must recognise the Lord I adore. In friend & stranger, in my lover & my slayer, I must see equally, since I also must be He, myself. This is the great secret of existence & the condition which we must first satisfy if we wish to live divinely & be divine.

This is, internally, our necessary attitude towards God & the world. But to translate an internal attitude into the terms of action, it is our experience that a rule of life is needed. The purpose for which a householder builds himself a mansion & dwells in it, can only be one; it is to live & enjoy. So it is with the Purusha & Prakriti; their relation is the enjoyment of the one by the other. God has made this world in His own being that He may in mind & other principles live phenomenally in phenomena & enjoy this phenomenal existence even while secretly or openly He enjoys also His transcendent existence. The Soul or God is, says the Gita, Ishwara, bharta, jnata, anumanta; the Master for whose pleasure Prakriti acts, the Indweller who fills her with his being & supports her actions, the Knower who watches & takes into His cognisance her activities, the anumanta who gives or withholds or after giving withdraws His consent and as He gives, continues or withdraws it, things begin, endure or cease. But He is also & preeminently bhokta, her enjoyer. For all this is bhogartham — for the sake of enjoyment. But in practice we find that we are not Ish, but anish, not master, but slave; not jnata & anumanta, but ajna, not knowing & controlling, but ignorant, clouded, struggling for knowledge & mastery; not an immortal enjoyer in delight, but victim of sorrow, death & limitation. Limited, we struggle to enlarge ourselves & our scope; unpossessed of our desire, we demand & we strive; unattaining, reacted upon by hostile forces, we are full of sorrow & racked by pain. We see others possess & ourselves lack & we struggle to dispossess them and possess in their stead. The facts of life as we live it contradict at every turn the sublime dogma of the Vedantist. What are we to do? To struggle with God in others & God in the world or live only for God in others & not at all for God in ourselves?

In his second line the Rishi utters his golden rule of life which supplies us with the only practical solution of the difficulty. To enjoy as we enjoy now is to lift to our lips a cup of mixed honey & poison; to abandon the world is to contradict God's purpose by avoiding the problem instead of solving it; to sacrifice self to others is a half solution which, by itself, limits the divine lila & stultifies our occupation of the body. The fulfilment of self both in our own joy & in the joy of others & in the joy of the whole world is the object of our life. How then is the problem to be solved? By that abandoned thou shouldst enjoy; do not thou covet any man's possession. Tena, that, refers back to yat kincha jagat. By that you have to enjoy — for the world and all in it is meant for the purpose of enjoyment, it is the means, movement & medium created by the Lord for the purpose, but by that abandoned, by that renounced. You have not to cast the world & its objects themselves away from you, for then you defeat your own object. It is a deeper, a truer renunciation that is asked of us. Everything in the world has to be renounced and yet, through the thing so renounced, tena tyaktena, you have to enjoy, bhunjithah.[2]

Shankara translates "possess", not "enjoy". Essentially this makes no difference, for possession implies enjoyment. But the

---

[2] *Sri Aurobindo wrote the paragraph that follows on a separate page of the manuscript but marked it for insertion here. Two other separately written passages whose points of insertion were not marked are reproduced as pieces [3] and [4] of the Appendix. — Ed.*

ordinary sense of the root is to enjoy, & it is clearly the sense which the Rishi intended; for the collocation of the strongly opposite ideas of tyaga & bhoga can no more be an accident than the significant collocation of jagati & jagat in the preceding lines. Nowhere in this Upanishad is there random writing; rather every word is made to carry its entire weight & even run over with fullness of meaning.

In order to make his meaning perfectly clear the Rishi adds "Do not covet". This then is the renunciation demanded, not the renunciation of the thing itself, but the renunciation of the attachment, the craving, the demand — when that is renounced, then only is enjoyment possible, then only can the bitterness be cast out of the cup & only the pure honey remain. For the reason that we are anisha is because we demand. He who is Lord & Master, does not struggle & demand; he does not need even to command; for Prakriti knows His will & hastens to obey it. If we would live divinely, we must realise the Lord in ourselves, we must have sadharmya with Him & be as He. What the Lord wills for His lila in this habitation, Prakriti will bring; what Prakriti brings for our lila, is what the Lord wills. That which struggles in us, craves, fights, covets, struggles, weeps, is not the pure Self but the mind, — which, as we shall find, weeps & struggles because ensnared in limitations it does not understand, — not Ish, but jagat, the movement, the whirl, one eddy in the shifting & struggling movement & clash of forces — perfectly guided by Isha, but to our human understandings unguided or ill-guided — which we call Prakriti. In this great knowledge & its practice we can become desireless & calm, august, joyous, free from anxiety, pain, grief, sama, udasina, yet full of delight in all that we here in Prakriti, — Purushah Prakritistha, — say, see & do.

Immediately the great recurring problem presents itself of works and the cessation from works, — the ancient crux which it is so easy to get rid of by a trenchant act of logic, so hard to solve in harmony with the actual facts of existence. To the ordinary mind action seems impossible or purposeless without desire; to the logical mind it seems inevitable that the more one penetrates into the supreme calm, the farther one must move

from all impulse to action, — that pravritti & nivritti, shama &
karma are eternally opposed. Shankara, therefore, deciding all
things by his triumphant & inexorable logic, insists that action
is inconsistent with the state divine. In practice the seeker after
perfection finds that calm, renunciation, joy, peace seem only to
be secure when one rests motionlessly established in the impersonal Brahman; freedom of desire is only easy by freedom from
activity. Does not then enjoyment without demand or craving,
does not enjoyment by the thing renounced mean enjoyment of
the renunciation & not of the thing itself? Is it not the enjoyment of the eremite, eremite in soul if not in body, the spectator
watching the action of the world but himself no part of it, that
is alone possible to the desireless mind? And even if it is not
the sole possible enjoyment, is it not the superior & preferable?
Who that has self-enjoyment in the soul, would condescend to
the enjoyment of external objects? Or if he condescended, it is
the greater bliss of other worlds that would attract him and not
the broken shreds which are all this world's joys, the hampered
fulfilments which are all this world's actualisation of infinite
possibility.

To all these ancient questionings the reply of the Upanishad
is categorical, explicit, unflinching. "Doing verily works here
one should wish to live a hundred years; thus it is with thee & it
is not otherwise than this; action cleaveth not to a man." It is not
surprising that the great Shankara with his legacy of Buddhist
pessimism, his rejection of action, his sense of the nullity of the
world, faced by this massive & tremendous asseveration should
have put it aside by his favourite device of devoting it to the
service of unenlightened minds, although it occurs apparently as
an integral portion of the argument & there is not a hint or a
trace of its being intended as a contradiction or qualification of
the main teaching, although too this interpretation is stultified
both by the run of the two lines & by the immediate occurrence
of the next verse, — but every incongruity & impossibility is to
be accepted rather than suffer such an assertion to stand as the
teaching of the Sruti. Nor is it surprising that Shankara's greatest
follower, Vidyaranya, feeling perhaps that his master's dealings

with the text in this commentary were of the most arbitrary & violent, should have preferred to exclude the Isha from his list of authoritative Upanishads. But to us, uncommitted to any previous theory, this sloka offers no difficulty but is rather an integral & most illumining step in the development of a great & liberating doctrine.

Kurvanneva, says the Rishi, having his eye on the great dispute. Thou shalt do works & not abstain from doing them and the works are the works of this material world, those that are to be done iha, here, in this life & body. Doing his works in this world a man shall be joyously willing to live the full span of years allowed to the mortal body. If he grows weary, if he seeks to abridge it, if he has haste in his soul for the side beyond death, he is not yet an enlightened soul, not yet divine. With this great admission the Vedanta can no longer be a mere ascetic gospel. Life — full & unabridged in its duration, — full and un-contracted in its activity is accepted, welcomed, consecrated to divine use. And the Rishi affirms his reason for acceptance — because so it is with thee & it is not otherwise than this. Because in other words this is the law of our being and this is the will of the Eternal. No man, as the Gita clearly teaches, can abstain from works, for even the state of withdrawal of the ascetic, even the self-collected existence of the silent Yogin is an act and an act of tremendous effect & profoundest import. So long as we are in manifest existence, so long we are in the jagati using, influencing & impressing ourselves on the jagat and we cannot escape from the necessity self-imposed on Himself by God within us. And it is so imposed for the reason already stated, because He has made this world for His habitation & as a means for His enjoyment & a thing for His delight — & this his great will & purpose no man can be allowed to frustrate. The wise mind, the illumined soul knowing this truth makes no vain attempt to square this circle; he accepts that which God intends fully & frankly and only seeks the best way to fulfil God in this existence which he occupies on the way to another. For he knows that bondage and freedom are states of the outer mind, not of the inner spirit; for there is none free & none bound, none panting after liberation

& none fleeing from bondage, but only the Eternal rejoicing secretly or manifestly in His innumerable habitations.

But in that case we are eternally bound by the chain of our works, nailed helplessly to the wheel of karma? Not so; for the wheel of karma is an error and the chain of our works is a grand illusion. "Action clingeth not to a man." Bondage is not the result of works, & liberation is not the result of cessation of works. Bondage is a state of the mind; liberation is another state of the mind. When through the principle of desire in the mind the soul, the Ish, the lord, mixes himself up in the whirl of Prakriti, he sees himself in mental consciousness as if carried forward in the stream of causality; he seems to the mind in him to be bound by the effects of his works; when he relinquishes desire, then he recovers his lordship — which in his higher being he has never lost — and appears to himself what he has always been in reality, free in his being, swarat, samrat. It follows then that the way to liberate oneself is not to renounce works but to rise from mind to Supra-mind, from the consciousness of mental being, sambhava, to the consciousness of self-being, swayambhava or asambhuti. It is necessary to remember oneself, but it is not necessary to forget phenomena. For action is the movement of Prakriti and the chain of action is nothing more terrible or mystic than the relation of cause & effect. That chain does not bind the Master; action leaves no stain on the soul. The works of the liberated man produce an effect indeed, but on the stream of Prakriti, not on the soul which is above its action and not under it, uses action & is not victimised by it, determines action & is not determined by it. But if action in its nature bound the soul, then freedom here would be impossible. It does not & cannot; the soul allows mind to mix itself up with its works, buddhir lipyate, but the action does not adhere to the soul, na karma lipyate nare. The fear of action is Maya; the impossibility of combining action with calm & renunciation is a false sanskara. Nivritti or calm is the eternal state & very nature of the soul, pravritti is in manifestation the eternal state and very nature of Prakriti. Their coexistence & harmony is not only possible, but it is the secret of the world obscured only by ignorance in the mind. The enemy therefore is not action, but ignorance; not works bind us, but works done in the state of ignorance give us the illusion of bondage. The idea of separateness, of limitation with its fruit of desire, internal struggle, disappointment, grief, pain, — this alone is our stumbling block. Abolish it, see God alone everywhere & all difficulty disappears. Nivritti & Pravritti, tyaga & bhoga move harmoniously to the perfect fulfilment of the divine purpose.

Those important enunciations completed, the Sage proceeds to a minor, but not inessential effect of the knowledge he is developing — the life after this one which we have to use here, our progress into worlds beyond. The gati, trans-mortal journey or destination of the soul, occupied profoundly the Vedantic mind as it has occupied humanity in all except in its brief periods of entire materialistic this-worldliness. As yet the Sage does not proceed to any positive statement; but by a negative movement he indicates the importance of the question. Our life here is only one circumstance in our progress — the fundamental circumstance, indeed, since earth is the pratistha or pedestal of our consciousness in manifest being, — but still the fundamental is not the final, the pratistha is not the consummation but only the means to the consummation. It is the first step in our journey, the initial movement in the triple stride of Vishnu. There is beyond it a second step, from which we constantly return till we are ready here for the third, for the consummation. Our future state depends on our fullness at the time of our passage, on our harmonious progress towards divine being. That is the hidden thing in us which we have to develop. We are to become atmavan, to possess our divine being, to disengage & fulfil our real self. Those who fall from this development, who turn aside from it are self-hurters or, to take the full vigorous sense of the word used, self-slayers. Not that God in us can be slain, for death of the soul is impossible, — but there may be temporary perdition of the apparent divinity by the murder of its self-expression. And to this we may arrive either by wilfulness of passion or by intellectual wilfulness. Instead of becoming gods, Suras, images of the Most High, the Paratpara Purusha in His effulgent glory, we may become misrepresentations of Him, false because distorted images, distorted by imperfection, distorted by onesidedness, Titans, Asuras or else souls unillumined by the sun of Knowledge & if illumined at all then only by false lights which eventually become eclipsed in darkness. Our after state will be Asurya, sunless, unillumined. To what worlds do we then journey?

The ordinary reading of the first word in the third verse of the Upanishad, is Asŭrya, Titanic, but there is a possible variation Asûrya, sunless. The substantial sense resulting from both readings is the same, but the colour given will be different. The Titans or Asuras of the Veda are souls of mere undisciplined might. They are those who found themselves not on light & calm but on asu, the vital force & might which is the basis of all energetic & impetuous feeling & action. The self-willed ones, who from temperamental passion wreck themselves by the furious pursuit in desire of a false object or from intellectual passion wreck themselves by the blind pursuit in belief of a false idea, they follow a path because it is their own from Titanical attachment, from an immense though possibly lofty egoism. Mole ruit sua. They fall by their own mass, they collapse by excess of greatness. They need not be ignoble souls, but may even seem sometimes more noble than the gods & their victorious legions. When they hack & hew at the god within them, it may be in tremendous devotion to a principle; when they subdue, cloud & torture themselves till they stumble forward into misery & night, till they become demoniac in nature, it may be in furious & hungry insistence on a great aspiration. They may be grandiosely mighty like Hiranyakashipu, ostentatiously largehearted like Bali, fiercely self-righteous like the younger Prahlada. But they fall whether great or petty, noble or ignoble & in their fall they are thrust down by Vishnu to Patala, to the worlds of delusion & shadow, or of impenetrable gloom, because they have used the heart or intellect to serve passion & ignorance, enslaved the spiritual to the material & vital elements & subordinated the man in them to the Naga, the serpent. The Naga is the symbol of the mysterious earthbound force in man. Wisest he of the beasts of the field, but still a beast of the field, not the winged Garuda revered to be the upbearer of divinity who opens his vans to the sunlight and soars to the highest seat of Vishnu. If we read Asŭrya we shall then have to translate "Verily it is to the worlds of the Titans, worlds enveloped in blind gloom, that they after passing hence resort who are self-slayers." Otherwise it is the worlds farthest removed from the Sun, our symbol & principle of divine Knowledge. There are materialised states of darkness in the conscious being in which they must work out the bewilderment & confusion they have fastened on themselves by an obstinate persistence in self-will & ignorance. In either case the intention of the Sage is evident from the later passages of this Upanishad. Whether we follow exclusively after Avidya or exclusively after Vidya, we go equally astray, exclusiveness means ignorance, exclusiveness means confusion & division of the indivisible Brahman, & persistence in such error is an obstinacy fatal to the soul in its immediate prospects. Temporarily — because eternal perdition is impossible, — it fails to cross successfully over death & enters into trans-mortal darkness. Those who accept the unity of the Brahman, who see in Vidya & Avidya only vyavahara, light & shadow reflected in Him for the use of self-expression in phenomena, who live in the knowledge of the One in the Many, embracing like Brahman all being in themselves, rejecting nothing, preferring nothing, bearing everything, effecting everything, infinite in calm by renunciation, infinite in might & bliss by enjoyment, they are men perfected, they are the siddhas. Even those who not yet attaining, follow faithfully this law & this ideal journey onwards in the way of their self-fulfilment and are lifted by all-purifying Agni to the regions of the Sun where they possess their perfect oneness & receive their consummate felicity.... With this warning (for the promise comes afterward) closes the first movement of the Upanishad.

III

God then & the world are before us, the Inhabitant to be recognised as the Lord of things even when He appears otherwise &

His habitation to be regarded merely as a movement set going by Him for phenomenal purposes, a stream of form & action by which He can enjoy His own conditioned being, — God & the world are to be possessed by a pure & infinite enjoyment, Ananda, or bliss which depends on a perfect renunciation not of the world, but of the limited struggle & the ignorant attachment, of the demand & the groping. These poor & imperfect movements [are] to be replaced by a mighty calm and a divine satisfaction. We are not to renounce works, which do not & cannot stain the soul or bind it, but to be liberated through acceptance of works in a luminous knowledge of their divine use & nature; not mutilation of life is to be our ideal, but fulfilment through life of the intention of the Most High in His phenomenal manifestation. If we mutilate life through self-will & ignorance we imprison ourselves after death in worlds of confusion & darkness and here like a ship befogged & astray in dense sea mists are hindered & long delayed in our divine voyage.

But now farther questions arise. Stated by itself & without development or qualification the first line of this great teaching, although fundamental to the practical living of the divine life and the sufficient & right attitude for its fulfilment might yet, like all trenchant assertions, too positively & exclusively taken, lead us into a profound error & misunderstanding. God & the World, the Movement & the Dweller in the movement, that is the practical relation between the unconditioned & the phenomenal which we have to accept as the unalterable basis of our rule of right living. But this general movement, with the particular knots in it of apparent movement & apparent status which we call formations or objects, — what is it? Movement of Mahat or movement of what nature, — real or unreal? And the inhabitant, is he different from His habitation? If He is different & the habitation is real, what becomes of the universal unity Vedanta teaches and how are we not handed over to duality and a fundamental disparity, if not a fundamental opposition? It is to remove this possible misunderstanding that the Rishi now proceeds to a completer though not yet entirely complete statement of universal existence. He has stated the practical relation, he now states the essential relation. It amounts in effect to the fundamental tenet of Vedanta in the Upanishads "Sarvam khalu idam Brahma." All this, in truth, is the Brahman. He says "There is One who unmoving is swifter than mind, neither have the gods reached It for it goes always in front. Standing, it outstrips others as they run. In It Matariswan sets activity. That moves & that does not move; that is far & the same that is verily near; That is within all this, the same that is outside all this."

Not only the stable but the unstable; not only the constant, but the recurrent; not only the Inhabitant but His habitation; not only Purusha but Prakriti. It is ekam, not a number [of] different beings, as in the dogma of the Sankhyas, but One being; not two separate categories, the real & the unreal, Brahman & Maya, but only One, the Brahman. That which moves not is the Brahman but also that which moves is the Brahman, not merely Maya, not merely a base & ugly dream. We know already by the first verse that the innumerable inhabitants of this moving universe are not essentially many, but are one Soul disporting in many bodies or not really disporting but supporting the multiform play of Prakriti; eko achalah sanatanah, in the solemn language of the Gita, one, motionless, without beginning or end. He is this man & that woman, yonder ancient leaning on his staff, this blue winged bird, that scarlet winged. But now we learn that also the name & form & property, the manhood & the womanhood, the age & the youth, the blueness & the scarlet hue, the staff, the attitude of leaning, the bird, the wing, all is the Brahman. The Inhabitant is not different from His habitation.

This is a difficult point for the ordinary mind to admit intellectually; it is difficult, even for minds not ordinary, really to grasp the intellectual conception, take it into the soul & realise it there in feeling & consciousness. Even the greatest materialist in theory regards himself in his feelings as a mind or a soul and is aware of a gulf between himself & the inanimate. His opinions contradict his heart's consciousness. In Yoga also one of our first realisations is the separateness of the body by the practical removal of the dehatmabuddhi, — a sensation the psychology of which is not well understood & being misunderstood gives rise to many errors. Hence we have a proneness to regard the inanimate as undivine, the material as gross & even foul and the objective as unreal — as if all this were not merely arrangement & vyavahara, as if the material was not also Atman & spirit, Brahman equally present in clod & man, body & soul, thought & action, as if all were not essentially equal in their divinity, and apparently so diverse merely because of the infinite variation of form & guna! By this cardinal error the intellectual man comes to despise & neglect the body, the religious man to treat the body & often the intellect also as an impediment, praising the heart only, the contemplative spiritual man to aim at casting out both mind & body & banishing from him the very thought & perception of the objective. All are ruled or driven by this dim sensation or clear belief that the subjective soul seated within them alone is God, alone the Self, that the objective movement of Spirit seeming to the movement of mind & senses to be outside & apart from us, is not God & is therefore worthless & evil. They all insist on a mental attitude to things, an attitude of analysis, separation & logical distinction instead of rising beyond mind-limitations & mind-methods to God's transcendent embracing vision which sees all things & states & is affected & bound by none. They all therefore make the essential error of duality, from which eventually every kind of ignorance & confusion arises. It is for this reason, to discourage this error that the Sage insists on his ekam in the neuter — not only is He divine, Sa, God regarding Himself subjectively as universal cognisant Personality, but That is divine, Tat, Brahman realising Himself by identity both beyond & in and as all phenomenal existences, at will & coexistently transcendental & phenomenal, conditioned & unconditioned, One in the One & One in the Many.

Brahman is spoken of here, not as the absolute Parabrahman outside all relation to life & phenomena, for to the unknowable utterness of Parabrahman such phrases as "swifter than the mind" or such ideas as outrunning the gods or going in their front cannot be applied, — It is the Brahman as we see It in Its relation to phenomena, God in the world, conditioned to our awareness in vyavahara, unconditioned to our awareness in paramartha, which is the subject of this & the following shloka.[3] That is the One & sole Existence which, though indeed It does not move, is swifter than the mind & therefore the Gods cannot attain to It because It goes always in front. For the mind served by the senses is the instrument which men use to grasp & measure the world & the gods are the presiding powers of all mental & physical functions, but neither the mind nor the senses, neither sensation nor reason can attain to the Brahman. It always goes far in front of any swiftest agency by which we can pursue It.

What is the precise significance of this imagery? The intention can only be understood if we remember the nature of mental action upon which such enormous stress is here laid and the limitations of that action. Mind always starts from a point, the thinker or the object of thought; it works in space or time on particular objects or groups of objects or at most on the sum of all objects known. It can only seek to know the movement & process of the world, but of that which is beyond & behind movement & process, what can it know? At most it can feel or be told that He the eternal & ineffable exists. Ordinarily, it can only go as far back as itself and say "I, mind, am He; because I think, I am; because I am & think, things are" — propositions which as the expression of a relative & intermediate fact have their validity but are as an universal & ultimate statement untrue. But even the movement of God in nature is too vast & swift for the mind to grasp. It catches at & seizes petty surrounding eddies or even great masses of movement at a little distance; it seizes, arranges to itself in its own terms of vision & classes them triumphantly as ultimate laws of Nature. But who has sailed all these waters or can tell where, if at all, they end? Who shall say that those laws are not byelaws only, or the charter & constitution of a single dependency only or province? Follow

---

[3] *The following sentence was written in the top margin of the manuscript page. Its place of insertion was not marked:*

Of the Absolute all we can say is "It is not that, it is not that"; it is unknowable in Itself, knowable only in our existence here or in relation to our existence here, not to be characterised by any epithet, description or suggestion.

God to the utmost confines of observable space, — He is sure to be whirling universes into being far in front. Pursue Him into the deepest recesses of experimentable being, there are unguessed universes of consciousness behind to which you have no present access. Infinity is only one of His aspects, but the very nature of Infinity is that the mind cannot grasp it, though the reason deduces it. Who measured Space? Can any vastest Mind find out when Things began or know when & how they shall end? Nay, there may be near to us universes of another Time, Space & arrangement to which our material dimensions & mind & sense limitations forbid us entrance. Even here who has traced out the purpose of creation or systematised the ways of Providence? Of a hundred things that happen immediately around us, can we even in a dozen instances tell more than fragmentarily & at a hazard why the thing has happened, to what end it conduced, or of what ordering of things it was a piece & movement? Yet, as the eye opens to the innermost secret of things, one realises that an infinite Wisdom presides over the smallest happening & eternally links today's trifling action to the grandiose movement of the centuries — nay, that every thought which passes through our minds however weak, trivial or absurd, has its mark, in the depths of itself its purpose, even its necessity. But of all this how much can the gods of mind, reason & sense ascertain? They run, they gallop, they outstrip the arrow, the bullet, the lightning, the meteor, all material swiftnesses, but That though it moves not, travels still in front. Yes, even when we think we are in front of Him, have fathomed His ways, classified His laws, understood existence, ascertained & determined the future by the past, suddenly we stumble & come across a new landmark or footprint which shows where That has passed; a touch of His finger surprises us as He speeds past & our theories crumble, our knowledge is turned into foolishness, our enlightenment becomes the laughingstock of better enlightened generations. It standing outstrips others as they run, yet all the time, had no need to move. Already God was in front of us, as He is behind, above, below, on every side. Our latest knowledge will always be a candle burning in the mists of the night; our discoveries pebbles picked up on the shore of a boundless ocean. Not only can we not know That in all Its absolute, transcendent reality, but we cannot know It in all the vastness of Its phenomenal workings. Much we may yet know by the mind, but not all, not more than a corner or a system. All that we can do is to seek the boundless Lord of a boundless universe & here & elsewhere to know each habitation and recognise its Inhabitant. The dweller is divine, but the house too divine, a temple of God, sukritam, well built, delightful & holy — my God Himself manifested as name & form.

That stands really & does not run. What then is the movement by which He outstrips others or is far in front? The clue is given in the expression swifter than mind. It is the mind that runs in us but what is it that runs swifter than mind just as mind runs swifter than any material force? Something of which mind & matter are lower movements, — that which is the essence of the jagati, the essential conscious being of which mind, life & matter are particular currents. This conscious-being is That — the sole Reality which assumes so many appearances. It does not run, for where should it run when it does not exist in time & space, but time & space exist in the Brahman. All things are created in God's consciousness which has no more to move than a man has to move when he follows a particular train of thought. He who was before Time, is still just what He was after Time is finished — drawn back, that is to say, into supratemporal consciousness. He has not moved in His being an inch, He has not changed in His being by the shadow of a shadow. He is still eko achalah sanatanah, one, motionless, without change or end. This side of the Sun or that side of Lyra are to Him one point, or rather no point at all. Space is a symbol into which Thought has translated an arrangement in supraspatial Consciousness. Time & Causality are not different. Therefore it appears that both jagati & jagat are no movement of matter or material force, (that is expressly excluded in the [eighth] verse), nor of mind, (that is expressly excluded here) but of Conscious being in itself, a mysterious activity the essence of which is limitless & absolute Awareness not expressible in language, but translated in the symbols of our Thought here into a movement in Time, Space & Causality. This universal tenet of Vedanta, although not expressly stated, is yet implied in the Rishi's thought & follows inevitably from his expression. He could very well in his age & surroundings take it for granted, but we have to state it explicitly; for, unless it is assumed, the second movement of the Sage's thought cannot be entirely understood by us. It is, indeed, the foundation of all Vedantic thinking.

In this Brahman Matariswan sets activity. Tasminn apo Matariswa dadhati. Tasmin, in the containing, stable & fulfilling active Brahman already described; Apas, work or activity (Latin opus), this Vedic word being used in preference to karmani, because karmani expresses individual actions & it is here the general universe-activity of Brahman that is intended, not indeed all Prakriti, but that which is manifest as work productive & creative, the movement of the sun & star, the growth of the tree, the flowing of the waters, the progress of life in all its multitude; Matariswa, he that rests in the matrix of things, that is to say Vayu, the motional or first energetic principle of Nature founded in Akasha, the static principle of extension which is the eternal matrix of things, working in it as Prana, the universal life-activity; dadhati, (τίθησι) establishes, sets in its place & manages. For the root dha has always the idea of arrangement, management, working out of things.

The reason for introducing this final and more limiting idea about the Brahman as the culminating phrase of this shloka, is the Sage's intention to emphasise the divineness of that particular movement of Prakriti which is the basis of karmani, human action in this mortal life. Matariswan is the energy of God in Prakriti which enters into as into a womb or matrix (Matar), is first concealed in, — as a child in the womb — & then emerges out of the static condition of extension, represented to our senses in matter as ether. It emerges in the motional principle of expansion & contraction represented to the senses as the gaseous state, especially as breath & as air, called by us therefore Vayu, which by disturbing the even, self-contained vibration (shabda) of the ether, produces vibratory waves (kshobha), generates action &

reaction (rajas) on which ether behind is continually impressing a tendency to equipoise (sattwa), the failure of which is the only cause of disintegration of movement (death, mrityu, tamoguna) & creates contact (sparsha) which is the basis of mental & material sensation & indeed of all relation in phenomenal existence. Matariswan, identifying himself with Vayu, supporting himself on these principles of wave-vibration, action-reaction & contact, valid not only in matter but in life & mind, using the other three elementary or fundamental states known to Vedic enquiry, — agni (fire), the formatory principle of intension, represented to our senses in matter as heat, light & fire, apas or jala (water), the materialising or outward flowing principle of continuation, represented to our senses in matter as sap, seed, rasa, & prithwi (earth), the stabilising principle of condensation, represented to us in matter as earth, the basis of all solids, — Matariswan, deploying existence in settled forms by the fivefold (panchabhautic) complex movement of the material Brahman, of conscious being as the essential substance of things, reveals himself as universal life activity, upholder of our vitality, prompter & cause of our actions. He as Life, is latently active in the utter inanimate, present, but unorganised in the metal, organised for life and growth only in the plant, for sense & feeling & thought in the animal creation, for reason & illumination & progress to godhead in man, for sempiternal immortality in the gods. But who, ultimately, is this Matariswan? Brahman himself, as the Rigvedic Rishis already knew, manifesting himself in relation to His other movements as the cause, condition & master of vitality.

Life-action, then, is not indeed the whole action of the universe; nor is our human life-action, our apas, work, task here, its culminatory activity. There are more developed beings, superior states, other worlds. But it is, whether here or in other planets, the central activity of this universe. It is of this apparently insignificant pebble, the stone that builders not Almighty, not All-wise would have rejected, that God has made the keystone of this work of His construction. In this the movement of our universe finds the means for its central purpose, through it fulfils itself, in it culminates or from it falls away. When God has fulfilled himself here, under these conditions, with prithivi as his pratistha, then we may pass away finally into other conditions or into the unconditioned, but till then, till God here is satisfied, Brahman here manifested, we come here to fulfil him. Till then, so it must be with us & not otherwise. And this principle is not undivine but divine, not something utterly delusive or diabolical, not the kingdom of a lower spirit or an aberration in knowledge, but God's movement, mahimanam asya, the manifest might, the apparent extension in Itself of the Brahman. Life here is God, the materials of Life here are God. The work is not separate from the worker nor the thought from the thinker. All is the play of a divine Unity.

We can now grasp what the Sage intends when he says, Tad ejati tannaijati. Tat or That, the suggestive vague name for the Brahman whether impersonal or above personality or impersonality, moves & That does not move. It moves or appears to move, — as action of Prakriti & the corresponding knowledge in Purusha, — in the conception of Time, Space & Causality; it does not move in reality, because these are mere symbols, conceptual translations of the actual truth, & movement itself is only such a symbol. The Habitation is the creation of a formative movement of Prakriti, who is indeed always recurrent in her doings because she & her ways are eternal, but also always mutable & inconstant because she works in Time, Space & Causality, terms of perception which have no meaning except as measures of movement or progression from one moment to another, one point to another, one state or event to another. Succession & therefore change is the fundamental law of God's ideative & formative activity in the terms of these three great symbols. But the inhabitant is one & constant, because He is beyond Time & Space. Surrounded apparently by the whirl of Prakriti, to the ignorant tossed about in it, He in reality exists both as its continent & creator as well as its informing soul, master & guide. That therefore in Itself is unmoving, immutable and eternal; in Its movement in Itself, Time-movement, Space-movement, Condition-movement (although as we shall see governed by durable patterns or general processes of conscious being which

ensure order & recurrence from one state or form to another)
That is mobile, active, inconstant & fleeting. Sooner or later, all
here passes out of our view, except the Inhabitant, the eternal
Existence-Consciousness, Him we see seated for ever. On Him
in this flux of things we have our sure foundation.

Thus we have the essential reality of things, we have the
practical relation of God in Impersonality or Personality as the
Inhabitant of His own objective being. We have the principle of
unity by which the practical relation refers back always to the
essential & derives from it. We have the fundamental justification of works briefly indicated in the identity of the working
principle with the eternal Reality behind our works. But the
justification of the harmony of tyaga & bhoga on this basis
has now to be prepared. After stating, therefore, the identity of
the eternal who moveth not, with the eternal who moves, of
the Timeless, Spaceless, Conditionless, with the Timed, Spaced
& Conditioned, the Sage proceeds with a consideration of the
latter only with which our vyavahara or practical life has to deal
& emphasises the unity of all things near & far, subjective &
objective. That is the near, the same That is the far. He is near
to us in our subjective experience, he removes to a distance in
the objective where our mind & senses pursue him until they
have to cease or return. In the subjective also, he is not only the
unknown, but the known, ourselves, that which is seated in our
hearts, not only the ungrasped, but the grasped, that which we
have & that which we seem not to have, that which we have
reached or passed or are approaching & that towards which
we vaguely or blindly move. Nothing should we think, feel or
observe without saying of it "It is He; it is the Brahman." That
is within every creature as all the continent of body & mind &
what is more than mind; That is outside every creature as that
in which it moves, lives & has its being; not only are our surroundings near or far but that which contains our surroundings,
is outside & inside them, alike their continent & their content,
sarvam Brahma. For That is the content of all this Universe; That
also exceeds & Is apart from every Universe. The Pantheism or
Monism which, unable to rise beyond the unity of attainable

data or manifest appearance, makes God conterminous with the world, is not Vedanta. The Pluralism which makes God merely a sum of realised experiences, a growing & diminishing, a fluctuating unknown quantity, X sometimes equal to a + b and sometimes equal to a - b, is not our conception of the Universe. These things are He, but He is not these things. To us the world is only a minor term in God's absolute & limitless existence. God is not even infinite, though finity & infinity both are He; He is beyond finity & infinity. He is sarvam Brahma, the All, but he is inexpressibly more than the sarvam. To our highest conception He is One, but in Himself He is beyond conception. Neither Unity nor multiplicity can describe Him, for He is not limited by numbers. Unity is His parabhava, it is His supreme manifestation of being, but it is after all a manifestation, not the utter & unknowable reality.

IV

The object of these two verses which have amplified the idea of monistic Unity in the universe, so as to remove any essential opposition between the world movement & the Inhabitant of the movement, is to lead up to the two verses that follow, — verses of a still higher importance for the purpose of the Upanishad. The Sage has laid down his fundamental positions in the first three verses, — (1) the oneness of all beings in the universe, (2) the harmony of renunciation & enjoyment by freedom from desire & demand, (3) the necessity of action for the fulfilment of the one purpose for which the One inhabits this multitude of names & forms, — the enjoyment of this phenomenal & in its consummation the liberated being. The remainder of the Upanishad is explanatory & justificatory of these original & fundamental positions. In this second movement the object is to establish the possibility of absolutely sorrowless & fearless enjoyment here in this world & in this body on the eternal & unassailable foundations of the Vedantic truth, sarvam khalu idam Brahma. For from that truth the Seer's golden rule of life derives all its validity & practical effectiveness.

These are the words, words of a rich & moving beauty, in which he discharges this part of his argument. "But he who sees all existences in the self and the self in all existences, thereafter shrinketh not at all. He who knows, in whom all existences have become the self, how shall he have grief, how shall he be deluded, who seeth all things as one."

The connecting word तु (the Greek δε) does not in Vedic Sanscrit always imply entire opposition, it suggests a new circumstance or suggests an additional fact or a different point of view. The new circumstance introduced in this verse is the idea of the Atman. The knowledge that the impersonal Brahman is all, need not of itself bring peace & a joyous activity; for the all includes sorrow, includes death, fear, weariness, disgust. Matariswan in establishing action, has also established reaction. He has established that inequality between the force acting & the force acted upon, that want of harmony which is the cause of pain, recoil, disintegration, mutual fear & oppression. We may recognise that all these are one coordinated movement in a single existence, are themselves all one existence but how does that help us if in the movement itself there are these inequalities, these discords, these incapacities which impose on us so much that is painful & sorrowful? We may be calm, resigned, stoical, but how can we be free from pain & sorrow? It is here that Mayavada comes in with its great gospel of liberation. "All this discord" it says in effect "is not Brahman, it is Maya, it is an illusion, a dream, it does not exist in the pure Atman. That is the unmoving; the movement is a cosmic nightmare affecting the mind only. Renounce life, take refuge in the pure, unconditioned, dreamless Atman, mind will dissolve, the world will vanish from you as a dream vanishes & with the world its pain, its useless striving, its miserable joys, its ineffugable sorrow." That is an escape, but it is not the escape which the Seer of the Upanishad meditates for us. He holds to his point. "All this is Brahman, the movement no less than the moving." A few may escape by the wicket gates of the Buddhist & the Mayavadin. Not by denial of fundamental Vedantic truth is mankind intended to be saved.

The worship of a Personal God different from ourselves &

the world brings with it a better chance of joyful activity in the world. "God's will, be it joy or sorrow; God's will, be it the triumph of good or the siege of the evil." This is a great mantra & has mighty effects. But it does not by itself give a secure abiding place. God's will may bring doubt & then there is anguish; may bring loss of the Divine presence, separation from the Beloved & then there is a greater agony. The intellectual man has the intellect God has given him to satisfy. The active man has the impulse to work, but at every step is faced with the difficulties of religion & ethics. He has to slay as a soldier, condemn as a judge, inflict pain, inflict anguish, choose between two courses which seem both to be evil in their nature or their results. Sin enters his heart, or there are ensnaring spirits of doubt which suggest sin where sin is not, he feels that he is acting from passion, not from God. His body suffers, pain distracts, his own pain, the pain of others. In this maelstrom it is only those whose hearts are mightier than their intellects & their devotion a part of their nature who can overcome all the winds that blow upon them. Therefore most devotees withdraw from life or from the greater part of life like the Mayavadin; those who remain have more resignation than happiness. They bear the cross here in the conviction that the aureole awaits them hereafter. But where then is that perfect bliss & that perfect activity which the Sage promises us, doing verily our works here in the ordinary life of mankind? The thing can be done on the devotional foundation, but only by a peculiar & rare temperament aided by God's special grace & favour. We need a wider pedestal, a securer foundation.

He finds that foundation who sees wheresoever he looks (that is the force of anu in anupashyati) only the Atman, only the Self. He watches the bird flying through the air, but what he is aware of is the Self watching the movement of the Self through the Self — air & bird & flight & watcher are only name & form, presentations of the one Reality to itself in itself by itself atmani atmanam atmana. He is stung by the scorpion but what he is aware of is only the touch of the Self on the Self; the scorpion that stings is Brahman, the stung is Brahman, the sting is Brahman, the pain is Brahman. And this he not only thinks as a metaphysical truth, for mere metaphysical opinion or intellectual attitude never yet brought salvation to living man, — but knows it, feels it & is aware of it utterly with his whole single & complex knowing existence. Body, senses, heart & brain are at one in that experience. Thus to the soul perfected in this knowledge everything that is, seems or is experienced, thinker & thought, action, doer, sufferer, object, field, result, becomes only one reality, Brahman, Self, God and all this variety is only play, only movement of conscious-self in conscious-self. That moves, God has His lila, the Self rejoices in its own inner experiences of itself seen & objectivised. There arises in the soul not merely calm, resignation, desirelessness, heart's joy in God's presence, but with the perfect knowledge comes a perfect bliss in the conditioned & the unconditioned, in the transcendent & in the phenomenal, in action & in resting from action, in Ishwara & in apparent anIshwara, in God's nearness & in God's remoteness, in what men call joy & what men call pain. Grief falls away from the soul, pain becomes rapture, doubt & darkness disappear in an assured & brilliant luminosity. Mukti is fulfilled, the soul is perfectly liberated here & in this body ihaiva, — for this & not renunciation of phenomenal existence is the true Vedantic moksha. This is what is meant by all existing things becoming the Self in a man, this is the result which is predicated of such a divine realisation. "Whence shall he have grief, how shall he be deluded who seeth all things as one?"

There are certain stages in the realisation, two of which are indicated in these slokas, and although the indication is only a minor & incidental movement of the Rishi's thought, the subject is of sufficient practical importance to be dwelt upon for a little even in this necessarily rapid examination. Brahman, Atman, Ishwara — these are the three great names, the three grand realisations we have here about the Absolute Existence. That existence, Paratparam Brahma, in its absolute truth (if such an expression is admissible where the ideas of truth & falsehood, absolute & relative no longer apply & knowledge itself disappears in an unconceivable & unimaginable Identity) — is unknowable by any, even the highest faculty of conscious mind. Arriving at the farthest limits of our existence here we may become & do become aware of it as a thing beyond our experience. It presents itself to us here as some ultimate shadow of itself which we feel sometimes as Sat, sometimes as Asat, sometimes as both Sat & Asat, & then we perceive that it is none of these things, but something beyond both existence & non-existence which are merely uncertain symbols of it & we end by the formula of the Rishis renouncing all vain attempts at knowledge, Neti, neti, not this not that. We must not go beyond this formula or seek to explain & amplify it. To describe It by negative epithets is as illegitimate & presumptuous as to describe it by positive epithets. We can say of Brahman that it is shuddha, pure; we cannot say of the Paratparam that it is shuddha. How can we know what It is? We can only say that here It translates itself into an utter purity. Neither can we say of It that it is alakshanam, without feature. How do we know what It is not? We can only say that we cannot describe It by any lakshanas, for the features we perceive here are those of a movement in which all opposites present themselves as equally true.

But here in this manifest universal existence we do perceive certain universal states & certain still more fundamental realisations which transcend all phenomena & all oppositions & antinomies. We perceive, for example, a state of Universal Being, the Sad Atman of the Upanishads, the goal of the Adwaitins; we perceive a state of Universal Non-Being, the Asad Atman of the Upanishads, Sunyam, the goal of the Madhyamika Buddhists. Then we perceive that both of these are the same thing differently experienced in the soul. It is That which expresses itself in our experience of Being & forgetfulness of Being, of Consciousness & forgetfulness of Consciousness, of Bliss & forgetfulness of Bliss, of Sacchidananda conditioned & Sacchidananda unconditioned. We call it the Brahman, that which extends itself here in space & time & fills its extension. We feel our identity with it & we realise that it is our true Self & the true Self of everything in the universe & of the universe both in its sum & in its entirety. We call it then the Atman, a word which originally meant true Being or true

Substance. We become aware of It as extending itself & filling its extension here for a purpose, the purpose of Ananda, delight in Vidya, delight in Avidya & governing all things towards that purpose, — self-aware as the One & self-aware as the Many, self-aware as Sat & self-aware as Asat. This great self-aware transcendent more than universal existence we call Sa, Ishwara, "He", God, the Paratpara Purusha, the Higher than the Highest. We see therefore that these three names merely try to express in human language certain fundamental conceptions we have here of That which is not perfectly expressible. The greatest names, tremendous as is their power, — how tremendous only those can know who have made the test without flinching — are only symbols, — I will not say shadows, for that is a word which may be misunderstood. But very great & blissful symbols in which we are meant to find a perfect content & satisfaction.

Through these symbols & the realisations which they try to represent, we have to work out our divine fulfilment here, & the Rishi gives all three of them to us in this Upanishad. For all three are supremely helpful &, in a way, necessary. Until we realise Ishwara, the mighty Inhabitant, as one with ourself, as the Atman, we find a difficulty in identifying Him with all that Is. We fall into these ideas of an extra-Cosmic God which satisfy the early & immature stages of soul development; or we see a God who pervades & upholds all existences but has put them forth in His being as eternally apart from Himself. That is a great practical realisation with immense results to the soul, the realisation of the Bhakta who rests in some kind of Dualism, but it is not the supreme goal which we are seeking. If we realise the Ishwara as the Atman, our Self, without realising Him as the Brahman we run, unless our souls have first become purified, another peril, the peril of the Asura who misapplies the mighty formula So Aham & identifies God with his own unregenerate ignorant Ego, — extending the Inhabitant only to some transient circumstances of the movement in which He dwells. He forgets the other equally important formula, Tat twam asi; he does not realise others as Narayan, does not become one self with all existences, forgets that the very idea of his egoistic self is inconsistent

with the true Adwaita and to extend that in imagination & call
it the whole Universe is a caricature of Adwaita. It is like the
error of the unphilosophical Idealist who concludes that the
objective Universe exists only in his individual Mind, forgetting
that it exists equally in other individual minds & not knowing
that in reality there is no individual Mind, but only one sea of
mind with its self-formed solid bed of sanskaras, waves of which
are constantly flowing through him, rising & breaking there &
leaving their marks in the sands of his mental, infra-mental &
supramental being. Even if we realise all beings as Narayan and
one Self, there is a difficulty in realising all things as God & self.
The Inhabitant is the Atman, good — but the name & form? We
can realise that God dwells in the stone as well as under the stone
& around it, but how can the stone be God, — this clod, that
rusty piece of iron, this clot of filth? With difficulty the mind
unreleased from dwandwa & sanskaras can believe that God
logically must be in the piece of filth He has created, but how
can He be that filth? The seeker can eventually realise God in
the criminal who is to be hanged no less than in the executioner
who hangs him & the saint who has pity for both, in the harlot
no less than the Sati, in all of the filth no less than in the glorious
star that shines in Heaven & the petals of the rose or jasmine
that intoxicates our soul with its fragrance, but the crime of the
criminal, the sin of the harlot, the corporeality of the filth, must
not that be kept separate? The sattwic mere lover of virtue, the
lover of beauty, the devotee reverently bowing before the throne,
must they not revolt eternally from such conceptions? We shall
see that for certain practical reasons we must in action preserve
a kind of separateness, — not only between the criminal & his
crime, but between the saint & his virtue, — for this reason the
Rishi has fixed on the relation of world of Movement & world's
Inhabitant as the basis of his system, — but the distinction must
be one of vyavahara only, for practice only & must not interfere
with our conception of All as Brahman. We must not yield to
the limitations of the sattwic mind, the moha or delusions of
the sattwic ahankara. For if we yield, we cannot proceed to that
greater goal of bliss, which attaining the soul shrinks not at all,

has no delusion, is not touched by any grief. Therefore we must realise the Ishwara not only as the true Self of things, but as Brahman, that which extends itself here equally in all things, in the beautiful but also in the ugly, in the holy & great but also in that which we look on as base & impure. Looking on Brahman moving & Brahman unmoving we have to say with the Mundaka Upanishad, Tad etat satyam (That yonder is this here & the Truth), & looking on Ishwara & Brahman moving & unmoving we have to say with the same Upanishad, "Purusha evedam sarvam karma tapo brahma paramritam." "It is the divine Soul that is all this, even all action and all active force and Brahman & the supreme immortality."

We have to realise the Self everywhere, but we have also to remember always in all our being, to feel always in every fibre of our existence that this Self is Brahman & the Lord. In the realisation of Atman by itself there is this danger that as we human beings stand in the subjective mind, that represents itself to us as our true Self and we are first in danger of identifying our subjective consciousness which is only one movement of Chit, with the Sarva Brahman. Even when we go beyond to the Sad Atman or Pure Existence, we, approaching it necessarily through our subjective being, tend to realise it as pure *subjective* existence & are in danger of not realising the real & ultimate Sat which is pure Existence itself beyond subjectivity & objectivity, but expressing itself here subjectively because of the Purusha & objectively because of the Prakriti, — the mingled strain of our subjective-objective existence here being the result of the interaction & mutual enjoyment of His Male & His Female principle. Hence arise the misconceptions of the Idealists, Illusionists & Mayavadins. If we halt in subjective mind, we see the objective world as a mere dream or vision of our conscious subjective activity. That is the dogma of the Idealist, nor can anyone fathom the depths of our mental being without passing through this experience. If we halt in our pure subjective existence, then not only the objective world, but the mind & its perceptions seem to be a dream, & the only truth is the subjective Nirguna Brahman aware only of his pure subjective existence. When this subjective

Nirguna Brahman looks out from the truth of himself & watches the perceptions of the mind, the great dream of the objective, then It alone as the sakshi seems to be real — but we get rid of the sakshi too & retire into the perfect samadhi in which Brahman is aware only of Itself as self-existent, self-conscious pure Atman. This is the dogma of the Mayavadin & no one can fathom all the depths of our subjective being who has not passed through this experience. Then comes the Buddhist, who turns upon this sakshi, this subjective Atman & says "Thou too art only a dream, for the same thing that tells me thou art, tells me the world is. I have no other evidence of the existence of Atman than I have of the existence of the world without, as both are equally dreams." And without going farther, he says with the Madhyamikas "The truth is the Asat, the Nihil, the universal Non-being", or he says with the Buddha — "There is Nirvana of all this subjective & objective; what there is beyond, we need not ask" — so as to say "we cannot know", "we need only to know that it releases from all pain & grief & death & all return of egoism." This experience too, if one can have it & not be bound by it, is of great use, of a rich fruitfulness to the soul. He can hardly gaze out of the manifest towards Parabrahman who has never stood face to face with the Asat & launched his soul into the fathomless & shoreless Negation. But we come back to the truth. That which is beyond is Parabrahman & that which represents Him here as the basis of our existence is the absolute existence, neither subjective, nor objective, turned both towards the world & away from it, capable of manifesting everything, capable of manifesting nothing, capable of universality, capable of nullity, capable of putting forth all antinomies, capable of reconciling them, capable therefore both of cosmos & chaos, which is expressed in the formula OM Tat Sat. But this is no other than the Brahman. Is it enough then to realise the Atman as the Brahman? Yes, if we realise that the absolute Brahman, who is rather beyond both Guna & absence of Guna than Nirguna, is also that which expresses itself as Guna, extends itself in space & informs its own extension. We must say with the Mandukya, Sarvam hyetad Brahma — Ayam Atma Brahma — So'yam atma chatushpat. All this world is Brahman, this Self is Brahman, & this Self which is Brahman is fourfold. Fourfold, not only the Transcendent Turiya, but also He who sees Himself the gross & sees Himself the subtle & sees His own single & blissful being in the states to which we have only access now in the deep trance of sushupti. Nor is this enough. For the realisation goes still too much towards abstraction, towards remoteness. It is necessary to remember that this great Self-Aware Being is the Lord, that He has created & entered into His own movement, with a mighty purpose & for the enjoyment of His own phenomenal being in the worlds. Otherwise we shall not be so much both spectators & masters of our worlds, but its spectators only — & a mere spectator tarries not long at a spectacle, he is soon sated of his inactive joy & withdraws. The movement of withdrawal is necessary for a certain number of souls, it is, so effected, a great, blissful & supremely satisfied movement, but it is not the purpose for which God is in us here. We must realise our true Self as Brahman-Ishwara. We must be one with the Ekah sarvabhutantaratma rupam rupam pratirupo bahishcha, the one Self within all existences who shapes Himself to form & form & is outside all of them, & understand the intention of the Aitareya in its great opening, Atma va idam eka evagra asit — Sa ikshata — Sa iman lokan asrijata. In the beginning this was all the Atman, He alone, He looked & put forth these worlds.

Finally, it is not even enough for the Sage's purpose that we should realise the Brahman except as the Atman & Ishwara. For if we do not realise Brahman as the Self & our Self we shall be in danger of losing the subjective aspect of existence & laying too much stress on That as the substratum of our objective existence in which I stand merely as a single unimportant movement. The result is a tamasic, an inert calm, a tendency to merge in the jada Prakriti, the apparent unintelligently active aspect of things which the Europeans call Nature or at the highest a resolution of our selves into that substratum of the objective in the Impersonal Brahman. The denial of the Transcendent Personality, the Parat-para Purusha is a strong tendency of the present-day Adwaita. "God", say these modern Adwaitins, "is a myth, or at most a

dream like ourselves. Just as there is no I, so there is no God."
Under this figure of thought, there lies a philosophical blunder.
Personality is not necessarily individual Personality, neither is it
a selection & arrangement of qualities, any more than existence
is necessarily individual existence or a selection & arrangement
of movements in our being. Personality can be & is Universal;
this Universal Personality is God in relation to our individual
experiences. Personality also can be & is Transcendent, self-
existent, beyond individuality & Universality, — this transcendent Personality, a blissful unlimited self-conscious Awareness in
self-existence is the Paratpara Purusha — adityavarnas tamasah
parastat, drawing us like a sun beyond the darkness of ignorance
& the darkness of the Asat. This is He — God universal, but also
God transcendent — the Lilamaya Krishna who transcends His
lila. Therefore the Upanishads everywhere insist not upon mere
Existence, like the later Adwaitin, but on the sole Existent; and
they speak continually on the Brahman as the creator, Master,
enjoyer of the worlds, by meditating on whom we shall attain
to perfect liberation. Neither Buddha nor Jada Bharata are the
true guides & fulfillers of our destiny; it is Yajnavalkya, it is
Janaka &, most of all, it is Krishna son of Devaki who takes us
most surely & entirely into the presence & into the being of the
Eternal.

Atman, Brahman, Ishwara, on this triune aspect here of the
Transcendent depend all our spiritual realisations and as we
take one or the other & in its realisation stop a little this side or
proceed a little to that side, our realisations, our experiences &
our creeds & systems will vary from each other; & we shall be
Buddhists or Adwaitins or Mayavadins or Dualists, followers
of Ramanuja or Madhwa, followers of Christ, of Mahomed, of
whosoever will give us such light on the Eternal as we are ready
to receive. The Rishi of the Isha wishes us to realise all three, but
for the sake of divine life in the world to dwell upon Ishwara, but
on Ishwara neither extracosmic nor different from His creatures
but rather in & about all beings as their indwelling Self, their
containing Brahman and that material Brahman also or Prakriti
which is the formal continent of the indwelling Self and the

formal content of the containing Brahman. In this realisation there are many stages of progress, many necessary first steps & later approximations; but the Rishi, his work being to throw out brief fundamental & important suggestions only & not to fill in details, to indicate & illumine, not to educate or instruct, gives us for the present only two of the final realisations which are the most essential for his purpose. We shall find, however, that there is more beyond.

We are first to realise this one divine Self, (which is *our*self also) in all existences and all existences in the Self. We have, therefore, in this realisation three terms, Self within, Self without, which are the same & invariable samam Brahma, & all existences, of which each separate existence is fundamentally the same, but in generic or individual play & movement different from other genera & individuals. All existences — not only animate but inanimate, for sarvabhuteshu does not mean sarvapranishu — not only the man, the animal, the insect, but in the tree, plant & flower & not only in the tree, plant & flower which have a sort of life, but in the mountain, the metal, the diamond, the pebble which seem not to have life, & not only in these bhutas which if they have not an organised life, have at least an organised or a manifest form, but in those which have no organised form, or no form at all to the eye or to any sense. The wind & sea also are He & the gases which constitute the air which moves as wind & the water which flows as the sea. He is ether that contains all & He is that which contains the ether.

Swami Vivekananda in a passage of his works, makes a striking or, as the French say better, a seizing distinction between the locomotive & the worm that it crushes, between the animate which has conscious life in it, however weak, & the inanimate which has only in it, however powerful, a blind & undeveloping power. But, however useful & true this distinction may be for certain practical purposes, certain vyavahara, it is not allowed us by the pure Adwaita of the Upanishads. God is not only in the worm that is crushed, but in the engine that crushes it — the engine too & the power of the engine are Brahman and as much Brahman as the life & consciousness in the worm. He is samam

Brahma. We have a right to make certain practical distinctions for vyavahara but none to make any essential difference. For the Vedanta is inexorable in its positiveness; as it will not spare us the most loathsome worm that crawls but insists that that too is Brahman, so also it will not spare us the most inert or sordid speck of matter, but insists that that too is Brahman. If we stop short anywhere, we create bheda & lose our full spiritual heritage. The seer anupashyati — he follows Prakriti in her movement from the greatest to the most infinitesimal, from the noblest to the meanest & everywhere finds only Brahman, God, the Self. Bhuteshu bhuteshu vichitya dhirah, says the Kena. We must have dhairyam, utter patience, utter understanding. To no weakness, no repugnance, no recoil even of the saint in us or the artist & poet in us, much less of our mere nervous & sensational parts or of the conventional mind with its fixed associations can we stop to listen, if we would attain. Love & hate, joy & grief must not interfere to warp our knowledge. All, all, all without exception is He. He breathes out sweetness upon us in the rose, He touches our cheeks with coolness in the Wind, He fills with His favouring breath the sails of the sailing-ship that carries our merchandise to its market, He tramples down into the Ocean depths the latest marvel & monstrosity of scientific construction in which travel the great ones of the world or in which our beloved are coming to our arms. The wrong that is done to us, it is He that does it — and to whom is it done? To Himself. The blow that is struck, is of His striking. Brahman is the striker, Brahman the instrument, Brahman the stricken. The insult that is cast on us, it is He that has flung it in our face. The disgrace, the defeat, the injustice are of His doing. That crime which we abhor, it is Brahman who has committed it, — it is our Self's, our own doing though we do it in another body. For the least sin that is committed in the world, each one of us is as responsible as the sinner. Our self-righteousness is a Pharisaical error, our hatred of the sinner & our contempt & loathing convict us of ignorance and limit, not increase our power to rectify or to help. The seer, the freed & illuminated soul hates none, condemns nothing but loves all and helps all; he is sarvabhutahite ratah, his occupation

& delight are to do good to all creatures. He is the Self seeing the Self in all, loving the Self in all, enjoying the Self in all, helping the Self in all. That is the ethics & morality of the Vedanta.

For what is the first result of this universal vision? Tato na vijugupsate. Jugupsa is not merely fear but includes all kinds of shrinking, fear, disgust, contempt, loathing in the nerves, hatred in the heart, shrinking of dislike or reluctance from thing or person or action. Raga & dwesha being the motives of all our ordinary feeling & action, jugupsa expresses that movement of recoil in the system which proceeds from dwesha of any kind, — the desire to protect ourselves against or ward off the unwelcome thing that presents itself to the mind, nerves or senses. We see therefore how wide a field the promise of the Upanishad covers. We shall not hate, fear, loathe, despise or shrink from anything whatsoever which the world can present us. It is evident, if this is possible, how all that constitutes real misery will fall from the soul & leave it pure & blissful.

We shall not have any contempt, hatred or disgust for any person, nor shall we fear anyone, however powerful or inimical; for in all we shall see Narayan, we shall know the Lord, we shall recognise ourself. One equal regard will fall from us on the tiger & the lamb, the saint & the sinner, the tyrant who threatens us and the slave who is subject to our lightest caprice. Squalor, sin, disease will not conceal from us the god within nor wrath & cruelty from us God's love working by strange ways under grotesque & fearful masks. No sort of foulness or ugliness will repel us. An universal charity, a wide & tolerant love, a calm & blissful impulse of beneficence to all will be the ethical first fruits of our realisation. We shall make no distinctions, we shall be no respecters of persons. We shall not despise the hut of the peasant nor bow down in the courts of the princes, neither shall we have wrath or scorn against the palace & partiality for the cottage. All these things will be equal to us. The touch of the outcaste will be the same to us as the sprinkling of holy water by the Brahmin — for how shall God pollute God? Every human or living body will be to us a temple & dwelling place of the most High. None shall be to us vile or contemptible. And yet none shall be too sacred for us, too dear or too inviolable; for it is the house of our Friend & Playmate; nay, it is our own House, for the Lover is not different from the Beloved, & it is a house, jagat not sthanu, a thing that can be changed & has to be changed, for which therefore we shall have deep love, but no fettering attachment. The sword of our enemy will have no terrors for us. For enmity is a play of the Lord & death & life make up one of His games of hide & seek. How shall God slay God? Even as our vision deepens, the touch of the sword shall be to us as much the kiss of His Love as the touch from the lips of a lover — one sharp, poignant & fierce, the other soft & wooing but the manner is the only difference. For we shall have torn aside the grotesque & unreal mask of hatred & seen in the apparent fulfilment of enmity & evil, the real fulfilment of love & good. By the divination of the heart & the vision of the higher knowledge we shall have found out the way of the Lord in His movement.

And because we shall have found out His way & seen everywhere Himself, things also will cause no kind of shrinking in us. We shall exceed the limitations of the senses & the ordinary aesthetic faculties, — we shall have gone beyond the poet & the artist. We shall know why the sages have called Him sarvasundara, the All-Beautiful. For things beautiful will have a more wonderful, intense, ecstatic beauty to us, but things foul, illshapen & ugly will also be to us beautiful, with a larger, more marvellous, more universal beauty than the artistic. We shall exceed the limitations of the mind & heart & conscience; we shall have gone beyond the saint & the moralist. For we shall no more be repelled by the sin of the sinner than by the dirt on our child who has fallen or wallowed in the mud of the roadside. We shall know why the Lord has put on the mask of the sinner & the perfect purpose that is served by sin & crime in the world's economy, & while knowing that it has to be put aside or transformed into good, we shall not be revolted by it, but rather view it with perfect calm & charity. This realisation, although it lifts us beyond the ordinary conceptions of morality & conventional ethics, does not incapacitate us for normal action, as it might seem to the thought which holds all action impossible except that which proceeds from desire & liking & disliking. Whatever morality the Vedantist practises will be based on a higher & truer ground than the ethics of the ordinary man in love, sympathy & oneness. For an ethics proceeding in its practical action on contempt, dislike or repulsion is an immoral or imperfectly moralised ethics which seeks to drive out poison by poison & it has always failed & will always fail to eradicate sin & evil, — just as the ordinary methods of society have failed to eradicate or even diminish crime & vice, because its method & its spirit are ignorant & paradoxical. Only perfect knowledge & sympathy can give perfect help and these are impossible without oneness.

At the same time it is true that the jivanmukta is not governed by ordinary moral considerations. He shrinks from no actions which the divine purpose demands or the divine impulse commands. He has no wish to kill, but he will not shrink from slaying when it is demanded, for he is bound neither by the rajasic ahankara nor by the sattwic; sattwic obstacles to slaying are therefore taken from him and his knowledge delivers him both from the desire to take life which is the evil of hinsa [and] from the emotional horror of taking life & the nervous fear of taking life which are the rajasic & tamasic basis of outward ahinsa. So also with other actions. For this morality or dharma is of the soul & does not depend upon the action which is a mere outward symbol of the soul & has different values according to the times, the social ideas & environments, the religious creed or the actual circumstances. To men who are not free a conventional morality is an absolute necessity, for there must be a fixed standard to which they can appeal. It is as necessary for the ordinary practice of the world as a standard value of coin for the ordinary commerce of a country. The coin has not really an immutable value; the pound is not perhaps really worth 15 Rs but fluctuates owing to circumstances; nevertheless to allow a fluctuating value is to bring a certain amount of confusion, uncertainty & disorder into finance & commerce. Therefore the liberated man though he knows the truth will not contravene the fixed rules of society unless he is impelled by divine command or unless the divine purpose is moving towards a change in the fixed morality. Then, if it is the part given to him, he will act as fearlessly against social rules as under ordinary circumstances he will adhere firmly to the law of the environment in which he dwells. For his one care & purpose will be to observe the divine purpose & carry out the divine will.

Neither will events bring to him grief or disappointment, fear or disgust with things, because he follows that divine will & purpose in himself & in others, in the inner world & the outer, watching everywhere the play of the Self. He has divined God's movement. Disgrace & dishonour, obloquy & reproach cannot move him. He is equal in soul to honour & dishonour, respect & insult, mana & apamana, because both come from himself to himself & not from another. Success & failure are equal to him, since he knows that both are equally necessary for the fulfilment of the divine intention. He will no more quarrel with them than with the cold of winter or the breath of the stormblast. They are part of the jagat, part of God's play, of the Self's action on the Self. He acquires a perfect titiksha or power to bear; he moves towards more than titiksha, towards an equal & perfect enjoyment.

Such, then, are some of the practical fruits of the realisation of God as the Self in all existences & the Brahman containing all existences. It raises us towards a perfect calm, resignation, peace & joy; a perfect love, charity & beneficence; a perfect courage, boldness & effectiveness of action; a divine equality to all men & things & equanimity towards all events & actions. And not only perfect, but free. We are not bound by these things we acquire. Our calm does not stay us from even the most colossal activity, for the calm is within us, of the soul & is not an activity in the jagat, in the movement. Our resignation is of the soul & does not mean acquiescence in defeat, but acceptance of it as a circumstance in the struggle towards a divine fulfilment; our peace & joy do not prevent us from understanding & sympathising with the trouble & grief of others; our love does not prevent an outward necessary sternness, our charity a just appreciation of men & motives nor does our beneficence hold back the sword when it is necessary that it should strike — for sometimes to strike is the highest beneficence, as those only can thoroughly realise who know that God is Rudra as well as Shiva, Chamunda Kali with the necklace of skulls no less than Durga, the protectress & Gauri, the wife & mother. Our courage does not bind itself by the ostentations of the fighter, but knows when flight & concealment are necessary, our boldness does not interfere with skill & prudence, nor our activity forbid us to rest & be passive. Finally our equality of soul leaves room to the other instruments to deal with each thing in the vyavahara according to its various dharma & utility, the law of its being & the law of its purpose.

These are the perfect results of the perfect realisation. But in practice it is difficult for these perfect results to be attained or for this perfect realisation to be maintained, unless after we have attained to it, we go farther & exceed it. In practice we find that there is a flaw, somewhere, which causes us either not perfectly to attain or to slip back after we have attained. The reason is that we are still removed by one considerable step from perfect oneness. We have realised oneness of the self within & the self without, of the self in us & the self in all other existences. But we still regard the jagat, the movement, as not entirely the Self — as movement & play of God, but not itself God, as action of the Lord, but not itself all the Lord expressed to Himself in His own divine awareness. Therefore when things come to us, when action or event affects us, we have to adopt an attitude towards it as something different from ourselves, something that comes, something that affects us. As the result of that attitude we have jugupsa. We have realised oneness, but by what kind of realisation? By seeing, — anupashyati, by action of the seeing faculty in the buddhi or the feeling faculty in the heart — for both these things are vision. Our realisation is a realisation of identity by attitude, not of absolute identity by nature, realisation through instruments of knowledge, not through our conscious being in itself. Subtle as the distinction may seem, it is not really so fine as it appears; it makes a wide difference, it is of first rate importance in its results. For so long as our divine state depends on our attitude, the least failure or deficiency in that attitude means a waning of the divine state or a defect in its fullness. So long as it rests on a continued act of knowledge in mind & heart, the least discontinuity or defect of that knowledge means a defect of or a falling from our divine fullness. Only if identity with all existences has become our whole nature & being of our being, is the divine state perfected, is its permanent and unbroken enjoyment assured. And so complete & exacting is the oneness of Brahman, so absolute is the law of this Adwaita that if even the name & form & the play & the movement are regarded as Brahman's & not themselves as Brahman, an element of bheda, difference & dissonance, is preserved which tends to prevent this absolute identity of being & preserve the necessity of attitude & the identity only through the instruments of knowledge.

Therefore in his next verse the Rishi gives us a higher & completer realisation which includes the missing elements & perfects the Adwaita. "He in whom Self & all existences have become one and perfectly he knoweth, how shall he be deluded, whence shall he have pain who sees in all things oneness." If we read this verse loosely, we may err by taking it as a justification of that Adwaita which denies the sarvabhutani and affirms only the Atma. In that case we shall have not only to translate "All existences have become Self", but to suppose that "become" means "disappeared into", "blotted themselves out in", — an extension of meaning which is justified by nothing, either in the language or in the context. It is contradicted by the immediately following passage in which the Seer insists on the necessity of the simultaneous view of Vidya & Avidya, while the exclusion of the world & its existences can only be effected in the state of sleep or trance and would be broken every time the mind returned to the state of waking. No such broken & truncated realisation is intended. The Mayavada demands that every time we look out on the world & its creatures, we shall say "This is not Brahman, it is a dream, a lie"; Adwaita of the Isha demands that looking out on the world & its creatures we shall say "This is Brahman, it is God, it is myself." There is a wide difference between the two attitudes. The one rests a metaphysical & argumentative Adwaita on a tremendous essential Dwaita of Satya & Asatya, that which is true & that which is false; the other rests a practical Adwaita on an apparent Dwaita, all being Satyam, eternal Truth, but Truth seen & recurrent presenting itself to Truth seeing & persistent — the sthanu & the jagat, an apparent difference of appearance to knowledge, not an actual difference of essential reality & unreality. Apart from this divergence, the language of the sloka is such as not to admit of the negation sought by the Mayavadin, but to contradict it. I have not translated the verse literally yet, but now I give the literal translation, "In whom the Self (of him) verily knowing by vijnana has become all creatures, there what delusion, what grief, of him seeing wherever he looks (anu) oneness." It is evident that the Mayavadin's position vanishes. The words are sarvani bhutani atmaivabhud — not sarvabhutani atmaivabhuvan — a singular verb demanding a singular subject. Therefore it is the Self that becomes, not the bhutas; and we cannot say that this is the attitude of a man still ignorant, ajna, for it is the Self of one who knows entirely, has that knowledge which in the Upanishads is called vijnana & who has attained to the vision of oneness. In him his Self has become all creatures.

Let us understand thoroughly the sense of this important sloka. Yasmin, in whom. The soul has become one with all existence, all existence it feels to be itself containing the creation & exceeding it, — therefore yasmin, not yasya. In him his Self, that which he feels to be his true I has become all creatures. Not only does he feel himself or perceive himself to be *in* all creatures as the divine presence in them & around them, but he is they, — he is each bhuta. The word bhuta means that which has become as opposed to that which eternally is & it includes therefore name & form & play of mind & play of action. The last barrier is broken; ahankara, the sense of separate self, utterly disappears & the soul is all that it sees or is in any way aware of. It is not only the seer in all, but it is the seen; not only the Lord, but his habitation, not only Ish but jagat. In fact, just

as the Lord himself, as Brahman itself becomes all things &
all creatures in itself, just as all creatures are only Brahman's
becomings, bhutani, just as Brahman is the ejat and the anejat,
the moving & the unmoving, God & his world, so is it now with
the soul that sees. Of it too it can be said Tad ejati tannaijati. It
moves & it moves not, it is the near & the far, it is within all
things & outside all things. The man thus liberated undergoes
a tremendous change of consciousness; he ceases to feel himself
as within his body & feels rather his body as within himself &
not only his but all bodies; he feels himself at the same time in
his body & in all bodies not separately like a piece of water in
a jar, but as an unity like one ether undivided in many vessels,
& at the same time he feels that they are not in him nor he in
them, but that this idea of within & without is merely a way of
looking, a way of expressing to the mind a truth in itself beyond
expression by space & time — just as we say "I have this in my
mind" when we do not really intend to express any location
in space but mean rather "This is my mental knowledge as it
just now expresses itself." Pashya me yogam aishwaram. For he
now feels that these things in which & outside which he seems
to be are himself, his becomings in the motion of awareness,
jagat, bhutani. This is the first important difference between the
preceding realisation of knowledge & this fuller realisation of
being. His self has become all existences; they & he are all merely
becomings of himself.

But if this realisation is only by the heart through love or
only by the purified reason through intellectual perception, then
it is not the realisation which this shloka contemplates. For so
long as we have not become that which we are realising, realisation is not complete & its moral effects cannot be securely held.
For what use is it if we merely understand that all is one when if
there is a touch from outside it, the body cries "Something has
struck me, I am hurt" or the heart says "Someone has injured
me, I am in grief" or the vital spirits cry "Someone means ill to
me, I am in fear"? And if the heart realises, but the reason &
other instruments fail, how shall we not, feeling one with the
grief of others, fail to be crushed by them & overborne? The

lower organs must also consent to the absolute sense of oneness or no sure and perfect result can be gained. How is this to be done? By the force of the vijnana, our ideal self. Therefore the Upanishad adds "vijanatah", when he knows, not by ordinary knowledge, jnanam, or by intellectual knowledge, prajnanam, but by the ideal knowledge, vijanatah.

What is this vijnana? Vedantic commentators have identified it with buddhi; it is, they think, the discriminating intellect or the pure reason. But in the psychological system of the Veda intellectual vichara, reason, even pure reason, is not the highest nor does it lead to the highest results. The real buddhi is not in mind at all, but above mind. For beyond & behind this intellect, heart, nervous system, body, there is, says the Veda, a level, a sea of being out of which all these descend & here take form, a plane of consciousness in which the soul dwells by the power of perfect truth, in a condition of pure existence of knowledge, satyam, pure arrangement of its nature in that knowledge, ritam or vratam, pure satisfying wideness in being of that knowledge-nature, brihat. This is the soul's kingdom of heaven, its ideal state, immortality, amritatwam. All things here are in the language of [the Vishnu Purana] vijnanavijrimbhitani; they live here in fragments of that wide & mighty truth, but because of bheda, because they are broken up & divide truth against truth, they cannot enjoy Truth of knowledge, Truth of Nature, Truth of being & bliss, but have to strive towards it with much failure, pain & relapse. But if man can rise in himself to that plane and pour down its knowledge upon the lower system, then the whole system becomes remoulded in the mould of the vijnana. Man can get himself a new heart, a new mind, a new life, navyam ayu, even a new body, punah kritam. This whole system will then consent & be compelled to live in the truth — & that truth to which vijnana itself is the door, is Brahman as Sacchidananda. All things here will be Sacchidananda. This is the second superiority of this high realisation as this shloka describes it, that it is vijanatah, attained not by intellectual discernment or feeling of the heart or concentration of the mind, not depending therefore on any state such as sushupti or on any attitude, but itself determining the attitude, & attained through direct ideal knowledge with the result of becoming all that is in our being, not merely the mind or thought or feeling, in our very nature. The practical consequence will be that body, mind & heart will no longer admit any bahyasparsha, but will utterly feel that nothing can come to them, nothing touch them but only Brahman. To every touch there will be but one response from heart & mind & nerve alike — "This is Brahman." Nanyat pashyati, nanyach chrinoti. They will see nothing else, hear nothing else, smell nothing else, feel nothing else, taste nothing else, but only Brahman. Of such a state it can be truly & utterly said, & not merely relatively, not subject to any qualification, ekatwam anupashyatah.

That oneness is the oneness of Sacchidananda, one being, one knowledge, one bliss, being that is consciousness, knowledge that is identity, both of them in their essence & reality bliss, — therefore not three separate qualities, but one existence, even though presented to the intellect as a trinity, yet always one. Whatever therefore is felt, seen, heard, thought, it will be bliss that is felt, bliss that is seen, bliss that is heard, bliss that is thought — a bliss which is in its essence & inseparably existence & knowledge. For the intellect we have to use all three words, for on the level of our mental action these three are or seem to be divided & different from each other, but to the illumined being of the Jivanmukta there is no difference, they are one. It is ekatwam. It is Brahman. The highest heights of this realisation are, indeed, not easily attained, but even on its lower levels there is a perfect freedom & an ineffable joy. Swalpam apyasya dharmasya. To these levels, tatra, neither fear, nor grief, nor illusion can come. Tatra ko mohah kah shoka ekatwam anupashyatah. How shall he be deluded, whence shall he have grief, to whose eyes wheresoever they turn all things are one? For grief is born of illusion, shoka proceeds from moha, & the essence of moha is that bewilderment, that stultification of the conscious mind by which we forget oneness. By forgetting oneness, the idea of limitation is fixed on our being; by limitation comes the idea of not being this, not having that; from this idea arises the desire to be this, to have that; by the disappointment of desire comes disappointment, dislike of that which disappoints, hatred & anger against that which withholds, fear of that which gives contrary experience — the whole brood of earthly ills. Moha shouts "Here is one I love, she is dying"; "Here is one who will kill me, I am terrified"; "Here is a touch too strong for me to bear, it is pain." "This is virtue, that is sin; if I do not gain one I am lost, if I fall into the other I shall suffer by God's wrath & judgment. This is fair, that is foul. This is sweet, that is bitter. This I have not which another has, I must have it, even if it be depriving him of his possession." But he who sees oneness sees only Sacchidananda, only bliss that is conscious being. Just as the mind that has taught itself to see only matter everywhere, says even of mind & soul, even of itself, It is not mind, it is not soul, it is matter, just as it sees everywhere only the play of matter upon matter, in matter, by matter, so the liberated soul says of body & nerve & mind, It is not mind, it is not body, it is not nerve, it is Brahman, it is conscious existence that is bliss and so he sees everywhere this bliss only & the play of bliss upon bliss, in bliss, by bliss. Ananda is the term through which he reconciles himself with the world. Into delight his soul is delivered, by delight he supports in himself the great world movement & dwells in it, in delight he is for ever one with, yet plays with God.

———

The second movement of the Upanishad is finished. In his first movement the Rishi advanced four propositions, — that the purpose of our existence is the fulfilment of God in the world, realising that the Lord & his movement alone exist, He is the only inhabitant, His movement the only cause of the forms in which He inhabits; secondly that the golden rule of life is to enjoy all God's movement or God in all his movement but only after the renunciation of demand & desire, for only so can it all be enjoyed; thirdly, that life & action in this world are intended, must be maintained & do not interfere with divine freedom

& bliss; fourthly, that any self-marring movement leads only to confusion & darkness here & beyond & not to our divine realisation. In order to lay down on a firm basis his justification of these teachings, he shows us first that God & the world are one, both are Brahman & therefore the world also is our divine Self compassing by a certain divine power movement of action & phenomenon in its still unmoving Self & without parting with its superiority to the movement, on this basis he shows us that existence & bliss not only can be made one, but if we realise this one Brahman who is our divine Self & God (antar asya sarvasya), all existence must necessarily become bliss & cannot be anything else; grief & fear & dislike & delusion have no farther place in us. It is to this realisation we shall arrive by realising God as we give up desire, renounce everything to Him and enjoy the world in Him & by Him, as His movement, as His enjoyment. For we shall then realise that all beings are one with ourself, the renunciation of desire will become possible and we shall not shrink from anything in life, because we shall know that it is God & his movement. Finally, the high & complete realisation will be ours in which the very cause of desire & demand will disappear & all will be utterly the Self, God, Brahman, Sacchidananda.

———

Chapter V

A question may arise. It is true then that enjoyment of all things here in oneness is possible; that renunciation of desire & self-surrender are the way & the realisation of the Lord in all forms & movements & self-surrender to him the method, — involving also action according to His will, enjoyment according to His will. But when the final realisation is accomplished, when oneness is utterly attained, then what farther need of enjoyment & action? The goal is realised, let the method be abandoned. Why keep the distinction of God & the world, why act any more in the world when the purpose of action is accomplished? It may still be possible, it is not necessary; it is not even desirable. Lose yourself in Sacchidananda, if not the impersonal unconditioned Brahman. Is it not that in which the vision of oneness logically culminates? Therefore not only the golden rule of conduct has to be justified, but the teaching of a liberated activity has to be justified. It is this to which the Sage next proceeds. He is about to establish the foundations of action in the liberated soul, to show the purpose of the One & the Many, — to reconcile Vidya & Avidya in God's supreme & blissful unity. The eighth verse is the introductory & fundamental verse of this movement.

APPENDIX

[1]

[*Bracketed and struck through in the manuscript. See the foot-note on page 378.*]

From the choice of terms in this opening line certain intellectual consequences arise which we have to accept if we wish to understand the teaching of the Upanishad. First, the Personality of God & His unity. Not only is the impersonal God one Brahman without a second, but the Personal God is one without a second. There is no other person besides God in the universe. Whatever different masks He may wear, from house to house of His habitation, it is always He. The disguises may be utterly concealing. He may manifest as Brahma & Vishnu, Surya & Agni or as the Yaksha & the Pishacha; he may dwell here as the man or dwell here as the animal; he may shine out as the saint or lust in Himself as the criminal; but all these are He.

[2]

[*Written on a separate sheet of the manuscript. See the footnote on page 378.*]

The world & God. What is the world? It is jagati, says the Rishi, she who is constantly moving. The essence of the world is not Space nor Time nor Circumstance which we call Causality — its essence is motion. Not only so, but every single force & object in it is of the same nature, it is a jagat, a knot of habitual motion. The ancient Hindus knew that the earth moves & therefore the earth also was designated in ancient times by a number of words meaning motion of which jagati itself is one — ga, go, jagati, ila. They knew of the physical movement of the universe. They would not have rejected the scientific hypothesis which sees in every object a mass & arrangement, a sort of cosmos of anus, atoms in constant movement with regard to [each] other. But the movement here contemplated is not, as we see in the fifth verse, tad ejati & the eighth verse, sa paryagat, movement of matter, but of divine being & conscious force of which matter is only an appearance. But for the present, the Rishi is content to envisage the world as a world of motion & multitude. In essence the kshobha or formative movement called active Prakriti, in universality it is this force ordering & arranging its objects by motion, jagati; in detail it is a multitude of single objects, forces, ideas, sensations etc, all in their nature motion of this moving universe, jagat, the apparently motionless stone no less than the ever circling & rotating earth. In this motion, in the objects, forces, sensations created by it He dwells who is its Lord.

[3]

[*Written in the top margin of two pages of the manuscript. Point of insertion not marked. See the footnote on page 380.*]

Moreover we must realise the Lord in others as one with Him in ourselves. Then we shall not need to covet any man's possessions. "Do not covet" says the Sage "the possession of any man whomsoever." Dhanam means any kind of possession whatever, not only material wealth — neither the glory of the king, nor the wealth of the merchant, nor the temperament of the sage, nor the strength of elephants, nor the swiftness of eagles. For whom are we envying, whose goods are we coveting? Ourselves, our own goods. If we realise divine unity, we can enjoy them as perfectly in another's experience as in our own. Moreover, being divine in power ourselves we can get them whenever our supreme self wills without anyone else in the world being the poorer for our gain. There must be no demand, no coveting. Not when or if the mind wills, but when or if He wills.

[4]

*[Written separately; point of insertion not marked. See the foot-
note on page 380.]*

Practically, therefore, the renunciation demanded of us is the renunciation by the lower unreal & incomplete self, mind, senses,
vitality, intellect, will, egoism of all that they are & seek to our
real, complete & transcendental Self, the Lord. And that renunciation we make not by substituting another demand, the demand
to be rid of all these things & released from the fulfilment of
His cosmic purpose, but in order the better to fulfil His purpose
& enjoy Him utterly in His movement, in all experience & all
action that He in us & through us is manifesting & perfecting.
For that which we have to enjoy is not only Ish but jagat, — for
as we shall see both are one Brahman & by enjoying Him entirely
we must come to enjoy all His movement, since He is here as
the Lord of his own movement. For this reason the word Ish has
been selected as the fundamental relation of God to ourselves
& the world — the master of all our existence to whom we
renounce, the Lord who for his purposes has made & governs
the world — for in this relation of "Lord" he is inseparable from
His movement. It is a relation that depends on the existence &
play of the world of which He is the ruler & master. Envisaging
the ruler, we envisage that which he rules, the habitation for
the sake of the inhabitant indeed, but still the habitation. We
get therefore in this first verse of the Upanishad the foundations
of the great principle of activity with renunciation with which
the teaching of the Gita begins & the still greater principle of
atmasamarpana or entire surrender to God, the uttamam ra-
hasyam with which it culminates. We get the reason & spirit of
the command to Arjuna from which all the moral teaching of
the Gita starts & to which it returns, jitva shatrun bhunkshva
rajyam samriddham, the command of activity, the command
of enjoyment — but activity for God only, yajnartham, without
ahankara, enjoyment in God only, mayi sannyasya, without desire or attachment, neither demanding what He does not take

for Himself in us, nor rejecting what He is here to enjoy, whether the enjoyment be of victory or defeat, of the patched loin cloth of the beggar or the imperial crown.

[5]

[Written in a different notebook; beginning lost or point of insertion unknown. Related thematically to Draft A of "The Life Divine".]

[.....] existence, lies the justification of all that is said in the scriptures of the liberated & perfected soul. He who would be free in this world, must be detached from it, though belonging to it, above it though in it, above it in his inward conscious self-being, though in it in his outward action of Nature. He must combine with a blissful enjoyment of all things in the world, a joyous indifference to all things in the world. He must be not un-mundane but supramundane, not inhuman but superhuman. In all his acts he must have in his soul the loud laughter, the attahasyam, of Kali. He must love with that inner laughter, slay with that laughter, save with that laughter, himself perish or reign, take joy or take torture with that secret & divine laughter. For he knows that the whole world is but a divine play of the eternal Child-God Srikrishna with Himself in the playground of His self-existence. All this he cannot have unless in the roots of his conscious being he feels not concealed or subliminal, but manifest & always present to him, the Bright, Calm, Unconcerned, Unbound, Unrelated Divine Existence.

This Pure Existence is not only an impersonal state of divine being, it is God Himself in His pure personality. For in all the divine manifestation, there is always this double aspect of Personality & Impersonality. God Impersonal manifests Himself, both in the universe & transcendent of the Universe, transcending it as infinite pure Existence, infinite pure Consciousness, infinite pure Delight, the triune Sachchidananda of our Scriptures, entering world existence. He manifests in it all this quality of existence, variation of Consciousness, multiplicity of delight which with its changes, perversities & apparent self-contradictions makes up the marvellous web of the world. But He is also, transcending existence, the infinite Pure Existent, the infinite Pure Conscious, the infinite Pure Blissful, — not anyone, no person or individual, for He alone is, but still neither a mere abstraction or state of Being. Entering into world existence, He is All-being, God, Shiva, Vishnu, Krishna, Kali, Allah, the Mighty One, the Humble, the Loving, the Merciful, the Ruthless. These things are aspects of Himself to His own consciousness. Just as Sacchidananda is Triune, — not three, but One, — for when we enter deep into the Trinity we find only Unity since Existence is Consciousness & nothing but Consciousness, & Consciousness is Delight & nothing but Delight, so the Personal & Impersonal God are Biune, not two, but one, since when we enter into the depths of this Biune, we find only Unity, Existence nothing but the Existent, the Existent nothing but Existence. The distinction between them is a necessary convention or arrangement of His truth for world manifestation; it does not amount to a difference. The metaphysician fixes his concentration of Will in Knowledge only on the Impersonal & pursuing it through the world & beyond, he affirms the Impersonal God but tends to deny the Personal. The devotee, fixing his concentration on the Personal & pursuing it through the world & beyond, affirms the Personal God but tends to deny or ignore the Impersonal. Both affirmations are true, both denials are false. Neither is one greater than the other, the Impersonal than the Personal, just as in the Personal, Shiva is not greater than Vishnu, nor Vishnu than Shiva, nor the All-Being than Krishna or Kali. Such exaggerated distinctions are the errors of partial or selective Yoga fastening on aspects & ignoring the true being of God in His self-manifestation. We must accept, for our perfection's sake, the multitude of His aspects & even of His divine impersonations, but we must not make them an excuse for breaking up the inalienable unity of God.

The Life Divine

[Draft B]

Part II
The First Movement

Chapter I
God and Nature

I

The Isha Upanishad opens with a monumental phrase in which, by eight brief and sufficient words, two supreme terms of existence are confronted and set forth in their real and eternal relation. Ish is wedded with Jagati, God with Nature, the Eternal seated sole in all His creations with the ever-shifting Universe and its innumerable whorls and knots of motion, each of them called by us an object, in all of which one Lord is multitudinously the Inhabitant. From the brilliant suns to the rose and the grain of dust, from the God and the Titan in their dark or their luminous worlds to man and the insect that he crushes thoughtlessly under his feet, everything is His temple and mansion. He is the veiled deity in the temple, the open householder in the mansion and for Him and His enjoyment of the multiplicity and the unity of His being, all were created and they have no other reason for their existence. Ishá vásyam idam sarvam yat kincha jagatyám jagat. For habitation by the Lord is all this, everything whatsoever that is moving thing in her that moves.

This relation of divine Inhabitant and objective dwelling-place is the fundamental truth of God and the World for life. It is not indeed the whole truth; nor is it their original relation in the terms of being; it is rather relation in action than in being, for purpose of existence than in nature of existence. This practical

relation of the Soul to its world thus selected by the Seer as his
starting point is from the beginning and with the most striking
emphasis affirmed as a relation not of coordinate equality or
simple interaction but of lordship and freedom on one side, of instrumentality on the other, Soul in supreme command of Nature,
God in untrammelled possession of His world, not limited by
anything in its nature or His nature, but free & Lord. For, since
it is the object of the Upanishad to build up a practical rule of
life here in the Brahman rather than a metaphysical philosophy
for the satisfaction of the intellect, the Seer of the Upanishad
selects inevitably the practical rather than the essential relation
of God & the world as the starting point of his thought, use
& subordination rather than identity. The grammatical form in
vásyam expresses a purpose or object which has to be fulfilled,
— in this instance the object of habitation; the choice of the
word Ishá implies an absolute control and therefore an absolute
freedom in that which has formed the object, envisaged the
purpose. Nature, then, is not a material shell in which Spirit is
bound, nor is Spirit a roving breath of things ensnared to which
the object it inspires is a prisonhouse. The indwelling God is the
Lord of His creations and not their servant or prisoner, and as a
householder is master of his dwelling-places to enter them and
go forth from them at his will or to pull down what he has built
up when it ceases to please him or be serviceable to his needs,
so the Spirit is free to enter or go forth from Its bodies and has
power to build and destroy and rebuild whatsoever It pleases
in this universe. The very universe itself It is free to destroy
and recreate. God is not bound; He is the entire master of His
creations.

The word Ishá, starting forward at once to meet us in this
opening vibration of the Seer's high strain of thought, becomes
the master tone of all its rhythms. It is the key to all that follows
in the Upanishad. For not only does it contradict at once all
mechanical theories of the Universe and assert the pre-existence,
omnipotence, majesty and freedom of the transcendent Soul of
things within, but by identifying the Spirit in the universe with
the Spirit in all bodies, it asserts what is of equal importance to

its gospel of a divine life for humanity, that the soul in man also is master, not really a slave, not bound, not a prisoner, but free — not bound to grief and death and limitation, but the master, the user of grief and death and limitation and free to pass on from them to other and more perfect instruments. If then we seem to be bound, as undoubtedly we do seem, by a fixed nature of our minds and bodies, by the nature of the universe, by the duality of grief and joy, pleasure and pain, by the chain of cause and effect or by any other chain or tie whatsoever, the seeming is only a seeming and nothing more. It is Maya, illusion of bondage, or it is Lila, a play at being bound. The soul, for its own purposes, may seem to forget its freedom, but even when it forgets, the freedom is there, self-existent, inalienable and, since never lost except in appearance, therefore always recoverable even in that appearance. This is the first truth of Vedanta assumed by the Upanishad in its opening words and from this truth we must start and adhere to it always in our minds, if we would understand in its right bearing & complete suggestion the Seer's gospel of life: —

That which dwells in the body of things is God, Self and Spirit; the Spirit is not the subject of its material, but the master; the soul in the body or in Nature is not the prisoner of its dwelling-place, but has moulded the body and its dharmas, fixed Nature and its processes and can remould, manipulate and arrange them according to its power and pleasure.

Idam sarvam yat kincha, the Seer has said, emphasising the generality of *idam sarvam* by the comprehensive particularity of *yat kincha.* He brings us at once by this expression to the Adwaitic truth in Vedanta that there is a multitude of objects in the universe, (it may be, even, a multitude of universes,) but only one soul of things and not many. Eko 'chalah sanátanah. The Soul in all this and in each particular form is one, still and sempiternal, one in the multitude of its habitations, still and unshifting in the perpetual movement of Nature, sempiternally the same in this constant ceasing and changing of forms. God sits in the centre of this flux of the universe, eternal, still and immutable. He pervades its oceanic heavings and streamings; therefore it endures. Nature is the multiplicity of God, Spirit is

His unity; Nature is His mobility, Spirit is His fixity; Nature is His variation, Spirit is His constant sameness. These truths are not stated at once; the Seer waits for a later verse to arrive at them. In this opening phrase he limits himself to the statement of the unity of God, and the multiplicity and mobility of Nature; for this relation in opposition is all that is immediately necessary to base the rule of divine living which it is his one object in the Upanishad to found upon a right knowledge of God & existence.

The self then of every man, every animal and every object, whether animate or inanimate, is God; the soul in us, therefore, is something divine, free and self-aware. If it seems to be anything else, — bound, miserable, darkened, — that is inevitably some illusion, some freak of the divine consciousness at play with its experiences; if this Soul seems to be other than God or Spirit, what seems is only a name and a form or, to keep to the aspect of the truth here envisaged, is only movement of Nature, jagat, which God has manifested in Himself for the purpose of various enjoyment in various mansions, — it is an image, a mask, a shape or eidolon created in the divine movement, formed by the divine self-awareness, instrumentalised by the divine activity. Therefore He is "this man and yonder woman, a boy and a girl, that old man leaning on his staff, this blue bird and that scarlet-eyed". We have, asserted in the comprehensiveness of the phrase, not only an entire essential omnipresence of God in us & in the world, but a direct and a practical omnipresence, possessing and insistent, not vague, abstract or elusive. The language of the Sruti is trenchant and inexorable. We must exclude no living being because it seems to us weak, mean, noxious or vile, no object because it seems to us inert, useless or nauseous. The hideous crawling worm or snake no less than the beautiful winged bird and the strong or gracious forms of four-footed life, the dull stone and foul mire and evil-smelling gas no less than man, the divine fighter and worker, are motions of the supreme Spirit; they contain in themselves and are in their secret reality the living God. This is the second general truth of Vedanta which arises inevitably from the pregnant verse of the Seer and, always present to him in his brief and concentrated thinking, must also accompany us throughout our pursuit of his sense and doctrine.

God is One; Self, Spirit, Soul is one; even when It presents Itself multitudinously in Its habitations as if It were many souls and so appears in the motion of Nature, Its universality and unity are not abrogated nor infringed. In all there is That which by coming out of its absorption in form of movement, recovers its unity. As the soul in man, though seeming to be bound, is always free and can realise its freedom, so, though seeming divided, limited and many, it is always universal, illimitable and one and can realise its universality and unity.

This creature born in a moment of time and bound in an atom of Space, is really in his secret consciousness the universal Spirit who contains the whole universe of things and dwells as the self of all things in these myriad forms of man & bird & beast, tree & earth & stone which my mind regards as outside me & other than myself. In the name of myself God inhabits this form of my being — but it is God that inhabits and the apparent "I" is but a centre of His personality & a knot in the infinite coilings of His active world existence. My ego is a creation of the Jagati in a form of mind; my Self stands behind, possesses and exceeds the universe.

II

This is Spirit in relation to Nature, one in multiplicity, the Lord of nature and process, free in the bound, conscious in the unconscious, inhabitant, master and enjoyer of all forms and movements of life, mind and body. Nature in relation to Spirit is its motion and the result of its motion, jagatyam jagat, phenomenon and everything that exists as phenomenon, universe and everything that constitutes universe. There are two terms in this brief and puissant formula, jagati and jagat. The second, jagat, is particular and multiple and includes whatsoever is separate existence, individual thing or form of motion, yat kincha; the first, jagati, is general and indicates both the resultant sum and the formative principle of all these particular existences, sarvam idam yat kincha. Sarvam idam is Nature regarded objectively as the sum of her creations; jagati is Nature regarded subjectively and essentially as that divine principle, expressed in motion of being and observed by us as force or Energy, which generates all these forms and variations. For Existence in itself is existence in a state of repose or stillness; indeterminate, infinite, inactive, it generates nothing: it is movement of energy in Existence which is active, which determines forms, which generates appearances of finite being and brings about phenomena of Becoming as opposed to fixed truth of Being. Therefore every objective existence in the world and all subjective forms, being forms of Existence in motion, being inconstant, being always mutable and always changing, progressing from a past of change to a future of change, are not truly different beings at all, but becomings of the one and only Being; each is the result of its previous motion, stands by its continued motion and if that motion were pretermitted or its rhythm disturbed, must change, disintegrate or transmute itself into some other form of becoming. Spirit or God is eternal Being, Nature in its sum & principle is the becoming of God and in its particulars a mass of His becomings, real as becomings, falsely valued as beings. The knowledge of the Upanishads takes its stand on this supreme distinction of Being and its Becomings; we find, indeed, in this Upanishad itself, another and more convenient collective term used to express all that is here defined as yat kincha jagatyam jagat, — one which brings us straight to this great distinction. The soul is Atman,[1] Being; everything else is sarvabhútáni, all becomings or, literally, all things that have become. This phrase is the common Sanscrit expression for created beings and though often referring in ordinary parlance to animate and self-conscious existences only, yet must in its philosophical sense and especially in the Upanishads, be accepted as inclusive of all existences whether they are or seem animate or inanimate, self-conscious or veiled in consciousness. The tree, flower & stone no less than the animal, heaven and wind and the sun and rain no less than man, invisible gas and

---

[1] The scholars hold erroneously that Atman meant first breath, then self; it meant, on the contrary, being, from the old root â, to be, still extant in Tamil, and the suffix tman, which expresses substance or substantial embodiment.

force & current no less than the things we can see and feel fall within its all-embracing formula.

God is the only Being and all other existences are only His becomings; the souls informing them are but one Spirit individualised in forms and forces by the play and movement of Its own self-consciousness.

We see, then, whose this energy is and of what the universe is the motion. But already from the little we have said there begins to emerge clearly another truth which in the Upanishad itself the Seer leaves in shadow for the present and only shapes into clear statement in his fourth and eighth couplets; he emphasises in the fourth couplet the unity of Soul & Nature, the stillness & the motion are not separate from each other, not one of them Brahman and the other an illusion, but both of them equally the one sole Existence, which moves & yet is still even in its motion, *Tad ejati tannaijati, anejad ekam manaso javíyas.* In the eighth verse he indicates that Brahman & the Lord[2] are not different from each other or from the motion, but are the reality of the motion as the motion itself is the play of the stillness; for to *Tad ejati,* That moves, comes as an echo & response, *Sa paryagát,* He went abroad. *Nature is motion of the Spirit, the world is motion of God; but also Nature is Spirit in motion, the world is God at play.*

All our inefficient envisagings of the world, all our ignorant questions fall away from this supreme Vedantic conception. We cannot ask ourselves, "Why has God brought about this great flux of things, this enormous and multitudinous world-movement? what can have been His purpose in it? Or is it a law of His nature and was He under an inner compulsion to create? Who then or what compelled Him?" These questions fall away from the decisive & trenchant solution, Ishá vásyam jagat. He has no purpose in it except habitation, except delight, an ordered and harmonised delight, — therefore there is what we call universe, law, progression, the appearance of a method

---

[2] The Mayavadins hold that God is only the first myth of Maya & not the truth of Brahman, — the language of the Upanishad shows that this was not the view of the old Vedantic Rishis.

and a goal; but the order effected feels always its neighbourhood
to the grandiose licence of the infinite and the harmony achieved
thrills at once with the touch of the Transcendent's impulse to
pass out of every rhythm and exceed every harmony. For this
is a self-delight which in no way limits or binds Him; He has
brought it about and He conducts it in perfect freedom; there is
no compulsion on Him & none can compel Him, for He alone
exists and Nature is only a play of time-movement in His being,
proceeding from Him, contained in Him, governed by Him, not
He by it or proceeding from it or coeval with it and therefore
capable of being its subject, victim or instrument. Neither is
there any inner compulsion limiting Him either as to the nature
of the work or its method. The movement of the universe is not
the nature of God, nor are its processes the laws of God's being;
for Spirit is absolute and has no fixed or binding nature, God
is supreme & transcendent and is not bound by state, law or
process, — so free is He, rather, that He is not bound even to
His own freedom. The laws of Nature, as we have seen, cannot
be laws of being at all, since Nature itself is a becoming; they are
processes which regulate the harmonies of becoming, processes
which are, in the Vedic image, chhandas, rhythms of the movement and not in their own being rigid, inexorable & eternal
because self-existent verities; they are results of the tendency to
order & harmony, not sempiternal fetters on Existence. Even the
most fundamental laws are only modes of activity conceived &
chosen by Spirit in the universe. We arrive then at this farther
all-important truth: —

*Nature is a divine motion of becoming of which Spirit is
the origin, substance and control as well as the inhabitant and
enjoyer. Laws of Nature are themselves general movements &
developments of becoming and conditions of a particular order,
rhythm and harmony of the universe, but not inexorably preexistent or recognisable as the very grain of existence. The Laws
of Evolution are themselves evolutions and progressive creations
of the Spirit.*

Since Spirit, transcendent and original of the universe, is the
sole existence, the motion of the universe can only take place in

the Spirit. Therefore the indwelling of the Spirit in forms is not only a free indwelling rather than an imprisonment, but also it is not the whole or essential truth of this mutual relation of God & Nature; indwelling but not confined, like the presence of the ether in the jar, it is symbolical and a figment of divine conception rather than the essential relation of body and spirit. We get the fuller statement of the truth in the fifth couplet of the Upanishad, Tad antar asya sarvasya tad u sarvasyásya báhyatah; That, the inexpressible Reality of things, is within this universe and each thing it contains, but equally it is outside of this universe and each thing that it contains, — outside it as continent, outside it as transcendent. The omnipresent Inhabitant of the world is equally its all-embracing continent. If form is the vessel in which Spirit dwells, Spirit is the sphere in which form exists & moves. But, essentially, It transcends form and formation, movement and relation, & even while It is inhabitant & continent, stands apart from what It inhabits and contains, self-existent, self-sufficient, divine and eternally free. Spirit is the cause, world is the effect, but this cause is not bound to this effect. Na cha mám táni karmáni nibadhnanti, says the Lord in the Gita; I am not bound by these works that I do, even while I do them. The soul of man, one with God, has the same transcendency and the same freedom.

Spirit contains, dwells in and transcends this body of things. It acts in the world but is not bound by Its actions. The same essential freedom must be true of this soul in the body, even though it may seem to be confined in the body and compelled by Nature's results and its own works. The soul in us has the inherent power not only of becoming in this outward & waking consciousness what it is in reality, the continent of the body which seems to contain it, but of transcending in consciousness all bodily relation and relation with the universe.

From the action of Nature in the Spirit, as from the action of the Spirit in Nature, the same formula of freedom emerges. I have, in God and by God, made myself and my world what we now are; I can, in God and by God, change them and make them what I would have them be. I am not the sport and puppet of Nature and her laws, but their creator and her master. She accommodates herself to me and pretends to herself & me that she is ruling my whole existence, when she is really following, however late, stumblingly and with feigned reluctance, the motion of my will. Instrument of my actions, she pretends to be the mistress of my being. The identity of the soul and God behind all veils is the Vedantic charter of man's freedom. Science, observing only the movement, seeing fixed process everywhere, is obsessed by what she studies and declares the iron despotism of mechanical Law. Vedanta, studying the Force that makes the movement and its cause, arrives at the perception and experience of Spirit everywhere and declares our eternal and indefeasible freedom. It passes beyond the Law to the Liberty of which the Law itself is the creation & expression.

III

It is not enough, however, to know the inner fact and the outer possibility of our freedom; we must also look at and take into account the apparent actuality of our bondage. The debit side of the human ledger must be taken into the reckoning as well as the credit account. The explanation and seed of this bondage is contained in the formula jagatyam jagat; for, if our freedom results from the action of Spirit in Nature and of Nature in Spirit, our bondage results from the action of Nature on all that she has created and contains. Every mundane existence is jagatyam jagat, not a separate and independent motion by itself, but part of and dependent on the universal movement. From this dependence by inclusion derives the great law that every form of things engendered in the motional universe shall be subject to the processes of that particular stream of movement to which it belongs; each individual body subject to the general processes of matter, each individual life to the general processes of vitality, each individual mind to the general processes of mentality, because the individual is only a whorl of motion in the general motion and its individual variation therefore can only be a speciality of the general motion and not contradictory of it.

The multiplicity of God in the universe is only a circumstance of His unity and is limited and governed by the unity; therefore the animal belongs to its species, the tree, the rock and the star each to its kind and man to humanity. If machinery of existence were all, if there were no Spirit in the motion or that Spirit were not Ish, the Master, origin, continent and living transcendence of the motion, this law is of so pressing a nature that the subjection would be absolute, the materialist's reign of iron Law complete, the Buddhist's rigid chain of causation ineffugable. This generality, this pressure of tyrannous insistence is necessary in order that the harmony of the universe may be assured against all disturbing vibrations. It is the bulwark of cosmos against chaos, of the realised actuality against that inconstant & ever-pulsating material of infinite possibility out of which it started, of the finite against the dangerous call and attraction of the Infinite.

The unity of God governs His multiplicity; therefore the more general motion of Nature as representative of or nearest to that unity governs the multiple individual products of the movement. To each motion its law and to each inhabitant of that motion subjection to the law. Therefore Man, being human in Nature, is bound first by Nature, then by his humanity.

But because God is also the transcendence of Nature & Nature moves towards God, therefore, even in Nature itself a principle of freedom and a way of escape have been provided. Avidyayá mrityum tírtwá. For, in reality, the motion of Nature is only the apparent or mechanical cause of our bondage; the real and essential cause arises from the relation of Spirit to Nature. God having descended into Nature, Spirit cast itself out in motion, allows Himself as part of the play to be bewitched by His female energy and seems to accept on Himself in the principle of mind isolated from the higher spiritual principles, her absorption in her work and her forgetfulness of her reality. The soul in mind identifies itself with its form, allows itself apparently to float on the oceanic stream of Nature and envisages itself as carried away by the current. Spirit veils itself from Mind; Ish wraps Himself up in jagat & seems to its own outer consciousness to be jagat. This is the principle of our bondage; the principle of our freedom is to draw back from that absorption & recover our real self-consciousness as the containing, constituting and transcendent Spirit.

Spirit, absorbed in the motion and process of Nature, appears to be bound by the process of becoming as if it were law of being; it is therefore said to be bound by Karma, that is to say, by the chain of particular cause and effect, the natural chain of active energy and its results. But by drawing back upon itself & ceasing to identify itself with its form, it can get rid of this appearance and recover its lordship and freedom. Incidentally, the soul of Man by drawing more and more towards God, becomes more & more Ish and can more and more control the processes of becoming in himself and in others, in the subjective and in the objective, in the mental and in the material world.

This final conclusion of freedom & power in the world is of the last importance for our immediate purpose. Merely to draw back from all identification with form is to draw away towards the Stillness, the Infinity & the cessation of all this divine play of motion. Ever since Buddhism conquered Vedic India and assured the definite enthronement of the ideal of Sannyasa in opposition to the ideal of Tyaga, this consummation has been constantly praised and held up before us in this country as the highest ideal of man and his only path to salvation. But even if for the few this goal be admitted, yet for the majority of men it must still & always remain God's ultimate purpose in them to realise Him manifest in the world, — since that is His purpose in manifestation, — & not only & exclusively unmanifest in His transcendental stillness. It must be possible then to find God as freedom & immortality in the world and not only aloof from the world. There must be a way of escape provided in Nature itself out of our bondage to Nature. Man must be able to find in Nature itself and in his humanity a way of escape into divinity & freedom from Nature, avidyayá mrityum tírtwá. This would not be possible if God and Nature, Brahman and the Universe, were two hostile & incompatible entities, the one real and the other false or non-existent. But Spirit and Universe, God and Nature are one Brahman; therefore there must always be a point at which the two meet; their apparent divergence in consciousness must be somewhere corrected in consciousness, Nature must at some point become God and the apparently material Universe stand revealed as Spirit.

In the profound analysis of the human soul built by the ancient Vedantic thinkers upon the most penetrating self-observation and the most daring & far-reaching psychological experiments, this point of escape, this bridge of reconciliation was discovered in the two supramental principles, Ideal Consciousness & Bliss Consciousness, both of them disengaged from the confusions of the mind involved in matter. Just as modern Scientists, not satisfied with the ordinary processes & utilities of Nature, not satisfied with the observation of her surface forces & daily activities, penetrated further, analysed, probed, discovered hidden forces & extraordinary activities, not satisfied with Nature's obvious use of wind as a locomotive force, found & harnessed the unutilised propulsive energy of steam, not satisfied with observing the power of electricity in the glare & leap of the thunderflash, disengaged & used it for the lighting of our houses & thoroughfares, for the driving of our engines & printing presses, for the alleviation of disease or for the judicial murder of our fellow-creatures, so the old Vedantic Yogins, not satisfied with observing the surface activities and ordinary processes of our subjective nature, penetrated further, analysed, probed, discovered hidden forces & extraordinary activities by which our whole active mentality could be manipulated and rearranged as one manipulates a machine or rearranges a set of levers; pressing yet farther towards the boundaries of existence they discovered whence this energy proceeded & whitherward this stir and movement tended & worked. They found beyond the manifest & obvious triple bond of body, life & mind, two secret states & powers of consciousness which supported them in their works — beyond this limited, groping and striving mind & life which only fumble after right knowledge & labour after the right use of power & even attaining them can possess & wield them only as indirect & secondhand agents, they discovered a principle of ideal consciousness, vijnana, which saw Truth face to face & unerringly, looking on the sun with unshaded eyes, and a principle of all-blissful power & being which possessed in itself, by the very right of its eternal existence & inalienable nature, right joy, right awareness & right action as the very self-atmosphere of its manifestation in the universe. Above this inferior trilogy of matter, life & mind (Annam Prana Manas), there is a superior trilogy of Infinite Being, Force & Bliss (Sat, Chit, Ananda) accessible to us & working on us inhabitants of the lower spheres from the symbol of divine beatific consciousness, the Anandatattwa, as its throne of world rule, the home & fortress of the divine Master, and employing as its distributing & arranging minister the truth-seeing ideal mind to feed, supply & compel the activities of the lower being. They saw, then, being arranged in seven stairs, seven worlds, seven streams of world movement, seven bodies of things, seven states of consciousness which inform & contain the bodies. They saw this material consciousness & this material world as the lowest stair, the least in plenitude & power & joy of these seven divine rivers. Man they saw as a soul dwelling in matter, deriving his activities from mind & holding them in mind but going back in the roots of his being to the divine trilogy. Earth, in the language of their thought, was the footing & pedestal of the human unit, but the heavens of Ananda concealed the secret & ungrasped crown of his world-existence. This conception of the sevenfold form of our being & of world-being helps to constitute the very kernel of the doctrine in the Upanishads. It is the key to their sense in many passages where there is no direct mention or precise reference to any of its seven terms. It is because we miss these clues that so much in these scriptures comes to our mind as a mystery or even as a vague & confused extravagance of disordered mysticism.

In this septuple system of our Scriptures every individual body obeys the laws of matter, every life the processes of vitality, every mind the processes of mentality, every ideal being the processes of ideality and every free soul the processes of Beatitude. The seven worlds are indeed different kingdoms, each with its own nations & creatures, prajáh, bhútáni. But since God is always one, each separate motion contains in itself the presence and potentiality of all the others; moreover, since it contains the potentiality, it is irresistibly led to develop under its own conditions that which it contains. For this reason Matter in the world tends to manifest Life, Life in Matter to rise into Mind, Mind in vitalised body to be released into Pure Idea, Pure Idea in matter-housed Mind to be consummated in divine Beatitude. The pervading law, therefore, which confines each species to the rule of its kind is only one general rhythm of the movement; it is crossed by a higher upward and liberating movement which leads the becoming we now are to strive for development towards that other, freer & larger scale of becoming which is immediately above it. This fresh rule of Nature, then, appears & constitutes the rule of our freedom as the other was the rule of our servitude.

The principle, "To each motion its law & to each inhabitant of the motion subjection to the law" is crossed and corrected by this other principle, "Each motion contains a tendency towards the motion above it and to each type of becoming, therefore, there comes in the progress of time the impulse to strain beyond the mould it has realised to that which is higher than itself."

In this complex arrangement of Nature where is man's exact position? He is a mental being housed in a vitalised body & he tends through pure idea towards divine beatitude. Now just as matter informed with life, no longer obeys the processes of matter only, but, even while it affects life-processes, is also affected by them and finds its complete liberation in the conquest of matter by life, just as mind in a life body is affected, limited and hampered by vital & bodily processes, but still governs them and would find its own liberation and theirs in the perfect conquest of life & matter by mind, so, since this mental being is really a soul imprisoned in mind, its perfect liberation comes by rising out of the mould of mind through pure idea into beatitude; escaping into beatitude, this mental existence is able to liberate the whole lower system of being by renewing every part of it in the mould and subjecting every part of it to the process of that which we have now become. The mould and process of Ananda

is freedom, God, bliss, immortality, universality, & these, therefore, are the laws of being, the *dharmas*, the sum of a divine
beatific existence which we put on by rising out of mental ego
into infinite Ananda. The motion of pure Idea, vijnana, is the
door of our escape in Avidya; for it is the kingdom within us of
Truth and Illumination, domain, in the Vedic symbol, of the god
of the Sun, the prophetic Apollo, the burning and enlightening
Surya. Sa no dhiyah prachodayát.

*The base of our being is in Matter, its knot is in mentality,
its escape into divine Bliss. Our aim as human beings must be to
rise through the pure Idea into divine bliss and there freed from
mental egoism & vital and material limitations spiritualise and
beatify our whole existence from the base to the summit.*

We are a double birth, God the Spirit, God in Nature, Ish
and Jagat. In Nature we are bound in our consciousness, because
we are there a whorl of its motion, a wave in its sea; in Spirit
we are free, for there we are a part of nothing, but one with the
indivisible Spirit. But this double is really biune. God, unbound
by His divisibility, unbound by His indivisibility, weds the One
to the Many in the play of His consciousness, in His ineffable
beatitude. There God and Nature meet, Vidya and Avidya embrace each other, our real freedom governs and uses consciously
our apparent bondage, the bliss of Transcendence joins hands
with the bliss of manifestation, God shows Himself in humanity
and man realises himself as divine.

The joy of that reconciliation dwells in the Immortality to
which the Vedanta is our guide and its starting point is the
recognition by mind of the one Lord in all bodies, the one
Spiritual Being in all becomings, átmánam sarvabhúteshu. Since
it is the all-blissful Lord who dwells within and Nature is for
His habitation and enjoyment, then a state of Nature which is
a state of bondage, sorrow-pursued, death-besieged, wrestling
with limitations, is convicted of being only a temporary mask
and a divinely willed starting-point for the Energy confined in
the triple bonds of mortal Mind, Life & Matter to work out
its own immortal freedom. The object of life is self-liberation,
the only aim of human existence consistent with the dignity and

fullness of our being is the escape through Nature to God, out of grief, bondage & death into joy, freedom and immortality. Avidyayá mrityum tírtwá vidyayámritam asnute.

APPENDIX

[*The following passage, written on a loose sheet, seems to be related to the above section.*]

In our observation of the workings of law & freedom in cosmic Nature we cannot fail to be struck by the principle of gradated and progressive freedom by which she climbs up from an apparent rigidity of law to an apparent elasticity of freedom. We observe that matter inert or informed only by an inert principle of motion is the field of rigid law & of fixed process. We observe next that in proportion as life develops in matter, the principle of variation, of flexible adaptability, even of instinctive, if unconscious self-adaptation manifests & increases in her workings. We observe that in proportion as mind develops in living matter this variation, this flexibility & self-adaptation grow into a conscious struggle with & partial domination of the life & matter in which mind operates. From this we arrive easily at certain large corollaries.

(1) Mind, life & matter are, in all probability, one essence, but not one principle. They are three different principles of Nature, each with its separate rhythm, principle of process & mode of working.

(2) Consciousness is the principle of freedom, form is the principle of law; the necessity of dealing with the rigidity of form and its processes is the cause of the limitations of the freedom inherent in consciousness.

(3) Consciousness and life evolve out of matter; they must then have been all the time inherent & involved in matter.

(4) Life itself seems to be an operation of involved consciousness working itself out of the imprisonment in matter. It is therefore conceivable that matter itself may be only a form of involved consciousness.

(5) Mind is a principle of mental self-conscious sensation, action-comprehension, reaction, attraction-repulsion rising into a luminosity (prakasha) we call knowledge of which thought is only the partial system or formula. In Life we notice in the plant & metal a vital sensation, action-comprehension, reaction, attraction-repulsion, essentially the same as the mental but expressed in a different system of values, — values of involved consciousness. In Matter we do not observe sensation, but we do observe the other common activities of Nature. Experimental Yogic psychists assert that matter does also receive & store blind sensations & that the mind of man can discover records of past events in material objects & convert them into values of knowledge. Science even goes so far as to assert that all sensations are an activity of matter & are stored in the brain & can always be turned by memory under some stimulus into values of knowledge. We may say therefore that the essence of consciousness is at least present in matter, but it only organises itself by evolution, through life in mind.

We cannot assert that the present state of consciousness [which is] the consciousness of limited freedom & derived knowledge in man is the last possible evolution of consciousness. It is at least possible that an entirely free consciousness bringing with it a spontaneous instead of a derived knowledge & an entirely free mastery instead of a partially free manipulation of mind, life & matter is concealed in Nature & its unveiling is the final goal of her evolution.

If such a free consciousness exists, there must be a principle in Nature superior to mind as mind is superior to life & matter & this can be nothing else than the Vedic principle called vijnana.

This free consciousness, entire mastery, must be a power of cosmic Nature & cannot be acquired by the individual except by breaking down the habits of consciousness & exceeding the fixed processes by which the individual action is separated & differentiated from cosmic action.

The ultimate evolution must therefore end in the openness of the individual for cosmic or infinite consciousness-being, not limited by individual ego-sense, the workings of free infinite cosmic force, not limited by individual will; possessing entire freedom, knowledge & mastery it must be in its nature an infinite joy & bliss in oneself & in all the cosmic workings which enter into our experience. The highest state of Nature & goal of evolution must be infinite Sacchidananda.

So much we can reasonably infer from the facts of the cosmos as we see them. We then arrive at the Vedanta results without starting from Vedanta; but if we accept the Vedantic premise that all world is only a formation & operation of consciousness, these inferences become inevitable conclusions.

Chapter II

The Golden Rule of Living —
Enjoyment & Renunciation

The first line of the Seer's first couplet has given us very briefly
and suggestively the base & starting point of the whole thought
of the Upanishad; the second line of the same couplet opens
to us, with equal brevity, with equal suggestiveness the consummation of the whole thought of the Upanishad. The rest
of the eighteen shlokas fill out, complete, play variations; they
add much thought that is necessary to avoid error, to perceive
supplementary and collateral truths or to guide oneself aright in
the path that has been hewn out or to walk with unstumbling
footsteps through the doors that have been opened to us; but
all the practical need of man and the central gist of the Seer's
thought about human life is compressed into these two lines
with their few brief words and their thousand echoes.

All the underlying Vedantic conceptions which we have had
to bring out in our first chapter, have had reference to the three
great practical factors of the human problem as it presented itself
to Vedantic thinkers, the reality of spiritual freedom, the appearance of material bondage and the means of escape out of the appearance and into the reality, out of matter into Spirit, out of Nature into God. But these expressions, freedom and bondage, are
intellectual, ideal or spiritual terms. This human being though he
lays hold on intellect as a guide and aspires to ideality and spirit,
does not live centred in those superior movements of consciousness; brain leads his thought when it can, but he lives in the heart
& lives in it, too, besieged by the nerves and body. His mentality
is, therefore, emotional, sensational and temperamental, not intellectual or ideal, and the practical aspect of his own problem is
not limitation or infinity, but the pressure of pain, grief, sorrow
and suffering and the possibility of escape from these his ruthless
and omnipresent persecutors. He could even be content for a
while with death and limitation if, free from this admixture of
pain & suffering, his short span of life & circumscribed sphere of

action could be assured of that limited happiness which the race at large is vainly pursuing. It was the agony of this problem that seized on Buddha and drove him from his kingly home & rich domestic joys to wander through the world as a beggar and ascetic; to escape from the insistent pain, grief and suffering of the world the Lord of Pity discovered for man the eightfold path, the law of compassion & self-sacrifice, the heavenly door of renunciation and the silent and blindly luminous haven of Nirvana. The Seer of the Upanishad sets before himself the same problem but arrives at a very different solution; for he proceeds not from pity, but from a clear strength and a steady knowledge, perceiving the problem but not overpowered by it, samáhita, dhíra. Dwelling in a world of grief, pain, death and limitation, anityam asukham imam lokam prápya, yet irresistibly impelled by Nature to aspire after joy, immortality and freedom, bound not to renounce that apparently impossible ideal on peril of forfeiting our highest, most consoling and most exalting impulses, how are we to reconcile this ineffugable contradiction or to escape from this unending struggle? This is the problem which the Seer solves in three brief words, tena tyaktena bhunjítháh, again a monumental phrase whose echoes travel the whole of existence. It is because it provides the true practical basis for the solution he is going to suggest that he has preferred to announce at the outset the immediate and active relation of our twofold existence, God inhabiting Nature, rather than the remoter essential relation, God and Nature one Brahman. For the first practical step towards freedom must always be to distinguish between the Inhabitant and the habitation and withdraw from the motion towards the Lord of the motion. It is in the motion that these shadows of limitation, grief and death appear; the Inhabitant is free, blissful and immortal. To escape, then, we must turn from the world to the Master of the world; in ordinary religious parlance, we must renounce the world in order to find and possess God. So also the Gita, after describing our condition, arrived in this transient and troubled world, anityam asukham imam lokam prápya, immediately points out the remedy, bhajaswa Mám. Turn & cleave rather to me, the Lord. But the world was made by its Lord for divine habitation & possession; the object of the renunciation, therefore, cannot be to turn away utterly from the world after abandoning it in itself & in the lower consciousness, but to conquer and repossess it through the divine Krishna and in the supreme & all-blissful conscious being of the Lord. Nivasishyasi mayyeva. Thou shalt dwell in Me utterly, in My illimitable being & not in a limited & mortal experience of the world. To form the basis of the rule of life which the Seer enunciates, we have, then, this practical corollary from the language of his first line: —

To escape from grief, death and limitation we must renounce the world, to enjoy bliss, freedom & immortality we must possess ourselves in the Lord; but since His object in manifesting is habitation of the universe and not its destruction, the bliss must be enjoyed in this universe, through the Lord, and not in the Lord apart from and exclusive of life in the universe.

This is the difference, the capital difference between the Buddhistic solution — with all those later solutions affected & governed by Buddhistic thought, such as Mayavada & monastic Christianity — and the ancient answer of Hinduism to the problem put to man by life. These say, "Abandon life, put away all possession & enjoyment; absolute asceticism is your only salvation"; that said "Abandon the world that you may possess and enjoy it." One is an escape, the other a recoil and an aggression; one is a divorce, the other a reconciliation. Both solutions are heroic; but one is a mighty heroism of difficult retreat and flight; the other a mightier heroism of self-perfection and conquest. The one is the retreat of the Ten Thousand; the other is Caesar's movement from Dyrrhachium to [Pharsalus]. One path culminates in Buddha, the other in Janaka and Srikrishna. The language of the Seer is perfectly framed, as in the first line, to bring about a confrontation of two giant opposites. Tyaktena in the instrumental case suggests a means, and the very first word after tyaktena, undivided from it by any other vocable or particle, the word which gives the object and work of this instrument, the word which sets ringing from the outset the conclusive note and culminating cry of the Upanishad and is suggested again and again in jijivishet, in ko mohah kah shokah, in amritam, in kalyanatamam, in raye, is the magnificent bhunjithah, Thou shouldst enjoy. Tyaga and bhoga, renunciation and enjoyment, have always been presented to us as the two conflicting ideals of human life & thought, — inevitably, for they are the two master impulses of Nature — both of them eternal — and through the ages they have perplexed and tormented humanity by their perpetual companionship in an always unfinished and inconclusive strife, dividing us into Puritan and Pagan, Stoic and Epicurean, worldling and ascetic, & perpetuating an opposition that rests on a false division of a double unity, maintaining a strife that can lead to no final victory. The Seer has deliberately brought these two great opposites & enemies together and using a pointed and unequivocal language, has put them side by side no longer as enemies but as friends and mutual helpers; his aim is by a fearless and puissant confrontation to reconcile and wed them eternally to each other, as he has already in the first line confronted, reconciled and eternally wedded the two apparent opposites, Spirit and world-Nature. Had he said not "Tyaktena" but "Tyagena bhunjithah", from which we might have concluded that he pointed us to renunciation of the world for the enjoyment of God aloof from the world, there would then have been no real confrontation & no great monumental phrase but only a skilful verbal turn of words pointing a contrast rather than effecting a reconciliation. But the instrument of the enjoyment is not renunciation in itself and for itself but the world we have renounced, tena, & the enjoyment is not the self-sufficient joy of renunciation & escape, but the enjoyment of Spirit in the world, the Lord in the motion. By means of all that is thing of world in this moving universe we are to enjoy God &, through Him, no longer as now apart from Him, to enjoy His universal motion, — all this that is moving thing in her that moves becomes the instrument of a divine delight, because the world is God and part of His totality, so that by possessing & enjoying Him we possess and enjoy world also. Enjoyment is to be reconciled then to renunciation & even wedded to it, made to depend upon it as the effect depends upon the cause, to stand upon it as a statue stands upon its pedestal or the roof of a house on its foundations, walls and pillars. Renunciation the means, enjoyment the end, but renunciation of the world as mere undivine, ignorant & fettered motion & becoming, enjoyment of God in Himself & of the world only as a symbol, a formal expression of God; this reconciliation founded on a knowledge of the true nature & purpose of existence is the gospel of the Seer.

The ascetic gospel of renunciation is incomplete by itself; the Pagan gospel of enjoyment is incomplete by itself. Renunciation and enjoyment of the world must be reconciled by substituting inward for outward bliss, the bliss that goes from within outward for the pleasure which seeks to appeal from without inward, joy of God in the form & name of things for joy of the finite appearance and the isolated idea. The reconciliation is to be effected through the consummate experience of Ananda, the divine beatitude at which we arrive by true seeing in the kingdom of the pure Idea, satyadharmena drishtyá.

Let us examine successively this renunciation and this enjoyment. We see, first, that tena refers back to the expression in the first line, so wide, so carefully comprehensive, idam sarvam yat kincha jagatyam jagat, by which the absolute unity of the Inhabitant is affirmed. We are to abandon utterly the world; we are to renounce every least or greatest detail of phenomenal existence, whether held by us in possession or aimed at in our desire; we are to surrender everything whatsoever that we have or may hope to possess or dream of possessing in the universe. We see that the demand in this second line is as sweeping and unsparing as the all-comprehensive description in its base & predecessor. We are to keep back nothing; all that is dearest to us in our outward environment, wife, children, home, friends, wealth, country, position, fame, honour, success, the respect of men, the love of those we cherish, — all that is dearest to us in our inward life; our loves, hates, jealousies, ambitions, sins, virtues, principles, opinions, tastes, preferences, ideals, — these and all we are, our body, life, mind, soul, personality, ego, all, all have to be sacrificed and laid upon a single altar. We must keep back nothing either of our outer or of our inner wealth; for if, professing to make the complete surrender, we consciously

& willingly keep back one doit or farthing, we are thieves before God, committing the Biblical sin of Ananias & Sapphira, — stena eva sah, — conscious or half-conscious hypocrites, — mithyáchárah sa uchyate, — and, even if the holding back be unwilled or unconscious, still are we imperfect sadhakas not yet having the right to grasp our crown. For the natural principle of this surrender is precise: —

As one gives so one receives. God is All & he who would gain all, must give all. The final sacrifice admits of no reservation and even a slight defect of renunciation, however seemingly lofty the scruple, vitiates the purity and effectiveness of the sacrifice.

But since the renunciation asked of us is not the objective renunciation, — although that too is not excluded so far as it is necessary for the real surrender, — since it is not an outward process of flight from the objects of pleasure, it can only be, in essence, an inner sacrifice to the Master of the world, to Ish, the Lord. Since there is only One Lord in multitudinous bodies & to Him the entire world belongs, everything that is offered to the enjoyment not of the one Lord of the world, but to the mind, senses, body as part of the motion, the jagat, is an ignorant sacrifice on a false altar. It may be justified by the great cosmic ignorance so long as that principle of consciousness keeps its hold on us, but it can never bring the supreme good or the divine bliss. A perverse & broken movement, it brings a perverse and broken result.[3] So long as we feel ourselves to be at all separate existences from God and others, anyán, we are here as His deputies and instruments to receive out of what the world possesses so much as the Lord of the world sends or brings to us, and to offer them up not to our mind and senses but to the Master of the Universe seated in ourselves and in others, bhoktáram yajnatapasám sarvalokamaheshwaram. He is the true enjoyer of all sacrifices and works of askesis, the mighty lord of all the worlds. For this reason the Gita directs us to offer up as an utter sacrifice to the Supreme all our actions, all our efforts, all our enjoyments, yat tapasyasi, yat karoshi yad

---

[3] Gita

aśnási. Demanding nothing for ourselves, but receiving for Him all that He wills to give us through the action of others or our own, we are to refer them all to Him again for His acceptance. Even what we do, we are to do not for our sake, but for God's sake, not for our personal & self-regarding aims, but for what we see, rightly or wrongly, in the light we have, to be His aim in us, concentrating on the action, not reaching out to its fruit. This rule of life is the greatest we are capable of while still at work in the ignorance and moving subject to the dualities; but if we wish to go beyond, we must proceed to a yet more unsparing sacrifice. The Gita begins with the sacrifice to God of our desires and the fruits of our action; but it goes on to the giving up *into* God, mayi sannyasya, of action itself and even the least internal or external movement towards action, sarvarambhah; it insists, above all & to the end, on the supreme renunciation of the ego-sense, the ahankara, as the one all-satisfying and divine sacrifice demanded by the ego-transcendent Universal Being from the ego-besieged and ego-ridden human soul. We must, in this consummation, fall perfectly passive in mind, life & body & allow the Divine Power to use them from above, as a man uses a machine, wields a sword or hurls a ball to its mark. These formulae of the Gita are, also, the true sense of the inner sacrifice imposed on the seeker by the Isha Upanishad. It is the sacrifice of the lower or motional parts of our being to the higher or divine part — the offering of jagat into the Lord.

The renunciation demanded of us is an inner sacrifice, effected in the surrender to God of all desire and attachment, of all self-will and self-action, and of all ego-sense and separate personality. Desire & attachment to possessions have to be cast & dissolved into the mould of a desireless and all-possessing bliss (Ananda or Jana); self-will & self-action cast & dissolved into the mould of a divine action of the universal Shakti or World Force (Chit or Tapas) which shall use the mind, body and life as a passive, obedient and perfected instrument; ego-sense cast and dissolved into the mould of divine & undivided being (Sat) which regards itself as one in all things & the multiplicity of minds, lives & bodies as only a varied motion of its own divine unity. This divine being, force & bliss constitute the higher part of man's being centred in the principle of Ananda; they represent the direct, unveiled and unperverted action of the free & blissful Sacchidananda. To this last and supreme Immortality (Amrita) these lower mortal parts of man must be given up as the victims of a high & ultimate spiritual sacrifice in the upward movement of world-Nature.

Renunciation once determined for us in its spirit & type, we arrive naturally at the other term of this great reconciliation, the enjoyment pointed at in bhunjítháh. To understand the place and relation of the Seer's gospel of divine immortality & bliss in the thought and development of Hinduism, we must return for a moment to the fundamental Hindu idea of sacrifice. For it is in the light of this original idea of sacrifice that we must understand the ancient transition from Veda to Vedanta. Sacrifice to the gods was from the earliest times the central idea of the Hindu religion, under the name of renunciation, sacrifice to God still remains its whole spirit and teaching. The gods, Masters of natural forces, act in Nature under God in the motional being of the Master of all and distribute their energies to individual movements and creatures; from their store, the individual receives whatever he possesses of capacities, desires & enjoyments; at their hands he must seek whatever, not possessing, he desires firmly to acquire. But the principle of Nature, that great motion and complex rhythm, stands in the harmony & interdependence of the individual & general, jagatyam jagat; the individual, therefore, can neither gain what he has not nor keep what he has except by sacrifice of his personal energies & possessions into the world-substance & the world-energies. By expenditure of what he has, offering it into the general stream of the corresponding force or substance in the perpetual flux and movement of Nature, he is kept safe by the gods or he increases. If it is my purpose to improve my muscular strength, I must first consent to an output, an expenditure in exercise of the strength I already have, allowing it to escape as energy into the world-sum of energy, sacrificing to Vayu and Prithivi; I must accept temporary loss of power, weariness and exhaustion, losing a little that I may gain more; then, what I have given is taken up by the deities in the Jagati and, if the sacrifice has been properly conducted, returned increased, doubled, trebled or even decupled to the giver. As it is in our physical, so it is in our mental & emotional being. I must pour love from myself in feeling & action into the world-stream of love, sacrificing to Mitra; then only what I have given may return to me increased, doubled, trebled, decupled in the love and affection of others or in my own enlarged capacity for loving. The rule, being fundamental & universal, holds good with all internal & external possessions and holdings, the dhanani of the Rigveda. "Foster by sacrifice the gods," says the Gita, "and let those gods foster you; fostering each other ye shall attain the supreme good, — param sreyah." Attaining the supreme good we pass beyond the gods and come to God; we leave Veda to arrive at Vedanta or, rather, fulfil Veda in Vedanta. Then we are no longer content to sacrifice this or that possession, giving a share, making reservations, but offer unreservedly & unconditionally the supreme sacrifice, yielding up on the highest of all altars all that we are and possess; we give no longer to Agni, Indra, Varuna or Mitra, but to the supreme & universal Lord, bhoktáram yajnatapasám. Then, too, we receive in return not wealth, nor cattle nor horses nor lands nor empire, not joys nor powers nor brilliances nor capacities, but God Himself & the world with all these things in them as trifles and playthings for the soul to enjoy as God enjoys, possessing them and yet not possessing, wholly unbound by possession.

Renunciation of some kind, voluntary or involuntary, is the condition of all growth and all existence; by expenditure acquisition, by sacrifice security, by renunciation enjoyment, this is God's universal law of sacrifice. The gods who are Powers of Nature, receiving our due sacrifice, give us the partial gains & enjoyments which come within their jurisdiction; God, receiving our due sacrifice, gives us Himself and in Himself everything that exists in Nature or beyond it.

There is a common agreement in the different schools of Hinduism that to the man who has renounced, God gives Himself in return for his renunciation; our difficulty has been to settle among our many conflicting conceptions what that is in soul existence which God intends to reveal as His very self and to what, therefore, we are called to aspire. The ascetic sees Him in impersonal Being and actionless peace; he believes therefore that we receive in return for renunciation release from phenomena and the bliss of the unconditioned Brahman. The devotee sees Him in divine Personality; he hopes to get, in return for what he offers, Shiva or Rama, Krishna or Kali. Some aspire to the Pure & Bright Stillness beyond, others like the Tantriks, seeing Him as Universal Power, attempt to acquire & feel Him here in a superior & divine power and mastery, yet others would have God in Himself and yet God playing also in His garden of the universe. The reason of these differences lies in our human variation of temperament — for we live in heart and temperament — and therefore of knowledge and approach — for with us mental being seated in the heart temperament determines our knowledge & action, — variations produced by the differently distributed motion in us of Prakriti, of Jagati, of the process of our world-nature. According to our nature we seek God. It is always, in fact, by some principle in Avidya itself that we are moved to exceed Avidya. Even as a man approaches me, says the Gita, precisely in that spirit & in that way I accept and possess him. Ye yathá mám prapadyante táns tathaiva bhajámyaham. The spirit in which the Seer would have us approach the Lord, is an all-embracing universality and the way he chooses for us is to embrace the all-blissful One in the world and in transcendence of the world, as the unity and as the multiplicity, through Vidya & through Avidya, in the Spirit and in the world, by God above Nature and by Nature in God. Ishwara, Brahman, the Life-principle Matariswan, the Bright and Pure Stillness, the supreme & absolute Personality, the triple Purusha, Surya, Sachchidananda, Agni, — successively he presents to us in the course of his thought these names, aspects or images of the Eternal, not that we may accept one and exclude others, but for our soul experience to embrace them all in a multiple & blissful unity. Everywhere he reconciles, everywhere he includes, seeking to understand and not to divide. In this world he gives us the supreme felicity and in that world our joy shall not be other. Why should we refuse to God in ourselves any form of His divine sweetness? There is no dragon watching at the gates of God to deny to us any of the fruits of Paradise; the law of divisibility and opposition ceases when we have shaken from our necks His leaden yoke of Avidya. But in these initial couplets the Seer is insisting especially on a divine life in this world, iha, as the necessary basis of the fulfilment which is held in store for us at the end of the utter & perfect sacrifice. All that we have renounced to Him, action and struggle, thought and knowledge, the rose and the breeze and the moonlight, bird and beast & human being, man and woman and children and land and houses and gold and silver and oxen and raiment, books and poetry and learning and science, mind, body and life are, when renounced, to become the material, instrument and medium of a divine enjoyment, objectively, by all that he keeps for us or gives back to us physically during and after the discipline of renunciation, subjectively, by the whole universe and all that it contains, possessed through a man's senses so far as God in him accepts their action and in a man's soul by sympathy and identity with all beings & with universal Nature. Still, these things will always remain the instrument of enjoyment; the object of the enjoyment, the true object of all bhoga, for the liberated soul, is God, — not Nature, although God in Nature & through Nature. We shall enjoy God in & through His universal manifestation, but always God and never the universe falsely experienced as a thing existent & enjoyable for its own sake, apart from God and different from Him.

The possession of God in the world-transcending height of His being does not exclude possession of God in His world-containing wideness. To the liberated soul there is no high and base, but only one equal divine bliss and perfection.

In the ideal of the Seer we do not cast away life and mind and body into an eternal sleep; removal from universe is not prescribed as a necessary condition before we can take possession of the supreme & ineffable bliss of the Brahman. The Seer asserts on the contrary a liberated bliss in the world and in human life. "He whose Self has become all existences, how shall he be deluded, whence shall he have grief", so rings his cry of triumphant freedom; it does not run "He whose Self is dead to the knowledge of all becomings". The most powerful support and argument of purely ascetic philosophies is the Buddhistic idea, foreign to Vedic Hinduism, that true freedom and true bliss are impossible in the universe and can only become possible if we escape out of it into some world-shunning secrecy of being, whether Nihil or Nirvana. The soul handling objects, it is thought, must be attracted to them; or else the freedom from attraction is so difficult and so rare that it is presumptuous to reckon on it as a practical possibility; in Samadhi the spirit is blissful & free, awaking from Samadhi it is bound to feel or be always susceptible to touches of limitation and of grief; the duality of pain & grief is an irrevocable law of the universe and where there is bliss in the world, there must also be as its companion grief in the world, for unmixed bliss is only possible where mind and its laws are excluded. These are the fundamental ideas of Asceticism and if they were true with this scope and this force, the very foundations of the thought in the Isha Upanishad would be vitiated and annulled; but, although generally held and insisted on by numbers of great saints and lofty thinkers, they are an instance of partial truths, perfectly valid, even perfectly general in their own province, carried in practice beyond their province and so by a false extension becoming, like all exaggerated truths, the foundation of error. They are perfectly true in the field where they apply but they apply only in the limits of mind & so long as the soul is subjected in the world to mind and its processes. But it is not a fact that mind is the supreme principle in the world and its movement & processes the dominant & ineffugable motion and process of the universe. It is only true that mind is the present centre of humanity & to humanity therefore seems, falsely, the supreme principle of the active universe. It is no doubt extremely difficult, without divine aid, for man to escape from mind & living in the world, yet to remain superior to the mental duality of joy & grief, pleasure & pain, which is the

ordinary law of our mundane existence. The difficulty of the
escape is the justification of Sannyasa. But the escape, though
difficult, is not only possible, it is the one real road to our self-
fulfilment as the human type of God-existence upon this earth,
evam twayi nányatheto'sti. It is possible because the supreme
principle and movement of the universe is not mind; the supreme
principle is Sat working out through Chit in Ananda, Infinite
Being working out through Infinite Force in Infinite Beatitude.
The Upanishads demand of us, and not only the Isha but the
Taittiriya & other Upanishads, not to dwell in mind untouched
by its laws, which would be a laborious & improbable achievement, but to raise ourselves beyond mind through Surya or
pure Idea into Ananda and live centred in that principle. From
this superior centre, seated free, imperial, Swarat, Samrat, in
the mountain citadel of our existence, we can, remaining in
the universe, yet govern our use of a subject and no longer
rebellious mind, life & body by the process and laws of our
blissful spirit and our divine Nature. The superior movement
then controls and uses the lower for its own purposes. But since
the principle of the superior movement is unmixed bliss, our
purposes and activities also must be purposes & activities of
unmixed bliss. If we are released only on the levels of mind,
then indeed sleep of Samadhi is our one safe & perfect state, for
coming out of that sure refuge & retreat, we are again naked in
mind and exposed to the efforts of mind to recover its natural
supremacy in its own kingdom. Rising to Ananda, liberated in
Ananda, living in Ananda, there is no such peril. The kingdom
of heaven imposes the will of God on the kingdom of earth,
the parardha takes possession of the aparardha, Sacchidananda
seizes & revels in the ecstasies of a liberated Manas, Prana and
Annam. In opposition, therefore, to the Buddhistic declaration
of the omnipresence of grief & pain outside Nirvana, we have
in the Vedanta the soul's declaration of its ultimate & eternal
independence: —

*To live in the world is not necessarily to live in the duality of
grief and joy. The soul seated in Ananda, even though it lives the
life of the universe, possesses as its dominant principle unmixed*

bliss and can use in this world & this human life mind, life &
body, sarvam idam, as instruments of God-enjoyment without
enduring the dominion of their dualities.

For the rest, these truths are a matter of experience. Those
who have attempted to enjoy the universe before renunciation
and, escaping from that error & delusion, have afterwards enjoyed God in the universe after renunciation, know, know with
a silent & inexpressible rapture, the alteration & seizing revolution, the immense and ineffable change, the seated sublimity and
all-penetrating intensity of that bliss of the Brahman towards
which the Upanishad points our faltering and doubt-besieged
footsteps. Before renunciation we enjoyed Nature ignorantly as
a thing in itself and we worshipped mind and the things of the
mind, followed after body and the things of the body, indulged
in life and the things of the life; after renunciation we enjoy with
knowledge, not the rose, but God in colour and petal and per-
fume, not a poem but God in the beauty of sound and the beauty
of words, not food, but God in taste and in vital satisfaction.
That which before renunciation was pleasure, has become after
renunciation bliss; pleasure which was transient, mutable and
fading, has become bliss lasting and inalienable; pleasure which
was uncertain, because dependent on circumstances & objects,
has become bliss self-existent and secure; pleasure which was
uneven, strained towards preferences, balanced by dislikes, has
become bliss equal and universal; pleasure which was even at its
highest impure and haunted, held with difficulty and insecurely
against a background of loss, deficiency and pain, has become
bliss pure, satisfying and perfect as God Himself. Before renunciation we besought objects to yield us a petty joy we did not
ourselves possess; after renunciation we perceive in the object
& receive from it the immeasurable bliss eternally seated in
ourselves. Before renunciation, we enjoyed with desire, seeking
and effort; after renunciation we enjoy desirelessly, not in the
satisfaction of desire, but in eternal possession, not as *anish*,
struggling to gain possession of what does not belong to us,
but as *ish*, already possessing all that the world contains. Before
renunciation we enjoyed, with egoism, only what the greedy

but easily tired mind and senses could grasp, possessing for ourselves and that too only with our own lame, limited and self-ish enjoyment; after renunciation we enjoy, without ego-sense, all that we outwardly possess, all that others possess and all that none but God possesses, and we enjoy it not only with our own enjoyment but with the individual and collective enjoyment of all our fellow beings animate and inanimate and with the divine enjoyment of God in the universe. Finally, we enjoyed before re-nunciation many separate things all of a limited pleasurableness; after renunciation we enjoy one thing in its multiplicity which is all-blissful everywhere. Such is the enjoyment in the world to which the Seer points us in the word, bhunjíthāh; and we have always in addition, — for that transcendence is the condition of this secure universality, — the bliss of the Lord's pure being in His self-existence beyond and above the motion of the universe.

Chapter III

The Golden Rule of Life —
Desire, Egoism and Possession

Ma gridhah kasyaswid dhanam.

Immediately after this great fundamental reconciliation, the Seer
proceeds to a phrase which under a form of familiar common-
ness conceals an immoderate wealth of spiritual suggestion.
"Lust not after any man's possession." Má gridhah kasyaswid
dhanam.

We seem to have stumbled out of deep and strange waters
into a very familiar shallow. Read superficially and without an
eye to the words that precede or to the whole serried thought of
the Upanishad, this closing cadence of the Seer's opening sloka
would suggest only a commonplace ethical suggestion identical
in form & spirit with the last of the Mosaic commandments, —
just as read superficially and apart from the coherent & inter-
woven thought of the Upanishad tyaktena bhunjíthái need not
go beyond a rule of moral self-discipline in which the aim of the
Epicurean finds itself married to the method of the Stoic. But the
Upanishads are never, like Greek epic & Jewish scripture, simply
ethical in their intention. Their transcendence of the ethical plane
is part of their profounder observation of life & soul-experience.
The Greeks sought always for a rule of moral training & self-
discipline; the Mosaic Law imposed always a rule of outward
conduct; and both aimed at an ethical balance of mind or an ethical balance of action; but the Vedanta rejects all mere balancing
and arrangement. The Vedic thinkers went straight towards
the soul and an inner rebirth. A radical change of outlook on
life was their motive force for the change, if any, of outward
conduct; a complete revolution & renovation of the soul was its
demand on the inner life of man. Troubling themselves little with
the management of conduct & feeling always for the springs
of life & action, they left the care of ethics to other Shastras;
neglecting comparatively the regulation of temperament, they

searched for that within from which temperament proceeds and by which it can be automatically regulated. When once that secret spring is touched, when once the soul is found & the lord of the temple manifests himself, ethics with its outer intellectual & emotional sanctions becomes superfluous; the outward life then flows spontaneously out of the sweetness, power & fullness of a supreme inner change. To the Vedantin the ethical stage is only important as a preliminary clearing in the jungle of desires & passions which prevents us from even attempting seriously to find our way through to the temple of the Lord.

Is there here the indication of such a preliminary ethical self-preparation? No; for it is the constant literary principle of these inspired writings that each phrase in Veda, as in the motion of the universe itself, lives not to itself but goes back to all that has gone before and reaches out to all that is coming; all moreover obey an unexpressed central unity which once grasped, illumines the whole text, but without which these writings break up into a mass of disconnected thoughts. In this Upanishad the one central thought is multiplicity of existence unified and freed from the sense of the dividing ego. The Seer does not allow himself for a moment either to ignore or to deny the multiple existences of the universe, but neither will he for a moment allow us to forget that all these many are really one, all this variety exists in its own unity, Jagat in Ish, the moving Brahman in the stillness, sarvabhutani in Atman, the many Purushas in the One. The present phrase, understood as an ordinary ethical rule, would be a contradiction and not an affirmation of the one ever-present and unifying thought of the Isha Upanishad. It would provide us with a preliminary rule of life founded upon the acceptance & not the denial of the dividing ego-sense. The ethical rule against covetousness is an ordinary human rule and stands on a strong affirmation of the ego-sense & it has no meaning in a gospel of divine life & universal consciousness. The phrase can only stand here, not as an ethical rule, but a rule of the inner life, tending not to the confirmation but to the annulment of the ego.

The Mosaic commandment is consistent in itself & with the spirit of the Decalogue. These Judaic moral Ten Tables start from an uncompromising dualism; their conception of righteousness is the straight road decreed for our walking by a personal Deity as different from His ephemeral creatures as the great eternal ocean from the soon-dried & inconsiderable puddles in a rainswept highway. The particular prohibition of covetousness stands partly on the idea of the morally seemly, the epieikes of the Greeks; much more (and in the Jewish temperament entirely) it rests on the stronger & more mechanical conception of legal justice between man and man, the Greek dikaion. In either case, it proceeds, like all ethics, from an original acceptance of the egoistic outlook on the universe; starting from the symbols I and thou, mine and thine, its aim and business is not to get rid of the ego-sense but to regulate and check those of its fierce and disorderly movements which poison individual peace and disturb social well-being. Even altruistic ethics starts from this fundamental recognition of egoism. Except in the Vedantised teachings of the Buddha, it does not seek to annul, — rather altruism lives & satisfies itself by an inverse satisfaction of the ego. But the whole aim and spirit of the Vedanta is to annul, to kill, to root out the ego-sense. Similarly ordinary ethics seeks to check, scold and limit desire, as an unruly servant, but would shrink from killing it as an enemy. We are, indeed, allowed by some systems to extend and pasture this eternal hunger, others permit us to satisfy it under severe restrictions; but always we must satisfy desire ethically, with justice & decency, with the sense of measure of the Greeks, avoiding the aischron, the adikon, the perversion, or with the religious enthusiasm of the Jews, shunning offence to the Lord of Righteousness. We must indulge it [in] what we possess or can lawfully acquire, our own wives, not the wives of others, our own wealth, not others' gold and silver and horses and cattle. But in Vedanta, it is wholly improbable that we should have any such ethical & social preaching of the epieikes & the dikaion. The principle of the Vedanta is to make no compromise with the inner enemy, but rather merciless war ending in its utter extinction, jahi shatrum durásadam.

In this Upanishad we have just had a tremendous and sweeping exclusion of all desire, an inexorable demand to give up the whole world spiritually to the Lord. It is incredible that immediately, without transition, warning or explanation of his purpose the Seer, this great master of language & its effects, should immediately weaken his thought & hamstring the great impulse he has created by the intrusion of a shallow and minor injunction, that he should say in effect, "Seeing God everywhere, abandon the whole world in Spirit that thou mayst enjoy the whole of divine existence, — but take care not to lust after other people's property." Such an interjection would be either a grotesquely unneeded warning to a soul free from desire and already enjoying the whole world in a free and pure satisfaction, or the suggestion of a preliminary discipline so awkwardly introduced as to break the effect of the great rule towards which it was intended to lead. We could have understood if the Seer had written, reversing the order of the clauses, "Covet not any man's possession, nay, abandon the whole world and all it contains", or even, though this would be contrary to his effective & cumulative style, "Abandon the whole world &, first of all, abandon the desire for other men's possessions." But he could not have written as it must stand now without link or clue; "Abandoning the whole world, enjoy by the whole world; covet not any man's possession." Even if permissible in any other style, such a vicious stumble is impossible to the divine Muse. The moment we read the line in the light of the whole structure & thought of the Upanishad, the difficulty at once vanishes, the real meaning of the clause emerges. Like all the others it is a smooth and clear surface covering many waters. In the careful structure of the Upanishad it starts naturally from the opening Ishá vásyam and its conclusion tyaktena bhunjíthádh and points forward to átmaivábhút sarvabhútáni of the seventh couplet.[4]

Thus understood in its right place as a link between this

---

[4] I have written on this point at a perhaps disproportionate length as an example of the great care necessary in studying the Upanishads. It is not enough to have a correct verbal rendering, everything must be understood in the spirit of the entire unity, not as a separate text apart from its setting. It is only by a strict adherence to this rule that we can really get the secret of the Upanishads.

starting point and the yet deferred conclusion, the thought of the Seer is seen, as he intended it, perfectly simple & straightforward in substance, admirably rich in suggestion. "All forms are various dwelling-places of one self; sorrow proceeds out of desire and egoism contradicting this truth of oneness, ekatwam, from the consequent lust of possession, from the sense that he is he, I am I, his is not mine, the sense that others are kaschid anyah and objects kasyaswid dhanam. This sorrow misbegotten of desire disappears if the mind's outlook on world can be remoulded in a form of the truth of things & not their false appearance, if it can be made to see that these others, anye, are not at all others, but entirely myself in the world-supporting reality, &, here in world, becomings of myself. Atmaivábhút sarvabhútáni. The decisive mental step to the true perception and practical sign of the true realisation is the selfless purity of the once impure & desiring heart when, possessing by abandonment of desire and by realisation of the one Inhabitant in all persons & bodies, — for person is only persona, a mask, a dramatic role of the sole & universal Personality, — it has ceased to hunger & thirst after what others have in their keeping from the false idea that they are different from myself and their possessions are not already my possessions." The difference of ideas between the Jew & the Indian becomes at once palpable. "Lust not after thy neighbour's goods," says the Jewish lawgiver in effect, "for he is he, thou thou, and thou hast no righteous claim to another man's possessions." "Lust not after thy neighbour's possessions," cries the Vedantic Seer, "for he is not thy neighbour other than thou, he is thyself & in him it is thy own self that already possesses. Thou hast no need for this desire & this lust." The object of the injunction is not to accept right ego-sense & discourage greed as wrong ego-sense, but to persuade & lead us to denial of the whole attitude of egoism implied in the lusting after possessions which this particular mind & body do not in the apparent movement of Nature possess, but which are so possessed by us in another mind & body, another habitation of our indwelling Self. In the words of men the letter is nothing. It is the spirit, the supporting stress of thought & the

temperament behind which give to the spoken symbol its import
& its effect.

Let me observe in passing, for the observation is needed
in these days of the siege of our religion and philosophy by
inadequate European conceptions, that we have here the key to
an important difference between Vedantic & Western thought,
which is not to the discredit of our great national Scripture.
We need not be too sensitive to the reproach that the Vedanta
is non-ethical or too eager to vindicate an ethical intention for
its teachings. Non-ethical may be either infra-ethical or supra-
ethical. Let us beware lest in vindicating the claim of Vedanta to
an European eminence & elevation, we bring it down from its
own heaven touching domain upon its Asiatic and Himalayan
mountain tops. Ancient Indian thought and life regularised in
teaching a practical difference which the West admits in practice
and denies in theory; it admitted three distinct standards deter-
minant of conduct, the customary law, ethical rule and spiritual
state; the mass of our pre-classical literature with its greatness of
law & custom, its rich abundance & delicacy of moral aspiration
& perfection & its great spiritual altitude faithfully reflects this
triple recognition. But in the many provinces, the varying levels
of human conduct the Vedanta seeks always the summits; its
consistent search is for spiritual truth and spiritual standards.
Seeking always that which exceeds & includes the lower life, it
exceeded also the limits of ethics, finding Brahman in the all &
not in the part, *anyatra dharmád anyatrádharmát*, otherwhere
than in virtue and otherwhere than in unrighteousness, & it
fixed its eyes only on so much of conduct as helps us to realise
the universality of God, the divine oneness of mankind & the
unity of all existences. Avoiding these modern pitfalls, we find
the full and profound sense of this final phrase disengaging itself
naturally by the light of its surroundings.

In this path the cessation from all lusting after things as the
possessions of others is the sign of the dissolution of ego in the
heart; for it proceeds from the heart's recognition of the truth
that one Lord inhabits all bodies. It shows that the truth is no
longer only an idea in the intellect but is being lived in the whole

being. The possessions of the one and only Self in one body are also his possessions in all other bodies; what the self in Shyâma owns, that the self in Râma possesses.

The exhortation to freedom from the desire of the heart, Ma gridhah, is the answer to all practical difficulties that may arise from the initial teaching of the Seer. Enjoyment by the world precludes physical abandonment of the world; yet physical abandonment is what we usually contemplate when we use the term renunciation; for although we are mental beings, yet ours is a mentality emmeshed in matter and impelled by that physical Maya to give a materialised or sensible value and a material expression to all our mental conceptions. We hardly admit a truth until we see it cloaked in an outward form or in an outward event & action. What then is this new rule of abandonment which impels not to denial and cessation of world-life, but to a free and perfect enjoyment? We have, at once, the answer in this phrase of the Seer, Ma gridhah. Thou shalt not have the greed of desire in thy heart, — that is the practical effect of the call to renunciation. Mental beings, souls throned in mind, it is in mind our centre not in matter which is to us a mere case, circumference and result of mind, that we should seek our secret of bondage and our means of deliverance. All outward material action is in itself Maya, a thing without self-existent reality. Action is effected only as the outflow and physical symbol of mind; it has no inherent moral or spiritual value, but is capable only of bearing such values as are put on it by the manomaya purusha, the spirit centred and veiled in mind. Humanity still imprisoned in its surroundings, servilely reflects in its mind the habitual impact of outward things, the bahya-sparshah, & gives to them a fixed & conventional mental value. The more humanity moves towards freedom & perfection, the more it will live in the mind itself, use outward circumstances of life & matter only as symbols of a free mental existence & fix their values by the mentality they express and not by some conventional standard determined by the action itself in its outward appearances. Therefore tyaga, the inner renunciation, is preferable to sannyasa, the physical renunciation; for the latter takes resignedly account of the present weakness of humanity and its false preoccupation with body and helps indeed that weakness to pass out from itself by the extinction of active existence, freeing us from life, but not freeing life for us; but the inner renunciation leads us through our real nature as mental beings, takes account of our strength and teaches us to insist upon it and realise its perfection in God. Sannyasa is a rapid road of escape for our self-accepted weakness; tyaga is a path of fulfilment, the strait and narrow road, for our slowly-realised divine strength. By this road, supathá, Agni Vaisvanara, God's pure force in man, leads us to our felicity. Nayati ráye asmán.

Bodily action is useful as a pressure on the materialised mind, but the better way is to act from within outwards, not from outwards within. To the man who lives the inner life, mind-state is all-important, bodily action only a variable symbol or a theatrical demonstration. Great spirits have yearned after Sannyasa as a symbol of inner renunciation and freedom; but the truth that has to be symbolised is selflessness in God, not renunciation, which is only a means towards that selflessness.

When desire is driven from the heart, the only necessary renunciation is already accomplished; all other self-mortification is, then, a superfluous austerity which may be severely lofty or even gracious, but can no longer be serviceable for the perfect aim of human existence.

The main intellectual difficulties opposed to the practice of renunciation disappear before this but there is also a more concrete obstacle. We have this high doctrine that the soul in itself is free and God, but bound and divided in world-motion; in the sense of division from God and its fellows it is bound and by its realisation of oneness with God and all beings it recovers its freedom, — ekatwam anupashyatah. But in practice some obscure obstacle interposes itself and baffles of their expected results the intellectual recognition and the emotional surge towards unity. Mankind has constantly been groping for this obscure and elusive knot of our bondage; but though it plucks at this twist and loosens that complexity, it reaches no better result than a temporary easing of the strings of that disastrous net in which the world-Magician has caught our labouring minds. In the midst of our unprofitable labour we hear the inspired voice and receive the illuminating word of the Vedantic Seer, "Má gridhah. Desire founded on egoism is the knot of your bondage; cut through that complexity, undo that twist and you are free." All other loosening of knots is a fumbling search or an incidental labour; desire and egoism slain, every other knot is of itself dissolved and collapses. We have seen that by our very nature as human beings, the knot must be hidden somewhere in our minds, and, particularly, it should be sought in the emotional part of our minds. For where the centre of our active being is, there must be the knot of our bondage, and there also must we seek for the secret of its unloosing. If we had been material beings or centred in matter, the knot would have been in some material habit and the release dependent on a material adjustment; for the individual, perhaps, Hathayoga and the conquest of the body by the physically effective Will would have been the one effective instrument. If we had been vital beings or centred in vitality, the knot would have been some vital obstruction and the release dependent on a vital adjustment; perhaps, then, Pranayama and the conquest by the vitally effective Will of the dualities which affect the nervous life and energy of man would rather have been the true instrument of our freedom. But our centre is mind and especially that part of mind which is sensational in its reaction to outward things & emotional in its valuation of them & in its moral response. We live in that subtle heart in us which taking up into itself the lower bodily and nervous impacts turns them into objects and media of dislike and desire, pleasure and pain and bringing down into itself the higher formations of thought and reason makes them subservient to the same imperative emotional & sensational dualism. We get therefore this law of disciplinary practice: —

Although ego-sense is the cause of the soul's bondage, yet the knot of the bondage in man is in the subtle heart where his active being is centred and it consists in the emotional egoism of desire. To get rid of ego-sense, we must, practically, labour to get rid of desire, for until that liberation is accomplished, the mere intellectual rejection of ego-sense, from which we have to start, cannot be perfectly operative upon the lower mentality and the vital and bodily existence.

Desire, the cause of our pain, has itself its cause or rather its secret essence in the ego-sense transferred from the discriminating mind to the responsive heart. Vedantic psychology sums up the motion of the Jagati in our mentality, — the complex thing we call mind, — in a quadruple knot; — the nodus of sense-forming mind reactive to outward impacts, the nodus of discriminating mind receptive and critical of these reactions, the nodus of responsive & formative heart or temperamental mind setting in motion waves of emotional or temperamental consciousness which first forms the stuff of the others & shapes itself out as their reaction and their criticism, the nodus of ego-sense which centralises & relates to one mental self-idea all these functionings; — buddhi, manas, chitta, ahankara. Formed in the discriminating mind, egoism enslaves its creator & descends to dominate the heart. "I am I" cries the discriminating mind, enslaved by egoism, "he is he; mine is mine & not his; his is his & so long as I cannot have or take, I can never regard it as mine." Thus discriminative ego shuts up man in his one bodily habitation and prevents him from enjoying his proper estate, the rich universe, rájyam samriddham, full of beautiful and noble possessions. Egoistic reason turns man into a sort of monomaniac emperor self-confined & limited who fancies himself a prisoner in his single palace, although, really, & if he chose, the wide earth is freely his and all that it contains. The heart accepts from the discriminating mind this false limitation & delusion, undergoes sense of want, sense of confinement, sense of difference & is tortured by their evil emotional results. While desire is our counsellor, pain and suffering must always be our heritage.

We must always remember that if ego were the truth of our being, limitation would not be painful, grief would not be the reaction of our activity. The heart, incapable of excessive yearnings, would rest in its proper circle. But we are capable of excessive yearnings because we ourselves exceed our bodies & circumstances. We are driven by an infinite stress towards increase, because we are ourselves elastic and really infinite. There is always something within us which is dissatisfied with the Is & gropes for the May be, something which is soon tired of present accomplishment & possession & reaches out for something larger, better or at the lowest new. It is the universe, it is infinity that the hidden Angel within us seeks. The Self within us knows its own infinity & sees itself as the lord of its [creation] [.................................] the heart, more passive & therefore more responsive, receives dimly & without understanding — for it is not its function to understand, but to feel — the silent message. Hence it has this striving, this dissatisfaction, this torture of pain, unease & grief. God puts the heart upon the rack of desire so that it may not be satisfied with smallness. He forces it to aspire towards the greatness & infinity of the Spirit, the mahat, brihat, bhúmá. "Nalpena sukham asti, bhumna sukham asti," cries the Upanishad. There is no abiding happiness in the small; happiness comes by the vast & free.

From the strife of this secret truth & this open falsehood desire in the heart contracts its disquieting double nature of wants terribly unlimited & capacities for enjoyment & satisfaction terribly limited & soon exhausted. The Nature-force available to the individual through his ego-centre is normally confined to the small amount of energy necessary for the maintenance of body, life & mind in their habitual & indispensable activities; there is no real provision in this limited nature for the greater things to which man in his expansion aspires. That he must seek from the infinite; that he must acquire from God or the gods, by effort, by sacrifice. The sound, sane, normal, animal man hardly aspires, perhaps would not aspire at all, but for the stress of hunger, the irritation of other men pressing upon his little share of the world & above all the stimulus of that class of beings just above him whom God has partially or entirely awakened to the beyond. But when we strain beyond the normal circle of our energies, — unless we have sought refuge in God first, — then, after the first fervent joy of struggle and partial success, our instruments begin to fail us, the pleasure we are seeking loses itself or turns into pain, pain of effort, pain of longing, pain of

disappointment, pain of incapacity. We advance by suffering, &
water the tree of our growth with our blood & tears.

All this pain would be unnecessary, the journey as well as the
goal would be Ananda, not suffering but delight, if the ego-sense
had not taken possession of our heart & reason. We seek our
infinity not only through the finite, but by insisting on the conditions of the finite & exaggerating them. Physical, vital & mental
man, acting & striving under these conditions, must always be
limited in his realisation and in his best satisfactions never entirely or permanently satisfied. He reaches towards physical,
vital and emotional satisfactions which, in the quantity, range
or intensity he covets, are & must be forbidden or opposed by
his habitual capacities, by his imprisoning & determining environment and by his constant clash with the equally outreaching
egoistic desires of other men. He escapes perhaps into mind
and seeks an unlimited satisfaction in the enjoyments belonging
to that more elastic principle, in art, science or literature; but
there too, though freer & better satisfied, he is both fettered
by his nerves and body and hedged in by the limitations of the
mind itself. The mind in sensational & vital man, incapable of
an universal catholicity of possession and enjoyment, measures,
divides, erects standards & hedges, rooted customary habits of
capacity, fixed associations of enjoyment and fixed associations
of failure in enjoyment, till we have built up a whole system of
conventional values of pleasant and unpleasant, good and bad,
beautiful and ugly, attractive and repellent, and in this mighty
forest of conventions, this jungle of dualities move & live; as
the forest is unseen for its trees so the fictions of mind, — mind,
the purblind stumbler among details, — obscure from us the
truth and real bliss of existence. The mentalised body, too, has
its own habitual standards of contacts which it can bear and
contacts which it cannot or does not wish to bear; therefore we
are divided between bodily pleasure and pain and those neutral
sensations which conform decidedly to neither of these values.
The mentalised nervous energy has, no less, its standards of
contacts which it can assimilate and contacts which it wishes to
reject, and we have, therefore, to reckon among the links of our

life-chain vital enjoyments & vital sufferings, these also divided by their neutral borders. Even when busy with its own proper experiences, the mind has its standard of contacts with which it can harmonise itself and contacts with which it is at discord or else remains unattracted, — grief, joy and indifference are the resultant emotional responses. Based upon these standards each individual or species has built up its own system of habitual wants & cravings and its own arrangement of accumulated conventions. So has grown the huge tree of desire and its associations, sanskaras as they are termed in our philosophies, which has grown out of the seed of ego-sense in the heart and conceals that seed in every part of its flowerings and branchings. Nor is the uprooting of that upas tree a facile undertaking. For desire does not perish easily by enjoyment; it seeks always to renew enjoyment or go beyond; hardly it perishes by surfeit, for it revives or it seeks other objects; nor is it, either, readily slain by coercion, for it sulks concealed in some invisible den awaiting for a treacherous or violent re-emergence and revenge. To finish with desire altogether by attacking & destroying its seed of ego-sense in the heart, is our only escape from present pain and our only safety from renewed suffering.

Man desires because he is infinite Self seated in the ego-ridden heart. The self is one in being and its nature is bliss; therefore the heart confined by ego seeks to reach out to the unity & to realise the bliss but it seeks, mistakenly, through physical and emotional enjoyment in the jagat. Man desires illimitably because he is universal and illimitable; he cannot satisfy his desires illimitably because egoistic self-division persuades him to limit himself to his individual mind, life and body. Man desires with pain & weeping because by creating habitual wants, conventional dualistic standards of delight and false values of grief and joy, pleasure and pain he has bound himself not to recognise infinite Ananda in the world, not to perceive that to the secret self, because it is unegoistic, all things are delight, even those touches which to the mind and body present themselves falsely & unnecessarily as grief and pain. While he persists in these conditions, desire, failure, discontent & pain must be always his portion. He must recognise the Truth, for the Truth only can set him free.

Throughout the human ages we seek an escape or a remedy, but all our solutions fail because either they seek escape from the results of ego by affirming the ego or else deny or unduly limit God's purpose in the ego. "Accept your limitations, work and enjoy as perfectly as you may within boundaries," is the creed of a practical Paganism. For a century or two it may serve man's need indifferently, but he is infinite and universal and after a time Nature in him heaves restlessly and strains out towards its element. She accepted the Greek ideal for a century, then rose up and broke it to pieces. "Recognise that you are yourself, others not yourself, and make a rule of life out of the moral consequences of that distinction; desire only that to which you have a right," — this is the solution of ordinary ethics. But still man remains universal; if egoistic vice is the poison of his life, egoistic virtue is not its fulfilment; he breaks back towards sin and unregulated desire or forwards towards something beyond vice and virtue. "Desire what you please, enjoy what you can, but without violating my laws and conventions," is the dyke raised by society; but man is a universal as well as a social unit and the societies he creates are a Procrustean bed which he moulds and remoulds without ever finding his measure. He supports himself on social conventions, laws & equities, but cannot limit himself by his supports. "Desire is sinful; observe duty and the Shastra, discourage & punish enjoyment," is the Puritan's law of self-repression; but duty is only one instinct of our nature and duty satisfied cannot eradicate the need of bliss. Asceticism digs deeper into the truth of things, "Compromise will not do" it cries; "flee utterly from the objects of desire, escape from the field of ego, shun the world." It is an escape, not a solution; God in man may admit escape for the few, but He denies it to the many, for He will not allow His purpose in life and world to be frustrated. Religion digs still deeper: "Replace many desires by one, drive out the desires of this miserable earth by the desire of God and of a future world not besieged by these unsatisfied yearnings." But to postpone the problem to another life is not to solve it; and to desire God apart from life and not in life is to divide the unity of His being. He will indulge a few in that evasion, but not the mass of mankind; therefore the many have to return with hearts still hungry from the doors of the temple; therefore the successive moulds of religion fail, lose their virtue and are cast away and broken. For Truth is imperative and demands inexorably its satisfaction. And the truth is always this that man is universal being seeking an universal bliss and self-realisation and cannot repose permanently on the wayside, in hedged gardens, or in any imperfect prison whatsoever or bounded resting place.

Universal Ananda & possession is our secret nature, to move towards it till it is reached, God's inexorable impulse in His creation. All solutions that deny or conflict with our nature, can only be palliatives, evasions or individual remedies.

It remains, therefore, to accept the two factors of the problem in their entirety and work out a solution on the basis of a reconciliation. This is the aim of the Seer. By the enjoyment of the whole of universal being in God, the legitimacy of the secret demand in us is recognised, by the renunciation of the attempt to enjoy through egoistic desire and in physical possession, the stumbling-block in the way of fulfilment is distinguished and removed. Mind and heart desire the universe; Self alone can possess it and already possesses it. Therefore the whole secret is to shift our centre from mind and heart to the all-blissful Self, from Jagat to Ish, from our temporary place in Nature besieged by the movement, to our eternal seat in the Godhead possessing, overtopping and controlling the movement. We can take the universe and all it contains into our self and possess it, — nay, we need not take, for it is already there; we have only to reveal it to ourselves; but we cannot take it into our hands or permanently keep any slightest part of it in our personal possession. It is too vast for our grasp and too slippery. We can possess the joy of the whole world physically, mentally & emotionally only by possessing it in the Spirit and through the Spirit; the desire to possess its form instead of its joy, or to claim it for the heart, mind & body in us and not for God in heart, mind and body, indriyartham and not atmartham, is the capital error of our egoism. The remedy therefore is to get rid of this desire of false possession and ascend into the truth of real possession. Were we to put this in modern language we should say: Man is evolutionary, not evolved; his present state of mentality in heart guided by reason is a transition, not his final nature; in mentality he is tied to desire, in body to limitation and in both to suffering, but when he evolves from the mental into the spiritual being, he will be free from grief because, living in infinite Spirit, he will have done with desire and limitation. In the true Vedantic view of things we must express it otherwise.

Man is Anandamaya Purusha not yet or always manifested, but in course of manifestation. At present he is manomaya, tied to mind and living by desire; he is besieged therefore by pain and limitation, from which, so long as he remains on the mental level, he can only escape entirely by Sannyasa. But if he has the will, he can even in this life and body manifest his true anandamaya self and become in Nature all-possessing & in life all-blissful.

Since then desire is the knot of our bondage and the seat of our sorrow, the seat must be abolished, the knot cut through or loosened. Chidyate hridaya-granthih, says the Upanishad, speaking of the state of liberation, "the knot of the heart is cut asunder." For the heartstrings are the cords that bind us through emotions of love and hate, attraction and repulsion, to the desire-created falsehoods of the world and hold back the soul from rising to its throne in the Vastness, the natural Righteousness of things, the Love, the Bliss. Desire binds to sorrow because it is the sentinel of egoism, the badge of the soul's subjection to its self-created environment and the veil of our absorption in the limited and fleeting. Egoism is the cause of sorrow, but desire is its seat. "I am I, thou art thou, mine is mine, thine is thine"; this false conception of things is the seed of all evil; but its hold would be transitory, if there were not this compelling emotion of desire which adds, "Thou art not I, therefore thee I must control or possess; mine is mine, therefore mine I must cling to and keep; thine is not mine, therefore thine too I must acquire or seize." If this reaching out to our not-selves is inevitable because our nature is a seeming particularity reaching out to its own real universality, if desire is the sign of the soul emerging out of matter and articulating, with whatever falsehood and stammering, its secret sense that it is the Lord of the universe, yet must it deny & transform itself, if it is to effect its grandiose object. The mighty Asura, Hiranyakashipu or Ravana, Attila, Alexander, Napoleon or Jenghiz, reaching out to possess the whole world physically as the not-self, is the Godhead in man aiming at self-realisation, but a godhead blind and misdirected. The Seer seeks instead to possess in the Spirit and through the Spirit; afterwards what shall be physically possessed or not possessed, is the Lord's business. The first step therefore must always be to get rid definitely of this craving for objects as the not-self in the possession of not-selves. Má gridhah kasyaswid dhanam.

Egoism, seated in the sense of personal difference, is the first element of the heart's error that has to be eliminated. Kasyaswid in the Seer's phrase is absolute and all-embracing like yat kincha and tena; there can be no limitation, no casuistry, no question of legal right or social justice, no opposition of legitimate claims and illegitimate covetings. Nor does dhanam in the Vedic sense include only physical objects, but all possessions, courage, joy, health, fame, position, capacity, genius as well as land, gold, cattle and houses. If we wish to understand the spirit of the rule, we may recall the example of the great Sannyasin who ran after the frightened thief with the vessels dropped in his flight, crying, "Lord, pardon me & take them; I knew not Thou hadst need of them." It is not, indeed, the form of this action that has to be observed and imitated, — the form is a mere symbol, — but the spirit it symbolises; for it breathes of the sense that there is one Lord only in all these habitations and nothing belongs to this body or to that mind or to the mental ego in which their motions are summed and coordinated; but all only to the Lord, one in all bodies. Ishá vásyam idam sarvam. It is immaterial whether a particular object belongs physically to myself or another, is kept with me or stolen from me, surrendered by me or recovered by me; that shall be according to the Lord's play and pleasure. Whether He plays in me outwardly the part of a beggar or the part of a king, of the philanthropist or the conqueror, is not the essential; the essential is that I should know Him in myself and others and live seated in His being and not in my mental ego. Then instead of coveting, enjoying with egoism & sorrowing over loss and disappointment, I shall desire nothing and possess everything in myself, in God and in others, freely, perfectly and universally.

Subjection, seated in the sense of non-possession, is the second element that has to be eliminated. The Lord, the Ish, does not desire, He possesses; desiring objects, we are anish, not lord, pursued by the false dream of non-possession; we see things withheld, things to be acquired, anaváptam aváptavyam. Regarding the object as not-myself, we struggle to possess it, against men, against circumstances, against forces of Nature in the midst of which our body is a straw in a whirlwind, our life an insect fluttering candlewards, our mind a bubble in an eddy. All the while, we are in our souls the Lord and possess everything; all this is our estate. Therefore we have to correct our false idea of not having and, shifting our centre from the anish to the Ish, replace temporary acquisition by eternal possession. Má gridhah dhanam. Liberated in Ananda, I cannot fail to possess all things in myself inalienably and eternally, without being bound to possession or loss as are those who seek & acquire only with personal possession & through the physical body.

The concentration of our vision on the form of things & in the outward motion of desire is the third element of error that has to be eliminated. We desire and suffer because we mistake form and name for essential existence; we fix on the perishable parts of things, a rose, a piece of gold, an acre of land, a horse, a picture, fame, lordship, reputation. All this is jagatyám jagat, myself an object in Nature reaching out to objects in Nature. But the principle of form and name in Nature is motion, separation, flux; therefore my desire & enjoyment in Nature must necessarily be limited, mutable & transient. It is only by shifting the motion of desire to whatever is eternal in the form and name that I can escape from this limitation and this mutability. But the eternal in the form & name of all objects is the eternal in myself

& need not be desired outside myself, or in each thing separately, since it has only to be found in myself to be possessed in all beings & objects. Once more, the universal spiritual possession proves to be all and to include or render immaterial the particular physical possession. Má gridhah kasyaswid dhanam. The treasure you have to seek is in yourself; its possession includes all other possessions. Not only the kingdom of heaven, but all the riches of the earth are within you.

At the same time we must not from this great & vital truth stride forward by a false rigidity of logic into the error of asceticism. Because universal spiritual possession renders immaterial and dispensable the material possession, we must not presume that material possession is worthless & evil. On the contrary by rendering it dispensable and immaterial, it renders it also good and worth having. For so long as the material possession is to our desires & knowledge indispensable for enjoyment, it becomes a bondage & renders life to us a curse & action in the world an evil; but once spiritual possession becomes the root of the matter to us, we become free in the material enjoyment of the object. It no longer binds us, since we no longer either strain after it or suffer by its absence or loss. By that abandoned we enjoy. Even our pursuit of objects becomes a play, the racing or wrestling of boys in a meadow in which there is no evil thought, no harm intended, no possibility of sorrow experienced. Material possession & enjoyment also is intended by God in the human being; for material enjoyment & possession He created this world and made matter its formal basis; but eventually He intends the enjoyment of the object as a symbol of the spirit in the spirit, freely. God in us is the poet, is the musician who throws out some few forms of the infinite world within him into symbols of word or sound, so that the material enjoyment of the sound ceases to be material & becomes a form of spiritual enjoyment and an extension of spirit into matter. I am free at any moment to begin it, at any moment to suspend it; & even when I throw away the temporary outward form of the enjoyment, I keep always the inward eternal form of it in my spirit. So a man who has once seen the Matterhorn rising into the Swiss heavens, keeps always that for which he was sent by the spirit within him to the toils & perils of Alpine climbing; he keeps in his soul the image of the white and naked peak, hard, firm and detached, a supreme image of matter which seeks to persist by solidity, yet is transient in the end like the rose and the insect, which rises towards but never attains that vaulted azure form above of the unsubstantial, unseen but eternal ether in which & by which it lives. He has done that for which the world of form was created. He has seen & enjoyed God in the symbol of the material object. He has embraced & possessed in his soul through the material organ one becoming of the only & eternal Being.

Chapter IV

The next stride of the Upanishad brings us to one of the greatest and most resounding controversies in Indian metaphysics, the quarrel between pragmatism & quietism, action and inaction, as the goal of man's existence or the condition of his highest self. Here, as always, the Seer solves the problem by a reconciliation of the two opposites. The substance of his teaching may be summed up in three mutually complementary & indispensable formulae, the one fulfilling utterly the pragmatic instinct in man, the other fulfilling utterly his quietistic instinct, & the third reconciling these ancient enemies.

In enjoyment continuance of action, in renunciation continuation of action; for continuance of action is the continuance of God's will in the universe.

The secret Spirit in man is always infinitely calm and free from the touches of its action; the sphere of disturbance is always on the surface only of the ocean of being in the waking consciousness. We should attain in waking mind, too, to that stillness; for without it there can be no freedom in our outward living. We should be perfectly & consciously still in the soul even though a whirlwind of action outwardly.

Since we are in the spirit inalienably free & untouched by action, but in the mind seemingly bound and subject to its stains, our true and only way is not to renounce action but to vindicate that secret spiritual freedom hidden within us as a possession for our outward and active mental consciousness. So shall a man be free, calm & joyous and yet through action accomplish God's purpose in him in the motional universe.

The strife between quietism and pragmatism in philosophy and religion is the intellectual symbol of an unaccomplished harmony in man. The universe and all things in it are the manifest Brahman and in the manifest Brahman there are always two eternal aspects, the aspect of incessant and all-pervading action and energy and the aspect of sempiternal and inalienable stillness and peace. The world of matter in which the mental being called man finds himself dwelling is a sensible manifestation of the principle of energy supported by the secret and non-manifest presence of the principle of rest and stability. This world is a manifestation of Force which is never at rest and even the apparent stabilities of Nature prove when analysed to be whorls of motion. All here is jagatyám jagat, motion in her that moves. Yet invisibly filling all her motion, supporting her activities and inspiring them, imposing an essential stability on the apparent flux and reflux of her infinite movement we perceive, not discoverable by the analysing reason, but real enough to the synthetic vision and the perceiving mind, the Sthanu, the eternal, imminuable immutable on which & from which all this motion works and in which all its actions result. Because this Eternal & Immutable is there, the parts & constituents of Nature vary, but its sum is unalterable; its appearances are a whirl of mutable forms, its essence is stable and immutable. Nature herself, manifest to the senses & the material reason only as motion and knowable only in the terms of motion, is equally manifest to the poised & considering soul, dhíra, samáhita, as an infinite power of peace & stillness. On a basis of eternal stability the world exists, to the expression of the stable Eternal it feels itself to be proceeding. Imperfection is its apparent starting point & medium, and the essential term of imperfection is mobility; perfection is its aspiration & goal and the essential term of perfection is acquired status. Through imperfection therefore Nature moves, in perfection it rests. But the perfections which are attainable in the movements of Nature are only perfections of the part and therefore their stability is temporary, illusory and precedent to a fresh motion. Only in an infinite perfection can there be an eternal stability. This perfection is a concealed completeness in us which we have to manifest; we are already an infinite perfection in our being, we have to manifest that hidden thing in our becoming. It is towards this infinite perfection that all things in Nature are, consciously or unconsciously, by her inborn tendency and movement irresistibly impelled. The whole problem of existence therefore resolves itself into some harmony or at least some settlement between these two terms. Whatever ignores either term, be it victorious Science or be it supreme Buddhistic Nihilism, has not understood the terms of the problem and cannot find its solution.

Man dwelling in Nature is compelled towards action and demands rest, lives in imperfection and progresses towards his ungrasped perfection; for action & motion are convertible terms. Action is the motion of man, motion is the action of Nature. All mobility, all change, all play of cause & effect, whether in the mind or the body, whether in animate or inanimate Nature, is therefore karma, action or work, — work is the essential characteristic of Jagati, universal Nature, infinite Force in its universal play. But where then in Nature shall man find rest? Lassitude is not the rest he seeks, sleep is not the rest he seeks; all lassitude, all inertia is still movement but movement of disintegration; sleep is a mass of dreams, sometimes half lit by fugitive and incoherent perceptions, sometimes shut up in a dark shell of bodily unconsciousness. Neither in his bodily nor in his subjective being is a man ever at rest while he lives in this body; what he calls rest is only a change of occupation or a shifting of the action from the waking to the subliminal sleep-consciousness which is always at work behind the waking self. Neither is death the rest he seeks; for death, like sleep, is only a shifting of the habitation, a transference of activity to another field. It is no more rest than the passing of a labourer reaping in a field of corn to work in a field of barley. His temporary & partial realisations of that he seeks are also not man's rest, for from these halting places he moves forwards towards a new activity and a continued journey. Like everything else in Nature man's motion, known to him or unknown, moves towards rest in a perfection which shall be eternal and really stable, not partial and apparently stable. To seek this higher perfection he is eternally moved and if he ever tries at all to rest in the material and temporary, he is soon driven forward again by the inexorable law of his nature to the old imperative endeavour. The frequent attempt of man to escape from his own soul by plunging his head into the running waters of Matter, is one of the recurrent jests, one of the constantly laughable mysteries of the universe. He cannot keep his head down in that alien medium; after some moments he must come up gasping for the necessary breath of his natural existence.

Since we cannot find a real & ultimate peace in material world, that great flux & whirl of movement, we are driven to look within for a principle of eternal stability. To look within is to look behind the veil of our material life. The very movement supposes that material existence is not everything, that our waking consciousness is not the whole field of our consciousness, but only one outward movement of our being & there is something more in us that is curtained and can be unveiled. This attempt necessitates in practice our acceptance of all subjective experiences as realities, not hallucinations, — as much realities as our experience, which is after all itself subjective, of life & death, of hunger & thirst, of wind & sun & rain. All experience, called by us subjective or called by us objective, corresponds in this view to some reality whether of this world or of another or of something beyond world, to some fact which it represents or misrepresents, and the truth of which has, in either case, to be discovered. Now in this inward looking, as we proceed from experience to yet deeper experience, we do come across a principle of eternal stability, a principle of eternal peace within ourselves which we perceive also to be omnipresent and pervasive of all time & space & to exceed & go beyond all time & all space, a principle we can not only perceive, feel & possess but in which we can live. Hallucination or no hallucination, this is a thing which can be seen, can be grasped, can be sensed by the mind, can be entered into, can be lived. Fact of material existence or no, it is an indubitable fact of spiritual experience and seems for a time to be the only wholly blissful fact, the one thing of which we can say Anandam Brahma, Delight is the eternal Reality, Bliss is Brahman. It is as described in the Upanishad, shukram akáyam avranam asnáviram shuddham apápaviddham, luminous, bodiless, invulnerable, without sinews of force & action, pure, unpenetrated by evil, — whether evil of sin or evil of suffering. The soul in this state has for the world, at first & inalienably, either a peaceful or a joyous indifference, — not a repugnance, but an equal-souled acceptance or an equal-souled rejection of all things in the world which it regards not as binding fact but as vision of form and name in itself. What has happened when the soul enters into this stable peace & quiet bliss? It has risen out of action into that principle of Brahman manifest in us which is essentially the principle of transcendent self-stability, Sthanu, anejad, fixed and unmoving, in which & by which this world of apparent motion exists. Passing into that inexpressible peace & stillness, we are liberated from the world; we have entered out of the whirling universe of Nature into Brahman's eternal calm.

The whole of our later Hindu philosophy is full of this mighty realisation of the still, self-luminous & inactive Brahman. In those preBuddhistic ascetics, naked of the world and utterly calm, whom the unresting Macedonian found in the Asiatic ultima Thule of his insatiable march, in the all-conquering soul of Buddha, in the victorious intellect of Shankara, in the aspiration and self-fulfilment of a million saints and hermits before and afterwards our race has aspired with an ultimate and limitless sacrifice, with a sovran self-giving, to the boundless Master of peace. Even the latest of the mighty Ones, the great Vivekananda, who was in outward seeming a storm of speech and thought & force and action, was yet reaching always to the rare, remote & icy-pure linga of Amarnath, the still & silent Mahadeva, as his inmost self & goal; in him too the millennial endeavour, the irresistible yearning endured. But is then this sacrifice really the ultimate sacrifice, this yearning the supreme human tendency, this goal the final & unsurpassable resting-place? If so, the gospel of the Isha Upanishad is either a vain message or a halting place for inferior souls. But the Seer will not have it so. Thou shalt act, he says; for thus has God made thee & not otherwise; other is the fruit of Vidya alone & not the supreme gain, the param sreyah. Nor is he in this insistence departing from the highest teaching of Vedanta. For this sacrifice is not really the ultimate sacrifice; the ultimate sacrifice is the renunciation even of mumukshutva, the giving up to God even of the desire for stillness & peace and of the attachment to inaction and the acceptance in its place, no longer with desire, attachment and passion, but with a free soul, of the Lila as well as the Silence, the great eternal play of the Ishwara no less than his vast eternal peace, the complex and progressively self-fulfilling movement of the Jagati no less than the single & ever-fulfilled immutability of the Ish, the joy of the ejad as well as the calm of the anejad Brahman. That, say the sages, is the final perception of the Vedantin and the supreme consummation of his knowledge when he discovers that there is none bound, none freed, none desiring freedom, but only Brahman variously manifesting, only God in the infinite rest & play of His own Being & becomings, — God & Brahman whom none can bind & who, therefore, even when figured to Himself as man in this apparent cage of a mind and body is still in Himself free — infinitely and for ever. The yearning towards stillness and peace is not then man's supreme tendency; not peace is his goal but divine Ananda of which peace is only the flooring and the threshold. If our ordinary world-existence is that of the Kshara Brahman, which seems to move & change, to be born & grow and perish, & our ordinary soul-state that of the Kshara Purusha who seems to lose himself in the world and to move and change with it, to be born and grow and pass with the mind and body, if the higher existence beyond the mutability of the world is that of the Akshara Brahman, calm, still, unmoving, indifferent, at peace and the soul-state through which we move subjectively to freedom is that of the Akshara Purusha who sits above all this flux & reflux of world-energy at its work, careless of it & untouched by it, udásínavad ásínah, yet is not that the last goal nor the unsurpassable resting-place. Beyond & containing the Kshara and the Akshara Brahman we perceive the supreme existence of the Param Brahma which, transcendent, realises in Itself the harmony of [the] stillness & the movement; beyond and containing the Kshara & the Akshara Purusha we arrive at & inhabit the supreme soul-state of the Purushottama, the Para Purusha, Ishwara & Bhagavan, who, transcendent, is the possessor, user and sovran reality of the movement and the eternal self of the stillness. In Him we find our rest and in Him simultaneously we find our active self-fulfilment; for He alone is our complete and utter being. Buddha and Shankara and our immense ascetic impulse of three thousand years are not the last word of our race nor of humanity; they are the expression of a salutary and violent necessity seizing on man & driving him to abandon utterly the world in its false appearances, by renunciation of all that here we perceive only as motion of Nature, sarvam idam yat kincha jagatyám jagat, they are a divine inspiration and a compelling impulse which will have us by any means and at any cost open our eyes to the truth that not in besotted attachment to the name and form of things, not in the blind, unillumined or falsely-illumined movements of the Jagati, not in that ignorant state of the soul in which it seems to the mind to be anish & not Ish and acts as anish, not Ish, subject and not Lord of the Jagati, is the ultimate fulfilment God intends for us, but there is a stillness beyond the movement which we have to reach, a self-luminousness of the soul in its true peace, freedom & wideness to which we have to aspire. Anyad áhur Avidyayá. But when we have obeyed the impulse, it should, normally, lead us beyond itself; for when we have conquered & transcended the movement, we have yet to surpass and transcend the stillness. Beyond the Kshara & Akshara we rise into the comprehensive infinity of the uttama; lifted above Buddha & Shankara stand Janaka & Krishna, the supreme Yogin & the entire Avatar; they in full action are in entire possession of peace and, conquerors of desire & ego or eternally superior to them, keep their hold on the real and divine bliss of God's triple self-manifestation; they know and exercise the simultaneous & harmonious enjoyment of His transcendent being, His universal Self and His individual play of becoming.

This then is the fundamental position assumed by the Seer, not denying the realisations of the quietistic sages but exceeding the goal of quietism, not preaching attachment to the world, but fulfilling desirelessly & happily, as eternal inhabitant & possessor, God in the world, it asks us to live in God's peace while embracing God's action. Kurvanneveha karmáni; thou shalt verily do actions in the world and not abstain from them; thou shalt not renounce thy human activity among these many kinds of races of thy fellow beings, for God's will in thee is towards action, kurvanneva, not inaction. Evam twayi nányathásti. Therefore, jijívishet shatam samáh, doing all human actions one should

accept the full term of human life, not seek to flee untimely
from the sambhuti, the birth & becoming in this world or in the
human body, not, like the Nihilist, mistake freedom for a silent
nothingness, not blindly & impatiently cut short by physical
or spiritual means one's full term of life or full measure of
human activity. For those who do these things are, inasmuch
as they maim the fullness of God's intended self-fulfilment in
man, átmahano janáh, self-slaying births, — not less, but in a
way even more so, bhúya iva, than the more numerous herd
of beings who by an ignorant attachment to bodily life and
outward objects maim that self-fulfilment on its other necessary
side. To renounce the condition of self-fulfilment is no less a
blind darkness, andham tamas, than to be bewildered by the
condition and by attaching oneself to the path, sacrifice the
goal. All exclusive knowledge is a form & manner of ignorance;
all narrow seeking is a mutilation of our secret and ultimate
vastness and infinity.

The emphasis with which the Seer enounces the necessity of
life and action, kurvanneva, nányatheto'sti, is demanded from
him by the truth of things as a necessary counterpoise to the emphasis with which he has declared the necessity of renunciation
and the abandonment of desire in the immediately precedent
phrases. For the first natural result of renunciation and the
abandonment of desire is a tendency to pure peace and stillness,
a disinclination to action as the source of all grief & disturbance
and an attachment to inaction as the condition of peace, the
sango akarmani of the Gita. Desire, in the ordinary machinery
of our nature, is the motive-spring to action; by the touch on
this spring the whole machine is set and kept working. Nor does
God slacken or destroy that human spring till the machine has
written out for Him in dual letters of pleasure & pain, joy &
grief, sin & virtue, success and failure, upward evolution and
backward sliding, the harmony of His inferior rhythms and His
lila as the Ego in the kingdoms of Ignorance. But if the spring
is destroyed or if the divine finger no longer falls upon it, then
the machine no longer works. Egoistic action, the only activity
to which mortal mind is habituated or which it understands, is

impossible without desire or at least without its essential feature, liking and disliking, emotional, sensational and intellectual preference and rejection. Hence, the first result of unsparing inner renunciation, is not only peace & calm, but inaction. If, departing from that calm of inaction, we seek again to act, the force of habit in past Nature associates with that rhythm of action its old triple gamut, ego, desire and suffering. It is the old keys that again are struck, the old painful music that again quivers through our being. This force of habit in past Nature mistaken for ineluctable law of eternal Nature, this obstinately persistent experience mistaken for ultimate and imperative experience is the root and basis of the quietistic gospel which declares action incompatible with peace & joy in Brahman, the false music of an original Illusion, the morbid throb of a great cosmic disease or, in its law, the ordering link of an incoherent series of sensations and to an unreal soul in its whirl of births a rigorous double chain. It is these phantasms that the Seer of the Isha Upanishad has to conjure, — phantasms of an overhasty metaphysical generalisation, imperfect conclusions of the soul escaping from its fever & mistaking the inactive repose of convalescence for its ultimate state of health. Not inaction & inert repose, but a healthful activity is our final state & release. We escape from this fever and struggle in which we live not by the drastic remedy of extinction but by emergence into right form of action and our true life in God. The Seer justifies God in the world to man by declaring His whole purpose in it, His complete action behind & beyond material appearances and our true infinite & cosmic being. The whole error arises from mistaking the root of our suffering and bondage; the doctors of metaphysics have deluded themselves and us with a false diagnosis. This error the Seer sets right in one of [his] brief, mighty and ample phrases, Na karma lipyate nare, Action cleaveth not to a man.

Action is not the cause of our bondage; attachment is the cause of our bondage. Inaction binds as much as action, if it is stained with attachment; action binds no more than inaction, if we are free from attachment to our works.

The constant association of ego & desire with action is due

*to the relapse of the mind back into its egoistic workings, sahan-
kara, sakama. It is this twin relapse which the seeker after perfection has entirely to overcome. We have not either to descend
back from non-ego into ego or to take refuge in world-oblivion,
but to ascend into God's infinity whose action is eternally unegoistic, cosmic & purely self-fulfilling, nirahankara and nishkama.
There we shall find & repeat in our own lives at once the utter
reality of His self-collected calm and the perfection of His divine
force at work, shama & tapas united in an action which is the
fulfilment of a mighty Silence expressing itself in waves of power
& bliss. That harmony & oneness of divine calm & divine work
is man's ultimate experience & the true nature of God active in
the world.*

This high teaching of the Seer, *na karma lipyate nare,* seems
to contradict violently the great current doctrine of the bondage
of Karma which Buddha found as an important but subordinate
tenet of our early Vedantic philosophy and brought forward
from the second to the first plane of our current metaphysical
ideas, impressing it in the process so forcibly on the general
Indian mind that it has left a dominant and indelible mark on all
our subsequent thinking. In order, therefore, to recover the early
thought of Vedanta, it is necessary to understand precisely the
intellectual basis of the great Buddhistic doctrine and the point
at which it separated from the lesser idea of Karma we find indicated in the Brahmanas and Upanishads. In the world as we see
it, there are two fundamental aspects or faces in which existence
presents itself to our ultimate mental perceptions, first, self-
conscious, self-governing existence, secondly, mechanical Force.
According to our view of the mutual relation of these two grand
entities will be the nature of our philosophy and our outlook
on life. If we hold the self-conscious, self-governing existence to
be subordinate to mechanical Force, contained in it and one of
its appearances and results, then we are naturally & inevitably
driven towards the conception of a tyrannous self-existent Necessity as the true nature & governing force of existence; the
self-conscious, self-governing entity dwindles into a side play
of that Necessity, governed by it & not really self-governing;

conscious only of its movement by that movement itself and not inherently, it yet mistakenly erects one nodus or one stream of mechanical Nature into the false idea of a self. This is the attitude towards life and existence of Buddhism, of materialistic Rationalism and, with one all-important modification, of Mayavada. On the other hand, if we hold the mechanical Force to be subordinate to the self-conscious, self-governing existence, contained in it and one of its appearances and conscious creations, then we are naturally & inevitably guided towards the conception of an all-constituting Self-Conscious Existence & Power, — Brahman, Ish, popularly conceived as Bhagavan, as God, which is the true being & governing force of existence, — then the apparent mechanical Force reveals itself as no blind or mechanical movement of dead life, that insoluble riddle, that ultra-Eleusinian mystery of modern Rationalism, but the conscious Will of the Sole Existence, its Tapas, its Atmashakti or Chit-Shakti which formulates itself freely into laws and processes — the daivyá adabdhá vratá of the Rigveda — for the ordering of the universe. This is the attitude towards life & existence of the Veda & Upanishads. All other philosophies are halting-places or compromises between these two master-conceptions of existence. The wide divergence between the Vedic & the Buddhistic conceptions of Karma arises as the inevitable result of this direct opposition between their fundamental conceptions of existence itself. Both admit that all active existence is of the nature of energy or work. Vedanta uses the terms Shakti, Force, Power, or Prakriti, Processive Working, for the energy, Karma, Apas, work, or the plural Karmani, works, for the activities & effects of the energy; Buddha ignores Shakti & Prakriti, because he denies the existence of God and soul or of any essential unity, but he sums up the work done in the general singular word Karma and elevates this ever indeterminate, ever increasing sum of work, into a determining conception which governs & constitutes our phenomenal existence. He is bound to this position by his idea of the world as void of unity & existence as consisting of a successive continuity of habitual subjective sensations, — sanskaras, — not an inherent continuity of self-existent Being, — whether that being be a self-conscious existence or unconscious Force. For Buddha therefore all phenomenal existence is determined by Karma, the sum of previous works; for the Vedanta all phenomenal existence is determined by the working of Shakti or Prakriti, Force of Nature, under the will & choice of Soul, Self or Spirit. This Soul or Spirit, variously termed Deva, self-luminous conscious Being behind the Force of Nature, or Purusha, informing Male inhabitant and possessor of this female executive Energy, or Ishwara, omnipresent Lord of this Will Power, this Shakti formulated in Force of Nature, is the beginning & end, the continent & inhabitant, the source & material of all objects & existences; for this Shakti, Prakriti or Nature produces all its works, objects & happenings only in the Ishwara's self-extended conscious existence. So, the Swetaswatara Upanishad defines Prakriti as Devátmashaktim swagunair nigúdhám, Self-Power of the Divinity concealed by its own modes of working. The Self in Vedanta is not only Swayambhu, self-existent; it is Swarat and Samrat, self-governing and world-governing. The Ishwara is master and user of his works, not Himself their slave, creature or instrument. Therefore, while Vedanta accepts the law of works as a subordinate and external instrument of rebirth and prolonged phenomenal existence, a bond unreal in itself & even in its action many-sided, elastic and flexible, Buddhism imposes it as the one cause of rebirth & a mechanical and in its action an ineluctable Necessity & rigid chain; while Vedanta becomes by its fundamental conception the gospel of a recovery by self-realisation in outward consciousness of an always existing freedom & mastery in a world which is secretly anandamaya, all-blissful, Buddhism becomes by its fundamental conception a gospel of escape by self-extinction from a sorrowful, intolerable & otherwise ineffugable bondage.

When we go behind metaphysical conceptions and look at the concrete facts of existence on which they stand, we shall find that the law of Karma is nothing else than a statement of the soul's entire subjection to the law of cause and effect. The idea belongs both to ancient Buddhism and modern Rationalism, but is stated in either philosophy on different grounds. Buddhism denies the real existence of soul, Rationalism denies it existence altogether, trenchantly & simply. To the modern rationalist the whole world is simply a working out of material Force and mind itself is a particular working of matter. Mind, in this conception, is a sort of automatical electrical apparatus which receives so many various kinds and degrees of shock, beats out mechanical responses & converts them, also mechanically, into so many forms of sound and idea. Ideas themselves must then be entirely material phenomena, although because they do not assume any of the ordinary visible objectual forms of matter, they falsely appear non-material to our consciousness. That consciousness itself is, indeed, only a subjective & quite subordinate activity of matter. Since the machine is automatic, there is no need to suppose the existence of an intelligent operator. Ego is a fiction of the mind, the soul an ignorant theory invented by the uninformed intellect to explain to itself its own existence. What then is the cause of these thinkings, doings, happenings? Obviously, they must be the workings of material Force of which the chief process is a mechanical causality. Previous workings produce as causes by an unchanging, inherent law of action other workings of Force which stand to them as effects; they in their turn join the general sum of causation, helping to produce new effects. The sum of past workings of Force yet in operation, — so far at least as they are concentrated round the object, — are figured for man as heredity, environment, education, past actions and produce a parent state of things or predisposing condition; its present workings, acting as immediate cause, or the sum of immediate causes, produce out of that condition all new states, actions & events, not intentionally but mechanically, by the joint force or interplay of cumulative and special causes. This is the modern materialistic theory of Karma to which, I presume, the majority of modern thinkers would give some kind of assent. Denying the survival of personality after death, it perceives no need to fathom deeper complexities or enter into more subtle problems. The bondage of Law is inexorable but need not greatly trouble us, since death after a short span of activity acts automatically as a release. To ego in the mind, to our falsely self-imagined soul, even if that ego be so foolish as to chafe and resent the bondage & limitation which is the law of all being, there is always this consolation of a speedy self-extinction in the sum of Matter. But any such resentment is a morbid folly of our intellect. To accept our chains, manipulate, rearrange and use them for our own welfare & that of the race is the gospel of scientific rationalism.

Buddhism views the same set of facts from the other end of thought. Not self-working material force, but a mass of subjective sensations is its reading of the universe. Material existence & action only exist in sensational consciousness and as terms of sensational consciousness; and sensational consciousness only exists as a phenomenon in the void. But behind this sensation-troubled void, there is another state, entity or what you will, Nirvana, in which there is neither this continual birth in phenomena, nor the sensational activity of which continual birth is the nodus. Later Buddhistic schools have supposed Nirvana itself to be void or Nihil, but it does not appear that this was the actual teaching of the Buddha. He left the ultimate metaphysical question aside and fastened only on the practical fact of this bound & troubled sensational existence and that ineffable bliss of release & escape. To escape, that is the goal & end of man. But who escapes? Buddhism denies God, denies the existence of the Atman. There is no one who escapes, only the escape itself. Buddha avoided always the logical difficulty & seized on the practical fact. There is here, undeniably, the phenomenal existence of something which feels, desires, sins & suffers, and the great principle of divine Compassion in him which far more than reason & logic was the master key of his thinking, compelled him only to take hold of this great sufferer, this tormented self-deluder & turn it into that path by which alone it could escape from its own false existence. The path of escape is that moral & intellectual discipline which leads it out of the dual stream of good and bad Karma. To Buddha also the sum of past workings still operative on us is the great preexisting condition which is causal of continued state, action & happenings, past working as cause produces fresh working as effect which again constitutes itself into fresh cause. From this chain there is no escape in

Nature except by perceiving existence as a streaming activity of successive sensational associations or sanskaras and climbing out of the stream by a supreme act of knowledge. For, unlike the modern Rationalist, Buddha's problem was complicated by the belief inherited from Vedic Hinduism that death is not a release; personality survives & in other states, other births, continues to suffer & enjoy, enjoy & suffer through unending Time unless & until the knot is cut, the renunciation of the self-idea envisaged and effected. Then we escape from these running figments of heaven & earth & hell, pleasure & pain, life & death, self & not-self into the shoreless & streamless peace of Nirvana.

Shankara, one of the mightiest of metaphysical intellects, a far greater intellect than the Buddha, though a less mighty soul, built up by his intuitions and reasonings a third position which reconciles Vedic Brahmavada and the Karmavada of Buddhistic rationalism & Rationalistic materialism. Shankara asserts the real existence of the Atman, self or soul which alone exists and is indeed the essential substratum & continent of this phenomenal universe. But he admits with Buddha the absolute rule of Karma, of the law of works, the law of cause & effect over the conscious soul immersed in the phenomenal universe. Is then the soul eternally coerced by its own phenomena, eternally bound to the revolving wheel of its own phenomenal manifestations? No, for freedom is the ultimate spiritual experience. Where then is the point of escape, the door, the egress? The point of escape is for Shankara, as for Buddha, in an ultimate act of knowledge which denies the real existence of the phenomenal world. He erects a rigid antagonism between essential truth and practical truth, paramartha & vyavahara, the one alone we must admit to be true truth, the other we must reject as only apparent truth. This world is a world of action, of karma, & in a world of action the governing practical truth is the law of karma which drives the soul through the endless chain of birth & death & rebirth, whirling for ever betwixt heaven & earth & hell, tossed from good to evil & evil to good, pain to joy & joy to pain, like a tennis ball kept continually at play between two equally skilful players. But all action depends upon and is only rendered possible by relation, and all relation depends upon and is only rendered possible by self-division, by bheda, by dwaita, by the false conception in the soul of itself as not one, but many, by Avidya therefore, by Maya, a great original sin of Ignorance, a mighty cosmic self-deception. Where there are many, relation and action are possible; where there is one, there can be no relation and therefore no action. Atman or Soul is one, therefore relationless and actionless, shantam avyavaharyam, therefore free from karma, from rebirth, from Maya. The rest is a phenomenon of creation produced by the play of active consciousness, jagati, & cast by it like a shadow or reflected image on the surface of the still, actionless & relationless soul. This play, this jagati is Maya which is and is not, — is in itself, for its works are there, but is not, for those works are unrealities; they are a mass of self-deceptions starting from an original self-deception rooted in the principle of mind. What the mind sees is a reality, it is Atman, Brahman, but the ideas, the terms in which mind sees it are falsehoods.[5] All practice therefore, however true for practical purposes in world, is really the plausible & well-arranged play of a falsehood; & practical truth & action are only so far useful that out of them, properly handled, emerges the impulse which leads to cessation from action & the knowledge which denies practical existence. In that cessation, in that denial is man's only escape from his false mental self into the calm essential reality, objectless bliss & relationless self-knowledge of the Atman. We see then that Shankara has practically transmuted or replaced Buddha's vague & undefined Nirvana by this actionless & peaceful Atman, the shanta akriya Sacchidananda, substituted for Buddha's false world of subjective sensations a false world of erroneous ideas starting from the original self-deception of duality, and accepting Buddha's law of karma as applicable only to this false world and Buddha's means of escape

---

[5] The explanations given by modern Adwaitins of Shankara's views, their interpretations in modern thought of his philosophical formulae, are so various & mutually contradictory, that it is becoming as difficult to know the real truth of his views as to know the real & original teaching of Buddha. I give what seems to me to be his teaching & at any rate it is the only logical basis for Mayavada.

by an ultimate act of knowledge, substituted knowledge of real self for Buddha's knowledge of non-self as the essence of that act & the true culmination of inner experience & meditative reason. Shankara like Buddha refuses to explain or discuss how active consciousness came at all to exist on the surface of a sole Self-existence which is in its very being shanta and inactive; he drives, like Buddha, straight at the actual fact of our bondage, the practical cause of bondage and the most direct path of escape from the bondage. These he states for us as he holds them to be established by Scripture, experience & reason & then, the fact once thus triply established, our business is not to account for its existence, which, moreover, must in the nature of things be inexplicable to the mind, since Maya is an original mystery & therefore incapable of solution, but to grasp at the one means of escape, of release, of the great & final liberation. The intellectual difference between the two systems is immense, their temperamental kinship is close. Yet we have this curious result, due to Buddha's stress on the means of self-denial provided by life & its ethical & altruistic possibilities as a preliminary training, that Shankara's system, less intellectually Nihilistic than Buddha's, has been practically more fatal to the activities of the divine power & joy in life in the nation which has so largely accepted his teachings. By denying God in life, by withdrawing the best souls from life, by discouraging through their thought & example, — the thought & example of the best, yad yad acharati sreshthah, — the sraddha of life, the full confident self-acting of Matariswan even in those who have practically accepted & cling to the burden of worldly existence, he has enlarged the original Vedantic seed of ascetic tendency into a gigantic growth of stillness & world-disgust which has overshadowed for centuries the lives & souls of hundreds of millions of human beings. On one side the race & the world have gained immensely, on the other it has suffered an immense impoverishment. The world-fleeing saint & the hermit have multiplied, the world-helping saint & the divine warrior of life come rarely & fail for want of the right atmosphere & environment. The Avatars of moral purity & devotional love abound, the Avatars of life, Krishna

& Balarama, manifest themselves no more. Gone are Janaka & Ajatashatru, Arjuna & Vyasa, the great scientists, the great lawgivers. The cry of OM Tapas with which God creates has grown faint in the soul of India, the cry of OM Shanti with which He withdraws from life alone arouses & directs the best energies of a national consciousness to whose thought all life is sorrow, self-delusion & an undivine blunder. Chilled is that marvellous & mighty vigour which flowed out from the Veda & Upanishads on the Indian consciousness & produced the grand & colossal forms of life eternally portrayed for us in the fragments of our ancient art & history & in the ideal descriptions of the Epics.

In Buddhism & modern Rationalism we have the denial of God, the grand negation, remedied for the purposes of life by a subordinate or substitutory conception which encourages the active impulses in humanity; in Rationalism the negation is corrected by a covert reaffirmation of Him in the disguise of a blindly purposeful Nature full of a supreme mechanical intelligence and working out an evolutionary intention in humanity, in Buddhism, by the strong & fruitful affirmation of Karma and of Dharma or ethical religion as the indispensable first condition of escape from Karma; in Mayavada we get back to the affirmation of God, but an ill-balanced affirmation ending for the purposes of life in a practical negation, since God in the world is presented to us as a dream of Maya and God aloof from the world as the only real reality. To get back to the full affirmation we have to return to the ancient Veda. There, we find stated or indicated in every Upanishad, but most succinctly and practically in the Isha Upanishad, Ish, Purusha, Deva as the supreme good; we recover there the perfect affirmation of God & return to the grand, original & eternal negation of all these succeeding negations. There can be no more direct contradiction to the negative element in Shankara's teaching than the uncompromising phrases of the Isha Upanishad, kurvanneveha karmani, nanyatheto'sti, na karma lipyate nare. Both Shankara and the Seer of the Upanishad start from the same premises, the universality of Brahman, the bondage of desire and ignorance,

the necessity of escape through the dissolution of the dividing
ego-sense in our mentality; but the practical conclusions they
draw from these premises reveal somewhere an abyss of divergence. Abstain from actions, cries Shankara, except, for a time,
from those that are indispensable and Shastra-enjoined, — and
even these do with a view to their early cessation; for action is
the master-key of the chain of Maya and only by ceasing from
action can a man escape from the grand Illusion of things; only
by cessation in relationless knowledge & the eternal stillness of
the actionless Brahman can there come the great release from
good & evil, from joy & pain, from birth & death, from living
& non-living. Verily do actions, cries the ancient Seer, accept thy
full term of human life and endeavour; for action is not in itself
a chain nor a result of ignorance, but rather a manifestation of
the Most High. Action cleaveth not to a man. The difference
arises from a divergence in the fundamental conception of God
in the world. To the Mayavadin, Ishwara, God in relation to the
world, is a supreme term of Maya and therefore like all things
in Maya existent yet not existent; to the Seer God is an eternal
reality standing behind Chit-Shakti in its works, embracing it,
possessing it, fulfilling Himself in it through the world rhythm.
Action to the Mayavadin can only be motived by individual
ignorance and must always be a knot of that ignorance; action to
the Seer can even in our outward consciousness be motived & in
the secret consciousness of God always is motived by the divine
& universal Force & Bliss at free play in the divine & universal
Being. The world is to the Mayavadin a freak of knowledge,
an error on the surface of Self, a misconception of mind about
Brahman; the world to the Seer is a running symbol of God and a
means for His phenomenal self-manifestation in His own active
being & to His own active knowledge. God, being unbound by
His own activity and its free lord & disposer, man also, being
one in self with God, is unbound by his works and, in God, their
free master and disposer. Na karma lipyate nare.

Yet, in this divergence of views the dominant sense of
our later Indian spirituality has been with the conclusion of
Shankara and against the conclusion of the early, the inspired,

the suprarational Vedanta. To the modern Indian mind unaffected by European pragmatism it has been untrue that action cleaveth not to a man, — na karma lipyate nare — ; & it has been true that all action results imperatively in bondage, — yah karoti sa lipyate, whoever acts is entangled in his action. The reason for this preference is obvious. Bondage & sorrow in the world are a fact of our daily experience, withdrawal from life an obvious and logical escape; freedom & bliss in the world are only a statement of Scripture, an experience abnormal to ordinary humanity and if eternally existent, then existent in our supraliminal self and not in our waking consciousness. Therefore India failing in the ancient power of Vedic tapasya has inertly accepted & combined the Buddhist Law of Karma & Rebirth & Shankara's gospel of cosmic Illusion & actionless Peace.

We have seen that the statement of the law of Karma is, at bottom, an assertion of the supremacy, complete & effectual in all forms of activity, of the grand cosmic principle of cause & effect. It formalises the subjection of the human life or even the human soul, at least in all its active parts, to the ineluctable dominion of an unending causality. If it can be shown that the dominion is not ineluctable or man himself is or may be above causality, its master and not under its control, then the whole elaborate chain forged for us by outward world-appearances crumbles in a moment to pieces. For Indian philosophy the main practical application for man of the chain of causality was the Law of Rebirth, — a law of the Soul in Nature; for modern Science, which denies the soul and knows nothing about rebirth, its practical application for man as for plant & stone & animal is, simply, the invariable working of material Force or, using a more popular language, mechanical Law of Nature. Even if the soul exists & rebirth be proved a fact, the Law of Rebirth can be to modern conceptions nothing but a particular working of Force, one, therefore, of the many subordinate Laws of Nature. As locomotion is the effect, electricity or steam the cause or motive force, so rebirth, continuity of personality in a material form, is the effect, past action is the cause; it is a law of Nature, on a par in the psychological field with the law of gravitation in physical Nature, that the soul which acts shall be subjected to rebirth as the ineluctable result of its actions.

So stated, and given the necessary premise that individual personality is itself no eternal mystery but only a result and a nodus of natural energies working through the mind, the Buddhists' ineffugable law of Karma becomes a luminous, simple, rational, rigidly logical solution of the problem of personal existence, and like all that is simple and trenchantly logical, it attracts sovereignly at the first glance & tempts the thought to find rest in its symmetry & security. But to a mind on the alert for the infinite surprises of our complex world-existence this simplicity, this rigid logic is itself a danger signal, a warning of error. The more largely & patiently we consider existence, the more we perceive its extraordinary complexity, the multitude of its strands and the variability of its formulae, the more we begin to distrust all simple & onesided conclusions. Even though the world be one in substance and unitarian in principle, it is always infinitely manifold in manifestation and infinitely complex in working. When therefore we have arrived at a conclusion which, attracting by its simplicity, convincing by its force of logical dogmatism, coerces all these complexities to fit a single formula, yet we shall do wisely if we survey our position once again, if we ask ourselves what side of the truth we have omitted from our review of things and whether there are not somewhere incompatible facts which we have too forcefully dismissed or too dexterously got rid of in the haste to reach some goal. As Buddhism by logical dexterity got rid of the human perception of self-existence or Mayavada of the human perception of world-existence or Rationalism of the human perception of a psychic life in us & outside us that overtops our material and bodily activities, our thought can only arrive at the whole truth of things when it learns to ignore and evade nothing, to leave out nothing that God has included but rather to give patiently, justly, dispassionately every fact & every aspect of existence its right value and full place in His scheme of things. If we do not perform the necessary work of self-criticism for ourselves, mankind will eventually do it for us and cast away as falsehoods those exclusive religions or those onesided philosophies which on their too narrow pedestals we have erected with so much & so immature a fervour of self-satisfaction. For Truth in the end is invincible and gets the better of all mankind's temporarily triumphant violences upon her. There are already signs that the mind of the race in India is beginning to react against the exaggeration of the Buddhistic generalisation of Karma to which modern Hinduism has been so long subjected both in life & in thought. The weakness of the Karma theory lies in its absolutist & exclusive generalisation of a great, a fundamental, but still a partial truth, — its overstress on outward human action as a determining factor of the soul's experiences, its insufficient stress on those vaster & more subtle workings of God in man of which outward action is only the partial symbol and the external machinery. It is here that the Upanishads recall us to a wider & sounder view of God in the world & His purpose in action & birth.

Not action but our past soul-states are the womb of our future; not action but desire, attachment and self-immersion of the individualised Soul in mind in a limited stream of the workings of its own executive Nature form the knot in the bondage of rebirth; action, whether of the thought, the speech or the body, is only an outward mechanical process by which the soul-state shadows out or symbolises itself in material life. It has no essential value of its own, but only the value of what it expresses; it can therefore have no binding power upon the soul which originates & determines it. What it does and can help to alter, are merely the mental & emotional values & terms in which soul-state expresses itself and even this function it performs as a partial agent and not as the real determining factor.

If that be true, then we have been grossly exaggerating the power of our actions over our souls, grossly & wilfully accepting in our mental & outward life the tyranny claimed over us by our individual nature, when our hidden relation to her & God's open ultimate intention in us is the very opposite of such a submission to the brute & despotic control of Matter. The relation of the

Swarat to his being, of the Samrat to his environment is our secret & true relation. To conquer one's own nature & fulfil God in world-nature, standing back from her in the soul, free & desireless, but not turning utterly away from her, is the true divine impulse of God in humanity. Life of Nature is intended to be to the soul of man as the Indian wife to her husband, not all in all, for it is to God that he should turn supremely & live in God perpetually, but yet always the half of himself through whose help alone as his sahadharmini, his comrade in works, he can fulfil the divine purpose of his living. The soul to Prakriti is intended to be as the Indian husband to his wife, the image of God in life, for whom she lives & through whom she arrives at the Divinity. We should seek first & live always in God beyond Nature, but God as Nature we should also cherish & enjoy as His symbol of that which is beyond & the appointed means of His active self-manifestation.

In Vedanta, therefore, the true & early Vedanta, the practical freedom of the soul is not to be gained as in Buddhism by self-abolition, — for the ego alone can be abolished, the soul is eternal, began not and cannot end, — nor, as in Mayavada, only by extinction of its activities in actionless self-knowledge, — for God expresses Himself in action no less than in rest; — but rather the soul is eternally free in its nature and its freedom has only to be entirely realised by the mind in all its parts in order to be possessed, whether in action or in inaction, in withdrawal from life or possession & mastery of life, by this outer consciousness which we call our waking self as it is eternally possessed in our wide & true effulgent spiritual being which lives concealed behind the clouded or twilit shiftings of our mental nature and our bodily existence.

Chapter V

The Soul, Causality and Law of Nature.

What then of this causality that we see everywhere? What then
of this law and fixed process in all Nature which is at least
the indispensable condition of all human activities? How can
the supposed freedom of the soul be reconciled with the actual
despotism in fact of an ordered Cosmic Energy?

Vedanta does not deny either Law of Causality or Law of
Nature nor their fixity nor their imperative control over individual activities; it rather affirms them categorically and, as we
shall see, with an inexorable thoroughness far more unsparing
than the affirmations of modern Rationalism. But it states these
laws in a formula far wider than the rationalist's; it sees not
only law of life & law of matter, but law of mind and law of
supermind; and it bases the stability and imperative force of all
law in the world on an ultimate truth & source of freedom. It
is this ultimate conclusion that gives to the Vedantic conception
of Causality and Law of Nature an entirely different force and
essential meaning from the vast generalisation of mechanical
Energy popularised by modern Science. Law of Nature is to
Science the tyranny of a self-existent habit in mechanical World-
Force which Intelligence, the indulged & brilliant youngest child
of material Energy, can use indeed, can convert in its forms or
divert in its processes, but from which it has no door of escape.
Law of Nature in Vedanta is the normality of a regular or habitual process in self-intelligent World-Force; in other words, — for
Chit-Shakti, self-intelligent World-Force can mean nothing else
than this, — in the cosmic Will-Power of universal self-existent
Being, — of God, of Brahman. The process of Force, then, however fixed, however imperative, is neither mystically self-existent
nor mechanically self-determined. On the contrary it depends
upon certain relations, exists in certain conditions, amounts to
certain fixed motions of the cosmic Will-Power which have been
selected from the beginning in the universal Wisdom and, once
selected, are manifested, evolved, established and maintained in

the workings of cosmic Energy until the fixed moment arrives for their variation or for their temporary or final dissolution. Laws of Nature are, in the pregnant phrase of the Rig-Veda, adabdhá vratá dhruvá yá devá akrinvata; they are the rules fixed and unovercome of active world-being which the gods have made and which they maintain eternally against the powers of dissolution. For the world in the old Vedic conception is a rhythm of action and movement in God's conscious being; or rather it is a combination and concord of rhythms; it is chhandas, it is metre, it is a choral symphony of Jagati & Gayatri, Brihati & Pankti, Tristubh & Anustubh; it is Vak, a formation of His Word, a formal harmony of His self-expressive consciousness, a harmony discovered and selected out of God's infinite possibilities and exposed therefore to the perpetual attack of those infinite possibilities. Therefore even the most well-established laws of Nature, the most general, persistent, apparently eternal and unvariable processes of world-Force, being formations of Jagati, being rhythms and harmonies of God's active Energy, truths of recurrent motion and not truths of eternal status, are none of them indestructible like the sempiternal Being out of which they emerge, but alterable and dissoluble and, since alterable and dissoluble, therefore ever attacked by powers of disorder and world-dissolution, ever maintained by the divine Powers consciously obedient to eternal Will & expressive of It through whom Ishwara has manifested Himself in material, moral and spiritual Nature.

Law of Nature is in God's being what social Law is in man's action & experience, not indestructible essence of that being or indispensable condition of that action, but formed, evolved and willed condition of a regular, ordered, complex and intricately combined self-expression in a harmony of various relations and grouped workings of energy. All existing natural conditions express a realised status and frame and base a farther evolution out of realised status.

Nature itself is Prakriti, working (literally, forward working) of world-Force, called by us Shakti, the cosmic or divine Power of cosmic or divine Will. And because that Shakti is, in the phrase of the Swetáswatara Upanishad, Devátmashaktih swagunair nigúdhá, the self-power of Divine Being hidden by the modes of its own workings, because it is, to use another Sanscrit formula, Chit-Shakti of the Sat-Purusha, Conscious Power of Conscious Being, & because that Conscious Being is infinite, absolute and unlimited in its possibilities and its Conscious Power infinitely, absolutely and illimitably a Free Will choosing freely Its own harmonies and not bound in their rhythms as though in fetters imposed by an alien will, forming, observing and using Its own laws and not compelled, enslaved and used by them, therefore is Prakriti or working of Nature in its laws a self-imposed system, a mighty and ordered Wisdom and not an eternal and inexplicable mechanical necessity. Its laws are formed & fixed processes of world-Force, selected and "loosed forth" by God, srishta, (created, as we loosely say,) out of the illimitable potentialities of self-existence, brought into play out of the depths of His self-being as a rhythm of music is brought out, manifested and arranged, srishta, vyakta, vihita, out of the infinite possibilities of indefinite sound. Self-luminous conscious being precedes, contains and manifests in self-intelligent & self-effective Force; self-intelligent and self-effective Force at once conceals and manifests itself in the mask of Prakriti, the mask of a motional and mechanical working of Nature. We arrive then at this formula of the conception of Law in Nature.

Law of Nature is a fixed process formed by the universal self-conscious Will of Ishwara; it is in its nature a particular or a general movement of that Force. So long as it is maintained, it is binding on things in Nature, but not binding except by His own Will on Ishwara. Fundamental or "eternal" Laws of Nature are those general processes or movements in Conscious Being in which the rhythm of the universe is framed and they would naturally endure unabrogated so long as that rhythm itself is sustained, as it is, in the Will and Being of God.

The Vedantic conception of Causality is equally determined by this initial and fundamental idea of the relation between mechanical process of Nature and the living Will of God. Cause, to the Vedantin, is nimitta, determining means, special determining factor; it is the particular manipulation, impact or application of motive force which brings out of a preexistent arrangement or condition of things new or modified condition and arrangement, the difference effected constituting result. Oxygen & hydrogen as separately manifest gases, the atmosphere, the ether, — or to put it in the old concrete symbolical language of Indian philosophy, the combined presence of Agni, Vayu and Akasha, form in their arranged shapes & relations the preexistent condition; contact & mixture of the two forces with the new vibrations set up by the new relation, sparsha and shabda, are the nimitta, the determining means; the new apparent condition of things, the rupa, shape of water, is the result. Agni latent in the ether & atmosphere is the preexistent condition; friction of the two aranis and the resultant vibrations, sparsha & shabda, are the nimitta; the sacrificial fire is the result. A seed planted in favourable ground is the preexistent condition, sun & rain, agni & jala, are the nimitta; the appearance of an oak tree is the result. In each case what has really happened is that in a certain arrangement of the current workings and a certain relation of the worked out shapes of Force — in this case of the active Life-Energy in the material world — a new arrangement was always potential and latent, water involved in hydrogen, fire involved in the tinderwood, the oak tree involved in the seed and a particular process, that is to say a particular working (karma or apas) of the same Force, the same Life-Energy, has been used to evoke the new shape of things out of latency, out of avyakta, and bring it into manifestation, into vyakta. The previous existence of the oak tree in the seed is not admitted by us because it is not there in realised form and to our erroneous notions realised form is alone reality. But realised form is only the material appearance of a truer reality which is not shaped in matter but only in consciousness: the oak tree is in the seed not in form but in being; for the form is only a circumstance of being and it is contained & latent in the being out of which it is born & which it expresses to formal vision. This latency and this process of manifestation in varying time and place by varying nimitta is, says Vedanta, the whole sense of phenomenal existence.

*All cause and result are merely the evocation of a latent
and potential shape or condition of things out of the previous
condition or status in which it was latent, by some particular
movement of a Conscious Force which is progressively passing
from status to status and thus manifesting in form all that it
holds in itself in being. Cause is only a means of manifestation
and not itself a creative power. The real cause is only the Will of
God working through its own fixed and chosen processes.*

Are we to say, as it is often said, that the preexistent condition of things or arranged sum of force is the real cause out of
which the event, the change, the new appearance must inevitably
come and the advent of the nimitta a sort of accidental or at least
subordinate & variable factor by which the inevitable result
happens actually to be induced to manifest itself in outward
eventuality? We have no right to say so; for it is not true as a
matter of perceived fact that a given preexistent condition of
things must lead inevitably in its own nature to a fixed result.
In all the cases we have cited the preexistent condition did not
necessitate the result and could not have produced it, but for
the interference of the nimitta or determining factor, just as the
determining factor could not have produced the result but for
the preexistent condition. Shall we say, then, that granted a
given preexistent condition and a given determining factor we
shall have with mechanical certainty a given inevitable result?
Again, we have no right to say so. The formula seems at first
to hold good where the material of the workings of Force is
the most rigid & unpliable and the workings themselves are the
most mechanical & regular in their recurrence. But even there
the inevitability of things is illusory. The aranis may be to hand,
the friction occur, yet the sacrificial fire may never be lit; the
seed may be planted, the soil favourable, sun and rain perfectly
adjusted in their bounty, but the oak tree may not appear. We
cannot even say that any given preexistent condition of things is
the sole condition under which a given result can be effected. We
say, indeed, taking actual fact for necessary fact, that only by the
incubation of favourable soil on the right seed can an oak tree
appear; but what we are justified in saying is only that, as yet, we

know no other conditions under which an oak tree has appeared. So also we thought that only by the incubation of the earth on the carbon could the diamond be produced; now, other conditions have been found under which this rare formation can be effected. Where the material which the force of Nature uses is more pliant and flexible, the idea of a mechanical Necessity becomes still less credible, is even more feebly substantiated by facts or is directly contradicted. A nation is in its last stage of moral and material decline; the preexistent conditions are precisely the same as in a score of instances in which destruction has followed or are even worse and more favourable to dissolution; the same determining nimitta is applied; but whereas in the previous score of cases the shock of the new impact has determined the anticipated result of destruction, in this worse case the selfsame shock, baffling anticipation, determines the entirely contrary result of rejuvenation, restored strength, energy of expansion, energy even of domination. Either some new factor has entered in unexpectedly or was already existent and even active, but concealed, or else a latent potentiality, which in the other cases remained latent, has here unexpectedly reacted, risen into the active superficial movement and become its dominant and deciding factor. Looking at these things, we are tempted sometimes to say that the whole sum of the past and the whole sum of the present was necessary for any given result in the world to be brought about; we are tempted to speculate that the whole cumulative stream of past active forces, past Apas or Karma, is the one real and inevitable cause of the future. But this is really only a statement of our ignorance; it is only an assertion that what has been, has been and since it has been, must, in any case, have become. It is an attempt to disguise from ourselves a fact that it really confesses, the fact that an infinite possibility of negation or modification, of non-happening or otherwise happening pursues and surrounds every actuality & eventuality in the universe and that we can relate how and under what conditions a thing has happened once or repeatedly and may be expected, if nothing interferes, to happen again, but we cannot fix inevitable cause to inevitable effect.

All event and all process of event is a selection out of infinite possibility which surrounds the actual past as the Might Have Been and the actual future as the May Be. Of every cause, process & result we can say justly that the result might have been otherwise or the same result spring from some other cause or be effected by some other process. This perception in mind of an omnipresent infinite possibility is a shadow of the soul's perception of the infinite freedom of God.

What then is it that in any given working of result out of precedent condition by nimitta, fixes the combination of the forces at work, governs their manipulation, selects in one case to be the determining factor a force which in other cases was impotent to decide the eventuality? Is it Chance? Is it Fate? Is it some inexplicable mechanical self-guidance? Or is it supreme intelligent Will, Will that is in its nature Intelligence? Is there a conscious Will or rather a Will-Consciousness which contains, informs, constitutes these apparent forces and objects, but is hidden from our eyes by their multitudinous whirl of motion, by their clamorous demand on the attention of the mind and senses, by their insistent claim that we should submit in thought and act to the tyranny of their workings? This last answer is the solution proposed by Vedanta. It rejects the concept of Chance as only a specious name covering our self-satisfied ignorance of the cause and process of things; Chance is really the free action, not pursuable by us in its details, of a mighty cosmic Providence which is one with cosmic Force. It accepts the reality of Fate, but rejects as a void and baseless imagination the idea of an inexplicable mechanical Necessity; Fate is merely the inevitable working out in itself by a cosmic Will of its own fixed and predetermined self-perceptions. It accepts the idea of a principle of unerring self-guidance in Nature, but is unable to regard that principle as in any way a mysterious agency or an inexplicable birth; Nature guides itself unerringly only because Nature is the self-working of a Self-luminous conscious Existence formulating its Will in fixed processes of things and combined arrangement of event actualised in its own eternal and illimitable being. Nature to Vedanta is only the mask of a divine cosmic Will, devátma-shaktih swagunair nigúdhá; Prakriti of Vedanta is no separate power, no self-existent mechanical entity, but the executive force of the divine Purusha at once self-revealed and self-concealed in the mechanism of its own workings. Purusha, conscious Soul, is the divine Poet and Maker; Nature, conscious Force, is His poetic faculty; but the material of His works is always Himself and their stage & scene are in His own conscious being.

Pre-ordered selection out of infinite possibility is the real nature of the power we call Fate. Chance is a secret Providence and Providence the constantly active Self-Knowledge of cosmic Existence and cosmic Will always fulfilling in actuality its foreseen selection of event and means, — foreseen in knowledge, — and preventing the pressure of infinite possibility from disturbing that pre-ordered arrangement. So a poet might work out in execution the original plot and characters as arranged in his mind and reject at every step the infinite possible variations which suggest themselves to him as he writes.

Law of Nature is the fixed system of conventional or habitual relations under which the Purusha has agreed with Himself to work out His pre-ordered selection and harmony. Causality is the willed arrangement of successive states & events and the choice of particular means in accordance with this fixed system of relations by which pre-ordered Fate of things is worked out in actual event.

Fate, Law and fixed Causality bind things in the movement of the Jagati; they do not bind the Purusha or conscious Soul but are the modes and instruments of His free self-working.

We must be on our guard against the idea that in this statement of the problem of predestination the infinite possibility we assert is an otiose and practically non-existent conception, — a thing that Is Not, a mere mental perception, — or that because the course of the world is fixed, the infinite freedom of God which supports and contains that fixity, is an abstraction of no practical moment or no practical potency. Among the many superficial fallacies of the practical man, there is none more superficial or fallacious than the assumption that in face of what has been, it is idle to consider what might have been. The Might Have Been in the past is the material out of which much of the future is shaped. It would not be so if the material life were a self-existent thing, proceeding out of itself, sufficient to itself, ending with itself. But the material life is only a selection, a formation, a last result of an infinite conscious life behind which far exceeds the sum of all that actually exists in form and happens in event. Infinite Possibility is a living entity, a positive force; it is the material out of which God is constantly throwing up the positive and finite actuality. It is therefore all-important for a full and real knowledge of the world to know & see this infinite material as well as the actual finite result and ultimately determined shape of things. God Himself in His foreknowledge foresees the infinite possibilities that surround the event as well as the event itself. The forces that we spend vainly for an unrealised result, have always their ultimate end and satisfaction, and often form the most important determinants of a near or a distant future. The future carries in it all the failures of the past and keeps them for its use and for their success in other time, place and circumstance. Even our attempts to alter fixed process, when that process seems to be a fixed & unalterable law of Nature, are not lost & vain; they modify the active vibrations of the fixed current of things and may even lead to an entire alteration of the long-standing processes of things. The refusal of great minds to accept the idea of impossibility, with which they are not unoften reproached by the slaves of present actuality, is a just recognition of the omnipotence divinely present in us by right of the one supreme Inhabitant in these forms; nor does their immediate failure to externalise their dreams prove to the eye that sees that their faith was an error or a self-delusion. The attempt is often more important than the success, the victim more potent than the victor, not to the limited narrowly utilitarian human mind fixed on the immediate step, the momentary result, but to God's all-knowing Fate in its universal and millennial workings. From another standpoint, it is the infinite possibilities that surround the act or the event which give to act and event their full meaning and value. It may be said that Arjuna's hesitation and refusal to fight at Kurukshetra was of no practical moment since eventually he did take up his bow and slay the Dhritarashtrians & the otiose incident might well have been omitted by God in His drama; but if it had not been possible for Arjuna to hesitate, to fling down the bow Gandiva or to have retired from the fight but for the command of the incarnate God beside him, then his subsequent action in fighting & slaying would have had an entirely different value, the battle of Kurukshetra would have meant something entirely different to humanity & its results on the future life of the nation & the world would have been, comparatively, almost a zero. We can see this truth even with regard to slighter incidents. The fatality which in Shakespeare's drama wills the death of Romeo & Juliet as the result of a trivial and easily avoidable accident, receives all its value from the possibilities surrounding the actual event, the possibilities of escape from fate, reconciliation & for these tragic lovers the life of an ordinary conjugal happiness. These unrealised possibilities & the secret inevitability — of Spirit, not of matter, — which prevents their realisation, which takes advantage of every trivial accident and makes use of it for the swift & terrible conclusion, make the soul of the tragedy. A mechanical fatality must always be a thing banal, dead, inert and meaningless. It is their perception of these things behind the veil, their transcendence of the material fact, their inspired presentation of human life that ranks the great poets among the sophoi, kavis, vates, and places poetry next to the Scriptures & the revelations of the Seer and the prophets as one subtle means God has given us of glimpsing His hidden truths.

The unrealised possibility is as much a part of Fate as the actual event. The infinite possibilities surrounding an event are not only the materials out of which the event is made and help to modify or determine the more distant future, but alone give its true & full value to every human or cosmic action.

God or Spirit then is the Master of His processes and their results; He is the law of natural law, therefore free from that law, nityamukta, the cause of Fate, therefore not bound by Fate but its ruler. Action is the free play in His eternal Being, therefore that Being is not bound by the action. Action does not compel in Him any results which He is not free to accept or to avoid;

it does not entail fresh action unless He so chooses, nor does it produce any modification either in His conscious existence or in the modes & phenomena of His conscious existence except so far as He allows those modes or phenomena to be affected or varied. In His essential being God or Spirit is ever immutable, since nothing ever essentially changes even in the universe, much less beyond the universe; and it is only phenomena in the cosmic motion of consciousness that seem to change. Here too sages have perceived that the change is not really a change, but only a successive presentation of ever recurrent phenomena to the Time-governed eye of conscious Mind. These changes are a play of self-ideas in Conscious Being existing for ever beyond Time & Space, but represented for us in the symbols of Time & Space. Such as they are, the succession of these changes affected by action of man or action of Nature are not binding on Spirit, not an inexorable stream of cause & result which Spirit has passively & helplessly to endure, but a harmony or progressive rhythm of successive states which Spirit has freely arranged in itself. Na karma lipyate.

God acts or rather produces action, produces, that is to say, process & succession of manifested energies in His own being without being bound either by the action itself or by its process or by its succession or by its causes or by its results. In action or out of action He is entirely, infinitely & absolutely free.

But then there arises the difficulty caused to our darkened minds by the false conception that God & world, God & the human soul are different entities. From this division of the indivisible there arises the notion, the fatal noumenal error, the illogical logic, that God beyond the world is free but God in the world is bound, bound to action, bound to sorrow, bound to death and birth, — the great fundamental error which seals our eyes & creates needlessly the insoluble problem of suffering & evil and death and limitation, — insoluble because we have created a false first premise for all our conclusions about the world. God in the world is not bound, but only pretends to mind that He is bound. Mind so envisages Him because it sees Him observing freely the arrangements & processes that He has made &, always associating fixed observance in Nature with inevitable observance, supposes Him to be observing His own laws inevitably, helplessly, not freely. All the more then is man, apparently limited, apparently bound in the meshes of a hundred woven laws, supposed to differ precisely in this from the transcendental Being that That is free & untouched by the world & its works, he a slave and moulded by their pressure into what he is now & will hereafter become. Thence the conclusion of so many philosophies that man here can never be anything but a suffering victim of his works & slave of illusion & only by annulling his existence in cosmos can become free, — free not in the cosmos but from the cosmos. But it is not so. For man is the Lord inhabiting His human temple, enjoying his own play in this mortal mansion built by himself out of his own cosmic being; he has determined what he is and is determining now by his play in works as he has previously determined by his play in internal consciousness what he shall become.

God in the world is not different in nature from God beyond the world but the same. Yad amutra tad eveha. God beyond is eternally free; God here is also eternally free. Spirit in all things & spirit in man are one spirit and not different entities or natures; therefore all spirit being eternally free, the soul of man also is eternally free. Mind in its multiple and dual play is, by its non-illumined state, the creator of this illusion of bondage.

We have in the Gita a striking illustration of God's workings in man which raises in a concrete instance and drives home to the mind the whole difficulty with an incomparable mastery and vividness. The armies of the Pandava and the Kaurava stand facing each other on the sacred plain of Kurukshetra; the whole military strength of India & all its political future have been thrown down upon that vast battlefield as upon a dice board. On one side we see the eleven mighty armies of Duryodhana, greatly superior in numbers, led by the three most renowned warriors & tacticians of the day; on the other the lesser host of Yudhisthira commanded indeed by notable fighters but fixing all its hope of eventual victory on the strong arm and invincible fortunes of Arjuna with Krishna, the incarnate Lord of the

world, as his charioteer. But Arjuna, their supreme hope, is on
the point of failing them; he is overcome by the magnitude of the
approaching slaughter, afflicted by the fratricidal nature of the
conflict he has cast down his bow; he has refused to fight. In the
great colloquy that follows & forms the substance of the Gita,
the incarnate Master of things, among a host of profound &
subtle reasonings, uses also this striking exhortation which has
become a commonplace of Indian thought, Mayaivaite nihatáh
púrvam eva, Nimittamátram bhava, Savyasáchin. "By Me are
these already slain & dead, do thou become only immediate
means & determining cause, O Savyasachin." The Universal
Will has seen and arranged from the beginning of this great
world-act, this vastly planned cycle of natural happenings, the
bodily destruction of Duryodhana and his mighty captains; the
bow Gandiva in the hand of Arjuna is only the predestined
nimitta. By the stream of successive events it has brought about
an arrangement of forces in which the nimitta can become operative. There is the preexisting condition; there is the arranged
result; there is the determining factor. But supposing this human
instrument Arjuna, rejecting the command of the Lord of all
things, preferring some hope of spiritual weal, preferring his
own moral self-satisfaction, obstinately refuses to be the engine
of God's will in him, in a work so thankless, bloody & terrible.
What if he listens only to the natural cry of the human heart,
Kim karmani ghore mám niyojayasi Keshava, "Why dost Thou
appoint me, O Lord, to a dreadful work?" We say from our
human standpoint, that even then the Will of God can & will
inevitably be fulfilled by Bhima, by the combined exaltation of
the Panchala heroes, by the sudden greatness, even, — for "He
makes the dumb man eloquent & the lame to overpass the hills",
— of some inferior fighter; and, in the thought & language of
the great infinite Potentiality that stands behind the material
actuality of things, this would be the truth, — but not in the
actuality itself. For in the God-foreseen actuality of things not
only the event, but the nimitta is fixed beforehand. The Cosmic
Being is no blind & chance bungler who misses His expected
tool & has gropingly to improvise another. Arjuna, too, is the

vessel of the universal Will and can only act as It chooses. "The Lord is seated in the heart of all existences, O Arjuna, and He whirls round all existences mounted upon a machine by Maya." Even if Arjuna's mind resists, even if his heart revolts, even if his members fail him, eventually there is a Force greater than the individual & mental will which will, if so destined, prevail upon his mind, his heart, his members. What is that Force? "Prakriti", answers the Gita, "Prakritis twám niyokshyati." The phrase is nowadays ordinarily interpreted to mean that Arjuna's warrior nature will whip him back to the fight. But the thought of the Gita is more profound & far-reaching. By Prakriti is meant the executive World Force, agent of the will of the Ishwara seated in the heart of all existences, that compels the tree to grow, man to think, the king to rule, the poet to create, the warrior to fight. The character of Arjuna is only one means towards her action, & even that acts not by itself, but in conjunction with the character of Duryodhana, of Karna, of Bhishma, of a million others even to the meanest soldier in either army. Yet left to itself the warrior nature of Arjuna might drive him back indeed to the fight but too late to determine its issue; even, it might be, his personal nature, were that God's will, would abdicate its functions, seized & overcome by universal nature, by pity, by vairagya, by fear of sin, and the fateful battle lose its fated nimitta. What is it that, not in free universal potentiality, but in the fixed fact must inevitably determine his return to his normal action? It is the executive Force of the universal Will which not only fixes personal nature, swabhava or swa-prakriti, but fixes too its working in each individual case, not only prepares the circumstance & the means but determines the action & the event. We seem to have here an overriding Fate, an ineluctable Ananke, even a self-acting mechanism of Nature; but it is not a mechanical inevitability, the result of the sum of our & others' past actions, not even a natural inevitability, the result of either a habitual or an ingrained working of our individual nature moved complexly by internal impulses, outward events & the actions of others; but a willed inevitability, seen beforehand in Its universal pre-knowledge by that sole Existence which is expressing itself

here in mind & body, in event & circumstance, and executed by
It as its own Will-Force & universal Nature which works out
automatically through arranged process & perfectly managed
interaction of individual forces that which was foreseen by It &
fixed from the beginning of things, vyadadhách chháswatíbhyah
samábhyah.[6]

We see then that working of Law of Nature & succession
of cause & effect are the process of fulfilment of a Will, a self-
effective Intelligence which is superior to working of law &
governs, not obeys, succession of cause & effect. That Will is
the Lord who inhabits all these animate & inanimate existences,
hriddeshe tisthati, the one universal Soul & is master of the
Jagati, not bound by her motions & actions. Na cha mám táni
karmáni nibadhnanti Dhananjaya. All these actions, O Arjuna,
of which I am the cause, bind me not at all; actions do not cleave
to me, na mám karmáni limpanti. Still, in the universal Soul
of things, we can understand such a freedom & omnipotence;
but the affirmation of the Seer has reference not only to the
universal Ishwara, but to the individual soul, na karma lipyate
nare, action fastens not on the man. How can it be affirmed that
man, the individual soul, has any control over the activity of
the universal Prakriti of which his action is a part, if that action
is predetermined, as the Gita asserts it to be determined, by a
higher all-knowing Will? And if he has no control of any kind,
what freedom can he have from his actions, from their subjective
pressure, from their objective results except the inner freedom of
renunciation, of quietism, of indifference? Man, it would seem,
can only be free by sitting still in his soul and allowing the great
executive world-Force to act out the predestined Will of God,
himself caring not for it & in no way mixing himself in the

---

[6] *The following paragraph was written at the top of the manuscript page. Its place of
insertion was not marked:*
Causality consists merely in the successive conditions of things in the world, one emerging out of another, & the successive groupings, relations & interactions of forces &
processes, by which the Will acts out its rhythm [of] prearranged eventualities. The
mechanism is a mechanism of self-possessed & continually waking consciousness that
knows its whole future, present & past. The fixity of things & events is merely the term
of practical executive wisdom in an original & inalienable freedom.

action. Is it not this freedom that the Gita recommends & is not this the action that the Upanishad enjoins, — action worked out mechanically by Prakriti while the soul watches only & knows that it is not the actor? And as for any other & greater freedom, it can only be the freedom by self-extinction of Nara in Narayana, of the individual man in the universal all-inhabiting Ishwara — if indeed the real goal be not some transcendental Impersonality in which man & world & God are all & for ever extinguished.

We might accept this conclusion but for the distinct injunction of the Seer, bhunjíthāh, thou shouldst enjoy. Divine Ananda in God at play & God at rest, not loss of interest and a quietistic indifference is the human fulfilment contemplated by the Upanishads. The first error of the human mind is to suppose that because our emotions, our desires, our personal will have an apparent effect upon event & fruit of action, they are themselves the real determinants of those events & the sufficient winners of that fruit; they are neither of these things; they are only one spring of the machinery, only one subordinate working of the universal Will. It is what the universal Will beyond all mentality decides & works out, not what the personally acting will in the material brain & heart hungers after, that determines event. Karmanyevādhikáras te, says the Gita, mā phaleshu kadáchana, Thou hast a right to action, but no claim at all on the fruits of action; for the fruits belong to God, they belong to the world-working, they belong to the universal will, they belong to the great purposes of the cosmos & not to any clamorous individual hunger. The second error of the human mind when it perceives itself to be the instrument only of a supreme universal Force or Will, its action to be only a whorl in the stream of universal energy and result to be a predestined event of universal Will partly executable by us, but not independently governable or alterable by our effort, is to argue falsely, confusing the Purusha with the Prakriti, that because our action is subject to universal Nature, therefore the soul also is subject to law of Nature & its only refuge is in quietistic renunciation, in indifference or in the withdrawal from phenomenal living. The real refuge is altogether different; it is the blissful withdrawal from personal hunger & desire, it is the detached but joyous contemplation of individual will as a working of divine or universal Will, it is the withdrawal from egoistic being & the perception of the individual as only a convenient term of the universal Ishwara, of the Jiva as only a form in consciousness of the Ishwara, it is the equal enjoyment of the fruits favourable or adverse not only of individual will, but of the universal will, not only our own joys, but the joys of all creatures, not only the gains which come to our minds & bodies, but those which come to the minds and bodies of all existences; it is to make the joy & fulfilment of God in the world our joy & fulfilment, it is to see one Lord seated in all creatures. This is the delight-filled equality of mind, anandamaya samata, that is in the world our ultimate prize & supreme state in mortal nature, fulfilling itself in a divine freedom equally from desire for the fruit of the action and from attachment to the action itself; the fruit is to be what the Lord has willed, the action is God's action in us for His great cosmic purpose. God Himself, the Gita tells us, has essentially this immortal freedom from desire, & yet He acts entirely; He has this divine non-attachment to the work itself & yet He works & enjoys in the universe & the individual, na me karmaphale sprihá, asaktam teshu karmasu, varta eva cha karmani; for in Purusha He contemplates, blissful & free, Himself in Prakriti executing inevitably His own eternal will in the universe known to Him before the ages began in that timeless, time-regarding conscious self of which we all are the habitations. So is the divine attitude towards existence constituted, the attitude of the Ishwara; a perfect & blissful calm & quietism of the divine soul harmonised & become one with a colossal activity of the divine Power driving before it the ordered whirl of a myriad forces occupying limitless Space & Time towards an eternally predestined end.

It may be objected, that while the divine Purusha standing back from the workings of His Prakriti, not only can be the free upholder, enjoyer & giver of an original & continued sanction to the world-workings, bharta bhokta anumanta, but also, by His eternal immanence as Master of the Will everywhere, is the present Ishwara, the controlling Lord of the action, man, by standing back from the Prakriti as the Soul or Purusha, may be indeed, secondarily to God, the upholder of his individual system, — that formal vessel, adhara, of his soul-states, — may be in some sort sanction-giver to its activities, may be, secretly always & here eventually, the free enjoyer of all world-activities that come within its experience, but is not & because of his individuality cannot be or ever realise in himself the Ishwara, the present Lord and master of Nature. He has freedom, not lordship, — the passive freedom of God in the unmoving Brahman he may indeed acquire or share, but not His active lordship in the moving Brahman. To be mukta but never *ish* would seem to be his destiny. Yet the Gita asserts that the Jivatman also is the Ishwara and the Upanishad declares the identity of the human soul with the divine Lord who inhabits all these motion-built forms of Nature.

In this disparity there is no contradiction. There are two aspects of all existence, the Being & the Becoming, Atman & Sarvabhutani. According as the soul of man either stands out in its human becoming & lives in the twisted triple strand of the mind, body & vital being, of which we are conscious now & here, or, on the contrary, stands back in the divine unity of Sacchidananda, it enjoys either of two states of conscious experience, the individual self-consciousness of the separate Jivatman or the universal divine consciousness of the Jivatman merged or dwelling in God. In the former & inferior self-poise, our status is that of a separate soul, different from the Ishwara & always in some personal relation with Him; a type usually of our human connections with each other & the world, connection of child with parent, servant with master, teacher with taught, friend with friend, enemy with enemy, mechanist & instrument, harp & harpist, or a combination of several kinds of interplay at once, answering to the tangled relations we see in our human existence. This relation, created by the fundamental duality of God's play with His becomings, can be realised by us in our waking consciousness or exist unconscious in our secret soul; but in any case it is a condition of subjection, conscious or unconscious, to the sole Ishwara, since even as enemy or rebel we can act after all only as He chooses, however much, for the delight of the play, He gives us a certain length of rope, a certain range of subjective freedom and lets us believe that we are acting independently of Him or in opposition to His will. But what is it that builds up or constitutes in us these relations of the duality? It is not the soul itself but the activities of the mind, life, body, our thoughts, emotions, sensations; it is not the Purusha but our parts of Nature or parts of Prakriti. The soul or Purusha enjoys these relations because it identifies itself with the activities of Nature working in a special name & form & regards all her other workings from that centre of special consciousness; but since that nature, subject to the universal mechanism and a part of it, is anish, not lord, the soul in mind identifying itself with it is also to its outward consciousness anish, not lord. Nevertheless all the time the soul itself is aware, — not in mind, but beyond it, superconsciously in the veiled, secret & higher parts of our nature where it lives guhahita, — of playing a play, of being itself universal, one with God and lord of Nature as well as its enjoyer. The more we detach ourself from Nature, the more, even in Nature itself, our lordship over her increases, our lordship first over her in our own being, our lordship, secondly, over her in her world-actions. We become more & more in our outward consciousness what the soul really is in the secret caverns of its luminous self-concealment, Swarat Samrat, Self-Ruler & Emperor of existence. Still, until the veil is entirely removed, we are indeed the Ishwara by the present immanence of our will in Life, but partially only, and not only secondarily to God, but in a limited degree. We are indeed always subject entirely to the universal Will or Shakti in Prakriti even when we are increasing our individual control over the processes of her individual and universal working. Still as we become purer channels, more & more of the divine Power pours through us & our motions are invested with a more swift, easy & victorious knowledge & effectiveness upon their environment. But it is only when we stand entirely apart from Nature, yet entirely immanent in her by conscious identification with the universal being, power & bliss of God that we become also entirely Ishwara; for then all walls break down, then with the false separation of individual being from God-being breaks down also the false separation of individual power from God-power and it becomes possible for that divine Knowledge-Will working in us to fulfil infallibly & inevitably its foreseen & intended result, as it fulfils it in the universal working of Nature — foreseen & intended in our waking consciousness, always indeed with a less extended working but still essentially & typically as God works, with a divine science if not the extended divine omniscience, a partial divine victoriousness if not the extended divine omnipotence.

We shall be able to arrive at the precise & practical meaning of this identification & this separation, this detachment & freedom & shall discover the secret of action & rebirth if we look at the actual facts of material life & then at the Vedantic explanation of our conscious existence. We have, to start with, this fundamental divergence already noted between ordinary psychology & the psychology of Vedanta, — the former recognising only three principles, Mind, Life and Matter, or adding at most a fourth, Soul or Spirit, while the latter, with a deeper in-look, a wider outlook, a firmer foundation of daring experiment and probing analysis, distinguishes between various workings of the supra-mental or spiritual principle and encounters in its search seven in the place of three prime elements of conscious being. Sat, Chit, Ananda, Vijnana are four divine unmodifiable principles; they constitute the divine being, divine nature & divine life, and are called in their sum Amritam, Immortality; Manas, Prana, Annam, Mind, Life & Matter, are inferior & modifying principles constituting in their sum in this material world mortal being, mortal nature, mortal life and are called Mrityu or Martya, mortality. The doctrine and instruction of the possibility, the means and the necessity for man of climbing from Mrityu to Amritam, out of Death into divine Life, — mrityum tírtwámritam asnute, is Veda & Vedanta.

The world in which we live seems to our normal experience of it to be a material world; matter is its first term, matter is its last. Life-energy and mind-energy seem to exist as middle terms; but though their existence and activity cannot be denied or ignored, so omnipresent, insistent & victorious is the original element out of which they have emerged that we are led to view them as terms of matter only; originated out of matter, formulated in matter, resolved back into matter, what else can they be than modifications of the sole-existing material principle? The human mind seeks a unity always, and the one unity which seems reasonably established here, is this unity of matter. Therefore, in the fine & profound apologue of the Taittiriya Upanishad, we are told that when Bhrigu Varuni was bidden by his father Varuna to discover, entering into tapas in his thought, what is Brahman, his first conclusion was naturally & inevitably this that Matter is the Sole Existence, — Annam Brahma. "For verily out of Matter are these existences born, by Matter they live, into Matter they pass away and enter in." We arrive, then, by reason considering only the forms of things and the changes & developments and disintegrations of form, at the culmination of materialistic Rationalism and a Monism of Matter. Annam Brahmeti vyajánát.

But here we cannot rest; driven by the Tapas, the self-force of the eternal Truth within, to an ever increasing self-knowledge & world-knowledge, we begin to analyse, to sound, to look at the insides of existence as well as its outsides. We then find that Matter seems to be only a term of something else, of Force, we say, or Energy which, the more we analyse it, assumes a more & more subtle immateriality and at last all material objects resolve themselves into constructions & forms of this subtle energy. Hoping to reconcile our old conceptions & our new results, we make, at first, a dualism of Force & Matter, but we know in our hearts that the two are one & we are driven at last to admit that ultimate unity. But what is this energy? It is, says the Vedanta, Prana, Matariswan, Life-Force or Vital Energy, that which organises itself in man as nervous energy & creates & carries on the processes & activities of life in material form. We find this same nervous & vital energy present also in the animal, the plant; it exists obscurely, it has been discovered, even in the metal. We have, therefore, in the world we inhabit, a unity of Life-Energy in its actions as well as a unity of matter in its formal changes. For modern thinking the problem is complicated by the narrow restriction of the idea of life first, popularly, to the material vessels of a conscious nervous activity, man, the animal, the insect, & then, more widely, to all forms of which organic growth and nervous response are the characteristic activities. Vedantic thought sees, on the contrary, that all energy apparent in matter is one Life-energy; nervous force, electric force, even mental force so far as it works in matter are different forms of one working, which it calls Pranashakti, Energy of Life, formulated force of Existence throwing itself out in the currents & knotting itself into the vessels of its self-adaptive material workings. Life, as we know it, is the characteristic fulfilment of this stream of being. According to the Vedantic idea the characteristic form of any energy is to be recognised by us not in its lowest, but in its highest expression. The higher form is not a new-creation of something previously non-existent out of the lower form, — for such a principle is essentially Nihilistic & leads inexorably to Nothingness as the starting point of existence, and to the Vedantic idea nothing can be created which does not already exist, nothing can be evolved which is not already involved. Life-energy of man is involved in life-energy of plant, metal and sod; it is that which manifests itself by veiled and obscure workings in these more imperfect vessels. We see, then, by closer scrutiny, Matter as only a form of Life, organic or inorganic, perfected in nervous action or obscure in mechanical energies. Obsessed by this discovery, living in this medial term of our consciousness, seeing all things from our new standpoint we come to regard Mind also as a term or working of Life. Bhrigu Varuni, bidden by his father back to his austerities of thought, finds a second and, it would seem, a truer formula. He sees Life as the Sole Existence, Pranam Brahma. "For from the Life, verily, are all these existences born; being born they live by the Life, to the life they pass away and enter in." Our physical body at death is resolved into various forms of energy, the mind which inhabits the nervous system dissolves also and is or seems to be no more, except in its posthumous effect on others, an organised active force in the material world. We arrive, then, by reason considering the energies of things in their forms & the movement [of] forces that constitute their changes, activities, development & disintegration, at the culmination of Vitalistic Rationalism and a Monism of the Life-Energy. Práno Brahmeti vyajánát.

Here too the mind of man, after finding this second goal of its journeyings, discovers that which it took for a final haven to be only a resting place. Life-Energy & Material Form or Substance of Life-Energy constitute together the outward body of sensible things, the sthula sharira or gross body of Brahman. But, as we pursue our analysing and probing, we begin to suspect that Mind is an entity different from either Matter or Life-Energy. Matter & Life reveal themselves to the mind through the senses. Mind, self-existent, self-perceptive, has on the contrary two evidences of its existence; it knows itself by the senses through its own results & outward workings, — it knows itself also both independently of the workings & in their more subtle movements, by itself, in itself, atmanyatmanam atmana. We perceive, besides, that man is essentially a mental and not a vital being; he lives for himself in the mind, is aware of his existence through the mind, knows & judges all things only as they form themselves to his mind. The speculation then inevitably arises whether as we found Life to be concealed in apparently inert matter and eventually knew Life to be the parent & constituent of material forms, we shall not, as the next step of knowledge, find Mind to be concealed in apparently unconscious forms of life-matter, the parent, constituent & motor impulse both of all life-energies & of all forms & forces in which Life here is either formulated or embodied. But there are difficulties in the way of this conception. First, mind knows itself by itself only in the individual body which possesses it; it is unable, normally, to watch itself in other bodies or perceive there, directly, its own presence & workings, it only knows itself there by analogy, by deduction, by perceiving through the senses the outward or formal effects of its presence & workings. All that is outside the individual form it inhabits, my mind knows by the senses only, & its own workings seem to consist simply of the nervous reception of this sense knowledge, the nervous reaction to it, the formulation of this experience in mental values & the various arrangement & rearrangement of the values formulated. Secondly, these values do not appear to be fixed independently by mind, as they would be if mind were the creator of forces and objects; mind appears to us to be not their master but their servant, although sometimes a rebellious servant, not their creator, poietes, but their translator and interpreter. Thirdly, mind seems unable to create life or to create or change material forms by its direct action. I cannot, by willing, add to my stature or change my features, much less alter forms external to my own. Just as it knows only by the senses, the jnanendriyas, so mind seems able to affect life & matter only through its bodily instruments of action, — the karmendriyas. The instances to the contrary are so exceptional, obscure and fragmentary that no conclusion can be formed upon such scattered & ill-understood data.

Nevertheless Vedantic thought insists. Knowledge, taught by experience, distrusts all first appearances & looks always behind them for the true truth of things. What is exceptional we must examine, what is ill-combined we must arrange, what is obscure we must illuminate. For it is often only by pursuing & examining the obscure & exceptional action of a force that we can come to know the real nature of the force itself & the rule of its obvious & ordinary action. It is not through the leap of the lightning, but through the study of the electric wire & the action of the wireless current that we get near to the true nature & the fixed laws of electricity. As life is obscure & imperfect in the plant & metal & its full character only eventually appears in man, so also mind is imperfect, if not obscure in man's present mental workings; its full character can emerge only in a better evolved humanity or else in a more developed &, to present ideas, an abnormal and improbable working of its now hampered forces even in our present humanity. The ancient Vedantins therefore experimented as daringly & insatiably with mind as modern scientists with life-force; they deployed in this research an imaginative audacity & a boundless credulity in the possibilities of mind as extreme as the imaginative audacity &

the boundless credulity in the possibilities of force working in matter deployed by the modern in his more external experiments & researches; they had too the same insatiable appetite for verification & more verification, — for without this harmony of boundless belief & inexorable scrutiny there can be no fruitful science; reason in man cannot accomplish knowledge without force of faith; faith cannot be secure in knowledge without force of reason.

Thus experimenting, the Vedantin discovered above mind in life the principle of pure Mind. He found that mind exists in the cosmos pure & untrammelled, but manifests in material forms imprisoned and trammelled. Mind subject to life & matter, erring in the circle of life & matter, he perceived as mortal mind, martya or manu of the Veda, the human thinker; mind pure & free he perceived as divine mind, deva or daivya ketu of the Veda, the divine seer & knower. He found first that mind really exists in man in its own self-sufficient consciousness, independently of the sense life turned upon the outer material world, even when it can only work or actually only works through the senses. Secondly, he found that mind in one form or body subconsciously & superconsciously knows & can watch mind & mind's working in other bodies directly or by means independent of sense-communication & the watching of speech & action, and can, more or less perfectly, bring this subconscious & superconscious knowledge into the field of our waking or life-consciousness. He found, thirdly, that mind can know external objects also without using the ordinary channel of the senses. He found, fourthly, that the values put by mind upon outer impacts & its reactions to them are determined not by the impacts themselves but by the general formulations & habitual responses of Mind itself in the universal Being and these fixed & formulated values & reactions can be varied by it, can be suspended, can be entirely reversed, can be infinitely combined at will in the individual vessel called the human being. Fifthly, mind can & does by will, ketu can by kratu, used actively or passively, consciously, subconsciously or superconsciously, without the aid of the karmendriyas, modify even life-forms &

action of life-forces, & does it even now, swiftly or slowly, to a greater or less degree, — as is evident from the phenomena of heredity & hypnotism, — can determine directly the action of energy in other bodies, animate or even inanimate, can modify existing forms of things and can even arrive, though with much greater difficulty, at the direct creation of forms by the mental will. All these powers, however, are powers of the pure or divine mind and can only be consciously exercised in our mortality, so long as they are abnormal to it, if & so far as the universal Being originates & sanctions their use in the individual; they can be possessed as normal faculties only by a humanity which has climbed out of its present struggling entanglement in mortal being & the subjection of the motion of mind to the motion of life & matter, by a humanity in other words which has divinised itself & reached the high & free term of its evolution. If these ancient results are at all correct — and the whole trend of modern scientific experiment as soon as it consents at all to dissect practically & analyse and manipulate experimentally mind as a separate force, tends, however dimly and initially, towards their confirmation, — then we can enter on a third stage of the march of knowledge. The intellectual difficulties in the way of our surpassing the vitalistic conception of world have disappeared. We begin to move, at first, towards a noumenistic monism of the universe. For if mind in man can determine, manipulate, modify & create not only the sensational values of forms and forces and impacts, but the forms and forces and impacts themselves, it is because in the universe these values, these forms, these forces have, originally and secretly, been fixed, created and moved by universal mind and are really its evolutions & formations. All forms of life-energy in this world are thus formations of mental force in which the principle of mind broods self-absorbed in work of life and concealed in form of life to emerge in man, the mental being. Just as life, working but form-absorbed and concealed in the clod & metal, has emerged in the plant and the animal to organise its full character and activity, so it is with mind. Mind is omnipresent; it does mechanically the works of intelligence in bodies not organised for its self-conscious workings;

in the animal it is partly self-conscious but not yet perfectly able to stand apart from its works and contemplate them; for the animal has more of sanjna than of prajna, more of sensational perceptive consciousness than of contemplative conceptual consciousness. In man first it stands back, contemplates & becomes truly "prajna", knowledge working with its forms & forces placed before it as objects of its scrutiny. But this evolution is the result and sign of a previous involution. Mind in the universe precedes, contains & constitutes life-action and material formation. Bhrigu Varuni, once more bidden by his father back to his austerity of thought, perceives a third and profounder formula of things. He sees Mind as that Sole Existence, Mano Brahma. "For from mind these existences are born, being born by mind they live, into mind they pass away & enter in." For as all forms that dissolve go back into the life-forces that constitute and build their shapes, so all forces that dissolve must go back into the sea of mental being by which and out of which they are formulated, impelled and conducted. We arrive, by reason investigating the essential causes, governance and constituting intelligence of all these energies & forms which determines & manifests in their functions, methods and purposes, at the culmination of pure idealistic Rationalism & the Monism of mind. Mano Brahmeti vyajánát.

But Vedanta is not satisfied with the noumenal conception of being; it journeys yet farther back. Studying & experimenting with mind it perceives that mind, too, is a special force manifested out of being and not itself the ultimate nature of being. Moreover it sees that we have crudely put together in the single confused concept of mind, a number of very different principles of which the one common characteristic is the possession of a luminous instead of a darkened consciousness informing its waters, not hidden in the cell of its own forms & motions. We have then still to analyse & probe the nature & limits of mind, & we have to sound and discern the nature & limits if any of what is beyond mind. Carrying the conception of knowledge far beyond the mental principle, discovering a Force more puissant and essential than mind-force, arriving at an essential existence other and purer than the mental self-consciousness which is, at present, man's ordinary & common subjective experience of himself, Vedanta finds that Life & Matter are not so much developments of universal Mind, as the subordinate formations and movements, — cooperative with it, although evolved out of it and formed by it, — of a supramental, supravital, supramaterial Something which no terms we have yet understood can describe to our intelligence. In the noumenal conception, the formula of the mental Brahman, we have not, then, yet reached the essential term of the reality of things.

Still, we have already in this triple formula of Mind, Life and Body, corrected by the statement of a more real and potent existence behind them, a sufficient present clue, at least, to the nature, the workings and the goal of mental life in this material universe. The basis of our existence here is Matter, but Matter with life and mind involved in it. Every cell of the human body, every fibre of bark & leaf, every grain of earth treasures in itself a secret life & mind, is the hiding-place of Prajapati, the cocoon of the eternal butterfly. In the lowest inert or inanimate status of matter just so much & such a nature of life-energy has been at work as is sufficient for the creation of its different forms and their maintenance & functioning in the convergent & divergent whirl and shock of all these cosmic forces, and this multiform correlation of an inert substance of energy and an apparently inanimate driving force of energy has constituted material being & established for its purposes both a general nature, swabhava or own being of matter and particular fixed processes of inherent self-action, the vratáni of the Veda, which present themselves to us as the eternal laws of physical Nature.

But since Life is involved in Matter, things cannot rest here: the Truth within things, the pure Idea at work in the world which, secret as well as mind & life in force of matter and form of matter, originates & guides evolution, demands & compels, perhaps by the pull from a higher world where life is the predominant power and basic principle, the evocation of an organised & self-fulfilling Life out of this inert substance and inanimate Life-force. That Life then eventually appears, but naturally &

necessarily, it comes as a stranger into its surrounding. Confronted there with a set of laws imposed by the native sovereign, not at ease with them as it would be with the processes of a world of which it was itself, from the beginning, the sovereign and omnipresent ruler & lawgiver, it has to work on the unfit & rebellious material to raise, vitalise & fit it for its own workings as a slave power or a subordinate energy. It has come in that process, like an alien invader & conqueror, to give and take, to make concessions, to conciliate its stubborn material in order eventually to dominate & use it. By slow processes, by long evolution, by multitudinous experiment Life arrives at the creation of a myriad forms of organised vitality in matter, in which the form has been trained & accustomed to bear & to answer to the workings of life in many varying degrees of intensity or complexity. But, in the end, Life itself has come to be fettered by its material. The processes of matter pursue it, enter into its action, encase and limit its processes. They are intolerant of any attempt to increase the complexity of the life-workings or to raise the intensity of its shocks beyond the limit of the rhythm already established between the form & its inhabitant. As a result of this resistance, the form tends to deteriorate or break in any upward or extensive endeavour. Ordinarily also, it comes about that the more intense & organised the life, the more brittle & easily disturbed in its functions becomes the material form which contains it, unless & until a new harmony is established, a new & higher or subtler rhythm effected.

But the upward evolutionary movement has only begun with the appearance of life; it is not ended. The Truth of things, the pure Idea at work in matter knows that Mind also is involved in Matter & the Truth of things demands & compels its evolution. It procures, again perhaps by the pull from a higher world where mind is the predominant power and basic principle, the liberation of this second and greater prisoner. Mind, like Life, appears but as a stranger and invader in a world in which it has to deal with already established processes of matter and already established processes of life in matter, and is not at ease with them as it would be with the processes of a world in which it was from the beginning a sovereign and omnipresent ruler. Mind, like Life, has to raise its material, mentalise it & make it fit for its own workings, Mind, like Life, to make concessions & conciliate its material. By long evolution, by slow process & multitudinous experiment it arrives at the creation of manifold forms of organised mind consciousness in vitalised matter, which have been trained to harbour & bear its workings. But in the process Mind, like Life, has become to a large extent a slave to its instruments; the processes of matter & material life enter into its action, encase, condition and limit its workings, are intolerant of increasing complexity & intensity, tend to damage or break the form & the functions when subjected to the increasing demand, resist rapid progress. Here too, ordinarily, the more intense the mental action, the more highly organised its faculties, the more brittle and easily disturbed in their functions become the material form and the nervous life, its case & instruments, unless & until a new harmony is established & a new & higher or subtler rhythm effected.

It is now clear that the entire freedom and lordship in Nature of life over matter or of mind over living body can only come if one or more of three essential conditions is satisfied. The inhabitant principle must either develop such a form or establish such an essential harmony with its case & instruments or else get such a hold upon the lower principles that it can at once maintain them in perfect undisturbed existence and compel them to bear a wide, vast, richly filled, even perhaps an infinite intensity & complexity of the functionings of cosmic life-energy or cosmic mind-energy rushing upon its instrument, informing it and using it for its own delight of self-fulfilment. Such a form, such a harmony, such a hold, life would presumably possess in a world where it was the dominant factor, mind in a world similarly subject to its sovereignty. The Veda supposes such worlds to exist; it perceives several births, dwelling places, kingdoms, jana, kshitayah, rajansi, — to the kingdom of matter it gives the name of Bhu, to the kingdom of Life or Life-Consciousness the name of Bhuvar, to the kingdom of pure Mind the name of Swar. It supposes also that the powers of the higher worlds, figured in the three & thirty gods of the Veda & their subordinate deities, support their representative and instrumental beings in Bhu and favour their attempt to establish an increasing & ultimately perfect similar mastery here for Life or Mind over the material world. For such a growth, such a perfection, the invasion [and] subjection of the lower by the higher principle is the first necessity. For we see that Matter here only realises its highest and most complex potentialities even of material development & organisation when it is invaded, possessed & raised by life, Life its highest & most complex potentialities even of vital development & organisation when it is invaded, possessed & raised by mind, and, — although, owing to our clumsy conceptions about mind, this is not so apparent to us, — Mind also can realise its highest & most complex potentialities even of mental development & organisation only when it is invaded, possessed & raised by that which is higher than itself.

Man is, here, the typical mental being. Imprisoned in the vitalised matter he has invaded & struggling, with his real being in Swar and aided by the gods of Swar, to impose the mastery of Mind on the material world, he has, for the achievement of his object, two alternative principles to follow, either to conquer matter by matter, life by life or else to get behind both of them, discover pure mind & its powers & apply them to his eternal object. His achievements in the struggle with the laws of physical Nature on the physical plane itself are even now considerable; he has been able to seize on her physical forces & harness them to processes & results which she with all her large & gigantic movements has never attempted, — and these processes & utilities are all of them stamped with the subtlety, regularity, & conscious purposefulness of liberated mind. Modern man has not yet succeeded in discovering or using the laws of Life, but there is no reason to suppose that he will not one day make that discovery also. The day must inevitably come when he will be able even to originate no less than to modify freely both plant life & animal life in matter & govern them for his purposes as he now originates mechanisms of material force and modifies & governs its currents, combinations and separate workings so as to abridge distance, to invade the air, to economise the expenditure of his own life-energies or to serve a hundred other purposes of human construction, destruction or development. All these efforts are marked, however, by one characteristic & pregnant limitation — they proceed on the assumption that we can only master physical Nature by manipulating & turning against her laws, movements & processes which she herself has originally established for very different objects & to suit a very different status of world-existence. Even, therefore, in conquering, he is compelled to obey and to confine his achievement within the limited capacities of the physical instruments and the physical processes. Having passed in a curiously imperfect & illegitimate fashion beyond his original slavery to her simple & elemental workings, he is menaced with a worse slavery to his own monstrous mechanisms & in danger of missing the path of the Gods, following only the path of the Bhutas. The true process of enfranchisement is rather, having discovered [and] separated the life-principle & its workings from the material processes in which they are fettered so that our vital life & forces may be raised into a sufficient instrument for infinite Mind, having the true pranayama or control of his vital being, to discover & separate also the principle & workings of pure mind from both life & matter and use them for the attainment of an entire mastery over our internal & our external world. In the eyes of the Vedantin a little progress, a minor achievement on the real path is of more value in the end than the vastest & most airy achievements of modern Science. For the latter is only clanking of gymnastics in self-multiplied chains by a strong and agile prisoner, the former is a step, however faltering, on the true path of freedom.

Nevertheless, even if we could so master the laws of mind as to entirely control our vital & physical being & its environment, the end of God in man is not achieved; for we ought not only to control life & matter by mind, but mind by a higher principle. Mind can only become free by self-subjection to God above mind and without freedom there is no true mastery. Samrajya is unreal without Swarajya. Mind that has mastered its inferior principles without obeying the law of a higher Truth, is figured for us in epos and Puran as the victorious Titan, Hiranyakashipu or Ravana, — victorious but doomed in the end to a sudden successful revolt of the lower principles or to direct destruction by Power descending from on high because the mastery it holds is artificial, mechanical, not the aim of Nature in the world & therefore, if eternalised, bound to obstruct the higher destinies of the race. What though it has enslaved the god to its will and compels fire to come at its need or wind to blow where it lists, what though it can control despotically men & things & events? It is not for all that divine nor free nor supreme. Essentially, it does with higher instruments what modern man is now accomplishing with lower instruments; it is using a mental instead of a physical machinery to establish a precarious, temporary & apparent mastery over Nature which only veils a more subtle & tyrannous form of subjection. The Daedalus who multiplies machines, is dependent on his creations, bound by his engines, often destroyed by them and in any case limited & shackled & his gains of one kind balanced by pauperisation in other directions. Not until we have gone beyond machinery, gained self-power, self-being, self-bliss of God, can we hold ourselves secure in the right path and fulfilled in the right object of our ascension. And for this reason, that mind is in its nature bound up with limitation & form and dependent on the centre from which it works. Universal Manas, like universal Life & universal Matter, exists indeed & contains all things in itself, but it contains without comprehending. Its nature is not comprehension, but division, & what it calls comprehension is merely the seizing on details, on fractions and arriving by addition or multiplication at their sum. The integer as mind sees it is not a true integer, for mind is essentially manas, that which measures, contains & is bound by its function of containing. It can by itself arrive only at a pluralist, not an essential unity, or else at a zero. If it passes out of limitation, out of its form, out of its centre, it must be either dissolved into Nirvana, dispersed into the chaos of its unformed & discriminate mental nature or reduced to quietism & immobility. Mind can either rest voiceless & actionless, lost to itself, in the shantam Brahma or it can find itself in the ejad Brahma; but it cannot combine the two opposites, it cannot at once live in the silent stability of God & throw itself into the voiceful motion of things. That is a privilege of the divine and not of the mortal nature. Acting, mind must use the machinery of the triloka, the triple system of mind, life & matter & must submit to it while using it; it can get behind life & matter, it cannot get behind itself into the true & essential infinity. Therefore, of the soul seated in the triple principle, Shankara's dictum is entirely true that it can escape from bondage only by actionless quiescence of the mental self; Buddha's dictum is entirely justified that it cannot find any ultimate solution except by denying & annulling itself in an ineffable Nirvana. Bhrigu Varuni was not allowed by his father Varuna to rest in the formula of the mental Brahma. Sent back to the austerity of his self-contemplation he had to arrive at the perception no longer of the mind but of the pure Idea as the Sole Existence, Vijnanam Brahma.

We arrive, now, at states of being, consciousness & living experience which are far remote from ordinary human life & thinking, for the expression of which human language has neither been framed nor yet adapted. These higher states of being are the guha, the cavern or secret place, of Vedic imagery, and to express their knowledge & experience of them men have always been compelled to resort to arbitrarily conventional word symbols, parables or concrete metaphors which can only serve as hints, signposts, hieroglyphic figures, not as a means of adequate expression. Those who can divine & follow these signposts find the path for themselves & arrive in experience at the truths the figures are meant to indicate. We can only form some idea of the Vijnana by the use of language & terms which properly belong to mental being and thinking and may therefore when applied to another order of facts quite as easily mislead as help to right understanding. Experience is here the only sure means of knowledge; for we have reached a kingdom of being where already nature of knowledge is beginning to pass into nature of identity, separate consciousness of things into luminous oneness with things, basis of external or sensuous observation into basis of internal self-identification and comprehension in a common self-existent & self-same truth of things.

Vijnana, like mind, is a principle fundamentally of knowledge, & not like life a principle of force, or like matter, a principle of substance. Force, knowledge & substance of being are the trinity constituting the activity of the divine Bliss of Being & Will to Becoming in the universe. In the system of Vedanta, pure Being exists as the background, beginning & foundation of all cosmic existence, containing in itself in eternal latency & potentiality of becoming all things that become or do not become in this universe. Becoming, or becoming of any form or force in the cosmos, is subject to the will of God or Brahman, that Unknowable which has manifested Itself in this fundamental term of Atman, Pure Being, Sad Brahman. Pure Being is Pure-Self-Awareness; Sat = Chit, — this is the first formula on which becoming depends. Atman extends itself in the secondary terms of Space & Time, which are conscious values of this biune Being that is Consciousness, Space in this formula representing the term of Being, Time the term of Consciousness; but when analysed or realised, they inevitably reduce themselves back into mere figures of extension of this Being-Consciousness & are seen to have no real existence in themselves. In an universe of consciousness-symbols, they are the first symbols. Chit or Self-Awareness of Brahman has again a double status, a status of rest in self-conscious being and a status of apparent motion in self-conscious being. In this double status it has the value in Conscious Being of a self-existent omnipotent Will manifesting in the extension of Brahman or retaining concealed in its unextension whatever it chooses in whatever process or order of things it prefers. Nimitta,[7] process or order, figured in relation, succession & causality, is the third symbol of consciousness by which cosmos is rendered possible; for it makes possible arrangement of things in the idea of Space & arrangement of happenings in the idea of Time. Will is in its nature Power of Knowledge or Act of Knowledge; therefore,

---

[7] The word nimitta means literally, measured arrangement; ordering in time & space is the essence of the concept of nimitta.

when analysed and realised, divine or cosmic Will is perceived to be Chid Brahman, self-conscious Being, Chaitanya, conscious Spirit, which takes into its possession in being of cosmic self-knowledge and effects in force of self-knowledge figures of Its own concealed & unknowable reality. We see, then, that all becoming in universe is a formal or symbolic manifestation of unknowable God or Brahman effected by Tapas, by the dwelling of self-knowledge on latent truth of being & the consequent forcing it out of its latency in figure of truth for the joy of God's cosmic self-knowledge. That which is to us unknowable X beyond thought & sensation is expressed here by Tapas of cosmic consciousness in theorem & formula of progression constituting the order of forms in the universe. The loosing of the latent out of latency by Tapas is the whole nature of creation in the idea of the Vedantin. The symbol of the creative Ishwara is always the Kavi, the poet-seer who by Tapas, by concentration of self-knowledge figured as creative Will, brings out from latency in his infinite unmanifest consciousness varied forms of himself. Therefore, it is said that when Brahma the Creator was born on the sea of essential substance, the kshirasamudra, it was in answer to a cry of OM Tapas, pealing out over the moveless ocean, that he set himself to the work of creation. The Kavi creates for his self-delight in self-expression and for no other reason. For when we say that the Will chooses, the Will prefers, when we speak of the icchashakti or omnipotent Will of God, we are expressing in terms of Force what is fundamentally in consciousness a movement of Delight or Ananda. For the nature of conscious-Being is bliss. That which the pure unrelated Sad Brahman, not looking towards cosmic self-expression, is aware of about Itself is unrelated self-Bliss; that which the creative Chid Brahman, looking towards cosmos, is aware of in the Sat, is the cosmic delight of self-expression in general & in particular symbols of consciousness, in extension of infinite being & conscious force & in their concentration into determined form of being & determined action of force. When we say that Brahman as Chaitanya, as Consciousness, dwells upon a figure of Itself & brings it out of its latency there where it dwells cavern-housed, guhahita, we imply, — Chaitanya & Ananda, Consciousness & Bliss being one entity, — that Brahman as Ananda, as Self-Delight, fixes on that figure for Its symbolic self-expression. What God delights in, that is His will-to-be in cosmos, that becomes. In the more ancient Vedic terminology this divine principle of Ananda was designated sometimes as mayas, a word which means both love or joy and creative comprehension and sometimes as jana, a word which means at once delight, especially the delight of procreation, productiveness, birth and world. God's delight in things is their birth, their seed of production, their coming into world. Chit Tapas, Consciousness working as Will is the condition & agent of cosmic existence, Ananda is its cause.

Still, we do not yet see clearly what it is that brings about the difference between self-being & symbolic being or becoming. Where is the principle that bridges the gulf between the pure & the figured Brahman? Or what power of consciousness enables the formless to pour itself into forms? It is, says Vedanta, a special principle, a selective power of pure consciousness which all Being possesses, the principle, the faculty of Vijnana. Sacchidananda is a Trinity; Being is in its very essence Bliss [&] Consciousness, Consciousness is in its very essence Being & Bliss, Bliss is in its very essence Consciousness & Being. It is the faculty of Vijnana which, while always resting in their eternal, indefeasible & indivisible oneness, yet casts them into triune figures of being & originates in world their mutual play & their multiplicity. It is vijnana that expresses & arranges the cosmic self-expression of being by looking at Brahman now predominantly in one aspect, now predominantly in another aspect even while it perceives all the others inherently contained in the predominant self-conception. When the vijnana in us dwells thus on the principle of divine Ananda, we see & we work out all things in terms of Ananda; still we are aware all the time of the nature of Ananda as infinite Conscious-Being and the ideas of Consciousness & Being attend & support the Ananda & work themselves out through its workings. When the divine Idea dwells rather on the principle of divine Force or Will in us, then we see & we work out all things in the terms of Force or Will; still the ideas of Consciousness & Bliss always attend & support Will & work themselves out through its workings. We see, then, that essentially Vijnana when analysed & realised reduces itself to the selective & disposing self-action of Chit-Tapas omnisciently aware of the eternally stable unity & eternally potential multiplicity of Brahman and omnipotently able to arrange the terms of that multiplicity from any & every standpoint of Brahman's self-consciousness. It is essential act of knowledge in an essential status of knowledge; its movement is not in the veiled objective manner of mental knowing, but a primary & comprehensive subjective movement in which universal Knowledge sees objects of itself within itself without any veil by reason of an essential identity in motional difference, self-aware self-existent inalienable identity manifested & not contradicted or abrogated [by] difference of form and action, just as a man sees his thoughts & his actions as movements of himself, as self-expression of himself in his own being. There are therefore three essential attributes of the Vedantic conception of vijnana. Vijnana is satyam; it is knowledge proceeding out of an essential identity of being & consciousness between the known & the knower, — the true ideal knowledge may come to a man either through identity of being with the object contemplated or through unity in consciousness with the object or through self-delight in the object, but always it will be self-revealing truth of fact, self-existent truth of being & not formed truth of thought or opinion. Vijnana is also brihat; it is knowledge comprehensive of & containing the object of knowledge in the knower; it possesses, it does not approach — its process moves from the essence to the appearance, from the unit to the parts, from the greater unit to the lesser unit, not from the attribute to the thing, from the fraction to the integer. Vijnana is ritam, is knowledge perfectly self-arranged & self-guided; spontaneously self-arranged in perception & in action spontaneously self-fulfilled through the law of inevitable manifestation of the Truth in its own nature & by its own force, it is the faultless instrument of an unerring omnipotence & omniscience. Satyam ritam brihat, the True, the Right, the

Large, describes God in His being of pure ideal knowledge and self-efficiency.

What is the practical value of this conception of vijnana? The thing we call mind is the knowledge of the individual about himself and of the world only as it affects or reaches his individual consciousness. It is the view of things which a man shut up in a dungeon with glazed & coloured windows may have about the world and his own dwelling place. In the colours of the senses he sees the objects outside, in the light of the few objects it sees through its small & scanty windows & by reasoning from their appearances mind forms its idea of the world; even of this house which it inhabits, it knows only one room with a locked door & all that is outside that door it can only guess at by analogy or infer from the sounds, smells, vibrations which come to its senses from the rest of the building or the occasional visits, messages & descriptions which it may receive from its other inhabitants. For it is now an ascertained truth even to modern psychological observation & experiment, — and was known thousands of years ago to the Vedantin, — that only a small part of our active conscious being is revealed to our waking mental consciousness; a vast amount of work of action, work of impulse, work of knowledge goes either under or above the lower & the upper level of our waking existence and faculty. In the nature of things, therefore, mental knowledge starts from limitation, lives in limitation & ends in limitation. It is dabhram, alpam, says the Veda, not, like the vijnana, brihat; in its nature truncated, oppressed, little. We know nothing certainly except that certain phenomena present themselves in a certain regular way to our senses and are valid within certain limits for our life; on the basis of that sensational experience we can make out a practical rule and order of living. All the rest of mental knowledge may be described [as] a selection of probabilities out of a mass of possibilities. But because mental knowledge is limited & subject to mixed truth & error, therefore also the feelings & impulses of mind in man are subject to falsehood, error, wrong placement, corruption & perversion; in a word, to evil & sin. And since action is only a mechanical expression of mind and feeling, his action also is subject to a resulting falsehood and wrong placement, to evil and sin. Ignorance of self & world is the original error; out of that seed proceeds all evil & suffering. Man, born as a mental being, cannot arrive at right action, right feeling, right knowledge; he can only struggle towards them and approximate to some blundering, limited & imperfect standard of right & truth formed by him out of his fixed notions and habitual feelings. These standards he is continually changing according to the shiftings of his knowledge & the circlings of his knowledge in pursuit of that eternal self-existent Truth & Right which the soul in him knows to exist but the mind & body in him fail to find and accomplish. For mind cannot see the Truth, — the goal & the condition of our journey, — it has to grope after it & feel it; for it has sense of things but not vision of things, mati, not drishti. It does not know the Right, the way of our journey, but has to seek for it; therefore it cannot proceed straight to its goal, but follows a devious & wandering journey. The lower mental life is not only dabhram & alpam, says the Veda, but it is hvaram & vrijinam, in action of knowledge & action of heart & action of body a crooked going, not like the action of vijnana, riju, straight-moving.

We distinguish then between vijnana & manas. Vijnana is brihat, limitless & comprehensive in its nature and process, because free from individuality, apaurusheya, and universal in its movement and origin; therefore it is true, satyam, in essence and true, ritam, in arrangement. Mind is alpam, limited in its nature because proceeding from an individual centre [and] standpoint and bound in its movement and origin; therefore it admits of asatyam and anritam, error & falsehood or misplacement, — for all falsehood & error is misplacement of truth, all manas diverted action of vijnanam — in the essence & arrangement. Vijnana is, because ritam, therefore riju, right or rectum, the straight — because it is in its nature right arrangement in right being, therefore it proceeds straight by the right way to the right goal with an assured, luminous & self-existent rightness of impulse, rightness of feeling & rightness of action. Mind is hvara; not knowing but seeking, it gropes & circles through falsehood either to truth or a worse falsehood; through sin & stumbling either to righteousness or to a worse sinfulness. Vijnana has for its process of knowledge drishti; thought of vijnana sees, it does not search; it starts from knowledge, it does not start from ignorance; it starts from the essence, not from the appearance; it begins with the essential truth, Brahman, & sees in it the general truth, the idea, the kavya of the kavi, which creates the mental, vital & material symbol, from the general truth it proceeds to detail & particular, from the idea to the working out of the idea in process, attribute, quality & variation. Reasoning in vijnana is only an arranged statement of already possessed knowledge; it is not a means of arriving at truth, but only of orderly stating of truth. Mind has for its process, mati; mind feels & senses, it does not see, for what it calls sight is only a form of touch or contact with its object from outside, not the internal knowledge of the object as a thing contained in the knower. It starts from ignorance & struggles towards knowledge, it grasps only appearance and can do no more than speculate about essence; starts from the fragments & pieces the whole, starts from the particular & perceives the general as a mental abstraction, not a living reality; proceeds from its abstract generalisation & infers essence but cannot come into the real presence of Being. Reasoning in mind is a statement of successive perceptions of data to arrive at a conditionally valid inference, not at a self-existent and for ever indubitable truth. Mind starts with a dark ignorance in the shape of non-knowledge or false knowledge & ends with a twilit ignorance in the shape of agnostic uncertainty.

Clearly, then, if this faculty of vijnana exists, is of this nature & has these relations to mind, then the path of our evolution and, consequently, also the right direction of our efforts is clear; it is, having exceeded nervous life & body, to exceed mind also and arrive at the culmination of right knowledge, right feeling, right works in the spontaneous & infinite mastery & liberty of the vijnana. It is rational to suppose that such a principle exists; for, given the existence of a self-existent Truth at all, supposing that all is not, as the Nihilistic Buddhist contends, a sensation-troubled void, then a self-acting faculty of knowledge responding to & perceptive of the self-existent Truth is at least probable and seems to be demanded. If, moreover, we consent to the Vedantic idea of the world as a creative form & rhythm of consciousness, this logical probability becomes an obvious and inevitable necessity. Self-existent Truth of things can in that theory be nothing else than self-perceptive Truth of conscious being. The existence of a world of objects of universal consciousness arranged in fixed relations & processes presupposes the existence of this principle of Vijnana & therefore of the faculty of Vijnana. It may, however, be reasonably questioned whether, even if the faculty exists, it is not a divine privilege denied to man as much as to the tree and the insect. Is not man unchangeably a mental being, not only at present fixed in mind as his centre, but eternally imprisoned in it as his element, continent and condition of existence? But such a rigid limitation is inconsistent with what we know of man and of Nature. Nature moves by steps & gradations out of one stream of her movement into a higher law. She has established a rudimentary reason in the animal which has perfected itself in the supreme animal, man. Equally she has established a rudimentary form of vijnana in man which has to be perfected in the inevitable course of her evolution, and must perforce be perfected here in no other being than a supreme humanity or supreme man. She has first arranged an illegitimate form of vijnana in the intellect, the mental buddhi or human reason, which has all the movements of the vijnana, perception, arrangement, synthesis, analysis, but is unable to arrive at its proper methods & results because it limits itself to the province of the senses and has for its one right function to train these mental servants & purify them from the control of yet lower elements of our being, the grosser life functions, the body, the nervous heart-movements. Above the reason & sending down its higher rays into the human intellect she has seated the vijnana-buddhi, the intuitional mind. Animals have an intuitional sense, they have not the intuitional intellect; man has access to a true intuitional mentality, and there is his right door to release from subjection to the sensational mentality he shares with the lower creatures. When he has fulfilled reason,

—not before,—he has to surmount reason, to silence it just as reason has silenced the brute passions, and lift up its faculties nearer to their true nature, mode and function, to the intuitional mind, which then, unbesieged by the sense mind & the erring intellect, can receive the pure rays from above of the luminous & divine Vijnana.

The evolution of vijnana out of mind is inevitable for the same reason that the evolution of life out of matter was inevitable or the evolution of mind out of life, because the vijnana or pure Idea, already involved in matter, life and mind, demands & will procure, perhaps by the pull from a higher world where the Idea would be the dominant power & basic principle, its own release out of the limitations of sensational mentality. Just as we found matter to be a formation out of life-energy, & life-energy to be a formation out of mind, so mind is a formation out of vijnana. That which has constituted & governs stone or tree, animal or man, is not matter, nor life, nor mind, but the Idea involved in these three masks of conscious being. The idea of the tree in Brahman's consciousness is hidden involved in that form of life-energy which our senses see as a seed. In reality, the seed of the oak tree holds at the back of its intended evolution the potential seminality of all trees that have existed or can exist, because the Idea, the Brihat, by which it exists, is the Brahman in all Its vastness, Brahman whose process in Nature is to dispose variously one seed of things so as to form a myriad various existences. Ekam bījam bahudhā vidadháti. But by successive selective processes of vijnana the form specially fixed in the seed, inherent & latent in it & bound to develop out of it, is first tree and then oak tree. For this reason and no other, an oak tree & no other existence must develop out of the seed the earth has received. It is the involved Idea, is the Vijnana Consciousness of God, which dwells in the seed, has chosen and prepared this form and supports, governs & directs by the mere fact of its inherent existence there the processes, arrangements, life & functionings of the oak tree. We do not see this truth because the form God takes is still a material form without an organised mental consciousness. It is only when we arrive at human life that, a little more clearly, & yet still very dimly, this truth begins to show itself. To our lower or material mind, for instance, a nation is an intellectual fiction; the reality is only a number of men agreeing for certain material ends to call itself a nation and living in an artificial idea of unity created by the associations born of a mere word. But, first, the intuition-sense we share with the animals by means of the emotional heart, then the reason seeking to find a cause, a formula and justification for the vitality of the nation-idea and, finally, the intuitive mind, looking behind the phenomena of the senses, begin to draw near to the real truth. In real truth a nation is an existence in the universal Consciousness, an Idea-Force in the universal Will that is knowledge, not constituted by geographical boundaries, nor by a given sum or combination of human units, nor by a common language, religion, custom, laws, government, — for all these conditions may be satisfied without a nation existing or dispensed with or exceeded without the nation ceasing to exist, — but created by the idea & living in the idea. Born of the idea in the Brahman, it exists by the force of the idea and only so long as that force supports it & needs the form for its self-fulfilment; the force withdrawn, the form departs into the general Idea force which is constantly grouping men and animals, plants & worlds into figures of corporative Brahman-consciousness, and entering into it either there dissolves or waits for fresh emergence in other time, place & conditions. What is true of the corporate mind-life of the nation is true of the individual mind-life also, of man, the animal, tree, stone, insect. "From the Idea all these existences were born; being born, by the idea they live; to the idea they pass away & enter in." But not till man appears in the material world, does it begin to be possible for the Idea to produce a form of mind, life and body which will be able to house & express the vijnanamaya ideal being, the god in the universe and can be prepared to bear the activity of a divine force & divine joy and, breaking the walls of the mental ego, enlarge into the wideness of a cosmic consciousness. The gods, it is said in the Upanishad, presented by the Spirit with successive forms of animal life for their habitation, returned always the answer, "This is not enough for us." Only when human life appeared, did they utter the cry of assent, "This indeed is well & wonderfully made," and enter satisfied into their fit dwelling. But to fulfil the great purpose of its being, humanity has first to learn how to break down the dungeon of mind and unlocking the doors of the one room in its dwelling-place vindicate for himself a free movement in his seven storied mansion. By passing from mind to vijnana, he will possess in his nature that toward which he now only gropes & aspires, a being that has conquered the limitations of ego, a cosmic knowledge that looks at truth direct & unveiled, a perfectly tuned heart whose emotions & impulses are in harmony with the diviner truth of things, an inner & outer action which, free from the duality of sin & virtue, is unstumbling in its spontaneous movement, confident in its pure & inalienable joy, self-effective of its own God-given objects without passing through the pangs of personal desire, straining and disappointment born of wrong aim, wrong method or wrong emotional reaction. Human life & being will then be moulded into the forms of the satyam, ritam, brihat. For man knowing himself & the world, man will work out his life spontaneously as the sun moves or the oak tree grows, by the force of the idea working out the swabhava, own nature, own or proper becoming. For dharma, right life & action in man and in every other existence, is swabhavaniyatam karma, works directed & governed by the inborn nature to fulfil the divine idea symbolised in the type & embodied in the individual. But in the sun & oak tree it works mechanically without an organised consciousness & joy of the work expressed in the form inhabited. Man fulfilled will enjoy consciously the perfect workings of God's Prakriti in him.

The Life Divine

[Draft C]

Chapter II

The perfect truth of the Veda, where it is now hidden, can only be recovered by the same means by which it was originally possessed. Revelation and experience are the doors of the Spirit. It cannot be attained either by logical reasoning or by scholastic investigation, — na pravachanena, na bahuná srutena . . . na tarkenaishá matir apaneyá. "Not by explanation of texts nor by much learning" . . . "not by logic is this realisation attainable." Logical reasoning and scholastic research can only be aids useful for confirming to the intellect what has already been acquired by revelation and spiritual experience. This limitation, this necessity are the inexorable results of the very nature of Veda.

It is ordinarily assumed by the rationalistic modern mind, itself accustomed to arrive at its intellectual results either by speculation or observation, the metaphysical method or the scientific, that the sublime general ideas of the Upanishads, which are apparently of a metaphysical nature, must have been the result of active metaphysical speculation emerging out of an attempt to elevate and intellectualise the primitively imaginative and sensational religious concepts of the Veda. I hold this theory to be an error caused by the reading of our own modern mental processes into the very different mentality of the Vedic Rishis. The higher mental processes of the ancient world were not intellectual, but intuitive. Those inner operations, the most brilliant, the most effective, the most obscure, are our grandest and most powerful sources of knowledge, but to the logical reason, have a very obscure meaning and doubtful validity. Revelation, inspiration, intuition, intuitive discrimination, were the capital processes of ancient enquiry. To the logical reason of modern men revelation is a chimera, inspiration only a rapid intellectual selection of thoughts or words, intuition a swift and obscure process of reasoning, intuitive discrimination a brilliant and felicitous method of guessing. But to the Vedic mind they were not only real and familiar, but valid processes; our Indian ancients held them to be the supreme means of arriving at truth, and, if any Vedic Rishi had composed, after the manner of Kant, a Critique of Veda, he would have made the ideas underlying the ancient words drishti, sruti, smriti, ketu, the principal substance of his critique; indeed, unless these ideas are appreciated, it is impossible to understand how the old Rishis arrived so early in human history at results which, whether accepted or questioned, excite the surprise and admiration even of the self-confident modern intellect. I shall try to show at a later stage what I hold to be, in the light of the psychological experience of Yoga, the exact processes involved in these ancient terms and their practical and philosophical justification. But, whatever the validity attached to them or the lack of validity, it is only by reproducing the Vedic processes and recovering the original starting point that we can recover also whatever is, to the intellect, hopelessly obscure in the Veda and Vedanta. If we know of the existence of a buried treasure, but have no proper clue to its exact whereabouts, there are small chances of our enjoying those ancient riches; but if we have a clue, however cryptic, left behind them by the original possessors, the whole problem is then to recover the process of their cryptogram, set ourselves at the proper spot and arrive at their secret cache by repeating the very paces trod out by them in their lost centuries.

All processes of intellectual discovery feel the necessity of reposing upon some means of confirmation and verification which will safeguard their results, deliver us from the persistent questioning of intellectual doubt & satisfy, however incompletely, its demand for a perfectly safe standing-ground, for the greatest amount of surety. Each therefore has a double movement, one swift, direct, fruitful, but unsafe, the other more deliberate and certain. The direct process of metaphysics is speculation, its confirmatory process is reasoning under strict rules of verbal logic; the direct process of science is hypothesis, its confirmatory process is proof by physical experiment or by some kind of sensational evidence or demonstration. The method of Veda may be said to have in the same way a double movement; the revelatory processes are its direct method, experience by the mind and body is the confirmatory process. The relation between them cannot, indeed, be precisely the same as in the intellectual methods of metaphysics & science; for the revelatory processes are supposed to be self-illumining and self-justifying. The very nature of revelation is to be a supra-intellectual activity occurring on the plane of that self-existent, self-viewing Truth, independent of our searching & finding, the presumed existence of which is the sole justification for the long labour of the intellect to arrive at truth. In Veda drishti & sruti illumine & convey, the intellect has only to receive & understand. Experience by the mind & body is necessary not for confirmation, but for realisation in the lower plane of consciousness on which we mental and physical beings live. We see a truth self-existent above this plane, self-existent in the satyam ritam brihat of the Veda, the True, the Right, the Vast which is the reality behind phenomena, but we have to actualise it on the levels on which we live, levels of imperfection & uncertainty, striving & seeking; otherwise it does not become serviceable to us; it remains merely a truth seen and does not become a truth lived. But when we moderns attempt to repeat the Vedic revelatory processes, experience by the mind and body becomes an indispensable confirmatory process, even a necessary preliminary process for their acquisition; for the use of these supreme instruments of intuitive & revelatory knowledge is naturally attended, for those to whom the intellect is and has always been the chief and ordinary mental organ, by dangers and difficulties which did not to the same extent pursue the knowledge of the ancient Rishis. To them it was natural in its possession, easily purified in its use; to us it is a difficult acquisition, hampered in its use by the interference of the lower movements. Experience is, for us, indispensable; we may not be certain of excluding by its means all false sight and false intuition, but we can correct much that has been imperfectly seen

and confirm beyond the possibility of all intellectual scepticism
that which does clearly come down to us as illumination from
our Higher self to be confirmed in life & experience, constantly
and regularly, by our lower instruments.

We have, for instance, the remarkable passages in the Isha
Upanishad about the sunless worlds, the luminous lid concealing
Truth, the marshalling & concentration of the rays of Surya
& his goodliest form of all, that form which, once seen, leads
direct to the supreme realisation of oneness, So'ham asmi. Our
intellect sees in these expressions a brilliant poetry, but no deter-
minable philosophical sense; yet no one can follow thoughtfully
the succession of the phrases without feeling that the Seer of the
Upanishad did not really intend to lead up to the direct clarity
of his supreme philosophical statement by a flight of vague poetical images; he has a more serious meaning, detailed, definite,
precise, pregnant, in the carefully arranged procession of these
splendid images. How are we to discover it? Using the scholastic
method we may hunt for a clue in the other Upanishads; we may
find it or imagine we have found it and by the aid of speculative
inference and a liberal dose of fancy we may construct a brilliant
or even a plausible theory of the Rishi's meaning. Or, without
any such clue, by the aid of a clear intelligence and putting
together of the ascertainable ideas of Veda or Vedanta, we may
fix a meaning which will adequately explain the text, fit into
the course of the argument and, in addition, justify itself by
shedding light on other passages where there is a reference to
the Sun, to its rays or to its revelatory function. These means,
however, can only conduct us to a plausible hypothesis, a twilight certainty, or at most a convincing probability. Nor, in this
passage at least, will the metaphysical methods of Shankara at
all assist us; for it is a question not of metaphysical logic but
of the meaning of an ancient symbol, the connotation of certain
antique figures. On the other hand, if we have been able to
revive by Yoga the old methods used by the ancients themselves,
we may, either in the ordinary course of our experiments or
guided by the suggestion of the Upanishad, arrive at the actual
experiences on which, in Vedic times, the use of this symbol and

these figures was founded. We may perceive in our own selves the interposition of the golden vessel, the action of the rays, their disposition, their concentration; we may have the vision of the goodliest form of all, tejo yat te rupam kalyanatamam, and know, by luminous experience, the link between that vision and the realisation of the supreme Vedantic truth, So'ham asmi. We shall then be certain of our knowledge, our unity with the one & only existence. If the ancient ideas of our psychology are correct, by process of revelation and intuition we could have arrived at the same results; the old Rishis, accustomed to use that process habitually and follow its progressive action with as much surety and confidence as we follow the steps of a logician, would have needed nothing more for certainty, though much more for realisation; but we, habitually intellectual, pursued into the higher processes, when we can arrive at them, by those more brilliant and specious movements of the intellect which ape their luminosity & certainty, could not feel entirely safe & even, one might say, ought not to feel entirely safe against the possibility of error. The confirmation of experience is needed for our intellectual security.

This method, by which, as I hold, the meaning of Veda can alone be entirely recovered, is, then, a process of psychological experiment and spiritual experience aided by the higher intuitive or revelatory faculties, — the vijnana of Hindu psychology, — of which mankind has not yet, indeed, anything but a fitful and disordered use, but which are capable of being, within certain limits, educated and put into action even in our present transitional & unsatisfactory stage of evolution. It differs from the method by which the ancient Rishis received Vedic truth, — revelation confirmed by experience, — only by the side of approach which must be for us from below, not from above, and the weight of the emphasis which must rest for a mentality preponderatingly intellectual and only subordinately intuitional, on experience more than on intuition. For the rest, the common consent of humanity has agreed that only by higher than intellectual faculties can the truths of a supra-human or supra-sensuous order, if at all they exist, be really known. Religion, except in ethical & rationalistic creeds like Buddhism and Confucianism which have put aside all such questionings as outside the human domain, has always insisted that revelation is the indispensable angel and intermediary and the intellect at best only its servant, assistant and pupil. Science & rationalism have virtually agreed to this distinction; they have accepted the idea that all knowledge, which does not reach us through the doors of the senses and, on its arrival, submit its pretensions to the judgment of the reason, is incapable of solution by the intellect; but they add that, for this very reason, precisely because the senses are our only doors of experience and the reason our only safe counsellor, the questions raised by religion and metaphysics are utterly vain and insoluble; they relate either to the unknowable or the non-existent; either the material only exists, or, if there is any other existence, the material only can be known and therefore alone exists for the purview of humanity. As man marches upon the dust and is circumscribed by the pressure of the terrestrial atmosphere, so also his thought moves only in the material ether and is circumscribed within the laws & results of material form and motion. Recently we see, even in Europe or chiefly in Europe, — for Asia is too busy imitating Europe of yesterday to perceive whither Europe of today is tending, — a revolt against this arbitrary denial of the rarest parts of human experience. The existence of the supra-sensuous & the infinite is reconquering belief and, at the same time, it is coming again to be admitted that there are faculties of intuitive & supra-rational knowledge which answer in the domain of Consciousness to these supra-sensuous facts of the domain of Being. The belief & the admission go together rationally. For to every order of facts in Nature there should be in the same Nature, inevitably, a corresponding order of faculties in knowledge by which they can be comprehended; if we have no certain knowledge of the facts, it is because we have not as yet the clear and steady use of the faculties.

In three of the external aids by which Veda has been perpetuated in India, religion, Yoga, the guru-parampara, this fundamental principle is amply admitted. Religion starts from revelation; it rests upon spiritual and moral experience. Yoga, admitting the truth of verbal revelation, the word of God & the word of the Master, yet starts from experience and rises, as a result of experimental development by fixed methods, to the use of intuitive and revelatory knowledge. The Guru-parampara starts with the word of the Guru, accepted as the knowledge of one who has seen, and proceeds to personal mastery by the experience of the disciple who may indeed go beyond his master & even modify his knowledge, but is not allowed to disown his starting-point. But there is one of our great Indian spiritual activities which has developed progressively in the direction of rationalistic methods and given the responsibility for nine-tenths of its work in these supra-sensuous fields to the very organ, pronounced by the consensus of human opinion insufficient for such inquiries, — the intellect. It is in Darshana, in the path of metaphysics, that this paradoxical phenomenon has been permitted. It is true that our metaphysical thinkers, unlike the European, do not launch themselves into the full flood of metaphysical rationalism; they hug the coast. They admit the supreme authority of revelation, but only of verbal revelation, of the spoken Veda. But the sense and the bearing of the Vedic text has long been doubtful and warring philosophies have founded themselves on the sacred Word; how is doubt to be resolved, dispute to be decided? By appeal to other texts? But if there is still dissonance, not entire consonance? By the aptavakya, the word of the fit authority. If that fails or there is, here also, a conflict? By logic; the intellect is called in as the arbiter of the sense of the Sruti. The word of the adept, the aptavakya, is admitted; but different Masters seem to have taught different doctrines. Who or what is to decide? Let it be settled by logical argument. Once more the intellect is called in as supreme judge; neither the Sruti, nor aptavakya, but logical judgment becomes the real master of our knowledge. Psychological experience also is admitted in certain fields of the argument; but men have different experiences, even different ultimate experiences. Adwaita asserts the pure self as an ultimate experience of consciousness; Buddhism denies it, holds it to be an illusion and goes beyond to the experience of psychological Nothingness. Yet again, logical argument is called in to decide the question. Therefore we find that our metaphysical method of arriving at the higher truth is practically, — though in theory this is subject to certain qualifications, — as much an intellectual & logical method as the method of European metaphysics or the method of scientific rationalism. Only, the Indian metaphysician admits certain data, values certain orders of evidence, which are ruled out of court as invalid or irrelevant by European thinkers. The scientific rationalist observes the sensible facts of life & Nature; these are the data on which alone he feels himself entitled to build his conclusions. The European metaphysician observes the general facts of sensible existence and adds to them the study of words, abstract concepts & categories which answer to no concrete existence, but are the general forms into which human thought has cast itself; these vast nebulae are the metaphysician's data. It is in this ethereal void that he disports himself in a grandiose freedom. The Indian thinker adds to the generalities of natural phenomenon and the abstractions of thought two other classes of evidence, the facts of psychological experience and the word of the revealed Scripture or of competent authorities. But he uses them sparingly & as a last resort. All that is really solid in our metaphysics (I except Patanjali's Yoga Shastra which stands by itself in the six Darshanas,) consists in its parts of logical inference and analogy; — we value in it not what it builds on revelation & experience, but its strenuous manner of justifying certain great assertions of Veda & high experiences of spiritual seekers by the reason and by logical disputation. The method of Darshana, the way of Shankara and Buddha, although it works round and upon certain grand psychological experiences, Maya, Nirvana, is essentially speculative and logical, not intuitive and experiential.

How came this method to be substituted for the old Vedic tradition and what is its real validity? The question has a great practical importance; for every Indian thinker[1] who approaches

---

[1] The only exception, to my knowledge, is Swami Vivekananda and even he has not entirely escaped the necessity of his environment.

these questions feels himself naturally impelled to be metaphysical in his method or his atmosphere and follow, with whatever modern variations, the path of Shankara, Buddha and the Sankhyas. The way of knowledge has become in India the way of metaphysical disquisition. Are we really bound to continue this tradition or is the more ancient method also the right method, to which humanity must eventually return; and, if so, what have we gained or lost by this more than millennial substitution of speculation for revelation and verbal logic for actual experience? The substitution itself has come about by a powerful general movement of humanity, simultaneous throughout the world, although it most thoroughly affected Greece and through Greece extended to the general temperament & thought of modern Europe. It cannot quite be said that Greece invented the intellect or the intellectual temperament, but it is certain that the Hellenic race first began the application of reason, inexorably, to the remoulding of thought & life in the temperament of intellectuality. Mankind can never be wholly rational, because our race is essentially built up of various elements, none of which can be eliminated from its system of being. It is our nature to be physical, animal, emotional & sensational as well as intellectual and the coldest thinker or most inexorable rationalist cannot escape from the constitution of our common nature. But mankind, under the great impulse which overtook it at a certain stage of its conscious activity, felt the need of rationalising, as far as that could with safety be done, its other irrational members, the heart, the senses, the life-action, even the body. This tendency, pursued simultaneously by Graeco-Roman civilisation, by Confucian China, by philosophical & Post-Buddhistic India, combated in India by the vitality of Yoga and religion, in Europe by the great united floods of barbarism and Catholic Christianity, has finally triumphed and reached a pitch of success, an extent of victorious propagation which, in human movements, is usually the precursor of arrest and decay. The movement of pure intellectualism has itself, indeed, no clear premonition of its own end. It hopes to conquer, to perpetualise itself, to bring under its sway the nations that are still exempt from its yoke or only imperfectly subdued to it; outwardly it seems to be on the point of success. It still holds the mind of Europe, although the soul of Europe begins to attempt uneasily an escape from its narrowing rigidity & dryness; it has seized on Mongolian Japan & is revivifying the traditional intellectualism of China by a flood of fresh ideas, by the inspiration of a new & wider horizon; it has touched already the Mahomedan world; the political subjugation of India has been followed by a pervasive invasion of European intellectualism which is striving hard to substitute itself progressively for the ancient law & nature of our Indian temperament and being. But these manifestations, however overwhelming in appearance, however conclusive they seem of approaching victory, conceal the seeds of a profound revolution in the inverse sense. An outward conquest is often the means of an inward defeat. What is happening now, has happened before on a smaller scale and under less developed conditions. When the combined intellectuality of Greece and practical materialism of the Latins, supported by the conquering military force of the Roman Republic and Empire, came into contact with the old tradition of Asia, the result was the collapse of the politically victorious civilisation under the assault of an Oriental religion which in its tenets & methods not only exceeded but trampled alike on the vital force of the body & on the free play of the intellect, alike on Greece & on Rome. And it was from a part of Asia which underwent directly the Roman yoke, but persisted with the most deep-rooted perseverance in its spiritual traditions that the revanche proceeded; conquered Judaea took captive the victorious civilisation. Once more Europe, much more profoundly intellectualised, much more profoundly materialised in its intellectualism, throws itself upon Asia with a yet more supreme military force, compelling a yet more widespread political subjugation; once more a penetrating eye can discover the preparation of the same result obscurely outlining itself behind the deceptive appearances of the moment. The first effect on the West from this impingement of the mental atmosphere of Europe on the mental atmosphere of Asia and the breaking down of the walls that separated them has been the revival of the invincible intuitionalism of the Aryan or Aryanised races. The philological tripartite division of the Old World into the Aryan, Semitic & Mongolian peoples, even if it be ethnologically untenable, does correspond roughly to real divisions in the cultural temperament of the human race, the result much less of original race than of historical formations & past influences. The Mongolian is predominantly intellectual, his lower nature is largely tamed & rationalised, the intuitive parts of his mind are slow and their beats tepid in their impulse; there is much less in his temperament to resist the intellectualising process of rationalism than in any other portion of humanity; in the Semite intellect is subordinated, he is intuitional, but intuitional through his lower members only, with as much of the higher activity as the heart & senses allow; the Aryan is intuitional either directly or through and by the heart and the intellect. The Aryan is therefore unfitted by his temperament to persevere in the relentless rationalising of our whole being; always there comes a time when he pauses, listens to a voice within that he has disregarded and, convinced by that inner daemon, departs from the paths hewn for him by the sceptical intellect with the same speed and enthusiasm with which he has followed their straight & level vistas. The very nations which are today the hope of a purely intellectual civilisation, hold in themselves that which can never remain satisfied with the pure reason, and this ineradicable betraying force is now being powerfully stimulated by the mental currents which for almost a century have been consciously or subconsciously reaching Europe with a slowly increasing force from the East. Therefore, the repetition, no doubt in a very different form & to very different issues, of the miracle of Christianity is psychologically inevitable.

If indeed, as modern thought imagines, intellectual reason were the last & highest term of evolution, this consummation need not have been inevitable, or, if inevitable, it would have been deplorable; for perfection depends on the rule of our highest member over its inferior cohabitants. But our evolution is only the progressive unfolding of our nature and faculties, & in the list of those faculties reason does not hold the highest place; it is not even a separate and independent power, but a link, servant and intermediary. Its business, when it is allowed to rule, is to train the lower man so as to make him a fit vessel for an activity higher than its own. The animal is content to follow his impulses under the flashlight of instinct. If ever, as is likely, there was a time when man also was a supreme animal, he must have been guided by an instinct different, perhaps, in its special kind but as trustworthy as animal instinct & of the same essential nature. It was, then, the development in us of that reason which we see ill developed in the animal which deprived man of his sure animal instinct & compelled him to seek for a higher guide. Everything goes to show that he must have sought it at first in the lower intuition & revelation which works in the heart, the aesthetic impulses, the senses. Again, it is the insistent development of reason that has served to make him dissatisfied with these powerful, but still inferior guides. But not until reason, without lapsing back to the lower movements, yet becomes permanently dissatisfied with its own limitations, can it fulfil its work of preparation. For there is a faculty in us superior to the rational, there is that direct seeing & touch of things which shows itself in the higher revelation & intuition & works obscurely, like a fire enveloped in smoke, in the phenomena of intellectual genius & unusual personality. Beyond direct seeing there is a faculty of direct being, if I may so express it, which, if we can entirely reach & hold to it, makes us one with God, brahmabhúta, can reveal in this material life the perfection of Brahman as it is intended to be manifested in humanity, so that man on the human level, in the human cadre, becomes perfect as God is perfect. The intellect itself cannot reach these heights. It can only discipline, chasten & prepare the lower members to receive & hold without harm or disintegration that higher force which has alone the power to raise us to the summits. In the intellectual ages of mankind, reason forgets these limitations; it tries to do a double work, to judge correctly all the knowledge which presents itself to the sensorium & its instruments and also to know things directly & in their essence. The former is its legitimate work & deserves the name of Science; the latter is an illegitimate attempt to go beyond its sphere and conceals an error under the name of Metaphysics. The intellect can know & judge phenomena; by its labour in examining them it arrives, in spite of much presumption & error, at a considerable number of phenomenal certainties; but it cannot know & judge the essence of things; by attempting to examine that field, whether unaided or as the principal inquirer, it only arrives, if it is honest with itself, at this one truth, that it can be certain of nothing; — all the rest is appearance, asseveration or opinion. We can know things as they seem to be in the order of the physical Nature in which they live; by the reason we cannot be sure what anything is, in itself, in that order of realities of which physical Nature is only the external seeming. Therefore the last refuge of reason, when it becomes conscious of its blunder, is to deny that such an order of realities exists at all, & to confine itself to the knowledge of material & phenomenal certainties. But such a restriction of knowledge brings with it a lowering, narrowing & petrifying of our humanity, because contrary to the whole nature and ineradicable tendency of our kind & sure therefore to falsify & slow down the springs of our action & being. Therefore Nature, mightier & wiser than the Scientist, compels man to revolt against the cold & debasing tyranny of a negative scepticism. She compels him back to the way to his internal skies & compels him to recover, in whatever new terms, the promise of his Scriptures & his Gospels. She makes him listen again for some indirect echo, if not for the actual resonance of the eternal, immutable chant, the ever-rhythmic unwritten Veda.

The European attempt must, therefore, come to nought the moment it is brought face to face, as daily it is being brought more & more nearly face to face with its own inalienable insufficiency. The tradition of Asia will again impose itself on humanity, & it is probable that it will be again a country politically subject to Europe but more than any other tenacious of its spiritual temperament & tradition, which will be the instrument of the revanche. But the revelation that will conquer this time the forces of material rationalism must be one which includes the intellect in exceeding it, fulfils, not annuls it; for the conditions demand this greater consummation. In the Roman days the intellect was attacked before its constructive work had proceeded beyond the first insufficient paces; today the intellect has done its constructive work and the work must be accepted. It is India alone that can satisfy this double claim of the human reason & the divine intelligence; & the new reconquest will differ as much and in the same way from the old as India differs from old Judaea.

It is true that in this country the reason has never fulfilled itself, triumphed & held undisputed sway to the same extent as in modern Europe. If we take in its general results in India the great intellectual movement of humanity, we see that it broke up & scattered about in fragments the ancient catholic tradition & knowledge, placed its stamp on much that yet remains, destroyed a great deal which it could not assimilate, left a little surviving under veils & in our remote & secret places. On the mental temperament of our people, the long struggle had a disastrous effect; for it has deprived all except the few of the higher supra-intellectual inner life of our forefathers, it has made impossible any general resort to that discipline which gave them the use to a certain extent, at least, of the higher intuitive mentality, the satyadrishti, the direct sight, and has driven the many to be content rather with the irregular intuitions of the heart, the aesthetic faculties & the senses; we have kept those faculties which receive the actual touch of the higher truth obscurely, with the eyes of the intellect closed but lost those which receive them directly, with the eyes of the intellect open and luminously transmitting them to the mind imprisoned in matter. We have therefore neither been able to organise the intellectual efficiency of the Europeans, nor retain the principles of inner greatness known to our forefathers. Nevertheless, we still have among us important remnants of the old knowledge & discipline & we have firm hold in our schools of Yoga on the supreme means by which its lost parts can be recovered. The key of a divine life upon earth lies, rusted indeed in an obscure corner of our mansion, used only by a few, but still it lies there & is still used. It has to be singled out from amid much waste matter, made fit for complete & general use and given freely to mankind. We have kept, fortunately, the intuitional temperament to which its use is easy & natural. The failure of the intellect to assume complete sway and entirely rationalise our life, was a necessary condition for the preservation of that temperament, itself necessary for the appointed work & God-decreed life of our nation. On the other hand, the indispensable work of Buddha and his predecessors & successors has not been entirely lost on our nation. Their great movement which denied, limiting itself in rationality, the capacity or the need of the human mind to know beyond the laws of phenomena, seized in metaphysical philosophy upon only so much as was necessary for conduct, sought to establish on pure logic & reason the few fundamental principles it needed and, feeling obscurely the necessity of completing itself by physical science, as soon as it entered that field, far outpaced the accomplishment of Europe or Arabia, ended in a defeat & collapse necessary for the final salvation of humanity. Its defeat necessitated in the divine scheme the later arrival in India of an intellectual & rationalistic civilisation, armed, organised, politically dominant, culturally aggressive, so that we might be forced, against our will & natural tendency, to hear from the rational intellect that which it was entitled to say to us & to perceive at last that the indirect & inferior intuition, great, divine & inspiring as it is in its more intense individual results, is still insufficient for humanity & that we must turn back to a higher guide & recover a lost & superior state. When, without falling into the European error, we have recognised this truth, — and the logical & rationalistic capacity developed in us by Buddha & Shankara gives us the power to recognise it & the tendency, — we shall be ready both for our national survival and for that greater world-work for which, alone among the nations, we keep still the necessary materials and the necessary capacity. Children of the Rishis, not entirely disinherited, repositories of the Veda, still clinging to our trust, we alone can recover in our experience its half lost truths for the growing need of humanity. We have acquired, too, by our long philosophical discipline, the power of stating supra-intellectual knowledge in that language of the intellect on which the modern world insists as the proper vehicle of understanding and the first condition of acceptance. We can see, from this point of view, the causes of the general substitution of the logical & speculative method for the intuitional & experiential; it was an incident in the inevitable recurrence of one of those periods in which pure intellectuality dominates & which have for their function to refine & chasten the lower nature in the general mass of humanity. We can see what we have gained, — the power of ratiocination, the openness to the processes of reason, the ability to express intellectually — so far as that is possible — supra-intellectual knowledge & experience, the control of the lower members by the reason. We can see, too, the natural limitations of the intellect & the inevitably inferior validity of the metaphysical method to the experiential in the attempt to grasp the truths of Veda, in that the certainty of these truths cannot be acquired either by speculation or logic. We can see how this inferiority has worked for the obscuration or elimination of much that was potent, active & living in the more ancient knowledge; for the intellect tends to reject in its self-confidence what it cannot grasp & define, just as the heart tends to reject in its self-will what it does not desire or enjoy; yet what the intellect cannot grasp & define, includes often the most valuable parts of experience and knowledge.

The seeds of this movement of the intellect are contained in the Sanhitas & Upanishads themselves, although the movement itself is foreign to the Scriptures. The Sanhitas are Karmakanda; their object is not the enunciation of the general Truths of Brahman, but the practice of its particulars; they are the perfect monuments, sufficient to themselves, of especial moments, stages, movements in the progress of the individual towards his divine goal; they are instruments by thought & speech for the stabilisation of his increasing gains in light, force & joy; they are the praise & invocation of the gods who preside over particular functionings in our nature & in world-nature; they are statements of experience packed full of psychological detail and minute spiritual realisation, which confirm the seer & help the seeker. They are truth of experience & have therefore no room for speculation; they are ascertained truth & give therefore no room to doubt, debate & logical reasoning. But there are passages, rare seeds of the method pursued by the Upanishads, in which a general question is put and the suggestion of an answer offered. The Upanishads, on the contrary, are Jnanakanda; they have for their object the enunciation of the Truth of Brahman & the fundamental principles of Brahman's self-manifestation in universe. But with one remarkable exception they do not use, in order to arrive at this truth, these principles, the method of logical reasoning. Unlike the Sanhitas, they admit, not so much of doubt, as of debate; they move by positive questioning and the positive answer to questioning. But, again, the answer to questioning does not move by logic either in its inception, in its process or in its consummation. When Yajnavalkya holds his grand debate with the Brahmavadins at the court of King Janaka, when the proud Balaki vails his pride to the superior knowledge of King Ajatashatru, it is not by the field of logic or with the arms of metaphysic disquisition that they encounter each other. The question one puts to another is not "What thinkest thou of this?" but "What dost thou know?" and he whose knowledge proves to be deeper than his adversary's, is the conqueror in the discussion. Nor has this superior knowledge been arrived at by a more just or a more brilliant speculation, but by deeper sight, by a more powerful concentration. He has arrived at it, tapas taptwa; that is the method laid down by Varuna to his son Bhrigu in the Taittiriya Upanishad; for, he adds, tapo Brahma, Tapas is Brahman. Tapas, in other words, is the dwelling of the soul on its object, by which Brahman originally created the world through vision — sa ikshata — saw Itself, that is to say, as world & what It saw, became, — the dwelling of the soul on its object whether, prospectively, in creative vision, outwardly realising, as the poet & the genius of action dwells, or, retrospectively, in perceptive vision of the thing created, inwardly realising, as the prophet dwells; tapas is the very foundation of the method of revelation & intuition. Therefore, as in the acquisition of knowledge, speculation & logic are not used, so also in the imparting of knowledge, disquisition and logic are not used.

The thing has been seen by the seer, he is the drashta & to him Veda is drishti; it is spoken to the hearer & he sees, indirectly, through the medium of the word what the seer has seen by the self-vision, directly; to the hearer, Veda is Sruti. Yajnavalkya speaks his knowledge, his adversaries do not dispute it; they, too, see, being themselves habituated to these supreme processes, and the thing seen they silently & without debate acknowledge. If they are to dispute, since dispute is only a comparison of knowledge, of sight, of Veda, of drishti,[2] they must themselves first see farther, more profoundly, more subtly; and to see farther, they must first plunge into farther tapas, remain long constant in a farther dwelling of the soul on its object.

Still, just as in the Sanhitas there is the seed of the Upanishadic method, so in the Upanishads there is the seed of the later philosophical & intellectual method; we have, very occasionally, an obscure & casual preparation for the Darshanas. One passage, indeed a line, entirely typifies this secret bridging of the two methods; by a slight glance at it we can see how the mighty many-branching tree of the metaphysical philosophies burgeoned out from a very insignificant grain of tendency. Gautama in the Chhandogya, declares to his son Swetaketu the fundamental principle that all existence apparent to us here comes out of one anterior & ultimate existence, and he immediately notices the opposite appreciation, accepted as a starting point in the Aitareya, that existence originally emerges out of an original state of non-being, but only to reject it on the ground of a logical difficulty, "How could existence be created or create itself out of the non-existent";[3] it is the earliest statement of the metaphysical principle common to all our positive & orthodox philosophies that nothing comes out of Nothing. The logic is large, axiomatic & elemental; we have a perception of logic

---

[2] The word for knowledge, vid, veda, is the Latin word for sight &, for the early Rishis, had probably not yet lost entirely all colour of its physical & more primitive meaning.

[3] The language of the Sruti is remarkable, Asat ekam evadwitiyam, Non-Being one without a second, & shows that the old use of not-being differs essentially from our idea of nothingness.

rather than a process of logic or a generalisation from one perception & a priori exclusion of another as evidently impossible, not a logical demonstration of the impossibility. We are still within the four walls of the Upanishadic process, but stand already in the cadre of the doorway leading out into metaphysical disquisition. When we come to the sermons of Buddha, one knows not how many centuries later, and the formal foundation of the six orthodox philosophies we see, in spite of an immense logical & rationalistic development, that they proceed, initially, on this method of Gautama; they start from an act of logical discrimination, the acceptance of one statement of general perception & the rejection of another which seems to be inconsistent with the first or its contrary. All the ancient philosophies refer back to the Veda for the justification of the fundamental formulas in which they differ most obstinately & irreconcilably from each other. They are right in their positive claim; where they are wrong, where Shankara himself goes so hopelessly astray, is in founding on the same authority not only their own ultimate justification, but the confutation of their adversaries. The Veda is not logical, does not really confute anything; its method is experiential, intuitional; its principle is to receive all experiences, all perceptions of truth about the Brahman, and either to place them side by side in order of experience & occasional relation, as in the Sanhitas, or to arrange them in order of perception and fundamental relation, as in the Upanishads, putting each in its place, correcting misplacement & exaggeration, but not excluding, not destroying. This is admirably seen in the colloquy of Ajatashatru & the proud Balaki; Ajatashatru does not deny the experiences & perceptions of Balaki; he accepts them, denies only their claim to represent the ultimate truth, gives them their true character, puts them in their right place & leads up by this purificatory process to his own deeper knowledge. Harmony, synthesis is the law of the Veda, not discord & a disjection of the members of truth in order to replace the manysided reality of existence by a narrower logical symmetry. But the metaphysical philosophies are compelled by the law of their being to effect precisely this disjection. Veda can admit two propositions that are logically contradictory, so long as they are statements of fundamental experience & perception; it does not get rid of the contradiction by denying experience but seeks instead the higher truth in which the apparent contradiction is reconciled. Logic, by its very nature, is intolerant even of apparent contradiction; its method is verbal, ideative; it accepts words & thoughts as rigid & iron facts instead of what they really are, imperfect symbols & separate sidelights on truth. Being & Non-Being are ideas opposed to each other; therefore, in logic, one or the other must be excluded. The One cannot be at the same time the many; therefore, in logic, either the Many is an illusion, or Duality is the fundamental reality of things. Brahman is Nirguna, without qualities, beyond definition; therefore, to the rigid Adwaitins, the Saguna Brahman, the Infinite Personality of God becomes a supreme myth of Maya, a basic & effective fact indeed, but basic & effective only in and of the grand cosmic illusion which It directs. Logic, the tyrant of the metaphysician, is satisfied by these abstract processes, but Truth is hurt & dismembered. Illusions of truth, dogmas of syllogism, take its place, and war upon each other, as indeed, so long as they live, they must go on warring for ever, since none can ever be established as undisputedly true, resting, as they do, on pure opinion of Smriti poured into the mould of Opinion, having, as they all have, a part only of Truth which they pretend vainly to be the whole.

We see, as a result, a progressive disjection of the fundamental truths of Veda, &, curiously enough, a disjection of the various parts of method which make up the totality of the Veda. The totality of Vedantic knowledge consists of several processes; first, Vedanta, the direct perception of the fundamental reality out of which all emerges & to which all returns; secondly, Sankhya, the analysis, by the discriminating perception, of the fundamental principles of being & knowledge in which the Reality manifests itself as world, as subject, & as object; thirdly, Yoga, the psychological basis of experience, experiment, practical analysis, synthesis which verifies the discriminative analysis; fourthly, Vaisheshika, the physical analysis of the form or matter in which the manifesting world-energy is expressed & established to our outgoing perceptions; fifthly, Nyaya, the analysis of the processes of discrimination whether by the intellect or by higher functions; sixthly, Karma of Veda, the application of the knowledge acquired in formulas of life-action by which the individual & the community can ensure the highest phenomenal expression of the fundamental Reality of which their special nature is capable, — by which, let us say, man can express Brahman in his superior & more plastic kind as the bee or the ant expresses Brahman in its inferior & more rigid & limited nature; — these six rank among other processes, — for life of Veda is supple, flexible and wide, — some of which are the foundation of Purana & Itihasa. The fundamental perception, separating, narrowed itself and became the Uttara Mimansa of Badarayana; the discriminative analysis, separating, narrowed itself and became Sankhya of Kapila; the psychological experimentation, separating, narrowed itself & became Yoga of Patanjali; the physical analysis, separating, narrowed itself and became Vaisheshika of Kanada; the analysis of discriminative processes, separating, narrowed itself and became Nyaya of Gautama; the application in formulas of life-action, separating, narrowed itself extremely & became the Purva Mimansa of Jaimini; yet each of the six arrogated to itself the functions & the sufficiency of the other five. Other parts of knowledge & process, ejected by the ever-narrowing tendency of logical exclusiveness, established themselves in other philosophies and branches of practice & knowledge and have come down to us, changed, often disfigured, in Shastra, in Purana, in legend & history, in different schools of Yoga.

The original method of all these differences was the method of Gautama in the episode of the Chhandogya, the exclusive affirmation of one's own seeing, the logical exclusion, by process of verbal & ideative distinction, of that which has [been] seen by others. We perceive very well this root of the evil in the grand example, supreme in its kind, of the Buddha. Unhelped by the conflicting philosophies of the schools, dissatisfied with the too rigorously materialised methods of the Yogins, he takes the right, the supreme step, he retires into himself & gives his soul the charge of the Truth. Sa tapo atapyata. He emerges from this concentration of soul, tapas taptwa, with the great illumination received in the ever-memorable night under the Bo tree. What is this illumination of Buddha? It is the perception of the chain of Karma, of the impermanence of sanskaras, of the illusoriness of the mental ego, of the release into the motionless peace of Nirvana. There was nothing new in these things considered merely as tenets; they belong, in one form or another, to Vedanta; they cannot have been unknown to the philosophers of the age. What was new in them was their puissant revivification in a supreme soul and a great personality, their removal from the category of metaphysical dogmas & abstractions, into realities of life, concrete, human, vivid, which could once more be pursued by all, realised, practised and lived. It was this return to the sources, this puissant reconnection of Vedanta with ordinary life which was the secret of the Buddha's tremendous effectuality. New also was the particular connection & interlinking of all these central ideas in the thought of the Buddha, the singular cast given to them by his unique, yet universal temperament & the formulation in the mould of that temperament of a system of Vedantic ethics. Still, in his fundamental method, in his approach to truth & his handling of truth, Buddha had not, so far, gone beyond the method of the Vedantic Rishis; Yajnavalkya or Pippalada would have so sought in themselves for the truth, received illumination in the same fashion, equally cast that knowledge into well-linked formulae of experience which could be lived and practised. But Yajnavalkya or Pippalada would not have shot the iron bolt of logic on the knowledge they had gained and shut themselves in a prison of ratiocination to the experiences of others and to fresh vision. It was here that, owing, perhaps, to the very strenuousness of Buddha's search as well as to the limits of the question with which he had started, "How shall one escape from the pain & grief of the world," he turned from the ancient path and allowed the metaphysical & logical training of his past [to] lay its heavy hand upon him. He built up walls of logic; he shut himself up in a creed. Thus it came about that this great destroyer of the ego, sanctioned in his disciples the supreme act of intellectual egoism and this giant render of chains imposed on his Sangha, without positively intending it, deprecating it indeed, the bondage to a single personality & the chain of a specific formula of thought. The movement of the metaphysical philosophies, more purely intellectual, far less temperamental & personal than the Buddha's, yet followed the same limiting process. They obeyed not a personal illumination, but the logic of their starting point. Sankhya, for instance, proceeded on a discriminative analysis of the world, proceeded indeed to the last limit of that analysis and found that, fundamentally, Existence starts & maintains its manifestation of world on the basis, first, of the Unity of Nature, — the unity, the Yogin would say, of the energy of the Lord, — and, secondly, of the multiplicity of souls observing & reflecting the works of Nature, — the multiplicity, the Vedantin would say, of the individual souls, in which Brahman, the Lord, the one Supreme soul, puts Himself forth to enjoy the works of His energy. Of these two fundamental principles the Sankhya metaphysician made a formula, an ultimate perception; he refused to go beyond; he built up a wall of logical disquisition to shelter himself from wider perceptions and a more complex experience. Such was the method of all these schools, the developed method of which we find so indistinct a seed in the Upanishads.

Still, it was from some fundamental experience or revelation that the metaphysicians started; the logical element intervened only as a second term of knowledge. Moreover, the method of the aphorism preserved the suggestive profundity of the intuition or revelatory experience & tended to maintain in the practice of knowledge the original closeness of the intellectual concept to that vision in the soul which thought can only translate very imperfectly to the reason. But about a thousand years later we find a new movement of the intellect in force, illustrated by the names of Shankara, Ramanuja, Madhwa, in which logic covers the whole field, leaving only a narrow corner to experience & intuition; but, for that very reason, the experience, the intuition assumes a character of much more eager intensity, exclusiveness, monotone of emphasis and steeps itself more fervently in the personality & temperament of the thinker. Hence a passion of dispute, an intolerance in logomachy which leaves far behind the measure of more ancient disputants. The battle is, finally, a civil strife between Vedantist & Vedantist; temporarily victorious over rival schools, they turn to rend each other; but the strife is still mainly about fundamental perceptions. The great question now is the fundamental unity or difference between the supreme soul & the individual or another, which would have astonished greatly the ancient Rishis, the question whether the world is false or real, — false, not only in its appearance to the senses, but per se, in itself, in its essence & its being. In the Mayavada of Shankara, Buddha, the rationalist, completes his work in India. He has led the reason to a great act of self-slaughter, the denial of existence to the world which alone it can study, more, the denial of Brahman in the world on the authority of that very Veda which spends so much time in affirming & elaborately explaining Brahman in the world. In other countries, in other ages, the Buddhistic agnostic train of thought led to a still more supreme suicide of reason; for it came to the denial of its own power to know anything real & fundamental, came almost, like Buddhistic Nihilism, to deny the existence of anything real & fundamental. In India the farther advance after Shankara & his successors has been mechanical & practical rather than theoretic; it has led towards the final divorce of intellect from experience. The metaphysician, devoted to intellect, has abandoned experience in favour of the authority of departed Acharyas. The schools of Yoga devoted to experience, have practised their psychological methods according to a fixed tradition without the harmonising touch, the generalising light; Sankhya dispensed with Yoga, Yoga divided itself from Sankhya. Thus has the spiritual life of India, by a misplaced & intolerant action of Intellect & its servant, rash-moving, light-winged, — the chameleon-hued phantasm Opinion, been shredded, parcelled out, narrowed into many streams & shallows, like the Oxus of the poet. Thus has it come down to our own age, ever narrowing more & more, shorn of its victorious streams, awaiting its return to a wider flood and a more grandiose motion.

Chapter III

We have, then, to choose between two methods, one historic &
modern, in possession of the field, easily applied in its fullness,
the other ancient, difficult to employ, impossible indeed for us to
utilise safely except by an inversion of the process of knowledge
known to the Rishis. According as we choose the one or the
other, we shall arrive at a logical and symmetrical result, a
private room hired for ourselves in the mansion of Truth &
marked out by us as her sole temple, or shall be free to range
in all her domain, gleaning wide & various results, but not
soon or easily sure of possessing her entirety. I have indicated
the disadvantages of the intellectual & logical method for the
interpretation of Vedanta, but, in view of its long dominion
& wide acceptance, it will be as well to consider & convince
ourselves of the more important of them clearly and in some
detail before we proceed.

In the first place, by the method of intellectual reasoning we
are compelled to apply the processes of logic to entities which are
beyond the grasp of logic. A single instance will suffice. We find,
as a matter of experience, that existence is one and yet existence
is multiple; everywhere, to whatever nook or corner of being
we penetrate, we find this riddle presenting itself, undeniable &
ineffugable, of a multiplicity which appears, a unity concealed
which yet the mind insists on as the sole truth of the multiplicity.
Nor is the unity which our mind thus asks us to perceive, a
sum of factors; that oneness exists, but behind it there is an
essential unity out of which both the sum & its factors emerge.
Yet, divorce that essential unity from all notion of multiplicity
expressed or latent, & it ceases to be unity; it becomes something
else of which unity & multiplicity are mutually related aspects.
But when we have arrived at this coexistent & coincident unity
& multiplicity, before we can proceed to the something else
which is neither one nor many, logic has already taken alarm. It
cannot be, it says, that two opposites really coexist & coincide
as the nature of Being. If we ask why not, — since after all,
it is an universal experience, — the answer is that the thing is

illogical & irrational; — unintelligible & contradictory to the
view of logic & reason, it is, therefore, to them impossible of
credence. A sum and its factors, may & must coexist, but not
a thing which is at once one and many. Therefore Logic sets to
work to get rid of one or both of the two irreconcilable, yet
strangely reconciled opposites. Buddhism dismisses the Many
as phenomena of sensation, the One as an ideative illusion of
sensation; it gets rid of the unity in sum as a mere combination
of sensational factors in the figure of the chariot and its parts,
having no existence apart from the factors, no real existence at
all; it gets rid of the essential unity as a mere illusion of continuity
created by the uninterrupted succession of sensations, in the figure of the flame & the wick. It drives by logical process towards
a Nullity, although not all its schools are bold enough to arrive
at that void & yawning haven. For the rest, its final conclusion is
illogical, for though it claims to be the pure concept of Nullity,
it is in reality, when examined, a something that is nothing.
Therefore, originally, Buddha seems to have turned aside from
the problem and declared to his disciples, Seek not to know, for
to know, even if it be possible, helps not at all & leads to no
useful result. Buddhism was satisfied with having got rid of the
original, actual & pressing contradiction in this world here &
now which it had set out to destroy. Adwaita asserts the One on
the ground of ultimate experience; it dismisses the Many as an
illusion; yet since both are ineffugable, since the soul escaping
from the illusion, escapes from it merely & does not destroy it,
it has to be admitted that the substratum of multiplicity exists
eternally. Here again we are led by logical process to a result
which is illogical; we have, in the end, a Maya that at once
exists and does not exist. This difficulty is at once put aside as
beyond enquiry; the contradiction exists, inexplicable but true;
we need not enquire farther, for we have got rid of the original
contradiction in which we were entangled & cutting through this
Gordian knot of Nature, we have released the individual soul
from the illusion of multiplicity & therefore from the necessity
of phenomenal existence. In both cases the process & result are
similar & a like subterfuge is utilised. In both cases Logic, like

Cato at Utica, has committed suicide in order to assert its rights & liberties; but it has died, as the patients of Molière's doctors had the felicity of dying, according to the rules of the science; therefore it is satisfied. It is not, however, Buddhism & Adwaita alone, but every logical philosophy that arrives at a similar result; we find always that when we would explain existence in an ultimate term which shall be subject to logic, we fail; we arrive either at a term which is plainly illogical, or at an explanation which fails to explain or a success which seems to succeed only because it ignores or suppresses or juggles away an important part of the data. The suggestion irresistibly arises whether this is not so, whether it must not be always so merely because the formulae of logic, a creature as it is & a limited movement of intellectual ideation, which is itself a creature and a limited movement of existence, useful enough within the sphere of their birth & movement, & in the circle of their jurisdiction, cannot control that which is beyond & wider than ideation, yet farther beyond & wider than its creature logic? Invaluable in relating correctly the particulars of the universe and purging our ideas about them, it may be of less sovereign efficacy in dealing with the fundamental things which underlie phenomena and of no efficacy at all in discovering the Reality which lies farther back behind phenomena.

Much of the luminous confusion of Metaphysics is due to the self-satisfied content with which it leans upon words & abstract ideas & uses them not merely as instruments, but as data, forgetting that these are merely useful to symbolise & formulate very imperfectly truths of experience & perception. Therefore in dealing with abstract ideas & conceptions we are unsafe unless we insist always on returning to the thing itself which they symbolise. Otherwise we lose ourselves in facile words or in confusing abstractions. For instance, in order to get rid of the anomaly of a Maya that exists & exists not, we say sometimes that the Many have a relative reality, but no essential reality. But what have we said, after all? Merely this, that we do not find the Many existing except in some relation to a unity behind, established in that Unity and, as far as we can see, existent by that unity, as indeed the unity itself exists in a certain relation to the eternally existent Many either in their manifestation or in their substratum of Maya. How much farther have we got by this manipulation of words? We have found a fresh formula which expresses the difficulty, but does not solve the difficulty. We have taken refuge in a disingenuous phrase which suggests [to] us that phenomena are unreal, but tries to escape from the consequences of its admission. As well may we say, that water is in any sense unreal because it only exists by the mixture of oxygen & hydrogen; oxygen & hydrogen unreal, because they only exist by the congregation of atoms; atoms unreal because they only exist by some obscure principle of the transformation of energy into forms; energy unreal because it exists to us only in its works & manifestations. In all this we are playing with words, we are making an argument of our own ideative limitations. So again, in a different way, with the question of the Personality & Impersonality of God. Personality is to us a word which we use too lightly without fathoming the depth of the thing which it indicates. We confuse it perhaps with the idea of a separate ego, we imagine God in His personality as one Ego among millions separate from all the others, superior & anterior to them; we refuse to extend or to subtilise our conception, and according to our personal predilections we argue that such a Personal God cannot exist or that He must exist. But the whole method was illegitimate. We ought rather to fathom in experience all the possibilities of human personality & of divine personality, if such a thing exists, in order to know them & arrive at sure results about them instead of battling over a verbal symbol or an arbitrary abstraction & ending only in an eternal war of ill-grounded opinions.

This danger of intellectual predilections thrusting out Truth is the third disadvantage of the logical method. Logic claims & even honestly attempts to get rid of predilection and to see things in the sure light of truth, but it is not equal to its task; our nature is full of subtle disguises and, the moment we form an opinion, attaches itself to it & secretly takes it under its protection under pretence of an exclusive attachment to Truth or a militant zeal for reason & the right opinion. We come to our subject with a predisposition towards a particular kind of solution established either in our feelings, in our previous education & formed ways of thinking or in our temperament & very cast of character. We seize passionately or we select deliberately & reasonably the arguments that favour our conclusion; we reject, whether with impatience or after scrupulous & fair attention, the arguments that would shake it. Logic, a malleable & pliant servitor behind all its air of dry & honest rigidity, asks only that it should be provided with suitable premises, unsuitable premises excluded or explained away, & its conscience is entirely satisfied. We perform the comedy with perfect sincerity, but it is still a comedy which Nature plays with us; our garb of intellectual stoicism has concealed from ourselves, the epicure of his own dish of thoughts, the mind enamoured of its favourite ideas. Shankara comes to the Upanishads with a judgment already formed; he is an Adwaitin, his temperament predisposes him to Mayavada. But the Sruti does not contain the Mayavada, at least explicitly; it does contain, side by side with the fundamental texts of Adwaita, a mass of texts which foster the temper & views of the Dualist. But the Sruti is the supreme & infallible authority; it contains nothing but truth; it can inculcate, therefore, nothing but Adwaita. Obviously, then, these dualistic texts must have a meaning & a bearing different from their surface meaning or their apparent bearing; it is Shankara's business, as a commentator in search of truth, to put always the right, that is to say always the Adwaitic interpretation on Sruti. Watch him then seize the text in his mighty hands and, with a swift effort, twist & shape & force it to assume a meaning or a bearing which will either support or at least be consistent with Adwaita, — a giant victoriously wrestling with & twisting into a shape a mass of obstinate iron! There is no insincerity in the process, rather the fervour of a too passionate sincerity. Still, Truth often veils her face with a tear or a smile, when Shankara comments on the Sruti. He is the greatest; the others are not likely to escape from the snare into which he casts himself headlong. Nor do I think the philosopher has yet been born who has escaped from these original meshes of intellectual preference, predestined belief & ineffugable personal temperament.

In fact, the supreme failing of the metaphysical method is that, owing to the paucity, abstract uncertainty and doubtful bearing of its most essential data, it becomes almost entirely a domain of opinion. The absolute contempt of scientific rationalism for metaphysics which for a long time past has conquered general opinion in Europe & put an end to fruitful philosophical thinking, is almost certainly exaggerated & unjustified. The emergence of a new metaphysical thinking, more practical & realistic than the old abstract philosophies, presaged by Nietzsche, fulfilled in James & Bergson, is a sign at once of the return of Europe upon this dangerous error and of a perception, subconscious perhaps, of that real defect in the character of metaphysics which gave a hold to the destructive criticisms of modern realism. The long and imposing labours of the highest human intellects in the region of metaphysics, has not been a vain waste of priceless energy. Nature makes no such mistakes; her glance, though it seems to rove & fall at random and vary capriciously, is surer & more infallible in its selection than our human reason. Metaphysics have fulfilled a necessary and, when all has been said, a right & true function in our evolution; the materials of the great systems she has built have been general truths and not abstract errors. But the systems themselves are not final expressions of truth; they are the mould of the philosopher's personality, the stamp of his temperament and type of intellect. If we examine the method & substance of our own philosophies, we shall see why this must be so and cannot be otherwise. Their most important data are vast & vague conceptions, infinite in their nature, Being, Non-Being, Consciousness, Prakriti & Purusha (Nature & Soul), Mind, Matter. How can these entities be compelled to give us their secret except by a profound & exhaustive interrogatory such as modern Science has applied to the lowest principle of Being, analysing & experimenting in every possible way with Matter? But the metaphysician does not base his process on the sure steps of experience. He starts with an ideal definition of these great indefinables and he argues logically from the abstract idea to results which are faultless, indeed, in logic; — but how can we be sure of an equal faultlessness in the reality of things which is after all our proper business? We cannot be; for each thinker handles according to his own light this vague & plastic material of ideas: there is nothing to check him; he asserts his opinion & his opinion is dominated by his education or his temperament. Shankara asserts that works are incompatible with salvation, Jaimini that works are indispensable to salvation. Who shall decide, when each proceeds with a perfect logic from his premises? Therefore, a second class of data have to be called in, the texts of the Sruti. But Jaimini & Shankara appeal equally to the texts of the Sruti; for there are some which, if pressed in their separate meaning, seem to declare the inutility of works, there are others which, if pressed in their separate meaning, seem to declare the indispensability of works. It is a question of interpretation and, where different interpretations are possible, we interpret, again, according to our opinion which is decided, as we have seen, by our education or our temperament. Even when an interpretation in the sense of our opinion seems to be impossible, an ingenious scholarship, a curious & intrepid learning can make it possible. Sa atma tattwamasi Swetaketo, cries Gautama to his son; "That is the Truth, that is the Self, that art thou, O Swetaketu." The evidence of Revealed Scripture seems to be conclusive for the Adwaitic view of existence. No, cries the Dualist, you have read it wrongly, you have separated átmátattwam into three distinct uncompounded words when there is really an euphonic combination of átmá atat twam, which gives us this result, "Thou art *not* that, O Swetaketu." Our inalienable perception of right, the satyam ritam in us, tells us that the Dualist's device is wrong, a desperate expedient only; but how shall we convince the Dualist, whose business it is, as a dualist, not to be convinced? For grammatically, textually, he is within his rights. Nor can Shankara at least complain of this amazing tour-de-force; for he himself has used the very same device, in his commentary on the Isha Upanishad, in order to read, for the convenience of his philosophy, asambhútyá, by the not coming into birth, where tradition, metre, sentence-structure & context demand sambhútyá, by the coming into birth. In this confusion, is there any other class of data handled by metaphysics which will help us out of the difficulty? Certain psychological experiences are so handled; notably, the phenomena of sleep, the phenomena of samadhi, the phenomena of ultimate experience in consciousness. But how are we to know that these experiences bear the construction put on them or justify the conclusions drawn from them? how are we to know, for instance, that the experiences in consciousness which we find advanced as ultimate are really ultimate or even that they are not entirely illusory & deceptive? As metaphysics handles them, isolating them from each other, advancing them to demonstrate particular views & opinions, we cannot have any certainty. And, indeed, we find that each builder of a metaphysical system has a different formula of ultimate consciousness, ultimate to him, from which he starts; this difference of the ultimate step in experience which is also the starting-point for the chain of our logical systematising, is the strong foundation of all these age long jarrings in religious sect and school of philosophy. Here again opinion is master, very clearly founded not on data, not on pure truth, but on truth as seen in the colouring & with the limitation of our education & temperament. We can see from examples in modern Science how these differences work out & where their remedy is to be found. Physicists & geologists have disagreed in their view of the age of the earth; the geologists had certain data of experience before them which pointed to one conclusion, the physicists had a different set of data before them which pointed to a different conclusion. The difference here [is] a difference of education; the education of each had trained his mind to look only at a certain set of considerations, to move only in a certain way of thinking & reasoning. If physicist & geologist are combined in one mind, the age of the earth will not even then be indisputably fixed, for the necessary data are still wanting, but a juster perception will be gained, a better preparation for considering the problem, a superior chance of arriving as near to the truth as is now possible. Again, we see two scientists, absolutely agreed on all positive physical problems, confronted with the phenomena of the psychical world, partly true, partly the conscious or half conscious frauds of exploiters & illusions of enthusiasts. One turns eagerly to the new subject, examines widely, believes readily, is discouraged by no disappointments; the other refuses contemptuously to investigate or, if he investigates, hastens as rapidly as he can to the conclusion that the whole business is a sink of fraud, imposture & mystification. It is difference of temperament, not of the facts, that has determined these conflicting opinions. In the positive questions on which they are agreed, in the conclusions of their respective sciences where the geologist & physicist would not dream of disputing each other's conclusions, intellectual type & temperament are by no means entirely banished as factors, but their play is restricted, a mass of actual fact & experience is there to check them & keep them in order. It is this check that is wanting to the method of the metaphysicians.

If, then, our object is to take a number of general truths, a number of abstract conceptions, a few general statements of Vedanta and wide facts of consciousness, and out of these materials build ourselves a bright, aerial house of speculation in which our intellect can live satisfied with the sense of finality and our personal temperament assert itself as the ultimate truth of things, the method of abstract speculation supporting itself on logic will be sufficient for our purpose. But if we wish rather to know anything for certain about God & the ultimate reality of the world and the foundations of our life & existence, it is not by logic and speculation that we shall arrive at our desire. Experience is the first necessity; an experiential method, not a speculative & logical method. What is the utility of logical discussion & the marshalling of Vedic texts to decide whether works are incompatible with salvation or indispensable to it or neither incompatible nor indispensable, but only useful & permissible? What we need is experience. If once it is established by the experience of the Jivanmuktas that works & salvation are compatible, by the experience of the Karmayogins that works also lead to freedom in the Infinite & Divine Existence, — although they need not be the only path, nor the only requisite, although, even, it may be difficult to harmonise an active existence with the calm & peace of Infinity, — then no amount of logic to the contrary can be of any avail. Nor will Vedic texts avail, since the bearing of the texts has itself to be first decided. And what is the use of proving by logic & a curious scholarship that Tattwam asi should be read atattwam asi or that Vidya & Avidya in a particular Upanishad do not mean what they mean in every other Upanishad or that amritatwam in one text means the state of the gods & in others the state of Brahman? We need rather to experience always, to experience our unity with the One Truth of things and our difference from it and the relations of the unity to the difference; having experienced we shall understand. We need by practice & experiment, under a fit human guide or guided by the Divinity within, if we have strength & faith in Him, to fathom the outer dissonances & the secret harmonies of Vidya & Avidya, to achieve & enjoy immortality instead of arguing about immortality, to realise the thing the Veda speaks instead of disputing about the words of the text. In the absence of knowledge of the object, touch with the object, direct experience of the object, argument tends to become a vain jangling and speculation a highsounding jargon. These things may be useful to awaken our intellectual interest in the subject and move us to the acquisition of knowledge, but only if we become dissatisfied with them & see the necessity of proceeding farther. The Greek philosophers argued, of old, that the world was made out of water or made out of fire, and their speculations & the logical ingenuities of the sophists awakened a widespread curiosity on the subject; but the moment the experimental methods of physical science give us actual experience of the constituents of the material world, such speculations become valueless; the simple relation of connected facts takes the place of abstract logic. No one would dream of trying to settle the constituents of water or the processes of water by speculative logic; the experiential method is there to forbid that inutility. Even if the right experiential method has to be found, it is still by progressive experience step after step aided by the eye of intuition that it has to be discovered. Argument from first principles can only be of a minor and almost an accidental assistance; its function is always to awaken the mind & attach it to the object, so that the intuition attracted by the mental demand may fall upon the point desired with its light & bright electric shock and its divinely illuminating swiftness.

It might seem to follow that as the scientific method has been used to elucidate the problems of matter, so it should be used to elucidate the problems of mind & spirit. Certainly, in the absence of another, the scientific method would be the best, — the method of patient and courageous experiment & observation aided by a scrupulous use of hypothesis & exact reasoning. A beginning has been made in this direction in Europe by the examination of the abnormal conditions of hypnosis, divided personality & rare mental & psychic phenomena as well as in the tendency of psychology towards the abandonment of the superficial, academic and unfruitful methods of the past. But it is doubtful whether the scientific method will bear as great fruit in the things of mind as it has borne in the things of matter; it is certain that it is wholly unsuited to the investigation of the things of the spirit, because here we come into touch with Infinity & even cross the borders that divide the definite from the indefinable. The more we progress in that direction, the more the methods of scientific reasoning become inapplicable, unfruitful & misleading. Even the Mind gives a very limited hold to the scientist. In the first place, experiment is much more dangerous & difficult than in the physical sciences; in the latter we risk death & suffering, in the former we have to go out of the normal, face the dangers of the beyond from which man draws back shuddering, risk even the loss of that very reason which we have chosen for our instrument. The repugnance of mankind to take this step is much greater than that fear & repugnance which set the mass of mankind against the early experiments of science as diabolical sorcery & magic. Similarly, we find denounced as quackery, dupery, hallucination, superstition, the modern attempts to deal with the obscure phenomena of mind, — those in which observation of the familiar & normal is not enough & experiment with the abnormal is necessary. But the difficulty of convincing the ignorant or the reluctant is here infinitely greater, because of the elusive nature of mind as compared with matter. This is the second capital disadvantage of the scientific method, — that our only field for full experiment is ourselves. In matter we can examine any object by bringing it sufficiently near to be within the vicinity of our senses; but in mind we are unable to see the movements & processes of the minds of others except in so far as we can judge them from their gestures, action & physical expression, — indices unutterably perilous to the reasoner, inconceivably misleading. Unless, therefore, we can discover & use mental instruments, answering to the microscope, telescope, retorts of the astronomer, chemist & physicist, by which we can see, study & analyse the mental processes of thought, feeling & sensation in others as well as in ourselves, we may know indeed the physical movements & organs corresponding to some of the motions of mind, but we shall never know mind itself. It is an obscure perception of this truth that explains the powerful revival in our own day of the occult. Erratic & ignorant as much of it is, it was inevitable & it is salutary. Nature, unerring in her action, is filling mankind with an instinctive sense, a sort of dim subterranean intuition that, now that Science has almost completed its analysis of Matter, the next subject of inquiry must be Mind & Mind cannot be known except by as yet undiscovered or little-used introscopic instruments. Even if these are found, the most dangerous, intricate, difficult & varied experiments will be necessary; for mind is infinitely more elusive & elastic than matter. Where physical Nature confines herself rigidly & stubbornly to a single process, psychical Nature uses, versatilely & intricately, a hundred. To have sufficient experience, to be sure of one's results, one must take oneself & others experimentally to pieces, combine & recombine, put in order & put in disorder one's mental & emotional functions in a way & to an extent which humanity of the present day would pronounce chimerical and impossible. Still our own philosophy founding itself on experiments repeated continually through many millenniums declares that it is possible. Our Yoga, if its pretensions are true, enables us to do these things &, given certain difficult precautions, to do them with an eventual impunity; it separates the various functions, keeps some inactive while others are acting, experimentally analyses & creates new syntheses of mind and feeling, so that we are able to know the constituents, process & function at least of our own internal forces, with some perfection. Certain forms of Yoga claim to develop faculties by which we can not only know & watch the internal processes of others, but silently control them. If these pretensions are found to be justified, if we can really master & use such methods & instruments, a scientific knowledge & control of the forces of mind may become as possible as our present scientific knowledge & control of the forces of Nature. But how much shall we have gained? A knowledge of constituents, processes, functions we shall have, not, any more than in physical nature, a knowledge of things in themselves. The reality & spirit of objects & forces will still escape us, leaving us only their forms & phenomena. Reason will once more find herself baffled; with regard to the one thing that really matters, the one thing humanity is driven eternally to seek as necessary, supreme & the highest good, we shall have to return, as now, to the sterile result of agnosticism.

Experience, yes; but experience illumined by Veda & vijnana. We must by experiment & experience develop those faculties which see the Truth face to face & do not have to approach it indirectly & by inference only. The results of experience will then be illumined by this higher truth; the truth acquired will be confirmed & enlarged by experience. We shall be able to recover our lost kingdoms of the spirit, know the unknowable, enter into relations with the Infinite, be ourselves the reality of the Infinite as well as, if we so choose, its expression in the apparent Finite. We shall not be confined to the silver & copper of mind & matter, but handle also the gold of the Spirit. We shall use indeed the smaller currency in which the Spirit makes itself negotiable in material form & mental impression, not despising even the most apparently insignificant cent or cowrie, since all are divine, but shall use them only as lesser symbols of the higher currency which is alone of a true & self-determined value. This knowledge & possession of the things of the Spirit is the promise of Veda &

Vedanta, — a promise not delayed for its fulfilment to another life & world, but offered, ihaiva, in the present life & in this perishable body, nor only offered, but continually realised since prehistoric times by elect spirits in our Indian generations. Yoga, which offers us the knowledge & control of mental processes & forces in ourselves & others, offers us what is infinitely more valuable & the one thing worth pursuing for its own sake, the knowledge & possession of the truth of forms mental & material in the reality of the Self and the realisation of life in the world as the phenomena of a divine epiphany. We can know God, we can become the Brahman.

This promise long confined to the few, to the initiates in India, is once more being placed before the whole world for its acceptance. Of this supreme offer a life recently lived in an obscure corner of the earth seems to me to be the very incarnation & illuminating symbol, — the life of the Paramhansa Ramakrishna of Dakshineswar. Not for any body of teachings that he left behind, not for any restricted type of living, peculiar system of ethics or religious panacea for the ills of existence, — but because it brought once more into the world with an unexampled thoroughness & liberality the great Vedantic method of experience & inner revelation & showed us its possibilities. An illiterate, poor & obscure Bengali peasant, one who to the end of his life used a patois full of the most rustic forms & expressions, ignorant of Sanscrit, of any language but his own provincial dialect, ignorant of philosophy & science, ignorant of the world, yet realised in himself all the spiritual wisdom of the ages, shed in his brief sayings a light so full, so deep on the most difficult profundities of our inner being, the most abstruse questions of metaphysics that the most strenuous thinkers & the most learned Pandits were impressed by his superiority. By what process did he arrive at this great store of living knowledge? Never by any intellectual process, by any steps of reasoning. In all the things of the intellect, even the most elementary, he was as simple as a child, more unsophisticated than the most ignorant peasant of his native village. He could turn indeed an eye of infallible keenness on the hearts & intentions of men, but it was the eye of vision, not the eye of thought. Never indeed, in modern times or since the intellectualising of mankind began were reasoning & intellectual processes so rigidly excluded from the process of knowledge with such astonishing results. The secret of his success was that always he lived & saw; where most men only reason and translate thought into sentiment, feel and translate emotion into terms of thinking, he saw with the heart or a higher faculty & threw out his vision into experience with a power of realisation of which modern men have long ceased to be capable; thus living everything to its full conclusion of mental & physical experience his soul opened more & more to knowledge, to direct truth, to the Satyam in things, until the depths hid nothing from him & the heights became accessible to his tread. He first has shown us clearly, entirely & without reserve or attenuating circumstance, the supreme importance of being over thinking, but being, not in terms of the body & life merely, like the sensational & emotional man or the man of action, but in the soul as well and the soul chiefly, in the central entity of this complex human symbol. Therefore he was able to liberate us from the chains imposed by the makeshifts of centuries. He broke through the limitations of the Yogic schools, practised each of them in turn & would reach in three days the consummation which even to powerful Yogins is the accomplishment of decades or even of more lives than one; broke through the limitations of religion and fulfilled himself in experience as a worshipper of Christ and of Allah while all the time remaining in the individual part of him a Hindu of the sect of the Shaktas; broke through the limitations of the Guruparampara, &, while using human teachers for outward process & discipline, yet received his first & supreme initiation from the eternal Mother herself and all his knowledge from the World-Teacher within; broke through the logical limitations of the metaphysical schools and showed us Dwaita & Adwaita inextricably yet harmoniously one in experience, even as they are shown to us in Veda & Vedanta. All that at the time still governed our spiritual life he took typically into his soul & into his mental & physical experience, swallowed up its defects &

imperfections in the infinite abyss of his personality and brought out through these masks & forms always the something beyond that is perfect and supreme. Thus establishing experience and inward revelation as the supreme means of the highest knowledge, his became one of the seed-lives of humanity; and the seed it held was the loosening of the bonds of the rational intellect & the return of humanity's journey from its long detour on the mid-plateaus of reason towards the footpath that winds up to the summits of the spirit.

Note on the Texts

Note on the Texts

ISHA UPANISHAD comprises Sri Aurobindo's translations of and commentaries on the Isha Upanishad. His translations of and commentaries on other Upanishads, as well as his translations of later Vedantic texts and writings on the Upanishads and Vedanta in general, are published in *Kena and Other Upanishads*, volume 18 of THE COMPLETE WORKS OF SRI AUROBINDO.

Sri Aurobindo had a special interest in the Isha Upanishad, whose principle of "uncompromising reconciliation of uncompromising extremes" (p. 83) underlies his own philosophy as well. He first translated the Isha around 1900, and over the next fourteen years returned to it again and again, citing, translating, and writing commentaries on this eighteen-verse text. None of these commentaries was completed, but each served as a step in the development of his interpretation.

Between August 1914 and May 1915 Sri Aurobindo published a translation and analysis of the Isha in the monthly review *Arya*. These were issued as a book in 1920 or 1921; a revised edition came out in 1924. This work contains Sri Aurobindo's last word on the Isha Upanishad; it may also be said to represent the quintessence of his Upanishadic interpretation. His final translation and analysis are published in Part One of the present volume. Part Two contains the various incomplete commentaries he wrote before August 1914.

PART ONE: TRANSLATION AND COMMENTARY PUBLISHED BY SRI AUROBINDO

This part comprises Sri Aurobindo's final translation and analysis of the Isha Upanishad.

Isha Upanishad. This work, consisting of a translation (with Sanskrit text) and an analysis in four "movements", was published in the monthly review *Arya* in ten instalments between August 1914 (the

Arya's first issue) and May 1915. It was brought out as a book around 1921. New editions appeared in 1924, 1941, 1945, and subsequently. The 1924 edition contained some comparatively minor revisions by the author.

PART TWO: INCOMPLETE COMMENTARIES FROM MANUSCRIPTS

Before publishing his final translation and analysis in 1914–15, Sri Aurobindo made ten different efforts to write commentaries on the Isha Upanishad. The earliest dates from around 1902, the last from mid-1914, that is, just before the time he started publishing his final translation and analysis in the *Arya*. They are arranged here in approximate chronological order. Some of them are of considerable length but none was completed or revised for publication. All were discovered among his manuscripts after his passing and subsequently transcribed and published in various journals and books.

Isha Upanishad: All that is world in the Universe. Circa 1902. Sri Aurobindo abandoned this work after a few pages. There is no full stop after the last word written.

The Ishavasyopanishad with a commentary in English. Circa 1905. The title page of this work reads in full: "Materials for Bhavani Grantha-/Mala./1. The Ishavasyopanishad/with a commentary in English." The Sanskrit phrase "Bhavani Grantha-Mala" means "Garland of books for the goddess Bhavani". This commentary apparently was intended to be the first of a series of works for the use of students of Bhawani Mandir, a "temple to the goddess Bhawani" where young men would be trained to do selfless work for Mother India. The idea of Bhawani Mandir was primarily that of Barindra Kumar Ghose, Sri Aurobindo's younger brother, though Sri Aurobindo did write a manifesto setting forth its ideals around 1905 (see *Bhawani Mandir* in *Bande Mataram: Political Writings 1890–1908*, volume 6 of THE COMPLETE WORKS OF SRI AUROBINDO). Shortly after writing the pamphlet, Sri Aurobindo lost interest in the project, and does not appear to have written any other works for the proposed "Grantha-Mala".

The text of the commentary ends abruptly at the bottom of the last page of the notebook. It may have been continued in another notebook that has been lost. Inside the back cover, facing the last page of text, Sri Aurobindo wrote the following: "Hunger is in its nature cannibal, you eat protoplasm & nothing else because you are protoplasm".

The Karmayogin: A Commentary on the Isha Upanishad. Circa 1905–6. This lengthy but still incomplete commentary was written sometime after Sri Aurobindo took up the practice of yoga in 1905, and no later than May 1908, when the second of the two notebooks in which it is written was seized by the Calcutta police at the time of his arrest in connection with the Alipore Bomb Conspiracy. He began it, as he had begun "The Ishavasyopanishad", as a guru-student dialogue, but dropped this form after the first page. The commentary contains several passages, totalling around 400 lines or ten printed pages, that are the same as or very similar to passages in "The Ishavasyopanishad". He apparently copied them from that work while writing this one.

Sri Aurobindo modified the structure of the commentary while he was working on it. See the note on page 170 for details. The first two "Chapters", dealing with verses 1 to 3 of the Upanishad, occupy the first of the two manuscript notebooks that were used for writing the commentary. (For some reason Sri Aurobindo wrote "Chapters I to III" on the first page of this notebook. This may explain why the first "Chapter" in the second notebook is numbered "IV".) This second notebook contains the second "Part", which deals with verses 4 to 6 of the Upanishad.

Ish and Jagat. Circa 1912. Editorial title. This piece is quite incomplete.

The Secret of the Isha. Circa 1912. In the manuscript, "Chapter I" is written above the title. Only this fragmentary first chapter was written.

Chapters for a Work on the Isha Upanishad. Circa 1912. Editorial title. These six draft chapters for a proposed "book" (see the last paragraph of chapter [2]) have been reproduced in the order in which they occur in Sri Aurobindo's notebook. The chapters are numbered editorially [1] to [6]. Sri Aurobindo's own working titles and numbers are given. Although headed "The Isha Upanishad", the piece deals with the text of the Upanishad only in chapter [3] and more briefly in chapter [6]. Elsewhere it deals, among other things, with Puranic cosmology, the savage and the ascent of the human being, philology, the Veda, and Sri Aurobindo's method of Vedic and Vedantic exegesis. The suggestion on the scope of "dhanam" in chapter [3] may refer to

Sri Aurobindo's discussion of this word in Appendix [3] of Draft A of "The Life Divine" (see below). This would indicate that this chapter was written after that draft.

The Upanishad in Aphorism: The Isha Upanishad. Circa 1913–14 (placed before the next piece in order to keep the three drafts of "The Life Divine" together). The first paragraph of this "commentary" consists of a translation of the first verse of the Isha Upanishad. The rest is an exploration, in aphorisms, of various related ideas.

The Life Divine: A Commentary on the Isha Upanishad [Draft A]. Circa 1912. Sri Aurobindo wrote this draft in pencil on unused pages or parts of pages of two notebooks that he had used a number of years earlier to make fair copies of literary works. He originally headed the piece "The Isha Upanishad". Later he changed the heading to "The Secret of Divine Life/A Commentary on the Isha Upanishad", and still later to "The Life Divine/A Commentary on the Isha Upanishad". "Introduction", written below the heading, was at one point changed to "Foreword". In the 18 July 1912 entry of *Record of Yoga*, his yogic diary, Sri Aurobindo wrote: "the Life Divine commenced". It was probably to this draft that he was referring. Note also the indirect reference to the *Titanic* disaster, which took place in April 1912. Several passages written for this piece but not worked into the text are reproduced in an appendix published at the end of the text.

The Life Divine [Draft B]. Circa 1913–14. Sri Aurobindo wrote this draft in pen in three notebooks. The five chapters of which it is composed are the beginning of "Part II/The First Movement" of a planned complete commentary. The following outline, written on the first page of the manuscript, shows the structure of this proposed work:

Part I.   The Upanishad
Part II   The First Movement – God, Life & Nature
Part III   The Second Movement – Brahman Self Blissful and All-Blissful
Part [IV] The Third Movement – God in World – Vidya & Avidya
Part [V]   The Fourth Movement – Surya & Agni
Part [VI] The Divine Life

Of these six parts, only "Part II The First Movement" was worked on.
The Life Divine [Draft C]. 1914. This draft consists of two chapters, numbered II and III by the author. Although they have the same heading

as "Draft A" and "Draft B", they seem to be destined not so much for a commentary on the Isha Upanishad as for an independent philosophical writing. (They contain no direct commentary on the Upanishad but occasionally mention it.) They seem in fact to represent a transitional stage between the "Life Divine" commentary on the Isha Upanishad and *The Life Divine*, Sri Aurobindo's principal philosophical work, which began to be published in the *Arya* in August 1914. The first instalment of Sri Aurobindo's final translation and analysis of the Isha Upanishad (see Part One above) appeared in the same issue.

PUBLISHING HISTORY

Sri Aurobindo published a translation of the Isha Upanishad on 19 June 1909 in the first issue of the *Karmayogin*, a weekly review of politics and culture. This was a revised version of a translation he had completed and typed around 1900. He published his final translation and analysis in the *Arya* between August 1914 and May 1915. Around 1921, the *Arya* text was reprinted by the Arya Publishing House, Calcutta. The same publisher brought out an "authorised edition", which was said to be "revised and enlarged", in 1924. That edition in fact contained no real enlargement (other than the restoration of the analysis of verses 4–5, which had inadvertently been omitted in 1921) and only slight authorial revision. Two more editions were brought out by the Arya Publishing House during Sri Aurobindo's lifetime, in 1941 and 1945. These contained a few minor changes. Several more editions were brought out after 1950. In 1971 the work was included in *The Upanishads*, volume 12 of the Sri Aurobindo Birth Centenary Library. The text in the present volume has been checked against the texts printed in the *Arya* and in the first four editions.

None of the ten incomplete commentaries published in Part Two appeared during Sri Aurobindo's lifetime. All have been transcribed from his manuscripts. Four were published in 1971 in *The Upanishads*, one in the *Supplement* to the Sri Aurobindo Birth Centenary Library (1973), and the other five in the journal *Sri Aurobindo: Archives and Research* between 1977 and 1983.